MW00772319

THE NATIONAL SECURITY CONSTITUTION
IN THE TWENTY-FIRST CENTURY

HAROLD HONGJU KOH

The National Security Constitution in the Twenty-First Century

Yale

UNIVERSITY PRESS

NEW HAVEN AND LONDON

The National Security Constitution in the Twenty-First Century is a revised
and substantially expanded version of *The National Security Constitution:
Sharing Power After the Iran-Contra Affair,* first published in 1990
by Yale University Press.

Published with assistance from the Mary Cady Tew Memorial Fund.

Yale University Press books may be purchased in quantity for educational,
business, or promotional use. For information, please e-mail sales.
press@yale.edu (U.S. office) or sales@yaleup.co.uk (U.K. office).

Set in Scala and Scala Sans display types by IDS Infotech Ltd.

Printed in the United States of America.
ISBN 978-0-300-25310-8 (hardcover : alk. paper)
Library of Congress Control Number: 2023946112
A catalogue record for this book is available from the British Library.

This paper meets the requirements of ANSI/NISO z39.48–1992
(Permanence of Paper).

10 9 8 7 6 5 4 3 2 1

To Mary-Christy,
From This Day Forward

CONTENTS

PART THREE: A NATIONAL SECURITY CONSTITUTION
FOR THE TWENTY-FIRST CENTURY

ACKNOWLEDGMENTS

IN 1987, AS A YOUNG PROFESSOR watching the waning days of the Reagan presidency, I began writing a piece for the *Yale Law Journal* titled "Why the President (Almost) Always Wins in Foreign Affairs" (97 *Yale L.J.* 1255 (1988)). Having first seriously engaged with the law of U.S. foreign relations as a law clerk to Judge Malcolm Richard Wilkey of the U.S. Court of Appeals for the D.C. Circuit and Justice Harry A. Blackmun of the U.S. Supreme Court, then as an attorney-adviser in Reagan's Office of Legal Counsel at the Department of Justice, I wrote that article while teaching a Yale Law School course on foreign-relations law. These experiences forced me to explore the gap between what government lawyers argue and what the Constitution actually requires.

Soon thereafter, Yale University Press published an expanded version of that article as *The National Security Constitution: Sharing Power After the Iran-Contra Affair,* a volume intended to introduce lawyers and political scientists to the then-overlooked field of U.S. foreign-relations law. While finishing that book during the post–Cold War era, I took as my model Louis Henkin's classic *Foreign Affairs and the Constitution,* which some decades later he usefully revised and expanded. As I have lived and worked through six more presidential administrations—led by the two Bushes, Clinton, Obama, Trump, and Biden—I felt increasingly moved to similarly update my original volume into this book.

I am grateful to William Frucht, Amanda Gerstenfeld, Phillip King, and Karen Schoen at Yale University Press for helping me make that renovation a reality. Kris Krause, my friend and assistant for many years, dismantled an old hardback to scan in and reproduce the original text. As I revised and expanded, I wistfully recalled how this book was first written: on large floppy drives, with a tiny green-lit screen, and a toddler in the next room singing Disney tunes. The current volume incorporates much of the earlier version, but has been greatly expanded and rethought. This volume now proceeds chronologically from the Founding to the present. It places the Iran-contra affair in its historical context before describing the evolution of twenty-first-century national security law with new chapters that cover the presidencies from George H. W. Bush to Joe Biden's first presidential years.

Of course, no one ever steps into the same river twice. Between these two volumes, I spent the intervening decades as a scholar, commentator, lecturer, and practitioner grappling with these historical developments as they unfolded in real time. From many different angles, I have learned a huge amount that I simply did not know when I first tackled this subject. First, I have served four U.S. presidents during each of the past five decades in the Justice and State Departments, as a government policymaker and as a lawyer. Second, I have sued the U.S. government on several occasions and have filed briefs against it in dozens of lawsuits. Third, I have learned a great deal more about international law, as a scholar developing the transnational-legal-process approach described here, and representing the United States and numerous other foreign governments before international courts and tribunals. Fourth, I have served as an executive myself, both as dean of Yale Law School and as head of two State Department bureaus. Finally, innumerable conversations with judges and legislators have forced me to think hard about the current state of Congress and the courts. Not surprisingly, this intervening time has given me different perspectives on some of the issues addressed in the original book. Still, as the closing pages note, the core of my thinking remains the same. As Justice Blackmun used to say when accused of changing his views: "Life is long, and you learn things." I have tried to incorporate the most important lessons that I have learned into this revision.

While the chapters in part 1 recall constitutional history and institutional practice, the chapters in part 2 are partly told from the perspective of a first-person participant. I confronted the issues in chapter 5 in the 1990s, while litigating foreign-affairs cases for Yale's Lowenstein International Human Rights Clinic. We fought major cases involving Haitian and Cuban refugees, to the Supreme Court alongside the late Michael Ratner, Lucas Guttentag, Joe Tringali, a remarkable team of dedicated Cuban-American lawyers from Miami, and extraordinary Yale law students who formed both "Team Haiti" and "Team Cuba." One of those students, Professor Mike Wishnie, became my litigation partner and colleague on the Yale Law School faculty and, along with Phil Spector and Hope Metcalf, helped me found two successor law clinics when the times demanded: Yale Law School's 9/11 Clinic in 2001 and the Peter Gruber Rule of Law Clinic in 2017. Together, we litigated or advocated with respect to nearly every issue discussed in chapters 6 through 8.

Starting in the late 1990s, I took leave from Yale to serve under three more presidents and secretaries of state: as assistant secretary of state for democracy, human rights, and labor under the late Madeleine Albright in the Clinton administration (1998–2001), as Legal Adviser of the State Department under Hillary Rodham Clinton in the Obama administration (2009–2013), and as senior adviser (the only political appointee) in the same Legal Adviser's Office under Antony Blinken during 2021, the first year of the Biden administration.

The terrorist attacks of September 11, 2001, propelled foreign relations and national security law into every university and law-school curriculum. The national security blogosphere transformed this field from an academic backwater into grist for daily news stories by insightful national security experts. Since 2013, I have commented on any number of these issues as a founding editor and author for Professor Ryan Goodman's *Just Security* blog, now an invaluable tool for any national security law practitioner. I have served as an adviser and am now co-chair of the American Law Institute's forthcoming *Restatement (Fourth), Foreign Relations Law of the United States.*

The luckiest scholars are blessed with devoted partners and friends. Dean Heather Gerken and Yale Law School's faculty, students, and staff have made Yale my intellectual home these past four decades. I am so grateful for exceptional research assistance by Jack Baisley, Connor Brashear, James Janison, Grace Kier, Zoe Kreitenberg, Daniel Lipkowitz, Michael Loughlin, Maggie Mills, Eleanor Runde, and Mary Szarkowicz. After I left the Biden administration in October 2021, the Rhodes Trust (particularly my old friend Elliot Gerson), Balliol College, Oxford University (particularly Professors Timothy Endicott and Andrew Hurrell), and Fordham Law School (particularly Dean Matthew Diller) all gave me havens to write this book as George Eastman

Visiting Professor at Oxford and Bacon-Killkenny Distinguished Visitor at Fordham. Master Helen Ghosh and the Fellows of Balliol College, President Dinah Rose KC and the Fellows of Magdalen College, Professor Dapo Akande of the Blavatnik School of Government, Professor Kate O'Regan and the Bonavero Human Rights Institute, and Deans Mindy Chen-Wishart and Anne Davies of the Oxford Law Faculty all gave welcome friendship, sustenance, and support. The *George Washington Law Review* invited me to give the keynote address at its 2022 Symposium on Foreign Relations and National Security Law, which allowed me to organize my thoughts in part 3. The members of the Yale and Fordham Law School faculty workshops gave me insightful comments on that address. A great many friends helped me finish this book, including Rosalie Abella, Daniel Bethlehem, Tess Bridgeman, Jim Brudney, Anupam Chander, Jim Cooper, Laura Dickinson, Bill Dodge, Kristen Eichensehr, Russ Feingold, Mary-Christy Fisher, Marty Flaherty, Monica Hakimi, Rebecca Ingber, Christine Jolls, Kris Krause, Steven Arrigg Koh, Doug Kysar, Sean Murphy, Gerry Neuman, Lucie Olejnikova, David Pozen, Charlie Savage, Kate Stith, Phil Spector, Ed Swaine, Bill Treanor, John Witt, and Aaron Zelinsky. Joel Goldstein, an extraordinary constitutional scholar and my friend for nearly a half century, generously read multiple chapters, multiple times.

My family gives me daily reason to live and work for the rule of law. My siblings have been a source of constant inspiration and stimulation. My brilliant mother, Dr. Hesung Chun Koh, taught me scholarly values and reminds me every day of the ideals that brought our family to America. Although gone for more than thirty years, my late father, Dr. Kwang Lim Koh, lives in my heart, reminding me daily of the difference between the rule of law and the rule of individuals.

Between the two editions of this book, my children, Emily Jennings Youngyon Koh and William Hagan Wonlim Koh, grew into accomplished professionals and my finest teachers. I love them more than life itself. And through more than four decades, my wise, wonderful wife, attorney Mary-Christy Fisher, a role model for public-spirited lawyering, has made everything possible and joyous. It is to our past, present, and future together that I dedicate this book.

THE NATIONAL SECURITY CONSTITUTION
IN THE TWENTY-FIRST CENTURY

Introduction: Two Constitutional Visions

AS JOE BIDEN FINISHES FOUR YEARS as the forty-sixth president of the United States, memories of Donald Trump's tumultuous presidency have started to fade. But before those memories recede, it is worth asking whether the excesses of the Trump administration were an aberration, attributable to a single man, or the revelation of a deeper disorder in our constitutional system. This book suggests the latter: that the past several decades have witnessed the steady erosion of what I called more than thirty years ago the "National Security Constitution," the substructure of U.S. constitutional norms that protects the operation of checks and balances in national security policy.[1]

That National Security Constitution rests upon a simple notion: that the power to conduct American foreign policy is not exclusively presidential, but is a power shared among the president, the Congress, and the courts. As Justice Robert Jackson famously wrote in *Youngstown Sheet & Tube Co. v. Sawyer* (the *Steel Seizure* case), "[p]residential powers are not fixed but fluctuate, depending upon their disjunction or conjunction with those of Congress," with the legality of executive and congressional action reviewable by the courts. Simply put, the constitutional system of checks and balances is not suspended simply because foreign affairs or national security are at issue. In foreign as well as domestic affairs, the Constitution requires that we be governed by separated institutions sharing foreign-policy powers.[2]

But today's headlines teach daily that this original design no longer well describes how, after nearly 250 years, the constitutional system governing

1

national security now functions. When national security threats arise, weak and strong presidents alike have institutional incentives to monopolize the response; Congress has incentives to acquiesce; and courts have incentives to defer. This convergence of institutional incentives has fostered an interactive dysfunction that has disrupted the constitutional norm of shared national security policymaking power. In its place has arisen a dramatically different vision of the National Security Constitution. Instead of *Youngstown's* vision of shared powers, presidential defenders have repeatedly invoked an alternative vision of unchecked executive discretion. This unilateralist vision—captured in *United States v. Curtiss-Wright Export Corp.*—views virtually the entire field of foreign affairs as falling under an exclusive constitutional domain where the president acts as "defender in chief," without the meaningful participation of either Congress or the courts.[3]

This book addresses two questions: First, how did this constitutional transformation happen? Second, as we plunge deeper into the twenty-first century, what can be done to restore balance to this distorted constitutional system?

Part I addresses the historical question. Chapter I defines the concept of a National Security Constitution and explains how that vision has evolved throughout our constitutional history from the Founding. It explains how lurking within the text of the Constitution—as construed by Supreme Court decisions, legislative enactments, and historical practice—is a National Security Constitution that both facilitates and constrains the operation of our national security policy process. That constitutional framework dates back to the beginning of the Republic: a precarious infancy that ended with the Civil War; a heady adolescence terminated by the dawn of the twentieth century; an adulthood that stretched to World War II; and a post–Cold War hegemonic era. Through each of these eras, the nation managed to adhere to a foreign-policy decision-making structure premised on the balanced institutional participation of all three governmental branches. That "*Youngstown* vision" found its clearest expression in Justice Jackson's *Steel Seizure* concurrence in 1952. Although the National Security Constitution assigns the president the predominant role in making foreign-policy decisions, it grants him only limited exclusive powers. Thus, the Constitution directs most governmental decisions regarding foreign affairs into a sphere of *concurrent authority*, under presidential management, but bounded by the checks provided by congressional consultation and judicial review.

As part 2 reviews, the past fifty years—which ended the twentieth century and opened the twenty-first—brought that constitutional vision under constant attack. Ronald Reagan's Iran-contra affair illustrated the ascension of a unilateralist *"Curtiss-Wright* vision" of presidential power, crystallized in a robust theory of the "unitary executive" and a diluted role for congressional checks and judicial oversight in foreign affairs. The unilateralist presidencies of George W. Bush and Donald Trump doubled down on this vision, with a watershed coming as the twenty-first century dawned and became defined by the terrorist attacks of September 11, 2001. The claimed need for unrestrained executive power to fend off future attacks dominated the popular imagination and led many politicians, judges, commentators, and scholars to defend presidential and American unilateralism.

The ensuing era of unending threat and "forever war" represented not simply a collection of unconnected indiscretions or statutory violations, but an escalating assault on the National Security Constitution that we have inherited. George W. Bush's war on terror spawned Donald Trump's brutal immigration policies and the foreign-policy scandal involving Ukraine that led to Trump's first impeachment. The Democratic presidencies of Bill Clinton, Barack Obama, and Joe Biden have swung the pendulum partially and sporadically back toward shared power, but new external threats and the legislative weaknesses of all three leaders forced them to employ ad hoc unilateralist tactics as well. As terrorism gave way to climate change, global pandemics, and wars in Ukraine and the Middle East as the greatest existential threats, the perceived need for presidential unilateralism has accelerated.

Upon closer inspection, this steady march toward presidential power exposes not just a constitutional crisis but a pressing policy problem as well. Why, in recent times, have our national institutions failed to voluntarily preserve the core notion of the National Security Constitution: shared foreign-affairs decision-making? Why, despite the constitutional mandate of power sharing, does the president almost always seem to win in foreign affairs?

The answer to that question, chapter 4 explains, ultimately lies in three sets of institutional factors that currently characterize our branches of national government. First, the president has won because weak and strong presidents alike have institutional incentives to take the initiative in foreign affairs and have often done so by construing laws that were enacted to constrain executive authority as authorizing executive action. Second, the president has won because Congress, as an institution, has continually acquiesced in what presidents have done. Third, the president has won because the federal courts have tolerated presidents' acts, particularly in recent years, either by refusing to hear congressional or private challenges to presidential action or by hearing those challenges on the merits and ruling in the president's favor. It is not the actions of any one branch, but the synergistic interaction between executive initiative, congressional acquiescence, and judicial tolerance that has broadly insulated the president from foreign-affairs accountability. These factors have jointly operated to undercut the Constitution's mandate of balanced institutional participation in national security decision-making.

As chapter 8 describes, under Donald Trump, this institutional dysfunction reached unprecedented heights. His extreme unilateralism exploited both the eagerness of the Republican Senate to normalize his behavior and the impulse of a Supreme Court that he has transformed to defer to imagined claims of national security necessity. I have elsewhere chronicled the many "resistance measures" taken to challenge the Trump administration's illegal initiatives through "transnational legal process."[4] But we cannot restore constitutional equilibrium simply by "throwing the rascals out." This historical march toward unilateral presidentialism could slow if the next few administrations were to push the pendulum strongly the other way. But as chapter 9 shows, the Biden years have not yet signaled that this will happen. If the Democrats instead revert to their persistent political tendency to undercorrect, more and more of America's constitutional democratic institutions may be exposed to existential threat.

What policy prescriptions would most likely prevent future gross abuses of executive power? Part 3 argues that now is the time for systematic reconsideration of executive unilateralism, before it entirely guts core legislative prerogatives. In other areas of pressing national concern, such as budget, tax, and trade reform, we have not relied upon periodic voluntary commitments to bipartisanship as long-term solutions to recurring problems. Instead, Congress has enacted "constitutional 'framework' legislation [to] interpret[] the Constitution by providing a legal framework for the governmental decision-making process." More than seventy years ago, Congress enacted the first such statute to govern national security decisions, the National Security Act of 1947. After Watergate's malicious domestic election tampering, a bipartisan Congress enacted stiffer laws regarding campaign conduct and finance. To address the foreign-policy dysfunction of Vietnam, Congress also passed national security framework statutes to constrain war powers, intelligence oversight, emergency economic powers, and international agreement making. The Trump era confirmed that we need similar reforms in all three branches to govern national security decision-making in the twenty-first century.[5]

The closing chapters suggest a plethora of achievable reforms to redefine the role that all three branches play in our national security system. Meaningful national security reform should not just restrain executive adventurism, but should also attack the institutional sources of congressional acquiescence and judicial tolerance. Chapter 10 outlines a broad legislative strategy and particular proposals for attacking the institutional drivers of creeping executive unilateralism in all three branches. Chapter 11 suggests how these general principles can be applied to improve particular areas of foreign-policy decision-making: war powers, agreement making and breaking, emergency powers, intelligence oversight, information control, and democracy and human rights.

These recommendations build on Justice Jackson's axiom that the Constitution "enjoins upon its branches separateness but interdependence, autonomy but reciprocity."[6] The president must strengthen internal executive-branch checks and balances. To avert the recurring cycles of interbranch warfare that we have recently experienced, we must promote better institutional power-sharing procedures designed to more clearly define constitutional responsibility and institutional accountability. To level the playing field with the executive, the courts must exercise more meaningful oversight. Congress must create stronger central repositories of national security expertise and legal advice, as well as legal structures to promote the interbranch dialogue essential to any "'bipartisan foreign policy': [congressional] consultation on the formulation of policy, participation in its execution, and information about its operation."[7]

Finally, the concluding chapter anticipates and answers likely critiques of these reform proposals. Having worked for four presidents over parts of five decades, I obviously favor strong presidential leadership. Today's world, however, demands not simply a strong president, but one who operates within an institutionally balanced constitutional structure of decision-making. In all national affairs, Justice Louis Brandeis told us, our constitutional system of checks and balances was designed "not to promote efficiency but to preclude the exercise of arbitrary power."[8] Whether or not a national decision-making structure ruled by an unencumbered executive suited an era of world history marked by American hegemony, it invites only crippling interbranch strife in a globalized world, where the United States is only one of the major powers.

The recent past is not just aberrant history that we can safely forgive or forget. The institutional problems that caused recent presidential abuses exposed a serious and growing imbalance that infects our national processes of foreign-affairs decision-making. As president, Donald Trump revealed some of the ways that the president could himself become a national security threat. But he was not the worst national security threat one could imagine. He did not invade other countries and often stymied himself. But his presidency graphically illustrated how grave a national security threat could be mounted by a more competent and focused unilateral president. It would take only one election for this to happen again.

To prevent recurrence, we must look for structural solutions aimed at promoting regularized interbranch communication, encouraging executive accountability, and revitalizing Congress and the courts as institutional counterweights to the president. We cannot restore balance to our national security decision-making unless we redesign the institutional incentives facing all three branches. Admittedly, Congress cannot legislate executive self-restraint, legislative will, or judicial courage. But Congress can and should seek to alter recurrent patterns of wayward executive behavior by restructuring the institutional attributes that now create incentives for executive officials to overreach and for congressional and judicial officials to permit such actions. Only by so doing can we fulfill the promise of the National Security Constitution: that America's foreign-affairs power is a power shared.

PART ONE

THE *YOUNGSTOWN* VISION

From Founding to National Security Act

ONE CANNOT READ THE UNITED STATES Constitution without being struck by its astonishing brevity regarding the allocation of foreign-affairs authority among the branches. Nowhere does the Constitution use the words "foreign affairs" or "national security." Instead, it creates a Congress, a president, and a federal judiciary and vests in them powers, some of which principally affect foreign affairs. Only occasionally does the Constitution explicitly condition one branch's exercise of a foreign-affairs power on another's, as in its grants to the president of the powers, with the Senate's advice and consent, to make treaties and to appoint ambassadors.[1] More frequently, the document grants clearly related powers to separate institutions, without ever specifying the relationship between those powers, as, for example, with Congress's power to declare war and the president's power as commander in chief.[2] Most often, the text simply says nothing about who controls certain domains; for example, the exercise of international emergency powers or the conduct of covert action.

In the few cases in which a constitutional phrase clearly designates who shall exercise a particular authority—the president's power to "receive Ambassadors," for example—the textually granted power appears far more limited than what has been exercised historically. Article II, section 3, for example, grants the president the seemingly ceremonial power to "receive Ambassadors and other public Ministers." But over time that clause has been expansively read to grant the president not just the authority to admit ambassadors and examine their credentials, but virtually unfettered authority to recognize and derecognize foreign states and governments.[3] Perhaps most striking, the relative balance struck in the Constitution's text between the president's few and Congress's many enumerated foreign-affairs powers hardly matches our present-day sense of their relative preeminence.[4]

These incongruities suggest that we must look beyond the Constitution's cryptic text to discover the broader constitutional principles that govern how Congress, the courts, and the executive should interact in the foreign-policy process. This chapter argues that there lurks within our constitutional system an identifiable *National Security Constitution,* a normative vision of the foreign-policy-making process that emerges only partially from the text of the Constitution itself. Like America's fiscal constitution and administrative constitution, which other scholars have described, the National Security Constitution comprises that subset of our public law that governs America's national security decision-making.[5] The National Security Constitution creates the basic governmental institutions to deal with national security matters, defines the fundamental power relationships between those institutions, and places limitations on the power of each branch.

The sources of law that make up this National Security Constitution can be found at three hierarchical levels. First and most obvious, the *text* of the Constitution provides a skeleton for the National Security Constitution by creating the three branches of the federal government and assigning certain foreign-affairs powers to them. As Charles Black recognized, a constitution "constitutes" not merely by enumerating individual rights and institutional powers, but more broadly by declaring how an entire government is to be structured. Thus, ultimate judgments regarding how the Constitution allocates particular powers in foreign affairs cannot be reached solely by looking at constitutional text, for the problem is not simply one "of correctly discerning or stating the legitimate bounds of the presidential and the congressional powers respectively." Rather, allocations of authority must be identified by "reasoning from the *total structure* which the text has created."[6] Accordingly, at this first level, the core principles of the National Security Constitution must be ascertained through textual exegesis of particular constitutional clauses, as understood in light of the broader structure and relationships created by the Constitution. Authoritative declarations of these core principles can also be found in those relatively few *judicial decisions* that have construed the basic constitutional structure and text with regard to foreign-affairs matters.

Historical examination of constitutional structure and relationships suggests that our National Security Constitution rests on a simple notion: that the foreign-affairs power of the United States is a *power shared* among the three branches of the national government. As a whole, the Constitution rests on a system of institutional checks and balances. The National Security Constitution expresses the corollary principle that checks and balances are not suspended simply because foreign affairs are at issue. In foreign as well as domestic affairs, the Constitution requires that we be governed by separated institutions *sharing* foreign-policy powers.[7] Under this constitutional power-sharing scheme, the president, Congress, and the courts all play integral roles in both making and validating foreign-policy decisions. As it has evolved, the National Security Constitution assigns to the president the predominant role in that process, but affords the president only a limited realm of exclusive powers regarding diplomatic relations and negotiations and the recognition of nations and governments.[8] Outside that realm, governmental decisions regarding foreign affairs must transpire within a sphere of concurrent authority, under presidential management, but bounded by the checks provided by congressional consultation and judicial review. In short, the structural principle that animates our National Security Constitution is *balanced institutional participation.*

At a second, subordinate level, more specific rules governing the legal rights and duties of the three branches in national security decision-making can be found in a discrete number of "framework statutes": laws that Congress enacts and the president signs within their zone of concurrent authority, not simply to "formulate specific policies for the resolution of specific problems, but rather ... to implement constitutional policies."[9] Statutes such as the Judiciary Act of 1789, the National Security Act of 1947, the War Powers Resolution of 1973, the Congressional Budget and Impoundment Control Act of 1974, the National Emergencies Act of 1976, and the International Emergency Economic Powers Act of 1977 all "attempt to support the organizational skeleton of the Constitution by developing a more detailed framework for government decision making" in foreign affairs.[10] Such legislation thus reinforces and elaborates the constitutional foundation of power sharing by constructing a statutory superstructure that declares in greater detail how power should be distributed among institutions in specific areas of foreign policy. These statutes specify legal authorities and constraints for particular institutional acts; provide procedures to evaluate and control particular exercises of delegated powers; and foster institutional expectations about how those powers will be exercised in the future.

By enacting such framework statutes, the president and Congress jointly generate a body of "subconstitutional" law in foreign affairs, working together both to construe particular constitutional provisions and to effectuate the underlying constitutional principle of balanced institutional participation. Within the executive's limited zone of exclusive constitutional authority, presidents can also unilaterally "legislate" by issuing *framework executive orders.*[11] But because these framework statutes and orders purport only to declare or elaborate the Constitution and are not themselves constitutional amendments, the courts may hold them unconstitutional when they erect subconstitutional frameworks that the judges find incompatible with the text or structure of the Constitution itself.

At the third and lowest level in this legal hierarchy stands a body of precedents that may be thought of as *quasi-constitutional custom.* This term embraces a set of institutional norms generated by the historical interaction of two or more federal branches with one another. All three branches can generate such precedents. Thus, quasi-constitutional custom includes executive practice that Congress has approved or in which it has acquiesced, formal and informal congressional actions with which the president has consistently complied, and certain vacated judicial opinions that have acted as influential advisory opinions for the other two branches. Each of these historical sources has contributed to the creation of a customary constitutional law in the realm of foreign affairs, resembling the rules of customary law observed by nations in the international arena.[12] Such rules are followed as a matter of consistent institutional practice that the various branches of government believe they have a legal obligation to follow. As Justice Felix Frankfurter, concurring in *Youngstown Sheet & Tube Co. v. Sawyer,* famously declared, "a systematic, unbroken, executive practice, long pursued to the knowledge of the Congress and never before questioned . . . making as it were such exercise of power part of the structure of our government, may be treated as a gloss on 'executive Power' vested in the President by § 1 of Art. II."[13]

These customary rules represent informal accommodations between two or more branches regarding who decides with respect to particular foreign-policy matters. For that reason, they carry greater normative weight than self-serving justifications that one branch may offer, without another branch's endorse-ment, to defend its own actions as constitutional. At the same time, however, both the informal process that governs the creation of these customary norms and the difficulties inherent in establishing their existence suggest that they should have only persuasive, not conclusive, force regarding what the constitu-tional allocation of authority in foreign affairs should be. Congress and its com-mittees have sought to place similar glosses on other constitutional clauses by declaring norms of constitutional conduct through means other than legisla-tion.[14] The lower federal courts have sometimes rendered important opinions affirming on the merits one branch's claim of foreign-affairs authority that the Supreme Court has subsequently vacated for procedural reasons. Although, strictly speaking, such vacated lower-court opinions carry no precedential weight, the president and Congress frequently cite them against one another as predictions of how a court would rule were a particular constitutional claim ever to arise again in the future.[15] Among the most influential of these cases has been *Goldwater v. Carter,* a per curiam Supreme Court decision from 1979 vacating a D.C. Circuit ruling in a suit by members of Congress challenging President Jimmy Carter's unilateral termination of a bilateral treaty with Tai-wan. That case has been read, overbroadly, to acknowledge presidential author-ity to unilaterally terminate bilateral treaties in accordance with their terms.[16]

Although this large body of quasi-constitutional custom fills in the inter-stices of the textual and statutory skeleton of the National Security Constitu-tion, it is perennially subject to revision. Just as nations can modify customary rules of international law by establishing more formal rules in a particular area by treaty, so too can Congress and the president override quasi-constitutional custom by enacting a framework statute or issuing a framework executive or-der, which can in turn be invalidated or modified by a formal constitutional amendment or judicial decision. In enacting the Judiciary Act of 1789, for ex-ample, Congress and the president "executed" Article III of the Constitution by creating an organic, formal structure of decision-making for the federal judi-ciary. But in *Marbury v. Madison,* the Supreme Court invalidated section 13 of that act as unconstitutional.[17] Similarly, the Constitution's text gives little guid-ance regarding which branch of government should exercise international emergency economic powers in wartime or non-wartime situations, leaving that question to be resolved by institutional practice (quasi-constitutional cus-tom). In the twentieth century, Congress and the president finally addressed that question by enacting three framework statutes—the Trading with the Enemy Act of 1917, the National Emergencies Act of 1976, and the International Emergency Economic Powers Act of 1977—a statutory structure that the Supreme Court has repeatedly upheld against constitutional challenge, even while invalidating embedded legislative vetoes.[18]

In sum, the Constitution's structure and text, as construed by judicial decisions, legislative enactments, executive orders, and subsequent historical practice, describe a National Security Constitution whose animating principle is balanced institutional participation. That principle is more faithful than executive unilateralism to the Constitution's core principles of checks and balances and separation of powers. This legal structure both facilitates and constrains the operation of the national security policy process. As later chapters will show, as a way of conducting foreign policy, this approach better supports democracy, avoids authoritarian capture, and lowers the risks of militarism and catastrophic outcomes.

This structural vision of a foreign-affairs power shared through balanced institutional participation has inspired the National Security Constitution since the beginning of the Republic and received its most cogent expression in Justice Robert Jackson's famous concurring opinion in *Youngstown* from 1952.[19] Yet throughout our constitutional history, what I call the *Youngstown* vision has done battle with a radically different constitutional paradigm. This counterimage of *unchecked executive discretion* has claimed virtually the entire field of foreign affairs as falling under the president's inherent authority. Although this image has surfaced from time to time since the early Republic, it did not fully crystallize until Justice George Sutherland's controversial, oft-cited opinion for the Court in *United States v. Curtiss-Wright Export Corp.* in 1936.[20] As construed by proponents of executive power, the *Curtiss-Wright* vision rejects two of *Youngstown*'s central tenets: that the National Security Constitution requires congressional concurrence in most decisions on foreign affairs and that the courts must play an important role in examining and constraining executive-branch judgments in foreign affairs. By denying that the other two branches have a legitimate role in foreign affairs, the *Curtiss-Wright* vision rejects, in favor of the contrary notion of executive unilateralism, the principles of balanced institutional participation and power sharing that lie at the heart of the National Security Constitution. As the twenty-first century has unfolded, the *Curtiss-Wright* vision has gained momentum, with strong and weak presidents alike seizing more power and Congress and the courts receding into increasingly passive, reactive roles.

International Regimes and Constitutional Regimes

Because most constitutional-law casebooks begin their discussion of foreign-affairs powers with either *Curtiss-Wright* or *Youngstown,* a newcomer to the field might conclude that the struggle between the paradigms they represent did not commence until 1936.[21] In fact, one can trace six discrete historical eras in the evolution of the National Security Constitution that date back to the beginning of the Republic: (1) a pre–Civil War period of infancy when America operated on the world's periphery; (2) an adolescence that ended with the turn of the twentieth century, during which the United States rose to the status of a dominant regional power; (3) a heady adulthood stretching until World War II, which witnessed America's emergence as a global power; (4) a period of mature dominance in which America enjoyed the singular status of hegemonic power; (5) a post–Cold War period during which the United States appeared to lose hegemony through a combination of imperial overstretch and disdain for alliances; and (6) the first decades of the twenty-first century, when counterterrorism, pandemics, climate change, and regional wars all forced more power into presidential hands.

Through the first four eras, discussed in this chapter, *Youngstown*'s norm of balanced institutional participation remained the dominant constitutional vision. But proponents of executive discretion periodically launched challenges to it, which culminated in the period of executive dominance that bred the Vietnam War. Vietnam triggered a powerful congressional backlash against the imperial presidency that led to the enactment of framework statutes in virtually every field of foreign affairs. Yet even this extensive post-Vietnam legislative activity failed to reimprint the *Youngstown* vision firmly upon the National Security Constitution, and thus allowed *Curtiss-Wright* to resurface during the Reagan administration's Iran-contra affair. Following that episode, Congress missed a crucial opportunity to enact a new round of framework legislation, largely ignoring the struggle between the competing visions of our National Security Constitution. That allowed the battle of constitutional paradigms to revive repeatedly during the last two historical eras, which are discussed in part 2.

The pendulum swings that marked the transitions from George H. W. Bush (Bush 41) to Bill Clinton to George W. Bush (Bush 43) to Barack Obama allowed the *Curtiss-Wright* vision to reach its zenith during the extreme presidency of Donald Trump. Joe Biden's presidency—plagued with pandemic, economic crisis, Afghanistan, Russia versus Ukraine, Israel versus Hamas—has done relatively little to restore the *Youngstown* vision.

By sketching in broad strokes the life cycle of the National Security Constitution, this chapter does not aim to comprehensively redescribe the history of American foreign policy, a path that has been exhaustively traveled by political scientists and historians alike.[22] Instead, my goal is to examine how the structure of domestic constitutional law has interacted over time with the structure of international politics. My inquiry focuses on how successive regimes of American constitutional decision-making in foreign affairs have both influenced and been influenced by the evolving international political regimes in which the United States participates. A broad examination of that question demonstrates that in each succeeding historical era, judicial decisions, framework statutes, executive orders, and institutional practice have all amended our National Security Constitution to respond to evolving national perceptions of America's changing position in the international arena. Each successive era has embroidered the basic constitutional tapestry as the branches have struggled over whether to preserve or dilute the core constitutional principle of balanced institutional participation.

How the National Security Constitution Evolved

Precarious Infancy: America on the Periphery

From the very beginning, the U.S. Constitution has been obsessed with the idea of national security; that is, "the government's capacity to defend itself from violent overthrow by domestic subversion or external aggression [and its] . . . ability . . . to function effectively so as to serve our interests at home and abroad."[23] The term "national security" was not officially coined until the Cold War.[24] Nevertheless, no fewer than twenty-five of the first thirty-six *Federalist Papers* concerned national insecurity, with most linking the young republic's international weakness to the incapacity of the national government.[25] As John Jay put it, "a cordial Union, under an efficient national government, affords them the best security that can be devised against *hostilities* from abroad."[26]

Under the Articles of Confederation, the United States had suffered a string of failures in foreign policy attributable in good measure to the national government's impotence. In their zeal to avoid creating an American king, the authors of the Articles had unwisely vested executive as well as legislative powers in Congress. Congress was authorized to appoint and supervise ambassadors as well as to approve treaties and exercise "the sole and exclusive right and power of determining on peace and war."[27] Although Article VI purported to give "the united states in congress" control over the new nation's foreign affairs, the Continental Congress lacked a supremacy power that empowered it to enforce treaty commitments against the states.[28] Consequently, individual states regularly violated the Treaty of Paris, which had secured America's independence from Britain in 1783. Not only did this noncompliance raise the specter of renewed British intervention, it also jeopardized America's hopes of developing stronger treaty relations with Spain, France, and Holland.[29]

To remedy the Articles' defects, the Founding Fathers framed the constitutional provisions on foreign affairs with two goals in mind—fashioning a stronger national government, while holding each branch of that government accountable to the others through a strong system of checks and balances.[30] The two goals were closely related. On the one hand, the Framers overwhelmingly agreed on the need for increased national power in four areas: taxation, military establishment, regulation of foreign commerce, and treaty enforcement.[31] James Madison, taking notes on Oliver Ellsworth's observations during the Constitutional Convention, remarked that because the Articles of Confederation had rendered the new country vulnerable to foreign invasion, only a strong national government could ensure national security.[32] As Madison put it, "[t]he powers delegated by the proposed Constitution to the federal government are few and defined. . . . [They] will be exercised principally on *external objects,* as war, peace, negotiation, and foreign commerce."[33]

At the same time, however, the Framers rejected the option of centralizing the national government's foreign-affairs powers in the president alone. Even Alexander Hamilton, the strongest defender of executive power, dubbed Congress "that body which is constituted the guardian of the national security."[34] The Framers also did not intend the operation of the system of checks and balances to stop at the water's edge. On the contrary, the Framers fully intended the system to apply to both foreign and domestic affairs. In Professor Louis Henkin's words, "the Framers were hardly ready to replace the representative inefficiency of many with an efficient monarch, and unhappy memories of royal prerogative, fear of tyranny, and distrust of any one man, kept the Framers from giving the new President too much head. . . . Every grant to the President . . . relating to foreign affairs, was in effect a derogation from Congressional power, eked out slowly, reluctantly, and not without limitations and safeguards."[35]

Thus, the first three articles of the Constitution expressly divided foreign-affairs powers among the three branches of government, with *Congress*, not the president, given the dominant role. Article I bestowed upon Congress legislative powers to "lay and collect Taxes, Duties, Imposts and Excises . . . and provide for the common Defence"; to "regulate Commerce with foreign Nations . . . and with the Indian Tribes"; to "establish an uniform Rule of Naturalization"; to "define and punish Piracies and Felonies committed on the high Seas, and Offences against the Law of Nations"; and to "declare War, grant Letters of Marque and Reprisal, and make Rules concerning Captures on Land and Water"; plus all manner of powers regarding raising, supporting, maintaining, and regulating the army, navy, and militia, which could be exercised both domestically and abroad. The Framers embellished these congressional powers not only with other specific constitutional grants, but also with Article I's sweeping authorization to Congress "[t]o make all Laws which shall be necessary and proper for carrying into Execution the foregoing Powers, and all other Powers vested by this Constitution *in the Government of the United States, or in any Department or Officer thereof.*"[36]

In Article II, the Framers granted the president specific executive authorities: the commander-in-chief power, the power to receive ambassadors, and the power to appoint ambassadors and make treaties with the advice and consent of the Senate. But the Framers pointedly denied the president other grants—most prominently, the power to declare war, rejecting the English model of a king who possessed both the power to declare war and the authority to command troops.[37] Similarly, the *Federalist Papers* made clear that the Framers considered it "imprudent to confide in [the president] solely so important a trust" as the treaty-making power.[38] Although the Framers also vested the "executive power" in the president, they did not expressly incorporate within that nebulous grant an exclusive power in foreign affairs or a general war-making power. Nor, despite expansive claims later asserted by more recent advocates of presidential power, did the Framers intend by that grant to bestow upon the president an unenumerated inherent authority to take external actions.[39] Article II declared that the president "shall take Care that the Laws be faithfully executed," but by its own terms that phrase more clearly imposed on the president a duty, not a license.[40]

Finally, in Article III, the Framers created a federal judiciary and extended the judicial power of the United States to cases and controversies arising under treaties; affecting ambassadors and consuls; and involving foreign states, citizens, and subjects. As implemented by the first Congress in one of its first framework statutes, the Judiciary Act of 1789, these authorizations gave the Supreme Court (and such lower courts as Congress might create) an important checking function against the political branches with regard to a range of foreign matters.[41]

Thus, the linchpin of the entire constitutional scheme remained the notion that powers in foreign affairs should be *distributed* among the branches and exercised through balanced institutional participation. As Professor Arthur Bestor notes, "the documents of this formative period of American constitutionalism consistently treated the conduct of foreign relations as a *shared responsibility.*"[42]

Even though the Framers carefully refrained from giving the president elastic unenumerated constitutional powers, they fully recognized that "[e]nergy in the executive is a leading character in the definition of good government."[43] The Framers thus anticipated the creation of a cabinet government. Early drafts of the Constitution actually referred to the Department of Foreign Affairs and the Department of War by name. In yet another early framework statute, Congress created those two cabinet departments pursuant to the Constitution's explicit reference to "executive Departments."[44]

Equally central was the Framers' decision to establish civilian supremacy over the military. Enumerating the "history of repeated injuries and usurpations" visited upon the colonies by the king of Great Britain, the Declaration of Independence had prominently mentioned the king's efforts "to render the Military independent of and superior to the Civil Power."[45] The Framers therefore named the president—a political and not a military leader—commander in chief of the armed forces. As Justice Jackson later noted in

Youngstown, "[t]he [Framers'] purpose of lodging dual titles in one man was to ensure that the civilian would control the military, not to enable the military to subordinate the presidential office."[46] For similar reasons, the Framers endowed another civilian entity, Congress, with the power to declare war and to make rules governing the armed forces.[47]

Of course, the birth of this National Security Constitution did not occur in a geopolitical vacuum. America's geographical separation from the rest of the world, which played a crucial role in fostering its liberal political tradition, figured equally prominently in the development of America's constitutional traditions.[48] In giving Congress a dominant role in the making of foreign policy, the Framers were aware that "[t]he distance of the United States from the powerful nations of the world gives them . . . happy security."[49] The United States constituted its national government during a global era of nascent British hegemony, which did not fully ripen until 1815. Until then, the new country's survival was far from assured. The young republic's physical separation from the Old World and the power struggles that raged in Europe permitted the United States to pursue a largely isolationist foreign policy, one "made possible by the fact of isolation[,] . . . made necessary by the weakness, disunity, and vulnerability that rendered the fledgling state utterly unfit for the strenuous game of power politics[, and] made desirable for Americans by their sense of differentiation and moral separation from the European world, their conviction that they had created a fresh and innocent society that could only be sullied by close involvement in European politics."[50]

So when, in the early years of the Republic, foreign sovereigns inevitably began to breach the cordon sanitaire that the British Royal Navy had imposed between the Old and New Worlds, it quickly became apparent that the Congress was poorly structured to respond. The varied tasks of nation building—recognition of and by foreign states, establishment of diplomatic relations, and conclusion of treaties—all demanded a branch of government that could react more quickly and coherently to foreign initiatives. Not only was the office of the president ideally structured for such responsive action, it was filled during those early years by presidents of unusual personal force.[51] For that reason, the president's constitutional authorities grew rapidly during this first era, but the growth was confined principally to expansion of the president's textually enumerated powers: in the areas of recognition, treaty making, and appointment and reception of ambassadors. Significantly, little claim was heard in those years that the president conducted foreign affairs pursuant to *inherent* unenumerated constitutional authority. The era was marked by sporadic, not steady, aggrandizement of presidential powers in foreign affairs vis-à-vis the Congress, with the presidencies of George Washington, Thomas Jefferson, Andrew Jackson, and James Polk marking high points amid identifiable valleys of presidential power.[52]

It soon became clear that weak as well as strong presidents seize strands of unilateral power. An examination of executive practice during these early years reveals that most unilateral exercises of presidential authority were driven not by presidential ambition, but by external events—particularly the president's desire to preserve the young nation's neutrality from foreign struggles. President Washington consciously and prudently avoided substantive tests of presidential power.[53] Still, he took several notable actions in foreign affairs that appeared to challenge the Federalist vision of power sharing: rejecting the French diplomat Edmond Charles Genêt (Citizen Genêt) as a foreign emissary; employing special agents to conduct diplomacy; negotiating treaties without prior consultation; withholding documents regarding the Jay Treaty from the House of Representatives; and issuing the Neutrality Proclamation of 1793 without consulting Congress. Yet virtually all of these decisions were driven by his primary foreign-policy priority: "that we avoid errors in our system of policy respecting Great Britain."[54] Moreover, on examination, nearly all of these acts stemmed from Washington's determination to assert sole constitutional responsibility for *communicating* with foreign nations. For example, he based his decision to withhold information about the Jay Treaty from the House not on unanchored principles of executive privilege, but on the House's constitutional exclusion from the treaty process.[55] He took military action only once without express congressional authorization, and even then, Congress arguably endorsed his decision through subsequent acts.[56]

Washington's most controversial foreign-policy decision was the Neutrality Proclamation of 1793. Yet that proclamation, a response to Citizen Genêt's efforts to draw the United States into France's war with Great Britain, received overwhelming congressional support.[57] Equally important in gauging the incident's precedential weight as quasi-constitutional custom was the fact that Washington expressly conceded that Congress had the power to change the neutrality policy by legislation.[58] By so saying, he prompted Congress in the following year to pass another framework statute, the Neutrality Act, which remains on the books today. In that law, Congress by statute went beyond what the president had sought to do by proclamation. Engaging all three branches, that early framework statute imposed criminal penalties, enforceable by the courts, on persons within the United States who begin, or provide the means for, a military expedition against any country with which the United States is at peace.[59] The purpose of the law was to prevent individuals from taking actions to disrupt an official foreign policy set by the president and Congress. Thus, "this policy was not a presidential monopoly; it was shared with Congress."[60]

In short, the framework statutes and customary norms established during Washington's presidency worked as substantial de facto amendment of the National Security Constitution. Although the Constitution's drafters had assigned Congress the dominant role in foreign affairs, the president's functional superiority in responding to external events enabled him to quickly seize the preeminent role in the foreign-policy process, while Congress accepted a reactive, consultative role. In practical terms, this switch in roles placed the president in a position to propose, leaving Congress to dispose. But although the president, and not Congress, took the lead, the dominant constitutional notion remained one of separated institutions sharing foreign-policy powers. The framework statutes passed during this early period firmly entrenched Congress, the courts, and the cabinet departments in the foreign-policy-making process. Institutional practice during these years revealed that although Congress generally acquiesced in the president's initiating role, the president took equal pains to keep Congress informed and to secure its approval for his actions in foreign affairs.[61]

Yet even as the events of this period reaffirmed the notion of balanced institutional participation, the counter-principle of unchecked executive discretion began to surface. When Washington issued the Neutrality Proclamation in 1793, his act provoked a heated exchange of letters between Alexander Hamilton (using the pen name "Pacificus") and James Madison (writing under the name "Helvidius"). Hamilton stressed that the primary aim of the new government was to safeguard the national interest, understood largely as national prosperity and national security.

Foreshadowing *Curtiss-Wright*, Hamilton made the first sustained argument for the expansive interpretation of the president's foreign-affairs powers. His *Pacificus* series recited for the first time a broad argument that the president's "executive power" and duty to "take Care that the Laws be faithfully executed" in Article II of the Constitution carried within them the power to unilaterally proclaim neutrality and to prosecute private citizens who violate that proclamation. As one political scientist put it, "Hamilton's case rested upon an interpretation of constitutional powers concerning war and peace which all but excluded the legislative branch of government."[62] But once declared, Hamilton's vision was immediately challenged and not embodied in customary law. Madison responded by defending the Framers' original power-sharing principle, characterizing Hamilton's claim as "no less vicious in theory than it would be dangerous in practice" and nowhere "countenanced . . . by any general arrangements . . . to be found in the constitution."[63]

Significantly, the ensuing presidencies of John Adams, Thomas Jefferson, James Madison, and James Monroe did not fundamentally alter the basic pattern laid down in the Washington years. Admittedly, those presidents took numerous external measures that Congress had not previously authorized. Adams led the country into its first undeclared war, with France; Jefferson effected the Louisiana Purchase and authorized the navy to retaliate against the Barbary pirates; and Madison and Monroe worked aggressively to seize West Florida. But as the definitive study of the period, by Judge Abraham Sofaer (later Legal Adviser to the Reagan and Bush 41 State Departments), established, "[t]he full picture contains very substantial evidence of [presidential] concern for both the legislative and the popular will." Significantly, none of these presidents ever claimed that he possessed inherent constitutional powers as chief executive or commander in chief that lay beyond legislative control. Neither did any renounce the principle of shared power by claiming that he "may use whatever raw power he has—monetary, diplomatic and military—in the national interest."[64]

Proactive congressional management during this period largely reinforced the president's caution. As the nineteenth century began, Congress maintained strict control of the president's power to raise military forces. For example, in contrast to such twentieth-century statutes as the International Emergency Economic Powers Act, which delegated sweeping tools of economic warfare to the president upon his declaration of an emergency, a statute enacted in 1799 imposed strict limits on the size of cavalry and infantry regiments except in the extraordinary event that "war shall break out between the United States and some European prince, potentate, or state, in which case it shall be lawful for the President of the United States, at his discretion, to cause the said regiments . . . to be severally completed to their full establishment."[65] However, in other areas—particularly recognition, the use of special envoys, and other matters related to the conduct of diplomatic relations—Congress almost entirely acquiesced in executive prerogatives established during Washington's presidency. Thus, when the congressman (later chief justice) John Marshall rose on the floor of the House in 1800 to call the president "the sole organ of the nation in its external relations," his remarks were uncontroversial, not because Congress accepted the theory of a broad presidential monopoly over all foreign relations, but because Congress had largely acquiesced in the president's dominance over the far narrower realm of diplomatic communications.[66]

The constitutional requirement of balanced participation did not interfere with the president's freedom to declare guiding principles of foreign policy, as President Monroe did in 1823 when he announced to the world the Monroe Doctrine: his express rejection of European colonialism in the Western Hemisphere. Although Congress neither authorized nor ratified that unilateral declaration, Monroe never asserted that the doctrine carried with it a unilateral presidential right to commit military forces to protect the hemisphere. Indeed, just one year later, the secretary of state, John Quincy Adams, rejected Colombia's attempt to invoke the Monroe Doctrine to obtain U.S. joinder in a defensive alliance, stating that "by the Constitution of the United States, the ultimate decision of this question belongs to the Legislative Department of the Government."[67]

The populist presidency of Andrew Jackson did not fundamentally alter this balance of constitutional authority. In domestic affairs, Jackson was "an exception to the general rule of weak presidents in the nineteenth century. He asserted strong claims, only to see them denied to his successors."[68] But even as his presidency remarkably expanded the president's domestic authorities in foreign affairs, he institutionalized a practice of information sharing with Congress and frequently requested legislative authorization for particular external acts.[69]

The most striking feature of this first era of constitutional history is the extent to which the courts actively participated in the delineation and delimitation of the executive's authority in foreign affairs. In its decision in

Bas v. Tingy in 1800, the Supreme Court unanimously upheld President John Adams's undeclared war with France, relying not on findings of plenary presidential power, but rather on declarations that Congress had intended to authorize limited hostilities by means other than formally declared war.[70] In *Talbot v. Seeman,* decided the following year, a unanimous Court headed by the newly appointed Chief Justice Marshall found that Congress had authorized an American commander's capture of a neutral ship, reasoning that "[t]he whole powers of war being, by the constitution of the United States, vested in congress, the *acts of that body can alone* be resorted to as our guides in this inquiry."[71] Three years later, in *Little v. Barreme,* Marshall reiterated the point, holding that a naval officer who had executed a presidential order during President Adams's undeclared war with France was nevertheless liable to those he had injured in violation of a duly enacted statute. Because "the legislature seem[s] to have prescribed ... the manner in which this law shall be carried into execution," Justice Marshall concluded, the contrary presidential order could not legalize the officer's act.[72] In yet a third Marshall opinion, *Brown v. United States,* the Court invalidated an executive seizure of British property shortly before Congress declared the War of 1812.[73] On the merits, the *Brown* Court again ruled that the executive was powerless to take the challenged action without legislative authorization. In none of these cases did the Court suggest that a legislative effort to regulate the issue in question would unconstitutionally intrude on an exclusive or inherent presidential prerogative. Significantly, the Court also had no difficulty finding any of these four cases justiciable.

Perhaps the most dramatic illustration of the judicial role in foreign affairs during this era was *United States v. Smith,* a New York federal-court case from 1806 whose facts bear an uncanny resemblance to the Reagan era's Iran-contra affair (discussed in chapter 3).[74] The defendant, Colonel Smith, was charged with aiding a Central American rebel in planning an attack and an indigenous revolt against the rulers of Spanish America (now Venezuela). Smith and the rebel later alleged that President Jefferson and Secretary of State Madison had promised covert, but not overt, assistance for this expedition. Relying on these alleged promises, Smith recruited troops for the rebel enterprise and persuaded private sympathizers to contribute funding and transportation. When the rebel expedition failed, Smith was prosecuted in a New York federal court for violating the Neutrality Act of 1794. He defended himself by claiming that the president and cabinet had authorized his acts, and subpoenaed four cabinet secretaries to prove it.

Supreme Court justice William Paterson, sitting on circuit along with a district judge, neither quashed the subpoenas against the cabinet members nor dismissed the case as a nonjusticiable political question or for potentially revealing state secrets. Paterson rejected the claim that the witnesses' "peculiar privilege of office" immunized them from being called to testify. He further refused to dismiss the case either on the ground that Smith was immune from prosecution because he had followed superior orders or on the ground that the Neutrality Act had unconstitutionally invaded the president's prerogatives as commander in chief. When Smith asserted that the president had authorized him to violate the statute, Paterson ruled (as *Little v. Barreme* had earlier done) that "[t]he president of the United States cannot . . . authorize a person to do what the law forbids." The president could not exempt Smith from the Neutrality Act under any claimed constitutional power, because the war-making "power is exclusively vested in congress." Given that Congress and the president had enacted the Neutrality Act to avoid enmeshing the United States in foreign conflict, "[w]hoever violates the law becomes liable to its penalties."[75]

It is unclear how many of the rulings in *Smith* would be decided the same way by a federal court today.[76] But the crucial point is that even during America's infancy, the time of its greatest national insecurity, foreign affairs were not treated as exempt from the ordinary constitutional system of checks and balances. On the contrary, the Framers designed the checks-and-balances scheme to apply *principally* in the realm of foreign affairs. The three branches agreed that even governmental decisions regarding covert actions should be conducted through the scheme of balanced institutional participation mandated by the National Security Constitution—under presidential management, but subject to the checks provided by congressional legislation and judicial review. Congress could and did legislate in ways that imposed meaningful constraints on executive authority in foreign affairs. And courts reviewed executive conduct on the merits—undeterred by alleged barriers of executive privilege, nonjusticiability, superior orders, state secrets, or inherent presidential power—to determine whether such conduct was consistent with duly enacted legislation and the overriding constitutional plan.

By the close of this first historical era, the new nation had moved beyond the task of protecting itself from the outside world toward the affirmative goal of "consolidating the continent."[77] After Madison and Monroe completed the annexation of Florida, Presidents Tyler and Polk embarked on a frantic period of territorial conquest. During his presidency, Polk alone expanded the national territory by nearly 50 percent. President Polk dispatched troops to Mexico in 1845 and misrepresented evidence to Congress to provoke a declaration of war the following year. By midcentury, the executive branch was increasingly provoking external conflict, claiming an independent war-making capacity and restricting the supply of information to Congress.[78] As Professor Henry Cox notes, rather than protesting, "Congress assented retroactively to unilateral executive actions undertaken without its knowledge or consent, so long as the activities themselves were successful and did not involve fundamental abrogation of constitutional principle."[79]

During those years, the courts made fewer forays into the area, and their rulings grew increasingly deferential to executive prerogative. In *Durand v. Hollins,* for example, an American naval commander bombarded a Nicaraguan town to retaliate against an attack by local citizens on an American consul. When an injured American citizen sued the commander, Supreme Court justice Samuel Nelson stated that whether the president had a duty to protect American citizens in Nicaragua "belonged to the executive to determine; and his decision is final and conclusive." Thus, neither the president nor his authorized agent was held civilly responsible.[80] By 1861, the implications were clear: one era of American expansion had concluded, and another would soon begin—and with it, new and powerful pressures to bend and amend the National Security Constitution.

Uneasy Adolescence: America's Rise to Dominant Regional Power

Even before the outbreak of the Civil War, the United States had become an economic giant, but with relatively underdeveloped military resources. In the 1850s, the country was preoccupied with its domestic problems and its foreign-policy agenda was largely consumed by relations with its neighbors in Cuba and Central America.[81] Abraham Lincoln assumed the presidency as a critic of executive adventurism in foreign affairs, having opined in 1848 that Polk's military actions toward Mexico rivaled "the most oppressive of all Kingly oppressions" that the Framers had sought to suppress.[82] Nevertheless, Lincoln's own presidency became marked by well-chronicled usurpations of constitutional authority: suspension of the writ of habeas corpus; refusal to convene Congress; enlargement of the armed forces beyond congressionally authorized limits; large expenditures without congressional appropriation or authorization; and the blockading of Southern ports without a congressional declaration of war.[83] Lincoln invoked both the power of the commander in chief and his duty to "take Care that the Laws be faithfully Executed" to deal with the ongoing domestic rebellion. In the *Prize Cases,* the Supreme Court narrowly sustained Lincoln's Southern blockade. Although the cases were decided by a 5-to-4 vote, the Court's opinion evinced a growing judicial receptivity toward expansive claims of executive power. As noteworthy as the Court's holdings on the merits—that President Lincoln had inherent legal authority to suppress armed insurrection and that Congress had ratified his blockade by subsequent acts—was the Court's hint that the president's decisions could be considered political questions that the Court ought not review.[84]

But as activist as Lincoln's wartime presidency was, it did not amend the National Security Constitution. Lincoln never acted against the insurrectionist Southern states by invoking the president's foreign-affairs powers; instead, he expansively employed his domestic statutory and constitutional powers. Congress had passed statutes in both 1795 and 1807 authorizing the president to call out the militia and to use national military forces to suppress internal insurrection against the government of the United States (which Donald Trump cited two centuries later to justify deploying U.S. troops to contain domestic protesters).[85] Furthermore, Article II granted Lincoln the constitutional authority to take care that those laws be faithfully executed.[86] Although successive presidents liberally employed their powers as commanders in chief against rebels, Native Americans, pirates, brigands, and slave traders, they did not generally invoke those powers to initiate or make war against sovereign states without congressional approval and over congressional objection.[87] Lincoln's weak successors, Andrew Johnson and Ulysses S. Grant, were too beset by impeachment and incompetence, respectively, to continue exercising expanded presidential powers. And for the rest of the century, Congress responded to Lincoln's activism by reasserting itself against the relatively passive presidents who followed him into office.[88]

Much of this congressional reaction came on the domestic front, as the Reconstruction Congress battled with post–Civil War presidents over issues of removal, nominations, use of appropriations riders, and the president's use of the veto. Invariably, some of those domestic battles spilled over into the realm of foreign affairs. Yet, once again, this era did not generate new customary norms that fundamentally altered the National Security Constitution, but because the *president* refused to acquiesce in congressional assertiveness. In 1867, Congress passed two framework statutes, the Command of the Army Act and the Tenure of Office Act, which were designed to protect military and civilian officials from presidential removal without Senate approval. The impeachment indictment of Andrew Johnson later charged that he had removed his secretary of war in defiance of the latter act. Yet despite this threat, Johnson continued to assert his exclusive constitutional prerogative to remove subordinates, an intransigence that led to a weakening of the Tenure of Office Act by amendment in 1869 and its ultimate repeal eighteen years later.[89]

Similarly, in 1867, congressional hostility toward Secretary of State William H. Seward's acquisition of Alaska triggered a House resolution opposing future purchases of territory, which placed a damper on expansionist presidential plans. But although subsequent presidents did not annex any additional contiguous lands for more than a generation, they continued, notwithstanding the resolution, to make efforts to obtain land and bases in the Pacific, the Caribbean, Central America, and Greenland.[90] In 1869, the Senate rebuffed President Grant by refusing to advise and consent to his treaty permitting de facto annexation of Santo Domingo. But even then, Grant refused to withdraw the naval force he had previously ordered to implement the "inchoate treaty," and Senate resolutions condemning Grant's military actions failed.[91]

Thereafter, interbranch struggle shifted from the area of war making to treaty making, as the Senate refused to ratify any important treaty outside the immigration context for nearly thirty years.[92] Writing in 1885, Woodrow Wilson attacked this trend as illustrating the "treaty-*marring* power of the Senate." Wilson's famous book, *Congressional Government,* went on to decry the pattern of the preceding two decades, describing, in Walter Lippmann's words, "what happens when the President is weak and helpless . . . [and] how power and responsibility disintegrate when the members of Congress . . . are predominant."[93]

By the end of the nineteenth century, the effective institutional balance of power in foreign affairs had shifted far in Congress's favor. But international pressures were already forcing a transformation of American foreign relations that spurred the pendulum's return swing.

Although the Civil War had temporarily transformed the United States into a military nation, after the war extensive demobilization occurred. Low-wage

immigrant labor, the creation of an intercontinental rail system, and new in-
flows of foreign capital all enabled America to use its vast natural resources for
soaring economic growth. Yet as American economic production grew, domestic markets became glutted, leading to new American economic interest
in burgeoning markets in East Asia, Latin America, and Africa.[94] As American industrial power grew and extended to markets outside the Western
Hemisphere, naval officers and shipbuilders formed a lobby to demand modern naval power to protect global trading routes. Domestic interest groups
began urging the president to pursue a more activist diplomacy, and public
concern developed that congressional intransigence would interfere with the
swift conclusion of desired alliances.[95]

Driven in part by this private desire for markets, executive officials in the
1890s adopted interventionist measures in Brazil and Chile and clashed
with Great Britain over Venezuela's boundaries, actions that aroused little or
no congressional protest. By 1896, the United States had undeniably established itself as the dominant hemispheric power. Simultaneously, between
1870 and 1890, the United States fought a string of internal wars against
Native Americans: "the last step needed to unify and consolidate the United
States before Americans could go abroad to become the superpower of the
twentieth century," according to Walter LaFeber.[96]

As the president demonstrated his functional superiority to Congress in
responding to the twin trends of outward expansion and internal consolidation, these events served over time to replenish his store of power vis-à-vis
Congress. Thus, Professor Cox, summarizing the era, concluded that claims
of presidential impotence during this period had been overstated: "Each
branch found the necessary tools to strike a healthy balance of legislative and
executive powers. . . . [E]ach branch increasingly recognized that actions critical to national security and well-being should not be taken by either without
at least a well informed reaction from the other."[97]

In the era's closing years, however, administration supporters in Congress
began to reassert Hamilton's vision of unchecked executive discretion as a
means of reviving what they viewed as diminished presidential power. To
defeat statutory attempts to limit presidential executive authority over the
armed forces, they contended that the president's constitutional duty to execute the laws carried with it an inherent authority to use physical power to
protect the "peace of the United States."[98]

In 1890, the Supreme Court threw some support to this view with expansively worded dicta in *In re Neagle,* which addressed the fact-specific question whether the president had inherent constitutional power to protect federal judges.[99] Neagle, a United States marshal, had shot and killed the assailant of Supreme Court justice Stephen Field while acting as Field's bodyguard. But en route to predictably ordering Neagle's relief from state custody, the Court held that the president had inherent constitutional power to authorize the protection of federal judges, thereby validating Neagle's acts and allowing him to invoke the protection of the federal habeas corpus statute. In sweeping language, Justice Samuel Miller declared that the president's inherent constitutional authority to execute the laws encompassed not only the enforcement of acts of Congress or treaties of the United States according to their express terms, but also "rights, duties and obligations growing out of the Constitution itself, *our international relations,* and all the protection implied by the nature of the government under the Constitution."[100] Within five years, the Supreme Court had upheld President Grover Cleveland's use of this inherent-power rationale to enjoin the Pullman strike for the public good, even without congressional authorization.[101] Less than a century later, President Jimmy Carter would be citing *Neagle,* along with *Durand v. Hollins,* as "clearly establish[ing]" the president's "inherent" and "constitutional power to use armed forces to rescue Americans illegally detained abroad" in Iran, without ever consulting Congress.[102]

Heady Adulthood: America as World Power

With the dawn of the twentieth century, a new generation of strong leaders triggered both a resurgence of presidential power and America's increased participation in the global balance of power. The revival began in 1898 with the Spanish-American War and accelerated through Theodore Roosevelt's administration to Woodrow Wilson's administration and World War I. In the Spanish-American War, "Americans first committed themselves to a major role in the international politics of the Far East, first found themselves policing the affairs of the Caribbean, and first fought men of a different color in an Asian guerilla war."[103] With the quick victory of the United States came control over Cuba and the acquisitions of Puerto Rico and the Philippines, which elevated the United States to the status of an imperial power. Blocked by the Senate in his effort to annex Hawaii through an Article II treaty requiring a two-thirds vote in the Senate, President William McKinley accomplished the annexation by joint resolution supported by majorities in each house. Without consulting Congress, McKinley also implemented Secretary of State John Hay's open-door policy and dispatched troops to China as part of a "police action" to help put down the Boxer Rebellion. Although Congress encouraged the Spanish hostilities, the president largely excluded the legislature from the Philippines and China initiatives.[104]

Theodore Roosevelt, America's youngest and perhaps most aggressive president, sought to insert the United States into the balance of power in European affairs among Britain, France, and Germany. As he later acknowledged, Roosevelt denied "that what was imperatively necessary for the Nation could not be done by the President unless he could find some specific authorization to do it." Instead, he offered a "stewardship theory," seemingly drawn from Hamilton's views in the *Pacificus* letters and the Court's decision in *Neagle:* "that the executive power was limited only by specific restrictions and prohibitions appearing in the Constitution or imposed by the Congress under its Constitutional powers." As Roosevelt explained, "[m]y view was that every executive officer . . . was a steward of the people."[105]

Roosevelt's stewardship theory left open the question of what "specific restrictions" imposed by the Constitution or Congress might be placed on a president's powers in foreign affairs. But during his presidency, a compliant Congress and Court did little to test the limits of Roosevelt's theory.[106] Roosevelt intervened in Cuba and Santo Domingo, built the Panama Canal (in the process terminating a treaty with Great Britain), and sent America's fleet around the world over Congress's express threat to withhold funds. Roosevelt cast himself in the role of international peacemaker, winning a Nobel Prize for his mediation of the Russo-Japanese War and chairing the Algeciras conference to discuss France's future relationship with Morocco, neither of which bore any direct relation to American interests.[107] Finally, Roosevelt put executive agreements to unprecedented new uses. In addition to an accord with Santo Domingo asserting U.S. control over its customhouses (1904), he concluded three deals with Japan: the secret Taft-Katsura Agreement of 1905, which approved Japan's military protectorate of Korea; the Gentlemen's Agreement of 1907 limiting Japanese immigration to the United States; and the Root-Takahira Agreement (1908), which entrenched the status quo in East Asia. Of these, only the Gentlemen's Agreement was concluded with prior congressional authorization, and Roosevelt effected the Santo Domingo accord after the Senate had declined ratification of a similar treaty.[108]

For all of Roosevelt's efforts, in 1909 the United States still stood on the edges of the "great power" system.[109] Roosevelt's successor, William Howard Taft, took a far narrower view of the presidency. In words reminiscent of Madison's in the Pacificus-Helvidius debate, Taft called Roosevelt's willingness to "ascrib[e] an undefined residuum of power to the President ... an unsafe doctrine [that] ... might lead under emergencies to results of an arbitrary character, doing irremediable injustice to private right." Most telling, Taft, a future Yale law professor and Supreme Court chief justice, went on to declare that the

> true view of the Executive functions is ... that the President can exercise no power which cannot be fairly and reasonably traced to some specific grant of power or justly implied and included within such express grant as proper and necessary to its exercise. Such specific grant must be either in the Federal Constitution or in an act of Congress passed in pursuance thereof. *There is no undefined residuum of power which he can exercise because it seems to him to be in the public interest.*[110]

In accordance with this view, Taft substantially contracted unilateral foreign-policy initiatives, largely confining his "dollar diplomacy" to modest moves toward China and Latin America.[111]

Long before becoming president, Woodrow Wilson had espoused a different, far more executive-centric view: "When foreign affairs play a prominent part in the politics and policy of a nation, its Executive must of necessity be its guide: must utter every initial judgment, take every first step of action, supply the information upon which it is to act, suggest and in large measure control its conduct."[112] Inspired by his desire to "make the world safe for democracy," Wilson "became the greatest military interventionist in U.S. history[,] ... order[ing] troops into Russia and half a dozen Latin American upheavals," including Mexico, Haiti, Santo Domingo, and Cuba.[113] Because Wilson conceived of the presidency as a form of prime ministership, he generally sought congressional approval for his acts. But he did not hesitate to commit troops first and obtain approval later, as he did in 1914 during the U.S. occupation of the city of Veracruz, Mexico (the so-called Tampico affair).

After Congress declared war against Germany in 1917, Wilson announced his Fourteen Points to Congress and dispatched an expedition to Siberia under his commander-in-chief power, virtually without consulting Congress.[114]

Wars have proved to be a powerful engine for the growth of presidential power, and World War I was no exception. But once again, the president's activism failed to permanently imprint principles of presidential unilateralism on the National Security Constitution. As the war ended, a period of forceful congressional reaction set in, culminating in Wilson's repeated failure to win two-thirds approval in the Senate for the Treaty of Versailles, which established the League of Nations. Unlike President McKinley, who named three senators as members of the peace commission that negotiated the end of the Spanish-American War, Wilson took no senators with him to the Paris Peace Conference to negotiate the Versailles Treaty, a unilateralist decision that undermined his later efforts to rally sufficient congressional support to implement his plan. Moreover, Senate procedures allowed the Senate Foreign Relations Committee to adopt crippling reservations to the treaty by majority vote. Senate procedures also gave the committee's chairman, Henry Cabot Lodge, unusual power to undercut the treaty, which kept the United States in a legal state of war until 1921.[115] Much the same fate befell Wilson's attempt to win advice and consent to ratification of the charter of the Permanent Court of International Justice.[116]

During the interwar years, which straddled the Great Depression and the stumbling presidencies of Warren Harding, Calvin Coolidge, and Herbert Hoover, congressional government strongly reasserted itself. Wary of reliving Wilson's fate, the new Republican presidents prioritized an international economic diplomacy that focused less on negotiating treaties that would be subject to Senate approval than on securing arrangements with private banks that would rebuild a war-torn Europe. Congress took the lead in freeing the Philippines, passing one bill to do so over Hoover's veto, again expressing strong isolationist sentiments, which led to a series of neutrality statutes in the mid- to late 1930s.[117]

As in the post–Civil War years, the first decades of the twentieth century thus marked a modulation, but not a fundamental transformation, of the basic premises of the National Security Constitution. By executive practice, the president increasingly dominated foreign-affairs decision-making, but Congress's acquiescence in that trend was neither unequivocal nor permanent. Although Presidents Theodore Roosevelt and Wilson offered expansive views of their foreign-affairs authority, their successors did not accept those views uncritically either as constitutional orthodoxy or as guides to action. Congress and the courts continued to defer to presidential judgments, particularly when the president deemed swift military action necessary. But as John Hart Ely summarized, such decisions were

> subject always to the core command underlying the constitutional accommodation . . . that he come to Congress for approval as soon as possible and terminate military action in the event such approval is not forthcoming. . . . [T]his constitutional understanding was quite consistently honored from the framing until 1950. And when certain Presidents did play fast and loose with congressional prerogatives . . . they obscured or covered up the actual facts, pleading public fealty to the constitutional need for congressional authorization of military action. *It is therefore difficult to cite the occasional nonconforming presidential actions of this period in support of some adverse possession-type theory that they had gradually altered the constitutional plan.*[118]

Although Congress generally supported presidential activism during the early part of this period, it did not blindly acquiesce in those initiatives. Toward the end of the era, Congress fully exercised its power-sharing role, particularly in the realm of treaty ratification. Although the president resorted with increasing frequency to executive agreements over treaties, the vast majority were agreements that Congress approved by legislation or treaty, not agreements concluded under the president's sole constitutional authority.[119] Admittedly, in what lawyers call *obiter dicta* (general statements unnecessary to the decision of particular cases), judges occasionally flirted with notions that challenges to certain executive acts were nonjusticiable or that such acts could be sustained under inherent, unenumerated presidential power. But the Supreme Court neither declared a broad political-question doctrine in foreign affairs nor recognized a pervasive, inherent "executive power" in the key holding of any case. Indeed, although the Supreme Court had previously deferred when the president and Congress acted together in wartime—treating domestic wartime legislation that permitted Prohibition, press censorship, and the suppression of radicals as largely exempt from judicial review—the Court reversed that trend from 1919 to 1924, reasserting the principle that "the Constitution applies even to action taken in the name of war."[120]

In sum, by 1933, neither institutional practice, nor legislative act, nor judicial decision had fundamentally altered the shape of the National Security Constitution. The constitutional principle of balanced institutional participation continued to provide the president with considerable flexibility to act as the prime expositor and initiator of foreign-policy decisions. The constraining power that that principle gave the courts and Congress enabled them to adjudicate and legislate to redress presidential overreaching. Although the other branches had acquiesced sufficiently in presidential initiatives to establish the president's preeminent role in foreign affairs, none of the three branches had yet made what Charles Black called "[t]he one fundamental error . . . of supposing that the modern expansion of presidential power is based on the Constitution by itself, and is hence inaccessible as a matter of law to congressional correction."[121] But that was about to change, as the *Curtiss-Wright* Court launched a newly expansive theory of presidential power.

Mature Dominance: Curtiss-Wright and America as World Hegemon

Bruce Ackerman has spoken of 1937 as an American "constitutional moment," when the New Deal legitimated the activist state and fundamentally altered America's constitutional politics.[122] Yet the same era also redefined the constitutional politics of American foreign affairs. For it was during Franklin Delano Roosevelt's four terms in office that the president became the most prominent leader of the free world, not just America. As much as any other juridical event, *United States v. Curtiss-Wright Export Corp.*, a Supreme Court decision issued in 1936, helped consolidate Roosevelt's transformation of the president's authority in foreign affairs.[123] In *Curtiss-Wright*, private parties challenged the president's right, pursuant to a joint resolution of Congress, to prohibit arms sales to belligerents in Latin America. Writing for the Court, Justice Sutherland not only upheld the executive act, but also announced a most sweeping theory to support the president's unenumerated constitutional authority to conduct foreign affairs.

Justice Sutherland began with a historical examination of the origins of the foreign-affairs powers. Echoing Theodore Roosevelt, Justice Sutherland suggested that the "investment of the federal government with the powers of external sovereignty did not depend upon the affirmative grants of the Constitution. The powers to declare and wage war, to conclude peace, to make treaties, to maintain diplomatic relations with other sovereignties, if they had never been mentioned in the Constitution, would have vested in the federal government as necessary concomitants of nationality."[124] Quoting from John Marshall's speech to the House of Representatives in 1800, he went on to declare that this "extraconstitutional" power was vested entirely in the president.

> Not only, as we have shown, is the federal power over external affairs in origin and essential character different from that over internal affairs, but *participation in the exercise of the power is significantly limited.* In this vast external realm, with its important, complicated, delicate and manifold problems, *the President alone* has the power to speak or listen as a representative of the nation. . . .
>
> [W]e are here dealing not alone with an authority vested in the President by an exertion of legislative power, but with such an authority plus *the very delicate, plenary and exclusive power of the President as the sole organ of the federal government in the field of international relations—a power which does not require as a basis for its exercise an act of Congress,* but which, of course, like every other governmental power, must be exercised in subordination to the applicable provisions of the Constitution.[125]

In the years since the Court's decision, *Curtiss-Wright* has received appropriately withering criticism.[126] As the decision's numerous critics have recognized, Sutherland's key language was dicta, for Congress had passed a joint resolution that expressly authorized the president to take the challenged action.[127] These commentators have further demolished the historical accuracy of Justice Sutherland's extraconstitutional theory of paramount unenumerated presidential power in foreign affairs.[128] Carefully read, the opinion contains important words of limitation. Justice Sutherland's statement that "the President alone has the power to *speak or listen* as a representative of the nation" could be read as recognizing only the well-established exclusive presidential power to communicate and negotiate diplomatically, not a novel executive power to conclude agreements, on behalf of the United States. Similarly, his conclusion that the president's "sole organ" power "must be exercised in subordination to the applicable provisions of the Constitution" would suggest that the president's power does not override congressional powers granted by the Constitution or individual rights recognized in the Bill of Rights.[129]

Notwithstanding these obvious defects, later presidents have sought to treat *Curtiss-Wright* as what Ackerman would call an "amendment-analogue"—an effective *judicial* amendment of Article II of the Constitution to add to the powers enumerated there an indeterminate reservoir of executive authority in foreign affairs.[130] Among government attorneys, Justice Sutherland's lavish description of the president's powers is so often quoted that it has become known as the "'*Curtiss-Wright*, so I'm right' cite"—a statement of deference to the president so sweeping as to be worthy of frequent citation in any government foreign-affairs brief.[131]

I defer until part 2 a fuller description of the impact that *Curtiss-Wright* has had on the courts in recent foreign-affairs cases. But for present purposes, the significant point is that *Curtiss-Wright* painted a dramatically different vision of the National Security Constitution from that which had prevailed since the founding of the Republic. As elaborated by the Framers and construed through the first three eras of American foreign policy, the National Security Constitution envisioned a limited realm of exclusive presidential power in foreign affairs. This exclusive realm embraced the president's textually enumerated powers and "sole organ" power as John Marshall originally meant the term: namely, mastery of diplomatic communications with the outside world. Outside that realm of exclusive presidential authority, most decisions in foreign affairs would occur in a sphere of concurrent authority, under presidential management, but subject to congressional consultation and oversight and judicial review. Within that sphere of concurrent authority, the courts would closely examine congressional enactments to determine whether they permitted the president to undertake particular actions.

Curtiss-Wright, by contrast, posited that the entire field of foreign affairs fell under the president's inherent authority. While accepting the notion that the president should manage foreign policy—a tradition that had begun with Washington—the *Curtiss-Wright* opinion rejected the attendant condition of congressional consultation and participation. As one critic put it, Justice Sutherland's theory that the president "possesses a secret reservoir of unaccountable power" that flows from external sovereignty and not the Constitution represented "the furthest departure from the theory that [the] United States is a constitutionally limited democracy."[132] Indeed, if the president actually possessed such extensive extraconstitutional powers, it is unclear why his actions in foreign affairs should ever be subject to the consent of the governed.

Significantly, notwithstanding its expansive reading of executive authority, nothing in *Curtiss-Wright* itself suggested that executive actions in foreign affairs should be immune from judicial review. On the contrary, in *Curtiss-Wright,* Justice Sutherland reviewed the president's action and upheld it on the merits. Yet, as elaborated in chapter 4, over time the *Curtiss-Wright* vision would mysteriously come to embrace another notion previously suggested, but never broadly adopted, by the Supreme Court—that once courts have determined that foreign affairs are at stake, they should dismiss challenges to executive acts as political, not legal, questions.[133]

Curtiss-Wright was not the Court's only foray into foreign affairs during these years. The following term, in *United States v. Belmont,* Justice Sutherland upheld the constitutionality of the Litvinov Assignment, an executive agreement made by President Roosevelt in 1933, as part of the recognition of the Soviet Union.[134] Five years later, in *United States v. Pink,* the Court confirmed that holding, invoking *Curtiss-Wright* to declare that "[p]ower to remove such obstacles to full recognition . . . certainly is a modest implied power of the President who is the 'sole organ of the federal government in the field of international relations.'"[135]

When *Curtiss-Wright* and *Belmont* were decided, the president's power vis-à-vis Congress remained at a relatively low ebb. Yet combined with executive practice during the years leading to World War II, the decisions provided the constitutional rationale for another truly dramatic expansion of presidential power. Three years after *Belmont,* President Roosevelt concluded the notorious destroyers-for-bases deal with Great Britain, relying on a legal opinion by then attorney general Robert Jackson that invoked the president's commander-in-chief power, the president's *Curtiss-Wright* authority, and two statutes of dubious relevance.[136] In early 1941, Roosevelt employed executive agreements to send American troops to Greenland and Iceland, declared a state of unlimited national emergency, and ordered the navy to convoy American ships and to shoot Nazi U-boats on sight, all without express congressional consent.[137] After Pearl Harbor, Congress's declaration of war authorized FDR to lead the nation into an all-out war. That conflict did not conclude until after President Harry Truman had twice dropped the atomic bomb without congressional consultation and in reliance on his commander-in-chief power.

Looking back, it seems clear that Roosevelt's activist presidency triggered an extrovert phase in American foreign policy, which was marked by wars, military spending, treaty making, and international summitry.[138] During this era, which began before Pearl Harbor and ended with Vietnam, the United States assumed the unchallenged status as the world's "hegemon," its great power. During these years, the president emerged as America's leader, and America emerged as the world's leader. When World War II ended, America acted through its president to erect the entire postwar multilateral political and economic order. The era was marked by institutions and constitutions: the creation of international institutions governed by written constitutions. On the political side, to prevent the resurgence of war, the United Nations and its regional and functional agencies were created. On the economic side, to prevent future depressions, the United States helped establish the so-called Bretton Woods system, which provided the World Bank to stimulate international development and reconstruction, the International Monetary Fund to monitor the balance of payments, and the General Agreement on Tariffs and Trade (GATT) to manage international trade.[139] The president spurred an optimistic vision of world public order with an orgy of treaty making, which secured America's participation in international organizations and led us into the brave new world of multilateralism.

Yet even as the United States was seeking to transform the world, FDR was transforming the domestic structure of the presidency. Although, as we have seen, presidential power had sporadically expanded since the beginning of the Republic, FDR's presidency marked a change not simply of degree but of kind. FDR became our first "plebiscitary president," a term coined by Professor Theodore Lowi to describe a presidency in which "[t]he lines of responsibility run direct to the White House, where the president is personally responsible and accountable for the performance of government."[140] Roosevelt personalized his role in world leadership through summitry and personalized his role as America's leader through frequent press conferences and fireside chats.[141]

Equally important, FDR did not simply centralize national power unto himself, he institutionalized it into a bureaucracy that would wield executive power. When he took office, his personal staff consisted of only a press secretary and a few special assistants. But following the recommendations of the President's Committee on Administrative Management, Roosevelt created the Executive Office of the President, which would eventually embrace the Council of Economic Advisers (established in 1946); the National Security Council (established in 1947); the Special Trade Representative (established in 1963, then renamed the U.S. Trade Representative); the Council on Environmental Quality (established in 1969); the Office of Management and Budget (established in 1970 as the successor to the Bureau of the Budget); and the White House Office of Science and Technology Policy (established in 1976).[142] During Theodore Roosevelt's administration, the White House staff consisted of only 35 people; by the time Ronald Reagan left office, the White House staff had swelled to 3,366.[143]

In short, internal and external forces worked synergistically. Growing American hegemony and growing presidential power fed on one another. Together, they created strong pressures for the transformation of the National Security Constitution along the lines suggested in *Curtiss-Wright*. As America emerged from World War II, the question became how the courts and Congress would respond to the president's broad assertions of authority in foreign affairs. The initial answer from the courts was resounding deference. In *Chicago & Southern Air Lines, Inc. v. Waterman Steamship Corp.*, the Supreme Court refused to examine the basis for presidential orders under the Civil Aeronautics Act granting or denying licenses for foreign air routes. The Court announced broad dicta declaring that "the very nature of executive decisions as to foreign policy is *political, not judicial*. . . . They are decisions of a kind for which the Judiciary has neither aptitude, facilities nor responsibility and which has long been held to belong in the domain of political power *not subject to judicial intrusion or inquiry*."[144] But ruling against presidential prerogative in *Youngstown* only four years later, Justice Jackson, *Waterman*'s author, acknowledged that *Waterman* did not validate a presidential exercise of inherent constitutional powers, only a "wide definition of presidential powers under *statutory authorization*."[145] Nevertheless, like *Curtiss-Wright*, *Waterman*'s sweeping language has fostered a judicial-deference argument that has been urged upon federal judges ever since.[146]

Congress's reaction to the newly powerful presidency proved more complex than the Court's. In the initial postwar years, it appeared that Congress might recreate the Treaty of Versailles experience and reject multilateralism, thereby reprising the isolationist role that the Senate had played during the interwar years. At first, the Senate followed that pattern by refusing to ratify the Charter of the International Trade Organization, the Genocide Convention, or other conventions on human rights. In 1946, the Senate also imposed the notorious Connally Reservation on the United States' acceptance of the compulsory jurisdiction of the International Court of Justice.[147] Despite initial protests, the president ultimately abided by all of these congressional actions. But in other foreign-policy areas, Congress soon demonstrated that it could work together with the president to promote multilateral cooperation. Between 1947 and 1950, for example, while Arthur Vandenberg chaired the Senate Foreign Relations Committee, the Senate gave its advice and consent to the Charter of the United Nations, the Marshall Plan, the NATO treaty, and to the United States' entry into a host of other international organizations and security arrangements.[148]

The growing need for the United States to engage the world sparked legislative innovation, particularly in the field of international trade. America's experience with framework statutes in the trade field demonstrated that a domestic structure of balanced institutional participation could coexist with an international regime of multilateralism, even if both were dominated by the American president. The emerging archetype of executive-legislative cooperation during this period became the body of framework statutes enacted to govern U.S. participation in the international trading system.[149] This domestic legal regime revealed that executive practice and judicial decisions were not the only means available to amend the National Security Constitution. *Framework legislation* offered an alternative way to maintain executive flexibility in foreign affairs, while reducing congressional-executive conflict by promoting interbranch dialogue through enforced statutory consultation. Before 1930, Congress had largely refused to delegate responsibility for international trade to the president, instead insisting upon setting every tariff level itself. Because congressional logrolling and horse trading had contributed to every individual duty rate, the infamous Smoot-Hawley Tariff Act of 1930 had set the most protectionist tariff levels in U.S. history, triggering a series of retaliatory measures by U.S. trading partners that fueled the worldwide depression.[150] To avoid similar fiascoes, Congress enacted the Reciprocal Trade Agreements Act of 1934, which delegated broad advance authority to the president to negotiate and conclude reciprocal tariff-cutting agreements with foreign nations without further congressional reference. To preserve its check on presidential initiative, however, Congress legislated a "sunset" provision that terminated the president's negotiating authority after three years.[151]

The regime of the Reciprocal Trade Agreements Act proved successful both as a domestic political compromise and as a way to promote U.S. adherence to evolving norms and structures of international-trade law. Successive Congresses extended the president's authority under the act nine times between 1937 and 1958, each time extracting a variety of concessions from the president as the price of renewed negotiating authority. Meanwhile, the broad advance delegation permitted the president to negotiate and accept thirty-two bilateral agreements between 1935 and 1945 and to consummate the postwar entry of the United States into multilateral trade management through the acceptance of the General Agreement on Tariffs and Trade (GATT).[152]

But by 1947, the primary focus of American foreign policy was not on international trade, but on the perception of rising Soviet expansionism. In July of that year, under the nom de plume "X," George Kennan published a famous article in *Foreign Affairs,* contending that the only way to check Soviet expansion was by "containing" it through "the adroit and vigilant application of counter-force at a series of constantly shifting geographical and political points." Although later questioned by some, including Kennan himself, the policy of containment "quickly became the quasi-official statement of American foreign policy."[153]

The question then arose whether the existing structure of foreign-policy decision-making was adequate to implement that containment policy. After substantial deliberations, the legislative and executive branches produced a new framework statute designed to reshape the national security decision-making structure for the postwar years. Because that law was designed to unify the president's capacity to make and coordinate national security decisions, it was known informally as the "Unification Act."[154] Its formal name was the National Security Act of 1947, and, together with Justice Jackson's concurring opinion in *Youngstown* (1952), that framework statute would help shape the National Security Constitution into its modern form.

From National Security Act to *Youngstown*

BY THE END OF WORLD WAR II, the *Curtiss-Wright* vision of presidential unilateralism offered a significant constitutional challenge to the Framers' original vision of separated institutions sharing foreign-policy powers. But as our post–World War II national security system developed, complementary policy and constitutional visions of national security decision-making reaffirmed the core constitutional assumption of shared foreign-policy power. That postwar framework included a policy vision, embodied in the National Security Act of 1947 and the statutes that have built upon it, and a constitutional vision guided by those statutes and Justice Robert Jackson's seminal opinion in *Youngstown Sheet & Tube Co. v. Sawyer* (the *Steel Seizure* case) in 1952.[1]

The National Security System: The Policy Vision

In 1947, America emerged from World War II only to find itself enmeshed in a Cold War, the ideological and historical dimensions of which have been thoroughly examined.[2] The Truman Doctrine, the Marshall Plan, military alliances such as NATO, SEATO, CENTO, and ANZUS, the Inter-American Defense System, and the Mutual Defense Assistance Program all formed interrelated substantive planks of President Harry Truman's foreign-policy response. At the same time, however, World War II had revealed the need for greater centralized management of both military and intelligence services.[3]

The central innovation of the National Security Act was its recognition that the management of this complex structure of agencies and alliances required a unified national security system, centered in the executive branch. The act therefore sought to place American governmental decisions regarding war making, intelligence, covert operations, military sales, and military aid under the executive's unified and coordinated control. As originally structured by the act, the national security system had two key features. First, the system was designed to be personally managed by a strong plebiscitary president with the support of a bureaucratic institutional presidency. Second, the system was intended to operate not just in times of declared war, but also during a "false peace." Thus, the system was meant to be flexible enough not just to meet the pressing demands of the Cold War, but to cope with new and unknown challenges that were yet to come: for example, overt undeclared wars, such as the Korean conflict, and overt creeping wars, such as the Vietnam War, that start and build before anyone is fully aware.

In much the same way as the Administrative Procedure Act (1946) imposed the concept of due process of administration on the domestic actions of executive officials, the National Security Act formalized the principle of accountable, centralized presidential *management* of the external acts of national security officials.[4] The system envisioned that overt wars would be managed by military officials subject to civilians under the control of the president and that covert intelligence gathering would be carried out by agencies directed by the president, as advised by the National Security Council (NSC).

The statutory requirement that overt wars be conducted by military officials under civilian control simply reaffirmed one of the charter principles of the National Security Constitution. The National Security Act converted the Department of War into the Department of Defense, comprising all three military departments, and integrated all military services under the command of the Joint Chiefs of Staff. Even though the Constitution already implicitly obliges the president to preserve civilian control of the military, the act expressly subjected the Joint Chiefs to "unified direction under civilian control of the Secretary of Defense," who was in turn answerable to the civilian president.[5] In subsequent statutes, Congress forcefully legalized the principle of civilian control in prophylactic statutory requirements that the secretary of defense and the secretary's deputies be individuals "appointed from civilian life" who had not served as active military officers for at least ten years.[6]

Similarly, the statute effected a long-awaited institutionalization and consolidation of the intelligence-gathering function in the Central Intelligence Agency (CIA), directed by the president and advised by the NSC. Government spying had gone on sporadically since at least the days of Nathan Hale. By the 1880s, the armed services had established permanent intelligence units. Shortly before Pearl Harbor, President Roosevelt established the first central office to coordinate government intelligence, which he later named the Office of Strategic Services (OSS). But when World War II ended, that office was disbanded, only to be revived by executive order less than a year later.[7] By formally creating the CIA in the National Security Act, Congress finally gave its imprimatur to executive intelligence gathering, which had already been proceeding systematically for some sixty years. At the same time, however, Congress sought to preserve a crucial distance between the CIA and the military by mandating that the director and deputy director could not both simultaneously be military officers and that those officials could not, during their CIA service, operate within the military chain of command.[8]

What seems far less certain, however, is whether in 1947 Congress intended to authorize either the CIA or the president to exercise a covert *war-making* function as opposed to simply gathering intelligence. As an umbrella term, *covert operations* encompasses both covert military and paramilitary action (that is, clandestine warfare), as well as a range of nonviolent conduct that is distinct from simple intelligence gathering, such as spreading propaganda, political action (for example, bribing foreign officials), and economic covert action (for example, initiating foreign labor strikes).[9] In 1947 Congress charged the CIA principally with collecting, evaluating, disseminating, and advising on intelligence, but also gave the agency the ambiguous authority "to perform *such other functions and duties related to intelligence affecting the national security* as the National Security Council may from time to time direct."[10] A drafter of the National Security Act testified that, by this language, Congress intended the CIA to perform covert operations, but expected the operations "to be restricted in scope and purpose."[11] Yet Congress never formally acknowledged that the CIA engaged in activities other than intelligence gathering until 1974, when Congress enacted the Hughes-Ryan amendment.[12] Shortly thereafter, the Church Committee concluded that in 1947, Congress had not expressly intended to authorize covert action at all.[13]

Some executive-branch attorneys have responded by claiming that express congressional authorization of covert actions is superfluous because such activities fall within the scope of the president's exclusive constitutional authority and can be taken without legislative approval, pursuant to his independent directive.[14] But that claim mistakenly views intelligence gathering and covert activities as constitutionally identical. The president may have exclusive constitutional powers to gather intelligence through the diplomatic process, but many covert activities also fall within Congress's constitutional power over foreign commerce. When covert action takes military or paramilitary forms, it constitutes war making and would thus fall within the realm of the two branches' shared war-making powers.[15] Assuming arguendo that the National Security Act permitted the CIA to conduct covert operations at all, there seems little doubt that Congress expected such operations to be tightly controlled by the president and the NSC.

The act's most glaring omission was its failure to mention the role of either Congress or the courts in foreign-policy decision-making. Congress had partially addressed the issue the previous year by passing the Legislative Reorganization Act of 1946. That law restructured and reduced the number of standing congressional committees, directed them to exercise "continuous watchfulness" over executive agencies, and authorized committees to seek expert advice from appointed, professional committee staff and the Congressional Research Service. These organizational changes were necessary, a joint congressional committee argued, to counter "manifest growing tendencies in recent times toward the shift of policymaking power to the Executive, partly because of the comparative lack of effective instrumentalities and the less adequate facilities of the legislative branch." Thus, in James Sundquist's words, "[t]he picture was clear; the president would prepare the unified and coordinated [national security] policy; if legislation or appropriations were required, the Congress would review and respond."[16]

In the years after Vietnam, Congress enacted a wave of foreign-affairs framework statutes that dramatically reasserted its right to participate in nearly all arenas of foreign-policy decision-making.[17] Those framework statutes expressly allocated policymaking responsibility not just vertically within the executive branch, but also horizontally between the president and Congress. By imposing on the president a range of notification, reporting, and certification requirements, those statutes sought to ensure that the president and Congress would jointly agree upon broad foreign-policy objectives. Furthermore, the statutes envisioned that the president, with the aid of the NSC, would coordinate a full internal debate within the executive branch and secure a consensus among the major foreign-policy bureaucracies (particularly the Departments of State and Defense). Thereafter, the president would propose particular policy initiatives to Congress to carry out those objectives. Experts outside the executive branch—particularly the congressional committees and their staffs—would then consider and test the wisdom of those initiatives. With committee approval, the relevant executive agencies would then carry them out. The various requirements that the president make written "findings" to trigger authorities in the intelligence laws, the consultation provisions in the statutes on war making, emergency economic powers, arms sales, and military aid, and the omnipresent legislative-veto provisions were all designed to ensure that policy execution would be subject to congressional consultation, oversight, and a meaningful opportunity for objection. While a particular policy initiative was being executed, the president was expected to seek political support for it from both Congress and the public, giving each access to all the information necessary to evaluate the wisdom and legality of that initiative.

Youngstown's Constitutional Vision

Justice Jackson's famous concurring opinion in *Youngstown* (the *Steel Seizure* case), issued five years after the passage of the National Security Act, complemented this policy vision of the national security system by articulating a parallel constitutional vision of how Congress, the courts, and the executive should interact in the foreign-policy process. In subsequent decisions, the full Court went on to embrace Jackson's concurrence as the lodestar of its separation-of-powers jurisprudence. In the *Nixon Tapes* case (1974), "the unanimous Court essentially embraced Mr. Justice Jackson's view," and seven years later, in *Dames & Moore v. Regan* (the Iranian hostages case), the entire Court united behind the assertion that Jackson's *Youngstown* opinion "brings together as much combination of analysis and common sense as there is in this area."[18] But the opinion's enduring value derives less from its precedential weight than from the unusual clarity with which it articulates the concept of balanced institutional participation that underlies the National Security Constitution.

By the time *Youngstown* reached the Court, the Cold War had markedly intensified, with both the national and the international mood reflecting the change. President Truman had actively implemented the containment policy in Greece and Turkey and, after the fall of Czechoslovakia in 1948, had authorized the CIA to conduct covert operations in Italy.[19] The national mood had become one of perpetual crisis.[20] In that atmosphere, it grew increasingly difficult for the president to reconcile basic constitutional principles with George Kennan's recommendation favoring "adroit and vigilant application of counter-force" wherever communism should rear its head. Walter Lippmann wondered, in his biting response to Kennan's "X" article, "is [the president] going to ask Congress for a blank check on the Treasury and for a blank authorization to use the armed forces? Not if the American constitutional system is to be maintained."[21] In an influential book published in 1948 entitled *Constitutional Dictatorship,* Clinton Rossiter countered that the Cold War had made constitutional revision necessary: "[I]n time of crisis, a democratic, constitutional government must be temporarily altered to whatever degree is necessary to overcome the peril. . . . [The government] is going to be powerful or we are going to be obliterated."[22]

By the time North Korea invaded South Korea in June 1950, world politics had become firmly bipolarized and nearly zero-sum. Almost by definition, any world event that engaged the national interest of either the Soviet Union or the United States automatically engaged the opposite interest of the other. Thus, although Secretary of State Dean Acheson had pointedly excluded Korea from America's "line of defense" in the Pacific only five months earlier, President Truman responded to the Korean invasion by committing American troops to combat without consulting Congress; he relied not on a declaration of war, but on his constitutional powers as president and commander in chief.[23] Senator Robert Taft declared that Truman "had no authority whatever to commit troops to Korea without consulting Congress," and one member of Congress even introduced a funding restriction to terminate the conflict. But Congress could generate no binding resolution to challenge the president's act, and a major undeclared war then ensued for three years, claiming the lives of millions of Koreans and some thirty-six thousand American soldiers.[24]

By April 1952, tens of thousands of U.S. troops had been killed in Korea, General Douglas MacArthur had been fired, and no end to the Korean "police action" was in sight. Fearing that a nationwide steel strike would stop the flow of war matériel to Korea, President Truman ordered his commerce secretary to seize the steel mills. Once again, Truman cited his inherent powers as president and commander in chief. When the steel companies' challenge to that action arrived at the Supreme Court, the president was strongly favored to win. As one contemporaneous commentator suggested, the president could cite in his favor language from federal-court decisions ranging from the *Prize Cases* to *Curtiss-Wright* that suggested that he possessed inherent constitutional authority to protect the "peace of the United States" from external threat.[25] As William Rehnquist, who was Justice Jackson's law clerk, later recalled, all nine of the sitting justices had been appointed by either FDR or Truman and "had swept aside past decisions that had limited the power of government, whether federal or state, to regulate economic and social affairs."[26] Indeed, the most likely candidate to support the president's decision appeared to be Justice Jackson himself. Not only had Jackson written the pro-executive *Waterman* decision just four years earlier, but as FDR's attorney general, he had written numerous opinions upholding presidential actions, including the controversial opinion from 1940 that supported the destroyers-for-bases deal with Great Britain.[27]

Despite the president's advantages, the *Youngstown* Court rejected his constitutional claims by a clear 6-to-3 vote, invalidating the seizure as an unconstitutional usurpation of legislative authority. After the fact, some have sought to minimize *Youngstown*'s relevance for foreign affairs by characterizing it as a domestic labor dispute.[28] Yet even assuming that foreign and domestic affairs could ever be so neatly compartmentalized, each of the participating justices plainly recognized the external implications of the decision. After a lengthy catalogue of "our responsibilities in the world community" and past exercises of presidential authority, Chief Justice Fred Vinson's dissent recalled Theodore Roosevelt's stewardship theory of presidential power. Vinson concluded that a "practical construction of the 'Take Care' clause . . . [as] adopted by th[e] Court in *In re Neagle, In re Debs* and other cases" should authorize Truman's acts.[29] Justice Hugo Black's opinion for the Court squarely rejected that view, declining to adopt as a holding the "inherent power" dicta of the cases relied upon by both the dissent and the president. The Court also declined to sustain the president's actions under Article II's grant of "executive power" or the president's commander-in-chief power, or any other constitutional claim of exclusive executive authority.[30] Instead, in a strangely formalistic opinion, Black held that Congress had the exclusive constitutional prerogative to engage in lawmaking and that the president's acts—which were not authorized by any congressional statute— transgressed that prerogative.[31] The *Youngstown* majority opinion reduced to an unpersuasive labeling exercise that has given the opinion limited long-term resonance in the decades since.

But each of the separate concurrences in the case took a more flexible, organic view of separation of powers, reaffirming the basic understandings underlying the National Security Constitution. Justice William O. Douglas, in particular, denied that either the press of international events or the president's institutional superiority to respond could justify a deviation from the constitutional principle of shared power. "All executive power . . . has the outward appearance of efficiency," Douglas acknowledged, "[b]ut . . . '[t]he doctrine of the separation of powers was adopted . . . not to promote efficiency but to preclude the exercise of arbitrary power.'" Similarly, Justice Felix Frankfurter read the Constitution's structural principle of separation of powers as a limit on the breadth of the president's unenumerated powers. He thought the answer rested less in judicial precedents than in dissection of past customary practice. After examining past instances of similar executive practice, he found that they did "not add up, either in number, scope, duration or contemporaneous legal justification[;] . . . [n]or do they come to us sanctioned by long-continued acquiescence of Congress" sufficient to accord them "decisive weight" as quasi-constitutional custom.[32]

It was Justice Jackson's now-classic concurring opinion, however, that most cogently expressed the core notion of the National Security Constitution—a flexible theory of decision-making premised on *separated institutions sharing powers:* "Presidential powers are not fixed but fluctuate, depending upon their disjunction or conjunction with those of Congress." Using congressional action as a guide, he went on to establish the three-tiered hierarchy of presidential actions that all first-year law students must commit to memory:

   1. When the President acts pursuant to an express or implied authorization of Congress, his authority is at its maximum, for it includes all that he possesses in his own right plus all that Congress can delegate. . . .
   2. When the President acts in absence of either a congressional grant or denial of authority, he can only rely upon his own independent powers, but

there is a zone of twilight in which he and Congress may have concurrent authority, or in which its distribution is uncertain. . . .

3. When the President takes measures incompatible with the express or implied will of Congress, his power is at its lowest ebb, for then he can rely only upon his own constitutional powers minus any constitutional powers of Congress over the matter.[33]

This framework is neither perfect nor complete and, chapter 11 argues, is now particularly obsolete with respect to the making of international agreements.[34] But read against the constitutional history and practice described in the previous chapter, Jackson's *Youngstown* concurrence squarely rejected the *Curtiss-Wright* vision and powerfully reaffirmed the National Security Constitution as it had evolved to that point. Read together with the Constitution's text and subsequent framework statutes, Jackson's opinion specifies enduring principles regarding Congress's role in the foreign-policy decision-making process and the role of the courts, and also sets out normative principles to guide foreign-policy decision-making within the executive branch.

Justice Jackson's opinion first defined Congress's role in national security decision-making by specifying what powers Congress does not have. In essence, Jackson's three-part schema recognized that the Constitution grants the president "conclusive and preclusive" power in certain limited areas. Although Jackson did not attempt to precisely define the scope of the president's sole constitutional authorities, he included within them the president's textually enumerated powers, as construed with "the scope and elasticity afforded by what seem to be reasonable, practical implications instead of the rigidity dictated by a doctrinaire textualism."[35] Outside of these narrow pockets of exclusive presidential authority, he suggested, Congress must have an opportunity to participate in the setting of broad foreign-policy objectives, or else those objectives cannot genuinely be called policies of the *United States*. Indeed, Jackson's tripartite categorization—which turns crucially on the degree of congressional endorsement of executive acts—would become meaningless if the president could constitutionally deny Congress the opportunity to approve or disapprove presidential actions taken within the scope of concurrent congressional-executive authority.

When the president and Congress jointly agree on broad foreign-policy objectives in a particular area and Congress has by statute expressly authorized the president to proceed, presidential initiatives taken to implement those broader objectives fall within Jackson's category one: "supported by the strongest of presumptions and the widest latitude of judicial interpretation, and the burden of persuasion would rest heavily upon any who might attack it." But when Congress has not specifically authorized a particular initiative, the case drops down to Jackson's category two, where the dispositive questions become whether the initiative has occurred within a constitutional zone of concurrent congressional-executive authority and, if so, whether Congress and the president have in fact agreed about the broad policy objectives that the initiative was designed to serve. Here, Jackson suggested, both constitutional text and congressional and executive practice are relevant. For in cases in which the president and Congress share "concurrent authority, or in which its distribution is uncertain[,] . . . congressional inertia, indifference or quiescence may sometimes, at least as a practical matter, enable, if not invite, measures on independent presidential responsibility."[36]

When Congress has expressly or impliedly objected to the president's actions, presidential authority is at its "lowest ebb." In most cases of this type, Jackson's category three would require presidents to abstain from acting (as the Court ordered in *Youngstown*) and to either modify their policy initiative or seek additional congressional support for their proposal. The exception would be the rare case in which the Constitution expressly grants the president exclusive constitutional power to execute a foreign-policy initiative without congressional approval, as, for example, in exercising the president's plenary power to unilaterally recognize a foreign government.[37] In such a case, Justice Jackson suggested, a court could "sustain exclusive presidential control . . . [but] only by disabling the Congress from acting upon the subject."[38]

Having defined Congress's role in the national security process, Jackson's opinion defined a pivotal role for the courts as arbiters within the process. When others challenge the president's sweeping claims of exclusive control over matters of foreign affairs, Jackson suggested, the courts should not abstain, but "must . . . scrutinize [those claims] with caution, for what is at stake is the *equilibrium* established by our constitutional system." Furthermore, he intimated, courts should not invoke constitutional bases to uphold presidential actions when express statutory authorization is present. Thus, Jackson read *Curtiss-Wright* not as a constitutional decision raising the broad "question of the President's power to act without congressional authorization," but rather, as a case of statutory interpretation raising the narrower "question of his right to act under and in accord with an Act of Congress."

Finally, even while recognizing the dramatic accretion of presidential power in the postwar era and the peculiar need for flexibility, secrecy, and dispatch in foreign affairs, Justice Jackson rejected the president's "[l]oose and irresponsible use of adjectives" such as "'[i]nherent' powers, 'implied' powers, 'incidental' powers, 'plenary' powers, 'war' powers and 'emergency' powers."[39] He did not find foreign-policy matters so different from domestic affairs that the courts must necessarily defer whenever presidents invoke their commander-in-chief power, their general executive power, or their inherent emergency powers in foreign affairs.[40] Thus, far from excluding the judiciary from the national security process, as the *Curtiss-Wright* vision would have done, Justice Jackson reaffirmed the vital role of the federal courts in maintaining institutional balance within the national security system.[41]

Also noteworthy is Justice Jackson's suggestion of quasi-constitutional principles regarding lines of authority and internal accountability *within* the executive branch: what I will call "internal checks and balances." These principles may be thought to describe a *"due process of foreign policy administration"* parallel to the due process of administration found in the Administrative Procedure Act—namely, rules to constrain the discretion of executive foreign-policy-making officials.

In 1947, Congress designed the National Security Act to consolidate the president's control over the national security apparatus by establishing "a clear and direct line of command."[42] By always speaking in terms of "the president," Jackson's tripartite analysis implicitly assumed that the executive acts being challenged were either the president's own or those carried out in the president's name with the president's clear approval. Under this assumption, an act of an executive official cannot carry the weight of presidential authority unless the president directly controls or approves that act through a clear line of authority. Thus, individuals on the NSC staff could not lawfully invoke the president's constitutional authority to justify their own covert actions unless they could also demonstrate that they were acting under a line of executive supervision that led directly to the president. Nor could the executive defend, as "presidential," decisions that were in fact reached by an unsupervised entity within the executive branch rather than through a genuine process of intra-branch debate.[43]

In the National Security Act, Congress directed the president not only to co-ordinate through the NSC the development and implementation of national-security policy, but also to keep subordinate foreign-policy bureaucracies carefully separate. Coupled with the president's constitutional responsibility to "take Care that the Laws be faithfully executed," that legislative directive im-poses on the president a solemn duty to maintain civilian control of the mili-tary and to establish intra-branch procedures to supervise the foreign-affairs bureaucracies.[44] In addition, subsequent developments in administrative law may be read to bar executive-branch agencies created by Congress from subdel-egating to inappropriate entities their governmental responsibilities for mak-ing or executing foreign policy. Under this reasoning, both the NSC and the CIA act unlawfully when they deviate from those foreign-policy tasks that Con-gress expressly created the agencies to perform. Similarly, the president and his subordinates act unlawfully when they delegate their national security functions to private citizens or governmental entities that were created to oper-ate outside the existing national security apparatus.[45]

Justice Jackson concluded his opinion by adding to these principles of inter-nal accountability a rule of *public* accountability. When the president acts in ac-cordance with authority delegated by Congress, "[t]he public may know the extent and limitations of the powers that can be asserted, and persons affected may be informed from the statute of their rights and duties." This language suggests an obligation of the president to preserve the accountability of execu-tive bureaucracies to Congress and an obligation of transparency: to provide the people and their representatives with at least as much information as is neces-sary to evaluate the wisdom and legality of the president's actions.[46] Far from being onerous, this requirement is critical to the making of sound foreign pol-icy. Eugene Rostow, a strong advocate of executive power, rebutted George Ken-nan's claim that Congress's constitutional role "makes it impossible for the United States to function effectively as a great power" by saying: "Our constitu-tional system for developing and carrying out our foreign policy rightly requires the cooperation of the President and of Congress, *and the full understanding of the people*. . . . [N]o nation, and surely no democratic nation, can carry out a sus-tained policy of any importance, especially one that may involve the catastrophe of war, unless public opinion understands and accepts it."[47]

Simply put, Justice Jackson's *Youngstown* opinion reaffirmed the centrality of "the *equilibrium* established by our constitutional system."[48] Jackson

firmly rejected *Curtiss-Wright* and embraced the principle of balanced institutional participation in foreign affairs that has guided the National Security
Constitution since the Founding. In the years since *Youngstown* was decided,
congressional framework statutes have confirmed Congress's constitutional
right both to participate in the setting of foreign-policy objectives and to receive the information and consultation necessary to make its participation
meaningful. The proliferation in the post-Vietnam era of statutes mandating
some form of reporting and consultation and the high degree of executive
compliance with those mandates buttress the claim that reporting and consultation requirements have now attained quasi-constitutional status. For
example, even when President Richard Nixon vetoed the War Powers Resolution in 1973, he expressly approved the act's consultation requirements as
"consistent with the desire of this Administration for regularized consultations with the Congress," not only with regard to troop commitments, but
"in an even wider range of circumstances." Although subsequent presidents
have not treated these reporting requirements as legally binding as a matter
of institutional practice, they have almost invariably complied with them as
a matter of custom.[49] Similarly, Congress has required the president not just
to report but also to consult, by embedding in the post-Vietnam intelligence
and arms-export-control statutes "presidential finding" requirements that
eliminate the possibility of presidential deniability.[50] An executive branch
that ignores those reporting and finding requirements, as the executive
branch did, for example, during the Iran-contra affair (discussed in chapter
3), violates a quasi-constitutional customary norm of reporting and consultation in foreign affairs.

    In sum, although the Cold War, the National Security Act, and *Youngstown*
all embroidered the National Security Constitution, its core principles remained intact to protect and facilitate the constitutional functioning of the
new national security system. Justice Jackson's *Youngstown* opinion rejected
the *Curtiss-Wright* vision of unrestrained executive discretion in favor of a
normative vision of the policymaking process in which the three branches of
government all play integral roles. In zones of concurrent constitutional authority, the president and Congress must transparently share information
about and jointly agree on the broad foreign-policy objectives of the United
States. The president must then coordinate full internal debate among the
decision-formulating entities of the executive branch in order to propose par-

ticular policy initiatives to Congress to fulfill those broad objectives. When Congress has endorsed particular initiatives, the appropriate decision-executing agencies must execute them in accordance with the law, under direct presidential supervision, and subject to the watchful eyes of Congress, the public, and the courts.

Competing Visions

Curtiss-Wright and *Youngstown* sketched dramatically different visions of the National Security Constitution. But by the mid-1950s, clarity had finally emerged on both a policy and a constitutional framework for the exercise of balanced institutional participation in national security affairs. *Youngstown* reiterated limits on exclusive presidential powers in foreign affairs and specified roles for congressional consultation and judicial review in distributing concurrent constitutional authority. It imposed a constitutional vision that fostered both dialogue and consensus between Congress and the president about substantive foreign-policy ends. In *Youngstown* itself, both Justice Black's opinion for the Court and Justice Jackson's concurrence read *Curtiss-Wright* as resting not on inherent presidential power, but on whether Congress had authorized the executive action under challenge.[51] Both opinions suggested that, even in foreign affairs, executive decisions based on legislative consent will better express the consent of the governed than those generated by the executive bureaucracy alone.

During the Warren Court years, an era that drew new attention to judicial protection of individual rights, the *Youngstown* theory took powerful hold. The administrations of Dwight D. Eisenhower and John F. Kennedy provoked relatively few conflicts with Congress in foreign affairs. President Eisenhower generally acted on the philosophy "that the Constitution assumes that our two branches of government should get along together," as illustrated by his decision to seek authorizing joint resolutions before he dispatched troops to the then Formosa (now Taiwan) Straits in 1955 and to the Middle East in 1957. Although President Kennedy clashed with Congress over international-trade matters, he conducted his blockade of Cuba during the Cuban missile crisis with the blessing of a congressional resolution.[52]

Most of the foreign-affairs cases that came before the Court during this era involved not interbranch conflicts but allegations that government conduct had infringed on individual rights. In such cases, the Warren Court carefully scrutinized statutes cited by the executive not only for signs of legislative consent to the president's actions, but also to determine whether Congress and the president acting together had encroached upon protected constitutional rights.[53] Justice Douglas most clearly articulated this judicial method in *Kent v. Dulles,* declaring that judges must find a clear statutory statement that Congress has authorized the executive act in question before deciding whether to condone an executive infringement on an individual's constitutional right to travel.[54] Fourteen years earlier, in *Ex parte Endo,* Justice Douglas had presaged this "clear-statement" principle, saying that judges "must assume, when asked to find implied powers in a grant of legislative or executive authority, that the law makers intended to place no greater restraint on the citizen than was clearly and unmistakably indicated by the language used."[55]

This clear-statement principle underscores the importance of legislative consent to executive acts in foreign affairs, particularly when individual rights are at stake. As Professors Harold Edgar and Benno Schmidt recognized, the clear-statement principle demands that rules regulating individual rights "reflect the political consent and public participation embodied in legislation, rather than the self-interested bureaucratic discretion that is likely to be the character of executive action."[56] But the rest of the Cold War, and the Vietnam era that followed, disrupted this vision with resurgent unilateralism inspired by *Curtiss-Wright.*

3

From Vietnam to the Iran-Contra Affair

DESPITE THE VISION OF SHARED POWER set forth in *Youngstown* and the National Security Act, the 1960s and 1970s unveiled a consistent pattern of executive circumvention of legislative constraint in foreign affairs that emerged unmistakably during the Vietnam War. A survey of the congressional-executive conflicts that spanned the U.S. foreign-policy horizon during those years reveals the inexorable rise of *Curtiss-Wright*'s counter-vision of unchecked executive discretion. These conflicts traverse the landscape of war making, treaty affairs, emergency economic powers, arms sales, military aid, and covert operations.

War Powers

The pattern of executive circumvention emerged most clearly in the realm of the war powers. In August 1964, American ships conducting covert operations were attacked by North Vietnamese torpedo boats in the Tonkin Gulf. America's response, allegedly in self-defense, was followed by another reported attack only days later, which inspired President Lyndon Johnson to order the first aerial bombing of bases in North Vietnam. President Johnson then asked Congress for the Tonkin Gulf Resolution, a joint resolution of support that he subsequently construed as broad congressional authorization to escalate the Vietnam War.[1] By 1973, that foreign-policy nightmare had triggered the passage, over President Richard Nixon's veto, of the War Powers Resolution, a statute imposing consultation and reporting requirements as well as a sixty-day limit on the president's commitment of troops overseas without express congressional authorization.[2]

Congress passed the War Powers Resolution to prevent future Vietnams— undeclared creeping wars that start and build before Congress or the public are fully aware. Yet by three crucial omissions, Congress markedly undercut the resolution's effectiveness. First and most obviously, as Charles Black noted, it is a peculiar war-powers act indeed that defined how many months U.S. troops may stay abroad but "utterly refus[ed] even to begin the task of defining the conditions under which the president should not commit troops for even ten minutes—the really crucial matter."[3] Second, the resolution regulated only "United States Armed Forces" and thus did not reach alleg- edly private activities or covert wars in which intelligence operatives acting under civilian supervision conduct paramilitary activities against foreign governments.[4] Third, Congress said nothing about short-term military strikes that could be completed well within the resolution's sixty-day limit. Congress's silence on these critical points freed the executive branch to treat that statutory limit as de facto congressional permission to commit troops abroad for a period of up to sixty days.

Thus, by its own terms, the resolution failed to address new types of mili- tary action that soon came to dominate the war-making landscape. In 1975, President Gerald Ford sent troops briefly to Vietnam to evacuate American citizens and to Cambodia to free the *Mayaguez,* an American merchant ship. President Jimmy Carter attempted an abortive military rescue of American hostages in Iran in April 1980. President Ronald Reagan dispatched forces to Grenada in October 1983, authorized a "surgical" strike against Libya in April 1986, and ordered attacks on Iranian oil platforms in the Persian Gulf in October 1987 and April 1988. President George H. W. Bush sent U.S. troops to El Salvador, the Philippines, and Panama, in each case avoiding full compliance with the resolution's consultation and reporting requirements.[5]

Ironically, the resolution arguably failed to prevent even the type of creep- ing escalation that it was expressly enacted to control. For example, President Reagan sent U.S. troops to Lebanon in August 1982 without prior consulta- tion with Congress and kept them there until February 1984. When Con- gress finally sought to force the removal of those troops after more than two hundred combat fatalities, the president successfully bargained for a joint resolution extending the deadline of the War Powers Resolution from sixty days to eighteen months, without ever articulating the policy that the U.S. military presence was meant to serve.[6]

Similarly, in the 1980s, American ships continued to patrol the Persian Gulf, convoying reflagged Kuwaiti tankers. Fearing Iranian attacks on U.S. ships, which might have prompted President Reagan to ask Congress for another joint resolution of support, the Senate passed a bill in the fall of 1987 that imposed a new sixty-day reporting requirement on the president and contemplated a future resolution setting durational limits on the commitment of troops in the Persian Gulf without express congressional authorization.[7] The House took no action on this de facto proposal to reenact the War Powers Resolution because more than one hundred of its members had filed suit in federal court to force the president to acknowledge the applicability of the existing War Powers Resolution to his Persian Gulf activities. But when the 100th Congress concluded, no new law had been passed, the congressional suit had been dismissed as a nonjusticiable political question, and an American naval ship acting out of perceived self-defense had shot down an Iranian jetliner in the Gulf.[8]

Long after the War Powers Resolution first became law, scholars and legislators continued to debate whether Congress should enact a new variant of it to enforce the resolution's original purpose.[9] Years of congressional-executive struggle over the war powers had only brought us from the Tonkin Gulf to the Persian Gulf. And by the 2020s, the loopholes in the resolution's text had gutted its constraining effect on the use of emerging modern methods of twenty-first-century warfare: drones, artificial intelligence, cyber conflict, and short-term operations by Special Forces units and private military contractors.

The Treaty Process

By the 1960s and 1970s, a similar historical pattern of executive circumvention of legislative constraint had emerged in the field of agreement making. During the years before the Vietnam War, the president asserted increasing control over one discrete phase of the treaty process, namely, treaty making. But in the post-Vietnam years, the president extended that control to treaty breaking and what might be thought of as "treaty bending," a category that encompasses both treaty modification and reinterpretation.[10]

Just as the years leading up to Vietnam witnessed dramatic presidential domination of the process of agreement making, the years since Vietnam have marked a parallel era of executive aggrandizement of the coordinate phases of agreement bending and breaking.

The Constitution speaks about international agreements only in sparing terms. Article I bars the states from entering treaties or "Agreement[s] or Compact[s] with . . . foreign Power[s]"; Article II authorizes the president to "make Treaties, provided two thirds of the Senators present concur"; and Article VI declares that "all Treaties made . . . under the Authority of the United States, shall be the Supreme Law of the Land."[11] While vague, the historical record suggests that the Framers drafted these provisions first, to ensure that the federal treaty power would prevail over state actions, and second, to require that within the federal government both the president and the Senate would participate before a treaty was concluded.[12] Although the Constitutional Convention considered at various points granting either the president or the Senate "the sole and exclusive power to . . . make treaties," Hamilton and Madison urged the adoption of Article II's current language, reasoning, in Hamilton's words, "that the joint possession of the [treaty] power, by the President and Senate, would afford a greater prospect of security than the separate possession of it by either of them."[13] Notably, neither the constitutional text nor constitutional history speaks specifically to treaty breaking or bending. But a close reading of John Jay's *Federalist* No. 64 reveals that the Framers intended the constitutional design to reflect a prudential as well as a legal judgment—that a wise treaty process would give the president the lead in all treaty matters but would require him to act in consultation with the Senate.[14]

During the Constitution's first century and a half, controversy swirled mainly around the supremacy of federal treaties and executive agreements over state law, questions the Supreme Court did not conclusively settle until the early 1940s.[15] Thereafter, battles between the branches of the federal government for dominance over treaty making took center stage. President Franklin Roosevelt quickly followed his famous destroyers-for-bases deal with Great Britain in 1940—a "transaction . . . sustained under statutes which hardly bear the construction placed upon them"—with two executive agreements in 1941 that sent American troops to Greenland and Iceland without express congressional consent.[16] By the end of World War II, advocates of presidential power were urging broad use of the executive agreement instead of the treaty to pave the way for the United States' entry into the United Nations and Bretton Woods multilateral treaty systems.[17]

By the mid-1960s, the president had firmly asserted his prerogative to conclude international accords through means that avoided prior congressional consent. During the nineteenth century, the United States had entered approximately one executive agreement and three treaties per year, a number that rose to twelve agreements and twelve treaties annually by 1933. But even though the annual average of treaties thereafter remained at twelve, the number of agreements rose to nearly 183 per year.[18] With few exceptions, however, Congress acquiesced in that trend. Congress generally authorized the president's pre-Vietnam agreements, whether by Senate ratification, prior or subsequent statutory approval, or the appropriation of funds to implement the country's participation in international organizations. Moreover, the Supreme Court largely validated the president's use of the executive agreement, enabling postwar presidents to lead the United States into the brave new era of multilateralism.[19]

During the Vietnam War, however, fears that the president would employ secret executive agreements to make binding commitments about overseas bases and troop deployment multiplied congressional objections to solo presidential agreement making. In 1969, the Senate adopted Senator J. William Fulbright's National Commitments Resolution, which expressed the sense of the Senate that promises to assist foreign states with American armed forces or financial resources could be made only by treaty or act of Congress.[20] Soon thereafter, Congress considered stringent legislation calling for the legislative review of all executive agreements.[21] When the president opposed that legislation, Congress enacted a less restrictive version, the Case-Zablocki Act, which required the president to notify Congress of any recently concluded international agreement.[22]

Until 2021, the Case-Zablocki Act constituted a high-water mark in congressional efforts to reassert control over the agreement-making process.[23] In the years following Vietnam, successive administrations developed a host of subtle and innovative methods to create or amend international obligations without congressional review. Presidents Nixon and Reagan employed the technique of "nonagreement agreements"—characterizing some executive agreements as "voluntary export restraints"—to avoid notifying Congress of trade accords on steel, automobiles, machine tools, and semiconductors.[24] To accept some, but not all, provisions of unratified treaties, Presidents Carter and Reagan selectively complied with those treaties by issuing "parallel unilateral policy declarations." In 1977, President Carter unilaterally declared that the United States would comply with the expired SALT I (strategic arms limitation talks) treaty so long as the Soviet Union did the same.[25] The Reagan administration similarly complied with the warhead limits in the unratified SALT II treaty until the administration chose to "breach" them in December 1986.[26] President Reagan also refused to sign the United Nations Convention on the Law of the Sea but announced that the United States would comply with nearly all of the convention's provisions as a matter of customary international law.[27] This technique, again used by President Reagan with regard to the Protocol II Additional to the Geneva Conventions of 1949, enabled the president to "get the international law we want without having to undergo the 'give' part of the 'give-and-take' of the [international] legislative process."[28]

The most creative post-Vietnam technique of executive treaty making proved to be the method of "reinterpretation." Under this technique the president sought to give an existing agreement a reading different from that accepted by the Senate when it gave its original advice and consent, thereby effectively amending the treaty without congressional approval. The best-known case of treaty reinterpretation transpired in October 1985, when the Reagan administration sought to unilaterally reinterpret the Anti-Ballistic Missile (ABM) Treaty from 1972, broadening its terms to accommodate executive planning for the Strategic Defense Initiative (SDI). The controversy over reinterpretation of the ABM Treaty sparked the sharpest conflict between the two political branches over treaty matters since the Vietnam era. Congress issued a threefold response to the president's actions, declaring that no funds from the 1988–1989 fiscal year defense appropriation could be used for new SDI tests; reporting a Senate resolution reaffirming the Senate's understanding of the so-called narrow interpretation of the treaty; and attaching to the Senate's resolution of ratification of the Intermediate-Range Nuclear Forces (INF) Treaty the "Byrd amendment," which declared that the United States shall not adopt a treaty interpretation that differs *from the common* understanding of that treaty shared by the executive and the Senate at the time of Senate advice and consent.[29] President Reagan responded by ratifying the INF Treaty and by challenging the Byrd amendment's constitutionality, stating that he could not "accept any diminution claimed to be effected by such a condition in the constitutional powers and responsibilities of the Presidency."[30]

During the years leading to Vietnam, presidents avoided securing Congress's prior consent in order to enhance international mechanisms of multilateral cooperation. The post-Vietnam years, by contrast, have witnessed the reverse trend: America's flight from international organizations and multilateral cooperation. If the early postwar years were America's era of treaty making, then the post-Vietnam years began an era of treaty bending and breaking that reached its zenith in the Trump administration. Once again, the president led the way, but now by unilaterally breaking or modifying preexisting international commitments, usually without consulting either Congress or the country's treaty partners.

But presidential efforts to bend and break existing treaties without Congress's prior consent differed from the presidential agreement making in the pre-Vietnam era in another crucial respect. Although the Supreme Court generally validated the expansion of the president's agreement-making authority in the pre-Vietnam years, the Court has not similarly endorsed the president's more recent techniques of treaty bending or breaking on the merits. In its decision in *Goldwater v. Carter* in 1979, the Court summarily dismissed Senator Barry Goldwater's challenge to President Carter's decision to unilaterally terminate a mutual-defense treaty with Taiwan in accordance with its terms. Yet no justice wrote in favor of a general unilateral presidential power of treaty termination, and only one justice voted to uphold the president's treaty-termination decision on the merits. Even that solitary vote rested on the fact that the case involved the recognition of foreign governments, an issue over which the Constitution has been read to grant the president plenary power.[31]

Nevertheless, executive-branch lawyers have gone on to read *Goldwater* to authorize a general unilateral presidential power to terminate any and all international agreements. Since *Goldwater*, if presidents have not liked existing treaties, they have unilaterally terminated the treaties without congressional consent, as President Reagan did, for example, when terminating the country's acceptance of the compulsory jurisdiction of the International Court of Justice (also known as the World Court), the bilateral Treaty of Friendship, Commerce, and Navigation with Nicaragua, and the country's membership in the United Nations Educational, Scientific, and Cultural Organization (UNESCO).[32] When a treaty's terms have required the United States to give six months' notice before terminating the treaty, the president has evaded that restraint by purporting to temporarily "modify" the treaty without congressional consent, as occurred, for example, when President Reagan modified for two years the United States' acceptance of the World Court's compulsory jurisdiction.[33] Whenever the president has proposed to ratify a multilateral treaty without fully subjecting U.S. conduct to international examination, he has used a line-item-veto approach or selective-nullification technique—employed, for example, with regard to both the Genocide Convention and the Convention Against Torture—whereby the president attaches so many conditions to the request for Senate advice and consent that those exceptions have significantly altered the terms of U.S. acceptance.[34]

With some judicial support, the president has asserted a sweeping power "to disregard [rules of customary] international law in service of domestic needs."[35] And the executive branch has adapted its novel method of unilateral reinterpretation to break as well as modify preexisting commitments. For example, the Department of the Navy reinterpreted a treaty with Iceland to the detriment of a U.S. shipper that sought to carry military cargo between the two nations. In enjoining the navy from implementing its reinterpretation, a federal judge announced that "[t]he arrogance of power has seldom been displayed in more telling fashion."[36]

I will defer until chapter 11 a fuller discussion of how U.S. foreign-relations law should address modern issues of agreement making and breaking. Chapter 11 argues for a different way of looking at both agreement making and breaking. It suggests a different way to understand when the president may constitutionally enter an international agreement, one that depends on both the subject matter of the agreement and the degree of congressional approval for it. As that chapter further suggests, when the president seeks to break an agreement, an overbroad "transsubstantive" unilateral presidential termination rule is not and cannot be the law. Instead, chapter 11 suggests application of a constitutional "mirror principle"—which requires the same degree of congressional input for exiting an agreement as was required for initial entry. This more nuanced conceptual framework for both agreement making and breaking better reflects how the current process of congressional acceptance of executive-branch international lawmaking actually works.

Emergency Powers

The vast majority of the foreign-affairs powers that the president exercises daily are not inherent constitutional powers, but rather, powers that Congress has expressly or implicitly delegated to the president by statute. Yet closer examination of the areas of foreign affairs in which Congress has extensively legislated reveals a pattern of executive ascendancy in statutory realms even more striking than the president's continued domination of the constitutional realms of war making and treaty affairs. In particular, in cases short of war, Congress has charged the president with imposing an astonishing array of economic sanctions in the name of exercising "emergency powers."

In the early 1970s, the Vietnam debacle stimulated a powerful congressional reaction against executive dominance in foreign affairs. During those years, dramatic institutional changes substantially transformed the seniority system in the House and altered congressional rules to enhance the independence of subcommittee chairs and the influence of rank-and-file members. The Vietnam- and Watergate-driven congressional election of 1974 brought to power an extraordinarily large number of reformist liberal Democrats. Congress made efforts to close the expertise gap between itself and the executive branch in foreign-policy matters, augmenting its committee staffs with foreign-policy specialists (the so-called S. Res. 4 staffers). And recognizing the institutional imbalance of foreign-affairs expertise with the executive branch, Congress took important first steps to develop a robust in-house research capability in foreign affairs.[37]

During the immediate post-Vietnam years, a rare synergy between these internal institutional reforms and external circumstance drove Congress to enact statute after statute subjecting the president's delegated foreign-affairs powers to stringent procedural constraints. The names of these curative statutes are familiar. In addition to the War Powers Resolution and the Case-Zablocki Act, the list included the International Emergency Economic Powers Act and the National Emergencies Act to govern exercises of emergency economic power; what has become the Arms Export Control Act of 1976 to regulate arms sales; the International Development and Food Assistance Act of 1975 and the Hughes-Ryan amendment to the Foreign Assistance Act to regulate foreign and military aid; the Trade Act of 1974 and the Export Administration Act of 1979 to manage import and export trade; and the Foreign

Intelligence Surveillance Act of 1978 and the Intelligence Oversight Act of 1980 to oversee intelligence activities.[38]

These enactments followed a template that could be called "finding, report, consult, legislative veto." They typically conditioned presidential exercises of delegated authority on executive adherence to elaborate statutory procedures, including factual findings; public declarations; committee-oversight, prior-reporting, and subsequent consultation requirements; and the legislative veto, the congressional control technique of choice in the post-Vietnam era. With few exceptions, however, the president's acceptance of statutory procedural constraints in this generation of statutes unlocked substantial fresh delegations of foreign-affairs authority.[39] By the late 1980s, it had become clear that the executive branch had successfully tapped into many of these broad new authorizations while paying only lip service to the accompanying procedural strictures.

The most glaring example of this trend has been the International Emergency Economic Powers Act (IEEPA).[40] Congress enacted the statute specifically to limit executive abuses of the national emergency powers that the Trading with the Enemy Act (TWEA) had conferred on the president sixty years earlier.[41] That earlier statute had authorized the president to wield an enormous store of delegated power in both wartime and non-wartime situations by simply declaring the existence of a national emergency. But TWEA's subsequent history demonstrated that presidents rarely terminated such emergencies once they had been declared. While Congress was considering IEEPA's enactment in 1977, for example, members were shocked to learn that both President Franklin Roosevelt's declaration of a national banking emergency in 1933 and President Truman's declaration in 1950 in response to the Korean conflict were still in force. As Justice Harry Blackmun later recognized, "TWEA emergency authority operated as a one-way ratchet to enhance greatly the President's discretionary authority over foreign policy. . . . [T]he President retained broad authority of indefinite duration to respond to anything that logically could be related to the general threat of the spread of Communism."[42]

Stung by perceived presidential abuses of its delegated TWEA power, Congress drafted IEEPA specifically to narrow the president's authority in non-wartime situations. The main distinction between IEEPA and TWEA was that the former authorized the president only to freeze, not seize, foreign assets.

Although Congress sought to ensure that the president would have sufficient emergency powers to deal with unforeseen circumstances, it conditioned the president's exercise of emergency powers on prior congressional consultation, subsequent review, and legislative-veto termination provisions.

Yet three successive Supreme Court decisions quickly eviscerated IEEPA's various congressional control devices.[43] In 1981, the Court generously construed IEEPA as authorizing the president to settle the central aspects of the Iranian hostage crisis. Two years later, the Court's sweeping opinion in *INS v. Chadha* invalidated the legislative-veto provision that had allowed Congress to terminate presidentially declared IEEPA emergencies. And in a dubious opinion the following term, the Court weakened IEEPA's statutory requirement that the president declare a national emergency when the Court upheld the president's authority under TWEA's "grandfather clause" to exercise preexisting statutory emergency powers against Cuba without declaring a new national emergency.

Those rulings freed the president to use IEEPA to conduct widespread economic warfare merely by declaring a national emergency with respect to a particular country, as Presidents Carter and Reagan subsequently did with respect to Iran, Libya, Nicaragua, South Africa, and Panama.[44] Moreover, despite the insistence of the House of Representatives that "emergencies are by their nature rare and brief, and are not to be equated with normal, ongoing problems," the president has made and sustained such declarations virtually without regard to whether bona fide "emergencies" have existed.[45] Of the many nations against which the president has imposed IEEPA sanctions since 1979, only a few have posed an "unusual and extraordinary threat" constituting a national "emergency" in the layperson's sense of those terms.[46] Nevertheless, the courts began regularly to rebuff challenges to the president's declarations of emergency under IEEPA on the ground that such determinations constitute nonjusticiable political questions.[47] Thus, like the TWEA national emergencies that preceded it, the Iranian emergency has now continued unterminated for more than four decades.

Perhaps most troubling, the Reagan administration initiated the practice whereby the president would declare national emergencies under IEEPA in response not only to hostile foreign action, but also in response to *Congress's* failure or unwillingness to act in accordance with his will. In 1983 and 1984, the president twice triggered IEEPA to sustain the existing export-control laws and foreign-boycott restrictions after Congress had failed to reauthorize the Export Administration Act.[48] When the House of Representatives rejected covert aid for the Nicaraguan contras in the spring of 1985, the Reagan administration again declared a national emergency. In an action later sustained by the lower federal courts, the president applied IEEPA sanctions against the Sandinistas as a substitute for congressional action, even though the alleged emergency conditions had persisted for many months.[49] Later that year, President Reagan abruptly declared a national emergency and imposed IEEPA sanctions on South Africa in an unsuccessful effort to preempt Congress's eventual enactment of comprehensive anti-apartheid legislation.[50]

By the end of the Reagan administration, executive officials were branding as "draconian" even the statutory requirement that the president declare a national emergency before invoking the delegated IEEPA powers.[51] With the help of the courts, the president had won broad discretion to decide how strictly to comply with IEEPA's procedural requisites. Although avowedly passed to limit the president's discretion, IEEPA, along with the plethora of statutory emergency powers enacted by Congress during the 1980s, had unwittingly enhanced executive power by fostering the "routinization of crisis government."[52] In only one decade, the executive branch had succeeded in extracting from IEEPA the same sweeping delegation of emergency authorities that Congress had expressly sought to remove from the president after Vietnam. As we shall see in later chapters, recent presidents like Joe Biden have come to use this authority to engage in the largest peacetime exercise of sanctions authority in history, wielded against Russia following its invasion of Ukraine in 2022. And prominent constitutional scholars have argued that the president could use IEEPA authorities to go beyond freezing Russian assets to seizing them for the use of the Ukrainian people.[53]

The Iran-Contra Affair

In an episode that became known as the "Iran-contra affair," the Reagan administration brought forth a bold new assertion of executive authority in foreign affairs. Starting in 1981, a team of White House staff members, charged with supporting the covert war in Central America, began illegally selling arms to Iran and diverting the proceeds to the Nicaraguan resistance (the "contras") in an apparent effort to trade arms for seven American hostages detained in Lebanon by Hezbollah. National Security Council staffer Lieutenant Colonel Oliver North confessed to diverting proceeds in 1985 from the Iranian weapon sales to fund the insurgency of the Nicaraguan contras in their struggle against the socialist government of Daniel Ortega.

It was initially unclear which higher-ups, if any, had authorized the transfers, and if they had, under what legal authority. But the report of the congressional committees investigating the matter later revealed that President Reagan had authorized the initial arms sales to Iran and ordered his subordinates to keep the contras together, "body and soul." CIA director William Casey then directed Lieutenant Colonel North to coordinate both sets of activities and endorsed the diversion of the proceeds from the sales into an "off-the-shelf, self-sustaining, stand-alone" covert organization staffed by private citizens and run with private monies. The president authorized the first shipments of arms to Iran in August and September 1985 (which took place through Israeli intermediaries) by "oral" findings that were nowhere authorized by the intelligence statutes. The second shipment in November 1985, which was executed in part by the CIA, was subsequently deemed to be authorized by a novel "retroactive" finding generated by the CIA's general counsel (which the national security adviser, Vice Admiral John Poindexter, later admitted destroying). A third finding, on January 6, 1986, and its amended version eleven days later were admittedly signed by President Reagan—who eventually died with Alzheimer's—but he later claimed that he had never actually read them. These obfuscations clouded the fact that none of these shipments had been authorized in the manner required by law.

Parallels were immediately drawn to Nixon's Watergate, in which a team of White House "plumbers," formed to plug government leaks regarding the Vietnam War, was discovered illegally breaking into Democratic National Headquarters. During both episodes, high-ranking executive officials stretched or disregarded the rule of law. In both cases, funds of unaccountable origin and private agents were used to conduct covert actions directly from the White House. Both incidents ultimately stemmed from executive efforts to sustain a war in a Third World country by bypassing established channels of command.[54] In both cases, congressional committees concluded that the president's staff had been running an illegal secret operation out of the White House, and placed ultimate blame on the president himself.[55] And in both cases, a presidential commission (the Tower commission for the

Iran-contra affair) and a special prosecutor were convened to question the president's staff about their activities, asking what the president knew and when he knew it.

But the two affairs differed in a crucial respect: unlike Watergate, the Iran-contra affair was implemented not simply by a covert operation, but by a *covert foreign policy*. That policy was apparently determined by a private cadre, upon whose decisions neither Congress nor the people had an opportunity to pass judgment. Moreover, the cadre's members thought their actions were legally justified. Expressly invoking *Curtiss-Wright,* they read the Constitution as giving the executive branch unfettered discretion to make national-security decisions and denied that such decisions need be shared with Congress.[56] Thus, whereas the Watergate investigations revolved principally around a factual question—What happened?—the Contragate investigations raised the question central to the National Security Constitution: In foreign affairs, who decides?

One might have expected the latter question to have been closely scrutinized by one or all of the governmental entities created to investigate the affair: the Tower commission, the Iran-contra committees, or the independent counsel Lawrence Walsh.[57] As a special review board created by executive order, the Tower commission had a mandate from the president to recommend changes in *executive policy* regarding the roles and procedures of the NSC staff. As select committees chosen by the House and Senate leadership, the Iran-contra committees were charged by congressional resolution not only to uncover the factual outlines of the affair, but also to recommend *legislative action*. As a special prosecutor appointed by a three-judge court pursuant to a post-Watergate congressional enactment, the independent counsel had a *judicial directive* to investigate individual wrongdoing, bring indictments, and obtain convictions.[58] But this division of labor never occurred, as each of the Iran-contra investigators pursued only its assigned role and avoided grappling with the heart of the constitutional crisis.

Had the investigators placed the Iran-contra affair against the broader historical background reviewed here, they would have recognized that it represented not just a passing historical aberration, but the latest act in a foreign-policy drama that had been playing out since the early 1970s. Indeed, far from being unprecedented, each of the four elements of the Iran-contra tableau—the covert sale of arms to Iran, the diversion of funds to the contras in apparent violation of the funding restrictions known as the "Boland amendments," the "operationalization" of NSC staff, and the abuse of covert operations—repeated historical events that had first occurred during the Nixon era. Viewed against the history of the early 1970s, the Iran-contra affair can best be understood as an extreme, but foreseeable, episode in the continuing post-Vietnam flow of foreign-affairs power from Congress to the executive.

The Arms Sale

The Reagan administration was not the first to sell weapons systems secretly to Iran. In May 1972, President Nixon sold fighter aircraft and associated equipment to the shah of Iran over the opposition of both the State and Defense Departments. Because that sale was primarily for cash on commercial terms, it evaded the legislative controls built into the Mutual Defense Assistance Act of 1949, which authorized the president to sanction government-to-government cash sales to foreign countries without congressional approval.[59]

The Iranian transaction in 1972 marked an important turning point in both the nature and direction of American arms-sale policy. Although massive private American arms sales had occurred during World War I, the American government's modern role as an international arms supplier began with the Lend-Lease Act of 1941. Before 1970, most American governmental arms supplies were directed toward developed nations, principally NATO allies, and included surplus or obsolete, as well as sophisticated, military weapons. Although the Foreign Military Sales Act of 1968 created a formal procedure for cash and credit sales of large quantities of weaponry, it left executive discretion largely unconstrained, freeing the president to use arms sales as an ad hoc tool of foreign policy.[60]

In the early 1970s, supplying modern arms to South Vietnam formed an important component of President Nixon's program to "Vietnamize" the war. The Nixon administration hoped to preempt the need for future direct American troop support to threatened Third World nations by supplying them with arms, with the expectation that those nations would then assume primary responsibility for their own defense.[61] As part of this global plan, in 1972 President Nixon promised the shah of Iran open-ended access to state-of-the-art nonnuclear weapons in the American arsenal in exchange for the shah's commitment to accept the lead role in protecting Western interests in the Persian Gulf. As the former NSC aide Gary Sick recounted, "[i]n the next four years after the Nixon-Kissinger visit, the Shah ordered more than $9 billion worth of the most sophisticated weaponry in the U.S. inventory, and the arms sale program quickly became a scandal."[62]

The public furor over these and later weapons sales to Saudi Arabia and Kuwait stimulated congressional concerns that secret arms sales to Third World nations would unavoidably escalate into more unwanted overseas commitments, such as in Vietnam. Those concerns encouraged Congress to pass, in 1974, new arms-export legislation that required the president to give Congress advance notice of any offer to sell to foreign countries defense articles or services valued at $25 million or more; the legislation further authorized Congress to veto all such sales within twenty calendar days by a concurrent resolution (which is not subject to presidential veto).[63] Congress later incorporated this two-house legislative-veto provision, along with numerous reporting and certification requirements designed to reach commercial sales and third-country transfers of U.S. arms, into the comprehensive International Security Assistance and Arms Export Control Act of 1976. That scheme subjected certain presidentially initiated arms sales to congressional disapproval, but only if a sale both exceeded certain dollar amounts and could not muster majority support in either legislative house.[64]

Although Congress never exercised its legislative veto in the arms-export laws, executive-branch officials conceded that the veto imposed "important discipline on all who administer the system—the State and Defense Departments, the White House and National Security Council staffs, ambassadors in the field, and the manufacturers of defense equipment, as well as foreign military leaders."[65] But the Supreme Court's watershed decision in *INS v. Chadha* in 1983 swept away not only the legislative veto in IEEPA and the War Powers Resolution, but this congressional veto as well.[66] Several years after *Chadha,* Congress amended the arms statute with a much softer "report and wait" provision. That amendment imposed on the president a much looser obligation—to report to Congress about planned arms sales and to wait to see whether Congress would nullify the sale by passing a joint resolution of disapproval (a two-house resolution subject to presidential veto).[67] Yet this option—barring a presidential action essentially by passing a new law that the president could veto—had always been available to Congress. Moreover, executive-branch lawyers successfully embedded in the successor legislation numerous provisions giving the president greater freedom of action if the president found certain proposed transfers to be "in the national security interests of the United States." The revised legislation left ambiguous whether the executive branch could transfer weapons abroad secretly if the transfer occurred as part of an intelligence operation conducted under other laws.[68]

As a result, even a joint resolution of disapproval did not bar the president from openly selling arms abroad, so long as he could veto that resolution and then defeat an override of that veto by securing more than one-third of the votes in either chamber of Congress. Nor was the president clearly barred from selling arms abroad covertly, as long as he could claim to be acting under intelligence, rather than arms-control, laws. This precise scenario materialized in 1985 and 1986, when the Reagan administration covertly sold some $30 million in missiles to Iran. At virtually the same time, the executive branch overtly sold nearly nine times that dollar volume in advanced missiles to Saudi Arabia over the objection of large majorities in both houses of Congress. A joint resolution disapproving the Saudi deal had passed the House by a vote of nearly six to one and the Senate by a vote of more than three to one. But after vetoing the resolution, President Reagan persuaded twelve additional senators to support his position, averting a veto override by a single vote.[69] Similarly, two years later, President Reagan successfully concluded a sale of nearly $2 billion in arms to Kuwait over the initial opposition of a Senate majority.[70]

Although members of Congress proposed an amendment to the arms-export laws "designed to restore a balance between the executive and legislative branches on foreign arms transfers," the bill died with the 100th Congress.[71] The Iran-contra furor likewise failed to trigger a substantial strengthening of the laws governing covert arms sales. Less than two weeks after taking office, the George H. W. Bush administration proposed new large-scale arms sales to Bahrain, Egypt, Israel, Kuwait, Morocco, Saudi Arabia, and the United Arab Emirates.[72] Thus, fifteen years after controversial Middle Eastern arms sales had first spurred Congress to enact restrictive arms-export legislation, the president retained largely unaltered discretion to conclude controversial arms sales to the exact same countries, even over substantial congressional objection.

Funding Secret Wars

Congress's most visible tool in foreign policy is its power of the purse. Prominent examples of that power were the Boland amendments, which were named for their sponsor, Representative Edward Boland of Massachusetts, and attached to successive appropriations bills between 1982 and 1986. Directed against Reagan's secret war in Central America, those amendments barred any "agency or entity of the United States involved in intelligence activities" from spending funds available to it "to support military or paramilitary operations in Nicaragua."[73] Yet those amendments did not mark the first time that Congress had invoked its appropriations power to harness executive funding of secret war making. Once again, the prototype for such legislation had been aimed not at Central America, but at Southeast Asia. The unmasking of the Nixon administration's secret Cambodian incursions in 1970 revealed that the president had used his special funds and transfer authorities to allot millions of dollars in secret military aid to Cambodia without prior congressional approval. At one point, the Nixon administration sent Cambodia $7.9 million in military aid and justified it after the fact, on the basis of a novel "retroactive presidential finding" that closely resembled one later made by the general counsel of the CIA during the Iran-contra affair.[74]

In 1971, Congress debated the famous Cooper-Church amendment to the Foreign Military Sales Act, which would have cut off funds for U.S. ground troops, advisers, and air support in and over Cambodia. The similar Hatfield-McGovern bill, introduced at roughly the same time, would have terminated the use after December 1970 of any appropriated funds in Vietnam for purposes of military conflict. Although Professor Bickel, for one, expressed no "doubt under the sun, . . . on the constitutional foundation for either the Cooper-Church or the McGovern-Hatfield amendment," neither became law.[75] As opposition to the expanding war in Indochina grew, in 1973 and 1974 Congress finally enacted seven separate provisions denying the use of funds authorized or appropriated pursuant to various laws to support U.S. military or paramilitary forces in Vietnam, Cambodia, or Laos.[76] Moreover, as CIA involvement in the Cambodian operations became public, Congress enacted the Hughes-Ryan amendment of 1974, which imposed reporting requirements on the CIA as a prerequisite to its expenditure of appropriated funds.[77]

Yet even these Vietnam-era statutory funding limitations did not totally curtail the executive's foreign military and paramilitary campaigns. Notwithstanding express statutory funding prohibitions barring the use of U.S. forces to carry out military operations in, over, or off the shores of Cambodia or South Vietnam, within a year President Ford had sent U.S. armed forces to rescue the *Mayaguez* and to evacuate personnel from Vietnam and Cambodia.[78] Even after the Hughes-Ryan amendment became law, secret U.S. paramilitary aid to Angola persisted. Already "[t]raumatized by Watergate and Vietnam," Congress finally passed the Boland amendments' direct ancestor, the Clark amendment to the Arms Export Control Act of 1976.[79] Until its repeal in July 1985, the Clark amendment did exactly what the Boland amendments later sought to do: it barred aid to private groups that would have the purpose or effect of aiding military or paramilitary operations in Angola.[80] Yet even after the Clark amendment became law, then director of central intelligence George H. W. Bush refused to concede that all U.S. aid to Angola had stopped.[81] During the Iran-contra hearings, allegations persisted that Oliver North had not only supported the Nicaraguan rebels while the Boland amendments were in force, but had also supported the Angolan rebels while the Clark amendment was in place.[82]

In his famous Iran-contra congressional testimony, Oliver North criticized the Boland amendments by highlighting what he viewed as the inadequate U.S. support for democratic movements in Vietnam, Angola, and Nicaragua. "[O]nce we made the commitment to support the democratic resistance" in each country, he argued, "we should have made that commitment a consistent one."[83] His interrogators could have responded that that was not his call; Congress and the president share the decision on whether to sustain U.S. "commitments" by appropriating funds. During each of the three conflicts, Congress had enacted, and the president had signed, a statute that explicitly barred continued U.S. military support for the resistance movement. Debate should then have ensued over a broader constitutional question: whether executive officials may unilaterally disregard funding decisions that Congress and the president have jointly made regarding U.S. commitments abroad. Instead, the Iran-contra investigators overlooked that point and the affair's deeper historical roots.[84]

The NSC Staff Operationalized

Similarly, the operationalization of NSC staff commenced not with the travels of Oliver North (whom the affair propelled to new roles as a news commentator and head of the National Rifle Association), but with Henry

Kissinger's secret trip to mainland China nearly two decades earlier.[85] The National Security Act of 1947, which had established both the NSC and the CIA, did not create the NSC as a decision-making or decision-executing body. Congress no more designed the NSC to execute national security policy than it designed the Council of Economic Advisers to print the nation's money. Instead, the act unambiguously provided that the NSC's function "shall be to . . . *advise the President* with respect to the integration of domestic, foreign, and military policies relating to the national security."[86] Accordingly, Congress made the president, the vice president, and the secretaries of state and defense statutory NSC members, with the director of central intelligence, the chairman of the Joint Chiefs of Staff, and the attorney general attending NSC meetings only by invitation.[87] Until the Korean War began, President Truman employed the NSC and its small staff solely as an information-gathering and policy-coordinating entity.[88]

Similarly, the staff position of assistant to the president for national-security affairs was not originally designed to act as a policy advocate or executor. In 1947, Congress established no position called national security adviser, authorizing only the creation of a small executive secretariat to serve as the NSC's staff.[89] In 1953, President Eisenhower invoked an obscure statute authorizing the appointment of "employees in the White House Office" to create the position of national security assistant to set the council's agenda, to brief the president on national security matters, and to supervise the NSC staff.[90] Throughout the Eisenhower era, the president, and not the national-security assistant, presided over NSC meetings; presidential decisions were transmitted for implementation to a separate operations coordinating board, chaired by the undersecretary of state.[91]

By the same token, in 1947, Congress never envisioned that the CIA would formulate, as opposed to execute, intelligence policy. Instead, Congress authorized the CIA to perform only such "functions and duties related to intelligence affecting the national security as the *National Security Council* may from time to time direct."[92] In the CIA's early years, Congress and the NSC mandated that the agency follow three internal control principles. First, Congress expressly denied the CIA "police, subp[o]ena, law-enforcement powers, or internal-security functions," to ensure that it would act as a national security agency, not as a domestic law-enforcement unit.[93] Second, an early NSC directive instructed the CIA to employ covert means only in pursuit of announced American foreign-policy ends. Third, subsequent NSC directives established that the CIA's covert activities should proceed only after full consultation and coordination with other executive-branch agencies and Congress.[94]

By the early 1960s, however, both the NSC and the CIA had deviated noticeably from their original organizational mandates. In accordance with his personalized leadership style, President Kennedy deinstitutionalized the NSC and incorporated NSC personnel into his personal staff. Kennedy's national security assistant, McGeorge Bundy, soon emerged as one of the president's principal policy advocates and public spokespersons in foreign affairs. Deinstitutionalization continued under Lyndon Johnson with informal Tuesday lunches gradually supplanting the NSC system as the forum for coordinating and supervising particular national security programs.[95] Within this flexible structure, the national security assistant's peculiar political and legal status effectively immunized his activities from congressional examination. The national security assistant maintained the protocol rank of a deputy undersecretary, thereby escaping Senate confirmation by being an "inferior Officer" whose appointment Congress had vested "in the President alone" for purposes of the appointments clause of the Constitution.[96] No statute required the assistant to report to Congress, and until the Iran-contra affair, each president refused to allow the national security assistant to testify before Congress, claiming executive privilege.[97]

During his 1968 presidential campaign, Richard Nixon hearkened back to the Eisenhower years, vowing to "restore the National Security Council to its preeminent role in national security planning."[98] In his initial presidential press conference, Nixon for the first time referred to national security assistant Henry Kissinger as "my *Adviser* for National Security Affairs."[99] Kissinger organized and chaired an NSC review group that oversaw a succession of top-level interagency committees charged with developing policies for particular geographical regions and subject matters, an arrangement that effectively replicated the State Department's own bureaucratic structure. Before Kissinger became secretary of state in name as well as in fact, the NSC staff had expanded to some 120 members, accumulating extraordinary decision-making, then decision-executing, power at the State Department's expense.[100]

Under Kissinger's leadership, the NSC's policy-formulating functions expanded to include numerous policy-executing activities. Kissinger's own operational activities began with his dramatic secret negotiating missions to Vietnam, China, and Berlin, the details of which he kept even from the secretary of state. Kissinger announced the decision that placed American military forces on worldwide alert during the Yom Kippur War in 1973 and opened the back channel to the Soviet leadership that ripened into the policy of détente. During the Indochina conflict, Kissinger and his deputy, Major General Alexander Haig, directly supervised the secret bombing of Cambodia over the defense secretary's initial objections.[101]

Yet even while the NSC began assuming these operational duties, the CIA started playing a greater role in policy formulation. Active CIA intervention in Iran began in the early 1950s with the reinstallation of the shah as national leader. Even before the Bay of Pigs, the agency began executing and formulating policy in Guatemala and Cuba that governed not just intelligence gathering, but covert operations and covert war.[102] The Gulf of Tonkin incident in 1964, by most accounts, resulted from overaggressive espionage by a naval destroyer working for a U.S. electronic surveillance unit.[103]

By 1974, the CIA had violated each of the three internal control principles that had guided its creation: to work internationally, follow foreign-policy directives, and consult and coordinate with other foreign-policy entities. During the Vietnam War, the agency conducted secret illegal domestic break-ins, mail intercepts, wiretaps, and surveillance. Congressional investigations uncovered CIA death plots against foreign leaders in Cuba and the Congo and secret CIA military and paramilitary activities in Chile. Not only were these activities contrary to stated U.S. foreign-policy objectives, but the agency conducted them without accountability to either Congress or the rest of the executive branch.[104] By the early 1970s, it was an open secret that the CIA was running secret wars in Vietnam, Laos, and Cambodia.[105] Indeed, Watergate itself ultimately grew out of our Southeast Asian foreign policy. The now-infamous office break-in was executed by the "plumbers," a White House unit that was funded with private campaign contributions and that was partly staffed by former CIA agents, supported by the CIA, and formed for the purpose of "plugging leaks" by governmental officials suspected of having exposed the secret bombing of Cambodia.[106]

In short, by 1974, the NSC had taken on significant operational responsibilities and the CIA was firmly entrenched as an important national security policy player. Although both trends subsided during the Ford and Carter years, the Reagan administration reinvigorated them. In a foreign-policy reorganization announced shortly after he took office, President Reagan installed William Casey as CIA director and gave him a status equal to that of the secretaries of state and defense. William Clark, President Reagan's second national security adviser, abandoned neutral brokering of interagency differences in favor of an active role in developing Middle East, Latin American, and international economic policy. Clark's interventions helped force Alexander Haig's resignation as secretary of state in 1982, which created a vacuum that propelled Director Casey into a primary role in directing Central American covert-operations policy.[107] As Robert McFarlane, and then John Poindexter, became national security adviser, the NSC maintained dominance over covert operations and crisis management (particularly with regard to counterterrorism), two war-making areas that Congress had left unregulated by the War Powers Resolution.[108] As a carryover from the Carter years, the NSC's crisis management–counterterrorism portfolio afforded the council principal custody of governmental policy regarding Iran, which effectively deprived top-level decision makers of the State Department's Iranian expertise.[109] Meanwhile, the NSC's covert-operations duties gave the council increasing line responsibility for managing the secret war in Nicaragua.

The Iran-contra investigations revealed that the NSC and CIA had finally swapped roles. The NSC staff had linked its operational relations with both Iran and the contras by conducting a covert policy that the director of central intelligence had helped formulate. Contrary to the internal agency control principles described above, the NSC's actions during the Iran-contra affair ran counter to announced U.S. foreign-policy objectives and were conducted without the knowledge of either Congress or most of the rest of the executive branch.[110] By trading places, the two agencies brought full circle an inversion of institutional responsibility that first began during the Vietnam era.

Covert Operations

Once the executive's Vietnam-era abuses came to light, Congress sought to prevent future executive adventurism by amending existing intelligence legislation to reach covert activities. Yet even a brief review of this revisionary movement again unveils a recurring pattern. In late 1974, as revelations of executive misconduct multiplied, the president declared that he would not tolerate illegal activities by intelligence agencies and formed a presidential commission to investigate hidden abuses.[111] Congress enacted the Hughes-Ryan amendment to the Foreign Assistance Act of 1974, which sought to ensure future account-ability for covert operations through stiffer certification and reporting require-ments.[112] The president then replaced the director of central intelligence, and Congress established select, and later permanent, House and Senate commit-tees to study governmental intelligence operations.[113]

On the basis of those investigations, oversight advocates offered a compre-hensive 263-page charter for the intelligence community. But following ex-tensive debate, opponents trimmed it down to the two-page Intelligence Oversight Act of 1980, which made only two significant changes in the law.[114] The Hughes-Ryan amendment had already precluded the pre-Vietnam prac-tice of denial of presidential responsibility by instead requiring the president to make an explicit statutory "finding" that each covert operation is "impor-tant to the national security of the United States." The new oversight law stiffened that reporting requirement by mandating that the executive pro-vide the intelligence committees with prior notice of any "significant antici-pated intelligence activity" (including covert operations).[115] In exchange, Congress reduced from eight to two the number of congressional commit-tees to which the president was required to report. In the case of "extraordi-nary circumstances affecting vital interests of the United States," Congress further reduced the members to be notified of pending covert actions to a "Gang of Eight" congressional leaders and allowed the president to act with-out prior notice as long as he reported "in a timely fashion."[116]

By requiring only that Congress be informed of intelligence activities, the new oversight act "hardly satisfied those who preferred a major statutory charter." The act "carried a certain ambiguity permitting the president to skirt prior notification; it placed no time limit on covert actions[;] and [it] did not provide for a congressional veto."[117] As finally enacted, the oversight act did little more than codify the executive practice followed by the Carter ad-ministration over the previous four years. The act included almost verbatim the provisions for intelligence oversight contained in President Carter's ex-ecutive order issued in 1978 restricting intelligence activities.[118] Even so, the Carter administration opposed legislative enactment of those provisions "be-cause the President did not want to give those restraints the force of law."[119] The act's effectiveness therefore hinged on informal congressional-executive accords and the president's willingness to issue and enforce the executive orders and national security decision directives necessary to discharge his statutory responsibilities.

In the Reagan years, this choice of informality proved costly. The fall of the shah of Iran and the Soviet invasion of Afghanistan—both viewed as intelligence failures—helped dampen public concern over CIA misconduct.[120] As memories dimmed, the administration began to protest the stringency of existing statutory reporting and consultation requirements. In addition, the new president began to unilaterally modify his predecessor's intelligence directives. For example, President Carter's executive order governing intelligence had required consistency between covert and overt policies by defining "special [that is, covert] activities" as secret "activities conducted in support of national foreign policy objectives abroad *which are designed to further official United States programs and policies abroad.*" In 1981, President Reagan's succeeding executive order quietly amended that order, dropping that important limiting language.[121] Although the new administration issued a national security decision directive requiring that the president approve covert actions by means of written findings, the Justice Department later opined that such executive directives were merely procedures instituted for the "internal use" of the president and his intelligence advisers and could not legally bind him.[122]

Similarly, the committee oversight mandated by the Intelligence Oversight Act of 1980 softened as the intelligence committees gained familiarity with the agencies they were regulating. Like governmental agencies "captured" by the private industries they regulate, all "federal agencies exist in a symbiotic relationship with the congressional committees and subcommittees to which they report. . . . [An agency] purchases freedom . . . by playing ball in the areas that are of concern."[123] The comparative laxity of the reporting requirements in the oversight act forced the House and Senate intelligence committees, like other congressional oversight committees, to pay for CIA information by affording the agency greater discretion. Before long, the Senate Intelligence Committee's vice-chair was charging that the committee, "[l]ike other legislative committees, [had come] to be an advocate for the agency it was overseeing."[124]

By 1984, revelations of covert CIA activities in Central America were quickly multiplying. Nicaragua brought an ultimately successful suit against the United States at the International Court of Justice, charging the Reagan administration with actively supporting military and paramilitary activities against it in violation of international law.[125] Intelligence committee hostility toward Director Casey peaked with the revelation in April 1984 that the CIA had secretly mined Nicaraguan harbors without giving the committees the statutorily required notice.[126] In response, the Senate initially passed a non-binding resolution proclaiming that no money could be spent for such purposes. But rather than embody that resolution in binding legislation, the Senate compromised and settled for the so-called "Casey accords," which required the director to give the committees notice of new covert actions as soon as practicable. Within days after accepting those "voluntary" reporting requirements, the Reagan administration began planning its secret arms sale to Iran.[127]

In the wake of these disturbing revelations, one might have expected Congress to have learned the lesson of the last war. But in covert operations, as in other fields, the post-Vietnam era largely repeated itself. The president declared that he would not tolerate illegal activities by his national security agencies and formed the Tower commission to investigate the abuses. Congress established House and Senate select committees to study the events. To forestall future Iran-contra affairs, both houses considered amendments to the Intelligence Oversight Act that would have required the president to inform Congress in writing about all new covert operations within forty-eight hours after they began.[128]

Congress's action prompted a predictable executive reaction. To quell public outcry, President Reagan appointed a new CIA director pledged to internal procedural reforms but opposed to any legislative reform of the agency.[129] The president's lawyers hinted that Reagan would veto the new reporting measure as an unconstitutional limit on his prerogative to initiate, direct, and control sensitive national security activities.[130] And his lawyers did not foreclose the possibility that if the legislation passed over his veto, the president might nevertheless order his director of central intelligence not to implement the law, citing the statute's alleged constitutional infirmities.[131] Needing to secure a two-thirds majority in each house to enact the proposed amendments, the congressional leadership settled for yet another interim informal accord with the president to achieve the same result. Although Reagan promised that his administration would abide by that accord, he did not purport to bind his successor with it, reiterating his belief "that the current statutory framework is adequate."[132] After the new CIA director had disciplined the officers responsible for the Iran-contra affair, public interest in restrictive intelligence oversight legislation subsided and did not revive until after the terrorist attacks on September 11, 2001.[133]

As the presidency of George H. W. Bush began, the new Senate majority leader reiterated his desire to enact the covert-action bill. But in the first days of the new Congress, Speaker James Wright voluntarily shelved the legislation as "an opening gesture of good faith on our part" toward the new president. In return, President Bush agreed to abide by the spirit and letter of the legislative proposal, but did not commit himself to accept the terms of President Reagan's informal covert-action deal. Following Speaker Wright's departure, the intelligence committees and the new president finally concluded yet another set of informal accords.[134]

In sum, the history of the covert-action field from Vietnam to "Contragate" repeats the pattern found in other foreign-policy arenas. Scandals regarding executive misconduct have proceeded from revelation to public outrage to blue-ribbon investigations. Those investigations have inspired restrictive legislative proposals that the president has opposed, with the president offering instead temporary informal accommodations and pledges to replace the responsible officials. As the scandals have faded from public consciousness, those pledges have weakened even as legislative solutions have grown increasingly difficult to secure. Congress has found itself left without adequate statutory remedies to prevent or redress the inevitable recurrence of the so-called aberrational event.

The Iran-Contra Trials

The assigned institutional task of the Iran-contra independent counsel, Lawrence Walsh, was to prove the defendants' criminal responsibility, not to expose underlying defects in the legal structure of our foreign-policy decision-making. But the independent counsel's thwarted prosecution, like the Iran-contra report before it, exposed two competing constitutional visions of the foreign-policy decision-making process: the defendants' *Curtiss-Wright* vision of unchecked executive discretion versus the prosecutor's *Youngstown* vision of balanced institutional participation. As originally conceived, Walsh's prosecution charged that defendants Oliver North, John Poindexter, and their private contractors, Richard Secord and Albert Hakim, had conspired to conduct a covert foreign policy (which they called "The Enterprise") in violation of federal laws. But Walsh was ultimately forced to dismiss those broad conspiracy charges during pretrial proceedings in the first three cases, returning them to a narrower focus on whether the individual defendants had committed particular crimes beyond a reasonable doubt. The resultant winnowing of the indictment converted the independent counsel's trial of North from a public debate over the prerogatives of Congress and the president in foreign affairs into a relatively straightforward case about North's private enrichment, lying, and cover-up to Congress.

North, the most notorious defendant, rejected the prosecution's theory that foreign-policy power is a power shared. Instead, he argued that the constitutional principle that guides foreign-policy decision-making is the *Curtiss-Wright* vision of unchecked executive discretion. Under North's reasoning, neither the courts nor Congress may restrain the president or his subordinates in foreign affairs. The diversion of profits from the Iran arms sales to the contras did not constitute "theft of government property," North claimed, because his acts were all known and authorized by other executive officials.[135] Nor could the courts pass judgment on those acts, because they were immune from judicial review under the political-question doctrine.[136] Under North's view, executive circumvention of the Boland amendments, which had barred any "entity of the United States involved in intelligence activities" from spending available funds to assist the Nicaraguan resistance, could not constitute "conspiracy to defraud the United States," because Congress never intended those statutory provisions to apply to the NSC. Even if Congress did so intend, North argued, those laws constituted unconstitutional congressional attempts to use the appropriations power to usurp the president's foreign-affairs authority.[137] Finally, North asserted that exigent political circumstances—"weigh[ing] in the balance the difference between lives and lies"—justified both his private conversions of property and his decisions to mislead and withhold information from Congress and the attorney general.[138]

The able trial judge, Gerhard Gesell, denied that the political-question doctrine barred the court from passing on the legality of North's conduct. He squarely rejected North's *Curtiss-Wright* theory of unchecked executive discretion and reaffirmed *Youngstown*'s principle of balanced institutional participation. The laws that North was alleged to have violated represented not congressional usurpation of presidential power, Judge Gesell wrote, but proof that "[t]he affected Branches have accommodated to each other's interest to establish the manner in which government will function."[139] Rejecting North's "constitutional argument . . . that the asserted primacy of the White House in foreign affairs precludes officials working for the executive from being prosecuted for false statements made to Congress," Gesell declared: "Congress surely has a role to play in aspects of foreign affairs, as the Constitution expressly recognizes and the Supreme Court of the United States has affirmed. . . . Where, as here, *power is shared among the branches,* willful and deliberate deceit such as North allegedly espouses cannot be excused on constitutional grounds."[140]

In striking contrast, Reagan's Justice Department filed an extreme *amicus curiae* (friend of the court) memorandum echoing North's sentiments and repeatedly invoking *Curtiss-Wright:*

> The President has plenary authority to represent the United States and to pursue its interests outside the borders of the country, subject only to the powers assigned Congress and the limitations specifically set forth in the Constitution itself. Moreover, it follows that Congress cannot through its appropriations or other powers invade any sphere of constitutional authority granted exclusively to the President. In particular, the President has plenary power which Congress cannot invade to conduct diplomacy, including covert diplomacy that seeks support (including financial contributions) for the foreign policy he articulates on behalf of the Nation.[141]

The Justice Department baldly asserted that, "[c]ontrary to the [independent counsel]'s suggestion, there is a sphere of presidential activity that could not constitutionally be limited by any congressional enactment" and denied that courts have any significant role to play in examining executive conduct in foreign affairs.[142] But Judge Gesell's final instructions to the jury rejected that theory, directing that "[n]either the President nor any of the defendant's superiors had the legal authority to order anyone to violate the law. [O]ur country is governed by the rule of law."[143] His instruction reaffirmed the Founders' original notion that the foreign-affairs power is a power shared; that even the highest-ranking executive officials must share vital foreign-affairs information with Congress; and that intentional distortion or concealment of such information from Congress, even under orders from the president, is a crime punishable in a court of law.

After extensive deliberations, however, the jury voted to convict North on only three of the twelve counts charged, acquitting him of those he claimed to have committed under superior orders. In December 1992, just before leaving office, President George H. W. Bush pardoned the other six Iran-contra defendants—most notably former defense secretary Caspar Weinberger and former national security adviser Robert McFarlane—even though four of the six defendants had already either pleaded or been found guilty. By pardoning these defendants, Bush violated a central norm of the National Security Constitution: that foreign-policy exigencies do not authorize a president to nullify the rule of law for the president's own administration. Nearly thirty years later, that pattern of pardoning was revived, with pronounced intensity, under Donald Trump.

The Pattern of History

The road from Vietnam reveals that the Iran-contra affair was only the tip of a much larger iceberg that crystallized during the Vietnam War. All of the congressional-executive struggles that surrounded the affair merely replicated battles that had transpired during that earlier period. History repeated itself across many spheres of foreign affairs, even after Congress had passed numerous statutes to avoid repetition of the Vietnam-era evasions. This suggests that the Iran-contra affair exposed systemic, not aberrational, problems in the American foreign-policy process.

The historical pattern is familiar to any student of regulation. Congress's postwar efforts to enact legislation that would stop the last war simply channeled executive action into new, unregulated forms of warfare. It was Vietnam that originally spurred Congress to pass the War Powers Resolution in an attempt to regulate overt executive war making. Yet far from eliminating such war making, the War Powers Resolution only drove it underground. The resolution stimulated the executive to substitute emergency economic sanctions for military warfare, to replace overt with covert operations, and to transfer the control of covert operations from the military establishment to the less heavily regulated intelligence agencies.

Abuses by those intelligence agencies then increased congressional regulation of the CIA through special oversight committees, which led to both the partial capture of those committees by the CIA and a shifting of the CIA's

activities during the Iran-contra affair toward an unregulated alternative, the
NSC staff. When the NSC found its own resources inadequate to execute covert operations, it subcontracted its duties to private agents and financed the
payments with contributions from private parties and foreign governments.[144]
Statutes requiring the disclosure of public international agreements caused
government-to-government deals to be struck privately.[145] Laws limiting overt
arms sales inspired NSC officials and their delegates to sell arms covertly.
After the Boland amendments restricted any official U.S. funding to the contras, military aid was privatized. In a familiar regulatory pattern, each succeeding congressional effort to catch up with executive evasion of legislative
controls served only to shift executive activity into a new pattern of evasion.

   Given this history, the Iran-contra affair represented nothing less than a
covert attempt to rewrite the National Security Constitution. During the
Iran-contra affair, the Reagan administration conducted a major foreign-
policy initiative that was contrary to the constitutional and policy vision set in
place by *Youngstown* and the National Security Act of 1947. The Iran-contra
affair occurred in two constitutional areas of shared congressional-executive
authority—military aid and covert operations. Before the affair began, the
president made two deals with Congress in each of these areas that set the
nation's broad foreign-policy objectives. Acting together, the president and
Congress reached substantive policy agreements not to negotiate with terrorists over hostages and, through congressional passage and presidential signature of the Boland amendments, not to fund military activities by the
contras. Furthermore, by congressional enactment and presidential signature of the arms-export and covert-operations statutes, the branches reached
a related procedural accord: that the president would personally participate
in decisions authorizing covert operations and arms sales and that he would
always keep Congress informed of those decisions. Yet during the Iran-
contra affair, Reagan secretly breached both the substantive and procedural
accords. Without consulting Congress, he unilaterally endorsed two opposite
policy objectives—release of the hostages in Lebanon by virtually any means
and private support for the contras. By so doing, he denied Congress its constitutional entitlement to participate in the setting of broad foreign-policy
objectives as well as its attendant rights to information and consultation.

   After authorizing the initial phases of the Iran-contra initiative, President
Reagan disengaged from the process of decision-making. Acting without the

knowledge of the major foreign-affairs bureaucracies and allegedly without the awareness of the president or the vice president, the CIA (a decision-executing entity) then helped formulate the details of a policy initiative to meet Reagan's objectives.[146] The national security adviser and his staff (an advisory entity that included active military officers) then executed that initiative with the aid of private parties and third countries, without meaningful internal debate within the executive branch and in violation of internal agency control principles. All of these actions were taken without the legally required congressional notification, knowledge, or oversight. The executive branch then concealed the existence of the entire affair from both Congress and the public, manipulating information to dampen public debate.

The Iran-contra affair thus ran afoul of both the constitutional and policy visions of the national security process described in chapter 2. The affair proved remarkable not simply because the president failed to take care that individual laws were faithfully executed, but because he condoned a near-total subversion of the U.S. foreign-policy process. By the president's own account, the only constitutionally authorized players in that process—the president, the vice president, and Congress—as well as the only other statutory NSC members, the secretaries of state and defense, were almost entirely excluded from decision-making. Both secretaries later testified that two nonstatutory NSC members, the CIA's director and the national security adviser, had supported the secretaries' exclusion from deliberations regarding an operation that was central to the mission of both of their cabinet departments.[147]

Moreover, within the executive branch, the decision-making and implementation process was turned upside down, as the CIA formulated and the NSC executed policy without presidential supervision. The two central actors in the affair, North and Poindexter, were both active military officers; two others, McFarlane and Secord, were recently retired military officers. Thus, the affair violated each of the legal principles that make up the due process of foreign-policy administration described in chapter 2. Executive officials claimed presidential authority for actions that the president had not directly approved; foreign-policy making and execution were delegated to private entities and foreign governments; military personnel ran foreign policy; and the president failed to either supervise his own foreign-affairs apparatus or preserve that apparatus's accountability to Congress and the people.

Once the constitutionally prescribed foreign-policy process became inverted, it was only a matter of time before the letter and spirit of particular laws that were meant to constrain that process were also violated. And the outcome of such an inverted, unilateral process was fundamentally unsound foreign policy. As the House select committee chair pointed out at the close of the congressional hearings, the arms-for-hostages "policy achieved none of the goals it sought. The Ayatollah got his arms, more Americans [were] held hostage . . . than when [the] policy began, [and the] subversion of U.S. interests throughout the region by Iran continues."[148]

In short, the Iran-contra affair represented a frontal assault by the executive branch upon the principle of power sharing that underlay the National Security Constitution. Congress's ambitious attempts during the post-Vietnam era to reassert its constitutional role in foreign-policy making yielded limited success. In statute after statute enacted during that period, Congress sought to impose on the president restrictions whose fundamental premises later presidents apparently did not accept. Although those presidents signed nearly all of those statutes, executive officials later exploited real or perceived loopholes in the statutes or simply defied them. The repeated willingness of presidents to break their deals with Congress undermined Congress's post-Vietnam attempts to increase its participation in foreign-policy making, and thereby disrupted the institutional equilibrium envisioned by the National Security Constitution.

4

Why the President Almost Always Wins

BEFORE TURNING TO RECENT HISTORY, we must ask some deeper questions: Why, after the post-Vietnam reforms, did America's national institutions fail to preserve the balanced institutional participation envisioned by the National Security Constitution? Why has Congress not been able to force the president to keep his bargains in foreign affairs? Whenever Congress and the president differ over foreign policy, why does the president almost always seem to win? In the end, these structural inquiries, not questions of individual responsibility, remain the real unanswered questions. Left unaddressed, they virtually ensure that similar crises will happen again.

Why does the president almost always seem to win in foreign affairs? For three reasons, which not coincidentally mirror general institutional characteristics of the executive, legislative, and judicial branches: executive initiative, congressional acquiescence, and judicial tolerance. First, and most obviously, the president has won because weak and strong presidents alike have taken the initiative in foreign affairs and have often done so by construing laws designed to constrain their actions as authorizations. Second, the president has won because, for all of its institutional activity, Congress has usually acquiesced in what the president has done, through legislative myopia, inadequate drafting, ineffective legislative tools, or lack of political will. Third, the president has won because the federal courts have usually tolerated the president's acts, either by refusing to hear challenges to those acts or by hearing those challenges, but then affirming the president's authority on the merits.

This simple, three-part combination of executive initiative, congressional acquiescence, and judicial tolerance explains why the president almost invariably wins in foreign affairs. Indeed, this three-part reasoning enters directly into the calculus of an executive-branch lawyer asked to draft a legal opinion justifying a proposed foreign-affairs initiative. If asked, for example, whether the president can impose economic sanctions on a foreign country, the president's lawyer must answer three questions: (1) Do we have the legal authority to act? (2) Can Congress stop us? and (3) Can anyone challenge our action in court? Or, to use the framework outlined above: (1) Do the Constitution and laws of the United States authorize the president to take this executive *initiative*? (2) If the executive acts, will Congress *acquiesce*? and (3) If Congress does not acquiesce and challenges the president's action (or if a private citizen sues), will the courts tolerate the act, either by refusing to hear the challenge or by hearing it and ruling in the president's favor? Time and time again, the executive-branch lawyer's answers to all three questions is yes.

Executive Initiative

What drives the executive branch to take the initiative in foreign affairs? Most critics of executive power simplistically assume that the entire answer is that presidents and their teams are overzealous, foolish, misguided, or evil. However true these explanations may be in particular cases, two deeper institutional explanations—based on domestic constitutional structure and international regime change—supplement them.

Structural Superiority

The simple yet sensible domestic explanation, offered by Charles Black, attributes executive seizure of the initiative in foreign affairs to the structure of the Constitution. As we have seen, Article I gives Congress almost all of the enumerated powers over foreign affairs and Article II gives the president almost none of them. But Congress is poorly structured for initiative and leadership because of "its dispersed territoriality of power-bases and . . . its bicamerality." The presidency, by contrast, is ideally structured for the receipt and exercise of power: "[W]hat very naturally has happened is simply that power textually assigned to and at any time resumable by the body structurally unsuited to its exercise, has flowed, through the inactions, acquiescences, and delegations of that body, toward an office ideally structured for the exercise of initiative and for vigor in administration. ... The result has been a flow of power from Congress to the presidency."[1]

The notion that the presidency is institutionally best suited to initiate government action is nothing new. The notion dates back to Hamilton's statement that "[e]nergy in the executive is a leading character in the definition of good government."[2] Nor, in theory, is there anything wrong per se with the president initiating international action. As in the domestic context, a plebiscitary president is uniquely visible, and hence accountable, to the electorate. The president is the only individual capable of centralizing and coordinating the foreign-policy decision-making process. The president can energize and direct policy in ways that could not be done by either Congress or the president's own bureaucracy.[3] The president's decision-making processes can take on degrees of speed, secrecy, flexibility, and efficiency that no other governmental institution can match. As Justice Sutherland declared in *Curtiss-Wright* (quoting from a Senate Report): "The President ... manages our concerns with foreign nations and must necessarily be most competent to determine when, how, and upon what subjects negotiation may be urged with the greatest prospect of success. ... The nature of transactions with foreign nations, moreover, requires caution and unity of design, and their success frequently depends on secrecy and dispatch."[4]

Most crucially, over time, the executive has gathered resources: a treasury assembled from a tax base; information—often classified; staff; various kinds of hard power, including weapons and troops; and soft power—a bully pulpit, public visibility, and moral standing. Taken together, these structural considerations help explain why the president has assumed the preeminent role in foreign affairs, despite the Framers' clear textual preference for congressional leadership.

Domestic Regimes and International Regimes

The structural fact that the president can more easily exercise foreign-affairs power than Congress does not explain why presidents *choose* to wield it. I suggest that the explanation lies not simply in constitutional structure, but rather in the complex relationship between domestic constitutional regimes and international regimes.[5] Theorists of international relations explain the president's activist choices in terms of the rise and fall of American hegemony during the postwar era. Franklin Roosevelt's personalization and institutionalization of the presidency initiated an extrovert phase in American foreign policy that marked America's emergence as the world's hegemonic power. During those years, which began before Pearl Harbor and ended with Vietnam, the president led America to erect the entire postwar multilateral political and economic order. An entire generation of Americans grew up and came to power believing in the wisdom of muscular presidential leadership in foreign policy.[6]

The activist logic of this extrovert era made presidential initiatives virtually inevitable. Yet Vietnam caused an entire generation to rethink its attitude toward foreign policy. National elites became less willing to intervene to defend other nations and to bear the costs of world leadership.[7] Why, then, have presidential initiatives not only continued, but appeared to accelerate, during the post-Vietnam era?

Many distinguished scholars have made the claim that America is losing its hegemonic grip on the world. The political economists David Calleo, Robert Gilpin, Robert Keohane, and Stephen Krasner, the historian Paul Kennedy, and the economists Charles Kindleberger and Mancur Olson have all explained the implications for the world order of declining American hegemony. Although other distinguished scholars have questioned the empirical basis underlying these claims of lost American hegemony, several policy analysts have steadfastly asserted the same claim.[8] The common strand that runs through this literature is the conclusion that the United States has entered a fifth, post-hegemonic era in its relationship with the rest of the world. In this environment, in which it remains a leading power, the United States acts as an engaged global participant, but without its former power to singlehandedly dominate the flow of international events.

Put simply, America's declining role as world hegemon has forced changes in the postwar structure of international institutions that have not reduced, but stimulated, further presidential initiatives. In the place of formal multilateral political and economic institutions that enact bodies of positive international law through treaties, new, informal regional and functional regimes have arisen. Those regimes, which the United States does not dominate but in which it must participate, now manage global economic and political events through bargaining and "soft," quasi-legal pronouncements. Examples on the political side include the international human-rights regime, the international peacekeeping and nuclear-nonproliferation regimes, and an evolving international dispute-resolution regime. On the economic side, the United States participates in the Group of Seven (G7) to manage exchange rates; in the Coordinating Committee on Multilateral Export Controls to manage strategic export trade; and in a debt regime that includes private bankers, multilateral organizations, and the informal Paris and London clubs for debt rescheduling, to give just a few examples.[9] Within these regimes, the United States can no longer simply suppress conflicts of national interest; it must constantly manage relations even with close historic allies through repeated applications of economic carrots and political sticks. For example, developments in the world trading system have stimulated the United States to turn to an array of unilateral and multilateral economic sanctions, bilateral free-trade agreements and investment programs, and plurilateral monetary bargaining in addition to (or in lieu of) its traditional multilateral bargaining within the framework of the World Trade Organization. The rise of new and unanticipated problems not subject to the control of any nation-state—such as global terrorism, debt crises, global pandemics, climate change, and unanticipated wars—have increasingly forced the United States into a reactive international posture.[10]

The Reactive President

In such a global moment, given the president's superior institutional capacity to initiate governmental action, the burden of generating reactive responses to external challenges invariably falls on the president. As post-Vietnam congressional reforms stimulated a resurgence of congressional interest and activism in foreign policy, the presidency was forced to react to that too. Key foreign-affairs committees dramatically regained both expertise and influence, and the number of informal congressional foreign-policy caucuses rose dramatically. Yet those same reforms left Congress too decentralized and democratized to generate its own coherent program of foreign-policy initiatives.[11] Increasingly, Congress exhibited its interest and activism in foreign affairs by exerting pressure on the president through means short of legislation. Particularly in fields such as international trade that directly affect congressional constituencies, Congress forced the president into a range of preemptive actions to respond to or forestall more-drastic congressional activity. Well-publicized examples included the executive order imposing sanctions on South Africa to preempt congressional enactment of comprehensive

WHY THE PRESIDENT ALMOST ALWAYS WINS

anti-apartheid legislation; executive decisions in response to congressional pressures to close Palestine Liberation Organization (PLO) offices in the United States and to deny PLO leader Yasir Arafat a visa; the expanded use of section 301 of the Trade Act of 1974 and so-called Super 301 of the Omnibus Trade and Competitiveness Act of 1988 to open foreign markets; and the reluctance to fund the United Nations, a reflection in part of pressure imposed by Congress's enactment of the Kassebaum amendment.[12]

The same public opinion that empowered the plebiscitary president simultaneously subjected presidents to almost irresistible pressures to act quickly in times of real or imagined crisis. "Mass pressure on plebiscitary presidents requires results, or the appearance of results, regardless of the danger."[13] Reagan's wave of treaty breaking and bending discussed in chapter 3 reflected a reactive presidential role in leading both America's flight from international organizations and its movement toward alternative mechanisms of multilateral cooperation. Similarly, the president's use of short-term military strikes and emergency economic powers (to respond to terrorism); longer-term military commitments in Lebanon and the Persian Gulf (to respond to requests for peacekeeping); arms sales (to respond to military tensions in the Middle East); and covert actions (to effectuate neo-containment policies in Central America) all reflected the post–Cold War American perception that crisis situations uniquely demand a presidential response.

Thus, the relative weakening of America in the world arena promoted an increase, rather than a decrease, in executive initiatives. Once such crises were thrust upon the president, powerful domestic factors such as ideology, political philosophy, or bureaucratic politics combined to help drive his response.[14] But a pervasive national perception that only the president can act swiftly and secretly to respond to fast-moving international events repeatedly forced the executive branch into a pattern of evasion of congressional restraint.

This pattern has afflicted presidents of both political parties, without regard to whether the presidents have been viewed as weak or strong, reckless or law-abiding. During the Iranian hostage crisis of 1979–1981, for example, President Carter reacted to both international and domestic pressures by conducting one of the most dramatic peacetime exercises of presidential power in foreign affairs in American history. During the 444 days that the U.S. hostages were held captive, he declared a national emergency under the

International Emergency Economic Powers Act (IEEPA); imposed a trade embargo and an extraterritorial assets freeze; cut off lines of communication and embargoed travel to Iran; sued Iran in the International Court of Justice; expelled Iranian diplomats; forced Iranian students to report to local immigration offices for visa checks; made a disastrous attempt to rescue the hostages by force; and concluded a wide-ranging executive agreement that suspended all private property claims against Iran and consigned American commercial claimants to arbitration for the next half century before a newly established international tribunal. Carter left office, however, viewed not as an imperial president but as the weakest, most reactive president in recent memory. As one commentator observed, describing Carter's disastrous military attempt to rescue the hostages, "[p]ublic opinion had forced upon the president an act of the sheerest adventurism."[15]

This unholy synergy between the executive branch's ideological imperatives, international incentives, and domestic latitude to act helps explain the Iran-contra affair. A president dependent on public opinion and sensitive to congressional pressure sought to respond to two perceived external threats—the taking of American hostages in Lebanon and the rise of a communist regime in Nicaragua. In the same way as Oliver North saw the choice as one between "lies and lives," President Reagan saw the choice as between lives and law. As he reportedly told his secretary of state, "the American people will never forgive me if I fail to get these hostages out over this *legal question*."[16]

As with earlier presidents, Reagan's commitment to action led him to condone an errant flow of decision-making power, not just from Congress to the executive branch but *within* the executive branch.[17] In his administration, power flowed away from the larger, more accountable yet cumbersome foreign-affairs bureaucracies, such as the State and Defense Departments, toward institutions such as the CIA and the NSC, which are closer to the Oval Office and more capable of swift, secret, and flexible action. But the same covert transfer of power to sub-executive entities that facilitated swift and secret action inevitably sacrificed even more: the technical expertise, institutional judgment, bureaucratic support, and bipartisan political approval that would have come from consultative inter- and intra-branch decision-making in accordance with the National Security Constitution.

As the Iran-contra affair further revealed, the executive branch never thinks of itself as dangerous. Invariably, it views itself as beleaguered and put-upon, obliged to serve, yet underappreciated, under-resourced, and mis-understood by those who do not recognize its worthy motives. In a bubble of "groupthink," executives tend to grow isolated, which breeds a temptation to act alone, sometimes in secret.[18] When their capacity to act is constantly tested by their perceived duty to react, executives begin to see the advantages of acting without prior consultation. They can more quickly respond to crises if they do not take time to talk to others who do not work for them. Those outsiders often lack the information or overall perspective that the leaders have and may not share their views. It becomes easier to act than to persuade. And so, executives dispense with prior consultation because it is easier to seek forgiveness than to ask permission.

Finally, the executive branch tends to assert exorbitant claims of executive authority not at times of political strength, but rather at times of intense political weakness. Weak executives assert unilateral power because they feel unsure that Congress will endorse, or the courts will ratify, what they feel inexorably pressured by circumstance to do. Take, for instance, Harry Truman's decision to seize the steel mills during the unpopular Korean War, Richard Nixon's illegal actions during Watergate, or Ronald Reagan's privatization of foreign policy during the Iran-contra affair. In each case, the executive branch asserted expansive constitutional justifications for unconstitutional actions.

Taken together, these factors help explain why executive power so often creates a problem for the law. Over time, a growing sense of feeling put-upon and misunderstood makes it easier for executive actors to convince themselves that their authority derives from their greater competence, or popular or legal legitimacy. And so, executives begin to confuse the "ought" with the "is." They come to believe that they exercise executive power because they *ought to* exercise executive power, which means they must have a "right" to do so, rooted in competence, law, or democracy. From this reasoning, it is just a short step to the notion that the exercise of executive power can validate itself. All of which, of course, brings back eerie memories of Nixon's famous remark: "When the President does it, that means that it is not illegal."[19]

Congressional Acquiescence

It takes all three branches, however, to create a constitutional crisis. Even the most expansive theory of presidential power cannot carry the day unless the checks and balances against such overreaching prove ineffective. When presidents overreach, they can remake the law to justify their actions only if Congress lets them.

Given the president's strong institutional incentives to take initiatives, why has Congress so consistently failed to check or restrain the president? Despite the initial flurry of post-Vietnam legislation, Congress has persistently acquiesced in executive efforts to evade that legislation's strictures. That acquiescence has institutional roots in legislative myopia, porous drafting, ineffective legislative tools, and an institutional lack of political will. The case in point is the War Powers Resolution of 1973, which has failed in its intended purpose for each of these four reasons.

Legislative Myopia

The first reason, already illustrated, is that Congress legislates to stop the last war. As explained in chapter 3, the War Powers Resolution was drafted principally to halt creeping wars like Vietnam, not short-term military strikes or covert wars of the kind that dominate modern warfare.

Why does Congress legislate this way? All explanations of congressional behavior, of course, must begin and end with politics. The institutional roots of congressional myopia lie in each phase of the legislative process.[20] As Professor Morris Fiorina has observed, Congress legislates retrospectively in large part because voters vote that way.[21] Like other legislation that attempts to be public-regarding, proposed foreign-affairs legislation is fully subject to undue influence or political veto by special-interest groups. The trade field, of course, is the most extensively studied arena of private-interest-group influence on Congress in foreign affairs. But in other areas, the defense and foreign-aid lobbies have proved to be highly successful in promoting the maintenance of military spending and military aid. The Israel lobby has exercised well-publicized influence over Middle East, Arab-boycott, and arms-sale policy. Even the intelligence committees are subject to lobbying by interest groups such as the Center for National Security Studies and the Association of Former Intelligence Officers.[22]

Occasionally, these interest groups will press for, rather than against, legislative action. The international human-rights lobbies, for example, successfully pressed for legislative action in obtaining the ratification of the Genocide Convention and the enactment of the South Africa anti-apartheid bill. An influential ad hoc national interest group composed of students, parents of potential draftees, and alumni of the 1960s civil-rights movement rose up to demand legislation to end the Vietnam War.[23] But more frequently, powerful interest groups will press to defeat or narrow pending legislation, thereby burying broader public-policy reform objectives amid a welter of provincial or ethnic-group concerns.

The result of these institutional influences is that Congress regularly lags public opinion in enacting major legislation and wraps its policies in largely symbolic packages that offer particularized benefits to organized interest groups. Even when interest groups successfully press individual members of Congress to act, rather than refrain from acting, there is no assurance that those members will take the broad view. The electoral need for members to be seen as addressing this year's problem encourages them to address last year's problems by tinkering with existing statutes rather than investing energy in introducing and passing large-scale reforms. In 1973, for example, Senator Thomas Eagleton attempted to expand the War Powers Resolution to reach paramilitary forces under civilian command, but his efforts failed because his colleagues did not wish to legislate against "speculative" problems. As Professor David Mayhew noted, the desire of congressional members to choose legislative devices that can be easily explained to constituents leads to a "congressional penchant for the blunt, simple action," which may be insufficiently sensitive to the complexities of the underlying problem.[24] Congress's taste for the symbolic, easily comprehended legislative fix explains its decisions to enact a War Powers Resolution with an automatic sixty-day withdrawal provision; to consider carefully the Gephardt amendment to the trade bill of 1988 (which, like the Gramm-Rudman-Hollings budget-balancing act, took an automatic phased, numerical approach to reduction of the trade deficit); and, after the Iran-contra affair, to propose intelligence-reform legislation that declared a simple, mandatory forty-eight-hour notice rule for all covert operations.[25]

Even when more-farsighted congressional members overcome this institutional particularity and introduce sweeping legislative reforms, they must deal with committees. The competing objectives of the committees sharing jurisdiction over any omnibus bill or of members within particular committees may impede the coalition formation necessary to bring that bill to the floor. Committee chairs, who are generally chosen on the basis of seniority, may be less ready to challenge the president than more junior members, who may be subcommittee chairs at best. Thus, as in the case of the Boland amendments, several years of internal committee battles may ensue before the committee chair is willing to support, much less lend his or her name to, legislation that restricts presidential prerogative.[26]

Thus, bills can be long delayed in coming to the floor, especially if they are referred for markup to multiple committees. Even after the committees finally report out the bill, it may not be brought to a floor vote if the leadership shelves it for extraneous political reasons. Even in the rare case in which a floor vote occurs and floor majorities can be mustered in support of a bill, the Senate's rules require only forty-one votes to sustain a filibuster and defeat the legislation.[27] Should the president veto the bill, as presidents have threatened to do with most proposed legislation that would limit the president's freedom in matters of foreign affairs, the number of senators required to sustain the veto drops even further, to thirty-four. The supermajorities needed to overcome a filibuster or veto rarely coalesce, and when they do, they address only the most specific incremental changes that would correct the most egregious known policy defects.

Porous Drafting

Even when enacted, legislation expressly designed to check executive adventurism has often failed because of faulty draftsmanship. The War Powers Resolution, the most ambitious piece of foreign-affairs framework legislation enacted in the post-Vietnam era, offers five particularly glaring examples. First, the resolution's consultation requirements oblige the president to consult "in every possible instance," but then allow the president to decide what that phrase should mean. Thus, although prior consultation was clearly "possible," neither President Carter nor President Reagan consulted Congress before sending troops to Iran and Grenada.[28] Second, the resolution requires the president to consult "Congress" before sending troops abroad, but nowhere specifies how many members must be consulted or how far in advance. When President Reagan sent warplanes to bomb Libya in April 1986, for example, he consulted with only fifteen congressional leaders and even then only after the planes were already in the air.[29] Third, the resolution covers only U.S. "Armed Forces" physically "introduced" into foreign territory, airspace, or waters while equipped for combat, and thus arguably does not apply to private contractors acting under covert governmental instruc-tion, let alone twenty-first-century drones, robots, or cyber conflicts. Fourth, depending on the situation, the resolution permits the president to file three different types of reports to Congress upon committing armed forces abroad—whenever U.S. armed forces are introduced "into hostilities" or im-minent hostilities; into foreign territory, airspace, or waters equipped for combat; or in numbers that substantially enlarge a preexisting combat unit. Yet the law's sixty-day clock for removing those troops runs automatically only from the date when a so-called hostilities report is submitted or "re-quired to be submitted" and not when one of the other two types of report has been filed.[30] Thus, simply by the choice of report, the president can sat-isfy the resolution's procedural reporting obligation without triggering the resolution's substantive obligation to remove those troops within sixty days. Fifth and finally, the sixty-day limit means that the president can take short-term military actions of less than sixty days with little check or oversight.

Some of these drafting errors are simply inadvertent. The legal counsel to the Senate Foreign Relations Committee during consideration of the War Powers Resolution recalls that the fourth drafting error described above was simply "unnoticed at the time the resolution was enacted."[31] But such inad-vertence also has institutional roots. As Professor Mayhew has observed, once members decide to vote for a bill and exhaust its "credit-claiming" pos-sibilities, they often "display only a modest interest in what goes into [the] bill[] or what [its] passage accomplishes."[32] Other drafting errors—the per-petuation of the "in every possible instance" language, for example—have resulted from the legislative tendency to draft new laws simply by transplant-ing boilerplate language from other statutes.[33]

Most frequently, what appears to outsiders to be poor drafting stems, in fact, from the constructive ambiguity forced by political deals or compro-mises struck between members of Congress; between staffers; between members and staffers; between congressional and executive staffers; be-tween members and executive officials; or between the drafting entities within the executive branch itself. Particularly when the president threatens a veto, there often transpires a peculiar Capitol Hill ritual known as "being pecked to death by ducks," whereby more stringent procedural provisions are watered down in conference in an often futile effort to avert the presi-dent's veto. This phenomenon accounted, for example, for the numerous loopholes in the South Africa anti-apartheid bill, which passed into law in 1986 over a presidential veto.[34] Similarly, although the Intelligence Oversight Act of 1980 (described in chapter 3) was originally drafted to require prior notice in all cases, the act was watered down to require only "timely" notice, language that lent itself to easy evasion during the Iran-contra affair.

Whatever the cause, the cumulative effect of these drafting failures has been to prevent the War Powers Resolution from being self-executing. Although the resolution puts pressure on the president to start thinking about removing armed forces sixty days after committing them to a hostile situation, the resolution also puts pressure on *Congress* to declare that U.S. forces are "in hostilities" in order to trigger the sixty-day clock for troop removal. If Congress as a whole is unwilling to make that declaration, aggrieved members must file suit in federal court seeking a judicial declaration that the War Powers Resolution has been triggered, an option that thus far has yielded them no relief.[35] So although Congress designed the War Powers Resolution to stop the last war—escalating conflicts like Vietnam—the resolution's drafting flaws have undercut its effectiveness in restraining just such creeping escalation, as in Lebanon, Central America, and the Persian Gulf.

Ineffective Tools

Many of Congress's legislative solutions have not worked even when Congress has both foreseen a problem and properly drafted provisions to address it. As chronicled in chapter 3, statutes enacted in the post-Vietnam era applied an array of innovative procedural devices to bring executive action under control, including statutory sunset provisions, reporting and consultation requirements, committee oversight procedures, legislative vetoes, and appropriations limitations. Each of the statutes whose enactment has been described—the War Powers Resolution, the Case-Zablocki Act, IEEPA, the Arms Export Control Act, the Hughes-Ryan amendment, and the Intelligence Oversight Act—was designed not only to restrain executive discretion, but also to increase congressional input into key foreign-policy decisions. But if the Iran-contra affair teaches anything, it is that most of these procedural devices simply have not worked, particularly when executive officials are intent on evading them and courts are unwilling to enforce them.

Each of these devices has its defects. As Judge Guido Calabresi has recognized, mechanical sunset laws force Congress to redo its work every few years and "give[] a tremendous weapon to those who oppose regulation itself; the force of inertia shifts to their side." Not only does time not serve as an adequate measure of how obsolescent a statute may be, but complex legislative compromises will inevitably be difficult to replicate when a statute is sunsetted.[36] The War Powers Resolution experience shows that reporting and consultation requirements lack teeth and are all too easily evaded. Committee oversight invites committee capture and can usually be conducted only after the executive action has been completed.[37] The only supervisory methods that have proved to have bite in foreign affairs—particularly in the areas of arms sales, the transfer of nuclear materials, and covert action—have been the now-banned legislative veto and the appropriations cutoff.[38]

Legislative vetoes are simple or concurrent resolutions that have been approved by a majority of one or two houses, respectively, but that have not been presented to the president for signature or veto.[39] As we saw in chapter 3, these provisions were the linchpins of the post-Vietnam-era framework legislation. Yet in 1983, the Supreme Court issued a sweeping decision in *INS v. Chadha* that denied the legislative veto legal effect.[40] *Chadha* announced wide-ranging separation-of-powers language that could be read to restrict Congress's authority to use methods functionally similar to the legislative veto to check presidential discretion in foreign affairs. In the first years after *Chadha*, the Court embroidered the case with a series of formalistic rulings whose broad language, read literally, would limit any congressional attempt to regulate executive exercises of delegated power by means other than legislation.[41]

As the Iran-contra saga of the Boland amendments has revealed, the alternative technique of appropriations cutoff does not necessarily ensure good executive behavior. When tacked to massive continuing appropriations measures, such limitations carry the political advantage of being nearly veto-proof.[42] At the same time, however, they possess the disadvantage of being subject to yearly reconsideration and modification. When, as in the case of the Boland amendments, the language of the restriction becomes more and less inclusive over time, executive officials can claim that the provision's vagueness impairs their ability to determine whether particular activities are proscribed.[43]

More explicitly drafted appropriations limits do not necessarily have more teeth. Two inconclusive Supreme Court rulings have left unclear how far Congress may go in exercising or enforcing its appropriations power to constrain the president's authorities in foreign affairs. In *United States v. Lovett,* the Court held that Congress could not use its appropriations power to effect a bill of attainder under Article I, section 9, clause 3 of the Constitution.[44] Although the Court has never extended *Lovett* beyond the bill-of-attainder context, presidential supporters have argued by analogy that the Boland amendments placed overly strict conditions on presidential expenditure of authorized funds and thereby unconstitutionally encroached on the executive's inherent authority to conduct foreign affairs.[45] Some commentators have argued that Congress may not constitutionally refuse to appropriate funds for the execution of the president's exclusive enumerated authorities in foreign affairs.[46] But until the late 1980s, no federal court had ever invalidated an appropriations statute on the ground that it unconstitutionally impinged upon the president's ill-defined *unenumerated* foreign-affairs authority, as described in *Curtiss-Wright.* In *National Federation of Federal Employees v. United States,* the District of Columbia federal district court invoked the amorphous "role of the Executive in foreign relations" to invalidate a statute precluding the use of appropriated funds to implement or enforce governmental nondisclosure agreements. The Supreme Court vacated and remanded that judgment for procedural reasons, which removed the district-court precedent from the books. But the Court's ruling left the underlying issue unresolved and the president free to challenge future appropriations limitations on executive-branch actions as unconstitutional exercises of Congress's power of the purse.[47]

As the Iran-contra affair revealed, the executive branch may also seek to escape Congress's power of the purse altogether by soliciting private entities to support U.S. foreign-policy initiatives with wholly private monies. Although the Iran-contra committees concluded that the Constitution prohibits such private solicitations *"where the United States exercises control over the receipt and expenditure* of the solicited funds," executive-branch officials could foreseeably circumvent that conclusion by soliciting third parties to directly support foreign initiatives and by arguing that the solicited private monies never became part of the "public fisc" that is subject to Congress's appropriations power.[48] Indeed, Oliver North made such a claim during the congressional hearings into the Iran-contra affair when he acknowledged urging private citizens to support the contras but maintained that "[w]e lived within the constraints of Boland, which limited the use of *appropriated* funds."[49]

Even when undeniably managing government monies, presidents have developed over time a whole range of devices to exploit spending loopholes in the appropriations process. When Congress grants the president statutory "drawdown" authority, the president may withdraw certain funds simply by determining that such withdrawals are vital to the security of the United States. Similar statutory provisions allow the president to access special or contingency funds on the basis of nebulous findings that the use of those funds is "important to the security of the United States" or "to the national interest." When given statutory "transfer" and "reprogramming" authority, the president may transfer to one appropriations account funds initially appropriated for another or may reprogram appropriated funds *within* a single appropriation account, often without specific statutory authority.[50] The Reagan administration showed that these authorities could be used in combination to sustain the Central American conflict without seeking new appropriations. In the early 1980s, the Reagan administration used drawdown authority over special funds to increase military aid to El Salvador by nearly five times the amount actually appropriated in a given year and routinely used the reprogramming authority to fund Central American projects that Congress had not approved.[51]

For all of these defects, the appropriations limitation remains one of Congress's few effective legal tools to regulate presidential initiatives in foreign affairs. Even the most creative president cannot exploit spending loopholes indefinitely. Moreover, each of the open legal questions described above should, in my judgment, be resolved in favor of Congress's appropriations power if Congress's exclusive power over the purse is to have continuing meaning in foreign affairs. But even if the courts eventually rule for Congress on these matters, the litigation may take so long that the president's administration ends before the challenge can be fully decided.[52] Indefinite judicial resolution has kept suspended constitutional objections not just to Congress's creation of appropriations limits, but also to the enforcement of such limits by the comptroller general.[53]

Ultimately, for purposes of Justice Jackson's category three—where presidential power sits at its "lowest ebb" because exercised against express legislative will—Congress retains only two meaningful ways to oppose a presidential initiative. Congress may disapprove the president's action by joint resolution or vote an unambiguous and complete denial of appropriated funds for the disfavored program. But in either case, Congress would then need to override the president's inevitable veto by a two-thirds vote in each house. In the end, both solutions only trade one problem for another, for each requires Congress to exercise a sustained measure of political will that it has only rarely been able to muster.

Political Will

Congress could regularly block executive decisions by joint resolution or appropriations cutoff, so long as it could override a presidential veto by a two-thirds vote. Yet over the years, Congress has overridden only about 4 percent of the presidential vetoes (excluding pocket vetoes) exercised since 1789.[54] Why not more often? In many cases, a critical mass of congressional members have simply been unwilling to take responsibility for setting foreign policy, preferring to leave the decision—and the blame—with the president. As Senator J. William Fulbright recalled, long before the mid-1970s, "[a] majority [of Congress] may have wished to end the war [in Indochina], but less than a majority of the two Houses were willing to take the responsibility for ending it."[55]

The precise critical mass necessary to kill legislation varies from bill to bill. In committee, sometimes even a single member can prevent a bill from reaching the floor; in the Senate, forty-one votes (less than a majority) can defeat cloture. Even in those cases in which a majority in both houses are willing to take a stand against the president, Congress often falls victim to simple numbers. For if Congress must muster a two-thirds vote in both houses to override a veto, only thirty-four senators can undercut those efforts. Even politically weakened presidents can usually muster at least thirty-four votes for something they really want, especially in foreign affairs. In the waning days of his administration, for example, President Reagan secured forty-two votes for the unsuccessful confirmation of Robert Bork as a Supreme Court justice; and early in his term, President George H. W. Bush won forty-seven votes for the ill-fated nomination of John Tower as secretary of defense. President Reagan also succeeded in defeating Congress's effort to override his veto of trade-reform legislation in 1988, essentially by securing the votes of two senators, even though the House had voted overwhelmingly for an override.[56]

At this writing, President Joe Biden's Republican opposition falls more than sixty votes short of the number needed to override a veto.[57] In theory, all members would have an incentive to enhance the power of Congress by enforcing an alternative solution—a binding political agreement to override any presidential veto regardless of its substance.[58] Yet even in a repeat-player game, such an accord simply would not hold up; those members who favored the president's position on any particular bill would always have an incentive to defect and support the president, even if their defection would weaken Congress's strength vis-à-vis the president in the long run. For precisely this reason, Congress was unable to circumvent the Supreme Court's decision in *Chadha* by entering a political compact to reenact all legislative vetoes by joint resolution regardless of their content.[59]

Collective-action problems aside, individual members of Congress face voting dilemmas when the president violates congressionally imposed procedural constraints in pursuit of substantive policies that the members favor. When the Reagan administration sent troops to Grenada and bombers to Libya without complying with the terms of the War Powers Resolution, for example, advocates of his policy decision remained quiet rather than contest his procedural violation.[60] Similarly, parliamentary manipulation by the president's congressional allies may force objecting legislators into untenable voting postures. In 1987, for example, Senator Lowell Weicker, an opponent of the president's Persian Gulf policy, initially voted against a weak resolution protesting the president's acts, on the ground that it implied that the War Powers Resolution was not self-enforcing. He ultimately decided to vote for the resolution, simply to ensure that Congress would register some objection to the president's noncompliance with the War Powers Resolution in the Persian Gulf.[61] It also is not unprecedented for members who led a drive to override the president's veto to vote to sustain the veto, simply to preserve their right to call for the bill's reconsideration.[62]

Some legislative restraints are rarely applied, simply because they leave members too vulnerable to political criticism. Appropriations cutoffs, for example, expose legislators to charges of having stranded soldiers in the field. Even though Congress had constitutional authority through its power of the purse to terminate the United States' involvement in Vietnam long before 1973, "a large majority of Congress felt it could not break with the President without jeopardizing the lives of American troops."[63] Even when Congress has successfully forced the president to the bargaining table on a question of foreign affairs, as it did with regard to the commitment of forces to Lebanon in 1982, the president has usually been able to demand concessions or future support in exchange for agreeing to modify the conduct at issue.[64] Thus, once again, presidents remain largely free to execute their initiatives without congressional check, except in those rare cases in which the president is politically weak and Congress's political will is unusually unified.

Judicial Tolerance

Neither the executive's lack of self-restraint nor Congress's failure to directly enforce its will on the president precludes third parties from enforcing that will through the federal courts. But however attractive this strategy may be in theory, it fades in light of the Supreme Court's pro-executive record on questions of foreign affairs. Since Vietnam, the Supreme Court has intervened consistently across the spectrum of U.S. foreign-policy interests to tip the balance of foreign-policy-making power in favor of the president. Whether on the merits or on justiciability grounds, the courts have ruled for the president in these cases with striking regularity.

The Merits

The history of the National Security Constitution has been a tale of three branches, not two. The player whose role in this foreign-policy drama has most frequently been overlooked has not been Congress or the president, but the federal judiciary. Given the outcome in *Youngstown*, one might have expected subsequent presidents to have encountered less universal success in the courts. But an examination of the president's judicial victories since Vietnam reveals that the president owes much of this success to a judicial revival of the *Curtiss-Wright* theory of the National Security Constitution. *Curtiss-Wright* has not only survived *Youngstown*, but now aggressively challenges it once again.

As chapter 1 explored, during the first era of our constitutional history, the courts played an important and active role in preserving the constitutional principle of balanced institutional participation. Through the next two eras, the courts grew increasingly deferential toward presidential power, at times issuing expansive dicta in support of inherent executive discretion. That trend culminated with the Court's recognition of the president's unenumerated sole-organ power in *Curtiss-Wright* in 1936 and the Court's validation of the president's exclusive recognition powers in *United States v. Belmont* in 1937 and *United States v. Pink* in 1942. Yet even through those years of deference, the Court remained willing to review the president's conduct on the merits, despite occasional hints that political decisions should not be subject to judicial review. One year after the founding of the national security system in 1947, dicta in *Chicago & Southern Air Lines, Inc. v. Waterman Steamship Corp.* strongly asserted the nonreviewability principle, but in *Youngstown*, both the Court and Justice Jackson, in his concurrence, announced a renewed commitment to the principle of balanced institutional participation.

In the decades since, however, the pendulum has swung back in the opposite direction. Particularly since the Vietnam War, the federal courts, through both action and inaction, have adopted an increasingly deferential attitude toward presidential conduct in foreign affairs. By applying a *Curtiss-Wright* orientation to tip particular decisions in favor of executive power, the courts have repeatedly upheld the president's authority to dominate foreign affairs.

Curtiss-Wright and *Youngstown* described sharply divergent visions of the National Security Constitution. *Curtiss-Wright* was decided during the rise of the imperial presidency and the American empire. By giving constitutional legitimacy to the concept of presidential dominance in foreign affairs, *Curtiss-Wright* forcefully contributed to the activist-presidency model fostered by Franklin Roosevelt. The vision of *Curtiss-Wright* carried the nation through World War II, a time when the nation drew together of necessity and Congress and the president shared a consensus about national ends. The president and Congress then designed the national security system in 1947 to sustain that national consensus in the Cold War years through a model of management by an institutional and plebiscitary presidency. But when President Truman used that system to extend the national security state and lead the nation into the unpopular, undeclared Korean War, the *Youngstown* Court reaffirmed the limits that the National Security Constitution placed on his authority.

Youngstown both reiterated limits on exclusive presidential powers in foreign affairs and specified roles for congressional consultation and judicial review in distributing concurrent constitutional authority. Both Justice Black's opinion for the Court and Justice Jackson's concurrence read *Curtiss-Wright* as resting not on inherent presidential power, but on whether Congress had authorized the executive action under challenge.[65] Both opinions suggested that, even in foreign affairs, executive decisions based on legislative consent will more likely express the consent of the governed than those generated by the bureaucracy alone.

As chapter 2 described, during the Warren Court years, the *Youngstown* theory largely held sway. But the Vietnam War disrupted both the dialogue and the foreign-policy consensus between Congress and the president that *Youngstown* had sought to foster. When Congress responded to the president's Vietnam-era abuses by embedding the *Youngstown* vision in a series of framework statutes, the Burger Court threw its weight toward *Curtiss-Wright*, which reemerged as the touchstone of the Court's foreign-affairs jurisprudence.

The first traces of this pattern appeared in 1971, when the Court rejected the efforts of the Nixon administration to enjoin publication of the Pentagon Papers without statutory authorization.[66] Although the votes of the First Amendment absolutists then sitting on the Court sealed the president's defeat in the *Pentagon Papers* case, the separate opinions unveiled a strong undercurrent favoring the *Curtiss-Wright* vision of executive supremacy in foreign affairs.

Three justices rejected the president's claims on First Amendment grounds, and a fourth did so primarily because congressional authorization was absent. But the three dissenters would have upheld the president's power, resting on *Curtiss-Wright*.[67] Moreover, the two swing justices, Potter Stewart and Byron White, not only acknowledged the need for executive supremacy in foreign affairs, but openly contemplated other situations in which they might be willing to approve a prior restraint against publication on the basis of national security claims. Justice Stewart declared that "[i]f the Constitution gives the Executive a large degree of unshared power in the conduct of foreign affairs and the maintenance of our national defense, then under the Constitution the Executive must have the largely unshared duty to determine and preserve the degree of internal security necessary to exercise that power successfully."[68] Less than a decade later, in a suit that the government later dropped, a lower federal court relied on Justice Stewart's opinion to enjoin publication of a magazine article whose subject matter later appeared elsewhere.[69]

Following the *Pentagon Papers* case, the executive-supremacy undercurrent resurfaced, as the Burger and Rehnquist Courts resurrected *Curtiss-Wright*, not so much in constitutional interpretation as in the realm of statutory construction. Against *Youngstown's* theme of legislative consent, *Curtiss-Wright* counterposed the principle of executive discretion: "congressional legislation . . . within the international field must often accord to the President *a degree of discretion and freedom from statutory restriction which would not be admissible were domestic affairs alone involved.*"[70] In the 1970s and 1980s, executive-branch attorneys urged that language upon courts construing statutes on foreign affairs as a canon of deferential statutory construction (what I call "statutory *Curtiss-Wright*"). Even when Congress has enacted statutes designed to limit executive power in foreign affairs, executive-branch attorneys have liberally construed statutory loopholes to permit or authorize executive initiatives that Congress never anticipated.[71]

The Burger Court had several opportunities to read *Curtiss-Wright* strictly and thereby rein in this executive practice. On each occasion, however, the Court ruled in the president's favor, approving rather than rejecting the president's self-serving construction of the statute in question.[72] Late in the Carter administration, the Supreme Court decided *Snepp v. United States,* in which the CIA sued a former agent for writing a book without the preclearance required under the terms of a nondisclosure agreement. Without briefing or oral argument on the question, the Court chose to award the government both a permanent injunction barring Snepp from speaking or writing without preclearance and an unprecedented post-publication constructive trust to recover the profits of the book. Without citing *Youngstown* or asking the *Kent v. Dulles* question—whether Congress had specifically authorized courts to restrain authors' rights by creating either pre-publication injunctions or post-publication constructive trusts—the Court dismissed Snepp's First Amendment claims in a footnote and inferred legislative authority for the CIA's acts from general language in the National Security Act.[73]

In the first foreign-affairs case of the Reagan era, *Dames & Moore v. Regan,* the Supreme Court upheld President Carter's authority to nullify judicial attachments, transfer frozen Iranian assets, and suspend private commercial claims against Iran as part of an executive agreement to free the American hostages in Iran. Dames & Moore, a company owed money by Iran, charged that the executive branch had violated the company's Fifth Amendment rights by taking its claims against Iran and voiding its prejudgment attachments on Iranian assets without paying just compensation. In an opinion issued barely a month after the complaint was filed, Justice William

Rehnquist, writing for a nearly unanimous Court, largely rebuffed these claims. The Court held that the International Emergency Economic Powers Act (IEEPA) had authorized the nullification and transfer, but could find no express authority in the act for the president's suspension of private claims. Nevertheless, Justice Rehnquist relied on the absence of express congressional disapproval of the president's action, the fact of IEEPA's existence, and a history of unchecked executive practice to conclude that Congress had endorsed the president's initiative, which brought the case within Justice Jackson's category one.[74] He further held that the nullification of the attachments did not constitute a taking and that the remaining takings claims were not ripe for judicial review.[75]

Justice Rehnquist's opinion purported "to lay down no general 'guidelines' covering other situations not involved here."[76] Nevertheless, his opinion introduced a three-part technique of statutory construction that the Supreme Court has since applied to many statutes on foreign affairs. First, notwithstanding *Kent v. Dulles,* Justice Rehnquist did not demand a "clear statement" that Congress had authorized the president to suspend individual claims, despite the undeniable impact of the president's act on individual rights. He thereby permitted executive discretion to override individual rights without a clear expression of legislative consent to do so. Second, he read IEEPA's language as unambiguously authorizing some of the executive acts under challenge, passing over the legislative history of the statute, which, as explained in chapter 3, clearly evinced a contrary legislative intent to narrow presidential power. Third, rather than construe IEEPA's silence regarding the suspension of claims as preempting the president's claim of inherent power to act, Justice Rehnquist construed a history of unchecked executive practice, the fact of IEEPA's existence, and the absence of express congressional disapproval of the president's action to demonstrate that Congress had *impliedly* authorized that action, thereby elevating the president's power from the twilight zone—Jackson's category two—to its height in Jackson's category one. He effectively followed the dissenting view in *Youngstown,* which had converted legislative silence into consent, and thereby delegated to the president authority that Congress itself had arguably withheld.[77]

It is hard to fault the result in *Dames & Moore,* given the crisis atmosphere that surrounded the decision and the national mood of support for the hostage accord. Yet given Rehnquist's own past experience as Justice Jackson's law clerk during *Youngstown,* in which the president had taken similarly drastic action without national support, one might have expected the Court to demand more specific legislative approval for the president's far-reaching measures.[78] The hostages had returned home months earlier, and the hostage accord had given the U.S. government six months before the frozen Iranian assets were to be transferred—plenty of time for the president to ask a supportive Congress for a swift joint resolution of approval. Yet by finding legislative "approval" when Congress had given none, Rehnquist not only inverted *Youngstown*'s holding—which had construed statutory non-approval of the president's act to mean legislative disapproval—but also condoned legislative inactivity at a time that demanded interbranch dialogue and bipartisan consensus.

Had the Court subsequently given *Dames & Moore* the narrow reading originally intended, its holding could have been limited to its highly unusual facts. But the decision effectively encouraged the president to act first and then search for preexisting congressional blank checks, rather than seek specific prior or immediately subsequent legislative approval of controversial decisions.[79] In later foreign-policy crises, *Dames & Moore* has encouraged executive-branch lawyers to play "find the statute," that is, to search the U.S. Code for preexisting statutes that they can claim already directly or implicitly authorized the challenged action. This has allowed the president to avoid asking the legislature for new legislative authority, which might be withheld. It has equally allowed Congress to act affronted, even when it holds hearings to complain or dissemble, while relieving Congress of public responsibility to back or oppose the policy. The courts can then invoke justiciability doctrines to avoid hearing challenges to the policy or, if forced to decide on the merits, can defer to executive discretion, citing the broad forms of congressional acquiescence described in *Dames & Moore.*[80]

In other decisions, the Burger Court chose to extend each prong of the generous statutory-construction method applied in *Dames & Moore.* In *Haig v. Agee,* a case decided less than a week before *Dames & Moore,* Chief Justice Burger upheld, on the basis of a dubious reading of the Passport Act, the secretary of state's revocation of an author's passport and gave similarly short shrift to the individual rights infringed by the executive action. Citing *Curtiss-Wright,* the Court ignored the principle of balanced institutional participation, suggesting that "in the areas of foreign policy and national security . . .

congressional silence is not to be equated with congressional disapproval."[81] Three years later, in *Regan v. Wald*, the Court applied the *Dames & Moore* technique of statutory construction to uphold President Reagan's power to regulate travel to Cuba under IEEPA's grandfather clause, despite unambiguous statutory language and legislative history to the contrary.[82] *Wald* went beyond *Dames & Moore*, insofar as it construed an ambiguous statute to override not simply property rights, but also the right to international travel guaranteed by the due-process clause of the Fifth Amendment. Although the Court of Appeals had properly applied *Kent v. Dulles*'s clear-statement principle and found insufficient evidence of legislative consent, Justice Rehnquist refused to do the same, now citing *Curtiss-Wright* to mandate "traditional deference to executive judgment '[i]n this vast external realm.'"[83]

What made the Court's deference in *Wald* remarkable was that the president could have sustained his Cuba travel restrictions without seeking renewed congressional consent simply by declaring a new national emergency under IEEPA (as he did shortly thereafter with respect to Nicaragua, Libya, South Africa, and Panama). Such a declaration would have occasioned national discussion about whether—after more than two decades of emergency controls—our relations with Cuba still constituted a national emergency warranting continued travel restrictions. That question was not merely academic, given that President Carter had licensed travel to Cuba for the five years before 1982, when President Reagan reimposed travel controls.[84] But by "grandfathering" preexisting statutory power, the Court again exalted executive discretion over legislative consent, once again allowing both the president and Congress to avoid making fresh judgments on that important foreign-policy question.

In 1983, the Court dramatically expanded the third prong of its *Dames & Moore* statutory analysis with its decision invalidating legislative vetoes, *INS v. Chadha*. *Chadha* construed Article I, section 7 of the Constitution to require that any congressional action that is "legislative in purpose and effect"—in the sense that it "alter[s] the legal rights, duties, and relations of persons . . . outside the Legislative Branch"—be both approved by a majority of both houses of Congress and presented to the president.[85] Because two-house vetoes (concurrent resolutions) meet only the first requirement and because one-house vetoes (simple resolutions) satisfy neither, the Court's reasoning invalidated both types of legislative vetoes. Although some commentators have suggested that some legislative vetoes survive *Chadha*, the Court's reasoning admits of no exceptions, thereby barring Congress from vetoing any presidential action in foreign affairs that it may disapprove of.[86] In the realm of foreign affairs, *Chadha* struck down, among other laws, the legislative-veto provisions in the War Powers Resolution, the Arms Export Control Act, the Nuclear Non-Proliferation Act, the National Emergencies Act, and IEEPA.[87] Thus, Congress may now disapprove an executive act in those areas only by passing a joint resolution in both houses and presenting it to the president, who would of course be entitled to veto it. As demonstrated in chapter 3 in the context of arms sales, the president may consequently make numerous major foreign-policy decisions under the cloak of congressional approval when in fact the president possesses support from only the thirty-four senators needed to sustain a presidential veto against an override.

Read together, *Dames & Moore* and *Chadha* dramatically altered the application of Justice Jackson's tripartite *Youngstown* analysis in foreign-affairs cases. As we have seen, Justice Rehnquist's *Dames & Moore* reasoning authorizes judges to construe congressional inaction or legislation in a related area as implicit approval for a challenged executive action. Yet under *Chadha*, Congress may definitively *disapprove* an executive act only by passing a joint resolution by a supermajority in both houses that is sufficient to override a subsequent presidential veto. These rulings create a one-way "ratchet effect" that effectively redraws the categories described in Justice Jackson's *Youngstown* concurrence. By treating ambiguous congressional action as approval for a challenged presidential act, a court can move almost any act out of the lower two Jackson categories, where it would be subject to challenge, and into Jackson's category one, where the president's legal authority would be unassailable. Yet because *Chadha* demands an extraordinary display of political will to disapprove a presidential act, Congress can only rarely return those acts to Jackson's category three, where a court may declare them invalid. Thus, these decisions effectively narrow Jackson's category three to those very few foreign-affairs cases in which the president both lacks exclusive constitutional powers and is foolish enough to act against congressional intent clearly expressed on the face of a statute.[88]

Coupled with *Chadha*, Justice Rehnquist's statutory interpretation in *Dames & Moore* enhanced the president's power against Congress by making it easier to find congressional approval and more difficult for Congress to express its institutional opposition to particular executive acts. The decisions simultaneously strengthened the president vis-à-vis the courts by effectively requiring them to apply special deference to executive acts in foreign affairs, a requirement that Justice Jackson had soundly rejected in *Youngstown* itself.

Chadha's broadest impact in foreign affairs derives not from what it says the president may do, but from what it implies Congress may not do. As construed in light of *Bowsher v. Synar*, decided two terms later, *Chadha* sketched a formalistic theory of separation of powers that rests on four basic premises: first, that constitutional powers are functionally definable as inherently executive, judicial, or legislative in nature; second, that the Constitution allocates certain powers exclusively to the executive branch, thereby denying them to the other two branches; third, that Congress has limited constitutional discretion to regulate executive action by means other than formal legislation; and fourth, that these separation-of-powers concerns require that specific constitutional provisions—such as the appointments clause or the presentment clause—be construed to invalidate even those legislative control devices that plainly promote administrative efficiency or political compromise.[89] To then read the power to conduct foreign affairs as an inherently executive one that Congress and the courts may not exercise or restrain by legislation or judicial decision—as *Curtiss-Wright* argued—would leave no room for the *Youngstown* vision of balanced institutional participation that is central to the National Security Constitution.[90]

Fortunately, in two follow-on cases decided outside the realm of foreign affairs, the Court cautiously retreated from *Chadha*'s formalism. In *Morrison v. Olson* and *Mistretta v. United States,* the Court declined to extend the formalistic separation-of-powers theory of *Chadha* and *Bowsher* to invalidate new laws—in *Morrison,* the independent-counsel provisions of the Ethics in Government Act, and in *Mistretta,* the new federal guidelines issued by the U.S. Sentencing Commission. In both cases, the Court's opinion eschewed *Chadha*'s formalistic approach in favor of a more flexible, functional separation-of-powers analysis that would permit a broader interbranch sharing of powers. Instead of asking the formalistic question, whether the powers being exercised were exclusively executive or legislative, the Court asked instead a functional question, whether the challenged legislation had aggrandized or encroached upon the president's ability to perform duties "central to the functioning of the Executive Branch."[91]

In important respects, *Chadha*'s formalism marked a Pyrrhic victory for the president. After all, it is the president, not Congress, who more frequently engages in foreign-affairs activities that are not authorized by the text of the Constitution.[92] Moreover, the president often promises Congress a measure of control as the price for winning desired statutory authority. By depriving Congress of formal devices such as the legislative veto that allow it to control delegated authority, *Chadha* encourages Congress to withhold future delegations, to take back statutory foreign-affairs powers that it has previously delegated to the president, or to construct informal, nonstatutory legislative vetoes of the type to which President Bush consented in March 1989 in his "Good Friday accords" with Congress to secure continued contra aid.[93] Finally, a strict application of *Chadha*'s formalistic reasoning would permit Congress to employ throughout its foreign-affairs legislation congressional control devices that are functionally more intrusive than the legislative veto— for example, a fast-track statutory approval device similar to the device found in the international-trade statutes—but that do not run afoul of *Chadha*'s literal holding.[94]

The Rehnquist Court's *Curtiss-Wright* orientation toward statutory construction challenged the *Youngstown* vision of balanced institutional participation. In *Weinberger v. Catholic Action of Hawaii/Peace Education Project,* decided one term after *Dames & Moore,* the navy refused to confirm or deny that it had stored nuclear weapons at a Hawaiian facility, claiming that the information was classified. Less than a decade earlier, in 1974, Congress had passed amendments to the Freedom of Information Act requiring the courts to make a de novo determination whether such a classification was proper. Nevertheless, Justice Rehnquist accepted the government's claim of a national security interest at face value, without conducting such a review or even considering Congress's intent that the executive's classification decisions receive close judicial scrutiny.[95] In *Japan Whaling Ass'n v. American Cetacean Society,* the Court similarly undercut legislation designed to place stringent limits on executive discretion.[96] Congress had passed two amendments to fisheries statutes, imposing a mandatory duty on the secretary of commerce to certify to the president any fishing operations by foreign nationals that "diminish the effectiveness" of an international fishery conservation program.[97] Although the International Whaling Commission had established a "zero quota" against the taking of whales in accordance with an international treaty, the commerce secretary chose not to certify Japan's whaling activities, in light of an executive agreement under which the United States permitted Japan to keep whaling at certain harvest levels for a fixed period of years. In a dissent joined even by Justice Rehnquist, Justice Thurgood Marshall charged that the secretary had "exceeded his own authority," had "substitute[d] . . . his judgment for Congress' on the issue of how best to respond to a foreign nation's intentional past violation of quotas," and had "flouted the express will of Congress."[98]

After *Japan Whaling,* the Rehnquist Court largely continued to support the expansive executive claims of foreign-affairs power. Even when the Court ruled against the executive in cases bearing on foreign affairs, it did not deny the executive's broader claim of substantive authority.[99] Its most expansive declaration of deference to executive discretion came in *Department of the Navy v. Egan,* in which the navy discharged an employee after revoking his security clearance without a hearing. As in *Curtiss-Wright* and *Waterman,* the Court's strict holding rested on narrow statutory grounds—that the statute empowering the Merit Systems Protection Board gave the board no authority to review the substance of the underlying security-clearance determination. But in ruling that executive agencies like the navy had inherent discretion to make judgments regarding security clearances, the Court issued broad pro-executive dicta, declaring that the president's "authority to classify and control access to information bearing on national security and to determine whether an individual is sufficiently trustworthy to occupy a position in the Executive Branch . . . flows primarily from . . . [the president's commander-in-chief power] *and exists quite apart from any explicit congressional grant.*"[100] The dissent, by contrast, found no evidence that Congress or the president had expressly agreed that alleged security risks should be discharged without a hearing, and objected to the Court's *Dames & Moore* technique to "assum[e] such a result from congressional 'non-action.'"[101]

Significantly, Congress designed none of these statutes to shift the balance of decision-making power in foreign affairs from Congress toward the president. Several statutes, such as the fisheries amendments and IEEPA, were enacted for precisely the opposite purpose. But the Supreme Court's reading of these statutes enhanced presidential power by encouraging lawyers throughout the executive branch to construe their agency's authorizing statutes to permit executive initiatives extending far beyond the intended scope of those statutes.

In reaching these decisions, the Burger and Rehnquist Courts rejected virtually every doctrinal technique offered them to narrow the substantive scope of executive power. When urged to apply the nondelegation doctrine to invalidate a grant of power to the president, the Court held that the doctrine does not apply equally to foreign affairs.[102] When asked to construe the existence of a statute in the field to preempt a claim of inherent presidential power to make foreign policy, the Court refused.[103] When asked to read narrowly a statute that impinged on constitutional rights, the Court refused to apply the clear-statement rule.[104] When urged to uphold the constitutionality of a congressional control device, the Court invalidated it.[105]

In short, far from maintaining a rough balance in the congressional-executive tug-of-war, the Court's decisions on the merits of foreign-affairs claims have encouraged a steady flow of policymaking power from Congress to the executive. Through unjustifiably deferential techniques of statutory construction, since Vietnam the courts have read *Curtiss-Wright* and its progeny to undermine the constitutional vision of *Youngstown*.

Justiciability

As important as these rulings on the merits have been, in many cases the Court has condoned executive initiatives in foreign affairs by refusing to hear challenges to the president's authority. In *Goldwater v. Carter,* the Court dismissed congressional challenges to presidential treaty breaking, with various justices finding the challenges not ripe or presenting nonjusticiable political questions.[106] In *Burke v. Barnes,* the Court dismissed as moot a congressional challenge to President Reagan's pocket veto of a foreign-aid bill that would have required him to certify El Salvador's progress in protecting human rights.[107] These Supreme Court decisions stand atop a much larger collection of lower-federal-court cases that, over the years, refused to hear challenges to the legality of the Vietnam War and to various aspects of the Reagan administration's support for the contras.[108]

Even when the courts have not relied on nonjusticiability doctrines tied to the nature, ripeness, or mootness of the question presented, they have invoked the identity of the plaintiff or the defendant, the cause of action, or the requested relief as grounds for dismissing the case. The Supreme Court has erected standing bars to suits regarding foreign affairs brought by aliens, citizens, taxpayers, and members of Congress.[109] Courts have held governmental officials immune from suits by citizens for monetary damages.[110] They have held the United States government, and private parties who contract with the government, immune from suits by members of the armed forces for all manner of injuries.[111] Courts have dismissed state, federal, and international-law claims against federal defendants for want of a cause of action.[112] Even when courts have conceded a right, they have denied claims for both mone-tary and equitable remedies on fuzzy "equitable discretion" grounds.[113] The lower courts have dismissed so many challenges to executive conduct by so many carefully selected plaintiff groups that the courts' opinions now seem to pick and choose almost randomly from among the available abstention ratio-nales.[114] In contrast, when Congress has raised similar defenses to suits brought by the executive branch, the Supreme Court has uniformly rejected them.[115] In short, the Court has been almost "totally deferential in reviewing challenges to executive conduct, but . . . very willing to declare unconstitu-tional congressional statutes as violating separation of powers."[116]

Chapter 10 addresses and challenges the prudential concerns that have led the courts to defer so broadly to the executive in foreign affairs. But however powerful these rationales may be, they provide no intellectual support for such sweeping statements of judicial abdication.[117] Nor do they explain the persistent reluctance of the courts to look behind talismanic executive asser-tions of national security, military necessity, or the need for judicial defer-ence to the political branches in matters of military discipline and military affairs.[118] Finally, those prudential concerns do not explain the troubling con-fusion that judges have exhibited in attempting to distinguish cases in which they find the president's conduct unreviewable from those in which they re-view the president's conduct and find it authorized.[119]

As the first two chapters reviewed, as the National Security Constitution has evolved since the founding, the courts have played a pivotal role in main-taining the constitutional equilibrium of the national security system. That role has required judges to police the boundaries of the branches' authority in foreign affairs to maintain the constitutional principle of balanced institu-tional participation. Particularly when Congress legislates a framework stat-ute governing executive decisions, those decisions should remain fully subject to judicial review.[120] Thus, the Burger and Rehnquist Courts' push toward executive insulation from judicial review in foreign affairs marked a relatively recent development, with little support in our constitutional traditions.

Why the President Wins

The broader lesson that emerges from this study of executive initiative, congressional acquiescence, and judicial tolerance in the post-Vietnam era is that under virtually every scenario, the president wins. If the executive branch possesses statutory or constitutional authority to act and Congress acquiesces, the president wins. If Congress does not acquiesce in the president's act, but lacks the political will either to cut off appropriations or to pass an objecting statute and override a veto, the president again wins. If a member of Congress or a private individual sues to challenge the president's action, the judiciary will likely refuse to hear that challenge on the ground that the plaintiff lacks standing; that the defendant is immune; that the question is political, not ripe, or moot; or that relief is inappropriate. Even if the plaintiffs somehow surmount each of these obstacles and persuade the courts to hear their challenge on the merits, the courts will usually rule in the president's favor. In sum, whatever the scenario, the bottom line has stayed the same: the president almost always seems to win in foreign affairs.

Over time, this doctrinal tangle has afforded presidential judgment in foreign affairs extraordinary insulation from external scrutiny. And as subsequent history shows, even though this trend was paused by a string of Supreme Court rulings against the George W. Bush administration's counterterrorism policy after September 11, 2001, the trend has renewed, if not intensified, in the decades since. The *Curtiss-Wright* vision has grown increasingly ascendant during the first quarter of the twenty-first century, to which part 2 now turns.

PART TWO

THE *CURTISS-WRIGHT* VISION

Bush 41 and Clinton: Globalization Dawns

"THE POST–COLD WAR ERA BEGAN," John Lewis Gaddis noted, "with the collapse of one structure, the Berlin Wall in November 1989, and . . . ended with the collapse of another structure, the World Trade Center on September 11, 2001."[1] That era spanned the presidential terms of two moderates, Republican George H. W. Bush ("Bush 41") and Democrat Bill Clinton. These years, which stretched from the end of the Cold War to the start of what the administration of George W. Bush ("Bush 43") dubbed the "global war on terror," were marked by the renewed rise of *Curtiss-Wright*.

Looking back, the closing decades of the twentieth century broadly reflected the optimistic dawn of the age of globalization, when barriers to trade, travel, finance, communications, and culture fell at an astonishing rate. The immediate post–Cold War era reflected a window of optimism about the constructive possibilities posed by the growing global networks to achieve global solutions to global problems. Empowered individuals could suddenly "cross borders" with a keystroke. Communications and commerce that previously had taken months could be transacted in moments, enabling reliance on global supply chains and global discussions about rights and democracy. South Africa, much of Central and Eastern Europe, and much of Latin America turned democratic, in what some called the "globalization of freedom": from fewer than 25 democracies worldwide in the 1970s, to more than 120 in the early 2000s.[2]

In 1992, Bush 41 became the first president in the age of email; the Clinton White House launched its first website in 1994. When Bill Clinton took office in 1993, just 24 percent of American households had computers; only ten million people worldwide were connected to the internet; and there were just fifty websites on the World Wide Web. But by the time he left office in the first year of the twenty-first century, the percentage of American households with computers and the number of people connected to the internet had doubled, and the number of websites had multiplied a million-fold. The "bridge to the 21st century" was well under way.[3]

Both Bush 41 and Clinton made visible efforts to adhere to the shared-power principles of the National Security Constitution. But in equally visible ways, the national security decision-making process continued to degenerate into one that forced the president to react to perceived crises; that allowed Congress to acquiesce in and avoid accountability for important foreign-policy decisions; and that permitted the courts to condone these political decisions. In a multimedia era, a plebiscitary president's capacity to address foreign affairs carries with it a perceived obligation to react to every new crisis. As media-driven presidents, Bush and Clinton became consumed in a perpetual reactive effort to "control the narrative" by appearing strong. Both presidents understood that their current popularity rating could vanish in weeks. Just after the Gulf War, Bush's popularity rating stood at nearly 90 percent; only ten months later, it had plummeted, and he lost reelection.[4]

The Bush 41–Clinton era also illustrated that divided government invites executive unilateralism. Particularly after a Republican Congress led by Bob Dole and Newt Gingrich seized power in the winter of 1995 and the Monica Lewinsky sex scandal drove Clinton's impeachment by the House, Clinton governed largely reactively in foreign affairs. The prospect of interbranch deadlock made it far more likely that the executive branch would resort to unilateralism in a crisis. Amid legislative gridlock, the president's difficulty exhibiting strength in domestic affairs—where Congress exercises greater oversight and must initiate funding proposals—makes it far easier for the president to show foreign-affairs leadership. At the same time, weak presidents may initially underreact to looming crises that demand strong action, for fear that they cannot muster the longer-term legislative support necessary to generate the appropriate response. But when weak presidents finally do respond, they tend to compensate by overreacting after an undermanaged foreign crisis has escalated into a full-blown crisis. From this era, the Balkans and Haiti became the most prominent examples. Reactive presidents

may also undercut their own foreign-policy program to preserve their domestic agenda, which usually determines both their reelection prospects and
their legacy. As Bush 41 and Clinton increasingly applied such tactics in the
closing decades of the twentieth century, the slanted incentives created by
divided government and reactive presidents only intensified the growing
dysfunction in our national security system. The synergy among these institutional incentives helped drive the steady migration of the national security
decision-making process toward executive unilateralism during these "post-
post–Cold War years."

George H. W. Bush and the "New World Order"

The one-term presidency of George H. W. Bush appears, in retrospect, to
be the last Republican administration generally accepting of *Youngstown*'s
constitutional vision of balanced institutional participation. Having previously served as a congressman, vice president, CIA director, and U.S. ambassador to the United Nations and China, Bush 41 possessed broad legislative
experience and confidence in the bureaucracy. He surrounded himself with
pragmatic, like-minded thinkers, including his national security adviser
Brent Scowcroft, Secretary of State James Baker, and former general and the
chairman of the Joint Chiefs of Staff Colin Powell. In his first inaugural address, Bush spoke aspirationally of a philosophy in which "our differences
ended at the water's edge" and called for the close cooperation between the
executive and legislative branches in foreign relations.[5]

Bush accompanied his call for domestic power sharing with an interna-
tionalist vision premised on international law. After the Berlin Wall fell, he
repeatedly called for a "new world order": "an historic period of cooperation"
in which "the nations of the world, East and West, North and South, can
prosper and live in harmony," "freer from the threat of terror, stronger in the
pursuit of justice, and more secure in the quest for peace."[6] Upon launching
the First Gulf War in January 1991, he again evoked "the opportunity to forge
for ourselves and for future generations a new world order—a world where
the rule of law, not the law of the jungle, governs the conduct of nations.
When we are successful—and we will be—we have a real chance at this new
world order, an order in which a credible United Nations can use its peacekeeping role to fulfill the promise and vision of the U.N.'s founders."[7] In the

years that followed, Bush 41 honored both multilateral decision-making and a significant congressional role in foreign affairs while addressing three major foreign-policy challenges: the collapse of the Soviet Union, the Chinese uprising at Tiananmen Square, and Saddam Hussein's invasion of Kuwait.

The First Gulf War

"Operation Desert Storm," the response to the invasion of Kuwait in 1990 particularly tested Bush 41's fealty to the *Youngstown* vision. Six days after Iraq invaded Kuwait, President Bush ordered the overseas deployment of nearly half a million U.S. combat forces, the largest military deployment since Vietnam. After an initial feint at both international and domestic unilateralism, Bush 41 ended up asking both the United Nations and Congress to approve his effort to use large-scale military force to oust Saddam Hussein from Kuwait. The president initially threatened to make war with U.N. Security Council approval alone, without seeking congressional consent. Congress initially avoided taking a stand, and the courts declined to enjoin an unauthorized war. But in January 1991, a constitutional crisis was narrowly averted as President Bush finally requested and Congress passed a joint resolution that authorized large-scale use of military force against Iraq.[8]

The Desert Storm episode revealed how a process of balanced institutional participation can ensure the power-sharing norm directed by the National Security Constitution. In ways not fully appreciated by the public, D.C. federal district judge Harold Greene's decision in *Dellums v. Bush* helped break the looming impasse between the political branches.[9] Although Judge Greene held unripe a request by members of Congress to enjoin an unauthorized war, he accepted two claims made both by plaintiffs and a law professors' amicus curiae memorandum: that the Constitution did not permit the president to order U.S. armed forces to make war without meaningful consultation with and affirmative authorization from Congress; and that the political-question doctrine did not bar a federal court from deciding that constitutional question in an appropriate case or controversy.[10] In what amounted to an unappealable declaratory judgment against the administration, Judge Greene concluded that "in principle, an injunction may issue at the request of Members of Congress to prevent the conduct of a war which is about to be carried on without congressional authorization." Had President Bush proceeded to wage war against Iraq without congressional authorization, he undoubtedly would have faced a string of suits citing that proposition, brought by soldiers asserting ripe claims not to fight and die in a constitutionally unauthorized war.[11]

Congress's eleventh-hour joint resolution averted that outcome and established a piece of "quasi-constitutional custom" around which future institutional expectations could coalesce. All three branches eventually acknowledged Congress's constitutional right to approve a war of this magnitude. Judge Greene found that "the forces involved are of such magnitude and significance as to present no serious claim that a war would not ensue if they became engaged in combat, and it is therefore clear that congressional approval is required if Congress desires to become involved."[12] Congress's authorizing resolution in Iraq expressly invoked the War Powers Resolution, and the president finally came to Congress and asked for its approval. The resulting military action was expressly confined to driving Saddam out of Kuwait, not engaging in offensive action against Iraq for purposes of regime change. Thus, Desert Storm joined the two world wars and Vietnam as one of four instances in the twentieth century in which the president sought formal approval for a major war—leaving Korea as the one glaring exception.

Extraordinary Rendition

But during those same years, Bush 41 also licensed a series of smaller-scale extraterritorial interventions without prior congressional or judicial approval. His administration argued that the president, acting through the attorney general, has constitutional authority to seize individuals abroad and "render" them to U.S. judicial proceedings, even if those actions violate international law.

During the Carter administration, only months after the United States and Mexico had concluded an extradition treaty that appeared to foreclose state-sponsored kidnapping of suspects on foreign soil, the Justice Department contemplated the extraterritorial abduction of the rogue financier Robert Vesco. But the department's Office of Legal Counsel (OLC) issued an opinion in 1980 concluding that "the FBI only has lawful authority [to engage in extraterritorial apprehension] when the asylum state acquiesces to the proposed operation." Given the contemporaneous understanding of the contracting parties, there was no need for the treaty to expressly prohibit state-sponsored kidnapping, because that conduct breaks one of the clearest rules of international law: that one sovereign shall not violate the territory of another. The opinion thus concluded that the FBI could not apprehend fugitives in contravention of international law under its general enabling statutes, reasoning that those statutes must be construed restrictively to prohibit any departure from the standards of international law. The agency reasoned that "a forcible abduction, when coupled with a protest by the asylum state, is a violation of international law. It is regarded as an impermissible invasion of the territorial integrity of another state."[13]

But when, in 1988, two grand juries indicted Panamanian dictator General Manuel Noriega for drug trafficking and racketeering, the Bush administration reviewed and secretly reversed the earlier OLC opinion. Noriega, who was prominently shipping arms to Marxist rebels in El Salvador, had harassed U.S. military personnel and citizens in Panama, and detained hundreds of American schoolchildren at gunpoint for hours in early 1989. Seven months after Noriega stole the presidential election in May 1989, the Bush 41 administration launched "Operation Just Cause" in Panama, inserting twenty-three thousand soldiers to seize Noriega and bring him to Miami, where he was tried, convicted, and sentenced to forty years in prison for drug trafficking, then extradited to France to face murder charges.[14]

The Noriega affair marked the first of what Professor Steven Arrigg Koh would later call "foreign affairs prosecutions": uses of military force and foreign-affairs authorities to pursue domestic criminal justice. This nascent trend toward what he has elsewhere called "the criminalization of foreign relations" would only expand and multiply during the first two decades of the twenty-first century.[15] Although the Noriega seizure seemed to flatly violate the 1980 OLC opinion, the Bush 41 administration justified the legality of its "snatch authority" in a secret OLC opinion that partially reversed that earlier opinion. The new opinion was issued in 1989, after the Noriega invasion, by then assistant attorney general William Barr, who later became attorney general in both the Bush 41 and Trump administrations.[16]

Less than a year later, again advised by Barr, Bush doubled down on this use of extraterritorial snatch authority. U.S. law-enforcement agencies orchestrated the kidnapping from Mexico of Dr. Humberto Alvarez-Machain forcibly bringing him to the United States on charges of participating in the torture and killing in Mexico of a Drug Enforcement Administration (DEA) agent. In secretly authorizing the seizure, Barr conceded that extraterritorial apprehension departed from customary international law, but argued that the president could override it, claiming that the "1989 opinion does not address the legal implications of deploying the FBI in violation of provisions of self-executing treaties or treaties that have been implemented by legislation," a category that includes extradition treaties.[17]

Over the next few years, the Office of Legal Counsel rebuffed repeated congressional efforts to obtain that secret opinion, citing both attorney-client and executive privilege. Barr's refusal to release the 1989 opinion left outsiders in the dark. They had no way to tell whether the secret opinion rested on factual assumptions that did not apply to the earlier situation; which part of the earlier opinion had not been overruled; or whether the overruling opinion contained nuances, subtleties, or exceptions that Barr's summary in congressional testimony simply omitted. In sum, the agency simply ignored its own prior opinion without ever explaining the factual basis for the later opinion or why the previous opinion was wrongly reasoned.

One might expect the Office of Legal Counsel to explain itself publicly when it overrules a prior opinion that is less than a decade old and claims for the first time general executive authority not simply to override customary international law, but to read a kidnapping exception into a ratified treaty. This is particularly true given that a related matter was pending before the Supreme Court in *United States v. Alvarez-Machain*. Even as the 1989 OLC opinion remained confidential, the *Alvarez-Machain* Court upheld the legality of this state-sponsored abduction, in a controversial 6-to-3 decision, deeply straining U.S. relations with Mexico and evoking widespread condemnation from foreign governments and legal scholars. Justice John Paul Stevens, writing for the dissent, called the majority's decision "monstrous" and accused the majority of unduly deferring to the executive branch's "intense interest in punishing [Alvarez-Machain] in our courts."[18] Nevertheless, both of the other branches of government acquiesced in the executive branch's reversal of position.

In congressional testimony delivered in November 1989, Barr continued to stonewall, testifying before a House subcommittee that "the content of the 1989 Opinion . . . must remain confidential." He added, however, that he was "happy to share with the Committee [OLC's] legal reasoning and conclusions" in summary.[19] But it came to light, when his opinion was finally declassified and made public in 1993, that Barr had performed a signature three-step lawyerly "move," akin to distinctive moves deployed by particular athletes and dancers. First, when asked by the congressional committee for the opinion, he refused and delayed. Second, when asked to release an opinion, he summarized. Third, he slanted that summary toward his client, and when the opinion was finally released three years later, it became clear that he had omitted those conclusions most unfavorable to his client, the executive branch. But Congress acquiesced and let Barr off the hook. By so doing, they effectively invited him later, as attorney general during the Trump administration, to repeat the same three steps—refuse and delay, summarize, and slant and omit—to mislead the public about the conclusions of the Mueller report regarding Russian interference in the 2016 presidential election.[20]

Unfinished Business

As the Bush administration reached its final year, its efforts foundered in Somalia, Yugoslavia, and Haiti. Each episode left difficult legacies with which the Clinton administration had to contend. In the waning months of his term, President Bush committed U.S. troops to Somalia, amid widespread famine, to help ease a humanitarian crisis. Although the operation enjoyed initial success, it quickly lost public support after the infamous "Black Hawk Down" episode during Clinton's term. Eighteen U.S. soldiers were killed after a helicopter—piloted by the same soldier who had transported Noriega to arrest just a few years earlier—crashed during a special-forces operation in Mogadishu. The disaster led President Clinton to order the withdrawal of U.S. troops from Somalia and to shy away from ground intervention to stop a genocide in Rwanda.[21]

Meanwhile, as Yugoslavia began to fragment, the United States unsuccessfully worked with the European Union and the United Nations to take political, diplomatic, and economic steps to keep the conflict from escalating. Had the United States launched a stronger military action earlier, it arguably could have prevented some of the atrocities that ensued. Instead, the crisis escalated until Clinton's Dayton accords finally clinched a cease-fire that lengthened into an uneasy peace. The two incidents left later administrations to decide whether and under what circumstances the United States would intervene in other countries for humanitarian ends, an issue that would later raise its head in Kosovo (for Clinton) and Libya and Syria (for Barack Obama).

The Haitian Refugee Crisis

In a third piece of unfinished business, Bush laid out the basic executive-branch blueprint for dealing with seaborne refugee crises. In a U.N.-monitored election in 1990, more than 67 percent of voters elected Jean-Bertrand Aristide as president of the first freely elected democratic government of Haiti. But after a brief, troubled presidency, Aristide was overthrown in a military coup in September 1991 and fled to the United States. Faced with boatloads of refugees arriving from Haiti, the U.S. government began administering brief screening interviews, with those Haitians who were found to have credible fears of political persecution being deemed "screened-in," making them plausible candidates for political asylum status. The Bush administration then directed the Coast Guard to bring the screened-in Haitians, not to the United States, but to the then little-known U.S. naval base in Guantánamo Bay, Cuba, where they were detained behind barbed wire in makeshift military camps without due-process rights.

In May 1993, the Bush administration issued the so-called Kennebunkport order requiring the direct return of fleeing Haitian refugees to their persecutors. The Kennebunkport order was plainly prompted at least in part by President Bush's election-year desire to avoid a replay of the Cuban Mariel boatlift crisis that had plagued the Carter presidency. These policies triggered litigation by refugee advocates in the Eleventh Circuit, followed by the case of *Haitian Centers Council, Inc. v. Sale* in the Second Circuit.[22] Over the course of sixteen months, the *Haitian Centers* case bifurcated around two issues: whether noncitizen detainees held on Guantánamo had due-process rights and whether the Kennebunkport order's direct return of refugees to their persecutors violated domestic statutory and international proscriptions against "refoulement."

Again, neither Bush practice—claiming that aliens have no due-process rights on Guantánamo or dispensing with asylum screening altogether—could be reconciled with past OLC opinions. In 1968 the United States had acceded to the United Nations Protocol Relating to the Status of Refugees, thereby accepting as domestic law article 33 of the Refugee Convention of 1951. That provision mandates: "No Contracting State shall expel or return ('refouler') a refugee in any manner whatsoever to the frontiers of territories where his life or freedom would be threatened on account of his . . . political opinion." In evaluating the legality of a proposed interdiction in 1981, the

Carter administration's Office of Legal Counsel concluded—in an opinion subsequently reaffirmed by another OLC memorandum written in the same year—that even on the high seas, article 33 strictly obliged the United States to ensure that interdicted Haitians "who claim that they will be persecuted ... [are] given an opportunity to substantiate their claims" through some kind of screening process. In a second opinion, the Office of Legal Counsel further determined that "[t]he base at Guantánamo Bay ... operates under an unusual international agreement with the Republic of Cuba which authorizes the United States to exercise complete jurisdiction and control" there, and thus concluded that the Anti-Slot Machine Act applied on Guantánamo.[23] From that conclusion, it would seem to follow *a fortiori* that the Fifth Amendment's due-process clause must also apply there.

The Second Circuit later agreed with the Office of Legal Counsel that the non-return principle applied on the high seas; after trial, the U.S. District Court for the Eastern District of New York ruled that the due-process clause applied on Guantánamo.[24] But neither ruling survived the Supreme Court's final resolution of the Haitian-refugee litigation during the first year of the Clinton administration. As a result, Bush 41's unilateral decisions to repatriate refugees to their homelands and to open offshore detention camps at Guantánamo continued to plague U.S. foreign policy more than thirty years later.

Clinton: Bosnia, Haiti, and Kosovo

Bill Clinton entered office believing that "globalization is about more than economics." "Our purpose," he said, "must be to bring together the world around freedom and democracy and peace and to oppose those who would tear it apart."[25] Because Clinton's presidency focused primarily on domestic economic recovery, some of the administration's most significant foreign-policy accomplishments were economic. Employing mostly executive tools, Secretary of the Treasury Robert Rubin orchestrated a legally controversial "peso bailout" in 1995 that averted impending economic collapse in Mexico; two years later, Rubin aggressively deployed executive tools to mitigate similar financial crises in volatile Asian markets.[26] Clinton narrowly concluded the North American Free Trade Agreement (NAFTA) with Mexico and Canada by congressional-executive agreement, over objections by a prominent

law professor that the agreement should have been concluded as an Article
II treaty (a legal choice that mathematically would have put congressional
approval out of reach).[27]

During the second Clinton term, Secretary of State Madeleine Albright
and her deputy secretary, lifelong Russia hand Strobe Talbott, strategically
engaged the newly independent states of the former Soviet Union to address
the crisis in the Balkans; they successfully pressed the Europeans to secure
the inclusion in NATO of Poland, Hungary, and the Czech Republic. Clinton's team also successfully worked with Congress through the provisions of
the Nunn-Lugar Cooperative Threat Reduction Program to give technical assistance and funding to the former Soviet states to help safeguard nuclear
power plants, dismantle nuclear weapons, and reduce the nuclear threat.

Clinton's other main foreign-policy accomplishments were diplomatic accords that did not require Senate ratification. These included the Holocaust
assets accords—negotiated by Deputy Treasury Secretary Stuart Eizenstat
with Switzerland, Germany, Austria, France, and other European nations to
cover the restitution of property, compensation to slave and forced laborers,
recovery of looted art and bank accounts, and payment of insurance policies—and the historic Good Friday peace accords between the Republic of
Ireland, the United Kingdom, and Sinn Fein, brokered by the former Senate
majority leader George Mitchell. As Clinton's eight years ended, his team
facilitated negotiations between Israeli and Palestinian leaders that narrowly
missed achieving a historic settlement in the Middle East.[28]

But Clinton also inherited Bush 41's foreign-policy crises and initially carried forward his policies in Somalia, Rwanda, Haiti, and Yugoslavia. Over
time, Clinton changed course on each, eventually engaging Congress in
many of his foreign-policy reversals. When the famous "Black Hawk Down"
episode in Somalia led to the horrific dragging of dead American soldiers
through the streets of Mogadishu, Clinton announced a full-scale withdrawal
of U.S. troops in March 1994. The failure to act against a low-tech genocide
in Rwanda led to nearly a million Tutsis being murdered by machete, which
helped convince many Clinton administration officials to urge stronger
humanitarian intervention several years later in Kosovo.

The administration's most significant diplomatic accomplishment was
the Dayton Peace Agreement. Orchestrated by Ambassador Richard Holbrooke without major legislative involvement, the Dayton accords finally

brought peace to the ravaged Balkans. After years of massive Serbian atrocities against Bosnian civilians, the Clinton administration pushed NATO to
begin bombing Bosnian Serb positions, creating a window for a strategy of
"diplomacy backed by force" that finally brought to the table the Croats,
Serbs, and Bosnian Muslims. Once the Dayton accords called a cease-fire,
Clinton enforced the peace without American casualties by dispatching
twenty thousand American troops as NATO peacekeepers, and free elections
were finally held in late 1996. The fragile peace forged by the Dayton accords
continued to stick decades later, during which time the United States worked
with the U.N. Security Council to erect an International Criminal Tribunal
for the former Yugoslavia. Over twenty-four years, that tribunal—acting pursuant to the Security Council's chapter VII authority in the U.N. Charter to
promote peace and security—indicted 161 defendants (including former Serbian president Slobodan Milošević) and sentenced nearly 100, including former Bosnian Serb leader Radovan Karadžić.[29]

The Haiti Paradigm

During his campaign, Clinton had criticized Bush 41's Haiti policy and
called the Second Circuit's decision invalidating Bush 41's direct-return policy the "right decision." But upon taking office, Clinton abruptly reversed
position. Clinton shifted to Bush 41's unilateralist approach to the Haitian
refugee crisis and Bush 41's pattern of executive reactivity, doubling down by
responding similarly to a parallel 1994 refugee outflow from Cuba. Some
ascribed Clinton's Haiti reversal to his retrospective desire to avoid a replay
of the "Fort Chaffee incident," when Mariel Cubans seized an Arkansas pen-
itentiary and doomed Clinton's first governorship. He clearly sought to avoid
a refugee inflow that might distract attention from his pressing domestic-
policy agenda.[30]

The advisers who helped Clinton make the decision included the incoming secretary of state, national security adviser and deputy, and secretary of
defense, but no one from Congress, from the Justice Department, or with
bureaucratic responsibility for the promotion and protection of human rights
or refugees. Lack of input by political appointees in the Justice Department
also helps explain why President Clinton reversed a long-standing campaign
position without ever explaining why a policy he had previously deemed unlawful had suddenly become lawful. And Clinton's own defense—that it was

more humanitarian to continue the forced-return policy than to lift it and thereby entice numerous Haitians onto the high seas to drown—did not fully explain why he could not have turned to a series of less harsh alternatives that would have protected Haitians from drowning without forcing them back into the repressive arms of the Haitian military.

Clinton's Justice Department persisted in defending Bush 41's Haiti policy in the courts through months of intensive litigation. The litigation, in two parallel cases, raised two main issues: whether noncitizen detainees held on Guantánamo have due-process rights and whether the direct return of refugees to their persecutors violates domestic statutory and international proscriptions against refoulement. Coincidentally, both tracks of the litigation were resolved on the same day in June 1993. In a landmark decision later vacated by settlement, Judge Sterling Johnson Jr. of the U.S. District Court for the Eastern District of New York issued a permanent injunction, ruling, among other things, that the government had violated the due-process rights of the more than two hundred HIV-positive Haitians being held on Guantánamo. The government's violations included denying the Haitians the procedures available to asylum applicants in the United States, showing deliberate indifference to their medical needs, and subjecting them to informal disciplinary procedures and indefinite detention.[31] Substantial congressional and public pressure after the court's ruling then forced the Clinton administration to decline appeal and bring into the United States the Haitians being held on Guantánamo, in exchange for their lawyers' agreement that Judge Johnson's ruling would be vacated in the settlement. But once the trade for the Haitians' freedom vacated that judicial precedent, the question of whether noncitizen detainees on Guantánamo enjoy any due-process rights would remain undecided for the next thirty years, well into the Biden administration.

Even as the airplane carrying the Guantánamo Haitians approached New York, on the direct return issue, the Supreme Court held, over Justice Harry Blackmun's dissent, that neither article 33 of the U.N. Refugee Convention nor section 243(h) of the Immigration and Nationality Act (INA) applied to protect refugees apprehended on the high seas.[32] Significantly, the Supreme Court refused to credit the government's various claims of nonreviewability, thus avoiding broad future insulation of similar executive conduct from judicial examination. But once the president acted and Congress stood by, it became almost inevitable that the Supreme Court would validate the president's actions. In various preliminary rulings over the previous two years, the full Court had voted against the Haitians no less than eight times. The Court directly foreshadowed its pro-government ruling in early 1992, when it denied certiorari to an earlier Haitian plaintiffs' petition, with only Justice Blackmun dissenting.[33] And by a 7-to-2 vote, the Court had stayed the Second Circuit's ruling blocking the Bush 41 policy of summary return, ensuring that the policy would continue for at least eleven months before plenary Supreme Court argument and decision.[34] In hindsight, the Supreme Court's decision was unsurprising. Once President Clinton changed his position, adopting the Bush 41 policy as well as its briefs, the potential swing votes—Justices Anthony Kennedy, Sandra Day O'Connor, David Souter, and John Paul Stevens—surely wondered why they should invalidate a policy of return that two presidents (including one who had once condemned it) had now embraced. Having essentially sanctioned a policy of refoulement for nearly a year, the Court was unlikely now to turn around and declare it illegal.

Still, the Court's decision was rife with legal flaws. As Justice Blackmun's dissent cogently observed, the Court's opinion in the direct-return case rested on three implausible assertions: that "the word 'return' does not mean return," that "the opposite of 'within the United States' is not outside the United States," and that "the official charged with controlling immigration has no role in enforcing an order to control immigration."[35] Although Justice Stevens, writing for the majority, construed the legal prohibition against the "return" of aliens as inapplicable to this kind of return, the Kennebunkport order itself authorized the Coast Guard "[t]o return" Haitian vessels and their passengers to Haiti. French newspapers contemporaneously reported that the United States had decided "de *refouler* directement les réfugiés," precisely the act that the law forbade.[36] The majority further held that Congress intended statutory protection to extend only to aliens physically present in the United States, even though Congress had deliberately dropped a geographic limit from the statutory language and provided that "[t]he Attorney General shall not deport or return *any alien*"—without regard to location—to conditions of persecution. Justice Stevens further concluded that the statute's directive to the "Attorney General" somehow did not limit the actions of the president and Coast Guard, even though article 33 of the Refugee Convention speaks of "[n]o Contracting State" and hence plainly bound the president as the head of state.[37]

The plaintiffs argued that the president's order could not grant the attorney general unreviewable discretion to return possible refugees, because the statute, treaty, and executive agreement all removed that discretion, just as the Taft-Hartley Act had removed President Truman's discretion to seize Youngstown's steel mills during the Korean War. But again, the Court rejected that claim, deciding that the presumption against extraterritoriality prevented the statute from removing that discretion even though the executive branch itself had cited the statute as the basis for its own extraterritorial authority to act. Properly understood, the president's direct return of the refugees should have fallen into the third category of Justice Jackson's *Youngstown* concurrence, where the executive's "power is at its lowest ebb" because the president is acting in a manner "incompatible with the express or implied will of Congress" that "[v]ulnerable refugees shall not be returned." But the majority simply rejected this *Youngstown* claim, predictably citing in dictum *Curtiss-Wright*.[38]

On reflection, the Haitian episode illustrated a recurrent pattern that I call the "Haiti paradigm" in U.S. human-rights policy. The United States proclaims a policy of supporting and promoting democracy and human rights abroad. Another nation, in this case Haiti, attempts to construct both civil society and political order against large odds, and fails because of a coup d'état, insurrection, civil strife, or an external invasion. The United States' initial response is largely executive inaction. Unchecked, human-rights abuses start to worsen and proliferate. Refugees begin to flee in increasingly large numbers. At this point, the executive branch finally reacts forcefully, but to the refugees, not the underlying political crisis. This period of executive action is followed by legislative inaction, in response to which nongovernmental organizations and human-rights advocates bring a transnational public lawsuit seeking to prod the government to more proactive, human-rights-sensitive measures. After initial court victories, the harsh executive position begins to soften, but that response ends when the Supreme Court legitimates the executive action. The net result is upside-down human-rights policy. The official U.S. position—now legitimated by judicial endorsement and legislative acquiescence—is anti-refugee and curiously tolerant of human-rights abusers. Through this circuitous route, the administration ends up endorsing a position that bears no resemblance to its officially enunciated policies of democracy and human rights.[39]

As the Haiti episode illustrated, even controversial presidential actions are usually followed by congressional acquiescence and judicial sanction. In the wake of the Kennebunkport order, for example, Congress introduced various bills, and various committees held hearings about the refoulement policy and the Guantánamo camp. In the end, the only legislative group to fight consistently for the Haitians, the Congressional Black Caucus, played a critical role in winning the release of the Guantánamo Haitians.

During the summer of 1994, this paradigm played out again when thousands of Cubans threatened by Castro fled by boat. Again, they were interdicted and held on Guantánamo as a result of an abrupt policy shift by the Clinton administration. These individuals fled in reliance on more than thirty-five years of consistent executive and legislative condemnation of Castro's Cuba, coupled with an essentially open legislative invitation for Cuban refugees to come to the United States. Playing the game of "find the statute" discussed in chapter 4, executive-branch lawyers reversed that policy without the benefit of legislative debate, new legislative action, or open public discussion. Again, the courts upheld the executive's reversal, until the attorney general finally exercised executive discretion to parole the Cubans in.

Taken together, the Haitian and Cuban incidents taught that in a human-rights crisis, neither legislative action nor private litigation will retrospectively cure initial failures of executive policy. In the end, both the Haitian and Cuban crises were resolved by reactive executive unilateralism. Public and congressional pressure finally forced Clinton to address the root causes of the Haiti crisis by intervening militarily to restore Aristide in the fall of 1994, without express congressional approval. To justify the intervention, Walter Dellinger, then assistant attorney general and head of the Office of Legal Counsel, played "find the statute." He argued that the Haiti invasion was, in part, authorized by a clearly more limited statute introduced the previous year by Senator Dole, one of the leading *opponents* of the Haitian action.[40] The episode revealed that even presidents who are sensitive to the rule of law are often forced into reactive, short-term, or covert uses of force to respond to perceived emergencies. The president perceives a threat, recognizes the need for American response, sincerely believes that he has a duty to act, but simultaneously realizes that he cannot get Congress to support him. So the president avoids raising the issue openly, to avoid forcing Congress to vote on the question of approval or disapproval. Instead, the president has powerful incentives to use short-term military strikes (of the kind that the Reagan and Bush administrations undertook in Grenada, Panama, and Libya), emergency economic powers (to respond to human-rights violations in South Africa or Myanmar), covert actions (as Reagan used in Central America), and arms sales (as the Biden administration later did, to respond to military conflicts in Ukraine and the Middle East).

Kosovo

As his administration ended, Clinton broke the cycle of the Haiti paradigm by taking proactive steps to end the bloody war in the Balkans. But in the process, he created an ambiguous legal precedent regarding humanitarian intervention. In 1999, Serbia's president, Slobodan Milošević, ordered his forces to begin attacking the citizens of the breakaway republic of Kosovo. Serb forces murdered thousands of ethnic Albanians and drove hundreds of thousands of refugees from their homes. A Russian veto rendered unobtainable the first-best option, a U.N. Security Council resolution. So in 1999, Clinton successfully urged NATO to begin a massive bombing campaign against the Serbian government without Security Council sanction, to end the Serbian government's "ethnic cleansing" of Albanians in the Kosovo region. To prevent those abuses, nineteen NATO countries finally chose to use force without U.N. Security Council authorization. The bombing for humanitarian purposes went on for seventy-eight days. With no American battle casualties during the fighting, U.S. troops joined British, French, and other NATO forces to occupy Kosovo as peacekeepers under an agreement worked out with Yugoslavia. Although the province nominally remained part of Yugoslavia, the Kosovars gained U.N.-sanctioned autonomy and eventually independence. So in the end, Clinton's formula of diplomacy backed by force again worked: Milošević was driven back and later deposed, and ended up dying in The Hague during his trial before the International Criminal Tribunal for the former Yugoslavia.[41]

Under domestic law, the Kosovo operation raised a constitutional question about the initiation of conflict and a statutory question about the continuation of conflict. On the constitutional, initiation issue, the question was whether this was "war" for purposes of Article I of the Constitution. On the statutory, continuation issue, the question was whether these were "hostilities" for purposes of the War Powers Resolution.

In his OLC opinion approving the Haiti intervention, Walter Dellinger had opined that the president may initiate a lawful use of force so long as the president cites a compelling national interest and the "nature, scope, and duration" of the action demonstrates that the president is not taking the country to a "war" that requires prior congressional approval.[42] As a constitutional matter, Congress has exclusive power to declare war; but if a use of force entails something less than "war," this reading gives the president authority to engage in the use of force abroad without prior congressional approval. Congress has since largely acquiesced in this interpretation. As we have seen, this reading would require prior congressional approval to initiate large-scale foreign conflicts like Bush 41's Desert Storm invasion in Iraq, but not to initiate more limited interventions of constrained nature, scope, and duration like that in Kosovo.

Once military intervention has begun, the War Powers Resolution moves to the foreground. Then, the statutory question becomes whether the United States is engaged in "hostilities." As discussed in chapters 3 and 4, the resolution imposes consultation and reporting requirements and a sixty-day limit (extendable under certain conditions) on the president's commitment of troops overseas without express congressional authorization. Although the resolution is triggered by the introduction of "United States Armed Forces" into the airspace and territory of a foreign country, the durational limit applies only if those U.S. forces are in "hostilities" or "imminent involvement in hostilities is clearly indicated by the circumstances." The question in Kosovo thus became whether the U.S. government was required to comply with the resolution's sixty-day limit after the bombing began.[43]

At the sixty-day mark, there was little doubt within the Clinton administration that the United States was engaged in "hostilities" in Kosovo. But the administration's policy determination was equally clear: they were close to success and they were not going to stop and allow Milošević to regain traction—particularly given that the sixty-day statutory limit had been arbitrarily chosen some twenty-five years earlier without this particular scenario in mind. So the Clinton administration continued beyond sixty days with bombing that clearly seemed to exceed the level of "hostilities." At seventy-eight days Milošević finally conceded which seemed to justify the U.S. military decision to keep bombing. But the lingering question was whether the last eighteen days of bombing had been lawfully conducted.

Shortly before the sixty-day mark, Congress passed a budget bill appropriating money for the military operation. The War Powers Resolution had carefully specified that legislative authority to introduce U.S. armed forces "shall not be inferred . . . from . . . any provision contained in any appropriation Act, unless such provision specifically authorizes" the use of such force. Nevertheless, at the end of 2000, the Office of Legal Counsel issued a detailed opinion that treated Congress's emergency supplemental appropriation for military operations as "authorization for continuing hostilities after the expiration of sixty days" under the War Powers Resolution. The opinion reasoned that the statute did not bar Congress from authorizing military operations through an appropriations measure, "but instead has the effect of establishing a background principle against which to interpret later acts of Congress."[44]

The legality of the Kosovo operation under international law was even more murky. Nineteen NATO members accepted the international legality of some form of humanitarian intervention in Kosovo even without U.N. Security Council approval. In October 1998, the United Kingdom publicly declared the legality of the operation, so long as the proposed use of process is "necessary and proportionate to the [humanitarian] aim" and "is strictly limited in time and scope to this aim." Seventeen other NATO members individually satisfied themselves of the legality of their participation in the operation. But curiously, the U.S. government never articulated a clear legal justification for its NATO actions. Instead, the United States relied on an amorphous listing of factors that together justified the intervention as a matter of policy. The Clinton administration never followed the British government in issuing an opinion explaining why its actions complied with international law. The administration simply asserted that the use of force was "illegal but legitimate." Secretary-General Kofi Annan captured the United Nations' ambiguity about a narrowly tailored form of humanitarian intervention in urgent situations by acknowledging that force might sometimes be necessary to serve humanitarian purposes. The entire incident catalyzed the ongoing international legal movement to explore whether there is an international "responsibility to protect" (thereafter dubbed, for shorthand, "R2P").[45]

As a policymaker in the State Department focused on human rights, I disagreed with the Clinton administration's decision to state no international-law rationale to justify its use of force for humanitarian intervention. I thought that the lack of a legal rationale was an egregious omission that would haunt U.S.

foreign policy for the coming decades. The omission was particularly glaring here, in a human-rights situation, where one never uses the rubric of "illegal but legitimate" to avoid stating the rules and principles that make that conduct (for example, same-sex marriage) lawful. As Professor Louis Henkin asked shortly after Kosovo, "Is it better [for us] to leave the law alone, . . . turning a blind eye (and a deaf ear) to violations that had . . . moral justification? Or should [these incidents] move us to push the law along, . . . closer to what [it] ought to be?"[46]

As a former head of the Office of Legal Counsel has argued, "the Executive Branch bears a responsibility to provide a public explanation for such a controversial and consequential action"; "the lack of public explanation completely undermines the precedential value of this intervention."[47] What gave the Kosovo episode precedential weight was that the United States maintained that it was acting lawfully, marking the episode as an instance of state practice under international law and a piece of quasi-constitutional custom under domestic law. For that reason, Kosovo has been cited as an international-law precedent by countries—such as the United Kingdom, Denmark, and Belgium—that have publicly explained their support for the international legality of humanitarian intervention.[48] Similarly, the OLC opinion has been cited as a domestic-law precedent for executive-branch reliance on an appropriations measure as a "background principle" to justify continuing humanitarian intervention past sixty days, notwithstanding the express language of the War Powers Resolution.

As chapter 7 will show, the Clinton administration's failure to articulate a clear legal rationale for its Kosovo intervention would haunt the Obama administration with regard to Syria fourteen years later. The Bush 41–Clinton era showed the difficulty of getting interbranch agreement on the substance of foreign policy, when the constitutional process fails to force the political branches into serious dialogue about which political ends they collectively seek. When interbranch dialogue occurs, it may produce consensus for war, as occurred, for example, during Desert Storm. But under the current process, interbranch incentives increasingly dictate that no such institutional dialogue ever occurs. The twentieth century thus ended with the executive continuing to seize initiative, Congress continuing to avoid collective responsibility for national security affairs, and judges becoming even more likely to accept specious claims of statutory authorization for acts taken on executive initiative. This recurrent pattern would only intensify during George W. Bush's "global war on terror."

6

Bush 43: 9/11 and Executive Power

IN DECEMBER 2000, THE SUPREME COURT opened America's twenty-first century by delivering the White House to George W. Bush (Bush 43), who had not won the popular vote. Given his razor-thin margin of victory, early expectations were that Bush would follow a moderate, shared-power foreign policy akin to that of his father, George H. W. Bush (Bush 41). But the terrorist attacks of September 11 gave Bush 43 a historic window through which he asserted unprecedented executive power.

If the Bush 41–Clinton years had reflected America's first, optimistic look at globalization, the September 11 attacks created a sharp cleft in that vision. During the decade following the fall of the Berlin Wall, the world had marveled at the possibilities of global travel, communications, and markets. But September 11 unveiled the same coin's dark side, taking the United States out of the light and into the shadows of a new age of global pessimism. Americans faced a collective, horrific realization that those same tools of globalization could be turned against them: terrorists could exploit the interconnectedness to turn airplanes into missiles destroying iconic buildings; use the global financial system to move and secret money; weaponize mail into a delivery system for biological weapons; and hack emails as a tool for cyberterrorism.

September 11, and the Iraq invasion that followed, brought upon the United States, like Achilles, a schizophrenic sense of exceptional power coupled with exceptional vulnerability. Given that Americans overnight had suffered some three thousand civilian casualties that some argued justified a war against terrorism, how to use America's superpower resources to reduce its vulnerability? The Bush 43 administration offered an overarching answer: *homeland security,* in both defensive and preemptive senses. In the name of forestalling future attack, the Bush administration instituted sweeping strategies of domestic security, law enforcement, immigration control, security detention, governmental secrecy, and information awareness at home, all united under the control of a sprawling, hastily assembled Department of Homeland Security.[1]

This approach was executed by a team of experienced, hard-core realists committed to executive power and skeptical of international law: Vice President Dick Cheney and his legal adviser David Addington, Secretary of Defense Donald Rumsfeld, Attorney General John Ashcroft, the deputy defense secretary Paul Wolfowitz, and the undersecretary of state John Bolton. These national security hawks formed Bush's de facto war cabinet, which soon dominated such moderates as Secretary of State Colin Powell and the national security adviser Condoleezza Rice.[2]

Congress and the courts responded with resounding deference. In 2001, only one senator, Russ Feingold of Wisconsin, voted against the Patriot Act, and only one representative, Barbara Lee of California, voted against the authorization for the use of military force against those responsible for 9/11. Until the Guantánamo cases, the Supreme Court set no limits on Bush's national security initiatives. And so Bush used the deference granted to him by Congress and the courts to fundamentally reshape America's national security philosophy. That philosophy was cited to invade Iraq, reopen Guantánamo for suspected terrorists, initiate extreme interrogation tactics that licensed torture, expand national security surveillance, and open CIA "black sites" abroad. Bush 43's eight years thus witnessed, as Charlie Savage of the *New York Times* subtitled his comprehensive national security chronicle: "the return of the imperial presidency and the subversion of American democracy." The extraordinary resources channeled toward the national security apparatus strengthened the government's kinetic muscles at the expense of diplomatic ones. The Bush 43 years left behind a career bureaucracy trained to see aggressive terror prevention as its raison d'être.[3]

Given this sea change during the Bush 43 years, and Barack Obama's control of both houses of Congress during only the first two years of his eight-year term, the cautious Obama administration succeeded in swinging the national security pendulum only part of the way back toward *Youngstown*. The only real constitutional check on executive power during the Bush 43 years came from four Guantánamo decisions by the Supreme Court, which had limited constraining effect on the march toward executive power. And so, the first decade of the twenty-first century gave the National Security Constitution a strong push in the *Curtiss-Wright* direction.

The Bush Doctrine

Taken collectively, the U.S. government's response to 9/11 signaled a "Bush Doctrine," with four identifiable elements. First, the Bush administration combined its unilateralist vision of constitutional law with a unilateralist approach to international law. Prior bipartisan policy (including Bush 41's) had emphasized using diplomacy first, with force as a last resort. But administration officials argued that the "global war on terror" had authorized them to use preemptive self-defense to force the disarmament of any country that appeared to pose a gathering threat. Bush 43's military actions against Afghanistan and Iraq exemplified a policy of force first, under which ad hoc "coalitions of the willing" preserved homeland security through discretionary war making on real and potential state sponsors of terrorism. This strategy was constrained not as much by international and domestic law as by the limits imposed by finite national resources.

Second, Bush 43's human-rights policy stressed American exceptionalism and elevated "freedom from fear" into the overriding human-rights value. When, sixty years earlier, Franklin Delano Roosevelt had summoned the Allies to arms against the original "axis of evil," he painted a positive vision of the postwar world. He evoked a world in which four fundamental freedoms could reign: freedom of speech, freedom of religion, freedom from want, and freedom from fear. His "Four Freedoms" speech generated a postwar human-rights construct enshrined in Eleanor Roosevelt's Universal Declaration of Human Rights and subsequent international covenants. For the next sixty years of human-rights policy, both Democratic and Republican administrations followed that construct's contours. The framework emphasized comprehensive universal protection of civil and political rights (freedom of speech and religion), economic, social, and cultural rights (freedom from want), and freedom from gross violations and persecution (for example, the

Refugee Convention, the Genocide Convention, and the Convention Against Torture).[4] But Bush 43 rejected human-rights universalism in favor of a two-pronged strategy: creating extralegal zones—most prominently the U.S. naval base at Guantánamo, where scores of security detainees were brought and held without legal recourse; and creating a category of extralegal persons—detainees labeled "enemy combatants," who, even if American citizens on American soil, were effectively accorded no legal avenue to assert substantive or procedural rights. Bush 43's administration scorned international criminal adjudication. It downplayed torture and violations of the Geneva Conventions committed by America or its allies as necessary elements of an all-encompassing global war on terror.

Third, beginning with Afghanistan and continuing with Iraq, the administration asserted a top-down strategy toward democracy promotion. From Ronald Reagan's famous Westminster speech in 1982 until September 11, successive administrations had supported as a fundamental goal of U.S. foreign policy "democracy promotion from the bottom up." During the Bush 41–Clinton years, the democracy-promotion strategy had widened into Bush 41's call for "a new world order." But after the U.S. invasions of Afghanistan and Iraq, democracy-promotion efforts shifted toward top-down militarily imposed democracy, characterized by U.S.-led military attack, prolonged occupation, restored opposition leaders, and the creation of resource-needy post-conflict protectorates. At the same time, the United States visibly reduced its efforts at bottom-up democracy promotion in Central and Eastern Europe (Ukraine), Africa (Côte d'Ivoire), Latin America (Venezuela), and South Asia (Pakistan).[5]

Fourth and finally, the Bush Doctrine flipped the traditional bipartisan script to emphasize strategic unilateralism and tactical multilateralism. Multilateralism became Bush 43's exceptional option, characterized by broad antipathy toward international law and global regime building through treaty negotiation. The Bush administration simultaneously disengaged diplomatically in key regions, creating a sharp contrast between America's military exceptionalism and its comparative diplomatic impotence. America's display of hard power in Iraq sharply contrasted with a striking decline in its diplomatic initiative in the Middle East. The administration withdrew from the activist, mediating U.S. role traditionally played in the Middle East peace process from the Carter and Clinton Camp David summits to the Madrid peace process of the Bush 41 administration. Bush 43 also abandoned the

"Agreed Framework" between the United States and North Korea that the Clinton administration had created in 1994 for multilateral diplomatic engagement and withdrew from direct engagement with North Korea. He did so over the objections not just of the South Korean president and Nobel Peace Prize winner Kim Dae Jung, but also those of Bush 41 and his key Asia advisers. By the time of his January 2002 state of the union address, Bush 43 had famously labeled North Korea part of the "axis of evil" along with Iraq and Iran. This prompted North Korean president Kim Jong Il to build more bargaining chips by lifting the freeze at the Yongbyon power plant, enriching plutonium to make nuclear weapons, ousting weapons inspectors, flouting other international agreements, and announcing North Korea's withdrawal from the Nuclear Non-Proliferation Treaty.[6]

The Bush 43 administration's disdain for diplomacy led it to unilaterally withdraw from treaties. The administration disregarded Clinton's signature to the Rome Statute of the International Criminal Court, disengaged from the Kyoto Protocol on climate change, and withdrew from the Optional Protocol to the Vienna Convention on Consular Relations. But Bush 43's abrupt disengagement fit awkwardly with the previous two centuries; since the Founding, the United States had become party to a global network of closely interconnected treaties enmeshed in multiple frameworks of international institutions. In an interdependent world, unilateral decisions to break or bend particular treaty commitments trigger vicious cycles of treaty violation and demoralize treaty partners. Repeated American treaty breaking undermined American "soft" power at the precise moment that the United States hoped to use that power to mobilize the same partners to help solve global problems that extended far beyond any nation's control. By contrast, the most enduring foreign-policy accomplishments of Bush 43's presidency came from soft-power initiatives undertaken in partnership with Congress and allies, such as the President's Emergency Plan for AIDS Relief and the Millennium Challenge Account.

Not surprisingly, Bush 43 could not execute this revamped foreign-policy vision—of unfettered executive power to use force in the war on terror, human-rights double standards, militarily imposed democracy, and strategic unilateralism—without recasting the constitutional vision within which foreign policy is made. As earlier chapters have recounted, national security policy had largely been based on the premise that executive power operates within the constitutional framework of checks and balances that animated *Youngstown*'s vision of shared institutional powers. Under that vision, a globalizing world demanded an energetic executive, but one checked by an energetic Congress and overseen by the judicial branch. Under this shared-power vision, there were no law-free zones, practices, courts, or persons; civil liberties could not be infringed without a clear statement by elected representatives; and except for some political rights, such as the right to vote or serve on a jury, aliens and citizens were to be treated largely the same.[7]

The Bush 43 administration inverted this constitutional vision. It asserted instead a theory of unfettered executive power based on sweeping interpretations of Article II and *Curtiss-Wright*'s vision of the president as the "sole organ of the federal government in the field of international relations." Treating the president's Article II powers as paramount, this vision dictated that Congress exercise minimal oversight over executive activity, and the Justice Department urged the courts to grant extreme deference to the president. The Bush 43 administration rejected human-rights universalism in favor of executive efforts to create extralegal spaces (Guantánamo), extralegal courts (military commissions), extralegal persons (enemy combatants), and extralegal practices (extraordinary rendition), all of which it claimed were exempt from judicial review. To insulate the U.S. government from charges that it was violating universal human-rights norms, the administration opposed judicial efforts to incorporate international and foreign law into domestic law. The executive claimed discretion to infringe on civil liberties without clear legislative statements, relying on broadly worded laws such as the authorization in September 2001 for the use of military force to justify secret National Security Agency (NSA) surveillance, indefinite detentions, and torture of foreign detainees. And the war on terror exacerbated already sharp distinctions between the rights of citizens and the rights of aliens in American society, particularly through scapegoating of Muslim aliens in American life.[8]

Three episodes most clearly illuminated the extreme face of the administration's post-9/11 legal vision: the claimed right to use preemptive self-defense in the invasion of Iraq; the Office of Legal Counsel's infamous "torture opinion"; and the administration's approach to detention on Guantánamo. The same three episodes revealed a glaring failure of governmental legal process. The Iraq invasion was based on a distorted reading of the international law of force. The military-commissions order later declared unconstitutional by the Supreme Court was drafted by the deputy assistant attorney general of the Office of Legal Counsel, supervised by the counsel to the vice president. Left out were the head of the Office of Legal Counsel, the attorney general, the national security adviser, the Departments of State and Defense, and their lawyers. Similar process fouls characterized the infamous torture opinion (also known as the "Bybee opinion" after its author, then OLC head Jay Bybee) and related OLC opinions, which helped lead to their withdrawal by later administrations.

Each episode illustrated the interplay among law, politics, and process in the national security space. Legality and sound process tend to promote more stable policy, whereas illegality and bad process foster policy disaster. Legal compliance and good national security process enable multilateral cooperation and accountability; they foster political agreement between the executive branch and Congress and U.S. allies about sensitive policies. But illegality combined with shoddy process enhances secrecy and cover-up and breeds a cascade of illegality that severely strains those relationships of trust. As later chapters will show, this trend ebbed during the Obama and Biden years, but sharply re-intensified during the Trump administration.

The Invasion of Iraq

The Second Gulf War in Iraq revealed how dramatically the Bush Doctrine had altered America's approach to the use of force. At the dawn of the post–Cold War era, the international-law rules for using force had seemed clear. One state could lawfully breach another's territorial sovereignty only in response to aggression, in self-defense, or as authorized by an explicit U.N. Security Council resolution. Bush 41's First Gulf War in 1991 had epitomized all three circumstances. After Saddam Hussein invaded Kuwait in August 1990, the United States under Bush 41 led a forty-nation coalition authorized by a U.N. Security Council resolution to drive Iraq from Kuwait. The action was authorized domestically by a congressional authorization for the use of military force to the extent permitted by a U.N. Security Council resolution. But when the Security Council resolutions after September 11 stopped short of explicitly authorizing military attacks on any particular country, the Bush 43 administration invoked a mixed humanitarian and self-defense rationale to strike back at Afghanistan. Having achieved impressive military success in the Afghanistan phase of its counterterrorism campaign, the Bush administration increasingly invoked arguments based on preemptive self-defense. The administration sent troops to the Philippines, geared up for a military campaign against Iraq, and claimed in a national security strategy paper that the United States had a customary right of preemptive self-defense to protect itself from attacks that had not yet occurred.[9]

Under the traditional international-law doctrine of self-defense, an aggressor must take unambiguously aggressive steps before the object of that aggression can respond proportionately in self-defense. But preemptive attacks cannot clearly distinguish between permitted defensive measures and forbidden assaults. Nor can preemptive attacks be meaningfully restrained by the doctrines of necessity or proportionality. Vice President Cheney's so-called one percent doctrine—"even if there's just a 1 percent chance of the unimaginable coming due, act as if it is a certainty"—significantly lowered barriers to executive initiative. This gave bureaucrats proactive license to thwart terrorism by any means. Combined with then defense secretary Donald Rumsfeld's maxim that "absence of evidence is not evidence of absence," that doctrine dictated a startling conclusion: that even without smoke, there must be fire, which then justified attacking preemptively with overwhelming force.[10]

Obviously, such a theory is deeply destabilizing. If international law is revised to authorize a nation to respond not just to perceived threats but to _premonitions_ that one's adversary might misperceive motives, hard evidence becomes displaced by conjecture. Down this hall of mirrors lies a doctrine that assumes necessity, then authorizes a disproportionate use of force to "shock and awe" a potential attacker into submission. If leaders believe that someone will likely attack their state with intent to kill, the leaders' best move becomes striking the potential attacker first with devastating force, à la Pearl Harbor. When that mindset prevails, evidence yields to hunches and the twisting of evidence. From there, it became a short step to the United States' intervening in Iraq in 2003, using overwhelming force to stop weapons of mass destruction that later could not be found.[11]

Preemptive-self-defense arguments also raise domestic constitutional-law challenges because they leave little room for shared decision-making about war. Congress's broad pre-approval of Bush 43's war effectively eliminated any meaningful input from private litigants or the courts. This time, Congress failed in Iraq by not following its First Gulf War sequence: demanding that the president first obtain nuanced Security Council authorization for force, and only then authorizing the president to use force to the extent necessary to enforce the Security Council resolutions. Such an approach would have forced Congress to clarify America's real goal in attacking Iraq. Was it promoting inspections, ensuring disarmament, forcing regime change, or imposing democracy by military force?

Instead, Congress gave the president a blank check to use force with or without U.N. approval and carte blanche to abandon his search for a second Security Council resolution at the eleventh hour.[12] In October 2002, the Bush administration won sweeping congressional approval for its proposed use of force by simplistically framing the issue in bipolar terms—either attack or accept a status quo in which Saddam builds unconventional weapons and brutalizes his citizens. By flattening the issue in this way, the Bush administration discouraged examination of an available third way: *disarm Iraq without attack*. The administration overlooked a multilateral strategy of disarmament plus enhanced containment plus more aggressive human-rights intervention. That strategy would have continued the Bush 41–Clinton approach of diplomacy backed by force: restoring effective U.N. weapons inspections, destroying Iraqi weapons of mass destruction, and cutting off the flow of weapons-related goods into Iraq. At the same time, this strategy would have pressed more aggressively for the insertion of human-rights monitors and support for the peaceful democratic opposition in Iraq. It would have developed the "Milošević-type" option of diplomatically forcing Saddam into exile and bringing him to justice before an appropriate international tribunal.[13]

Such a strategy would have avoided a bloody war, its financial and symbolic costs, and the ensuing decades of occupation. More fundamentally, it would have secured Iraq's compliance with international law at no cost to the United States' own appearance of compliance. It would have strengthened the United States' capacity to return to the U.N. Security Council for the lifting of Iraqi sanctions. Through continued multilateralism, Bush 43 could have secured U.N. support in identifying and destroying any Iraqi unconventional weapons, in planning a U.N.-supervised civilian reconstruction, and in creating an ad hoc criminal tribunal for Iraqi war criminals. But that multi-pronged strategy would have required sustained strategic multilateralism, the precise approach the administration had already rejected.

The Bush administration flipped the authorization sequence from the First Gulf War. It first secured sweeping congressional authorization to use force and only later pursued authorization under international law. In March 2003, Security Council Resolution 1441 afforded Iraq "a final opportunity to comply with its disarmament obligations under relevant resolutions" or face "serious consequences." Iraq reluctantly confirmed its intent to comply with the resolution, triggering a four-month public "trial" of disarmament facts à la the Cuban missile crisis. During these months, U.N. inspectors combed through Iraq, where Saddam was supposedly developing a "currently accurate, full and complete declaration of all aspects of [his] programmes" to develop chemical, biological, and nuclear weapons and long-range missiles. During this period, the administration waffled both on whether it would seek a second Security Council resolution before using military force and on whether its real goal was disarmament, regime change, or democracy promotion. The administration would not clarify whether its rationale for the use of force would be the breach of past Security Council resolutions, the continuing threat posed to peace and security, or the novel doctrine of preemptive self-defense.[14]

In the end, fortunately, the official legal justification for the Iraq War did not rest on preemptive self-defense. Instead, the administration made the much narrower claim that Iraq was in material breach of U.N. Security Council Resolution 1441; the administration also claimed a "revived" right to use force under older Resolutions 678 and 687, as well as Resolution 1441. Still, in my view, the Iraq invasion that followed violated international law. By not authorizing the member states to use "all necessary means"—the preferred term previously used to authorize the use of force under Security Council resolutions regarding Rwanda, Bosnia, Somalia, Haiti, and Iraq— Resolution 1441 deliberately avoided authorizing force. Some who supported that resolution apparently hoped that, when the time came, there would be a clearer political consensus to authorize "all necessary means." The United States also failed to make a plausible legal argument based on "revived authorization" for the use of force under Resolutions 678 and 687, passed more than a dozen years earlier. It was disingenuous to pretend that these past legal instruments somehow created a *present* political consensus within the United Nations that legally authorized the war, when it was manifestly clear that, in fact, none currently existed.[15] Left unanswered was whether and when the United States could justify using force collectively, without a Security Council resolution, to prevent human-rights abuses against innocent civilians: the so-called doctrine of humanitarian intervention. As chapter 7 shows, after September 11, the Kosovo debate over humanitarian intervention or the emerging international-law doctrine of "responsibility to protect" (R2P) largely hibernated, only to revive during the Libya and Syrian episodes of the Obama administration.

Finally, the Second Gulf War revealed that the Bush Doctrine had engendered a growing discrepancy between America's hard and soft power. At the same time as the United States was using stunning military technology to bomb Baghdad, it could not diplomatically secure the votes of even its closest allies on a matter that the president deemed to be of highest national importance. Bush 43's unilateralism raised new fears at home and abroad about the perils of a world dominated by a unilateralist United States and a unilateralist president. Those fears moderated, but did not disappear, during the Obama years and would revive with even greater alarm during the Trump administration.[16]

The Torture Opinion

The *reductio ad absurdum* of the Bush 43 administration's preemptive-self-defense argument was its embrace of illegal torture. The Justice Department's infamous torture opinion said, in effect, that if the United States could attack in preemptive self-defense, it could also torture in preemptive self-defense.[17] Unfortunately, that claim confounded a "zero tolerance" policy on torture that the United States had announced in 2000. As late as June 2004, Bush 43 reiterated:

> Today . . . the United States reaffirms its commitment to the world-wide elimination of torture. . . . Freedom from torture is an inalienable human right, and we are committed to building a world where human rights are respected and protected by the rule of law. . . . America stands against and will not tolerate torture. We will investigate and prosecute all acts of torture and undertake to prevent other cruel and unusual punishment in all territory under our jurisdiction. American personnel are required to comply with all

U.S. laws, including the United States Constitution, Federal statutes, including statutes prohibiting torture and our treaty obligations with respect to the treatment of all detainees.[18]

Yet even as Bush spoke these words, Human Rights Watch chronicled widespread acts of torture and cruel treatment by the U.S. Army's 82nd Airborne Division. Reports from foreign legal experts alleged that U.S. officials were using or supporting the extraordinary rendition of detainees to other countries where those detainees were being subjected to torture.[19]

The legal justifications for these activities were set forth in a memorandum opinion, dated August 1, 2002, from Jay S. Bybee, then the assistant attorney general for the Office of Legal Counsel, to then White House counsel Alberto R. Gonzales regarding coercive interrogation tactics. The Bybee opinion explored the question whether U.S. officials could use tactics tantamount to torture against suspected terrorists without being held liable under a federal statute that criminalizes torture. The opinion effectively answered that question yes: despite the established zero-tolerance policy, American officials could apply tactics tantamount to torture without being held liable. It took more than two years for the Office of Legal Counsel to withdraw the Bybee opinion, even though the opinion sparked a firestorm of criticism when it was leaked to the press in response to the exposure of grotesque abuses at the Abu Ghraib prison. For at least two years, then, the deeply flawed Bybee opinion stood as the official executive-branch interpretation of federal officials' non-liability with regard to torture and cruel treatment.[20]

By every measure, the Bybee opinion was disastrously wrong. Its most glaring error was its narrow definition of torture: "[inflicting] physical pain . . . equivalent in intensity to the pain accompanying serious physical injury, such as organ failure, impairment of bodily function, or even death." Ironically, this definition would have excluded a range of acts committed by Saddam's regime that Bush 43's administration had used to justify invading Iraq. These included "branding, electric shocks administered to the genitals and other areas, beating, pulling out of fingernails, burning with hot irons and blowtorches, suspension from rotating ceiling fans, dripping acid on the skin, rape, breaking of limbs, denial of food and water, extended solitary confinement in dark and extremely small compartments, and threats to rape or otherwise harm family members and relatives." Obviously, any number of these punishments would constitute torture long before they resulted in organ failure, bodily impairment, or death. Yet the U.S. government's own definition would have exonerated Saddam of most of his acts of torture.[21]

Second, the Bybee opinion declared that criminal prohibitions against torture do not apply to the president or to the interrogation of enemy combatants conducted under the commander-in-chief authority. "Any effort by Congress to regulate the interrogation of battlefield combatants would violate the Constitution's sole vesting of the Commander-in-Chief power in the President." The opinion goes on to claim that lower-level executive officials can escape prosecution for illegal torture because "they were carrying out the president's Commander-in-Chief powers." A "just following orders" defense would preclude the application of the federal criminal statute against torture "to punish officials for aiding the president in exercising his exclusive constitutional authorities." But if anyone who carries out the president's orders to torture cannot be prosecuted, then the Constitution immunizes from criminal prosecution underlings who torture in the president's name. Simply put, the Bybee opinion licensed the president to be "torturer in chief." Although a later memorandum opinion issued by the Office of Legal Counsel in 2004 withdrew this part of the Bybee opinion, that subsequent opinion did not formally repudiate the Bybee opinion's reasoning. This left open whether the withdrawal was warranted because the reasoning was wrong or because it was just unnecessary.[22]

In one step, the Bybee opinion moved the U.S. policy on torture from zero tolerance toward zero accountability. To resist accountability, the Bush administration executed a very simple strategy: first, try to block public release of more Abu Ghraib–type pictures; second, bring prosecutions against low-level officials; third, authorize multiple military investigations that place little blame on higher-ups or civilian officials; fourth, draw a false line between torture, which was nominally forbidden, and related cruel practices like waterboarding and extraordinary rendition, which the administration condoned; fifth, only use euphemisms for torture, like "extreme interrogation techniques" and "migration of extreme practices." This game plan gave the CIA de facto license to conduct unreviewed cruel and inhuman interrogations, so long as these interrogations were conducted by private contractors or civilian officials outside U.S. soil.[23]

By following this game plan, the U.S. government violated both international and domestic law. The Bybee opinion nullified the most basic international-law principles established at the Nuremberg war-crimes trials. Nuremberg changed the valence of personal responsibility. Before Nuremberg, gross atrocities could be committed and no one held responsible. Street-level officials who had committed torture and genocide could claim that they were "just following orders," while their commanders could pretend that they did not know what was going on. After Nuremberg, the law recognized that all participants were culpable. Commanders bore command responsibility because they were obliged to know what atrocities were being committed in their name; street-level officials could no longer escape accountability by claiming that they were "just following orders." These principles are now embodied in the basic instruments of international criminal law. Yet the Bybee opinion sought to reverse this half century of history.[24]

But this time, neither Congress nor the courts acquiesced. In 2005, led by a torture survivor, Senator John McCain, Congress enacted the McCain amendment to the National Defense Authorization Act. That amendment prohibited the use of cruel, inhuman, or degrading treatment against any individual in the custody or effective control of the United States. The amendment also required all U.S. troops to follow Army Field Manual procedures when detaining and interrogating military prisoners. Nearly thirty retired generals, led by former secretary of state Colin Powell, came forward to speak in favor of the amendment. And Judge Hellerstein of the Southern District of New York ordered the release of dozens of pictures of prisoners being abused at the Abu Ghraib prison. Despite vigorous lobbying from the White House, the Republican-controlled Senate and House voted overwhelmingly to strengthen the guidelines governing the treatment of prisoners in U.S. military custody. On December 30, 2005, President Bush signed the McCain amendment into law. Even then, however, his signing statement accompanying the act promised only to execute the new law "in a manner consistent with the constitutional authority of the president to supervise the unitary executive branch." But under intense public pressure, Bush 43 ultimately backed off such extreme claims, finally telling an interviewer: "I don't think a president can . . . order torture, for example. . . . Yes, there are clear red lines."[25]

The president's signing statement exposed the fundamental question: whether the U.S. president has constitutional power to authorize U.S. officials to commit torture and cruel, inhuman, or degrading treatment against detainees, despite an explicit legislative determination to the contrary. The *Youngstown* vision of the National Security Constitution would mandate that the answer be no. The text and history of the Constitution nowhere provide for a commander in chief to override the basic constitutional protections of due process and freedom from cruel and usual punishment. An originalist vision of the Constitution especially would not authorize the president to be torturer in chief. The Declaration of Independence attacked the king for mistreating captives and for engaging in cruelty unworthy of the head of a civilized nation.

The Constitution also does not grant the president an exclusive authority to sanction torture over which Congress lacks power to interfere. Congress enacted the Uniform Code of Military Justice, which prohibits the torture of interrogatees, under Congress's Article I constitutional power to "make Rules for the Government and Regulation of the land and naval forces."[26] Congress and the courts have exercised broad power to define and punish torture as an offense against the law of nations. In 1980, the Second Circuit famously declared that the torturer, "like the pirate and slave trader before him[, is] *hostis humanis generis,* an enemy of all mankind." Since then, Congress has ratified the Convention Against Torture and has enacted the Torture Victim Protection Act, the War Crimes Act, and the McCain amendment. Were a *Curtiss-Wright* vision applied here, the president would have sole constitutional authority to engage in genocide or to impose a system of apartheid over congressional protest.[27]

The authorization for the use of military force enacted one week after September 11 authorizes the president to use "all necessary and appropriate force" against "persons" associated with the September 11 terrorist attacks to protect the nation from the recurrence of such attacks. To accept the Bybee opinion's reading of those words, a court would have to conclude that by enacting the use-of-force authorization in September 2001, Congress silently repealed all previously enacted statutory prohibitions against torture. When the use-of-force authorization was being discussed, no member of Congress argued that it was either "necessary or appropriate" for the president to order torture and cruel treatment of detainees a part of the overall strategy for prosecuting a war on terror. The Bush administration claimed that torture could be justified by the defense of necessity. But, as Israeli chief justice Aharon Barak explained, the "necessity defense" does not constitute a source of authority. . . . [T]he very nature of the defense does not allow it to serve as the source of authorization." The Bybee opinion argued that we must torture someone to get information to defend the country, but "torturing in self-defense," on its own terms, is an oxymoron.[28]

When the president acts in a field in which Congress has legislated so comprehensively, of course, the acknowledged touchstone for constitutional analysis is *Youngstown*. Justice Jackson's concurrence had made clear that "[p]residential powers are not fixed, but fluctuate, depending on their . . . disjunction with those of Congress." The statutory debate over whether the use-of-force authorization authorized torture reflects the contrast between *Youngstown* as written and as executive-power advocates would rewrite it. To read this law as President Bush's lawyers did would recreate another Tonkin Gulf Resolution: a law construed after the fact to give the president a blank check to engage in broad activities never contemplated at the time of the law's enactment.[29]

Historically, the president has not been understood to be free on his own authority to violate a *jus cogens* norm: a fundamental preemptory norm of human rights. In *Committee of U.S. Citizens Living in Nicaragua v. Reagan*, decided by the D.C. Circuit in 1988, then circuit judge, formerly congressman, and later White House counsel Abner Mikva wrote: "Such basic norms of international law . . . may well restrain our government in the same way that the Constitution restrains it. If Congress adopted a foreign policy that resulted in the enslavement of our citizens or of other individuals, that policy might well be subject to challenge in domestic court under international law." In *Sosa v. Alvarez-Machain*, the Supreme Court, by a vote of 6 to 3, decided that when there is "a norm of international character accepted by the civilized world and defined by specificity comparable to the features of the 18th-century paradigms we have recognized," like torture, an alien can sue for that violation under the Alien Tort Statute. And in *Rasul v. Bush*, decided just one day earlier, Justice Stevens's majority opinion noted that people held on Guantánamo may also invoke the Alien Tort Statute. So under U.S. law, if the executive branch of the U.S. government violates a *jus cogens* norm, that violation should be actionable in a U.S. court.[30]

Most fundamentally, claiming a right to preemptively torture simply misunderstands the way in which torture and cruel, inhumane, and degrading treatment are really used. As assistant secretary of state for democracy, human rights, and labor in the Clinton administration, I learned about torture dens in Kosovo, Turkey, the People's Republic of China, and North Korea.

That experience taught me that torture rarely, if ever, yields reliable information. People being tortured do not tell the truth; instead, as one might expect, they will say whatever they think they must say to stop or minimize the torture. Neuroscientists make the obvious point that at a neurological level, every specific tactic used to extract information by torture—sleep deprivation, temperature changes, waterboarding, food restriction—inhibits rather than enhances the victim's ability to truthfully recall and convey accurate memories. So torturing prisoners in search of accurate information achieves the exact opposite of what it is intended to do.[31]

In sum, ordering torture is illegal. If ordered by a president sworn to uphold the Constitution and laws of the United States, it is a high crime and misdemeanor, and hence an impeachable offense. The Bush 43 administration's Bybee opinion—now withdrawn—is the most clearly erroneous legal opinion I have ever read.[32] It offered a definition of torture so narrow that it would exculpate Saddam Hussein. It read the commander-in-chief power so broadly as to remove Congress and the courts as meaningful checks on executive torture. It nullified Nuremberg by giving governmental officials a license to be cruel. Such an opinion must go down in history as an indelible stain on the National Security Constitution.[33]

Guantánamo Detention

During the early days of the Bush 43 administration, the Office of Legal Counsel, after reviewing existing case law, concluded that "[a] detainee could make a non-frivolous argument that [habeas corpus] jurisdiction does exist over aliens detained at [Guantánamo Bay, Cuba], and we have found no decisions that clearly foreclose the existence of habeas jurisdiction there." Still, after the terrorist attacks of September 11, 2001, President Bush chose to bring more than seven hundred alleged al Qaeda detainees held in Afghanistan to Guantánamo, with no apparent exit strategy.[34]

Guantánamo soon became the subject of a heated international and domestic legal debate that continues to this day. In November 2001, President Bush issued a military order, without congressional authorization or consultation, that declared that "[t]o protect the United States and its citizens, . . . it is necessary for [alien enemy combatants] . . . to be tried for violations of the laws of war and other applicable laws by military tribunals." The order was issued without the knowledge or consultation of the secretary of state, the national security adviser or her legal counsel, the general counsel of the CIA, the assistant attorney general for the Criminal Division of the Justice Department, or any of the top lawyers in the Judge Advocate General's Corps. But the Supreme Court, until then a bystander in the war on terror, stepped up in four plenary cases to place limits on the administration's extreme constitutional vision.[35]

In the first such case, *Hamdi v. Rumsfeld* (decided in 2004), the Court denied the president's claim that courts may not even inquire into the factual basis for detention of a U.S. citizen "enemy combatant" being held in the territorial United States. A plurality of the Court affirmed the *Youngstown* vision, reasoning that "[w]hatever power the United States Constitution envisions for the Executive in its exchanges with other nations or with enemy organizations in times of conflict, it most assuredly envisions a role for all three branches when individual liberties are at stake."[36]

Rasul v. Bush, decided the same day, was the Supreme Court's first Guantánamo case. The Court held that noncitizen detainees on Guantánamo have a right to file statutory writs of habeas corpus to challenge their detention. In so holding, the majority rejected the president's claim that it would be an unconstitutional interference with the commander-in-chief power to interpret the habeas corpus statute to encompass actions filed on behalf of Guantánamo detainees. Writing for the Court, Justice Stevens stated that "the United States exercises exclusive jurisdiction and control" at Guantánamo. The presumption against extraterritoriality of U.S. law did not apply at Guantánamo, he reasoned, because petitioners were being "detained within 'the [United States'] territorial jurisdiction.'" Thus, a majority opinion by the same justice who had previously written the direct-return decision against the Haitian refugees ruled that noncitizen detainees do in fact have legal rights on Guantánamo. Justice Kennedy, concurring, agreed that "Guantánamo Bay is in every practical respect a United States territory."[37]

Two years later, the Court decided *Hamdan v. Rumsfeld,* again in favor of an alleged "enemy combatant" held at Guantánamo. Hamdan, allegedly Osama bin Laden's driver, was charged with the nebulous crime of "conspiracy 'to commit . . . offenses triable by a military commission.'" The Bush administration urged the Court to accept an extraordinary constitutional presidential prerogative to deal with the war on terror, claiming authority based on the president's broad authority as commander in chief and Congress's terse use-of-force authorization in 2001. Justice Stevens's opinion for five justices called the military commissions an "extraordinary measure raising important questions about the balance of powers in our constitutional structure." Rejecting the administration's extreme constitutional theory of executive power, all the justices who addressed the merits again placed the case within the tripartite framework of shared institutional powers set forth in Justice Jackson's *Youngstown* concurrence. By enacting the Uniform Code of Military Justice, the Court reasoned, Congress had authorized the president to use commissions but had specified that, wherever practicable, the executive must follow the same procedural rules in military commissions as are applied in ordinary courts-martial. Accordingly, the majority placed this case within Justice Jackson's *Youngstown* category three, where "the President takes measures incompatible with the expressed or implied will of Congress."³⁸

Significantly, the Court refused to accept the government's claim that a new crisis paradigm somehow required that ordinary legal rules be jettisoned. As Justice Kennedy put it, "a case that may be of extraordinary importance is resolved by ordinary rules . . . pertaining to the authority of Congress and the interpretation of its enactments." He asserted that "[t]he Constitution is best preserved by reliance on standards tested over time and insulated from the pressures of the moment." As important, the Court rejected the government's attempted dichotomy between law and war by requiring consistent application of the law of war to Hamdan's case. As Justice Kennedy explained, "[i]f the military commission at issue is illegal under the law of war, then an offender cannot be tried 'by the law of war' before that commission."³⁹

To paraphrase Justice Frankfurter, *Hamdan* did not just decide a particular case: "It overruled a particular way of looking at law."⁴⁰ *Hamdan* underscored that the Constitution places clear limits on the president's capacity to act unilaterally, even in national security and foreign-affairs crises. The *Hamdan* Court resoundingly rejected the Bush administration's constitutional vision of the war on terror. It reaffirmed the core notion that constitutional checks and balances do not stop at the water's edge. The Court followed its earlier insistence in *Rasul* that Guantánamo be treated as a land subject to domestic and international law and that Hamdan was also a person subject to that law. Acknowledging that Hamdan might have committed serious crimes, the Court declared that "in undertaking to try [him] and subject him to criminal punishment, the Executive is bound to comply with the rule of law that prevails in this jurisdiction." *Hamdan* reaffirmed that interbranch dialogue, not presidential unilateralism, was the best way to develop a sustained democratic response to external crisis. Justice Breyer put it simply: "Where, as here, no emergency prevents consultation with Congress, judicial insistence upon that consultation does not weaken our Nation's ability to deal with danger. To the contrary, that insistence strengthens the Nation's ability to determine—through democratic means—how best to do so."[41]

When the president is conducting a war on terror, *Hamdan* instructed, the president may not go it alone by citing a broad constitutional theory and statutes that do not specifically authorize that conduct. Rather, the president should seek to fit any actions within the scope of enacted laws, like the Uniform Code of Military Justice and ratified treaties. By so saying, *Hamdan* disproved the Bybee opinion's exorbitant claims regarding the president's supposed freedom to authorize torture and cruel treatment. With respect to torture and cruel treatment, *Hamdan* confirmed that if the president does not act within the scope of a specific statute (in this case, the McCain amendment) or treaty (in this case, Common Article 3 of the Geneva Conventions), the president's actions will likely be invalidated under *Youngstown* category three. Finally, a majority of the Court denied the government's claim that enemy aliens could never enforce the Geneva Conventions in U.S. courts. According to a long-standing canon of statutory construction, courts must construe statutes, absent clear congressional intent to the contrary, consistently with international law. The majority held that Hamdan's proposed trial violated Common Article 3 of the Geneva Conventions. In both interstate conflicts and conflicts with terrorist groups, that provision prohibits "the passing of sentences and the carrying out of executions without previous judgment pronounced by a regularly constituted court affording all the judicial guarantees which are recognized as indispensable by civilized peoples."[42]

As Justice Breyer wrote for four Justices, "[t]he Court's conclusion ultimately rests upon a single ground: Congress has not issued the Executive a 'blank check.'" Given the individual liberties at stake, the Court demanded a clear congressional statement before the commander in chief could try even a suspected alien terrorist in a special military commission. In so doing, the Court followed a line of cases dating back to *Kent v. Dulles* that held that, even in times of war or national crisis, Congress must give a "clear statement" before the executive branch may deprive suspected enemies of their rights.[43]

Hamdan thus joined a long string of Supreme Court decisions rejecting the claim that the president may invoke his power as commander in chief to disregard an act of Congress.[44] By so holding, *Hamdan* also destroyed the legal case undergirding the NSA's sustained program of secret, unreviewed, warrantless electronic surveillance of American citizens and residents. On its face, the Foreign Intelligence Surveillance Act of 1978—a criminal statute—required the executive branch to seek a warrant within three days of commencing surveillance or within fifteen days after a declaration of war, which by their own admission, administration officials never did.[45] The administration claimed that the president has an implied exclusive constitutional authority over "the means and methods of engaging the enemy," including the conduct of "signals intelligence" during wartime. But *Hamdan* obliged the president to follow the Uniform Code of Military Justice, which similarly regulates the "means and methods of engaging the enemy."[46]

Congress responded to *Hamdan* by quickly passing the Military Commissions Act of 2006. That statute renewed the president's authority to try "alien unlawful combatants," including those held on Guantánamo, before military commissions.[47] But in *Boumediene v. Bush,* the Supreme Court once again ruled against the government, holding that Guantánamo detainees have a *constitutional* right to file writs of habeas corpus challenging their detentions. The Court acknowledged the long history of judicial precedent regarding Guantánamo. It held that fundamental constitutional limitations, particularly the suspension clause, apply to foreign nationals detained there. Writing for the Court, Justice Kennedy definitively rejected the notion that Guantánamo is a black hole. Accepting the government's argument that noncitizens have a constitutional right to the writ of habeas corpus only on the sovereign territory of the United States, he wrote, would effectively grant the political branches "the power to switch the Constitution on or off at will," by moving noncitizen detainees to wherever the Constitution did not apply. Justice Kennedy instead applied a "functional approach" based on "practical concerns, not formalism." That functional reasoning led him to conclude that provisions of the Bill of Rights—such as the suspension clause—should apply to Guantánamo unless it proved "impracticable or anomalous" to apply them. Going forward, then, *Boumediene*'s "impractical or anomalous" test should determine which constitutional rights aliens enjoy on Guantánamo.[48]

This quartet of 9/11 cases should have marked a major step toward rees tablishing what Justice Jackson's *Youngstown* concurrence called the "equilib rium established by our constitutional system." But for two decades after these landmark rulings, the Supreme Court essentially withdrew from decid ing post-9/11 cases. Since *Boumediene,* the Supreme Court has consistently denied certiorari to petitions from Guantánamo Bay detainees and in other national security and terrorism-related cases. It has repeatedly avoided op portunities to clarify the detainees' due-process and habeas rights. Mean while, the next three administrations continued to litigate these issues through the lower courts. Most striking, the Justice Department under the Obama and Biden administrations did not take markedly different positions from those of the Bush 43 and Trump administrations. And the D.C. Circuit visibly diluted the reach of *Boumediene* in subsequent Guantánamo habeas litigation.[49]

When I returned to the government in 2021, during the first days of the Biden administration, I was startled to see how little real impact these cases had made in checking the bureaucracy's orientation toward executive unilat eralism. At interagency meetings, military and security interests were regu larly double counted, and "kinetic" solutions privileged over diplomatic ones Throughout 2021, thousands of Americans were dying from Covid-19 and affected by climate change. Yet just weeks after an angry domestic mob at tacked the U.S. Capitol seeking to undo a presidential election, countless hours were still being spent contemplating the continued detention of a few dozen aging detainees on Guantánamo and potential terrorist threats origi nating in distant theaters. This institutional fixation on past threats resisted the Biden administration's efforts to turn the page to address newly pressing challenges. Much of the bureaucracy, and even younger Biden political ap pointees, had come to regard Guantánamo not as an aberration to be elimi nated, but as an accepted and inevitable feature of the American national security landscape.

Guantánamo stands as a monument to government inertia. After nearly twenty years, when the Biden administration began, the United States was still holding forty detainees at Guantánamo. In *United States v. Husayn (Zubaydah),* the Biden administration urged that the widely known location of the torture of a current Guantánamo detainee was a state secret and that the state-secrets privilege required dismissal of the plaintiff's claim. When a Supreme Court plurality accepted that claim, Justices Neil Gorsuch and Sonia Sotomayor dissented. They charged that dismissal of the plaintiff's claim "abdicat[es] any pretense of an independent judicial inquiry into the propriety of a claim of [state-secrets] privilege and extend[s] instead 'utmost deference' to the Executive's mere assertion of one." Remarkably, thirty years after Judge Johnson first decided—in a ruling in the Haitian-refugee litigation that was later vacated by settlement—that alien detainees on Guantánamo have constitutional rights to due process of law, that legal issue still remained unresolved.[50]

In short, the Bush 43 years marked a watershed. They began what may be an irreversible pendulum swing toward the *Curtiss-Wright* vision of executive power. That is a swing that neither the Obama nor Biden administrations seemed willing or able to undo.

7

Obama: Revision and Undercorrection

THE HISTORIC ELECTION OF BARACK OBAMA restrained and channeled, but did not fundamentally undo, all of the excesses of the Bush 43 administration. Obama had campaigned on a platform of "change you can believe in." But when it came to stemming the flow of power toward executive unilateralism, enduring change proved hard to achieve.

Obama genuinely believed in the interdependence of the global community. He was committed to principled engagement with allies based on respect for the rule of law. This faith came from being born of a Kenyan father and spending years of his childhood living in Indonesia. In a soaring speech in Cairo in 2009, Obama underscored his commitment to engagement through strategic multilateralism. Twenty-first-century challenges, he proclaimed, "must be [met through] partnership." Global problems must therefore be tackled by open dialogue and partnership between the United States and peoples and nations across traditional regional divides. He pledged that the United States' actions would be "based on mutual interest and mutual respect" and an acknowledgment of "the rights and responsibilities of [all] nations."[1]

To implement this return to strategic multilateralism, Obama's secretary of state, Hillary Rodham Clinton, called for the use of "smart power" to place diplomacy at the vanguard of U.S. foreign policy: "a blend of principle and pragmatism" that makes "intelligent use of all means at our disposal," including promotion of democracy, development, technology, and human rights and international law. As articulated by the president and his secretary of state, the Obama strategy could be summarized as what I have elsewhere called "engage, translate, and leverage": the United States would tackle global problems by engaging with its allies around common values; translating existing international law to legal rules suited to the new situations; and leveraging limited uses of force with diplomacy, development, and cooperative law enforcement to achieve enduring diplomatic solutions to global problems.[2]

Yet despite great effort, as a constitutional matter, Obama's eight years undercorrected for the excesses of the Bush 43 administration. This allowed the *Curtiss-Wright* vision to revive with even greater virulence under his successor, Donald Trump. Obama's undercorrection had many causes: his inherent caution; the commitment of many on his team to continuity; his overriding political priority on health care; his tenuous influence with Congress; and tenacious resistance from conservative courts dominated by judges appointed by the two Bush presidents. Previewing what his vice president, Joe Biden, would later face as president, Obama spent much of his presidency fighting uphill. He inherited the worst recession since the Depression; long-standing conflicts in Iraq and Afghanistan, and against al Qaeda; massive earthquakes in Haiti and Chile; and a fractured political environment that usually placed out of reach the sixty Senate votes needed for cloture, let alone the sixty-seven needed for treaty ratification. He confronted major challenges in closing Guantánamo and in resuming international engagement to tackle the twenty-first-century threats of climate change, cybercrime, terrorism, food security, and global health.

To avoid legal-process breakdowns of the kind that had often afflicted the Bush 43 administration, the National Security Council (NSC) under Obama revived the Clinton administration practice of convening an interagency group of general counsel known as "the lawyers group." Chaired by the NSC legal adviser (double-hatted as a deputy White House counsel), the group included the general counsels of the Departments of State and Defense, the Central Intelligence Agency, the Office of the Director of National Intelligence, and the Joint Chiefs of Staff, as well as the assistant attorneys general for either the Office of Legal Counsel or the National Security Division at the Department of Justice (and depending on the issue, the general counsels of the Department of the Treasury and the Office of the U.S. Trade Representative). The lawyers group held regular weekly meetings to spot in advance and answer issues bubbling out of each agency and ad hoc questions that arose from senior interagency policy meetings.[3]

This interagency legal mechanism proved simultaneously therapeutic and cumbersome. To its credit, the process ensured that the interagency policy-makers would deliberate only those policy options that a consensus of expert senior lawyers had already deemed lawful. This created what former Legal Adviser Abram Chayes had called "continuous feedback between the knowl-edge that the government will be called upon to justify its action and the kind of action that can be chosen."[4] To avoid process fouls of the kind that plagued the prior administration, the lawyers group thoroughly vetted essentially all legal decisions of import regarding U.S. national security issues—including confidential and covert operations—and any changes in legal positions. The lawyers group thereby offered an effective means for unearthing and system-atically answering national security legal questions and injecting the answers into the national security policy process. Along the way, it enabled the presi-dent and the national security adviser to ask and answer difficult national security and international-law questions in real time, and to work those an-swers smoothly into fast-moving policy discussion.

But this same process carried a downside: it reinforced Obama's own gradualist instincts. Government lawyers instinctively start with a presump-tion of *stare decisis*: that an existing executive-branch legal interpretation should stand unless, after careful review, a considered reexamination of the text, structure, legislative or negotiating history, purpose, and practice under the treaty or statute provided convincing evidence that a prior interpretation should be changed. This bias toward legal inertia preserved many question-able positions adopted by a Bush 43 administration that had largely ignored legal process to make aggressive policy and legal change in the *Curtiss-Wright* direction. The requirement of consensus before agencies could change the status quo created a strong default in favor of the previous administration's legal positions by empowering just one dissenting voice within the adminis-tration to keep a controversial legal position in place. This laborious process also explained the grudging release of the controversial OLC opinion autho-rizing the targeted killing of the terrorist Anwar al-Aulaqi, the Obama ad-ministration's unwillingness to seek stronger accountability for past acts of CIA torture, and the stubborn continuation of a Guantánamo detention pol-icy despite Obama's repeated insistence that it is not "who we are."[5]

Still, the Obama administration visibly differed from its predecessor in its attitude toward constitutional and international law. President Obama and

ecretary Clinton, both seasoned public lawyers, understood that acknowl-
dging legal constraints legitimizes and gives credibility to government ac-
on. As Obama emphasized in his National Archives speech in 2009, the
merican political system was founded on a vision of universal rights and
ne rule of law. "Fidelity to [these] values," he announced, makes us stronger
nd safer.[6] The Obama team—coordinated by the national security advisers
m Jones, Tom Donilon, and Susan Rice—included Clinton's (and later
iden's) national security adviser, Jake Sullivan, the deputy national security
dviser and deputy secretary of state (and future Biden secretary of state),
ntony Blinken, and the ambassador to the United Nations (and future Biden
dministrator of international development), Samantha Power. They shared
ne belief that obeying international law advances U.S. foreign-policy inter-
sts and strengthens America's position of global leadership. Vice President
ne Biden, Secretaries of State Clinton and John Kerry (later Biden's special
residential envoy for climate change), and Secretary of Defense Chuck Ha-
el were all former senators conscious of congressional prerogatives in for-
ign affairs. But the Democrats controlled both houses of Congress during
nly two of Obama's eight years in office, which severely hamstrung his abil-
y to secure legislative approval for key foreign-policy initiatives.

As a matter of law, Obama's eight years most visibly departed from the Bush
.3 years with regard to the use of force, particularly the law of counterterrorism
nd humanitarian intervention, and the making of international arrangements,
articularly the Paris climate-change accord and the Iran nuclear deal. In each
rea, Obama sought to reengage multilateral allies by making a visible effort to
econcile the United States' actions with international law. At the same time,
owever, he avoided seeking congressional approval that he knew he could not
ecure politically. Instead, he tried wherever possible to fit his initiatives within
reexisting statutory authorizations and interpretations of extant law. These
atterns most clearly emerged with respect to the law of counterterrorism, hu-
nanitarian intervention, and the making of international agreements.

The Law of Counterterrorism

Upon taking office, President Obama made clear that his goal was to obey
he law even in times of armed conflict. He repeated this commitment in his
nauguration speech, his National Archives speech in 2009, his Nobel Prize

speech in 2009, and a speech at the National Defense University in May
2013. Although some simplistically characterized the Obama administration's approach to post-9/11 national security issues as just continuing Bush
43's, the Obama administration painstakingly narrowed Bush's approach to
the "law of 9/11." Obama's administration deliberately embraced a more restrained *Youngstown* reading of presidential prerogative. The administration
asserted that the president could engage in appropriate and necessary use
of military force in a manner consistent with both the Constitution and the
congressional resolutions in 2001 and 2002 authorizing the use of force
against those responsible for the September 11 attacks and against Iraq. But
at the same time, Obama urged that those statutory authorizations should be
narrowed and eventually repealed.[7]

Under international law, the Obama administration first narrowed Bush's
legal theory by declaring that the United States was in a non-international
armed conflict with al Qaeda, the Taliban, and associated forces in response
to the 9/11 attacks and subsequent attacks. Under international law, Obama
asserted a right to use force in accordance with the laws of war and its inherent right to self-defense. In *Hamdan v. Rumsfeld,* the Supreme Court in 2006
had concluded that the United States was engaged in an armed conflict with
al Qaeda that crossed borders, but could still be called "non-international"
because it was not between two nation-states.[8] Within that armed conflict,
Obama reaffirmed the United States' commitment to follow both the international law of initiating war (*jus ad bellum*) and the international law of
conducting war (*jus in bello*).

President Obama further narrowed the scope of the claimed conflict by
rejecting an amorphous "global war on terror" for being as sprawling and
rhetorical as a "war against drugs" or a "war on poverty." This narrowed legal
theory allowed Obama to assert that the United States was not at war against
"terror" generally, but with the specific *transnational terror network* that linked
al Qaeda, the Taliban, and associated forces. Thus, sympathizers "inspired"
by al Qaeda, like the Boston Marathon bombers, were common criminals
not part of the particular terrorist network that the United States had declared
war upon. The Obama administration later construed ISIS (the "Islamic
State" or "Daesh") to be a "splinter" or "associated force" of al Qaeda operating as its "co-belligerent" by entering the fight alongside al Qaeda and against
the United States in active theaters of battle in Afghanistan, Iraq, and Syria.

As part of that narrowed armed conflict, Obama argued, a limited use of military tools could contribute to an integrated legal approach to targeting and detention, as an element of the broader national security strategy of "smart power." Within this diplomatic framework, he argued, the use of targeted killing by drones could be an effective, discriminating tool to help dismantle specific networks that threaten the United States. To win broader legitimacy, he insisted that U.S. targeting should be lawful; that detentions should be legally authorized and administered; that fruits of illegal detention or interrogation should not be used in subsequent proceedings; and that the United States should pursue multilateral, lawful cooperation with other states that were also fighting those terrorist networks, wherever possible relying on shared law-enforcement authorities.[10]

The Obama administration's legal interpretation did not follow verbatim from twentieth-century rules of international law. Instead, its interpretation derived from good-faith efforts to translate the spirit of those laws to current circumstances. To implement those international-law rules, Obama stated a clear preference for capture over kill and respect for the sovereignty of other states. At the same time, he endorsed the notion that self-defense may be invoked to use force against a continuing imminent threat. He deemed it necessary to apply an elongated notion of "imminence" when taking action in self-defense against senior terrorist operational leaders who were clearly determined to strike against the United States, so long as there is a "near certainty that no civilians will be killed or injured." Finally, Obama reaffirmed his absolute commitment to humane treatment in detention, interrogation, and targeting.[11]

Under domestic law, Obama did not assert that the United States was battling specified terrorist networks purely on the basis of the president's unenumerated constitutional powers under Article II of the Constitution. Instead, in all instances, his administration based its use of force on specific congressional authorizations—the use-of-force authorizations passed by Congress in 2001 and 2002. Even over the objection of some judges appointed by Bush 43, principally the future Supreme Court justice Brett Kavanaugh, Obama argued that these domestic authorizations should be informed by the international laws of war.[12]

With respect to domestic law, the Obama administration consistently asked the same two questions previously asked about the Kosovo intervention in chapter 5: the constitutional question whether a proposed military action rose to the level of "war" that Congress must declare, and the statutory question whether the conflict constituted "hostilities" that could continue past sixty days. With the exception of the Libyan intervention, discussed be low, the short-term nature of most military actions carried out under Obama rendered the War Powers Resolution's conditions largely inapplicable. The Obama administration also took great pains to meet the resolution's report ing and consultation requirements.

With respect to detention, President Obama made clear that his adminis tration would follow international law. Common Article 3 of the four Geneva Conventions, which is regarded as customary international law, states that there should be no violence to life and persons, including torture, taking of hostages, outrages on personal dignity, or sentences without due process. As I noted in congressional testimony, it does not matter that the "terrorists have not signed Common Article 3. . . . [W]hales have not signed the Whaling Con vention [either]. But it is about how we treat them and how we are obliged to treat them." Additional Protocol II amplifies these guarantees and outlaws all forms of violence against noncombatants. Civilian trials were to be preferred After the Supreme Court's invalidation of the first military-commission order in the *Hamdan* case, military commissions were required to comply with the Constitution. An executive order on periodic review was implemented to de termine which detainees should continue to be held and which should be re leased. And the National Defense Authorization Act came to incorporate an absolute statutory guarantee of humane treatment.[13]

Rejecting Bush 43's "war, not law enforcement" approach to counterter rorism, the Obama administration merged military and law-enforcement tactics into a hybrid antiterrorist approach. Obama's lawyers took pains to apply a fact-based, not label-based, approach to identifying the enemy. To la bel someone an "enemy combatant" did not suddenly mean that tools of war could always be used against him anywhere, anytime. What might be an ap propriate warlike response toward an ISIS leader found in an unstable part of Syria would yield to a law-enforcement approach if that same ISIS leader should be found instead in a robust law-enforcement environment like Paris. Hard cases thus called for a detailed fact-based inquiry to help determine whether a particular person could lawfully be the subject of military action.

This approach made legal analysis central to the exercise of the use of force. By declaring torture illegal under all circumstances, the Obama administraion reaffirmed what Bush 43's administration had resisted declaring: that the president could not constitutionally act as torturer in chief. The lawfulness of targeted killing in warfare depended on whether it was executed in accordance with the laws of war. This required case-by-case targeting decisions that included many government lawyers. Obama's national security lawyers had to draw lines regularly between legal and illegal uses of force. Unlike chemical weapons, for example, drones were not inherently illegal weapons. They could be deployed indiscriminately and illegally, but they could also lawfully be used for certain targeted operations that met carefully defined criteria.

So through the complex interagency legal process described above, the Obama administration's approach required its lawyers to engage weekly, at times daily, in discussions regarding the legality of particular targeting decisions. An interagency team of government lawyers had to decide in specific cases how likely it was that a particular person would order or participate in an imminent attack on U.S. persons or facilities, or on the homeland itself. They were required to precisely determine that individual's true identity, his history of past hostile acts, his position in the terrorist network chain of command, and the certifiable threat level he currently posed. As the administration closed, the president also issued an executive order calling for regular disclosure of civilian casualty statistics.[14]

In a series of speeches beginning in April 2010, Obama administration officials sought to make these rules more transparent, while defending the lawfulness of targeted killing when conducted against senior operational terrorist leaders who posed imminent threats to American security. As Aharon Barak, the chief justice of the Supreme Court of Israel, had previously suggested, targeted killing may in some cases be more consistent with human-rights norms than other forms of warfare because of the lower possibility of killing innocent bystanders. What is most necessary to make targeted killing lawful is that the action be duly authorized under both domestic and international law; that the targeted person's rights be adequately considered; and that the sovereignty of the country in which the action occurs be adequately respected. If all of this were done correctly, the Obama administration argued, targeted killing would not constitute unlawful extrajudicial killing, execution, or assassination. Instead, targeted killing could be lawfully carried out by drone or precise special operation, as occurred, for example, with the killing of Osama bin Laden in 2011.[15]

Through much of the Obama administration, it was widely assumed that a future president Hillary Clinton would carry on these efforts. But Donald Trump's surprise victory forced the Obama administration to publicize its understanding of the legal rules under which it was operating. In December 2016, just before Obama left office, the administration embodied these principles in a comprehensive "legal and policy frameworks" document, which the media dubbed "the playbook." The frameworks report detailed how the United States had sought to "ensur[e] that our uses of force overseas are supported by a solid domestic law framework and consistent with an international legal framework predicated on the concepts of sovereignty and self-defense embedded in the United Nations Charter." In an effort to "encourage[] future Administrations to build on this report and carry forward the principles of transparency it represents," President Obama issued a memorandum asking the NSC staff to update the report at least annually and the report was accompanied by President Obama's last national security speech. But as soon as Donald Trump became president, precisely how and whether these rules were still being followed became opaque. Trump reportedly abolished the interagency lawyers group and delegated targeting decisions to regional commanders, and away from government lawyers.[16]

Finally, in clarifying the law of counterterrorism, the Obama administration became the first to summarize the emerging state of the law of cyber conflict. Cyber intrusions run a wide spectrum of activity: from cyber monitoring, defense, and espionage to hacking, all of which can be done by private parties; to computer network exploitation (CNE), which is a form of espionage; to pernicious forms of computer network attack (CNA), which can have broader, physical consequences, such as using a computer to open a dam or to shut down a hospital. Given that these physical effects can be no different from simply bombing the dam or hospital, such destructive cyber acts should plainly be governed by the laws of war.

In 2012, as State Department Legal Adviser, I gave the first U.S. government speech setting forth ten agreed-upon international rules of cyber conflict. That speech made clear that international law applies in cyberspace that cyberspace is neither a law-free zone nor a black hole; and that cyber actions can, under certain circumstances, represent a use of force to which the laws of *jus ad bellum* and *jus in bello* apply. I made clear that states were responsible for their own actions, as well as the acts of proxy actors. Five years later, my successor as Legal Adviser made a follow-on speech promoting stability in cyberspace through international law. A series of legal experts simultaneously engaged in an extended exercise to produce the *Tallinn Manual,* which has elaborated these emerging rules in great detail. But further sustained efforts to legalize cyber conflict will be needed to promote official governmental standard-setting through ongoing diplomatic negotiation before such global forums as the Group of Governmental Experts and the U.N. Open-Ended Working Group on Cybersecurity. As U.S. military capabilities in the use of cyber tools and artificial intelligence accelerate, government lawyers must keep translating the laws of war to rapidly evolving technological capabilities. Such translation efforts make even clearer that advances in the ability to do harm in cyberspace must be matched by modern tailored rules to constrain that harm, developed under an evolving twenty-first-century law of war.[17]

Humanitarian Intervention

Probably the greatest unresolved legal area with respect to the use of force was determining whether and when the United States could engage abroad in humanitarian intervention or military exercises justified as a "responsibility to protect" (R2P) foreign civilians. Little noticed in President Obama's Nobel Prize acceptance speech in December 2009 was his declared "belie[f] that force can be justified on humanitarian grounds, as it was in the Balkans, or in other places that have been scarred by war." The president thus signaled early that, under appropriate circumstances, he was prepared to act to prevent civilian slaughter in a future Kosovo-type situation. This directly raised the question whether it was lawful for the United States to lead a collective effort to enter another state's territory or airspace to try to mitigate the humanitarian disaster.[18]

This issue, which raised complex questions of both international and domestic law, arose for Obama first in Libya, then in Syria. In 2011, a unanimous Security Council resolution gave the Obama administration clear authority to intervene in Libya, but controversy soon arose about whether the administration had violated the domestic War Powers Resolution. In 2013, the administration threatened to intervene in Syria but ended up backing off, even after Syria's leader, Bashar al-Assad, had crossed Obama's previously announced "red line" of using chemical weapons against innocent civilians. Although Obama decided as a policy matter not to use force in Syria, he expressly stated that under some circumstances, he would consider force or the threat of force to be a lawful option.[19]

I have argued elsewhere that the Clinton administration's failure to articulate a clear international-law rationale for its Kosovo intervention violated its "duty to explain." That failure came back to haunt the Obama administration with regard to Syria fourteen years later. As chapter 5 reviewed, as a matter of domestic law, the War Powers Resolution imposed a sixty-day limit on the president's commitment of troops to "hostilities" in Kosovo without congressional authorization. At the sixty-day mark, there was little doubt that U.S. military activity in Kosovo constituted "hostilities," but the policy question was whether the United States should cease bombing and thereby allow Milošević to regain traction, particularly given that the sixty-day statutory limit had been arbitrarily chosen a quarter century earlier, without this particular scenario in mind. Shortly before the sixty-day period expired, Congress passed a budget bill appropriating money for the Kosovo operation. So the operation proceeded, and a few weeks later, at seventy-eight days, Milošević conceded. At the end of 2000, the Office of Legal Counsel issued a detailed opinion that essentially justified bombing for the additional eighteen days. The opinion treated the supplemental appropriation for military operations as "establishing a background principle" that gave "authorization for continuing hostilities [even] after the expiration of sixty days" under the War Powers Resolution.[20]

With this background, roll the clock forward ten years, when suddenly across the Arab region, authoritarian governments were collapsing, confronted by rising popular movements. The Obama administration was forced to decide what happens when Arab Awakening meets the international-law doctrine of responsibility to protect. In 2011, Libya's dictator, Muammar Qadhafi, publicly pledged to lead "millions to purge Libya [of his opponents] inch by inch, house by house, household by household, alley by alley, and individual by individual until I purify this land." He promised that his opponents—whom he called "rats"—would all be executed. Less than a month later, in another televised address, Qadhafi threatened his enemies "We will come house by house, room by room. We will find you in your closets. And we will have no mercy and no pity." Inside the Obama administra tion, there was no doubt that his words were not just bombast; reports from defecting Qadhafi forces recounted rules of engagement ordering them to "show no mercy" to prisoners, and confirmed that Qadhafi's forces were using rape as a weapon of war.[21]

To prevent an imminent humanitarian disaster, President Obama rallied other NATO countries to join his coalition. Starting in late March 2011, the United States, the Arab League, and NATO secured two Security Council resolutions to enforce a no-fly zone to protect civilians. President Obama declared, "[W]hen someone like Qadhafi threatens a bloodbath that could destabilize an entire region, and when the international community is prepared to come together to save many thousands of lives, then it's in our national interest to act. And it's our responsibility." The United States asserted not just that preventing the slaughter of Libyan civilians was a compelling national interest, but also—in a claim then embedded in the two Security Council resolutions—that Qadhafi had forfeited his government's responsibility to protect Libyan citizens. Qadhafi's forfeit implicitly invited the United Nations to fill that void. Following the reasoning used by OLC head Walter Dellinger in approving the intervention in Haiti (the Dellinger test discussed in chapter 5), the Office of Legal Counsel stated in a written opinion by then acting assistant attorney general Caroline Krass that because the use of force contemplated was limited in nature, scope, and duration, it did not constitute a "war" in a constitutional sense. The Office of Legal Counsel thus concluded that prior congressional approval was not required for the use of force. During the first few weeks of military action, the United States established a no-fly zone over Libya, and neither the House nor the Senate objected. The United States took the lead among the NATO nations in establishing the no-fly zone, which required the United States, using its unique military capabilities among the NATO allies, to engage in extensive precision bombing at the front end. But President Obama made clear from the start that once the no-fly zone was established, the United States would shift to a backup role, primarily through refueling and aerial-reconnaissance activities, limited to supporting no-fly-zone patrols flown by other NATO countries.[22]

As day sixty of the intervention approached, an intense debate about next steps ensued inside the Beltway. Initially, the administration saw only three options. Option one: at sixty days, just stop. The widespread prediction was that Qadhafi and his forces would then recover, creating a real chance that the slaughter of innocent civilians would resume. Most in the administration thus deemed this option unacceptable. Option two: ask Congress to pass authorizing legislation, which of course was everybody's first preference. But quiet inquiry revealed that too many members of Congress who had felt politically burned by their votes authorizing the Iraq War were reluctant to have to vote publicly on war again. Accordingly, congressional leaders made clear that they would not pass legislation, expressing in every conceivable way that they wanted no public votes. So option two—seeking legislation—effectively reduced to option one: doing nothing and letting the slaughter of innocents resume. Senator John McCain and his congressional allies offered a third option: the president could simply declare the War Powers Resolution unconstitutional and force a showdown with Congress over that long-contested legal issue. But while the administration was focused on averting civilian slaughter in Benghazi, creating a separate, constitutional battleground for interbranch confrontation over the separation of powers was the last thing anyone wanted to do. So the question became whether these were in fact the only available options.[23]

As a legal matter, there was consensus that the force being used was so limited in nature, scope, and duration that it did not constitute a "war" in a constitutional sense. The question under the War Powers Resolution thus became whether the force actually being used was also so limited in nature, scope, and duration that it did not even constitute "hostilities" under the resolution. If that could be shown, the administration would have a fourth option: to accept the constitutionality of the War Powers Resolution but determine that the United States was not, in fact, engaged in "hostilities" that would trigger the resolution's sixty-day limit.[24]

To answer that question required the president's lawyers to explore a legal question: What did Congress intend "hostilities" to mean when it enacted the War Powers Resolution? They also had to answer a factual question: How much military action was actually transpiring in Libya? With regard to the first question, the term "hostilities" was not self-defining. As a federal judge had observed, "fixed legal standards were deliberately omitted from this statutory scheme," as "the very absence of a definitional section in the [War Powers] Resolution [was] coupled with debate suggesting that determinations of 'hostilities' were intended to be political decisions made by the President and Congress." The only relevant legislative history, found in the House report explained that "[t]he word hostilities was substituted for the phrase armed conflict during the subcommittee drafting process because it was considered to be somewhat broader in scope"; but the report provided no clear direction on what either "hostilities" or "armed conflict" was intended to mean. One of the resolution's main sponsors, Senator Jacob K. Javits, had stated that "[t]he bill . . . seeks to proceed in the kind of language which accepts a whole body of experience and precedent without endeavoring specifically to define it." As another witness testified, "there is peril in trying to be too exact in definitions," as "[s]omething must be left to the judgment, the intelligence, the wisdom, of those in command of the Congress, and of the President as well."[25]

As State Department Legal Adviser, I concluded as a legal matter that what constitutes "hostilities" for purposes of the War Powers Resolution was far from clear. That term had previously been studied by several legal offices within the U.S. government—including the Justice Department's Office of Legal Counsel—but none had clarified exactly what the term meant. The Dellinger test had specified a three-factor "nature, scope, and duration" standard for what constitutes "war," but executive-branch lawyers had never specified a similar test for what constitutes "hostilities." Accordingly, I testified to the Senate Foreign Relations Committee:

> [A]s everyone recognizes, the legal trigger for the automatic pullout clock, "hostilities[,]" is an ambiguous term of art that is defined nowhere in the statute. The legislative history . . . makes clear there was no agreed-upon view of exactly what the term "hostilities" would encompass, nor has that standard ever been defined by any court or by Congress itself. From the start, legislators disagreed about the meaning of the term and the scope of the 60-day pullout rule and whether a particular set of facts constitutes hostilities for purposes of the resolution has been determined less by a narrow parsing of dictionary definitions than by interbranch practice. The Members of Congress who drafted the War Powers Resolution understood that this resolution is not like the Internal Revenue Code. Reading the War Powers Resolution should not be a mechanical exercise. The term "hostilities" was vague but they declined to give it more concrete meaning in part to avoid hampering future Presidents by making the resolution a one-size-fits-all straitjacket that would operate mechanically without regard to the facts.[26]

Asked at a House of Representatives hearing whether the term "hostilities" was problematic because of "the susceptibility of it to different interpretations,"

Senator Javits had answered that this ambiguity was a necessary feature of the legislation: "There is no question about that, but that decision would be for the President to make. No one is trying to denude the President of authority."[27]

Thus, successive administrations had agreed that the term "hostilities" is "definable in a meaningful way only in the context of an actual set of facts." In Libya, the president had framed the military mission narrowly, directing, among other things, that no ground troops would be deployed (except for necessary personnel recovery missions). He further ordered that once the no-fly zone was established, U.S. forces would transition responsibility for leading and conducting the mission to an integrated NATO command. On April 4, 2011, U.S. forces did just that. They shifted to a constrained and supporting role in a multinational civilian-protection mission—in an action involving no U.S. ground presence or, to that point, U.S. casualties—authorized by a carefully tailored U.N. Security Council resolution.[28]

In comparing the situation in Libya with historic situations in which the "hostilities" question had previously been debated, we found that the Reagan administration had argued in 1983 that U.S. armed forces in Lebanon were not engaged in "hostilities," even though there were roughly sixteen hundred U.S. Marines equipped for combat on a daily basis and roughly two thousand more on ships and bases nearby; U.S. Marine positions were attacked repeatedly; and four marines were killed and several dozen wounded in those attacks. In the case of Grenada, the Reagan administration did not acknowledge that statutory "hostilities" had begun, even though nineteen hundred members of the U.S. armed forces had landed on the island, and combat claimed the lives of nearly twenty Americans and wounded nearly a hundred more. With respect to activities in the Persian Gulf in 1987–1988, the Reagan administration argued that the War Powers Resolution's pullout provision was inapplicable to a reflagging program that was preceded by an accidental attack on a U.S. Navy ship that killed thirty-seven crew members and that led to repeated instances of active combat with Iranian forces. And in the case of Somalia, the Bush 41 and Clinton administrations could not agree with Congress about when "hostilities" began, even though twenty-five thousand troops were initially dispatched by Bush, without congressional authorization, and ground combat eventually led to the deaths of more than two dozen U.S. soldiers.[29]

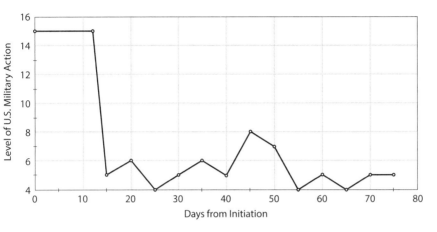

Fig. 1. Libya "hostilities" (figure by Bill Nelson)

Even if we did not accept any of these past executive-branch positions as correct, these historical precedents suggested that the *magnitude of the military engagement* is a key factor in determining whether the United States was indeed in "hostilities" for purposes of the War Powers Resolution. At that point, seeking the facts on the ground, my office asked for a chart showing the amount of bombing that had been taking place (figure 1).

The graph showed, on the x-axis, the number of days from initiation of the use of force. The y-axis measured the number of U.S. military strikes and amount of ordnance dropped. Because the United States was initially tasked with creating the no-fly zones, the number of strikes and amount of ordnance dropped was clearly above the "hostilities" level for the first fifteen days. But around day fifteen, the number of strikes by U.S. forces dropped dramatically. It stayed roughly at that lower level until past day forty, when a relatively low level of U.S. bombing was thereafter dictated by the limited, supporting nature of the U.S. mission as part of the multinational force in Libya. Around the fortieth day, after NATO had initially destroyed command and control of Libyan weapons in the opening weeks to establish a no-fly zone, Qadhafi's forces replicated command and control by "pairing" laptops on jeeps with remaining surface-to-air weapons. Those mobile platforms thus became capable of firing the very same surface-to-air missiles that had initially been immobilized by the first NATO strikes during the opening days of the operation. Because precision-targeted U.S. drones were the only available weapons that could pinpoint and eliminate those mobile platforms, the number of U.S. strikes ticked upward between roughly day forty and day fifty-five. Even so, as I later testified, "American strikes [were] limited on an as-needed basis to the suppression of enemy air defenses to enforce the no-fly zone and limited strikes by Predator unmanned aerial vehicles against discrete targets to support the civilian protection mission." I explained that "the bulk of U.S. contributions ha[d] been providing intelligence capabilities and refueling assets to the NATO effort," and that 75 percent of the overall sorties were "being flown by our coalition partners." "The overwhelming majority of strike sorties, 90 percent," continued to "b[e] flown by our partners." Most telling, "[b]y our best estimate," I testified, "since the handoff to NATO, the total number of United States munitions dropped in Libya has been less than 1 *percent* of those dropped in Kosovo."[30]

Although the overall magnitude of military strikes in Libya remained moderate, the statutory question remained whether that level of strikes, combined with other factors, exceeded the legal standard for "hostilities." In his exhaustive account of this period, the *New York Times* reporter Charlie Savage reported that the general counsel of the Defense Department circulated a "discussion paper . . . saying that the administration would have a stronger argument that it was complying with the [War Powers Resolution] if its military activity receded to a purely supporting role, like refueling allied warplanes and providing surveillance. That could mean no more American missile strikes at air defenses and returning to the rule that Predator drones were for surveillance only."[31] But even if this policy option had not been rejected by the Defense Department's policymakers, this legal distinction could nowhere be found in either the text or legislative history of the War Powers Resolution. The general counsel did not explain why the mere *availability* of missile and drone strikes against revived mobile platforms—no matter what the daily or overall magnitude of actual strikes might be—would suddenly transform the situation into "hostilities" and trigger the War Powers Resolution's sixty-day limit.

So in the end, the question became highly fact specific. The United States had no boots on the ground; ran no risk of escalation, because of the limited nature of the mission; flew almost exclusively support missions; did some precision bombing to protect civilians; and made drones available not just for surveillance but also for attacking replicated mobile platforms. Did the totality of those activities constitute "hostilities" for purposes of the War Powers Resolution? Under these circumstances, I argued, there was a solid case that this situation did not constitute statutory "hostilities" of the kind the resolution had envisioned.

On this point, the statute's text was deliberately ambiguous, from the passage of the War Powers Resolution to the present. Just one year before the Libyan crisis arose, the Supreme Court had directed that an interpreter engaging in statutory construction should focus not just on statutory text, but on the "focus" of congressional concern. Here, it seemed clear that the focus of the War Powers Resolution was as a "no more Vietnams" statute, not a "let's have more Rwandas" statute. Congress's focus was on preventing large-scale creeping wars, like Vietnam, that build and escalate to involve large numbers of ground troops. Congress's intent was not to truncate a U.N.-authorized humanitarian mission that had been carefully designed to limit U.S. military engagement and prevent both large-scale escalations and civilian slaughter.[32]

This reading seemed confirmed by a legal opinion issued just two years after the War Powers Resolution was enacted, when Congress had expressly invited the executive branch to provide its best understanding of the term "hostilities." The Legal Adviser of the State Department and the general counsel of the Defense Department jointly distinguished between full-scale military encounters and "intermittent military engagements" that did not require withdrawal of forces under the resolution's sixty-day rule. They suggested that the executive branch had traditionally understood "hostilities" to mean "a situation in which units of the U.S. armed forces are actively engaged in exchanges of fire with opposing units of hostile forces." Hence, they concluded, the term should not be read to include situations in which the nature of the mission is limited and does not "involve the full military engagements with which the Resolution is primarily concerned." Nor did "hostilities" contemplate situations in which the exposure of U.S. forces and the risk of escalation were limited, such as situations involving "sporadic military or paramilitary attacks on our armed forces stationed abroad."[33]

Given all of this analysis, I advised that under the particular circumstances prevailing in Libya, the administration could construe the facts and the law to conclude that the United States was not engaged in "hostilities" for purposes of the War Powers Resolution. As I later testified: "In light of this historical practice, a *combination* of four factors present in Libya suggests that the current situation does not constitute the kind of 'hostilities' envisioned by the War Powers Resolution's sixty-day automatic pullout provision."

First, the nature of the mission is unusually limited. By Presidential design, U.S. forces are playing a constrained and supporting role in a NATO-led, multinational civilian protection mission charged with enforcing a Security Council Resolution.

Second, the exposure of our Armed Forces is limited. From the transition date of March 31 forward [following the creation of the no-fly zone], there have been no U.S. casualties, no threat of significant U.S. casualties, no active exchanges of fire with hostile forces, no significant armed confrontation or sustained confrontation of any kind with hostile forces.

Third, the risk of escalation here is limited. In contrast to the U.N.-authorized Desert Storm operation, which presented over 400,000 troops, the same order of magnitude as Vietnam at its peak, Libya has not involved any significant chance of escalation into a full-fledged conflict characterized by a large U.S. ground presence, major casualties, sustained active combat, or an expanding geographic scope. . . .

And fourth and finally, we are using limited military means, not the kind of full military engagements with which the War Powers Resolution is primarily concerned. . . . The violence U.S. Armed Forces are directly inflicting or facilitating after the handoff to NATO has been modest in terms of its frequency, intensity, and severity. . . .

Had any of these elements been absent in Libya, or present in different degrees, a different legal conclusion might have been drawn. But the unusual confluence of these four factors, in an operation that was expressly designed to be limited— limited in mission, exposure of U.S. troops, risk of escalation, and military means employed—led the President to conclude that the Libya operation did not fall within the War Powers Resolution's automatic 60-day pullout rule.[34]

As the national security adviser Tom Donilon later confirmed, "the not-hostilities theory 'was on the table before the decision' and so was not an after-the-fact rationalization." By his own account, White House counsel Bob Bauer then advised President Obama that this was a reasonable legal interpretation of the War Powers Resolution. Given all of this advice, President Obama, himself a former longtime professor of constitutional law, "decided to go forward with the operation on that basis."[35]

In testifying before the Senate shortly thereafter, I took pains to stress the limits of our legal position:

Throughout the Libya episode, the President has never claimed the authority to take the Nation to war without congressional authorization, to violate the War Powers Resolution or any other statute, to violate international law, to use force abroad when doing so would not serve important national interests, or to refuse to consult with Congress on important war powers issues. The Administration recognizes that Congress has powers to regulate and terminate uses of force, and that the War Powers Resolution plays an important role in promoting inter-branch dialogue and deliberation on these critical matters. The President has expressed his strong desire for congressional support, and we have been work-ing actively with Congress to ensure enactment of appropriate legislation.[36]

At a press conference a few days later, President Obama reiterated this le-gal view as representing both his and the U.S. government's position. Con-gress could have responded by rejecting the executive-branch interpretation and asserting its war-making prerogatives at any time, if it could organize itself to do so. But significantly, Congress did neither; as Savage reported, "[t]he precedent Obama had carved out of the War Powers Resolution stood uncontested by Congress as an institution." The key congressional leaders—including Republican Speaker John Boehner, past and future Speaker Nancy Pelosi, Senate majority leader Harry Reid, Senate minority leader Mitch Mc-Connell, and Senate Foreign Relations Committee chair John Kerry—all agreed that the continuation of U.S. military action in Libya did not violate the War Powers Resolution. Thereafter, various House resolutions were in-troduced challenging the interpretations, but all failed to pass.[37]

Some academic commentators harshly criticized this approach, making much of reported disagreements among Obama administration lawyers. But other distinguished constitutional commentators—particularly Laurence Tribe, Akhil Amar, and Richard Pildes—supported the administration's view.[38] In the end, the joint NATO action achieved its goals: untold thou-sands of Libyan civilian lives were saved; the slaughter of Benghazi was averted; the United States maintained its supporting role in a multilateral humanitarian mission authorized by the U.N. Security Council; critical U.S. interests were protected in the region; and a message was sent throughout the Middle East and North Africa that the United States would stand with them at a historic moment of transition. Although Qadhafi's overthrow was not the stated goal of the joint NATO operation, he left office and went into hiding, and eventually was captured and killed by the Libyan opposition.[39]

The same use-of-force questions soon arose again in Syria. When the civil war first began in Syria, the initial U.S. diplomatic strategy was to achieve a ceasefire, oust Assad, secure chemical weapons, introduce humanitarian aid, and promote accountability. But the soft-power tools available were simply not sufficient to achieve those broad objectives. After Libya, the Russians made it clear that they intended to veto similar Security Council resolutions; the reason, they claimed, was that force had been overused in Libya to remove Qadhafi from power. For many months, Russia's recalcitrance placed Obama's diplomats in the awkward position of offering draft Security Council resolutions in search of a linguistic formula that the Russians would "abstain to" in the name of stopping the violence in Syria. The diplomatic goal was to get the Russians on board for something, and then escalate to stronger Security Council resolutions if the one that the Russians finally let pass did not succeed in stopping the violence. But that key first step never happened, notwithstanding Secretary Clinton's, and then Secretary Kerry's, repeated meetings with the Russian foreign minister and the U.N. special envoy in search of a Security Council resolution the Russians would permit.[40]

In August 2013, after I had left the government, the Obama administration received unmistakable proof that the Syrian leader Assad had launched a deliberate chemical assault on innocent civilians. Previously, President Obama had warned that Assad's use of chemical weapons would cross a "red line." A U.N. report concluded unequivocally that the Assad regime had used chemical weapons on a relatively large scale against innocent civilians near Damascus on August 21, 2013, and allied intelligence concluded that only the Assad regime could have carried out such a large-scale chemical-weapons attack. The Arab League endorsed international action but shied away from approving "all necessary measures," which made it difficult to invoke the U.N. Charter article 52 "regional organizations" route—famously deployed during the Cuban missile crisis—to skirt a Russian veto. The British attorney general issued a post-Kosovo legal opinion stating that humanitarian intervention without a Security Council resolution could be lawful under international law, but the prime minister failed to secure parliamentary support for intervention.[41]

Unfortunately, the Obama administration never publicly explained why use of force in Syria would have been consistent with either international or domestic law. To my knowledge, the only public legal position the U.S. government offered on the legality of intervention in Syria was a quote by the White House counsel to the *New York Times* explaining that, although an attack on Syria "may not fit under a traditionally recognized legal basis under international law," given the novel factors and circumstances, such an action would nevertheless be "justified and legitimate under international law" and so not prohibited.[42] I have elsewhere described in some detail a fuller international-law test that the administration could have offered.[43]

The administration also apparently concluded, as a matter of domestic law, that congressional approval was not required but, again, never issued an opinion explaining why. With respect to the possible initiation of hostilities, the White House counsel was almost certainly invoking Walter Dellinger's OLC opinion approving the Clinton administration's intervention in Haiti (described in chapter 5). Under Dellinger's reasoning, a large-scale offensive of the type initiated in Iraq in 2003 would plainly be "war," which would have required congressional approval. But prior congressional approval was probably not legally required for the limited strike against Syria that the president apparently contemplated, which Secretary of State Kerry called "incredibly small." Whether the Obama administration would have determined at the sixty-day mark that a Syrian action constituted "hostilities" under the War Powers Resolution would have depended on the application of the statutory test stated in my Libya testimony: whether there was again the unusual confluence of four factors, in an operation expressly designed to be limited in mission, in the exposure of U.S. troops, in the risk of escalation, and in the military means employed.[44]

But faced with weak support abroad and at home, President Obama pushed the pause button, not once but twice. He initially said that he would seek prior approval from a distracted and divided Congress, when he plainly had not secured the necessary House votes. Two weeks later, he postponed indefinitely that congressional vote—which he likely would have lost—to pursue diplomatic alternatives. Still, he reasonably deemed it politically prudent given the intense congressional questioning after the British parliamentary action.

In retrospect, President Obama erred, not by announcing a "red line" against the use of chemical weapons, but by failing to lay the political groundwork necessary to enforce such a ban. Starting in August 2012 and earlier, Obama failed to socialize first congressional leaders and then key allies to publicly commit to help enforce that red line once it was breached. He failed to make clear earlier that Assad's deliberate launch of chemical weapons against his own population would cross a near-century-old red line that had been drawn not by Obama alone, but by international law. Had the president seriously intended to use force to discourage a repeat use of chemical weapons, he should have engaged in better sequencing: he should have secured multilateral approval for the use of force ex ante, then sought a congressional use-of-force authorization up to the level of international approval. As chapter 5 described, this was the sequence secured by George H. W. Bush for his military action against Saddam Hussein in 1991 and initially attempted by Obama for his own prior military action in Libya. Instead, President Obama drew a red line without engaging in either the domestic or international politics needed to defend it. That made his abrupt threat of force in the late summer of 2013 seem more unilateral than principled. His threat also seemed strikingly inconsistent with his broader—generally successful—first-term "smart power" approach to foreign policy. Most disturbing, Obama's threat led to the spectacle of Vladimir Putin ostentatiously taking America to task for violating international law—even while he was himself flagrantly violating the sovereignty of Georgia, Ukraine, and Syria.[45]

Still, Obama's threat had a catalyzing effect. It extracted Assad's confession that he had a chemical-weapons stockpile and drew the Russians into a long-overdue diplomatic process. In his speech before the U.N. General Assembly in September 2013, Obama pushed back against Putin's dismissal of American exceptionalism. Obama "re-nested" his Syria policy amid two broader regional objectives: "Iran's pursuit of nuclear weapons, and the Arab-Israeli conflict." And he called on U.N. members to support a Security Council resolution on Syria and provide humanitarian assistance, thereby recalling international law to the historic task of meaningfully enforcing a ban against "the brazen use of chemical weapons."[46]

In effect, by putting the possibility of force back on the table, President Obama and Secretary of State Kerry were able to reenergize a stalemated diplomatic process. That process led to an internationally supervised removal of chemical weapons from Syria monitored by the Organisation for the Prohibition of Chemical Weapons. The incident shows that if invoking an international-law responsibility to protect is a legally available option, it can have a catalyzing effect in promoting diplomacy. The point is not that lawyers should provide excuses for unconstrained uses of force in places like Syria. Rather, the goal is to make legally available in particular cases the Dayton-like option of diplomacy backed by force, which would then motivate meaningful diplomacy more than diplomatic talk alone.

Given the importance of the issue, the Obama administration failed by not stating its domestic or legal position regarding the legality of humanitarian intervention as America's British, Danish, and Belgian allies have all done. The president's lawyers should have explained—not just in lay terms, as President Obama himself did, but in legal language that lawyers could debate—whether and when humanitarian intervention without a Security Council resolution would be legal or illegal under international law. Threatening military action in Syria without stating a public legal rationale created a dangerous precedent. As Abram Chayes argued after the Cuban missile crisis, "[f]ailure to justify in terms of international law warrants and legitimizes disapproval and negative responses from the other governments participating directly in the process." In the future, other less-humanitarian-minded states could cite President Obama's threat of military action in Syria to put their own broad spin on the legal interpretation, twisting the concept of an international-law responsibility to protect for their own self-interested purposes. Indeed, that came to pass only a decade later, when Putin's Russia invaded Ukraine, with Putin fraudulently claiming that he was acting to stop a genocide being committed by the Ukrainian government against its own people.[47]

The Making of International Agreements

The Obama administration also diversified the tools for international agreement making. As noted in chapter 3, hornbook constitutional law says that the United States can make law through international cooperation via one of three domestic legal devices: an Article II "treaty," advised and consented to by two-thirds of the Senate; a congressional-executive agreement, which involves passage of a statute by a majority of both houses of Congress and signature by the president; and, under certain circumstances, a sole executive agreement, concluded within the scope of the president's independent constitutional authority.[48]

These remain important categories of modern U.S. foreign-relations law. But in real life, I found during my years as the Obama State Department Legal Adviser, international legal engagement has become far more fluid and messy. International legal instruments do not come neatly packaged in tripartite constitutional boxes. In the twenty-first century, the United States has moved to a whole host of less crystalline, more nuanced forms of international legal engagement and cooperation that do not fall neatly within any of these three pigeonholes.

Increasingly, these traditional forms of international legal engagement no longer convey the full output of American legal diplomacy. As the Obama administration unfolded, it became painfully clear that the always-imaginary "triptych" of Article II treaties, congressional-executive agreements, and sole executive agreements had become overtaken by real-world events.

First, Article II treaties had gone from being the rule to the exception, neither the exclusive nor even the primary means for the United States to enter into international-law obligations. The growing partisanship over once-bipartisan agreements rendered the president unable to secure a two-thirds Senate vote for even the most uncontroversial international arrangements.[49]

Second, congressional-executive agreements had long been treated as legally interchangeable with Article II treaties for completing diplomatic deals. The last gasp for the legal indispensability of treaties came in the 1990s, when Laurence Tribe famously called unconstitutional the congressional-executive mechanism by which the Clinton administration joined NAFTA. Tribe's theory met near-universal rejection, including by the overwhelming majority of the legal academy. Scholars correctly reasoned that constitutional practice had developed sufficiently to permit binding agreements to be entered into by the executive and approved by majorities of both houses of Congress, particularly in such cases as NAFTA, in which Congress was exercising its foreign-commerce power. Indeed, in the second half of the twentieth century, the United States used congressional-executive agreements as its tool of choice to conclude a whole range of international economic arrangements: not just NAFTA but also the agreement establishing the World Trade Organization and the Bretton Woods agreement (1945), which "did nothing less than create the foundations of a new world economic order."[50]

But given successive administrations' political difficulty in securing congressional majorities even for previously uncontroversial trade agreements, formal congressional-executive agreements have ceased to be the sine qua non of international lawmaking. Under the political deadlock between the president and Congress during the Obama administration, the number of senators needed to block consideration of such an agreement declined from fifty-one (a majority of senators) to forty-one (the number needed to sustain a filibuster) to ten (the number usually needed to prevent a congressional-executive agreement from being voted out of the relevant committee) to one (a single senator) and finally to just one Senate staffer sending a nightly email to prevent an otherwise uncontroversial congressional-executive agreement from receiving unanimous consent.[51]

Third, agreements in the last triptych category—true "sole executive agreements" based solely on the president's plenary constitutional authorities—have become vanishingly rare. Legal scholars still cite a few iconic sole executive agreements, like Franklin Roosevelt's destroyers-for-bases deal in 1941 or the deals made as part of the recognition of the Soviet Union in the 1930s that were upheld by *United States v. Belmont* and *United States v. Pink*. But in practice, few modern-day presidents ever claim to be making a controversial agreement based solely on their own plenary constitutional authority, particularly when Congress has already legislated elsewhere regarding the same subject. Instead, the agreement-making president almost always—and usually for good reason—claims to be making the agreement with express or implied congressional approval or receptivity evidenced by other related congressional actions in the subject-matter field.[52]

Yet despite these undeniable trends, many foreign-relations scholars still fetishize the triptych. They sometimes argue that a particular international lawmaking arrangement they oppose must be unconstitutional because they cannot easily place it in one triptych box or another. Some formalistically suggest that innovative international arrangements not pre-approved by Congress must pose a "threat to the very idea of constitutional government."[53] But such hyperbole substitutes unnuanced pigeonholing for more nuanced understandings of the many complex real-world ways by which the executive seeks to make—and Congress now signals its acceptance of—international commitments with foreign partners.

In fact, the Obama administration pursued a range of international agreements that did not fall neatly into any of these boxes. Yet they were fully consistent with, and could be entirely implemented under, existing law. Take, for example, the controversy surrounding the executive's authority to enter into the Anti-Counterfeiting Trade Agreement, a multilateral agreement on enforcing intellectual-property rights. Clearly, some of that procedural controversy derived from policy disagreements with the substance of the agreement. But a surprisingly large number of law professors questioned the executive's legal authority to even enter into the agreement, saying, in effect, that since this agreement seems to fall between the wings of the triptych, that must mean the United States entirely lacks any authority to enter the agreement.[54]

In my experience, this formalistic theory grossly oversimplifies the reality of international cooperation. As Justice Jackson suggested in his landmark concurrence in *Youngstown,* and Justice Rehnquist affirmed in *Dames & Moore v. Regan,* legislative authority in the foreign-affairs area does not sit on isolated stools, but rather runs along a spectrum of congressional approval. Every year, the United States enters into a plethora of international agreements that are consistent with, and can certainly be implemented under, existing domestic law but that do not fall neatly into these three conceptual boxes. The problem is not the illegality of the agreement, but the simplistic way in which the triptych box has been conceived.

A survey of how the political branches had dealt with similar agreements in the past suggested that the Anti-Counterfeiting Trade Agreement was supported by "quasi-constitutional custom," a widespread and consistent practice of executive-branch activity that Congress, by its conduct, had essentially accepted. First, although Congress did not expressly pre-authorize the agreement, it did pass legislation calling on the executive to "work[] with other countries to establish international standards and policies for the effective protection and enforcement of intellectual property rights." Second, as the United States Trade Representative determined, and as I confirmed as State Department Legal Adviser, the agreement negotiated fit within the fabric of existing law, was fully consistent with existing law, and so did not require any further legislation to implement. Third, Congress's call for executive action to protect intellectual-property rights arose against the background of a long series of agreements similarly concluded to address the specific question of intellectual-property protection.[55]

In enjoying implicit legislative authorization, the Anti-Counterfeiting Trade Agreement thus resembled the Algiers Accords, which ended the Iranian hostage crisis and which the Supreme Court then broadly upheld as constitutional in *Dames & Moore v. Regan.*[56] The Supreme Court relied not on any particular express ex ante congressional authorization but rather on "closely related" legislation enacted in the same area and a long history of executive-branch practice of concluding claims-settlement agreements. The Algiers Accords, like the Anti-Counterfeiting Trade Agreement, did not fall neatly into any of the three traditional doctrinal boxes. Nevertheless, the *Dames & Moore* Court upheld their constitutionality by finding a "legislative intent to accord the President broad discretion," which in the words of Justice

Jackson's *Youngstown* concurrence "may be considered to 'invite' 'measures on independent presidential responsibility.'" In *Dames & Moore*, Justice William Rehnquist, who had previously served as Jackson's law clerk, concluded that because Congress had acted in the general area, Congress had given its implicit authorization, which raised the president's power to its highest.[57]

Dames & Moore de facto expanded *Youngstown* categories one and two at the expense of category three—the only category in which the president might be overruled. But whatever one may think of the original correctness of *Dames & Moore,* more than forty years later it seems unlikely to be rejected by the current Court, not least because the opinion was drafted in part by (now chief justice) John Roberts, who was then one of Justice Rehnquist's law clerks. Responding to a question at his confirmation hearing, Chief Justice Roberts said:

> I do know that when you are in the middle area where it's difficult to determine whether Congress is supporting the President's action or is opposed to the President's action, that the Court often has to try to read the tea leaves of related legislation. If you look at the *Dames & Moore* decision coming out of the Iranian hostage crisis, what the Court did in that case, applying the middle tier, was look at a vast array of legislation . . . to try and figure out what Congress's view was.[58]

What the Anti-Counterfeiting Trade Agreement episode shows is that *Dames & Moore* has now largely carried the day. When Congress has generally pre-authorized the agreement, the agreement fits within the legal landscape of related legislation, and the agreement is consistent with executive practice, the courts will likely sustain it, even in the face of public criticism. *Dames & Moore* thus authorizes the president to make international agreements when Congress has legislated general approval for the president to act in the area, and the overall tenor of that legislative activity and executive practice in that subject-matter area is consistent with the new presidential action.

Against this background, the two most important diplomatic arrangements concluded by the Obama administration were the Paris climate-change accord (the Paris Agreement) and the Iran nuclear deal (the Joint Comprehensive Plan of Action). Academic commentators have raised constitutional questions about each.[59] But significantly, each was concluded with almost no reference to the traditional triptych framework, suggesting the growing obsolescence of that framework. The Obama administration argued—and Congress did not dispute—that these arrangements did not create new legal obligations. Thus, they fell within the *Dames & Moore* zone of congressional authority and approval, indicated by general preauthorization, legal landscape, and consistent executive practice.

The Paris and Iran deals together illustrate the evolution of what Dan Bodansky and Peter Spiro have called "executive agreements plus." That category recognizes the intellectual limitations of the triptych. As executive agreements plus, both international arrangements were constitutional because they fit generally into preexisting legislative authorizations and conspicuously did not require the United States to undertake any new or legally binding obligations as a matter of international law.[60]

The Paris Agreement marked the culmination of the Obama administration's efforts to address the threat of global climate change. The seeds for that accord began in Copenhagen in 2009 and culminated in 2015 with the Paris Agreement, which entered into force in November 2016. The Paris accord was adopted within the framework of the United Nations Framework Convention on Climate Change, an Article II treaty with 195 parties that the Senate approved in 1992. In 2011, the parties to the climate-change convention adopted the Durban Platform, which launched a new round of negotiations to develop "a protocol, another legal instrument or an agreed outcome with legal force under the Convention applicable to all Parties." The Durban Platform specifically provided that this new legal or quasi-legal instrument would be "under the" United Nations Framework Convention on Climate Change. Hence, the subsequent Paris agreement was not based on sole executive power. Rather, it was preauthorized by a duly ratified Article II treaty and negotiated within the scope of the Senate's original advice and consent to that treaty.[61]

In addition, Congress had expressed its broad support for climate-change negotiations by enacting several laws: the Global Climate Protection Act of 1987, which asserted the need for "international cooperation aimed at minimizing and responding to adverse climate change"; the Clean Air Act, which allows the president to negotiate international agreements as a necessary adjunct to regulating domestic emissions; and section 115 of that act, which authorized federal action reciprocally with other nations to address "international air pollution," namely, transboundary pollution causing damage within the United States.

Finally, the agreement accorded with consistent executive practice, unchallenged by the legislature. Presidents of both parties had negotiated similar environmental agreements addressing pollution—including the Convention on Long-Range Transboundary Air Pollution (and multiple subsequent protocols), the United States–Canada Air Quality Agreement, and the Minamata Convention on Mercury—as executive agreements without express congressional approval.[62]

Operating under these precedents, the United States first unsuccessfully went down the road of seeking legally binding treaty commitments in trying to adopt the Kyoto Protocol. But in 1997, by a 95-to-0 vote, the Senate adopted the Byrd-Hagel Resolution, which declared that the United States should not join any new climate agreement that would mandate emissions reductions for developed but not developing countries. That made it clear that a follow-on Kyoto Protocol would be dead on arrival. In 2001, President George W. Bush announced that the United States did not intend to become a Kyoto party.[63]

This experience led to a daring change in the U.S. diplomatic approach to international legal commitments. At the U.N. Climate Change Conference of 2009 in Copenhagen, dramatic personal diplomacy by President Obama and Secretary Clinton forged a last-minute consensus among all the major economies on the Copenhagen Accord: a political, not legally binding, document that moved away from the more inflexible Kyoto Protocol paradigm. The Copenhagen Accord secured, for the first time in decades, meaningful commitments to address climate change from developed and developing countries alike. The accord included a global aspirational temperature goal, international assessment procedures, and a new "green" global climate fund. Although not legally binding, the Copenhagen Accord paved the way for the Cancun Agreements—which were negotiated the following year and, still in a non-legally-binding way, incorporated and elaborated the Copenhagen Accord's main elements—and then the Durban Platform.

These efforts culminated in the Climate Change Conference of 2015 in Paris, where the parties produced a historic agreement. Significantly, they worked hard to make most of the agreement not legally binding. The most dramatic moment of the conference came on the final day, when the United States hastened to "correc[t] an error in the text, which had converted a provision intended to be non-binding into a binding obligation, by using the verb 'shall' rather than 'should.'" As concluded, the Paris Agreement stated no legally binding emissions caps, declaring only that member states "should" meet such targets. The financial commitments of the accord also were not newly binding: they only "continu[ed] the existing obligations under the [United Nations Framework Convention on Climate Change]." The relatively few new "legally binding provisions [in the Paris Agreement] [we]re largely procedural in nature and in many instances [we]re duplicative of existing U.S. obligations under the UN Framework Convention on Climate Change." Thus, they could be fully implemented under existing U.S. law. In short, the Paris accord did not require formal congressional approval, because it followed broad congressional directives in an existing Article II treaty, in the Clean Air Act, and in the Global Climate Protection Act. Accordingly, it could be implemented by the president merely by carrying out preexisting legal obligations under domestic law.[64]

Even while the Paris accord was reaching completion, the Joint Comprehensive Plan of Action was being concluded between Iran, the P5+1 (the United Kingdom, France, China, Russia, the United States, and Germany), and the European Union. The Iran nuclear agreement, which consisted of the agreement itself and five technical annexes, envisioned actions by Iran, the United States, the International Atomic Energy Agency (IAEA), and key allies, including the other permanent Security Council members, Germany, and the European Union. After extended negotiation, Iran agreed to specified limits on its nuclear development program in exchange for the United States' agreement to lift unilateral U.S. sanctions and the other nations' agreement to lift international sanctions that had been imposed through the United Nations. Again, this agreement did not require fresh congressional approval given the pre-existing nature of the legal obligations being assumed.[65]

First, there was ample domestic legal authority for all the actions the United States committed to undertake under the agreement. In particular, statutes authorized the president to suspend economic sanctions pursuant to waiver authority provided by Congress, so long as Iran fulfilled its stated commitments. To be clear, this constituted not just "general preauthorization" but specific statutory authorization of the *Youngstown* category one kind.[66]

Second, as in *Dames & Moore*, the broader legal landscape clearly envisioned the president exercising these statutory authorities. Although the Constitution's allocation of substantive authority granted Congress express subject-matter authority over foreign commerce, and hence economic sanctions, Congress, through enacted statutes, had just as undeniably delegated to the president implementation of this authority with respect to the matters in question. Congress had thereby granted the president specific statutory authority to waive existing domestic-law sanctions against Iran when the president determined that it was in the national interest to do so. This included a waiver if Iran did what it had committed to do with respect to abating development of highly enriched weapons-grade uranium. Fittingly, the last Supreme Court precedent upholding the constitutionality of a commitment settling complex issues with the Islamic Republic of Iran—the Algiers Accords—became a precedent for defending the constitutionality of a new nuclear agreement with the same country.

Third, and crucially, the Iran nuclear agreement was a political, not a legally binding, commitment in both form and substance. As Duncan Hollis and Joshua Newcomer have detailed, such political commitments have long been common in executive practice. On matters of substance, the parties went out of their way to style the obligations as "voluntary." They carefully avoided all the procedural trappings of a binding international convention in favor of a political commitment to do something, so long as another strategic partner reciprocally took the steps it had agreed to take.[67] Under the agreement, the United States did commit to propose and vote for a new Security Council resolution, which changed the nature of other countries' legal obligations under chapter VII of the U.N. Charter to provide sanctions relief to Iran, with the possibility of "snapback" in case of Iranian default. But again, that is a subject-matter area where the U.S. executive branch already had considerable existing delegated legal authority to adopt sanctions and thus to modify them under appropriate circumstances.

Significantly, despite much congressional debate, Congress did not disapprove the Iran nuclear deal. On the contrary, the only new piece of legislation enacted in response to the agreement, the Iran Nuclear Agreement Review Act, did not undermine the president's legal authorities; if anything, it added to them. At its heart, that bill was a classic "report and wait" provision: the only effect the bill had on the president's existing statutory waiver authority over Iran sanctions was to postpone the exercise of that authority until sixty days had passed without Congress enacting a joint resolution of disapproval, which it never enacted.[68]

Some scholars have criticized the rise of nonbinding political agreements as a dangerous trend in foreign-relations law.[69] But in the end, the Iran nuclear deal is best understood as a confidence-building device designed to shift from a historical pattern of confrontation with Iran toward a halting pattern of reciprocal cooperation. The president had ample existing statutory authority to waive the sanctions in question; he also had clear constitutional authority to make a nonbinding political commitment that the United States would not reimpose such sanctions, so long as Iran kept its part of the bargain and did what it said it would do under the agreement.

Although some have decried this rise of executive lawmaking, the reality is that these variegated forms of agreement making are already here. They will not soon disappear. As a functional matter, the many legislative obstacles to concluding formal agreements have stifled the president's ability to build global regimes through multilateral cooperation and negotiation. For obvious reasons, the constitutional barriers to the president's conclusion of deals should not be dramatically higher than the relatively low barriers to the president's use of force. As chapter 11 argues, foreign-relations law today perversely makes it easier for the president to exit than to enter into international agreements, even though entry is far more likely to constrain presidential and American unilateralism. It is also not clear why modern foreign-relations law does not support the executive branch's capacity to fashion innovative accords that can build complex regulatory regimes or to grow bilateral confidence with longtime adversaries, such as the Paris and Iran deals. Robert Putnam and Nicholas Bayne described how the G8 summit evolved from an informal meeting into a quasi-international institution, without ever crossing the line into formal lawmaking. What they presaged is that international law is increasingly developed through "diplomatic law talk"—dialogue within epistemic communities of international lawyers working for diverse governments and nongovernmental institutions.[70]

While in government, I found myself regularly holding such meetings with groups of my foreign legal-adviser counterparts to discuss emerging legal norms in an array of areas, including use of force, cyber conflict, and the law governing private security contractors. We understood those meetings to be creating a record of state practice and a process of generating *opinio juris*. In such forums, states declare their intent to engage consistently in certain practices out of a sense of legal obligation, not just national convenience, with the understanding that those obligations might someday crystallize and become embodied in a multilateral treaty negotiation.[71]

The Obama administration thus pursued its foreign-policy objectives through an innovative array of methods. These included binding and non-binding arrangements, layered cooperation, normative dialogues, and hybrid public-private partnerships. Transnational cooperation became a living, breathing human tapestry of meetings, relationships, and other communications that moved beyond the wooden doctrinal triptych to focus on the broader policy tasks of promoting cooperation, monitoring, enforcement, and norm development. By so doing, Obama's administration broadened the traditional view of international lawmaking fixated narrowly on concluding particular treaties to include such innovative techniques of norm enunciation and forum creation based on important shared principles.

Twenty-first-century international lawmaking thus moved beyond static texts to a dynamic process. By building relationships to foster normative principles in new issue areas, this lawmaking led to "regime-building" and soft law that would eventually harden into more formal legal norms. As global regimes develop, they breed a life of their own—building consensus about what set of norms, rules, principles, and decision-making procedures should apply in a particular issue area. The stakeholders first seek to define new soft norms, which, through an iterative process, gradually harden. Intricate patterns of layered public and private cooperation develop, and formal lawmaking and institutions eventually emerge. These patterns create stiff paths of least resistance from which new political leaders can deviate only at considerable cost.

To be sure, I am opposed to secret dealmaking, but enhanced consultation and reporting requirements are the best way to promote transparency, accountability, and oversight.[72] Chapter 11 will discuss how these new international lawmaking techniques can be better incorporated into the framework of national security law. But upon entering office, Donald Trump and members of his administration sought to undo this development, not by secret dealmaking, but by focusing instead on the opposite end of the treaty process: treaty withdrawal and termination.

8

Trump: Extremism and Exit

HILLARY CLINTON'S UNEXPECTED DEFEAT IN 2016 abruptly ended the Obama era of constitutional accommodation and ushered in the most unilateralist presidency in American history. Donald Trump's mercurial presidency became unique as, over four years, the president daily combined dishonesty and ignorance with outright contempt for even the most basic rule-of-law values and institutions: peaceful transition, free and fair elections, an independent judiciary and civil service, nonpolitical prosecutions, inquiring media, and protections for racial, religious, and sexual minorities. Trump became the first president to be impeached twice by the House, both times escaping meaningful sanction when a sharply divided Senate refused to either remove him from office or disqualify him from future presidential service. After leaving office, he became the first former president to be indicted, multiple times, in both state and federal court.[1] But unlike disgraced past presidents such as Nixon, who had at least resigned under threat of impeachment, Trump showed neither shame nor any inclination to pay even lip service to constitutional requirements.

Baldly declaring that "Article II [of the Constitution] allows me to do whatever I want," Trump laid bare how the *Curtiss-Wright* national security vision could run riot within the U.S. government.[2] In episode after episode, Trump demonstrated that he was either oblivious to or contemptuous of fundamental norms regarding separation of powers and checks and balances, domestically and abroad. Trump's presidency pushed back against Obama's *Youngstown* leanings and institutionalized a *Curtiss-Wright* vision in all three branches. The sharp division and polarization of the legislative branch created a deadlock that invited repeated executive action, a vacuum that Trump eagerly exploited. Trump appointed a majority of pro-executive federal judges, installing for a generation a Supreme Court controlled by *Curtiss-Wright*–oriented justices.

Trump's four years amalgamated his predecessors' worst national security abuses. Like Nixon, Trump illegally used force abroad, ordering the killing of Iranian general Qassim Suleimani in Iraq in January 2020. Like George W. Bush, he claimed a right to make preemptive military strikes.[3] Like Nixon, he distorted law enforcement by influencing the attorney general and the Justice Department and composing an "enemies list" to target his critics. As in the Iran-contra affair, the president allowed foreign policy to be privatized by the intervention of unaccountable rogue agents like Michael Flynn, Roger Stone, and Rudy Giuliani. In his now-infamous call with Ukrainian president Volodymyr Zelenskyy on July 25, 2019, Trump diverted a bona fide national security request for arms toward his private political gain. In seeking damaging political information about his political opponent, he went beyond Lieutenant Colonel Oliver North's illegal diversion of proceeds from Iranian arms shipments to fund the Nicaraguan contras.[4]

Trump took executive unilateralism to new heights. For the first time, a president invoked *Curtiss-Wright* in an effort to nullify the rule of law for his entire administration. Trump claimed that all his actions were authorized and justified by his plenary constitutional authorities, which he claimed rendered his actions immune from interbranch interference. Under that claim, any restraints coming from inside the executive branch could be ignored under a theory of unitary executive; any restraints from outside the executive could be treated as unconstitutional intrusions into the president's plenary national security powers. By bringing back Bush 41's attorney general, William Barr, Trump installed a constitutional adviser philosophically committed to what Barr's own predecessor called "using the office he holds to advance his extraordinary lifetime project of assigning unchecked power to the president."[5] When Congress sought to investigate or call executive witnesses to testify, Trump asserted executive privilege and fought subpoenas endlessly through the courts. When his administration's abuses predictably triggered criminal investigations for violating national security laws, Trump pardoned the suspects or granted them clemency, often even before they came to trial. After Trump lost reelection, he engaged in an eleventh-hour "pardon whitewash." And even after leaving office, he continued to assert extreme claims of executive impunity, prompting an indictment by hoarding highly classified information regarding U.S. operations and assets abroad at his Florida home.[6]

Predictably, Trump's foreign policy evinced little respect for such rule-of-law values as due process, regulatory stability, and the protection of settled expectations. Geopolitically, Trump was most destructive when weakening the U.S. alliances, multilateral organizations, and international dispute-settlement mechanisms vital to facilitating solutions to global crises such as pandemics, forced migration, and climate change. Trump rejected the previously bipartisan global strategy of "engage, translate, and leverage." Instead, he pursued the opposite approach: "disengage, black hole, and go it alone." When in doubt, his administration disengaged, argued that new situations presented "black holes" to which no law applied, and substituted unilateral browbeating for negotiated solutions.

At the global level, Trump's obsession with "deals" led to a cascade of transactions—punctuated with threats, tit-for-tat retaliations, and abrupt reversals. His ad hoc transactional approach disrupted long-standing relationships and alliances built on bonds of mutual interest, confidence, trust, and sacrifice. At both the national and the multilateral level, Trump combined his contempt for relationships with a scorn for the truth, diplomacy, bureaucracy, and other essential ingredients of sound administration. When confounding a settled wisdom, he would regularly call the truth into question by challenging media reports as "fake news" and denigrating settled scientific knowledge. His disdain for expertise resulted in the degradation of such established national institutions as the U.S. Postal Service, the Centers for Disease Control and Prevention, the Environmental Protection Agency, the Food and Drug Administration, the FBI, and the U.S. intelligence community.

Trump's pattern was to act on instinct and impulse, following an approach best described as "extremism and exit." His pattern became: Whenever possible, disengage from globalism. Undermine international institutions and resign from global leadership. Reverse what Barack Obama did and what, as president, Hillary Clinton would have done. When in doubt, adopt an isolationist "hard power" posture. And when challenged, defend the president's legal right to act with extreme claims of presidential power, while demanding broad deference from Congress, the courts, allies, the media, and non-governmental organizations.

Trump's means to achieving these ends became equally predictable: Use unilateral executive actions to make radical shifts with little or no notice. "Flood the zone" with relentless initiatives so that the world quickly forgets yesterday's surprise because of this morning's tweet. Diminish diplomacy as a soft-power tool by demoralizing and gutting the career bureaucracy. And cloak discriminatory actions in the veil of presidential power to control the "national security process," which his underlings advised "will not be questioned."[7]

Trump offered a nihilistic vision of supplanting the post–World War II Kantian vision of a community of democracies cooperating on the basis of shared values with a values-free Orwellian vision of amoral spheres of great-power influence. This Orwellian vision was not only repugnant to core American values. It offered no answer to any of America's three looming reckonings: an economic reckoning over inequality; a cultural reckoning about diversity and inclusion; and a global reckoning calling for international cooperation to combat zero-sum nationalism. By trashing the long-standing U.S. tradition of constructive engagement with admittedly imperfect multilateral institutions, Trump encouraged a destructive race to the bottom on key economic and climate issues, and triggered both trade and vaccine nationalism.

The result was a harrowing decline in America's long-standing reputation for competence, reliability, and leadership. During Trump's fourth chaotic year, his disastrous response to the Covid-19 pandemic laid bare his flawed overall approach to governing. During most of Trump's presidency, America faced self-inflicted crises. But the Covid-19 disaster cast Trump's signature weaknesses in stark relief: topsy-turvy policymaking, mendacity, and conspiracy mongering. Trump's failure to implement a national plan to provide testing, protective equipment, ventilators, paycheck protections, contact tracing, or vaccine delivery intersected with his administration's efforts to undermine Obama's health-care program. Trump's deliberate disengagement from any coordinated global effort to tackle the pandemic virtually ensured that the dual public-health and economic crises would spin out of control.[8]

In the area of national security, four issues most sharply revealed these features of Trump's unilateralist presidency: immigration controls, trade sanctions, agreement breaking, and election interference.

Immigration Controls

Trump's greatest flurry of executive decisions imposed a harsh system of immigration controls. At the international level, citing concerns about U.S. sovereignty, the administration continued its treaty-breaking trends by ending participation in the Global Compact for Safe, Orderly, and Regular Migration. Trump's domestic actions included three successive travel bans directed primarily at travelers from Muslim countries. He sought to strip all federal funding from so-called sanctuary cities. And he issued strict border controls, illustrated by repeated calls for a border wall—allegedly to be paid for by Mexico, but which ended up costing U.S. taxpayers billions. The administration ended temporary protected status for thousands of Hondurans, Haitians, Nicaraguans, and Salvadorans. Declaring its hostility toward refugees, judges of foreign origin, and "chain migration," the administration unveiled a maximalist penchant for deportation, even of "Dreamers." The Department of Homeland Security adopted "shock and awe" raids in schools, businesses, and homes, as well as the heartless policy of separating migrant parents from their children to encourage "self-deportation."

In just four years, Trump's immigration team unilaterally adopted more than 450 administrative changes, all using executive power.[9] To close the southern border, Trump issued sweeping presidential proclamations and executive orders, departmental policy guidance, and myriad technical adjustments. These changes simultaneously transformed the U.S. immigration system and made it more punitive and less humanitarian. Trump's immigration policies revealed that in the immigration field, presidential power has gone from being the exception to the norm. Significantly, Trump's lawyers defended his sweeping immigration controls not on the basis of *Curtiss-Wright* claims of inherent Article II or stand-alone presidential power, but by invoking *statutory* authorities.

As Adam Cox and Cristina Rodríguez detailed in reviewing the evolution of America's immigration system, the major source of presidential power invoked by Trump was the implicit or explicit delegation by Congress of its supposedly plenary immigration power. Sometimes, Congress has delegated express discretion to the executive, for example, through statutory provisions setting annual ceilings on refugee admissions. But more frequently, Congress has de facto delegated enormous discretion to the executive branch through the "one size fits all" penalty of removal combined with a broad delegation of authority to the president to determine how the laws should be "faithfully executed." The net result has been a massive transfer of plenary congressional power to the president.[10]

This shift to a "statutory *Curtiss-Wright*" approach to immigration evolved during both Democratic and Republic administrations. For example, two Obama initiatives designed to provide young immigrants and parents of U.S. citizens with temporary stability and protection from removal—President Obama's Deferred Action for Childhood Arrivals (DACA) and Deferred Action for Parents of Americans and Lawful Permanent Residents (DAPA)—began as policy pronouncements made by secretaries of homeland security invoking their statutory authority to defer enforcement against classes of individuals. Although the Roberts Court later struck down Trump's DACA policies as arbitrary and capricious under the Administrative Procedure Act, it *sub silentio* supported this use of presidential power, so long as the proper bureaucratic steps have been taken.[11]

Three signature Trump initiatives were particularly intensely litigated: the travel ban against individuals from Muslim countries, the "remain in Mexico" policy (the Migrant Protection Protocols), and the use of Title 42 public-health authorities to crack down on immigration in alleged response to the Covid-19 pandemic.[12] These lawsuits revealed the Supreme Court's reluctance to oversee the legality of executive immigration-enforcement orders.

The most startling example of Trump-era judicial deference was the 5-to-4 majority opinion by Chief Justice John Roberts in *Trump v. Hawaii*, which upheld Trump's Muslim travel ban. The first version of that ban, issued on January 27, 2017, blocked entry into the United States by citizens of seven predominantly Muslim countries. The ban initially barred individuals from those countries with valid U.S. visas and green cards from reentering the United States, temporarily suspended entry of all refugees into the United States, and for an indefinite period, barred all Syrian refugees. But underneath, this travel ban amounted to a thinly disguised Muslim ban. On the campaign trail, candidate Trump had repeatedly promised to impose just such a measure, saying: "Islam hates us. . . . And we can't allow people coming into this country who have this hatred of the United States." Far from rejecting any parallel to the Japanese internment case, *Korematsu v. United States,* Trump invoked it to justify his call for a "total and complete shutdown

of Muslims entering the United States." President Franklin Roosevelt, he
said on the anniversary of Pearl Harbor, "did the same thing" by interning
Japanese Americans during World War II.[13]

On its face, this policy seemed illegal for at least four reasons. First, under
international law, such a ban affronted two treaties to which the United States
has long been a party: the Convention Relating to the Status of Refugees (the
"Refugee Convention"), which requires that "[t]he Contracting States shall apply the provisions of this Convention to refugees without discrimination as to
race, religion or country of origin," and the International Covenant on Civil
and Political Rights, which states that "[a]ll persons are equal before the law
and are entitled without any discrimination to the equal protection of the law."[14]

Second, these norms have been internalized in the domestic law of the
United States, a country founded on religious freedom. Even a sanitized
Muslim ban discriminated against one religion for the benefit of others, in
violation of the First Amendment's establishment clause. No ban so broad
had ever been authorized by statute. Key immigration laws instead expressly
forbade exclusion on the basis of national origin.[15]

Third, as a matter of policy, the ban was both over- and underinclusive.
None of the countries from which people were excluded had ever actually
produced a terrorist who had killed anyone on U.S. soil. Meanwhile, other
countries that had produced such terrorists were not on the list: for example,
Saudi Arabia, from which most of the 9/11 attackers hailed.[16]

Fourth, the travel ban emerged from a defective and arbitrary governmental process. Because it was rushed into operation, the executive order was not
vetted by knowledgeable governmental lawyers, the incoming secretaries in
the Departments of Defense and Homeland Security, or the key legislators
who oversaw counterintelligence and homeland-security issues.[17]

Yet despite this record, the Supreme Court upheld the ban. The Court
reasoned that over time, the ban had evolved into a lawful, "facially neutral"
policy denying certain foreign nationals the privilege of admission." But as
Justice Sotomayor's dissent clarified—citing chapter and verse from Trump's
Twitter logs—"[t]he full record paints a . . . harrowing picture, from which a
reasonable observer would readily conclude that the Proclamation was motivated by hostility and animus toward the Muslim faith."[18]

Still, the majority opinion upheld the revised travel ban by making errors of
fact and law. As a matter of fact, the majority claimed that there was "persua-

sive evidence that the entry suspension has a legitimate grounding in national security concerns." But as chronicled in the amicus brief of former national-security officials from Republican and Democratic administrations, throughout the fifteen months of the travel-ban litigation, the U.S. government never offered a sworn declaration from a single executive official willing to describe the national security need for the orders or the process that led to their adoption. Trump's administration never identified any new national security threat that justified shifting so abruptly toward such an overtly discriminatory policy, just seven days after he took office. On the contrary, the Trump officials' own dilatory actions in the wake of the original travel ban showed that even they never took seriously their own claims of national security urgency.[19]

As a matter of process, the Court did not say, as it later did in the DACA case, that the process that underlay the administration's actions was arbitrary and capricious. Instead, the Court chose to grant broad deference to an executive action that rested on ever-shifting, inconsistent rationales. As the briefing in the case showed, the policy did not emerge from the considered judgment of executive officials responding to a bona fide national security threat. The Court never acknowledged that the bigotry that had infected the original travel ban carried over to its successors. Notwithstanding the government's recitation of a subsequent "worldwide review process undertaken by multiple Cabinet officials," those processes were plainly designed to preserve, in dressed-up form, the original ban's group-discrimination template. As Justice Clarence Thomas acknowledged in *United States v. Fordice*, "if a policy remains in force, without adequate justification and despite tainted roots . . . it appears clear—clear enough to presume conclusively—that the [government] has failed to disprove discriminatory intent."[20]

As a matter of law, the Court majority applied an unusually deferential standard of review. The Court said that it would sustain a policy if the government could offer *any* rational national security basis for it, even if the factual record showed that the policy was actually motivated by blatant official animus against a particular religion. Ironically, the travel-ban ruling came just weeks after the Court had found that state officials' actions toward a baker who declined to serve LGBT customers violated that individual's freedom of religion. Yet in the travel ban case, the same Court found no similar violation, looking past far more overt and repeated hostile statements about Muslims from Trump and his senior advisers.[21]

In the process, the court over-read the pivotal statute, 8 U.S.C. § 1182(f)—the same statute invoked by the Bush 41 and Clinton administrations to win the Haitian-refugee case described in chapter 5—to "exude[] deference to the President in every clause." That description was better suited to the court's own opinion than to the law itself. The Court never plausibly explained why that law, which authorized the president to suspend entry of "immigrants or nonimmigrants," was not modified by a subsequent statutory provision that expressly prohibited nationality discrimination in the issuance of immigrant visas.[22]

In hindsight, the Court's 5-to-4 decision was predictable. The Court signaled its initial willingness to stay the lower court's preliminary injunction, thereby ensuring that the policy would continue for half a year before a final Supreme Court decision. Most troubling was the Court's blind acceptance, in Justice Sotomayor's words, of "the Government's misguided invitation to sanction a discriminatory policy motivated by animosity toward a disfavored group, all in the name of a superficial claim of national security," in effect "redeploy[ing] the same dangerous logic underlying *Korematsu*."[23]

Chief Justice Roberts pronounced that *Korematsu* "was gravely wrong the day it was decided, has been overruled in the court of history, and—to be clear—'has no place in law under the Constitution.'" Yet remarkably, in the same breath, he claimed that "*Korematsu* has nothing to do with this case" and called it "wholly inapt to liken that morally repugnant order to" Trump's travel ban.[24]

In fact, the wholly apt resemblance to *Korematsu*—drawn explicitly in Trump's own public statements—should have been enough to invalidate the travel ban. In both cases, the president invoked an amorphous national security threat to justify a sweeping discriminatory policy that significantly limited the freedom of a particular group. In both cases, the government invoked a grossly overbroad group stereotype that presumed that membership in that group, standing alone, signaled a potential hidden desire to harm the United States. In both cases, the government misstated key facts to the Court. And the manifest wrong of both policies rested on the government's insistence on inflicting harm on the basis of membership in a group—defined by descent, nationality, or religion—whose dangerousness the government never proved.[25] In the end, the government both judged and penalized a group because of their collective religious beliefs, without ever assessing the content of their individual characters.

In the end, the travel ban represented only the most prominent Trump administration policy that, in Justice Sotomayor's words, "now masquerades behind a façade of national security concerns." Although he harshly condemned and used military force in response to Syrian president Bashar al-Assad's use of chemical weapons against Syrian children, Trump was unwilling to lift his nationality-based ban against those same children entering the United States.[26]

As the Trump administration ended, many critics heralded the need for a new reform-minded administration to use its presidential power in the opposite direction. Initially, Biden sought to protect immigrants by assertively reversing Trump-era policies. But as the next chapter shows, the Biden administration found Trump's immigration policies hard to change, especially as it struggled to maintain control of the southern border. Although subsequent administrations may be able to rescind many of Trump's immigration changes, some of the policies will likely stay on the books for many years to come, significantly contracting the openness of the U.S. immigration system.[27]

International Trade

Many of Trump's unilateralist patterns in the immigration area simply replicated themselves in the field of international trade. As in the immigration area, Trump relied disproportionately on false linkages between trade and national security. In the trade field, as in other foreign-policy realms, Trump rejected the smart-power "engage, translate, and leverage" approach in favor of "disengage, black hole, and go it alone." Wherever possible, he sought to disengage from global alliances, claimed that no meaningful rules constrained his power, and eschewed cooperative diplomatic approaches. Most significantly, as in the immigration field, the Trump administration based its unilateral actions on claimed statutory authority, not solely on a *Curtiss-Wright* vision of the president's constitutional prerogatives.

As with immigration, the trade field has been marked by mass migration of plenary congressional power to the president.[28] The infamous Smoot-Hawley Tariff Act of 1930 triggered the Great Depression. This episode created the enduring impression that protectionism results from congressional micromanagement of tariff levels, and suggested that greater presidential control of trade policy was more likely to promote trade liberalization. Accordingly, over the balance of the twentieth century, Congress statutorily delegated most of its tariff-reducing authority to the president. Successive presidents used that delegated authority, as well as periodically delegated fast-track authority, to reduce both tariff and nontariff barriers through multilateral trade rounds, bilateral free-trade agreements, and regional pacts like NAFTA.[29]

Trump wielded this broad delegated statutory authority to engage in unilateralist acts that exploded the basic elements of the late-twentieth-century U.S. trade consensus. His trade policies deeply undermined three accepted bipartisan features of the post–Bretton Woods multilateral trading system: bilateral and regional diplomacy, the "trade rule of law," and respect for the World Trade Organization and its system of multilateral dispute resolution. President Trump wielded his delegated tariff power to restore tariff barriers to the center of public debate and to promote presidential trade protectionism. What made his trade policies particularly surprising is that Trump's nominally pro-trade Republican Party bent over backward to defend them. Instead of objecting to his actions in light of their long-stated commitment to trade liberalization as an engine of global and national economic growth, Trump's party quietly discarded the decades-old orthodoxies that had long been articles of faith for Republican free traders.[30]

Instead of trying to resolve disputes via multilateral cooperation within agreed-upon diplomatic frameworks, Trump abandoned multilateral forums and conducted destructive bilateral trade wars outside those frameworks. But although Trump sought to resign from global leadership, the United States proved so deeply enmeshed with existing laws, norms, and institutions of international-trade law that the new U.S. default became "resigning without leaving." The United States remained in the very multilateral institutions and alliances that Trump derided, but with the vastly reduced influence and legitimacy that inevitably follows when one becomes a lame duck.[31]

Because Trump regularly threatened withdrawal without a backup plan, in cases like the NAFTA renegotiation, the threatened exit simply led to a hasty negotiation that shallowly repackaged the status quo. In other cases, such as the Trans-Pacific Partnership, the United States did exit, misjudging that the regime would collapse without U.S. participation. The United States then found itself supplicating to reenter a deal that it never should have left in the first place. In an ironic twist, after loudly rejecting the Trans-Pacific Partnership, the Trump administration ended up quietly accepting many of its provisions in the new NAFTA, the United States–Mexico–Canada Agreement.[32]

Trump also launched an audacious frontal assault on the core norms and understandings underlying the World Trade Organization (WTO), the primary multilateral institution for trade liberalization and stabilization. Trump's administration attacked the WTO's strongest component—its binding dispute-settlement system—with no visible substitute in mind. To be sure, the WTO had been far from perfect: the Doha round of trade negotiations failed to produce fairer rules for developing countries; the WTO has no meaningful legislative body; and its Appellate Body has issued some questionable decisions. But the WTO's crowning achievement had been the development of a binding standing system of dispute settlement that is unique in the world of international law. Trump falsely proclaimed that "we lose . . . almost all of the lawsuits in the WTO." But he simply ignored data showing that the United States has arguably been the greatest beneficiary of that system; the United States had the highest win rate, prevailing on some 90 percent of the adjudicated issues, whereas by the same measures, China had the lowest win rate.[33]

Trump's decision to block all Appellate Body nominees, without regard to professional qualifications or accomplishment, was a classically overbroad effort to choke off third-party judicial-style dispute settlement. His retreat from the vision of an authoritative, quasi-constitutional international-trade tribunal to set precedents and resolve conflicts will almost surely damage the United States' long-term interests. Most fundamentally, Trump's opportunistic "pick and choose" approach to WTO rules—invoking its provisions when on the offensive, but disdaining WTO disciplines when on the defensive—sketched a chilling blueprint for China to follow. Under this blueprint, the largest trading powers can seek asymmetrically to embrace the gains of market competition without accepting neutral oversight over their own national compliance with global trade rules.[34]

Just two decades after major "trade rule of law" advances in the mid-1990s, Trump ushered in a sharp regression from, and potential dismantling of, a rule-oriented trade system. His trade agenda threatened the return of both multipolarity and territorialization. It splintered the inclusive WTO framework, in which disagreements between trade stakeholders can be debated and resolved, and revived the bitter North-South divides that had accompanied calls in the 1970s for a new international economic order.

At the same time, the Trump administration's disruptions diverted the multilateral trading system from a long-overdue effort to shift attention away from national security concerns, toward a twenty-first-century focus on equality and redistribution. Expansion of global trade had become a lightning rod for growing inequality. Technology had unsettled production practices in advanced economies, triggering middle-class anger toward the globalist forces. Workers came to believe that globalization had frozen their wages, stolen their jobs, and forced the migration of manufacturing. From country to country, the middle class was left feeling betrayed and abandoned, which fostered infectious nationalist counter-movements against perceived liberal orthodoxies, such as diversity, multiculturalism, and openness to immigration.

Instead of resigning from global leadership, both the Bush 43 and Obama administrations had sought to intensify U.S. participation in trade governance. They sought to engage like-minded trading partners to revamp trade rules. They sought to update trade norms, through the WTO where possible and through regional trade agreements where necessary. They tried to prove that trade expansion could make the U.S. working class better off, so long as America's integration with other economies was carefully managed through smart diplomacy abroad and wise domestic policy at home.[35]

Trump rejected this strategy because of his belief—sloganized at populist rallies as "America First"—that the United States had lost competitiveness vis-à-vis other countries in what he perceived to be a zero-sum game. Globalization, he insisted, had left the American working class behind by allowing immigrants and foreigners to steal their jobs. To "make America great again," the United States needed to offload the burdens of global leadership so that other nations would pay their fair share. According to Trump, bilateral "[t]rade wars are good and easy to win."[36] A strategy of trade unilateralism, he argued, would force exploitative trading partners to choose between mutually destructive tit-for-tat tariff escalation and coerced renegotiations that end up "getting us a better deal" on such agreements as NAFTA and the United States–Korea Free Trade Agreement.[37]

But in trade, as in other areas of international law, Trump's unilateralism did not foster enhanced cooperation, only reciprocal unilateralism and the erosion of collective norms. Trump's trade wars—again conducted in a constitutional zone of plenary congressional power—ended up diluting America's legitimacy within the world trading system. It poisoned the global trade atmosphere and deepened suspicion over the good faith and competence o

U.S. trade policy. Counterproductively, Trump's unilateralism delayed much-needed WTO reforms and undermined the long-term global framework for the trade rule of law.[38]

Agreement Breaking

During Trump's time in office, his administration announced the withdrawal of the United States from more than a dozen bilateral and multilateral agreements. He also threatened to withdraw from numerous others, including NATO, becoming the first Republican president, after six Republican predecessors, to threaten withdrawal from that organization.[39] Unlike Trump's other areas of unilateralism, agreement breaking raises few factual questions but a clear legal one: Does the president enjoy a general constitutional power to terminate, suspend, or withdraw from any and all international agreements to which the United States is a party? In particular, did President Trump (or would any future president) have legal authority—in a single tweet—to unilaterally withdraw the United States from every agreement, treaty, and international organization foundational to the postwar world order?[40]

Significantly, nothing in the Constitution's text or structure confers on the president a general unilateral power of treaty termination. Article II, section 2, clause 2 of the Constitution empowers the president to "make Treaties, provided two thirds of the Senators present concur," but says nothing about which branch of government may unmake those treaties. Neither can such a general unilateral power be derived from Supreme Court precedent. As chapter 3 reviewed, the only Supreme Court decision on this subject, *Goldwater v. Carter,* is a splintered nonjusticiability ruling, not a controlling precedent on the merits of this question.[41]

Fairly read, *Goldwater* does not support a general unilateral presidential power of treaty termination. *Goldwater* simply supports the nonreviewability of the attempted unilateral termination of one bilateral treaty, the mutual-defense treaty with Taiwan. Even then, the ruling was splintered: four justices found a political question and one concluded that the case was not ripe. Only one justice in that case, William Brennan, opined that the president had the constitutional power to terminate the particular treaty at issue in that case; significantly, he made no general statements about a broader unilateral power of treaty termination. Instead, Justice Brennan based his vote on the particular fact that the bilateral treaty happened to have been unilaterally terminated in accordance with international law and within the scope of the president's exclusive recognition authority.[42]

Even at the time, none of the nine *Goldwater* justices advocated a general unilateral transsubstantive power of presidential termination. On the contrary, four justices observed "that different termination procedures may be appropriate for different treaties." That statement hardly suggests a "one size fits all" general rule authorizing a general unilateral presidential power of treaty termination. Instead, it suggests a more context-dependent rule, such as the commonsense "mirror principle" described in chapter 11.[43]

The recent *Restatement (Fourth) of the Foreign Relations Law of the United States* (the *Fourth Restatement*) concedes that "[t]he Supreme Court has not resolved the constitutional authority to terminate a treaty." But in the next breath, a controversial provision broadly suggests that "[a]ccording to established practice, the President has the authority to act on behalf of the United States in suspending or terminating U.S. treaty commitments and in withdrawing the United States from [Article II] treaties." While the reporters cautioned that this section currently applies only to Article II treaties, one reporter recently wrote that "if presidents do have the legal authority to withdraw from Article II treaties, it is not clear why that authority would not extend to congressional-executive agreements" and presumably, other agreements as well.[44]

This claim of historical pedigree is of surprisingly recent vintage. To make its sweeping statement, the *Fourth Restatement* relied on relatively recent historical practice following *Goldwater v. Carter.* As one of the *Fourth Restatement* reporters summarized, after extensive historical review, "[w]hereas it was generally understood throughout the nineteenth century that the termination of treaties required congressional involvement, the consensus on this issue disappeared in the early parts of the twentieth century." By "the end of the twentieth century," Louis Henkin, the chief reporter of the *Third Restatement,* had concluded that "it is apparently accepted that the President has authority under the Constitution to denounce or otherwise terminate a treaty."[45]

The *Restatement* reporters also cited "structural and functional considerations" in favor of a unilateral presidential power to terminate.[46] But on its face, *Goldwater* says nothing at all about terminations of or withdrawals from agreements that are multilateral, not bilateral, or terminations or withdrawals that arguably are not implemented in accordance with the agreement's terms or that otherwise arguably violate international law. Thus, whatever unilateral termination power may be recognized by historical practice after *Goldwater,* it would not extend to unilateral acts by the president to suspend, terminate, or withdraw from treaties in a manner *not* in accordance with international law or the treaty's own terms.

Goldwater says nothing about terminations or withdrawals that are carried out within the scope of concurrent legislative-executive authority. Many such agreements were authorized by Congress's plenary authority over international trade or foreign commerce, and initially adopted against a general background of congressional awareness and approval. As the *Fourth Restatement* reaffirms, "[a]lthough historical practice supports a unilateral presidential power to suspend, terminate, or withdraw the United States from treaties, it does not establish that this is an exclusive presidential power."[47] Thus, if the president were to attempt a treaty termination within zones of either concurrent congressional-executive foreign-affairs authority or exclusive legislative power—such as the foreign-commerce power—the Senate could presumably limit executive discretion preemptively in its advice and consent to a particular treaty. Congress could also enact a general "no unilateral exit" statute, or a specific no-exit law with respect to any particular international agreement.

As noted in chapters 1 and 2, the Supreme Court has at times recognized "historical practice" as a basis for normative reinterpretation of structural constitutional provisions. But as Justice Frankfurter's famous discussion of historical practice in *Youngstown* made plain, "systematic, unbroken, executive practice" places a historical "gloss on the 'executive power'" in Article II only if—like adverse possession in property law—that practice has been "long pursued to the knowledge of the Congress and never before questioned."[48] Since the 1930s, presidents have unilaterally terminated several international agreements—"a few dozen" since *Goldwater*. But as the *Fourth Restatement*'s reporters correctly noted, "[m]ost of these terminations have not generated controversy in Congress."[49]

The fact that the president may have unilaterally terminated agreements that Congress did not care about tells us little about what would happen if

Congress were actively to contest a withdrawal. In fact, the appellate briefs in *Goldwater* debated whether there were genuinely more than three contested treaty withdrawals in all of American history. Even four decades of consistent executive practice would not rise to Justice Frankfurter's level of historical "gloss" unless the other affected branch of government affirmatively "acquiesced" in the legality of the executive acts. Again, this plainly would not be the case, for example, if the president now sought to withdraw from an important multilateral agreement that enjoys wide bipartisan congressional support, such as NATO.[50]

What makes reading congressional silence as "acquiescence" even more perilous is that there is no guarantee that Congress even knows about most agreement terminations. The Case-Zablocki Act of 1972 ostensibly requires the executive branch to notify Congress of all foreign agreements. But the act has prominently failed to ensure the complete reporting of all agreements and political commitments that presidents may actually make. No existing statutory provision even requires the president to notify Congress of an executive decision to terminate or withdraw from any treaty or international agreement. Nor is there any readily available listing of agreements or treaties that may have been unilaterally terminated. Although the annual *Digest of United States Practice in International Law,* published by the State Department's Office of the Legal Adviser, voluntarily reports on some terminations, there is no legal requirement that the Office of the Legal Adviser or the State Department report all such terminations, and the *Digests* are not published until *after* the incidents they describe.[51]

Apart from historical practice, the only other support offered for the *Fourth Restatement's* black-letter rule is that "structural and functional considerations are consistent with the general ability of the President to act unilaterally, as it has been exercised in practice." But looked at from a dynamic perspective, today such structural and functional considerations cut against, not for, rapid unilateral agreement withdrawals. As to constitutional structure, chapters 1 through 4 clarified that the foreign-affairs power is generally a power shared: unilateral powers are the exception, not the rule. So whenever the Constitution's text does not explicitly assign a plenary power to one branch, the multiple, overlapping grants of foreign-affairs authority should presumptively dictate that powers not be unilaterally exercised, but rather shared between Congress and the executive.[52]

In support of a unilateral executive withdrawal power, some commentators have made a functional "quick divorce" argument. They claim that foreign-affairs exigencies may require the United States to exit entangling alliances that were entered into deliberately, and with extensive congressional awareness and participation, over a much longer period. Under this functional theory, the president alone is best positioned to decide whether and when a quick divorce is demanded.

On reflection, the "quick divorce" rationale may apply in historically rare circumstances like those surrounding Jimmy Carter's termination of the Taiwan treaty, when quickly disentangling the country from a treaty had to be done rapidly to effectuate the unilateral recognition of one regime and the concomitant derecognition of another. But as a functional matter, an overbroad unilateral executive power to withdraw from any and all international agreements would risk overly hasty, partisan, or parochial presidential withdrawals. More fundamentally, it would also tend to weaken systemic stability and the negotiating credibility and leverage of *all* presidents. Take, for example, Trump's abrupt withdrawal from the Iran nuclear deal at the precise moment that he was attempting to negotiate a similar denuclearization deal with North Korea. Even if the short-term, first-order "functional" effect of more congressional involvement in the withdrawal process were to constrain the executive, the second- and third-order functional effects would strengthen the executive's hand in future international negotiations. The negotiating credibility of a future executive who wishes to enter into a new agreement would be strengthened, not weakened, if such agreements are made harder to break by the executive's successors. Negotiating partners would have far greater assurance that the proposed arrangement would enjoy continuity and stability.[53]

This concern has special force with respect to Article II treaties, which cannot be entered into on a whim. As we have seen, the constitutional barriers to entry into Article II treaties are considerable. The constitutional ratification requirement demands that two-thirds of the Senate consent. This entails a massive mobilization of executive-branch and legislative resources. Allowing Article II treaties to be so easily exited at the executive's whim could undermine legislative will to enter into such treaties in the first place. Legislators could too easily conclude that their politically safest posture would be never to take a tough, visible vote. Instead, they could comfortably stay on the sidelines with respect to all actions regarding international agreements. Their passivity would allow the president to unilaterally make and unmake *all* international agreements through executive action. This would lead to across-the-board diminution of legislative participation in and accountability for international lawmaking. In the long run, it would establish a strong de facto bias against the United States' ability to ever participate in formal treaties, which would greatly diminish the Article II treaty instrument.

Whatever functional sense a crosscutting *Goldwater* approach—strong unilateral presidential termination rights coupled with minimal judicial review—might have made in the 1970s, the world has plainly changed in ways that call that logic into question. As the United Kingdom has painfully learned since its Brexit referendum vote in June 2016, breaking up is hard to do. In the modern era, as a functional matter, international agreements are not just transactional but relational. These agreements do not authorize sequential, one-off transactions so much as they create organic, evolving *relationships* that generate an interconnected set of rights, duties, expectations, and reliance for all parties. As in any marriage, momentary lapses can be forgiven if a fundamental commitment to the enduring relationship has been demonstrated. But the disruptive act of termination engages the interests of all parties, both participating and represented, who accordingly should be as much involved in the decision to exit as they are in the initial decision to enter.[54]

Particularly in legal systems in which treaties are the supreme law of the land, treaties confer legal rights that have a direct effect on domestic actors. Those treaties lay a foundation upon which, over time, sedimentary layers of legal acts, executing legislation, and court decisions build a deeply internalized framework of transnational law. This process strongly embeds treaty membership into the domestic fabric of political life. Withdrawing abruptly from such an organic treaty framework is a destructive act akin to trying to pull out only the red threads from a multicolored tapestry. Withdrawal rips the fabric of domestic law and disrupts all manner of domestic rights and expectations.

Ironically, even while Trump was invoking a transactional approach to international affairs, condemning all manner of international agreements as "bad deals," his administration made the opposite, relational argument before the Supreme Court. In *Jam v. International Finance Corp.*, Trump's solicitor general did not reject international agreements and institutions as "bad deals." Instead, he stressed that the "United States' participation in international organizations is a critical component of the Nation's foreign relations [that] reflects an understanding that robust multilateral engagement is a crucial tool in advancing national interests."[55]

Back when "politics stopped at the water's edge," one could safely assume basic foreign-policy continuity even though the White House had changed hands. In that setting, academics and justices could well have believed that their approach would minimize foreign-policy conflict and make the United States more compliant overall with international norms. But the rise of a post–Cold War political era marked by dramatic foreign-policy discontinuities from Presidents Clinton to Bush 43 to Obama to Trump to Biden has dramatically undermined this assumption.

Unless somehow blessed by Congress, unilateral withdrawals based on presidential caprice will be highly disruptive to both foreign and domestic policy. That very disruptiveness and unpredictability will, in turn, make it harder for future presidents and Congresses to negotiate valuable international agreements. And whether or not one president could unilaterally terminate an Article II treaty without Senate participation, a constitutional question left open is whether a future president could reinstate U.S. participation in that agreement without new advice and consent, reasoning that the necessary legislative approval has already been obtained.[56]

In sum, the most accurate reading of historical practice is that *Goldwater* has functioned as a piece of what chapter 1 termed "quasi-constitutional custom" that is perennially subject to revision. Much of the more recent historical practice of unilateral presidential termination since *Goldwater* can be attributed to path dependence and conventional wisdom, not to serious substantive review of the constitutional arguments on the merits. Any rule suggested by the most recent historical practice could—and in my view should—be revised either by judicial decision or by altered interbranch practice going forward.

In *Goldwater*, D.C. Circuit judge George MacKinnon foresaw the dangers of the Trump era when he presciently warned against "an ambitious or unreasoned President disengaging the United States from crucial bilateral and multilateral treaties with the stroke of a pen." "In future years," he warned, "a voracious President and Department of State may easily use this grant of

absolute power [of unilateral termination] to the President to develop other
excuses to feed upon congressional prerogatives that a Congress lacking in
vigilance allows to lapse into desuetude."[57]

Until recently, this debate had been deemed moot because, as a practical
matter, no litigant could challenge on the merits a president's decision to
unilaterally terminate or withdraw from international agreements. In the
first few decades after *Goldwater,* few treaty terminations were contested on
the merits, because of the justiciability obstacles of standing, ripeness, and
the political-question doctrine. Several lower courts followed the lead of the
Goldwater plurality by finding that suits challenging executive power to unilaterally withdraw from treaties were nonjusticiable.[58]

But more recently, the law of justiciability has significantly changed. In
Zivotofsky v. Clinton (Zivotofsky I), the Supreme Court declined to apply the
political-question doctrine to bar review of the president's power to recognize foreign states in the face of a contrary congressional statute. When the
case returned to the Court in *Zivotofsky v. Kerry (Zivotofsky II),* the majority
held on the merits that the same statute was unenforceable because it was an
unconstitutional intrusion on the president's exclusive power of recognition.
Chief Justice Roberts's opinion for the *Zivotofsky I* Court called the political-
question doctrine a "narrow" exception to the general rule that the judiciary
has the "responsibility to decide cases properly before it." The opinion notably narrowed the six-factor political-question test originally introduced in
Baker v. Carr to its first two "textual" elements. *Zivotofsky* explained that a
political question exists only "[1] where there is 'a textually demonstrable
constitutional commitment of the issue to a coordinate political department;
or [2] a lack of judicially discoverable and manageable standards for resolving it.'"[59]

Under *Zivotofsky I*'s narrowed two-pronged political-question test, a contested treaty termination would not raise a political question. First, termination is not a decision "textually committed" by the Constitution to a branch
other than the judiciary. Article II, section 2 of the Constitution authorizes
the president to "make" treaties with the advice and consent of two-thirds of
the senators present but nowhere expressly authorizes any branch to *unmake*
such treaties, whether through suspension, termination, or withdrawal. Second, there is no "lack of judicially discoverable and manageable standards
for resolving" the question. A court need only decide whether the president's

action—standing alone—is legally sufficient to terminate an international treaty obligation. As Justice Lewis Powell argued in *Goldwater,* in such a case, "the Court would interpret the Constitution to decide whether congressional approval is necessary to give a Presidential decision on the validity of a treaty the force of law[,] an inquiry [that] demands no special competence or information beyond the reach of the Judiciary."[60]

The case for adjudicating a future contested treaty termination would be made even stronger if Congress were to enact a bipartisan bill preventing the president from withdrawing the United States from NATO, for example, without congressional consent.[61] Such legislation would eliminate any doubt that Congress, as a whole, had properly challenged the president's action, and would thereby create exactly the "constitutional impasse" between the political branches that Justice Powell's *Goldwater* opinion envisioned as necessary for ripeness.[62]

But if such a case were heard on the merits, a question would arise about what constitutional standard should govern agreement breaking. Chapter 11 will argue that there should be no transsubstantive unilateral presidential power of agreement termination. Instead, I follow the suggestion by four *Goldwater* justices that "different termination procedures may be appropriate for different treaties."[63] Instead of a rule of unilateral presidential termination, a constitutional "mirror principle" should apply, so that the same degree of legislative involvement would be required to withdraw from an agreement as was constitutionally required to enter into it in the first place.

Election Interference as a National Security Threat

Finally, no one should forget that both impeachments of Trump concerned electoral interference. The first addressed Trump's efforts to deflect attention from the Russians' attempted disruption of the 2016 presidential election, and his seeking to leverage national security commitments to affect the 2020 election. The second impeachment addressed Trump's effort to promote domestic disruption of the 2020 presidential election. Both impeachments highlighted Trump's broad willingness to condone electoral interference: first by the Russians, then by his own domestic supporters.

Both Trump's defenders and his detractors focused too narrowly on individual wrongdoing, not institutional failure. Although Trump characterized the long-awaited Mueller report as a "complete and total exoneration," it instead provided a detailed recounting of criminal activity that was deemed immunized from prosecution by executive-branch constitutional interpretation.

More accurately, the Mueller report described a thoroughgoing assault on the National Security Constitution. Volume one of the report exhaustively detailed a hostile foreign power's systematic initiative to infiltrate, influence, and support one side in a closely contested U.S. presidential campaign. This was an official foreign initiative that, by all accounts, the Trump campaign neither reported nor resisted, but welcomed. Volume two then chronicled the president's unrelenting efforts to cover up that infiltration. But when asked later whether he would again accept derogatory foreign opposition research in a future election, Trump responded that of course he would look to see whether it served his personal political benefit.[64]

The articles of impeachment voted by the House in 2019 flattened that episode into two counts: abuse of power and obstruction of Congress. The Democratic House charged and impeached President Trump for welcoming foreign interference in the tight 2016 election and, after the special counsel Robert Mueller declined to charge criminal misconduct, for seeking foreign interference to denigrate his 2020 electoral rival. When Congress investigated, Trump stonewalled subpoenas until they became irrelevant. He falsely claimed that he was blameless and had prevailed in the 2016 presidential election despite the interference of Democrats and corrupt Ukrainians.[65]

Like the Iran-contra affair and 9/11, the Russian hacking episode exposed a dire national security vulnerability: U.S. electoral processes are dramatically exposed to external attack. Indeed, the Mueller report's official title—"Report on the Investigation into Russian Interference in the 2016 Presidential Election"—described just such an urgent national security threat. Since 2013, Russia has conducted nearly forty election-influence campaigns targeting nineteen different countries. Mueller and other senior U.S. intelligence officials testified before congressional committees that Russia was poised to influence future elections.[66] Combined with daily expanding cyber capabilities, the historical anomaly of the Electoral College, and political manipulation of the electoral base through gerrymandering and census manipulation, future election-hacking episodes could easily call into question the very legitimacy of America's constitutional order.

After Trump was voted out of office in November 2020, his national security threats only accelerated. As the January 6 House Select Committee investigation and special counsel Jack Smith's indictment chronicled, after
losing decisively to former vice president Joe Biden, Trump became the first
president in 220 years to lead a concerted effort to disrupt the lawful and
peaceful transfer of power. Against even the advice of Attorney General Barr
and his acting successor, Trump pushed to overturn the free and fair election. He repeatedly lied, pressured multiple state and federal officials to
throw out contrary election results, and goaded his supporters to storm the
Capitol to block the seating of his constitutional successor. When his own
vice president, Mike Pence, refused to manipulate the electoral count to keep
him in office, Trump welcomed the thought that the mob should attack
Pence to change his mind.

During Trump's final days in office, his visible instability led cabinet members to contemplate invoking the Twenty-Fifth Amendment. Trump's escalating efforts to seize a lost election culminated in his public encouragement
of mob violence. Military officials and top generals feared that Trump would
improperly invoke his national security powers to create a foreign-policy crisis abroad or to order troops into American city streets.[67] All ten living former secretaries of defense signed a public letter attesting that any effort by
Trump to "involve the U.S. armed forces in resolving election disputes would
take us into dangerous, unlawful and unconstitutional territory." Yet when
Trump was again impeached without conviction, national security threats
were again underemphasized. The single article voted by the House charged
him simply with "incitement of insurrection" against the U.S. government
and "lawless action at the Capitol" on January 6. As the House changed
hands in 2023, ending the January 6 Committee's work, Trump announced
his candidacy once again to swear the presidential oath to "support, protect,
and defend, the Constitution." Not long after, he became the first former
president to be indicted, by several different courts. Yet Trump continued to
trumpet that his previous defeat constituted a "Massive Fraud of this type
and magnitude [that] allows for *the termination of all rules, regulations, and
articles, even those found in the Constitution.*"[68]

The first article of the first impeachment charged that "President Trump
used the powers of the Presidency in a manner that [1] compromised the
national security of the United States and [2] undermined the integrity of the

United States democratic process."[69] These twin threats are deeply interconnected. Whether from foreign or domestic sources, an attack on the integrity of our democratic process—and an administration's repeated willingness to encourage it—threatens our national security and constitutional stability as much as, if not more than, a terrorist attack on a major American city.

Whether from foreign or domestic sources, an attack on the determinants of our democracy constitutes a national security threat of the highest order. More fundamentally, the two impeachments showed that Trump had taken presidential extremism to an entirely new level. History has taught Americans to see their president as their main defense *against* national security threats. But Trump was impeached because he himself became a glaring *national security threat* who used his constitutional powers to normalize both election insecurity and an extreme form of executive unilateralism.[70] And as threatening as Trump was as president, Trump was not the worst national security threat that one could imagine. He did not regularly bomb or invade foreign countries; many of his efforts to exit multilateral treaties and institutions failed; and his ego and incompetence often blunted his effectiveness. Were he to take office for another term, without the further check of standing for reelection, there would be even fewer political checks against more extreme misbehavior.

Trump's presidency demonstrated unique contempt for the *Youngstown* vision of the Constitution. His presidential term exposed how dangerous executive unilateralism can be in the hands of a lawless executive. Executive unilateralism that may feel tolerable when leaders remain mindful of their constitutional oath directly threatens democracy when it empowers a lawless leader committed to election tampering. What made Trump singularly dangerous was that he used his constitutional powers to normalize executive unilateralism in a single-minded effort to undermine the integrity of American democracy. Elections cannot check autocracy if autocrats can use their powers to subvert elections. Trump's presidency thus gave a glimpse of how a more competent and effective unilateralist president could launch an even graver national security threat.

To be sure, Trump did not bear sole responsibility for his unilateralist project. It depended crucially on the eagerness of the Republican Congress to normalize his behavior and the willingness of a Supreme Court on which he filled three seats to defer to his claims of national security necessity. Not just one branch, but all three, contributed to the rise of this interactive institutional dysfunction.

In sum, we are only one election away from renewed crisis. If Trump, or another president in his unilateralist mold, were to enter the White House, this historical march toward unilateral presidentialism could sharply accelerate. This trend has increasingly exposed more of our constitutional democracy to existential threat.

To be sure, that historical march could also be slowed if Trump's successors were to strongly push the pendulum the other way. But as suggested above, the Democrats' persistent political response has been to undercorrect. Undercorrection occurs when a party newly in power does not push hard enough to reform the vulnerabilities exposed by its predecessor, or when the new administration's opponents systematically undermine its reform efforts. Trump's extreme contempt for the rule of law demanded an equally ambitious counter-agenda to avoid undercorrection. The next chapter explores whether Joe Biden's successor administration was able to deliver it.

9

Biden: Reengage and Rebuild

JOE BIDEN TOOK OFFICE AS PRESIDENT two weeks after the insurrection on January 6, 2021, and told a Trump-weary world, "America is back." He promised to restore respect for constitutional government, declaring: "What I don't want to do . . . [is] emulate Trump's abuse of the Constitution and constitutional authority."[1] Biden's first years proved far more respectful of checks and balances than Trump's, but his razor-thin legislative margins repeatedly forced him to take executive action without express congressional authorization. He could not fundamentally swing the pendulum back toward *Youngstown*. To take the dramatic steps necessary to restore the economy, public health, and democracy at home and abroad, Biden repeatedly fell back on executive unilateralism, again replicating the pattern of a Democrat undercorrecting for the extreme unilateralism of his Republican predecessor. His first years supplemented Trump's aggressive unilateralism with a series of ad hoc unilateralist steps that continued the unidirectional flow of foreign-policy power toward the presidency.

As the nineteenth-longest-serving senator in American history, Biden came to office with more high-level legislative experience than any U.S. president since Lyndon Johnson. But Trump's persistent public denigration of the 2020 election led many Americans to doubt whether Biden was the legitimately elected president. A Senate split 50–50 could not muster the 60 votes needed for cloture, let alone 67 for treaty ratification. The midterm election of 2022 helped Democrats gain slightly stronger control of the Senate, but they lost the House. So despite his four decades of congressional

service, Biden's first years as president saw relatively few legislative successes in the fields of foreign policy and national security.[2]

Although Biden achieved impressive success on the global front, especially in building and sustaining a coalition to oppose Russia's invasion of
Ukraine in 2022, he found far less success in achieving his domestic objectives. Biden had assumed, optimistically, that his long history of bipartisan
cooperation would enable his team to forge a new domestic and international consensus that could take concerted action to restore America's global
commitments and leadership role. To signal a change from Trump-like *Curtiss-Wright* extremism, Biden's lawyers (like Obama's) took pains to premise
his actions not on sweeping assertions of constitutional executive power, but
on past historical practice and statutory grants of delegated authority, administered consistently with international law.[3] But despite Biden's natural inclination to pursue a *Youngstown* course, nearly all of his foreign-policy moves
were accomplished by executive actions that could be reversed by his successor using the same unilateral legal tools.

Predictably, Biden's overall foreign-affairs orientation began as largely
continuous with that of Barack Obama, Bill Clinton, and the 2016 Democratic presidential candidate Hillary Clinton. This approach preached the opposite of the "disengage, black hole, and go it alone" philosophy of the Trump
administration. Biden's administration pursued the "engage, translate, and
leverage" strategy described in chapter 7: wherever possible, engage with
U.S. allies around common values; translate the spirit of the laws from traditional to modern settings; and leverage the core of a legal solution with other
available tools to try to achieve long-range, durable solutions.

To implement this approach, Biden appointed an experienced national-
security team, nearly all of whom had previously worked for the Obama and
Clinton administrations. His cabinet included seasoned lawyers and legislators, including the former senator and now vice president Kamala Harris
and, as chief of staff, the longtime Senate Judiciary Committee counsel Ron
Klain (replaced after two years by the former Covid czar Jeffrey Zients).
To maintain continuity with previous administrations, Biden appointed lawyers Jake Sullivan, Avril Haines, and Samantha Power as national security
adviser, director of national intelligence, and administrator of the Agency
for International Development, respectively. To ensure experience, he appointed the career diplomats William Burns as CIA director and Linda

Thomas-Greenfield as U.N. ambassador, and former general Lloyd Austin as secretary of defense. To restore human rights to the center of U.S. foreign policy, Biden appointed Antony Blinken, Wendy Sherman, and John Kerry— all committed human-rights professionals—as secretary of state, deputy secretary, and special climate envoy, respectively.

Biden had suddenly became the consensus Democratic nominee in early 2020 when his party challengers collectively conceded to him at the start of the Covid-19 pandemic. His early anointment freed him to spend far less time traveling, particularly because the pandemic made face-to-face campaigning nearly impossible, giving him more time to plan his transition. With the help of his closest friend, the former senator Ted Kaufman, Biden assembled the best-run transition team of any president in American history. He used the many extra hours he gained at home in Delaware planning his administration and talking to the leaders of his domestic and international transition teams. Dozens of detailed briefing papers were prepared on issues large and small, such as whether there should be a Biden doctrine and which of Trump's legal initiatives should be reversed in the first two hundred days.[4]

On Inauguration Day 2021, hundreds of new Biden administration officials across the country were sworn in virtually from their homes, via remote platforms like Webex and Zoom. These early entrants were assigned government ID cards and email addresses, and started working remotely with career members of the civil, foreign, and military services. Yet the pandemic intervened to centralize power in the White House. Many high-level agency officials were not quickly named or confirmed, let alone vaccinated, and agencies were instructed that no more than 25 percent of staff could report to work in person. Meanwhile, virtually everyone employed at the White House was called to work with a thrice-daily testing regime. Political appointees subject to Senate confirmation were confirmed at a snail's pace because of slow vetting and Republican senatorial foot-dragging. The absence of confirmed political appointees guaranteed that key national security decisions would be made at the National Security Council, not the foreign-affairs agencies. The Biden NSC also chose to replicate the Obama interagency lawyers group described in chapter 7—which had been largely discontinued during the Trump years—with virtually all national security decisions again being made through Obama's painstaking, meeting-filled interagency process.

Unlike Trump, who went through his first three years facing no real external crisis until the Covid-19 pandemic struck, Biden took office amid the worst American disease outbreak in a century. He responded by treating the fight against the pandemic as tantamount to wartime mobilization: what he called "the first priority, the second priority and the third priority" for his administration. In sharp contrast to Trump's Covid disorganization, Biden's team clarified the chaotic, unscientific messages that had come from the Trump administration and rapidly accelerated the pace of vaccinations. The White House Covid team deployed ventilators to places of need; invoked the Defense Production Act to accelerate production of Covid tests; made tests freely available to anyone who requested them; and opened myriad vaccination clinics to administer initial and booster shots. He used Covid tests and vaccines as tools of foreign aid. But as the pandemic wore on and public resistance to mandates grew, state governors ignored federal guidance and Covid variants multiplied. The pace of progress slowed, and the Biden administration found less success in persuading people to get booster shots, approving lifesaving treatments, and making Covid tests more widely available.[5]

Building Back Better

In the early months of the administration, Biden's team followed three basic principles. First, "from day one . . . tak[e] concrete steps to put human rights back at the center of our foreign policy and reassert our moral leadership on the global stage."[6] Second, prioritize diplomacy, democracy, and development as three means of achieving desired foreign-policy outcomes. Third, sequence priorities through "four Rs": reverse, reengage, rebuild, and reconceptualize. This meant: reverse Trump's policies; reengage with institutions the United States had left, but go beyond simply restoring a pre-Trump status quo; rebuild these institutions by promoting long-term structural change, or what Biden liked to call "build back better"; and reconceptualize a new agenda for international law and institutions. As the United States reengaged with U.S. partners and allies, the Biden administration saw an increasing need to give allies assurances that arrangements made in the next four years would survive into the future. To that end, Biden's legal team reengaged aggressively through nonbinding political agreements, memoranda of understanding, joint communiqués, and occasionally "executive

agreements plus" of the kind that President Obama had come to use for the
Paris climate and Iran nuclear deals: international compacts not expressly
approved by Congress but consistent with broader preexisting legislative
frameworks.[7]

Biden's first foreign-policy years recalled the heavyweight boxer Mike Tyson's famous maxim: "Everyone has a plan until they get punched in the
mouth."[8] By any standard, Biden's first two hundred days were remarkably
productive. But starting in 2021, Biden got "punched in the mouth," through
a sloppy exit from Afghanistan and the continuing migration crisis at the
southern border. In February 2022, Russia's invasion of Ukraine gave him a
defining new opening to demonstrate his foreign-affairs competence. But in
2023, his slim legislative majority forced him to act mostly unilaterally, as
Hamas attacked Israel, political polarization heightened, inflation spiked,
Covid-19 resurged, and his popularity plateaued.

Reverse and Reengage

With strong central direction, experienced teams, and little initial opposition, the Biden administration produced a striking amount of activity in its
first two hundred days. In the initial "reverse" phase, the administration
swiftly ended Trump's Muslim travel ban, which had been litigated for nearly
four years. The administration repealed the "remain in Mexico" policy and
the ban on service of transgendered individuals in the military, and established the White House Gender Policy Council. Biden "reengaged" with numerous international institutions and agreements Trump had withdrawn
from: rejoining the Paris climate accord and the World Health Organization
on the first day, and soon thereafter renewing the New START Treaty (which
Russia terminated in 2023). The administration sought and won reelection
to the United Nations Human Rights Council in October 2021 and rejoined
the United Nations Educational, Scientific, and Cultural Organization
(UNESCO). Biden's team reengaged with parties to the Iran nuclear deal and
resumed the process of closing Guantánamo, where, after twenty years, several dozen detainees still remained even though twenty of them had been
cleared for transfer if willing recipient countries could be found.[9]

After my tour as Bill Clinton's assistant secretary of state for democracy
human rights, and labor, I wrote an article arguing that U.S. human-rights
policy for the twenty-first century should follow three simple principles: tel

the truth; lead by example; and take a consistent position toward the past, present, and future. In the early months of the Biden administration, even without many confirmed political appointees, the Blinken State Department proactively followed that blueprint. To tell the truth, the Biden team almost immediately renounced Trump's unbalanced Commission on Unalienable Rights, which had focused disproportionately on anti-abortion and anti-LGBT+ issues and had privileged attacking political persecution against Christians over confronting persecution of other religious groups. Biden acknowledged that the United States would again lead by example, "not pretending that our history has been perfect but demonstrating how strong nations speak honestly and strive to improve."[10] With regard to the past, the Biden administration acknowledged, for the first time, the Armenian genocide in the Ottoman Empire (modern-day Türkiye) in 1915.[11] As to the present, the administration spoke out against ongoing abuses in Xinjiang and in Myanmar against the Rohingya. Blinken called for accountability for war crimes committed by all sides in the conflict over Ethiopian Tigray, and later strongly condemned Russia's war crimes and crimes against humanity in Ukraine.[12]

In the area of international criminal law, the Biden administration achieved a dramatic reversal of the hostile Trump-Pompeo-Bolton policies toward the International Criminal Court, adding the latest pendulum swing to that court's fraught relationship with the United States. After supporting war-crimes trials in Nuremberg and Tokyo and leading accountability efforts in Bosnia and Rwanda, in 1998 the United States famously declined to sign the Rome Statute creating the International Criminal Court. But in December 2000, just before leaving office, Bill Clinton signed the treaty. Three years later, the Bush 43 administration, in a letter from Undersecretary John Bolton to the U.N. secretary-general, "unsigned" the Rome Statute, and Congress passed the American Servicemembers Protection Act, which, in various ways, made U.S. government cooperation with the International Criminal Court difficult if not illegal. The Obama administration then rejected the Bolton letter, saying that what counted legally was President Clinton's continuing signature on the Rome Statute and reaffirmed that it was not U.S. policy to frustrate the object and purpose of the treaty.[13]

Initially, the Trump administration left the International Criminal Court alone. But when John Bolton briefly returned as national security adviser, he and Secretary of State Mike Pompeo renewed their assault on the court, prompting Trump to issue an executive order that attracted global dismay by sanctioning the court's prosecutor and deputy prosecutor. In April 2021, the Biden administration "reset" its relationship with the International Criminal Court. The Biden team lifted the counterproductive sanctions that had been imposed by the Trump administration on the outgoing prosecutor and deputy prosecutor, and supported the election of a new prosecutor, Karim Khan. Biden's support for international criminal justice included supporting the convictions of the Lord's Resistance Army commander Dominic Ongwen of Uganda and the Congolese exploiter of child soldiers Bosco Ntaganda in the International Criminal Court. The administration nominated law professor Beth Van Schaack to be the ambassador at large for global criminal justice and contributed funds to complete the prosecution of the assassins of the former Lebanese prime minister Rafic Hariri.[14]

Through all of these unilateral Biden steps, the United States warmed its relationship with the International Criminal Court without changing any laws. In the latest pendulum swing, just months after Russia's invasion of Ukraine in 2022, the administration began working closely with Prosecutor Khan, who found a reasonable basis to open an investigation into war crimes in Ukraine dating back to 2014. Longtime anti-ICC Republicans in the Senate and House began to favor cooperating with the International Criminal Court—and supported limited legislation to that effect—to promote Russian accountability for war crimes in Ukraine. The State Department supported an internationalized hybrid tribunal, rooted in Ukrainian law with international elements, to try Russian president Vladimir Putin and others for the crime of aggression. But old habits die hard: even after the ICC prosecutor issued an arrest warrant for Putin for committing war crimes, the Defense Department continued to oppose intelligence sharing with the International Criminal Court, until overruled by Biden's White House.[15]

The ICC episode revealed a recurrent pattern: Republican administrations have proved far more effective at expressing their hostility to international cooperation through legislation than later Democratic administrations have been in garnering legislative support to repeal those measures. This asymmetry then forces those Democratic administrations to take unilateral counter-actions *within* the contours of the restrictive Republican legal framework without ever changing it. For example, Biden's decision finally to share intelligence on Ukraine with the ICC prosecutor was apparently made partly to head off new legislation that, if enacted, would have mandated such intelligence sharing as a matter of law. But Biden's reversal of the ban on intelligence sharing was purely a temporary policy decision that amended no laws and thus could be reversed by any future president hostile to the court.[16] And so unless finally amended, the American Servicemembers Protection Act will continue to chill more proactive cooperation between the United States and the court and make possible a quick return to a hostile posture once the next Republican administration takes office.

Rebuild

With respect to the future, Biden's prime focus was on rebuilding democracy at home and abroad. Biden took office with an ambitious vision of restoring the postwar liberal order of international law and institutions. His theory was that renewed American leadership under his administration could deliver a lasting course correction and help restore a "thicker" version of the liberal international order. Since World War II, public international law had become notably more progressive, human rights oriented, and "owned" by multiple stakeholders, public and private. Kant's theory of global governance, set forth in his famous pamphlet *Toward Perpetual Peace,* called not for world government, but for a league of nations, a group of united nations sharing values, a de facto community of democracies. This vision of Kantian global governance had inspired the postwar order, from the United Nations to NATO to the Bretton Woods system, as well as a range of institutions and agreements designed to attack global problems, including the World Health Organization and the Paris climate accords. But Trump and his fellow authoritarians had all challenged this vision. As the previous chapter reviewed, their assault on democratic institutions and norms led, by the end of Trump's term, to the outlines of a counter-structure that started to look uncomfortably like the illiberal international order described in George Orwell's *1984.* In that barren world, authoritarian states would maintain spheres of influence by constantly shifting alliances, resorting to demagoguery, and disdaining the truth.[17]

Biden's antidote was to focus insistently on the restoration of democracy, at home and abroad. In foreign affairs, he convened the Summit for Democracy (held in 2021 and 2023, and scheduled to be held again in 2024 in Seoul,

Korea) to address three key determinants of democracy: judicial independence, human rights, and anti-corruption. By one year in, the Biden administration had refined the "engage, translate, and leverage" rubric, explaining that "this administration approaches . . . the great transnational challenges of our time: climate and COVID, nuclear proliferation, economic equality" in two parts. "First, deep investments in allies and partners so that we are addressing all of these challenges, leveraging the strength of friends, as well as our own strength," and second, by recognizing that "we are in a decisive decade when it comes to democracy proving that it is the form of government best suited to delivering for its citizens and for delivering against the great challenges of our time in a way that improves the lives of people."[18] In short, the administration had announced a two-part "Biden Doctrine": invest in alliances (that is, "engage, translate, and leverage") and show that democracy delivers.

Biden's team saw the need for the United States to strengthen democracy at home and abroad as both a means and an end. The administration plainly intended the Biden doctrine to fill the global governance vacuums created by Trump that Russia and China had eagerly exploited. China sought to supplant the U.S.-led Bretton Woods institutions with its own institutional creations, including the Asian Infrastructure Investment Bank and the Belt and Road Initiative. Speaking at George Washington University in 2022, Secretary Blinken treated China as a case study in the application of the Biden Doctrine principles. He reduced the Biden strategy on China to three elements. First, the United States would *invest* in democracy, infrastructure, innovation, and competitiveness to support common values. Second, the United States would *align* U.S. interests with the interests of its allies and non-state-actor partners by resolving trade disputes with Europe and creating—as regional counterweights to Chinese influence—new diplomatic platforms and alliances, such as the G7's Build Back Better World (an initiative aimed at countering China's Belt and Road Initiative), AUKUS (a new trilateral security pact uniting Australia, the United Kingdom, and the United States), and the Quad, or Quadrilateral Security Dialogue (QSD) between Australia, India, Japan, and the United States). Third, the United States would *compete* with China to defend alliance interests and build a vision for the future, pressing in such areas of disagreement as human rights and partnering in such areas of shared interest as climate change. On a level playing field, Blinken argued, the United States and its democratic allies could prove to the world that democracy delivers as the best form of government, both at home and abroad.[19] Significantly, these cooperative arrangements were not formalized in any legally binding international agreement that required congressional advice and consent. Instead, the Biden administration was seeking to rebuild a neo-Kantian community of cooperative democracies by using the kinds of informal nonlegal understandings, layered cooperation, and diplomatic "law talk" described in chapter 7.

Reconceptualize

Biden's greatest challenge came not in reengagement or rebuilding, but in reconceptualizing three defining issues: use of force, global health security, and climate change.

The most intractable issue proved to be use of force. When I returned to the government in 2021, after eight years away, I was startled to see that, in foreign affairs, the president now operates almost entirely by executive order or national security directive and rarely proposes national security legislation unless it involves appropriations. The White House had virtually given up on congressional-executive agreements or supermajority ratification of Article II treaties as ways of concluding international agreements. The president regularly imposes crushing trade and economic sanctions under previously delegated statutory authorities. As detailed below, he wields broad diplomatic tools justified by expansive readings of the recognition and foreign-affairs powers. And executive war making now proceeds by weaponizing artificial intelligence, cyber conflict, and special forces, under legislative authorizations enacted two decades earlier.[20]

The two decades since September 11, 2001, had transformed the national-security bureaucracy into an opaque behemoth that approached what Michael Glennon has called "double government": "a bifurcated system . . . in which even the President now exercises little substantive control over the overall direction of U.S. national security policy," at times evolving "toward greater centralization, less accountability and emergent autocracy."[21] I personally observed how deeply ingrained the 9/11 mentality had become in the U.S. bureaucracy, distorting priorities in favor of familiar threats. Even within the executive branch, national security bureaucracies had grown steadily richer, more powerful, and more opaque relative to their diplomatic and justice counterparts. Over the two decades since September 11, 2001, the military and intelligence budgets have swelled as if for years only one arm muscle had been given steroids. Those agencies' resources increasingly dwarf those of the State Department, and as a result there are now "about as many members of the armed forces in marching bands as there are American diplomats."[22]

The resulting bureaucratic structure too often resists new priorities in favor of combatting more familiar threats. Just weeks after the January 6 assault on the Capitol, with thousands daily dying from Covid-19 and harmed by climate change, we spent countless meetings contemplating such "legacy issues" as the continued detention of the few remaining detainees on Guantánamo and potential terrorist threats in faraway theaters. The institutional obsession with past threats made it much harder to address newly pressing challenges. So when new urgent crises arose—such as the exit from Afghanistan, Russia's invasion of Ukraine, the Hamas attack on Israel, climate change and global health—bureaucratic inertia slowed the Biden administration's aspirations to fulfill older promises, such as ending the "forever war," closing Guantánamo, and repealing the obsolete authorizations for the use of military force enacted in 1991, 2001, and 2002.

Biden sought to reclaim the United States' leadership role by convening world leaders to make progress together on shared global challenges. Biden proposed that America serve as the world's vaccine arsenal, driving the global economic recovery and restoring U.S. climate leadership. The Covid pandemic caused nearly eight hundred million cases worldwide and seven million deaths: more than had died in the United States from the Spanish flu a century earlier, long before there was either modern medicine or a modern international legal system. Biden's first U.N. General Assembly speech offered a three-part plan to enshrine public health as a human right: save lives now; vaccinate the world; and build back better.[23] His plan simply applied the "engage, translate, and leverage" strategy to Covid: partnering with public and private entities to deliver millions of doses of new vaccines to hundreds of countries, contributing to the global response, and translating new legal rules to public health. But despite a massive effort, Biden's global plan still left much of the global South unprotected.[24]

Biden's team offered an equally simple plan to repair the global health architecture: fix the leaky boat and build a better boat, but at least have one boat that floats. The first initiative was to "fix the leaky boat" through targeted amendments to the International Health Regulations (2005), the only meaningful treaty in this area. These regulations had visibly failed during the Covid-19 pandemic by ceding too much authority to the Chinese to keep outsiders from investigating the sources of zoonotic disease in Wuhan. The Europeans instead favored drafting a new pandemic instrument or treaty, which would likely take a decade to complete, focused on building "One-Health" to simultaneously improve both animal and human health— curbing the spread of zoonotic disease from animals to humans—and access and benefit sharing with respect to pathogens that could be used to develop effective vaccines. Unfortunately, many Europeans prefer that this new instrument be developed as a framework convention under the auspices of the World Health Organization. But because of the United States' inability to muster sixty-seven votes for Senate ratification, the last framework convention, on global tobacco control, has gone unratified by the United States since 2009. Another framework convention would have no reasonable prospect for Senate ratification in the foreseeable future. So once again, the political inability to produce legislative support for treaty ratification has forced the president to seek global health reform through non-treaty means that are subject to unilateral reversal by a hostile successor administration.[25]

Biden's third great conceptual challenge was to make up four years of lost progress on climate security under Trump. Biden appointed former secretary of state John Kerry as his special climate envoy and made three dramatic commitments: to reduce U.S. emissions by 50 percent by 2030, create a 100 percent carbon-free power sector by 2035, and achieve a net-zero-carbon economy by 2050. Under current policies, average global temperatures are forecast to rise 2.8 degrees Celsius. Biden's goal was to stay under a 2.0 degree Celsius rise from pre-industrial levels, which would still spark extreme heat waves, drought, and species extinction. The first U.N. Climate Change Conference of the Biden era, held in Glasgow in 2021 and commonly referred to as COP26, called for "keeping 1.5 alive," that is, returning to the Paris climate targets adopted in 2016. If that could be achieved, sea levels would rise much less dramatically, although even then, many low-lying island nations would still disappear. Accordingly, Special Envoy Kerry negotiated a series of ambitious pledges at Glasgow: a methane pledge; a deforestation pledge; a coal phasedown pledge (watered down by the Chinese from the original coal phase*out* pledge); a pledge to end oil and gas subsidies for fossil-fuel projects; and a joint pledge with the Chinese to limit the global average temperature increase to below 2 degrees, although China's own emissions would not start to fall until 2031.[26]

Yet once again, Biden's ability to act was hamstrung by his own tenuous influence with Congress. Biden initially proposed two infrastructure bills that would collectively provide close to $1 trillion to implement the U.S. climate pledges. Congress enacted the first bill for $270 billion, but negotiations with one pivotal senator (Joe Manchin) reduced the second much larger bill—originally intended for $550 billion—to $370 billion. Only through last-minute negotiations with Manchin was the Biden administration able to make credible pledges at the 2022 climate-change conference in Egypt (COP 27), which it renewed in 2023 in Dubai (COP 28). Thus, whether the Biden-Kerry climate plan can ultimately succeed in maintaining U.S. climate leadership will crucially depend on domestic politics.[27]

Biden's Challenges: Afghanistan, Immigration, Human Rights, and Ukraine

After a productive first six months, the Biden administration got "punched in the mouth" by its chaotic departure from Afghanistan, issues surrounding control of the southern border, human-rights challenges, and Russia's invasion of Ukraine in 2022. Despite Biden's pledge to return to greater interbranch collaboration on foreign affairs, he fell back to the constitutional default of executive unilateralism in addressing each of these four areas.

Exiting Afghanistan was long overdue. Twenty years earlier, in the aftermath of September 11, 2001, the United States had led an extraordinarily swift and successful military campaign to oust the Taliban and restore democracy. Yet a challenge far greater than winning the war became securing the peace. In Bosnia, the United States famously "went in heavy" after the Dayton accords, committing sixty thousand NATO peacekeepers, including some twenty thousand Americans. But in Afghanistan, the United States initially committed fewer than five hundred of six thousand NATO peacekeepers to a significantly larger geographic area. The predictable result: although Hamid Karzai nominally acted as president of the newly democratic Afghanistan, outside Kabul much of the country remained under the de facto control of warlords and drug lords. Karzai's vice president was assassinated, and Karzai himself narrowly avoided assassination, making a sus tained commitment of U.S. security personnel essential to ensure his safety. Human-rights abuses continued, under the name of some Northern Alliance leaders whom the United States supported during the war, and the Taliban continued to control critical areas. And instead of making the additional financial commitments necessary to secure Afghanistan and promote serious nation building, the Bush 43 administration initially allocated *zero* dollars in its 2004 budget for Afghan reconstruction, until embarrassed congressional staffers finally wrote in the paltry line item of $300 million to cover the oversight. So although the United States nominally "won" the Afghan war, it failed to make the necessary commitments to secure the peace. It failed to meaningfully build democracy in a country that has been ravaged by warfare for decades, even as Bush 43 moved on to a far more ambitious war and nation-building exercise in Iraq.[28]

President Obama, over then vice president Biden's objection, decided on a "surge" of troops in Afghanistan, but again without a clear or achievable long-term objective. After billions more were spent, and too little democracy or security achieved, the Trump administration negotiated an unrealistic, accelerated timetable whereby the United States was supposed to withdraw from Afghanistan by May 2021. The incoming Biden administration could only push that deadline to September 2021. Knowing that the United States had already decided to leave, the Taliban saw their opportunity and went on the offensive, seizing provincial capitals. The government of President Ashraf Ghani started to collapse, and finally did, in August 2021, one month before Biden's announced September 11 deadline.[29]

Simply put, no one has ever left anywhere a month early without disarray. But four additional factors contributed to the chaos. First, Ashraf Ghani's government pleaded with the Biden administration not to say publicly that the United States was leaving. The Biden team pledged to stand by Ghani, as it later did with Ukraine's Zelenskyy; but Ghani, unlike Zelenskyy, was not ready to stand and fight. Instead, Ghani himself secretly plotted to flee, and took much of his resources with him. Second, U.S. military intelligence consistently advised the Biden political leadership that they had at least six months before the Taliban would finally take over. Those estimates proved wildly over-optimistic as the Taliban swept across the country, seizing major cities in just a few weeks. Third, Congress had previously enacted into law an onerous fourteen-step legal requirement before any Afghan who had worked with the United States as an interpreter or otherwise could be admitted to the United States on a special immigrant visa. These fourteen steps, which were ostensibly put in place to prevent Taliban sympathizers from finding refuge in the United States, could not be completed quickly to facilitate the evacuation of large groups. Consequently, many Afghans who had made genuine sacrifices for the U.S. cause and military effort were tragically left behind. The United States did evacuate some 124,000 in less than three weeks, a logistical challenge comparable to the Berlin Airlift. But many needy Afghans were left behind and remain stranded still. Finally, the Biden administration consulted weakly with U.S. allies, who were caught unawares, which impeded cooperation and contributed to the fiasco.

As the Taliban oppresses Afghanistan and crushes human and women's rights today, the episode must be marked as a major human-rights failure, especially for those Afghans to whom America had made—as Biden entitled his memoir—"promises to keep." However poorly the exit from Afghanistan was handled, in retrospect, it was still probably the right thing to do. The upside was limited and the American investment in Afghanistan had been huge: twenty years of fighting; $2 trillion in U.S. aid; countless Afghan casualties, twenty-one thousand Americans wounded, and nearly twenty-five hundred dead, including thirteen service members killed by a suicide bomber in the last chaotic days at the Kabul airport. It is hard to imagine how the Biden administration could have successfully managed simultaneously the Afghan withdrawal and the Ukraine and Israeli crises, which became all-consuming only months later.[30]

Immigration and Human Rights

An even more desperate humanitarian situation unfolded at the southern border, where migrants continued to flow into the United States from Haiti, Mexico, Guatemala, El Salvador, and Honduras. The U.S. Court of Appeals for the Ninth Circuit declared illegal Trump's punitive "remain in Mexico" policy, which Biden ended soon after he entered office.[31] But Trump's belt-and-suspenders alternative was to use a public-health rationale to block migrants from crossing the southern border: Trump cited Title 42 (the Public Health Service Act), making the dubious claim that all migrants at the southern border should be denied admission on a blanket basis because they could transmit Covid-19. The Trump administration's first issuance of a Title 42 order in March 2020 in response to the growing Covid crisis marked the first time that the Centers for Disease Control and Prevention had invoked its authority under this statute. The extraordinarily broad order suspended the right to introduce certain persons into the United States from countries where a quarantinable communicable disease exists, but limited that suspension to persons traveling from Canada or Mexico. The Department of Homeland Security was made responsible for implementing the order at the border.[32]

The Title 42 policy authorized summary expulsion of aliens without access to asylum, even if those individuals had been vaccinated, tested negative for Covid, and presented themselves without documents at a port of entry. As the D.C. Circuit later observed, it was not "credibly disputed" that these expulsions have resulted in a "stomach-churning" pattern "of death, torture, and rape."[33] The breadth and implementation of Title 42 authority again raised significant concerns about whether the United States was living up to its binding obligations under international human-rights and refugee law. Those obligations particularly included the Convention Against Torture and the Protocol Relating to the Status of Refugees (the Refugee Protocol), which entered into force in 1967 and modifies and incorporates the terms of the 1951 Refugee Convention. Under those provisions, U.S. law directs that "the Attorney General may not remove an alien to a country if the Attorney General decides that the alien's life or freedom would be threatened in that country because of the alien's race, religion, nationality, membership in a particular social group, or political opinion."[34]

During the campaign, both President Biden and Vice President Harris had criticized the Title 42 rationale, but they maintained it once they assumed office. Reportedly, some migrants were not even told where they were being taken when placed on deportation flights, learning only when they landed that they had been illegally returned to their home country or place of possible persecution or torture. That is the exact act of refoulement that is forbidden by the Convention Against Torture and the Refugee Convention. The inadequate procedures employed by the administration created an unacceptably high risk that a great many people deserving of asylum would instead be returned to countries where they had a credible fear of persecution, death, or torture. Then, while the Afghan exit raged, more than ten thousand Haitians appeared under a bridge in Del Rio, Texas. The television images conveyed the public impression of an administration that could not control its own border. Many of the Haitians were rounded up by men on horseback, a horrifying spectacle that both Biden and Harris condemned. Biden said, "It's wrong. It sends the wrong message around the world and sends the wrong message at home. It's simply not who we are." Nevertheless, those same Haitians were then summarily expelled under Title 42 authorities.[35]

In October 2021, on my last day serving in the Biden administration, I wrote an internal memo (later leaked, not by me). The memo explained why maintenance of the Title 42 policy was both illegal and inhumane and "not worthy of this Administration that I so strongly support." I argued that the Biden administration's humanitarian actions toward Afghan refugees stood in stark contrast to its continuing use of Title 42 to rebuff the pleas of thousands of Haitians and others arriving at the southern border, who were fleeing violence, persecution, or torture. I opined that the Biden administration's continued implementation of the Title 42 authority violated the United States' legal obligation not to expel or return ("*refouler*") individuals who fear persecution, death, or torture, especially migrants fleeing Haiti. This concern was only heightened by recent tragic events in Haiti, which had led the Biden administration to extend temporary protected status to Haitians already in the United States. Moreover, lawful, more humane alternatives plainly existed, and there were approaching opportunities in litigation to substitute those better policy alternatives for the flawed Title 42 policy.[36]

Immigration has been one of the few areas in which the federal courts have resisted recent presidential initiatives. Democratic-appointed lower-court judges generally checked Trump's most extreme immigration actions until the cases reached the Supreme Court; Republican-appointed judges—often chosen by plaintiffs through careful forum shopping—have regularly blocked Biden's. Since Biden took office, judges across the political spectrum have largely declined to defer to his administration's immigration policies.

Several courts have declared unlawful the administration's continuing use of Title 42 public-health authorities to expel asylum seekers without adequate refugee screening. When a Trump appointee writing for a unanimous D.C. Circuit panel invalidated the Title 42 policy's absence of screening, Biden prepared to abandon it. But then a Louisiana federal court blocked Biden's actions, leaving in place a policy that the Biden administration had publicly committed to repealing. When the D.C. Circuit reaffirmed its ruling, the Supreme Court stayed that ruling and initially decided to hear the case. But in February 2023, when Biden mooted the case by declaring an end to the Covid-19 public-health emergency, the Court dismissed the case from its calendar, ending judicial oversight of this policy for the time being.[37]

Meanwhile, Biden announced that the United States would grant humanitarian parole to up to thirty thousand migrants per month from Cuba, Haiti, Nicaragua, and Venezuela. This announcement came as part of a new border strategy under which the Departments of Homeland Security and Justice would apply another revised Trump-era policy called the "transit ban." Under the new rule, migrants would be prohibited from applying for asylum in the United States unless they were first turned away for safe harbor by another country. The new transit ban deemed ineligible migrants who do not go through authorized ports of entry. The collective legacy of these policies has been grim. As of this writing, Title 42 has been used to expel migrants, many of them asylum seekers, some 2.5 million times since its inception under the Trump administration.[38]

Sadly, the episode again confirmed a phenomenon that I called in chapter 5 "the Haiti paradigm in U.S. human-rights policy." The Haiti paradigm illustrated the broader interactive institutional dysfunction described here: when a perceived national security crisis arises, the executive reacts, Congress acquiesces, and the courts defer. The perverse result is an upside-down human-rights policy in which the U.S. government's official positions, legitimated by legislative acquiescence and judicial endorsement, end up being anti-refugee and tolerant of human-rights abuse.[39]

Outside the immigration area, other geopolitical events caused the Biden administration to soften its initial strong support for human rights. In response to Russia's invasion of Ukraine in 2022, the NATO nations imposed sanctions on Russian oil. This fed inflationary pressures throughout the West and created political pressure on Biden to find alternative sources of fossil fuels. In response, Biden started softening his position regarding human-rights violators in order to keep oil flowing.

Unfortunately, many of those who control large percentages of the world's fossil-fuel production happen to be gross human-rights violators, not just in the Middle East, but also in Venezuela and Russia. Accordingly, despite Biden's pledge to make Prince Mohammed bin Salman (MBS) of Saudi Arabia a "pariah" for his undisputed planning of the execution and dismemberment of the *Washington Post* columnist Jamal Khashoggi, Biden and his team held a series of accommodating meetings with MBS and other high-ranking Saudi officials. When MBS was civilly sued in Washington, D.C., the Biden administration asserted MBS's absolute immunity to obtain dismissal of the federal lawsuit. The decision was questionable, given that the United States plainly had competing interests at the time. On one hand, the United States regularly asserts reciprocal principles of immunity so that its own head of state will be offered protection from foreign courts. But that consideration has to be weighed against the United States' interest in ensuring that autocrats understand that the president means what he says about the centrality of human rights to U.S. policy. All things considered, silence would have been the better way to balance those competing national interests. There were ample judicial precedents to support a State Department decision to stay silent. Even when the immunity determination is considered an exercise of presidential power, the State Department should have made more explicit that its determination in no way foreclosed the president's option to declare another sitting head of state, such as Russian president Vladimir Putin, not immune for *jus cogens* violations should he come to the United States in the future.[40]

With the deepening humanitarian crisis in Yemen, U.S. military participation in the brutal Saudi military campaign seems certain to grow more controversial as Biden's presidency continues. Similarly, the administration made accommodating gestures toward Nicolas Maduro, the Venezuelan autocrat who controls roughly 10 percent of the world's oil. In short, America's continuing addiction to fossil fuels put the United States in the awkward position of condoning human-rights violations and watering down Biden's repeated vocal commitments to keep human rights at the center of U.S. foreign policy.

Russia's Invasion of Ukraine: Economic Sanctions

During the Obama years, Biden had been the administration's point person on the U.S. response to Russia's invasion of Crimea in 2014. One year into Biden's presidency, in February 2022, Russia launched a full-scale invasion of its neighbor Ukraine. Putin used false claims that Ukraine had committed genocide against its own citizens as a pretext for committing atrocities against thousands of innocent Ukrainians. Putin's war displaced millions and inflicted tens of billions of dollars of destruction on Ukraine's infrastructure. Biden's team strongly rebounded from the chaotic Afghan withdrawal to orchestrate the most comprehensive display of multilateral cooperation and alliance management since the First Gulf War. Biden and his team galvanized NATO and the G7 to organize the Western alliance from Canada to Japan to help Ukraine protect its fledgling democracy. Supported by a rare bipartisan congressional vote, NATO was expanded to include Finland and Sweden. Through rapid deployment of Western trainers and massive transfers of precision weapons, Biden's coalition thwarted Putin's initial blitzkrieg strategy, isolated Russia economically, and empowered Ukraine to inflict significant losses on Russia's invading army, all without loss of American life.[41]

President Biden's simultaneous response to the twin Ukraine and Covid-19 crises marked perhaps the most dramatic peacetime exercise of presidential power in four decades. Particularly dramatic was the Biden administration's aggressive use of coordinated economic sanctions, enhanced almost weekly post-invasion. The administration imposed bans on the provision of technology for oil and gas exploration and on the provision of credit to Russian oil companies and state banks, and imposed travel restrictions and asset freezes on Russian oligarchs close to Putin, especially those connected to the Crimean annexation. In the wake of the invasion, Biden exploited congressional outrage by persuading Congress to enact statutes to enhance his authority to coerce. The United States invoked the Export Control Reform Act of 2018 to impose strict export controls on sensitive exports to Russia. But the vast bulk of the sanctions were imposed by executive orders and regulatory decrees under existing statutory authorities or directives.[42]

Biden's use of economic sanctions rested on the declaration of seven new national emergencies, which brought to more than forty the number of presidentially declared national emergencies in effect as of January 2023. Most of Biden's sanctions were conventional "blocking freezes" under the authority provided by the International Emergency Economic Powers Act (IEEPA) to freeze the assets of designated entities and block related transactions within the United States or by U.S. persons, including U.S. financial institutions. But Biden went further, blocking central bank assets to limit Russia's ability to secure funds through sovereign debt. The statute authorizes the executive to confiscate and take title to ("vest") assets only "when the United States is engaged in armed hostilities or has been attacked by a foreign country or foreign nationals"—which Russia had not done. But some prominent scholars interpreted that law to allow the United States not just to freeze, but to seize and liquidate Russian Central Bank assets because the statute gives the president authority to "nullify, void . . . or prohibit" any foreign country from "holding" or "exercising any right, power, or privilege" over property in which it has "any interest" and to "direct and compel" the "exportation" of such property. Others challenged that view, recalling that, unlike the powers granted under the Trading with the Enemy Act (TWEA), the president's peacetime statutory emergency economic powers authorized him only to "seize, not freeze" foreign assets.[43]

Biden's political strategy aligned with an aggressive "lawfare" strategy adopted by Ukraine and its lawyers, which supplemented Ukraine's military resistance and multilateral sanctions with international litigation before a plethora of international courts and tribunals.[44] As I have described elsewhere, that lawfare campaign grew out of Ukraine's five-part grand strategy toward Russia: information, isolation, illegality, diplomacy, and accountability.[45] Open-source information and a series of lawsuits consistently showed that Russia's actions are illegal, justifying the economic sanctions to make Putin an isolated outlaw in an interdependent world. By isolating Putin and stalemating his progress on the battlefield, Ukraine sought to provoke diplomacy—the sort of comprehensive process of peace negotiations that produced the Dayton accords that ended the Bosnian war—while leaving open the fifth and final element: criminal and civil accountability in domestic and international forums.

The U.N. General Assembly adopted a resolution recognizing the need to establish, in cooperation with Ukraine, "an international mechanism for reparation for damage, loss or injury, and arising from the internationally wrongful acts of the Russian Federation in or against Ukraine." More than one hundred thousand Ukrainians have already died in Putin's bloody war, and Ukraine estimates that it has incurred more than $150 billion in infrastructure damage, an amount that it hopes to reclaim from some $1.14 trillion in frozen Russian assets. So a critical question will be whether the Biden administration will seek to stretch the statutory limits of its emergency-economic-power authority to go beyond freezing to seizing Russian assets in order to compensate Ukrainian survivors.[46]

Bringing peace to Ukraine will sorely test not only the Biden administration's bandwidth, but also its diplomatic skills. Even though he has reunited the West to oppose Russia, Biden has proved far less successful in reuniting America to address such basic issues as climate change, gun control, and reproductive rights. The United States now stands out as the world's greatest superpower with one of the most dysfunctional domestic political systems. As the Ukraine crisis has worn on, it has become yet another "proof of concept" for Biden's grand strategy of investing in democratic alliances. Russia's brazen invasion of Ukraine has starkly raised the question whether the twenty-first century ushered in a renewed emphasis on a "thinner" approach to international law, under which law will play a more interstitial role. As the Israel-Hamas war deepens and Republican support for Ukraine softens, Biden may need to resort to even more unilateralism to manage an increasingly tumultuous foreign policy.[47]

Taking Stock: The National Security Constitution Today

The Biden era confirms that over the past five decades, the National Security Constitution has moved steadily away from *Youngstown* toward *Curtiss-Wright*. I have personally witnessed this transformation, which has affected all three branches of the federal government: first, while I worked in the federal courts and the Reagan Justice Department during the early 1980s, then at the State Department from 1998 until 2001, again from 2009 until 2013, and most recently in 2021, at the start of the Biden administration. On each return stint, I have observed how foreign-policy power has shifted further and further away from Congress toward the executive branch as a whole. The national security establishment has exploded in size, swallowing up resources at the expense of work in diplomacy and justice. The 9/11 mentality has reshaped the foreign-relations bureaucracy. The resulting bureaucratic structure too often resists new priorities in favor of combatting more familiar threats. Institutional obsession over past dangers has hindered the Biden administration's efforts to turn the page.

In foreign affairs, even the longtime senator Joe Biden—who widely proclaims his love of the Senate—now operates almost entirely by executive fiat. Executive war making continues to proceed on the basis of classified policy memoranda, with minimal congressional oversight, under broad readings of

Article II and decades-old legislative authorizations for the use of military force.[48] Biden has continued an era of shadow war making that has clouded his effort to end the "forever war." He has tried to pull back from Trump's growing military confrontation with Iran, but he has continued to use drones for out-of-theater targeting. He has launched targeted air strikes against senior al Qaeda leaders and targets in eastern Syria used by Iran-supported non-state militia groups, and smaller-scale military operations in Somalia against al-Shabaab, an associated force of al Qaeda. Although each strike has been legally justified on its own facts, the overall trend—without serious congressional debate or chance for the public to grapple with the president's reasons for striking—has reinforced the public impression that the forever war continues. In June 2022, a bipartisan group of nearly fifty members of Congress responded by reintroducing a bill similar to one vetoed by President Trump in 2019. That bill would end the U.S. logistical and personnel support and intelligence sharing that has enabled offensive strikes by the Saudi-led coalition in Yemen. In early 2023, the Senate, but not the House, enacted bipartisan legislation to repeal the 1991 and 2002 authorizations for the use of military force against Iraq, formally end the Gulf and Iraq Wars, and reassert Congress's constitutional role in deciding whether and when to commit U.S. troops to future conflicts.[49]

Whereas most recent Republican administrations have unabashedly seized power, successor Democratic administrations with slim legislative majorities have seriously undercorrected for past executive overreach. As described above, the Reagan and George W. Bush administrations trumpeted executive power as a defining feature of their constitutional vision. The George H. W. Bush, Clinton, Obama, and Biden presidencies—all afflicted by weak legislative support—also resorted to ad hoc unilateralism to respond to particular national security crises. Under Donald Trump's presidency, this interactive institutional dysfunction and executive unilateralism reached new and crisis levels. Until Trump, those who believed in constitutional government could assume that a president would have *some* internalized limit at which public duty or shame would dictate self-restraint. But Trump displayed no such limit, expressing unique contempt not just for the *Youngstown* vision of the Constitution, but for legal constraints of any kind.

At this writing, Biden has carefully avoided the most extreme constitutional claims of the Trump administration. He has not, for example, claimed the power to terminate long-standing international arrangements without paying lip service to interbranch consultation. Nor has he usurped Congress's power of the purse by claiming emergency powers to build a border wall using funds that Congress had expressly withheld.[50]

But Congress's general response to presidential initiatives continues to be institutional passivity and a focus on extraneous issues. Biden's first years witnessed only a few prominent pieces of foreign-policy legislation: a climate-change bill enacted on a party-line basis and bipartisan votes to boost U.S. competitiveness with China and to support Finland's and Sweden's admission to NATO. But generally speaking, the congressional process for international lawmaking has virtually broken down. As one long-serving congressman put it a decade ago: "Taxpayers are hiring mediocre talent, candidates who think their job is to ignore policy in order to get elected and reelected."[51]

Foreign-policy compromise has become a dirty word, as once-bipartisan issues have become deeply politicized. On the House side, starting in 1995, Newt Gingrich centralized power in a politicized Speaker's office, which he merged with the majority leader's and whip's offices, effectively gutting the role of committee chairs.[52] Opposition legislators began to see their role not as making bipartisan foreign policy, but as waging total war against the other party's president, even shutting down the government when expedient to score political points. As one departing member described it:

> Objective information sources such as the Democratic Study Group were banned. Leadership told members how to vote on most issues and force-fed talking points so that everyone could stay "on message." All major floor votes became partisan steamrollers with one big "yes" or "no" vote at the end of debate, with . . . no coherent alternatives . . . allowed to be considered, only approval of party doctrine. Instead of limited legislative freedom, a member's only choice was between being a teammate or a traitor.[53]

The national security consequences of polarization in the House were graphically illustrated in January 2023, when a small faction of the newly elected Republican majority blocked the House of Representatives from doing any business whatsoever, forcing four days of voting on electing the Speaker. During that period, no member of the House could be sworn in, obtain access to classified materials, or serve on any foreign-affairs or national security oversight committees.[54] The elected Speaker was then ousted, causing even more chaos. The Senate divide has become even more polarized, paralyzed, and zero-sum. Senate electoral outcomes now closely track presidential outcomes, which creates greater pressure for senators to vote with their party's president and less incentive to make deals across party lines.

Each party has been able to assemble a strong Senate majority only once in the last twenty years. Yet because the minority can always envision gaining legislative control in the next election, minority senators have become far less inclined to give bipartisan approaches any perceived victories. Votes across the aisle have largely given way to lockstep minority opposition, which hamstrings the majority from winning any opposition votes for any key initiatives by the other party's president. The majority can therefore legislate only when there is near-total unity within their own party. This gives a tiny number of "swing senators" disproportionate leverage to block or dampen their own party's legislative ambitions, but not enough leverage to ensure that the opposition party will join their initiatives. There are not enough of those swing senators, however, to build regular or reliable bipartisan coalitions that can overcome the sixty-vote threshold to end a filibuster. Finally, as America's population concentrates in the largest states, states representing a shrinking percentage of the national population have become even more over-represented in the Senate, with smaller segments of the electorate controlling more Senate seats. One experienced congressional observer called this "a distortion that is so great it puts into question the entire legitimacy of the Senate as a governing body." The overall result is far less foreign-policy legislation, and even less that truly represents the will of the people.[55]

As important, public perception has come to treat this reality as the new normal. In most foreign-policy situations, everyone now *expects* Congress to do nothing. Members never want to vote on war when such votes are among the only public acts sufficient to get legislators ousted at the polls. In America's sharply polarized polity, the legislature has become so narrowly divided that it has become nearly impossible to quickly compose legislative majorities capable of overcoming a filibuster, let alone confirm executive officials for key Senate-confirmed foreign-policy posts. Individual senators and individual staffers have been afforded extraordinary power to hold nominees for no good reason. So when a crisis arises in the world, the public, the Congress, U.S. allies, and the media all now demand *executive* action. This universal expectation has only furthered the centralization of foreign-policy power and initiative in the White House and the National Security Council. At the same time, it has dampened the incentives for political appointees to consult with a Congress to which they do not owe confirmation, or which unconscionably delayed their confirmation. Even executive-branch officials with instincts to consult or cooperate more with legislators increasingly find themselves facing a binary choice between unilateral action or no action. Because the executive is punished politically for passivity, not surprisingly, the executive branch usually opts for unilateral action.[56]

Finally, the judiciary has only modestly moderated these trends. As the executive has populated the courts, judges appointed by both parties have with striking frequency—except in the immigration area—either rubber-stamped executive actions or dismissed individual challenges to them on preliminary grounds. To be sure, the Supreme Court responded to the excesses of the George W. Bush administration by holding against the executive branch in a famous string of Guantánamo cases, discussed in chapter 6. But as chapter 7 noted, inside the government, these cases have had surprisingly little real impact in checking the migration toward executive unilateralism.[57]

Academic commentators have read great meaning into such cases as *Zivotofsky v. Clinton* (*Zivotofsky I*), discussed in chapter 8, in which the Supreme Court declined to apply the political-question doctrine to bar review of the president's actions in the face of a contrary congressional statute, and *Bond v. United States* (*Bond I*), which granted a criminal defendant civil standing to challenge, on Tenth Amendment grounds, a statute that implemented a major multinational treaty.[58] But these decisions notwithstanding, the courts of appeals have generally continued to rely on expansive understandings of justiciability doctrines, procedural obstacles, or immunity defenses to avoid reaching the merits of any civil dispute that arguably touches on national security. In military-contractor cases, for example, lower courts have continued to invoke the political-question doctrine to throw out ordinary tort suits. In others, the lower courts have shifted their focus from justiciability to dismissals for failure to state a claim, upholding statutes that strip jurisdiction from the federal courts to hear certain kinds of foreign-policy claims or that displace state law in the name of unspecified "foreign policy" interests.[59]

Commentators have also not fully acknowledged the extent to which the courts that do hear cases *on the merits* go on to hold for the executive. Two theories have emerged to uphold executive action in foreign affairs at the merits stage. First, as occurred in the *Zivotofsky* litigation, the courts may apply a "*Youngstown* category three" theory to find a legislative enactment unenforceable because it unconstitutionally invades the president's exclusive constitutional powers. Second, a "statutory *Curtiss-Wright*" theory of delegation authorizes a court to conclude that Congress has conferred a greater degree of discretion on the president through foreign-affairs-related statutes. Such a theory relies on *Curtiss-Wright*'s suggestion that the delegated statutory authority overlaps with or complements the president's foreign-affairs powers under Article II. This broad theory of statutory delegation now enjoys the support of at least five members of today's Supreme Court. This approach would effectively enshrine *Curtiss-Wright*'s dicta into holding. It would empower the president to operate virtually alone in such traditionally congressional fields as immigration and trade, invoking expansive claims not of constitutional power, but of broadly delegated statutory authority. Citing the executive's claimed functional monopoly of foreign-policy judgment, numerous circuit-level decisions have doubled down on granting the executive special deference to make foreign policy through self-serving interpretations of foreign-relations statutes.[60]

In short, because the president keeps reacting, Congress keeps acquiescing, and the courts keep deferring, the resulting process has created *unbalanced institutional participation* in foreign-affairs decision-making. This recent history teaches that we cannot count on America's National Security Constitution to protect itself.

Unfortunately, the current political environment gives no political actor either the tools or the incentives to address underlying systemic problems. Because impeachment was designed as an extreme constitutional remedy for individual unfitness in office, it was never intended as a substitute for ongoing interbranch accountability or as a tool for fixing deeper systemic malfunctions of our constitutional system. Before Trump, presidential impeachments had been rare and cataclysmic events in American political life and moments for intense national self-reflection. But the stubborn resistance of Trump's supporters converted both impeachment exercises into rote political exercises that ended in almost party-line votes of House impeachment and Senate non-conviction. As Senate minority leader Mitch McConnell's behavior revealed, even when the legislative leaders of a defeated president's own party disapprove his behavior, they may decline to support conviction because he is leaving office anyway. The person named the winner of the next presidential election, in this case Biden, will rarely wish to revisit such a backward-looking issue. When legislative control is closely contested, the ruling party will have strong political incentives to back the president and avoid seeking institutional fixes. When such gaps are exposed during a president's first term, even an aggressive opposition will hesitate to call for impeachment, opting instead to use any evidence unveiled to defeat the incumbent at the polls. For all these reasons, both of the impeachment efforts against Trump failed. Significantly, the impeachment efforts against Richard Nixon and Bill Clinton happened during their second terms, when no other political mechanism was available for their removal. After both Clinton and Trump survived impeachment and finished out their elective terms, it seems far less likely that, after impeachment, any future president with majority support in the Senate would ever resign.

The report by special counsel Robert Mueller further illustrated this recurring trend toward undercorrection, aided by expansive theories of presidential discretion, immunity, and exemption. Mueller clearly felt limited by the executive regulations constraining the special counsel and pro-executive-branch Justice Department opinions touting expansive claims of executive privilege and prosecutorial inability to indict a sitting president. Mueller's public presentations of his report's findings seemed chilled by his understandable desire not to emulate former FBI director Jim Comey's flagrant pronouncements elaborating his decision not to indict Hillary Clinton for her private emails. Popular disappointment in the report's carefully worded findings flowed from Attorney General Bill Barr's prerelease spinning, unrealistic public expectations created by media overhype, and a distinctively American tendency to expect the narrow prosecutorial tools that Mueller wielded to solve deeper structural problems.

Only when the January 6 House Select Committee was finally composed did the full scope of the constitutional violations committed come to light. But the January 6 Committee prominently included only two Republican members, who both later left office, having lost popularity because of their willingness to break from their party to investigate Trump's post-defeat abuses. The January 6 Committee found that "President Trump and a number of other individuals made a series of very specific plans, ultimately with multiple separate elements, but all with one overriding objective: to corruptly obstruct, impede, or influence the counting of electoral votes on January 6th, and thereby overturn the lawful results of the election." In light of that conclusion, the committee for the first time made four criminal referrals to the Justice Department regarding the conduct of a former president: the committee recommended that Trump be prosecuted for obstructing an official proceeding, for conspiracy to defraud the United States, for conspiracy to make a false statement, and for "incit[ing]," "assist[ing]," or "aid[ing] and comfort[ing] an insurrection."[61] But in early 2023, the January 6 Committee's work came to an abrupt end when the Republicans assumed control of the House.

Later that summer, a grand jury in Washington, D.C., indicted Trump on charges mirroring many of the charges made in the January 6 Committee's final report.[62] The indictment accused him of leading a conspiracy to subvert American democracy by repeating knowingly false claims of election fraud, encouraging false electors, pressuring the vice president, and directing a mob of supporters to the U.S. Capitol on January 6 to obstruct the congressional session certifying Joe Biden's election as president. But the president's party continued to brush both January 6 investigations aside, going to extraordinary lengths to normalize Trump's behavior with denialist apologies that continue to this day.

When our constitutional decision-making process has become so seriously imbalanced, we cannot hope to restore constitutional equilibrium simply by "throwing these rascals out." After Watergate—another case of deliberate, malicious domestic interference into electoral processes—a special prosecutor named President Nixon as an unindicted criminal co-conspirator. Congress enacted stiffer laws regarding campaign conduct and began impeachment proceedings against Nixon because of his extensive efforts to cover up, even though no one seriously claimed that Nixon had participated in the Watergate burglary itself. After both the Iran-contra affair and 9/11, bipartisan commissions and congressional investigations chronicled in detail what happened and made policy recommendations to avoid repetition in the future. To address the foreign-policy dysfunction exposed by Vietnam, Congress passed national security "framework statutes" to restructure war powers, intelligence oversight, emergency economic powers, and international agreement making. But none of the official responses to recent executive excesses were designed to make broad policy suggestions for institutional reform.

Were successor administrations or other governmental institutions to give the pendulum a strong push in the opposite direction, this historical march toward unilateral presidentialism could be arrested or slowed. But instead, America's persistent institutional political response has been to *undercorrect,* a pattern that, if repeated, can only license more nakedly unilateralist presidents.

In sum, the National Security Constitution hovers dangerously close to the precipice. It remains just one election away from constitutional calamity. Halting, incremental responses cannot repair the deeper structural problem. It is high time to pursue more urgent policy action. The national security danger posed by an executive's extreme contempt for the rule of law demands a more sustained and ambitious counter-agenda. The next two chapters sketch both an overarching strategy and a blueprint of specific reforms to prod our constitutional system to respond to the threat of executive unilateralism in the areas of war powers, international agreement making and breaking, emergency powers, intelligence oversight, and information control. The concluding chapter anticipates and answers likely critiques of these reform proposals.

PART THREE

A NATIONAL SECURITY CONSTITUTION FOR THE TWENTY-FIRST CENTURY

10

A Strategy for Reform

MORE THAN TWO DECADES AFTER SEPTEMBER 11, 2001, the National Security Constitution has taken on a strikingly unbalanced cast. In twenty-first-century practice, foreign-relations law has become national security law. Virtually all foreign-affairs issues have been reframed in national security terms. And because so much of foreign-affairs law seems to have become justification for unilateral exercises of executive power, at times it seems almost as if foreign-affairs law is not law at all. In the past five decades, our national security decision-making process has deteriorated into one that forces the president to react to perceived crises, that permits Congress to avoid accountability for important foreign-policy decisions, and that encourages the courts to condone these decisions on the merits or by avoiding judicial review.

A policy of balanced institutional participation in the making of foreign policy is not only more true to the U.S. Constitution. As a policy matter, the *Youngstown* vision better supports democracy, avoids authoritarian capture, and lowers the risks of militarism and catastrophic outcomes. History teaches that executive unilateralism has generally failed to advance our national interests in the international arena. The Trump era repeatedly showed that secretive or impulsive unilateral executive decision-making—missing the representative qualities derived from congressional participation and the legal constraints imposed by judicial supervision—guarantees neither wise nor effective foreign-policy making. Because the United States is a party to a network of closely interconnected treaties, for example, unilateral decisions to break or bend one treaty usually force the United States into vicious cycles of treaty violation, and thereby reinforce the country's reputation for lawlessness and diminish its soft power.[1] The American history reviewed in the first two parts shows that foreign-policy dominance by any single branch fosters reactive interbranch conflict that ultimately jeopardizes the long-term interests of the nation as a whole. Internecine political warfare plainly harms the national interest when interbranch disputes determine critical national positions in the international realm. As the House Foreign Affairs Committee chair Lee Hamilton pointedly told Lieutenant Colonel Oliver North at the end of his Iran-contra testimony: "You said . . . the Congress would declare itself the winner . . . but may I suggest . . . [w]e all lost. The interests of the United States have been damaged by what happened."[2]

As recently as 2001, the *Youngstown* vision of checks and balances held sway. But today's National Security Constitution looks dramatically different from its Cold War predecessor. During each of my four tours in government, I have observed how foreign-policy power has increasingly shifted toward the executive branch. Twenty-first-century national security threats have given weak and strong presidents alike institutional incentives to monopolize the foreign-policy response, a polarized Congress even greater incentives to acquiesce, and the courts continuing reason to defer or rubber-stamp. The interactive synergy between these institutional incentives explains the steady migration from a *Youngstown* vision toward a *Curtiss-Wright* vision of executive unilateralism in postwar foreign policy.

Judged strictly as constitutional law, *Curtiss-Wright* has not yet displaced *Youngstown* as the controlling vision of the National Security Constitution. Measured by the high standards for "constitutional acquiescence" set by Justice Frankfurter's *Youngstown* opinion, the observable historical practice over the past half century has not, as yet, resulted in a *permanent* redistribution of constitutional authority.[4] Since the Founding, the provisions of the Constitution regarding foreign affairs have never been subject to formal constitutional amendment. Instead, periodic framework legislation, judicial decisions, and executive practice accepted by the other branches have adapted our National Security Constitution to meet changing times. As chapter 1 recounted, the framework statutes and customary norms established during the early years of the Republic worked a de facto amendment of the National Security Constitution by shifting the president's role in foreign affairs from the secondary one assigned to presidents by the Framers to the dominant role presidents have since traditionally played. During succeeding historical eras, executive practice endorsed by judicial decision and congressional approval consolidated the president's exclusive authority over recognition, diplomatic relations, and negotiations, and ratified new constitutional modes of agreement making. But when *Curtiss-Wright*'s dicta, coupled with unprecedented presidential activism in the years after World War II, threatened to further expand those zones of exclusive presidential discretion, new framework legislation, namely the National Security Act of 1947 and the post-Vietnam foreign-affairs statutes, along with an authoritative Supreme Court decision in *Youngstown* in 1952, reaffirmed the constitutional primacy of balanced institutional participation.

As parts 1 and 2 recounted, since Vietnam, quasi-constitutional custom in this field has shifted decidedly in favor of executive dominance. But to allow executive practice to perpetually remake constitutional law in this area would authorize successive presidents to rewrite the National Security Constitution to fit their shifting views of the exigencies of the external world. More troubling, such a practice allows the president's agents to claim constitutional legitimacy for arbitrary, unsupervised, and even unauthorized exercises of executive discretion. As Justice Jackson observed, in the relatively rare foreign-relations-law case in which judges "review and approve [executive action that oversteps the bounds of constitutionality], that passing incident becomes the doctrine of the Constitution. There it has a generative power of its own, and all that it creates will be in its own image."[5]

But even decades of informal accommodations among the three branches have generated new pockets of quasi-customary constitutional law only in particular areas of foreign policy. Practice alone cannot permanently amend the National Security Constitution unless such practice is additionally blessed by authoritative judicial decision, framework statute, or constitutional amendment, none of which has yet occurred. Although the Supreme Court has trumpeted executive discretion in foreign affairs with broad dicta, the Court has supported that language with relatively narrow holdings and refusals to adjudicate on the merits. Congress has not repealed its framework legislation of the 1970s. No constitutional amendment formally increasing the president's power has been adopted, nor is one pending.

Before *Curtiss-Wright* becomes the new normal, we must define and implement a coherent menu of politically achievable acts for corrective national security reform. We must preserve a strong chief executive, of course, who operates *within* a strong system of internal and external checks and balances and is thus constitutionally accountable to the electorate. The goal of national security reform should not be just to restrain executive initiative, but to revitalize Congress, the courts, and other players as institutional counterweights to the presidency. This will require both a master strategy and a detailed blueprint of constitutionally appropriate responses to address the institutional defects that have been laid bare.

The next chapter reviews in more detail specific areas of law that deserve particular attention in the years ahead. This chapter sketches a master strategy based on commonsense principles: Break the interactive institutional cycle that leads to executive unilateralism. Reform the executive branch by strengthening internal checks and balances to discourage *Curtiss-Wright* and encourage *Youngstown* tendencies. Limit the resort by executive legal opinions to overbroad assertions of plenary constitutional power. Equalize the playing field with respect to expertise in foreign affairs through institutional reforms in Congress. Make the judiciary a more potent source of oversight by reducing barriers to justiciability and limiting doctrines that overly credit national security claims as reasons to defer to impulsive executive action. And create space for other actors—states and localities, the media, private-public partnerships, and alliance politics—to act as meaningful counterweights to executive unilateralism in foreign affairs.

Three decades ago, I urged Congress to enact a comprehensive national-security charter to accomplish this rebalancing.[6] If the political will could be mustered for such sweeping reform, recent bipartisan legislative proposals— like the Senate's National Security Powers Act and its House counterpart, the National Security Reforms and Accountability Act—offer a possible foundation on which to base broader structural reform to rebalance the institutional allocation of national security powers.[7]

But until such ambitious framework legislation becomes politically achievable, I propose instead a collection of changes—by the executive, legislative, and judicial branches—that can be implemented either as a package or piecemeal over time. Plainly, executive practice has gained undue predominance as the prime source of customary constitutional law in the area of foreign affairs. The process of reconstituting our National Security Constitution should be confided instead to all three branches working together: to a presidency that will accept internal and external constraints; to a Congress

hat enacts laws clarifying institutional responsibilities in foreign affairs; and
o courts that fulfill their duty to draw boundaries between lawful and unlaw-
ul conduct.[8] Such measures would supply much-needed counterweights to
unchallenged executive practice in this area. Even targeted legislation on
particular issues would replace outmoded parts of the barnacled National
Security Act of 1947 with more recent, considered statements of how na-
ional security policy should be made jointly by Congress and the president
and construed by the courts.

To be clear, the goal of such reform proposals would not be to encourage
congressional micromanagement or improvident judicial activism in foreign affairs, but rather to reduce the isolation that currently surrounds
executive-branch activities, to enhance internal executive-branch delibera-
ions, and to increase congressional-executive dialogue while foreign-policy
objectives are being set and initiatives implemented. By so doing, even piecemeal reform over time could modify normative expectations *within* each
foreign-policy institution and reduce cynicism about balanced institutional
participation in foreign-affairs decision-making. If some or all of these proposals were adopted over the next few decades, the interaction between these
revised incentives should generate a more virtuous circle of change in
nstitutional and interactive behavior.

Executive Restructuring

First and most obviously, the executive branch must address its own defi-
ciencies. The executive should recast its current structure to incorporate
more reliable mechanisms to ensure *internal* checks and balances. Reforms
should address internal legal review, law-enforcement independence, con-
licts of interest, and abuse of plenary constitutional authorities for military
action.[9]

Better Legal Advice

Since 1949, more than a dozen private and public studies have examined
how to better organize the foreign-policy apparatus of the executive branch.[10]
Alexander George has made the case for creating a decision-making system
hat encourages competing foreign-policy views to be presented to the presi-
lent for final decision.[11] This adversarial approach, extended also to test the

legality of foreign-policy initiatives, would have discouraged the kind of secret, unchallenged agency legal opinions that proliferated during the Reagan, Bush 43, and Trump administrations.[12]

Three changes should be made to ensure that the president receives loyal but impartial national security legal advice. First, the White House counsel's office should shrink in size, and the National Security Council legal adviser should no longer function as a "double-hatted" deputy White House counsel vulnerable to political oversight and influence. Instead, the NSC legal adviser, advised by a group of foreign-relations lawyers from the general counsels' offices of the participating agencies, should give independent advice directly to the national security adviser and deputy.[13]

Second, an adversarial process inside and outside the executive branch should test the legality of all proposed foreign-policy initiatives. To ensure that executive initiatives will not commence without genuine consensus, or on the basis of one general counsel's secret and self-serving invocation of "find the statute," a formal executive order should make permanent the requirement of the type of interagency lawyers group that was convened during the Clinton, Obama, and Biden administrations.[14] Such interagency review would mimic the centralized review of agency rulemaking that the Office of Management and Budget has conducted since the Reagan administration.[15] The task of obtaining and coordinating competing legal analyses could be confided to the NSC's legal adviser. As in earlier times, the legal adviser to the NSC should rarely generate written opinions, instead playing the roles of discerning consensus, breaking ties, and deriving the best advice available from the detailed analyses of the expert agencies. The participants in the interagency legal process must press the NSC legal adviser to ensure that public written rationales are offered for all major legal decisions.[16]

Third, we should return to the more efficient and effective system that functioned in the 1980s, when most detailed foreign-affairs legal advice came from two large, established foreign-policy offices with expertise in both foreign-affairs law and international and humanitarian law: the Legal Adviser's Office at the State Department and the General Counsel's Office at the Defense Department.[17] As one government practitioner has chronicled international-lawmaking processes and the United States' reputation as a law-abiding actor are particularly harmed when its covert and possibly illegal behavior later comes to public light. State Department review of executive initiatives in foreign affairs, for consistency with international law, would be fully consistent with statute and historical tradition.[18]

In the Judiciary Act of 1789, Congress authorized the attorney general to provide opinions on questions of law to the president and the heads of executive departments, a responsibility that the attorney general has over time delegated to the Office of Legal Counsel.[19] Despite that office's notorious failures during the Bush 43 era, over the last four decades academic scholarship—much of it written by OLC alumni from both parties (of whom I am one)—has continued to exaggerate the office's centrality in the giving of foreign-policy and national security legal advice.[20] In fact, in most of the interagency national security meetings that I attended since 2009, the Justice Department input came not from the Office of Legal Counsel, but from the National Security Division, which was created after September 11.

Many of the OLC opinions generated since the George W. Bush administration greatly exaggerate the breadth of presidential power in foreign affairs. They should be systematically reviewed for their correctness and withdrawn when found incorrect. The office should adopt public internal principles of "best practices" and apply them to this review. The office should publicly overrule a number of plainly incorrect OLC opinions from previous eras, some of which were apparently generated as post hoc justifications for controversial national security decisions.[21] The office should revise its opinions to clarify that no person is above the law with respect to investigation, indictment, conviction, or sentencing. Even as extreme an advocate of presidential power as the late former Whitewater prosecutor Ken Starr argued that the Office of Legal Counsel had incorrectly concluded that a sitting president is not indictable. The office should now review its precedent and clarify that a sitting or former president can violate federal criminal law and is in fact constitutionally indictable, even while in office, when he commits obstruction of justice.[22]

Even more troubling than bad advice has been no advice: when the Justice Department has not been consulted at all. As one former assistant attorney general recalled, the Iran-contra affair ensued after the Reagan administration unwisely restricted the attorney general's participation in the approval and review of sensitive foreign-policy and intelligence matters.[23] Congress should modify the findings requirements in all relevant intelligence statutes to require the transmission of such written findings to Congress not only with the president's signature, but also with the attorney general's certified approval as to form and legality, a prerequisite that already applies to all executive orders.[24]

Law-Enforcement Independence

The Biden Justice Department should revise internal regulations to protect the independence and integrity of the Justice Department and FBI by establishing institutional checks to ensure that the president does not abuse law-enforcement powers for partisan political purposes. Because the Constitution grants the president such broad pardon powers, the procedures for ensuring the constitutional exercise of those powers should be clarified and regularized through a combination of executive practice, institutional reform, and statute. The president could officially declare, for example, the norm that presidents may not pardon themselves. The federal government could establish the kind of independent clemency commission that many states have created. Congress could enact a statute, as a majority of states have recently done, to authorize federal prisoners to go back to court, not to the executive, to seek a reduction of their sentences.[25]

Special counsel Robert Mueller's investigation into Russian electoral interference revealed the weakness of the current special-counsel procedures when national security abuse by the executive is exposed. Trump showed that unrelenting threats to fire the special counsel, limit the scope of the counsel's investigation, spin the sealed findings to his advantage, and offer to pardon the targets of the investigation could intimidate and hamstring a special counsel's investigation. After a number of uncontrolled special- or independent counsel investigations in the late twentieth century, the Justice Department revised its regulations to prevent abuse of the special-counsel system. Past abuses by independent counsel had warranted some revision.[26] But those revisions went too far: the regulations now treat the special counsel as an internal Justice Department employee, barred by department rules from making public statements about ongoing investigations. The special counsel is authorized only to file an internal confidential report to the attorney general. These Justice Department regulations should be revised to instead authorize the special counsel to issue a public report similar to the bipartisan 9/11 Commission's report. That report should offer factual background, specific public recommendations to prevent recurrence, and a finding whether the fact gathered are sufficient to show that the president has committed a crime (whether or not the president may be indicted for it while in office).[27]

Conflicts of Interest

The Trump era also exposed conflicts of interest as a serious national security threat. Why should the Saudis, for example, ever deal with the U.S. embassy in Riyadh if they can simply do business directly with the White House by quietly meeting with the president's proxies at his local D.C. hotel?

The foreign-emoluments clause states that "no Person holding any Office of Profit or Trust under them, shall, without the Consent of the Congress, accept of any present, Emolument, Office, or Title, of any kind whatever, from any King, Prince, or foreign State."[28] But the Justice Department's current reading of that clause to allow private business deals permits foreign nations to curry favor with the president by purchasing real estate from one of his companies; to pursue an advantage by granting intellectual-property benefits to the president immediately upon his taking office; and to approve a regulatory deal that personally enriches the president. These are not just hypotheticals, but allegations in a congressional emoluments-clause suit brought against President Trump. Upon taking office, presidents should be required by law, enforced by criminal penalties, to put their holdings in a blind trust and expressly relinquish any supervisory role in their businesses. Reading the clause correctly—to prohibit private financial interactions with foreign governments unless the president first obtains the consent of Congress—would enable Congress to exercise its critical oversight role under the Constitution and thereby diminish foreign influences that improperly interfere with American national security and foreign policy.[29]

Moreover, that clause does not operate alone: it sits atop a broad web of governmental ethics rules designed to protect against undue influence in the making of national security and foreign policy. New transparency and disclosure mandates should expressly apply public-corruption and ethics laws to the president, senior executive officials, and legislators so they cannot mix foreign policy with private business. New laws should require the president and all presidential candidates to disclose their taxes for the previous decade and to account publicly for their income, holdings, and management of assets and investments. Congress should enact a bill, introduced by the chair of the House Ways and Means Committee, to amend the Internal Revenue

Code to provide for examination and disclosure of presidential income-tax returns.[30]

Restraining Military Adventurism

The next chapter broadly addresses the issue of executive war making. But to restrain impulsive and illegal presidential uses of military power, four urgent internal executive restraints should be immediately clarified by clearer executive interpretations of existing laws. These restraints could later be codified into legislation, if necessary, when doing so becomes politically possible.

First, in 1977, after the Church (Senate) and the Pike (House) Committee hearings revealed U.S. assassinations, President Gerald Ford issued Executive Order 11,905, which prohibits executive-branch personnel from engaging in, or conspiring to engage in, political assassination. In 1981, President Reagan issued Executive Order 12,333, which, as amended, remains in effect today and limits application of that prohibition to individuals "acting on behalf of" the U.S. government. That executive order should now be clarified to reinforce the ban on preemptive assassinations.[31]

Second, the Biden administration should promptly reissue and strengthen Obama's Executive Order 13,732, which, among other things, required all U.S. government agencies to publicly disclose the number of civilians killed in drone strikes, particularly if those killings occur outside areas of active hostilities.[32] In 2019, the Trump administration quietly revoked that reporting requirement; it should be promptly reinstated.

Third, the Office of Legal Counsel should draft a new opinion to prevent abuse of the Insurrection Act. One senator has incorrectly claimed that the Insurrection Act authorizes the president to launch an "overwhelming show of force" by state and federal troops against Americans "to protect law-abiding citizens from disorder."[33] In 2020, it was reported that President Trump "wanted to invoke the Insurrection Act of 1807 and use active-duty military to quell the protests. He wanted ten thousand troops in the streets and the 82nd Airborne called up." When the chair of the Joint Chiefs of Staff resisted, Trump reportedly asked, "'Can't you just shoot them? Just shoot them in the legs or something?'"[34] A correct legal interpretation of existing law would make clear that the president does not possess such legal authority. The president may not deploy military forces against domestic protesters in civilian streets over the objections of state governments when such deploy ment is unrelated either to enforcing a court order or to protecting civil rights. This clarifying interpretation should make clear that there is no "widespread public disorder" exception that somehow authorizes broad presidential deployment of federal troops into American city streets.[35]

Fourth, and finally, domestic regulations and processes must be strengthened to enhance internal controls over the use of nuclear weapons. If the United States or its allies have been attacked with nuclear weapons—a situation in which a decision about retaliating might need to be made within minutes—the president should retain the sole power to authorize the use of nuclear weapons. But in instances of first use, when the United States has time to decide whether to initiate an attack, Congress should invoke its textual war powers to enact legislation conditioning authorization on interagency dialogue and agreement among the president, vice president, and the secretaries of defense and state, as well as interagency legal review to determine that such a launch would comply with the Constitution and the international law of armed conflict.[36]

Congress's Article I "declare war" and "necessary and proper" powers should be sufficient to sustain the constitutionality of such consultation and approval requirements. Requiring the approval of the vice president would include in the decision-making process the individual who is first in the presidential line of succession and the only other politically accountable U.S. official elected by the entire nation. Requiring the concurrence of the defense secretary would ensure participation by the cabinet officer possessing the necessary military knowledge to understand the utility and consequences of deploying a nuclear weapon, the risks of further escalation, and the practicalities of ensuing armed conflict. Including the secretary of state, who negotiates nuclear-weapons treaties and monitors compliance with these agreements, ensures participation by the cabinet member most likely to assess and deal with the likely diplomatic fallout from any nuclear decision. The current process of interagency legal review, which already makes legal-compliance determinations regarding the use of force and conventional weapons targeting, could simply be extended to cover this situation.

Reforming the Bureaucracy

Finally, executive-branch reforms must address the growing autonomy of the national security bureaucracy, which has become a double-edged sword. Sometimes, entrenched national security bureaucracies can act as internal checks and balances, resisting rash political impulses from extreme leaders. But at other times, they may simply obstruct a new president from carrying out campaign promises that arguably are part of the president's electoral mandate. And so the "deep state" frustrated many extreme political initiatives during the Trump era. But during the Biden era, it has frustrated political directives by slow-walking such corrective reforms as closing Guantánamo, reversing draconian immigration policies, cooperating with the International Criminal Court on Ukraine, and issuing stricter guidance for drone strikes.[37] Even if today's sprawling national security agencies cannot be quickly downsized, they must be better shaped and their legal marching orders clarified. After September 11, for example, a huge and diverse number of agencies were urgently cobbled together to form a Department of Homeland Security. The resulting conglomerate has never been well streamlined or rationalized to perform its stated mandates.

The main challenge here is for conscientious political appointees to take more deliberate longer-term steps to restructure the "intentional bureaucratic architecture" in order to promote better national security governance. Successive political leaders of cabinet agencies have found it far easier to answer today's short-term fire drills than to attempt wholesale revision of how the bureaucracy should give, receive, and incorporate foreign-affairs legal advice. This has led to a shared bias among both politically appointed and career executive-branch lawyers in favor of legal positions that preserve and enhance executive power.

Citing internal executive *stare decisis,* the bureaucracy tends to entrench even legal decisions that were reached outside a well-functioning interagency legal process. Plainly, the national security bureaucracy can respond better to lawful political direction without becoming obstructionist. New political appointees to agency general-counsel positions should press for the internal overruling of defective prior positions. These political appointees should especially demand change when bureaucracies seek to preserve, on grounds of executive *stare decisis,* past legal analyses "that are not reached through cautious, deliberative, forward-looking processes, that do not appropriately buffer law enforcement or intelligence decisions from partisan politics, that do not appropriately marry expertise to authority, and that do not reflect well-considered rules for addressing conflict and reaching a clear output."[38]

Congressional Reforms

Congress must tackle the national security threat of executive unilateralism, which has stymied core legislative prerogatives. As John Hart Ely reminded us, foreign-affairs scholarship is full of "halftime pep-talk[s] imploring [Congress] to pull up its socks and reclaim its rightful authority."[39] But history also teaches that Congress legislates most strongly when it perceives that a salient crisis has occurred and demands a strong regulatory response.[40] Thus, a crucial first step would be for members to accept, as illustrated by the January 6 hearings, that we have reached a point of constitutional crisis. Biden's legislative successes in his second and third years offer some hope that under the right circumstances, foreign-affairs reform legislation could be passed.[41]

When Congress enacted the National Security Act in 1947, its greatest error was its failure to address its own role in the national security system. Although Congress partly redressed this oversight in the wave of statutes it enacted after Vietnam, the institutional changes that transformed Congress during those years diffused power in both houses. In the 1990s, Newt Gingrich consolidated power in the House, but power in the Senate remained relatively diffuse, doubly undercutting Congress in foreign affairs: first, by hampering Congress's capacity as a whole to confront the president, and second, by rendering Congress less able to withstand interest-group influence.[42] To level the playing field with the executive, Congress should now channel its reform efforts in three directions—toward creating counter-arenas of *centralized foreign-affairs expertise* within Congress that may act to oppose the president; building a central repository within Congress of *legal advice* regarding international and foreign-relations law; and developing *better tools to counter executive overreach.*

Core Consultative Group

Congress should create a joint committee on national security, akin to the Joint Committee on Taxation, that would become a core group of expert members on national security matters.[43] This new committee could have eight to twelve members, drawn from the leaders of the foreign-affairs, armed-services and intelligence committees in the House and Senate. The four congressional leaders, the Speaker and minority leader of the House and the majority and minority leaders of the Senate, could sit on the committee, ex officio, as needed. The committee could hire a bipartisan, expert, professional staff to consult, investigate, write reports and legislative histories, and meet regularly with staff from foreign-affairs agencies and the NSC to discuss national security matters. Through this core consultative group, Congress could provide the executive with the benefit of its deliberative judgments without demanding unacceptable sacrifices in flexibility, secrecy, or dispatch. Some thoughtful bills, never enacted, sought to achieve comparable centralization by requiring the president, before using force, to consult with a "permanent consultative group" composed of the majority and minority leaders of both houses of Congress, plus the chairs and ranking minority members of the armed-services, foreign-affairs, and intelligence committees of each house.[44] The bills required that this group be consulted to design legislative remedies to terminate or approve particular military involvements. Under the proposed bills, the group would have had formal authority to invoke the War Powers Resolution even if the president chose not to do so; its legislative proposals would have been accorded a special fast-track status in the legislative process.

Like the congressional "foreign policy monitor" that some have proposed, this core consultative group would play several functions: "to alert the Majority and Minority Leaders of both houses of impending issues and decisions regarding which they might wish to request full consultation [with the president]; to identify for senior executive officials potential problems on which they might wish to seek legislative counsel; [and] to brief appropriate congressional leaders in advance of major consultations in order to make such exchanges more focused and meaningful."[45] The creation of such a core consultative group would serve the long-term interest not only of Congress but also of the executive. It would eliminate the president's chronic complaint that in emergencies, statutory consultation requirements impose an intolerable burden on the president to find members with whom to consult.[46] In the most extreme situations, the number of members consulted could even be reduced to the subgroup of four ranking minority and majority leaders in each house. Even in the most urgent situations, however, the group consulted should never fall below this number, on the assumption that any action that could not secure at least their minimal backing should not proceed. Were Congress to mandate regular confidential meetings between its core consultative group and the president or his principal cabinet officers at the start of each new administration, we might return to true consultative decision-making between the branches.[47]

Even if consultation with such a group might marginally delay presidential responses, "[t]here are few crises short of battlefield disasters and the instant calamity of a nuclear strike in which properly briefed members could not play a valuable part."[48] Moreover, unlike a legislative committee that might be susceptible to capture by the executive entity or interest group being regulated, this core consultative group would consist of congressional leaders and experts who would be directly accountable to the entire membership; they would have the stature to express to the president views unlikely to come from the president's own subordinates. The fact that the group's members would be designated, not self-selected, would reduce the likelihood that members unusually prone to special-interest-group pressures would predominate.

The core consultative group would help rationalize the legislative process and make it more transparent. The group could propose hearings on bills that overlap committees but are clearly related and urge the formation of select committees when appropriate, not simply to investigate, but also to propose curative legislation. Finally, this core consultative group could centralize the legislative consideration of a particular national security problem by helping the leadership agree with the president to block floor consideration of bills, resolutions, and amendments that have not been reviewed by both the group and the executive branch. By so doing, the group could assure the president that congressional mavericks would not disrupt painstakingly drafted interbranch compromises.[49]

Because the core consultative group would be drawn from expert congressional leaders, its members would view themselves, like the president, as representing a broad national constituency and not just particular interest groups.[50] Over time, the group and its staff would develop a bipartisan overview of the policy terrain comparable to that of the president or the Joint Committee on Taxation, without forsaking the expertise of the existing specialized committees and committee staffs. Given that members of Congress now experience far greater longevity in office than executive-branch officials, the core legislative group could very well come to gain greater perspective and expertise than its executive-branch counterparts.[51] Just as earlier presidents have selected secretaries of state and defense from the Senate—for example, John Kerry, Hillary Clinton, Edmund Muskie, William Cohen, and Chuck Hagel—

future presidents could draw upon this core group for future cabinet officers, bringing the two branches even closer together.[52]

Congressional Legal Adviser

To get better legal advice, Congress should create, as legal counsel to the new consultative group that I have proposed, a central legal staff headed by a congressional legal adviser. This office would correspond to the Legal Adviser's Office in the State Department or the Office of Legal Counsel in the Justice Department and would be comparable to the Congressional Budget Office in the sense of independently monitoring and analyzing the legal output of the executive's national security apparatus.[53] The congressional legal adviser could be an elected officer of the House, like the clerk or the parliamentarian, or an attorney agreed upon by a consensus decision of both parties, similar to the director of the Congressional Budget Office. The congressional legal adviser's task would be to coordinate the work of the staff counsels to the various international-affairs committees, to act as a liaison between executive legal staffs, and to brief and advise the core consultative group on questions of international and foreign-relations law.

Far from being redundant, the congressional legal adviser would fill a role not currently played by any of the legal offices extant within Congress: the counsel to the numerous foreign-policy committees, the Office of Legislative Counsel, the Senate legal counsel and the general counsel to the clerk of the House, the legal and American government divisions of the Congressional Research Service, or the House and Senate parliamentarians. The congressional legal adviser's primary role would not be legislative drafting (the role currently played by the Office of Legislative Counsel), litigation (currently handled by the counsel to the House clerk and the Senate legal counsel), legal research (the Congressional Research Service's task), or interpretation of internal congressional rules (the job of the parliamentarians). Instead, the proposed congressional legal adviser would play a counseling function similar to that currently played by the staff counsels to the foreign-affairs or intelligence committees (who need not be lawyers) but would not be beholden to any particular committee or chair. The congressional legal adviser would represent Congress as a whole.

The congressional legal adviser would therefore exercise a jurisdiction encompassing all of the issues of constitutional, foreign-relations, and interna tional law that are currently scattered across a great many committees, including the judiciary, armed-services, foreign-affairs, intelligence, commerce, and government-operations committees. The legal adviser's central task would be to render legal opinions to Congress regarding both presidential and congressional conduct. By internal rule, Congress could both authorize and require the legal adviser to issue a "counter-report" whenever the executive branch transmits a declaration of national emergency, a war-powers report, or an intelligence finding. These counter-reports could then be subject to an immediate congressional vote (under the fast-track procedure described in greater detail below), which would establish a contemporaneous written record either accepting or rejecting the president's legal justification, against which any future executive claim of congressional acquiescence could be immediately tested.

Issuance of such counter-reports by a quasi-independent congressional entity would not be unprecedented. In effect, these reports would form legal analogues to the independent cost assessments of proposed administration programs that the Congressional Budget Office currently provides to the foreign-affairs committees.[54] Similarly, in 1986, Congress created an independent five-person commission to monitor Central American negotiations and the internal reform efforts of the contras and to submit reports regarding those matters for congressional comparison with similar reports statutorily required of the president.[55] The legal adviser's office proposed here would have a continuing institutional mission to prepare comparable reports but containing a legal, rather than a policy, analysis. This new entity would not require dramatic institutional changes. On the contrary, the legal adviser's office could be created by merging or affiliating existing congressional legal offices, thus centralizing and reorganizing much of the legal expertise that already exists within Congress. The long-term goal of the legal adviser's office would be to promote continuing interbranch dialogue by encouraging congressional and executive legal staffs to foster common constitutional understandings regarding issues of foreign affairs that would rarely be resolved in court.

The skilled legal staff of the legal adviser's office could be sensitive to the need for more carefully worded statutes (described in chapter 4 as the issue of "porous drafting.")[56] For example, that staff could advise the members of Congress to amend the War Powers Resolution to include more detailed definitions of the terms "armed forces" and "hostilities." Moreover, to give greater operative content to the notion that the president must genuinely consult with

Congress before committing troops abroad, Congress could also amend the resolution to require that the president consult with the core consultative group proposed here rather than merely brief a few selected members of Congress at the last minute.[57] To ensure that Congress withholds statutory authority from executive acts that it does not wish to authorize, this legal team could develop established terms of art specifying Congress's intent to preempt presidential claims of inherent constitutional authority, to declare that a court may not read statutory silences or limited delegations as congressional endorsement of related presidential initiatives, and to require "clear statements" to prevent executive action pursuant to the statute from infringing on individual rights.[58] Once the staff developed standard definitions of recurrent statutory terms, it could make sure that Congress's drafting unit—the Office of Legislative Counsel—inserts them in the modified International Emergency Economic Powers Act, the modified Arms Export Control Act, and other statutes, depending on the core group's assessment of the relative need for executive flexibility under each of these statutes.

Finally, Congress could enhance external legal accountability by requiring that executive-branch legal opinions justifying particularly controversial actions be submitted, confidentially, for adversarial review by the congressional legal adviser, or until one is created, by the committee legal staffs. For reasons of justiciability or classification, such opinions would almost never be tested in court. Far from being unprecedented, a version of this process was employed during the Iran-contra hearings and to review the State Department Legal Adviser's opinion advocating a broad reinterpretation of the Anti-Ballistic Missile Treaty.[59] Each house of Congress could modify its internal rules to set forth special threshold circumstances under which a committee, house, or both houses could demand an executive-branch legal opinion. By analogy, current rules define conditions under which these entities may demand factual information that lies within the control of the executive branch, and also impose stiff sanctions against congressional members or staffers who inappropriately release confidential information.[60]

Better Congressional Tools

Congressional movement toward each of these basic institutional reforms would go a long way toward curing two of the specific causes of congressional acquiescence identified in chapter 4: legislative myopia and porous draft ing. Congress can strengthen its tool kit by developing a constitutional substitute for the legislative veto; making more effective use of its appropriations power; imposing criminal penalties for extreme executive violations of key national security statutes; and more liberally exercising its impeachment power against executive officials.

Under the legislative-veto regime, Congress delegated statutory authority to the president while retaining a right of subsequent review in particular cases. In 1983, the Supreme Court held that legislative vetoes violate the bicameralism and presentment clauses of the Constitution. The legislative veto had numerous policy disadvantages, most prominently, the freedom it gave members to avoid visible responsibility for their actions by avoiding roll-call votes.[61] But despite these infirmities, the legislative veto effected a crucial political compromise. Although the president gained current legislative authorization for certain acts, the president's need to return to Congress for subsequent approval provided assurances that consultation would continue while those actions proceeded.

One alternative that would largely preserve the veto's beneficial political compromise, without its accompanying disadvantages, is the so-called fast-track legislative approval procedure. Unlike the legislative veto, which is not legislation jointly voted by the two houses and signed by the president, fast-track approval is a legislative process, albeit greatly expedited. It is found most prominently in the trade laws. Under this procedure, Congress authorizes the president to initiate a foreign-affairs action (for example, negotiation of a trade agreement) in exchange for a commitment that the president will submit the product of that action to Congress for final approval. Under modified House and Senate rules, Congress "promises" the president that it will require automatic discharge of the completed initiative from committee within a certain number of days, bar floor amendment of the submitted proposal, and limit floor debate, thereby ensuring that the package will be voted up or down, as is, within a fixed period.[62]

The fast-track procedure allows Congress to overcome both the political inertia and the procedural obstacles that most frequently prevent a controversial measure from coming to a vote at all. Furthermore, because one-fifth of the members present in each house retain constitutional power to require a roll-call vote on any matter, an individual member's vote on any particular fast-track approval resolution would almost invariably be made visible to the public.[63] If triggered by objectively determinable circumstances—for example, "exchanges of hostile fire"—fast-track procedures could be used to privilege certain joint resolutions introduced by any interested member and thereby compel Congress to vote up or down quickly on resolutions that challenge executive acts.[64] An alternative would be for the president and Congress to agree, for example, to a joint resolution that amends the War Powers Resolution so that Congress authorizes the president to carry on military actions in particular countries for, say, one year. But in addition, the law would state that that action shall cease upon a concurrent resolution of the House and Senate—that is, a bicameral vote not subject to presidential veto—and the president would agree ex ante, in the joint resolution, to abide by that concurrent resolution. The bill could also authorize Congress to declare its opposition to a presidential troop commitment by less than a two-thirds vote in each house and combine a fast-track procedure with an automatic appropriations-cutoff device and a judicial-review provision.[65]

The fast-track approval method has the advantage of versatility, inasmuch as it can be combined with "committee gatekeeping," point-of-order, and appropriations procedures to vary the intensity of its regulation. Under a committee-gatekeeping procedure, a majority vote of a single congressional committee may derail a presidential proposal from the fast track—and in many cases, effectively kill it—which gives the executive strong incentives to consult with the committee's members at each step of the process.[66] Similarly, when a House or Senate rule triggers a point of order, any member can raise that point of order to halt consideration of the bill until the presiding officer considers and rejects the matter.

If the president should seek to implement a program without satisfying a statutory requirement, such as notice or prior legislative consultation with Congress, these procedures could be used to temporarily block appropriations bills to fund the program.[67] Although members ought not use the appropriations process indiscriminately to accomplish what they cannot achieve through legislation, Congress as a whole could properly tie appropriations cutoffs to objectively determinable facts, and such appropriations cutoffs would then be enforceable through judicial-review provisions. Congress could also demand greater executive accountability earlier, when it is authorizing those programs that will later receive appropriations. As Senator J. William Fulbright once observed with regard to foreign aid, such authorizations "provid[e] the closest thing we have to an annual occasion for a general review of American foreign policy."[68] To use this process more productively, Congress could conduct a long-term-authorization review process, whereby the core consultative group that I have proposed could function like the Joint Committee on Taxation and regularly evaluate and review existing national-security programs. Alternatively, Congress may combine its authorization and appropriations powers to maintain control over executive-branch spending. Congress's ability to do so was shown, for example, in March 1989, when President George H. W. Bush and Congress signed "Good Friday accords" to ensure the release of $45 million in nonlethal aid to the contras.[69]

Congress could enforce its national security revisions through statutory criminal penalties, subject to good-faith immunity defenses, and more liberal use of impeachment for executive officials who have entirely lost the confidence of the Congress. Once Congress has determined to deny appropriations to a particular activity, "the specific activity is no longer within the realm of authorized government actions."[70] Thus, one of the original drafters of the National Security Act of 1947 proposed that criminal penalties be imposed on any governmental officer or employee who knowingly and willfully violates or conspires to violate an express statutory prohibition against the expenditure of funds for a particular foreign-policy purpose.[71] Congress could amend the Neutrality Act—an early framework statute described in chapter 1—to provide criminal penalties for private adventurism conducted at the executive's behest. To the extent that such an amended law were applied against U.S. government officials who order, plan, or initiate foreign activities, enforcement of all of these criminal provisions could be confided to a special counsel or departmental inspectors general.[72]

Finally, the Constitution declares that "[t]he President, Vice President and *all civil Officers of the United States,* shall be removed from Office on Impeachment for, and Conviction of, Treason, Bribery, or other high Crimes and Misdemeanors." The House has the sole power to bring impeachments, the Senate has the sole power to try them, and the president lacks constitutional power to pardon those who have been impeached.[73] Thus, Congress could declare certain clear violations of key national security provisions "high Crimes and Misdemeanors" that would warrant impeachment of the responsible officials and their removal from office. The impeachment remedy resembles criminal penalties inasmuch as it requires determination of individual responsibility. It differs, however, in the crucial respect that it was constitutionally designed to be exercised not by courts but by Congress against executive subversion of constitutionally mandated processes. In 1974, for example, the House Judiciary Committee famously considered, but did not report to the full House, a proposed article of impeachment that charged President Nixon with engaging in unauthorized secret bombing in Cambodia, which he had concealed from both the people and Congress, thereby preventing Congress from responsibly exercising its appropriations and war powers.[74] Impeachable acts would need to be proved to the satisfaction of two-thirds of the senators; and the judgment of impeachment would extend no "further than to removal from Office, and disqualification to hold and enjoy any Office of honor, Trust or Profit under the United States."[75] Thus, Congress could theoretically pursue the constitutionally authorized remedy of removal from office without risking subsequent pardon or prejudicing any subsequent criminal investigation.

Use of these tools would alleviate Congress's most intractable problem, namely, the problem of political will. Unlike the current regime, which requires a two-thirds majority in both houses to enforce existing laws, nearly all of these proposals (with the exception of the "crimes and misdemeanors" proposal) are designed to be enforced by a considerably lesser showing of congressional will. Many of these proposals—including the creation of the core consultative group and the congressional legal adviser, demands for executive-branch legal opinions, and use of the long-range-authorization process—could be implemented by concurrent resolution if necessary. The core consultative group and gatekeeping committees could express their will to the president even without formal votes. The fast-track, point-of-order, and confidentiality procedures could be adopted by modification of chamber rules and subsequently triggered automatically or by the action of a single interested member. The appropriations provisions could be made either self enforcing, enforceable through impeachment, or enforceable civilly and criminally by the courts. And despite their ability to regulate executive conduct, none of these devices would run afoul of the Supreme Court's ban on the legislative veto; in particular, the fast-track procedure is fully constitutional because it produces bona fide, albeit expedited, legislation passed by both houses and signed by the president.[76] Thus, even if Congress cannot create political will where none exists, it can modify existing institutions and procedures to give quicker and fuller expression to viewpoints that remain dispersed or submerged under its current institutional structure.

In addition to these larger changes, there are any number of smaller internal changes that Congress should adopt to reduce partisanship and restore a bipartisan spirit that is capable of swift action and unified appreciation of clear facts in national security situations. Congressional incentive structures should be revised to reward members for taking bipartisan foreign policy seriously, reducing political polarization, and challenging the opposing party with true facts rather than falsifiable sound bites. A simple, critical revision of the filibuster rule would require senators to appear on the floor *in person* if they want to block nominees or legislation. At present, they too often off-load these responsibilities onto low-level aides who can indefinitely block unanimous consent for treaties, bills, or key nominees, simply by sending a daily text from their subway ride home at night. Of course, "Congress will always be a sausage factory," one distinguished congressman observed, "but it can be a better sausage factory if we get the incentives right and if top-quality people volunteer or at least help those who do."[77]

Judicial Engagement

Because such legislative proposals require exercises of political coalition building that may not be possible in a sharply divided Congress, the courts have a crucial role to play. One need not advocate widespread judicialization of the field of foreign affairs to accept that the courts have excluded themselves too thoroughly from the national security area and have thereby removed a meaningful check on executive action. Aided by Congress—when it is willing—the courts should take three simple steps: reduce barriers to justiciability, clarify grounds for affirming on the merits, and modify existing foreign-relations doctrines to better adapt them to the age of globalization.

Justiciability

The courts should continue to reduce barriers to justiciability in foreign-affairs cases. Leading conservative judges, like Robert Bork and Antonin Scalia, have criticized the lower courts for treating the political-question doctrine as a catchall method to avoid deciding straightforward constitutional cases.[78] As Chief Justice Roberts recognized in *Zivotofsky I*, "[i]n general, the Judiciary has a responsibility to decide cases properly before it, even those it 'would gladly avoid.'" Exceptions to that responsibility should therefore be narrowly construed. In many cases, he noted, "[t]o resolve [a plaintiff's] claim, the Judiciary must decide if [the plaintiff's] interpretation of [a] statute is correct, and whether the statute is constitutional. This is a familiar judicial exercise." This task should not be shirked simply because some courts would prefer to avoid making those decisions.[79]

Reviewing the history of judicial precedent recounted in chapters 1 and 2, Justice William Brennan concluded: "Our cases in this field seem invariably to show a discriminating analysis of the particular question posed, in terms of the history of its management by the political branches, of its susceptibility to judicial handling in the light of its nature and posture in the specific case, and of the possible consequences of judicial action." Applying those standards to decided cases, Brennan uncovered a rich historical tradition of judicial decision-making in foreign affairs.[80] The evidence in the foregoing chapters confirms Justice Brennan's findings. Since the beginning of the Republic, federal judges have issued rulings that span the foreign-policy spectrum and involve interpretation of virtually all bodies of law. They have reviewed the legality of military seizures, presidential orders in wartime, retaliatory strikes, covert actions, executive agreements, and treaty interpretation. They have reviewed and rejected defenses of executive privilege, superior orders, and inherent presidential powers.

The Supreme Court's decisions of the early 1800s, coupled with its "recognition" decisions (culminating in *Zivotofsky II*), establish that a president's exercise of textually enumerated presidential authorities—for example, the commander-in-chief and recognition powers—are not immune from judicial review (although the court may construe those powers generously). Nor does any impediment to judicial review arise when the president construes an executive agreement, treaty, or customary international law. The political-question doctrine plainly does not bar review when executive conduct is directly contested by Congress acting as a whole. The courts have a special duty to look closely when executive conduct in foreign affairs infringes directly on individual rights.[81]

Since *Marbury v. Madison*, an American judge's job has been to evaluate the lawfulness of executive conduct. "It is the province and duty of the judicial department to say what the law is" by drawing the line between illegitimate exercises of political power and legitimate exercises of legal authority.[82] The Supreme Court drew precisely such a line in *Youngstown*. But the federal judiciary failed to perform a similar task during the Vietnam War, in no small part because Congress had largely failed to make its own intentions clear.[83] By now enacting national security legislation designed to encourage judicial decision-making, Congress would support the judiciary in performing its constitutionally assigned task of line drawing.

Whatever the general vitality of the political-question doctrine in constitutional cases, plainly it would not apply if Congress specified foreign-affairs responsibilities in various statutes. As Justice White put the point in the *Japan Whaling* case, "under the Constitution, one of the Judiciary's characteristic roles is to interpret statutes, and we cannot shirk this responsibility merely because our decision may have significant political overtones."[84] In 1988, the Court held that the National Security Act of 1947 was not intended to preclude judicial review of a constitutional challenge to an executive decision made under that framework law. Similarly, in *Curtiss-Wright* and *Dames & Moore*, the two cases most frequently cited by executive-power advocates, the Court reviewed on the merits the president's conduct under foreign-affairs statutes.[85]

Congress cannot legislate judicial courage any more than it can legislate executive self-restraint or congressional willpower. Congress can, however, seek to stem the lower courts' continued migration away from the *Youngstown* vision and toward *Curtiss-Wright* by embedding in legislation the judicial role described by Justice Jackson in his *Youngstown* concurrence. With respect to judicial abstention, Congress's central strategy should be to enact legislation that would override the abstention doctrines that the courts have wrapped around themselves and clarify which plaintiffs, defendants, claims, and forms of relief would be properly subject to adjudication.

To authorize challenges to executive conduct, Congress could first insert in its national security statutes provisions authorizing interested citizens or members of Congress to act as "private attorneys general" to police violations of national security laws but requiring that such suits not be brought by individual members of Congress until they have fully exhausted their legislative remedies.[86] Second, as Justice Scalia urged, Congress could amend or overrule the *Feres* doctrine, a judicially created doctrine that has effectively shielded the U.S. government from suits by service members by fashioning an exception to the immunity waivers in the Federal Tort Claims Act.[87] Although in 1982 the Court granted the president absolute immunity and granted high-level executive officials qualified immunity from civil damages for actions taken within the outer perimeter of their official duties, Congress could clearly state exceptions to the doctrine of official immunity for particularly egregious constitutional violations.[88] Third, Congress could modify the relevant provisions of the Administrative Procedure Act to afford private plaintiffs a cause of action under that statute, which arguably provides discretionary nonmonetary relief against federal officials who commit unlawful actions in foreign affairs.[89] Fourth, Congress could authorize courts to entertain injunctive suits against U.S. government officials who are alleged to have acted in excess of their statutory or constitutional powers, or could specify circumstances under which the president would be authorized to act but would be required ex post to pay just compensation to those individuals whose private property has been taken by the president's actions.[90]

As it has done in administrative-law statutes, Congress could lay statutory venue for all claims of statutory violation in one circuit—for example, the courts of the District of Columbia Circuit—to create a counter-arena of centralized foreign-affairs expertise within the federal judiciary analogous to the core group of foreign-affairs experts that I have encouraged Congress to create within itself.[91] To address the self-fulfilling claim that federal judges have little foreign-affairs experience, judicial selection should focus more on global, rather than merely local, experience. Federal Judicial Center and circuit-conference trainings on international law should continue to be held, as they have for many years, for both judges and their law clerks, and written guides to international-law doctrines should be improved, updated, and widely distributed.[92]

The Merits

The courts should revise several administrative-law doctrines that affect foreign affairs.[93] With respect to facts, courts should scrutinize and invalidate executive actions taken in the area of foreign affairs when the justifications offered in court by the U.S. government are manufactured motivations for the government's actions. In the travel-ban case (*Trump v. Hawaii*), Justice Sotomayor correctly called out the majority for deferring to the Trump administration's "masquerade[] behind a façade of national security con cerns."[94] The courts should build instead on the approach in the recent census case, *Department of Commerce v. New York,* in which Chief Justice Roberts wrote that the reasons proffered there by the Commerce Department "seem[ed] to have been contrived" and pretextual. The Court directed that under the Administrative Procedure Act, a court could demand that the relevant agency "offer genuine justifications for important decisions, reasons that can be scrutinized by courts and the interested public."[95]

In the same vein, courts should give far-more-skeptical scrutiny to Justice Department arguments based on the executive's "*Youngstown* category three" and "statutory *Curtiss-Wright* theory of delegation" arguments described in chapter 9. Recently, in *West Virginia v. EPA,* the Supreme Court rejected Obama's Clean Power Plan—a plan to implement the United States' Paris climate commitments—by applying the "major questions" doctrine. The Court described the doctrine as addressing a "particular and recurring problem: agencies asserting highly consequential power beyond what Congress could reasonably be understood to have granted," even in the face of congressional silence. The Court held that rather than treat such assertions of power as normal agency statutory interpretations to which judges should give broad *Chevron* deference, courts should approach them with a greater degree of skepticism and require a "clear congressional authorization" for "major" executive actions that have far-reaching consequences.[96] In the domestic realm, this major-questions doctrine remains highly controversial, probably overstated, and likely to be narrowed significantly in the years ahead.[97] But if the Roberts Court insists on demanding specific congressional authorizations for certain major executive actions that dramatically affect our climate security, why not also demand similarly specific delegations in other areas of foreign affairs?

I have also long argued that courts should exercise "procedural scalpels" rather than "jurisdictional meat cleavers." Well-established procedural doctrines requiring that administrative remedies be exhausted, that the forum be convenient, and that insubstantial claims be dismissed before discovery or on summary judgment would remain available to spare governmental officials the burden of unwarranted trials.[98] Sometimes citing their own self-reinforcing ignorance and institutional incompetence, courts have mechanically applied presumptions and canons to avoid engaging with our modern global environment.[99] Those applications have led to broad jurisdictional interpretations that

oust from the courts entire classes of cases, rather than more nuanced application of existing procedural doctrines to eliminate from dockets those *particular*
cases that truly do not belong in U.S. courts. As two justices put it in a recent
state-secrets case, the Court's overly exclusionary approach "abdicates judicial
responsibility to use ordinary tools of litigation management in favor of the
Executive's wish to brush this case out the door."[100]

Such rulings have licensed lower courts to use presumptions and canons
in a way that is overly deferential to executive-branch arguments—even
when those arguments are not backed up by well-documented foreign-policy
interests.[101] In the process, the courts have frustrated congressional intent to
regulate extraterritorially. These canons and presumptions have also limited
constructive judicial participation to better align U.S. and international regulatory interests, a task to which the American common-law case-by-case
method of judging is well suited.

As one corrective, the Supreme Court should soften its recent modification of the presumption against extraterritoriality. The Court has for many
years applied this presumption inconsistently, preventing statutes from
reaching extraterritorial conduct even in the face of legislative history evinc-
ing Congress's contrary intent to regulate such conduct.[102] Under the Court's
current interpretation, a statutory provision should not be considered extraterritorial if a judicially identified "focus" of that provision can be located in
the United States. Setting aside the difficulty of making that determination
with respect to many statutes, the Court's presumption unwisely removes
discretion from the lower courts. The presumption does so in the name of
safeguarding U.S. foreign-relations interests by avoiding unintended clashes
with the laws of other nations. But as modified, the presumption is too easily
misapplied.[103] It is not well suited to a global age, because it overprotects
foreign sovereigns even absent diplomatic protest and restricts judicial over
sight without clear proof of congressional intent. It is not clear why this pro
tective goal would not be better served by a case-by-case approach of the kind
that Justice Scalia applied in his dissent in *Hartford Fire Insurance Co. v. California*.[104] The courts should apply a more flexible reasonableness require
ment to the balancing of U.S. and foreign interests before hearing a case in
U.S. court, making the kind of nuanced assessment of the affected U.S. federal interests found in Justice Breyer's concurrence in *Kiobel v. Royal Dutch
Petroleum Co.*[105]

Adapting Doctrines to Globalization

The Supreme Court should also reexamine and modify several existing for-eign-relations doctrines to better adapt them to the age of globalization. The first and most glaring is the non-self-executing-treaty doctrine, a judicially cre-ated distinction between self-executing treaties and non-self-executing treaties that dramatically limits the enforceability of negotiated treaties in U.S. courts. The lower courts have over-read a footnote in *Medellín v. Texas* to read into the supremacy clause the notion that ratified treaties are presumptively non-self-executing unless the political branches expressly say otherwise. Given that the text of the treaty clause draws no such distinction and that the first treaties were all self-executing, it is not clear why any presumption should not run the other way. As currently applied, the doctrine undermines the diplomatic process by creating a glaring asymmetry in the negotiating process. Although other countries enter treaty discussions seeing themselves as "negotiating for keeps," they too often see U.S. negotiators as only committing themselves to conditional and limited domestic compliance with any treaty obligations concluded in the negotiations. The doctrine further undermines the treaty-making process by reserving, for later judicial interpreters, conclusions about national intent that are better reflected in the executive and legislative actions taken at the time when those treaties were originally negotiated, concluded, and ratified.[106]

The second doctrine requiring reform is the Court's unrealistic and ahis-torical mantra that judges should not look to foreign and international law to interpret the meaning of U.S. constitutional law. As I have argued elsewhere, that claim cannot be originalist, as the original American judges looked to foreign and international law on a regular basis. More fundamentally, it counterproductively cuts off American judges from learning from the expe-riences of neighboring courts that may have encountered legal challenges to global phenomena that will soon challenge the United States. In our diverse society, it runs deeply against our national nature to decree that any sector of American life—law, culture, or cuisine—is categorically barred from "bor-rowing" from foreign sources.[107] By their nature, Americans borrow. As a Korean American who has witnessed the importation into American cinema and music of such Korean influences as *Parasite* and "Gangnam Style" and the infusion into Americanized tacos of such Korean ingredients as *kimchi,* I can only marvel at the insularity of Supreme Court justices who claim that, in an age of globalization, we can maintain an "American rule of law" hermetically sealed from all foreign and international influences. As a jurisprudential matter, judges should candidly accept that borrowing is just as American as the hot dog (*Frankfurter*) or apple pie (*Apfelkuchen*).

Despite their contrary protests, no fewer than twelve Supreme Court justices have recently looked to foreign and international precedents as an aid to constitutional interpretation. These include, recently and ironically, Justice Alito in the *Dobbs* abortion case, Justice Gorsuch in *Buffington v. McDonough,* and Justices Gorsuch and Kavanaugh during oral argument in the census case.[108] The Court as a whole has regularly looked to foreign or international law in at least three situations, which for simplicity's sake I have elsewhere called "parallel rules," "empirical light," and "community standards." First, the Court has looked to foreign precedents when American legal rules parallel those of other nations, particularly those with similar legal and social traditions.[109] Second, as Justice Breyer has noted, the "Court has long considered as relevant and informative the way in which foreign courts have applied standards roughly comparable to our own constitutional standards in roughly comparable circumstances," reasoning that "their experience may nonetheless cast an empirical light on the consequences of different solutions to a common legal problem."[110] Third, the Court has looked outside the United States when an American constitutional concept, by its own terms, implicitly references a community standard: for example, "cruel and unusual," "due process of law," "unreasonable searches and seizures." The Court has recognized that in a global age, it makes sense to consult a broader set of community standards than just those found only within the United States.

The centuries-old *Charming Betsy* canon states that "an act of Congress ought never to be construed to violate the law of nations if any other possible construction remains."[111] In the late 1980s, Justice Blackmun built on that notion by presciently suggesting that domestic courts should look beyond the United States' immediate interests to the

> mutual interests of all nations in a smoothly functioning international legal regime . . . to consider if there is a course that furthers, rather than impedes, the development of an ordered international system. A functioning system for solving disputes across borders serves many values, among them predictability, fairness, ease of commercial interactions, and stability through satis-

faction of mutual expectations. These interests are common to all nations, including the United States.[112]

This suggests a different, more sensible kind of canon for the twenty-first century: when interpreting a statutory or constitutional provision—absent a convincing governmental showing that such a construction would genuinely interfere with the conduct of foreign affairs—judges should construe the provision in a manner most consistent with the modern consensus of the international legal community, if one can be clearly discerned. Judicial interpretation of the Constitution in light of international and foreign law is nothing more or less than an informed choice-of-law decision, but guided by an outward-looking, not inward-facing, canon of judicial interpretation.[113]

Taken together, these proposed doctrinal modifications would be far from radical. They would simply ask American common-law judges to seek to reconcile the legality of U.S. practices with those of a wider civilization tasked with tackling the same global issues. These transborder issues cannot be managed by the United States alone and are ones over which the United States can exert only limited regulatory control. Far from being radical, the overall judicial approach recommended here should be considered "originalist," inasmuch as it would emulate the efforts of the early Supreme Court to help manage the United States' legal relationship with a rapidly evolving world order. To recall Chief Justice Marshall's famous plea: "[We] must never forget that it is a constitution that we are expounding . . . intended to endure for the ages to come, and consequently, to be adapted to the various crises of human affairs."[114]

The obvious objection to my proposal is that it would push the courts to improperly intrude into the foreign-policy decision-making process. Over the years, many thoughtful constitutional analysts, including Alexander Bickel and Jesse Choper, have argued against such a judicial role. Professor Bickel articulated a philosophy of prudence, called the "passive virtues," under which the Supreme Court should be allowed to withhold constitutional judgment in cases raising concerns over separation of powers. Dean Choper reached the same conclusion by a different, "functional" rationale. He reasoned that because the branches of government possess adequate political weapons to protect their interests against one another, to husband their resources for individual-rights cases, courts should refrain from reviewing interbranch controversies involving separation-of-powers questions.

The judicial decisions chronicled in part I demonstrate that these three rationales have found expression in a wide array of justiciability doctrines, including the political-question doctrine, private and congressional standing, and
doctrines related to the immunity of defendants, nonripeness or mootness,
equitable discretion, and constitutional avoidance, under which courts decide
cases narrowly to avoid reaching constitutional questions. The most indiscriminately invoked of these doctrines had been the political-question doctrine, in
the words of one court, "a tempting refuge from the adjudication of difficult
constitutional claims [whose] shifting contours and uncertain underpinnings
make it susceptible to indiscriminate and overbroad application to claims properly before the federal courts."[115] But as chapter 8 reviewed, in *Zivotofsky I*, the
Roberts Court greatly narrowed the application of that doctrine.

I do not doubt that my statutory proposals would, at least in the short run,
increase the number of federal-court suits involving foreign affairs filed
against the government and its officials. But neither do I see that result as
permanently disrupting or impairing the operation of the executive branch.[116]
Even if litigation were to ensue, judicial resolution of those disputes would
help clarify currently ambiguous boundaries of constitutional responsibility.
If national security statutes were challenged, the Supreme Court could either
sustain the statute as written or strike the statute's unconstitutional parts and
stay its judgment pending congressional modification of the law to comply
with the Court's constitutional interpretation.[117] Once the Court had resolved
such initial disputes, an interbranch modus vivendi under the act could ensue, now guided by clearer judicial statements regarding which presidential
actions are or are not legislatively or constitutionally authorized. In the longer
term, the likelihood that executive officials would win most suits against them
on the merits would dampen incentives to bring frivolous statutory claims.

Finally, some argue against judicial review in cases involving foreign affairs
reasoning that judicial rulings against the executive would confuse our allies
and embarrass the president. If this claim rests on foreign confusion, it deni-
grates our allies' intelligence and assumes that they cannot comprehend a
constitutional system of shared powers. Even when the Senate refuses to ratify
a treaty that the president has negotiated, Professor Martin Redish notes
"other nations are asked to understand our complex constitutional system of
checks and balances, and we somehow manage to survive as a nation."[118] Likewise, it does not make sense to condone illegal executive conduct simply to

avoid embarrassing the president, particularly if the unlawfully acting party *should* be embarrassed. As the Trump era showed, this information will most likely emerge anyway during subsequent executive, legislative, or criminal investigations. To bar civil adjudication while the illegal conduct takes place only increases the risk that the unscrutinized conduct will become public later and cause even greater embarrassment to the United States.

However different foreign affairs may be from domestic affairs, that difference does not exempt them from our constitutional system of checks and balances, particularly the check of judicial review. If anything, meaningful judicial review is even more constitutionally necessary in foreign than domestic affairs, because the states do not play as great a role as a political check against presidential action. Even without new legislation, judges retain a duty to ensure that in the field of foreign affairs, legal authority does not become permanently decoupled from legal constraint.

When the courts systematically remove themselves from independent review of executive action, it is only a matter of time before clear lines of legality fade from the landscape of American foreign affairs. Left behind are temporary lines in the sand drawn by the latest interbranch turf battle, only to be redrawn by the next powerful president or Congress. The federal judge who said during the Iranian hostage crisis that "it is not the business of courts to pass judgment on the decisions of the President in the field of foreign policy" was wrong.[119] Precisely *because* federal judges enjoy life tenure and salary independence and owe nothing to those who appointed them, it is their business to say what the law is in the field of foreign affairs. In *Ramirez v. Weinberger,* then judge Scalia protested a federal-court decision restraining American military activities in Honduras. No "special charter," he argued, authorizes judges to keep the executive in line in the area of foreign affairs. Judge Malcolm Wilkey, a once and future executive-branch official, answered that "the Judiciary does operate under a 'special charter' to help preserve the fundamental rights of this nation's citizens. That charter is commonly known as the United States Constitution."[120]

Empowering Other Counterweights

It will not be enough, however, simply to strengthen the checking power of the coordinate branches of the federal government. Reforms are also needed to empower an additional set of counterweights capable of acting against a unilateralist executive. These include activist states and localities engaged in foreign-affairs federalism; an aggressive and persistent mainstream and social media; private-public partnerships; and alliance politics. Elsewhere, I have chronicled the role of these counterweights, individually and collectively, in supporting many effective "resistance measures" to challenge the Trump administration's illegal initiatives through participation in "transnational legal process."[121]

States and Localities

Further revisions in judicial doctrine will likely be required to enable these other actors to act as more effective counterweights to executive unilateralism in foreign affairs. Traditional judicial views of federalism have rigidly sought to bar states and localities from participation in foreign affairs with multiple doctrines of foreign-affairs preemption. In the early twentieth century, judicial negation of state roles in foreign affairs led to absolutist dicta pronouncing that "[a]s to such [foreign affairs] purposes, the State of New York does not exist." But today, such assertions seem rigid and anachronistic. In modern times, there seems little need for an overbroad theory of "foreign affairs preemption of state activity," à la *Zschernig v. Miller,* or of "dormant foreign-affairs preemption," which invalidates state policies that only potentially affect the United States' relationship with foreign nations, even where the U.S. government has not specifically protested the policies in question.[122]

The Constitution nowhere expressly excludes states from engaging in acts that affect U.S. foreign relations. Such acts now seem inevitable when a state like California ranks as the fifth-largest economy in the world. When Trump abandoned federal efforts to combat climate change, there seemed little reason why that decision required states to abandon their own ongoing climate-change abatement policies. When challenging California's cap-and-trade agreements with Canadian provinces, for example, the federal government could not demonstrate that those particular state policies would genuinely interfere with the conduct of national foreign affairs.[123] Nor is there a persuasive federal interest in truncating the recent wave of climate-change lawsuits that make state-law claims in state courts. Those cases seek remedies from major fossil-fuel producers that contribute to climate injury, asserting traditional state-law claims of public and private nuisance, negligence, fraud and misinformation, and defendants' failure to warn despite knowing about the likely harm flowing from their actions. With little disruption of the real-life status quo, these federal-state preemption doctrines could be narrowed to genuine issues of conflict preemption, which would give states and localities needed freedom to experiment on such issues as clean energy and local compliance with international human-rights treaties.[124]

Media

Traditional mainstream and social media have played an enormous role in exposing rule-of-law abuses in the Trump administration, including on national security matters. The Trump administration responded to that scrutiny through a series of petty punishments, for example, ostracizing particular journalists and barring others from receiving White House press passes. Executive abuses through media regulation in foreign countries make clear why such matters should not be subject to the discretion of any particular elected leader.[125] Instead, they should be regularized and distributed through an administrative process—managed, for example, by the Federal Communications Commission—that would meet due-process standards. To address individual violations, Congress should give the Justice Department inspector general authority to review credible allegations of executive retaliation against the news media. Finally, the courts can and should play a pivotal role. In one recent incident described as "the 'National Security Constitution' at work," the courts refused to defer to the president's claim of national security to ban a social-media company, on the grounds that the president lacked the statutory authority to implement such a ban.[126]

Allies

For alliance politics to act as a more effective counterweight to executive unilateralism, the courts will need to carefully scrutinize the limitations on the president's unilateral power to terminate international agreements. The next chapter argues that absent legislation restricting such termination, courts should apply a constitutional "mirror principle," requiring as much legislative input to exit an international agreement as was constitutionally required to enter it. The courts should give stronger weight to clear expressions of U.S. and foreign diplomatic interests in maintaining long-standing multilateral institutions, and demand proof that private lawsuits or intrusive state and local activity will genuinely disrupt foreign regulatory objectives.[127]

Private Actors

Similarly, private companies are engaging in more international lawmaking, for example, in the realms of global cyberlaw, artificial intelligence, and the use of private security contractors. The resulting norms can have important restraining and channeling effects on U.S. executive action. Increasingly, private-public partnerships have played an active role in helping shape governmental and corporate standards on climate change and environmental, social, and corporate governance. The private Facebook Oversight Board, for example, played a crucial role in limiting Trump's capacity to post in support of violence on January 6.[128] At a time when intergovernmental forums have moved slowly to articulate global cyber rules, private information and communication technology companies have convened productive discussions spurring the development of international-law rules restricting military use of cyber tools and artificial intelligence.[129] Global universities and hotel chains have helped set higher standards for smoke-free environments, recycling, plant-based cuisine, and Covid-19 protocols. As private American actors inevitably multiply their global contacts, foreign-affairs law must develop doctrines of delegation and discretion that will encourage this private experimentation. Without disrupting governmental policy, such actors can operate creatively and constructively to help set customary norms of best practice, which can then form the basis for emerging global legal standards.

Restatements

In the years to come, a prudent balance can also be struck and maintained by ensuring that the rules of foreign-relations law are clarified, restated, and fleshed out somewhere other than in the U.S. courts or in self-serving executive documents. This legal dialogue should transpire in a considered fashion over an extended period, with all stakeholders participating. One venue will be the American Law Institute (ALI), which will bring judges, academics, private and public practitioners, and foreign advisers together over the next decade to complete the *Restatement (Fourth) of the Foreign Relations Law of the United States*. These *Restatements*, which run on roughly thirty-year cycles, address rules of U.S. law with substantial significance for U.S. foreign relations and rules of international law that apply within the United States and to the United States in its relations with other states. After a nearly three-decade hiatus, in 2018 the ALI completed work on three selected topics: treaties, jurisdiction, and sovereign immunity. In 2023, the ALI authorized completion of the *Fourth Restatement*, which may take a number of years. Some of the topics addressed in the 2018 *Restatement (Fourth)* sections may need reexamination in light of more recent executive abuses.[130] Significant debate over the future shape of foreign-relations law will inevitably occur during these multi-stakeholder ALI discussions. The evolution of the *Fourth Restatement* project will clarify not just what the governing rules of foreign-relations and national security law are, but also how they should develop in contested areas.

Rethinking Foreign-Affairs Law

IN ADDITION TO THE INSTITUTIONAL REFORMS just recommended, key areas of foreign-affairs law deserve special attention in the years ahead. These include war making, international lawmaking, agreement breaking, emergency powers, intelligence oversight, information control, and democracy and national security. How might these areas be best addressed, especially if broader framework legislation cannot be enacted in the near future?

War Making

The previous chapter identified some key modifications needed to revise the laws on the use of force. But plainly, we need a better overall system of checks and balances to govern war making. After half a century, the War Powers Resolution of 1973 must be replaced.

To its credit, the resolution tried to define the respective roles of each political branch in a realm of shared constitutional power. Congress sought to do so by enacting a framework statute that aimed to promote interbranch communication, consultation, and cooperation. The law succeeded in forcing presidents to report regularly, albeit cryptically, on foreign deployments and to shorten sustained foreign interventions. But as chapter 4 described, successive administrations have increasingly skirted the resolution's textual restrictions on the sustained introduction of U.S. "armed forces . . . into the territory, airspace or waters of a foreign nation," by resorting to short-term insertions of special forces, drones, and cyber actions.

Apart from that, the resolution has largely failed to promote the inter-branch dialogue and cooperation about war making that it was designed to produce. The resolution was based on a gimmick: it "promotes" interbranch dialogue only indirectly, by threatening the president and Congress with a sixty-day statutory time limit to force them to talk to one another. But because the practice of all three branches has essentially rendered this "deadline" non-self-executing, that time limit has lost its power either to push the president toward consultation or to push Congress toward a prompt vote of approval or disapproval for the president's troop commitments. The resolution's legislative-veto provision runs afoul of the Supreme Court's decision invalidating legislative vetoes in *INS v. Chadha*.[1] At the same time, the substantive provisions of the resolution derogate from Congress's war-making powers by allowing the president too much freedom to make covert and short-term war and to commit military forces overseas without a clear purpose or an exit strategy. Finally, the resolution defines no role for the courts in forcing the political branches to engage in dialogue with one another about the reasons for engaging in armed conflict.

When the resolution was first enacted, Charles Black pointed out its most glaring omission: it defines how many months U.S. troops may stay abroad, but "utterly refus[es] even to begin the task of defining the conditions under which the president should not commit troops for even ten minutes—the really crucial matter."[2] As the Libya episode in 2011 showed, the resolution, as currently worded, does not encourage meaningful interbranch dialogue regarding the wisdom of any particular presidential troop commitment, for example, for urgent humanitarian intervention. Instead, the current law entrenches existing institutional inertia by condoning what Professor Richard Pildes has called "policymaking-by-silence." It frees Congress to take no position on the wisdom of any proposed conflict, to say nothing if the military action succeeds, but then to blame the president if it fails. "By design," Pildes explained, the resolution

makes Congress's silence . . . tantamount to a decision by Congress to prohibit the United States from continu[ing] to participate in 'hostilities' that the United States has initiated. Thus, Congress's failure to act has all the consequences, as a practical matter, of an affirmative decision by Congress to cut off the . . . operation, though without Congress actually making such a decision or having to take direct responsibility, through the act of voting, for such a decision and its ensuing consequences.[3]

As the twenty-first century proceeds, this kind of war-powers law will be-come increasingly obsolete. Russia's invasion of Ukraine in 2022 notwith-standing, large-scale manned interventions like Vietnam or Operation Desert Storm will become increasingly rare. As armed conflict is increas-ingly conducted not by massive air strikes or ground invasions but by the sporadic use of drones, artificial intelligence, special operations, and cyber weapons, the resolution's blunt, durational limit will become entirely inef-fective in forcing thoughtful interbranch dialogue about the goals of military operations.

Can this situation be fixed? In the current legislative environment, even modest legislative action may be politically unobtainable. But if Congress can muster the political will to enact a war-powers bill, the first-best option would obviously be general reform of the War Powers Resolution.[4] While myriad war-powers reform proposals have been floated over the years, any war-powers legislative strategy should incorporate the following elements.

First, by creating the kind of core consultative group (in the form of the joint committee on national security discussed in the previous chapter), a war-powers bill would devise a centralized repository of political expertise in Congress with continuing responsibility to deal with the war-powers prob-lem. Second, by requiring the president to consult regularly with that core consultative group, the bill would directly foster interbranch dialogue and attempt to equalize access to sensitive information that would otherwise lie exclusively within the president's control. In the process, thicker consulta-tion requirements would promote congressional involvement earlier in the decision-making process so that the president cannot simply commit troops first and then present Congress with a fait accompli.

Third, to encourage presidential signature, a revised law should define areas of legislative pre-authorization. The original Senate version of the War Powers Resolution laid out various circumstances under which Congress would approve in advance the introduction of U.S. armed forces into actual or imminent hostilities without a declaration of war. But this provision was dropped from the final version in conference.[5] The core consultative group and its staff, armed with a deep familiarity with the subtleties of past cases, could work with the executive branch to refine this provision for reinsertion into future legislation. In addition, the War Powers Resolution took no ac-count of either covert warfare or short-term military strikes. Again, the core consultative group could redress that omission by treating covert warfare as both a war-making and an intelligence issue and address the currently un-regulated problem of short-term military strikes. The revised law could ex-pressly authorize the president to engage in certain activities for which he currently lacks legislative authorization: for example, committing troops overseas for such limited, short-term purposes as rescuing American citi-zens endangered abroad. Not only would such provisions eliminate existing ambiguities regarding the scope of the president's statutory authorities, but they would also render Congress's legislative package more attractive to the president by unambiguously elevating the pre-authorized activities into *Youngstown*'s category one.

Fourth, a new law should create specialized legislative procedures for spe-cifically authorizing particular military actions. Using the legislative fast-track procedure described in chapter 10 could force Congress to vote on each particular troop commitment and thereby make a swift, specific public judg-ment approving or disapproving each proposed presidential military action.[6] To give a current example, Congress should adopt a stricter framework to regulate and oversee the use of force in Iran, Somalia, Syria, and Yemen and against emerging terrorist groups.[7] If the president proposed to commit U.S. armed forces to one of those regions, he could simultaneously have a bill introduced under expedited fast-track legislative procedures that would re-quire Congress to vote on a joint resolution of approval or disapproval of the action within ninety days. That fast-track action would force Congress to ap-prove or disapprove any particular intervention by action, not silence.[8]

Fifth, as chapter 10 discusses, any new war-powers bill should also grant individual members of Congress statutory standing to seek judicial enforce-ment of the act in the D.C. federal courts, which would develop a judicial counter-arena of legal expertise in that circuit with regard to war powers. As Professor Ely wryly observed, the same courts that have claimed separation-of-powers or judicial-incompetence reasons for refusing to decide whether "hostilities" exist for the purpose of triggering the War Powers Resolution have routinely decided, in insurance-contract cases, whether hostilities exist to determine whether a matter was insured for purposes of giving effect to a war-risk clause in an insurance policy. At the same time as judges have ab-stained from deciding whether our own government and officials have vio-lated international law and the constitutional law of foreign affairs, they have regularly passed judgment on whether foreign government officials have violated international and domestic law in transnational commercial and human-rights cases.[9]

Sixth, any new war-powers resolution should address the issue of humanitarian intervention, which, as chapter 7 described, has been a subject of considerable public debate. As I argued as State Department Legal Adviser during the Libyan war-powers episode, a humanitarian intervention would not be lawful under international law unless it met certain rigorous conditions. Under domestic law, in future cases, all three branches would likely read Congress's acquiescence in the executive's completion of the Kosovo and Libyan operations to support relaxation of the War Powers Resolution's strict durational limits for the limited purpose of completing the humanitarian mission in question. Under the test stated in my Libya testimony, the military operation would need to address Congress's main war-powers concerns: namely, curbing open-ended military missions, open-ended exposure of U.S. forces to foreign threats, open-ended escalation of the number of U.S. troops placed in harm's way in a foreign territory, and the uncontrolled use of military means in open-ended armed conflicts. If the facts showed that a particular intervention had become unreasonably prolonged, Congress or the courts could fairly conclude that the presidential use of force had become unlawful and must cease. To paraphrase Justice Breyer in *Zadvydas v. Davis,* in deciding whether the duration of any particular operation remained reasonable:

> [T]he court must ask whether the [operation] in question exceeds a period reasonably necessary to secure [the intended outcome]. It should measure reasonableness primarily in terms of the statute's basic purpose. Thus, if [completion] is not reasonably foreseeable, the court should hold continued [use of force] unreasonable and no longer authorized by statute.[10]

Seventh, any new war-powers resolution must consider targeted killing conducted via drone, artificial intelligence, or cyberspace. President Obama's speech at the National Defense University in May 2013 acknowledged that if Congress saw the need for judicial oversight as a more effective check on executive conduct than committee oversight, it could create a court to review targeted killing either before or after the operation occurred, along the lines of the Foreign Intelligence Surveillance Court. Congress could require intelligence officials to make ex parte, in camera submissions to the court of their evidence and justifications for action, with the court having discretion to deny that submission and order the release of the classified information to the oversight committees. Over time, such a court could become an expert referee between the intelligence agencies and the committees, while reducing the likelihood of leaks and offering greater protection of classified information.[11]

It may be some time before the emerging fields of cyber conflict, artificial intelligence, and private security contractors are ready for codification in either statute or treaty. But in each area, even without new legislation, the executive branch can continue to translate best practices into codes of conduct. As discussed in earlier chapters, cyber conflict is under active discussion in a variety of public and private lawmaking forums. Rules that are being negotiated have already become important reference points for U.S. interagency and allied legal discussions.[12] Public-private arrangements like the Montreux Document have produced an International Code of Conduct to govern private security practices. That code of conduct can be internalized into private behavior through contracts that govern the conduct of private security contractors.[13]

Similarly, as a recent U.S. political declaration showed, global laws regulating the use of artificial intelligence in warfare are being intensely debated.[14] The laws of war do not treat autonomous robots as per se illegal weapons. To the extent that many such weapons are only semi-autonomous, the human operators of such robots can program in controlling principles analogous to those stated in President Obama's Frameworks Report of 2016 to ensure compliance with international humanitarian, human-rights, and criminal law.[15] Following the Montreux model for private security contractors, the president could issue an executive order, to be reinforced later by statute, directing purchase-contract terms and updating policies, contracts, and regulations to ensure producer liability for legal violations.

These norm-setting exercises should clearly declare that fully autonomous robots that do not have a human operator in the loop when they select, acquire, and engage targets are per se illegal weapons of war. The problem is not the presence of technology to control navigation or movement, but the *exclusion* of human beings from algorithmic decisions to engage in offensive selection of targets that are then attacked with lethal force. A global consensus is emerging that relevant governmental personnel must require appropriate levels of human judgment in the development, deployment, and use of such artificial intelligence for military purposes. The U.N. Conference on Conventional Weapons in Geneva has stated general principles for maintaining meaningful human control in compliance with international humanitarian law and establishing a responsible chain of command with humans in the loop. But the evolution of these legal standards remains at a relatively early stage. As these standards mature and crystallize, they too can be embedded into private contracts, codes of conduct, political declarations, executive orders and statutes, and eventually intergovernmental legal agreements.

The final challenge in this area is ending the "forever war," which has been going on since September 11, 2001.[16] A generation of Americans has now grown up in a state of war, and thousands have served and paid in blood for that conflict. The Obama administration entered office with an ambitious plan to end America's wars. As chapter 7 described, in May 2013, President Obama committed himself to ending the "forever war" by disengaging from Afghanistan, closing Guantánamo, and issuing clearer drone rules. He promised to narrow the "war on terror" by embedding limited uses of force in a broader smart-power counterterrorism strategy against al Qaeda and its associated forces. But Obama left office three years later with Guantánamo still open; troops in Iraq, Afghanistan, Syria, and parts of Libya; creeping expansion of the armed conflict into Somalia and Africa; continuing criticism of his drone rules; and unrepealed authorizations for the use of military force.

Candidate Biden made ending the "forever war" a hallmark of his 2020 campaign, but continued threats from Iran and violence in Syria have kept him in the drone wars. As of 2023, however, he has left Afghanistan. The numbers at Guantánamo have dropped to a few dozen. Only a few hundred U.S. troops remain in Syria. His administration has now issued a new variant of Obama's counterterrorism "playbook."[17] And Congress is finally moving toward repealing the outmoded 1991 and 2002 authorizations for the use of military force and considering the repeal of other statutory use-of-force authorizations. I have written at length elsewhere about the specific steps the United States should now take to finish the job of ending the "forever war." In particular, Congress should enact recent pending proposals for new national security framework legislation to guide the winding down of perpetual conflict.[18] Both private and public actors must push, so that inch by inch, the administration can finally make visible progress toward this painfully delayed goal.

International Lawmaking

In the twenty-first century, how should the United States enter into its international obligations? Chapter 7 reviewed President Obama's diversified tools for making such agreements, including the Paris climate accord and the Iran nuclear deal. That chapter explained why too many foreign-relations scholars and pundits still fetishize the traditional constitutional "triptych"— Article II treaties, congressional-executive agreements, and sole executive agreements—over a more nuanced understanding of the complex real-world spectrum of techniques by which the executive now actually makes international commitments to the United States' foreign partners. Because American international legal engagement has transcended treaties and executive agreements, we need a better, more realistic way to describe the textured tapestry of modern international lawmaking.

Modern foreign-relations law should dispense with the transsubstantive triptych. It is no longer a meaningful—and at times it is a positively misleading—way of describing the multifarious ways in which the United States currently engages in international lawmaking. Instead, we should ask a prior question: Whether the proposed agreement actually entails any new, legally binding obligations at all. Only if we are making new legal obligations does an executive action have the potential to be like treaty making, which constitutionally requires congressional approval. If the only international obligations that the executive branch incurs are to carry out domestic legal obligations that already exist, new congressional approval should not be required. The United States is only reaffirming existing obligations to obey domestic law. If the international commitment being assumed is only political, and neither new, legally binding, nor domestically enforceable, the obligations being created are diplomatic and political, not contractual. They can lawfully be made by the president alone, operating against the background of legislative acceptance endorsed by the *Dames & Moore* case.

But once new legal obligations are actually entailed, we should shift to an issue-specific and agreement-specific framework that better reflects how the current process of congressional approval for executive international law-making actually works. Until now, the *Youngstown* framework has focused on one factor: whether Congress has approved, disapproved, or said nothing about the agreement in question. A better framework would weigh this as one of two factors: first, the *degree of congressional approval* for the executive lawmaking; and second, the *constitutional allocation of institutional authority* over the subject matter at issue. Whether a particular set of commitments is lawful should be both agreement specific (e.g., to what extent has Congress approved these particular provisions?) and subject-matter specific (e.g., is this agreement about war, trade, or intellectual property?). These inquiries reveal that a one-dimensional triptych is an inadequate proxy for representing the two-dimensional intersection of two spectrums of political interests.

Put together, the two spectrums form a grid with four quadrants (figure 2). The first, vertical spectrum—depicted by the y-axis in the chart—denotes the extent of congressional approval for a particular presidential action and runs from zero congressional approval (at the bottom of the chart) to unambiguous and widespread congressional approval (at the top of the chart). This vertical spectrum roughly parallels the traditional triptych because the triptych itself was a proxy for Justice Jackson's tripartite tiers of congressional approval in his *Youngstown* concurrence. That opinion, now enshrined in the majority opinion in *Dames & Moore*, famously describes a spectrum running from congressional disapproval to approval, with Article II treaties representing supermajority approval in the Senate as a valid constitutional alternative to approval by legislative majorities in both houses.

The greatest failing of Jackson's framework is that it purported to be trans-substantive. It overlooked the fact that the degree of congressional approval required to legalize any particular presidential agreement is *substance dependent*: it depends on which branch of government has substantive constitutional authority regarding the foreign-policy area in which the agreement is being made. The second, horizontal spectrum—depicted by the x-axis of the graph—runs from textual reservoirs of exclusive presidential authority under the Constitution (e.g., the recognition power) on the far left to countervailing zones of plenary congressional authority (e.g., the foreign-commerce power or the appropriations power) on the far right.[19]

Putting these two spectrums together, the graph shows that presidential lawmaking will be most constitutional when it is strongly supported by congres-

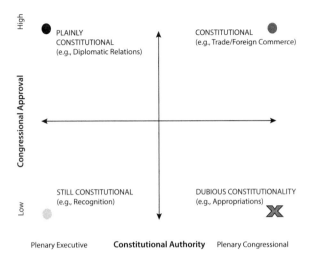

Fig. 2. Lawfulness of executive international lawmaking (figure by Bill Nelson)

sional approval. Indeed, the top half of the graph simply depicts *Youngstown* category one, where the president's "authority is at its maximum, for it includes all that he possesses in his own right plus all that Congress can delegate." Whether congressional support is even necessary will depend on whether the subject matter falls within a zone of presidential, congressional, or shared authority. Toward the left side of the graph, the president has powerful claims of plenary authority even without congressional action. In such areas, the president could conclude the agreement even in the face of express congressional disapproval if he has clear plenary power (e.g., the power to recognize or conduct diplomatic relations) that allows him to act even over congressional objection (*Youngstown* category three).[20] But if there is both low congressional approval and the subject matter of the dispute is within Congress's plenary constitutional authority (as in the lower right quadrant of the graph), the agreement will be unconstitutional.[21] Finally, the middle range on the y-axis reflects Justice Jackson's *Youngstown* category two: the president acts in the face of congressional silence with regard to the specific presidential action being contemplated. In this zone, the issue of constitutionality will probably be resolved by the courts, either by ruling on the merits of the president's action or by rejecting a challenge to it on the grounds of nonjusticiability.[22]

In sum, in evaluating the extent of congressional approval for an agreement of this type, one should look not to the triptych, but to factors similar to those applied in *Dames & Moore:* general pre-authorization, consistent executive practice, and legal landscape. If an agreement entails new, legally binding obligations, we should examine first the degree of congressional approval legally required to enter into an agreement—an assessment that roughly maps onto the three *Youngstown* categories. But whether that degree of congressional approval is constitutionally mandated depends on the second factor: which branch of government has substantive constitutional prerogatives regarding that area of foreign policy. In the area of recognition, for example, the president's plenary power obviates the need for congressional approval to enter into an agreement; but in the area of foreign commerce, his discretion is limited and would in some cases be barred by Congress's foreign-commerce powers.

Going forward, this approach offers a more realistic, issue-specific, and agreement-specific way to reflect how much political approval for executive-branch international lawmaking is actually necessary. If a particular agreement does not embody new, legally binding commitments, it will almost certainly be lawful even with little or no congressional approval. Under this analysis, as chapter 7 showed, President Obama's Paris climate accord and Iran nuclear deal were clearly constitutional. But if a particular agreement does embody new, legally binding international commitments, the constitutionality of that arrangement will depend on where the subject matter of the agreement and the degree of congressional approval fall on the graph. The further down an agreement falls in the bottom right quadrant—for example, a sole executive agreement attempting to mandate appropriations—the more dubious its constitutionality would be.

A final question is whether a more functional Congress should centralize its procedures for deciding whether particular substantive agreements should be ratified by treaty or executive agreement. Professor Louis Henkin once suggested that Congress address this "choice of instruments" problem by forming a joint committee on international agreements, similar to the core consultative group or joint committee on national security envisioned in the previous chapter. That group would consult with the executive during the negotiation process and advise the executive on whether the agreement should go to Congress for consent, and if so, whether to the Senate or both houses.[22]

Presidents since William McKinley have involved members of Congress in agreement negotiations. In the 1970s, a group of committee members and staffers observed negotiations and later helped secure congressional approval of trade agreements negotiated at the Tokyo round of the General Agreement on Tariffs and Trade negotiations. A similar bipartisan group, supported by staffers for the Senate Armed Services and Foreign Relations Committees, was instrumental in securing the speedy ratification of the Intermediate-Range Nuclear Forces Treaty.[24] As chapter 10 suggested, Congress should institutionalize this practice by statute, by creating a joint committee on national security as its standing core consultative group to monitor or appoint expert congressional monitors for each significant international negotiation. The monitoring group could then serve as a congressional liaison with executive-branch negotiators, help secure subsequent approval of the negotiated accord, and with executive permission, observe negotiations and receive information from the executive negotiators to ease executive-legislative tensions as the international agreement goes through the approval process.

Agreement Breaking

The Trump era revealed both the danger of mass agreement breaking and the weakness of the constitutional claim of a general presidential power for unilateral treaty withdrawal. But if the Constitution recognizes no such unilateral presidential power, what should be the alternative?

Significantly, only one U.S. court decision—the en banc D.C. Circuit decision in *Goldwater*—has ever endorsed an unnuanced rule of unilateral presidential termination on the merits, and that ruling was vacated a month later by the U.S. Supreme Court.[25] If and when the Supreme Court finally considers this issue on the merits, it should conclude that no single transsubstantive rule governs whether and how each and every international agreement may be terminated or withdrawn from as a matter of U.S. domestic law. Instead, the Court should apply a "mirror principle," whereby the degree of congressional approval required to exit from an international agreement mirrors the degree of congressional approval needed to enter into that agreement in the first place. Unlike an overbroad "unilateral presidential termination rule," the mirror principle would not mandate a "one size fits all" mode of agreement termination. Instead, the mirror principle would require varying degrees of congressional and executive participation to exit from various kinds of international agreements, depending on the particular subject matter and entry process of the agreement at issue.

U.S. constitutional jurisprudence has long acknowledged that withdrawals from international agreements should be dictated by a mirror principle. As a constitutional matter, the mirror principle is simply a variant of the famous "last-in-time rule," first stated in the *Head Money Cases* and *Whitney v. Robertson*. Those cases long ago settled that, however made, a binding international agreement can be superseded only by a later-in-time agreement or statute that is adopted with a comparable degree of legislative input.[26] Because the Court held that the last-in-time instrument controls—so that such a superseding legal enactment effectively exits the United States from a prior international commitment—the mirror principle became U.S. law long before *Goldwater* and remains so today. Moreover, self-executing treaties are the law of the land, no less than congressionally enacted statutes. If the president cannot alone enact or repeal a statute, why should the president be able to repeal the duly enacted law of the land—and its accompanying framework of internalized domestic law—just because the initiating juridical act happened to be in treaty rather than statutory form?

To escape this reasoning, executive-branch lawyers have tried to argue by analogy to executive appointments. They claim that the president alone should be able to terminate a treaty that was made with the advice and consent of the Senate because the president alone can fire a cabinet member appointed with the advice and consent of the Senate. But this analogy is inapposite, not least because firing a cabinet member is an internal matter within the control of the executive branch. The removal power rests on the Article II vesting clause and the take-care clause because presidents cannot properly discharge executive power or take care that the law be faithfully executed if they cannot use the threat of unilateral removal to hold subordinates accountable. Treaty abrogation, by contrast, runs afoul of the take-care clause because the president is unilaterally undoing—not enforcing—binding domestic and international law that has already been made.

I argued above that when making agreements, the president's lawyer should examine, first, the degree of congressional approval for the executive lawmaking and, second, the constitutional allocation of institutional authority over the subject matter at issue. Under the mirror principle, the degree of congressional and executive participation required to exit from an international agreement would turn on the same two factors: the *subject matter* of the agreement at issue and the *degree of congressional approval* involved in the

RETHINKING FOREIGN-AFFAIRS LAW

entry into that agreement. Thus, as with entry, the degree of legislative participation required to exit from an agreement would be *substance dependent*. Because the mirror principle requires for exit only the same degree of legislative participation as was required for entry, it is flexible enough to allow Congress's input into an exit decision to vary according to the subject matter.

Consider how the mirror principle would apply in a range of contemporary situations. First, under the mirror principle, agreements lawfully concluded with *no* legislative input—so-called sole executive agreements—could also be terminated by the president alone. But agreements initially concluded with *considerable* legislative input, such as congressional-executive agreements and treaties, would require a comparable degree of legislative input to terminate. This would be particularly true if the president tried to act alone to terminate an agreement that was made within the heart of Congress's concurrent or exclusive constitutional authority over a particular subject matter, for example, foreign commerce or government funding. If the president lacked the constitutional authority to make an agreement in a subject-matter area without congressional approval, the president would similarly lack authority to unilaterally *unmake* an agreement in the same subject-matter area. Thus, President Trump's threat to terminate or withdraw from NAFTA (which was later amended into the United States–Mexico–Canada Agreement) would have been barred by Congress's commerce-clause authority.

So-called executive agreements plus, such as the Paris climate accord—that is, agreements initiated by the executive with general congressional awareness and approval in a zone of congressional subject-matter authority based on a broader history of legislative authorization in a particular direction—could not be terminated by the president alone, as terminating such an agreement would disrupt legitimate congressional expectations. Finally, the president could not unilaterally terminate an agreement in violation of international law in an area of congressional subject-matter authority, such as the Iran nuclear deal.[27] Under that deal, the president was not exercising constitutional powers but, rather, exercising delegated congressional foreign-commerce powers to adjust sanctions when the agreement partner had complied with its international commitments. Instead of acquiescing in the withdrawal as it did, Congress could have instead revoked its delegation and used its foreign-commerce power to decline to reimpose economic sanctions on Iran, despite Trump's decision, because it saw no basis for an executive claim of retaliatory breach.

Thus, Congress could have cited the mirror principle to assert a constitutional right to participate in any final decision to withdraw from the Iran nuclear deal.

As Justice Breyer noted nearly two decades ago, the Supreme Court "has long considered as relevant and informative the way in which foreign courts have applied standards roughly comparable to our own constitutional standards in roughly comparable circumstances." In *Printz v. United States*, he elaborated that the "experience [of other nations] may . . . cast an *empirical light* on the consequences of different solutions to a common legal problem."[28] Of course, the constitutional issue of treaty exit arises not just in the United States, but in every other country in the world. The foreign decision casting the most relevant empirical light on this issue is the United Kingdom's famous Brexit case. The Supreme Court of the United Kingdom held that the U.K. government may not use its executive prerogative powers but rather must seek parliamentary approval to trigger article 50, the withdrawal provision of the Treaty on European Union. Similarly, the High Court of South Africa for the Gauteng Division held that the executive branch could not unilaterally withdraw from the Rome Statute of the International Criminal Court without the parliamentary approval previously required for accession. Similar mirror reasoning can be found in Canadian law. A recent survey reports that parliamentary approval for withdrawal is required by organic laws in ten Eastern European countries and by constitutional or administrative interpretation or presidential decree in nine others. The reasoning of these comparative precedents cuts strongly against the view that functional considerations should sanction a general unilateral termination rule. Instead, these cases suggest that U.S. withdrawal from a long-standing treaty or international organization—such as the United Nations or the World Trade Organization, whose rules have also been deeply internalized into U.S. law—should not become effective without congressional involvement, particularly since such a withdrawal or termination would similarly require the unwinding of many domestic laws that the executive could not repeal alone.[29]

To be workable, of course, the mirror principle would need to anticipate such political exigencies as the need for a "quick divorce" (as discussed in chapter 8). To accommodate bona fide emergency situations, the Supreme Court could recognize the president's unilateral authority to suspend U.S.

treaty obligations for a limited period, long enough for the president to make the case to Congress that withdrawal is warranted "for cause." But it would be wildly overbroad to allow such a rare exception to swallow the rule. Although in a genuine emergency the president may be best positioned to decide whether an exit from a treaty is urgently required, that in no way dictates the much broader rule that the Constitution authorizes any president, on impulse, to withdraw the United States from any and all bilateral and multilateral arrangements that it has joined over the centuries. Recognizing a very limited exception to the mirror principle for genuinely exceptional circumstances would acknowledge a functionally narrower and better tailored authority than granting one person blanket unilateral power to terminate, withdraw from, or suspend all treaties in all situations.

Finally, as chapter 8 describes, the Supreme Court's decision in *Zivotofsky v. Clinton* (*Zivotofsky I*) suggests that a litigant could challenge, in court, a future president's decision to unilaterally terminate or withdraw from an agreement.[30] The dismissal in *Goldwater v. Carter* had suggested that such cases were nonjusticiable, but in the four intervening decades, the law on the issue of justiciability has changed. In *Zivotofsky I*, the Court narrowed the political-question doctrine by declining to bar review of the president's power to recognize foreign states in the face of a contrary congressional statute. Thus, although recent historical practice recognizes that, in some circumstances, the president has the authority to act on behalf of the United States in suspending, terminating, or withdrawing from U.S. treaty commitments, courts may find that different termination procedures are appropriate for different agreements, depending on the degree of legislative input that went into the United States' original entry into the agreement. Congress should make this point explicit by enacting a statute requiring the president to come to Congress in order to withdraw the United States from particularly vital international agreements such as the U.N. Charter, NATO, the World Health Organization, the Paris climate accord, and the World Trade Organization.[31]

Simply put, it would be grievous error for the president, or the president's lawyers, to claim an uncontested general unilateral power to terminate or withdraw from any and all international agreements. Even a future extreme unilateralist president should not lightly assume that the U.S. Constitution confides in one person alone the power to entirely disengage the United States from the post–World War II legal order.

Emergency Powers

Apart from the right to suspend habeas corpus, the Constitution grants the president no inherent emergency powers. Congress has more than compensated for that omission by giving the president an array of statutory authorities. Justice Jackson's *Youngstown* concurrence explained that the Framers had omitted broader constitutional powers because "[t]hey knew what emergencies were, knew the pressures they engender for authoritative action, knew, too, how they afford a ready pretext for usurpation." And in a characteristically prescient twist, Jackson added: "We may also suspect that they suspected that emergency powers would tend to kindle emergencies."[32]

Recent decades have unveiled the myriad ways by which a unilateralist president could exploit his emergency powers. As chapter 8 described, Trump declared national emergencies to impose sanctions on prosecutors from the International Criminal Court and to build a wall that Congress had refused to fund. To impose trade sanctions, he declared Canada to be a "national security threat" and claimed national security "emergencies" to act unilaterally in such traditional congressional areas as immigration, military construction projects, warfare, trade, international agreements, and government funding. He claimed flimsy national security justifications to impose the travel ban, to separate infants from their parents at the border, and to expel transgender individuals from the U.S. military. He invoked a "public health emergency" under Title 42 to deny aliens their asylum rights at the southern border, a policy that Biden maintained during the first two and a half years of his presidency. And after Russia invaded Ukraine in 2022, Biden used sweeping authorities under the International Emergency Economic Powers Act (IEEPA) to impose crushing economic sanctions on Russia almost weekly, without a U.N. Security Council resolution.[33]

As with the War Powers Resolution, the possible amendment of IEEPA has been thoroughly vetted elsewhere.[34] Here, too, the law could be sensibly revised. The field of presidential emergency powers raises four issues: ensuring that they are not triggered on a pretext; coordinating them to ensure that they are effective, coherent, and lawful; terminating emergencies after crises have ended; and ending the use of secret emergency powers.

Under current law, presidents can too easily trigger their statutory emergency powers. The National Emergencies Act authorizes the president to declare an emergency simply by signing an executive order, then renewing that emergency yearly, without limit. As of February 2023, over sixty declared national emergencies, dating back over forty years, were in effect, nearly all based on IEEPA.[35] Because there are now so many national emergencies, declared over so many years to sustain sanctions against so many countries and entities, stronger principles of internal and external accountability are plainly needed.

Within the executive branch, internal accountability has been greatly enhanced by the creation and appointment of a series of able ambassadors-at-large in the State Department to coordinate sanctions. One of those sanctions coordinators has wisely recommended developing a "common law of sanctions" so that the timeline, severity, equity, and legality of different sanctions imposed on different countries at the same time will be properly coordinated within the U.S. government and between the United States and its allies.[36] To promote external accountability, interbranch dialogue, and explicit power sharing, an amended IEEPA could require the president to consult with a core consultative congressional group like the joint committee on national security discussed in the previous chapter, specifying the intended sanctions and the reasons why, before declaring such an emergency.

The president should be required to make a more detailed showing when invoking a "national emergency" to impose sanctions, and that showing could then be tested by interagency review at the Justice Department and adversarial congressional review (with the filing of a counter-report by the congressional legal adviser). If Congress wished to prospectively authorize the president to exercise sweeping powers for particular purposes—for example, to respond to aggression (as in Ukraine) or to rescue hostages (as during the Iranian hostage crisis)—it should give examples of such "national emergencies" in an amended IEEPA, specifying, for example, that manifest violations of international law or the seizure of American citizens would constitute factual triggers justifying the president's exercise of extraordinary statutory emergency powers.[37]

Current law allows Congress to vote to end an emergency, but only if it has a veto-proof supermajority in both houses to override the likely presidential veto. To ensure that Congress would expressly approve or disapprove the president's emergency actions before the emergency expired, an amended IEEPA would give fast-track legislative treatment to a joint resolution affirming the existence of the emergency and approving any executive orders issued under it. To end perpetual emergencies, a revised statute could sunset any declared national emergency by having it automatically expire within a fixed period, such as two years. The law could mandate renewed face-to-face consultation between executive officials and the core group before the emergency could be extended. These statutory revisions would allow the president to conduct emergency actions pursuant to express congressional approval at all times, but would require the president to return to Congress periodically to extend that emergency authority.[38]

Congress should also clarify two issues, discussed in chapter 9, that have faced the Biden administration during the Russia-Ukraine crisis. First IEEPA currently authorizes the executive to confiscate and take title to ("vest") assets only "when the United States is *engaged in armed hostilities or has been attacked* by a foreign country or foreign nationals"—which Russia has not done. But other language in the statute gives the president authority to "nullify, void, . . . or prohibit" any foreign country from "holding" or "exercising any right, power, or privilege" over property in which it has "any interest" and to "direct and compel" the "exportation" of such property.[39] Either a court or Congress should clarify whether, in peacetime, IEEPA provides the authority to seize foreign central bank assets held in the United States and to transfer them (for example, to Ukraine for reconstruction) or whether such sovereign assets are immune from attachment. If Congress were to specifically authorize such seizures and transfers, it would also need to provide the assets' owners with constitutional due process.[40]

Second, how to ensure that these authorities are being exercised lawfully under domestic and international law? As the discussion in chapter 3 revealed, domestic courts have rejected challenges to the president's exercise of statutory authorities under IEEPA. Nevertheless, to ensure that courts quickly dispel any doubts regarding the validity of the president's actions, a sanctions amendment bill could contain procedures for expedited judicial review of any challenged national-emergency declaration and sanctions order. Because any challenge to the president's IEEPA authority would involve statutory interpretation, the political-question doctrine should not bar judicial review. And because of the impact of statutory "travel transactions" (that is, financial transactions incident to foreign travel) on the First Amendment right to travel, courts should give special scrutiny to this individual-rights issue.[41]

Under international law, a tribunal could potentially find a variety of reasons why U.S. sanctions are illegal. It could rule, for example, that they exceed the scope of permitted countermeasures; violate accepted principles of sovereign immunity; are disproportionate or indiscriminate; violate due process; or exceed the scope of the security exception under international-trade law. Although European courts have largely upheld sanctions against Russia, Iran has challenged both U.S. and Canadian sanctions in the International Court of Justice as violations of international law.[42] Between 2016 and 2018, Iran brought two applications to the International Court of Justice against the United States under the Treaty of Amity, Economic Relations, and Consular Rights (1955), claiming that the United States had violated Iran's treaty rights through economic sanctions. At this writing, final judgment in the sanctions case is still pending. But even if the court should find that the U.S. economic sanctions were necessary responses to Iranian noncompliance with its nonproliferation obligations, it could still hold that U.S. measures are illegal if they directly interfere with basic human needs like food, medicine, and transportation safety.[43]

Finally, any new legislation in this area should clarify that there should be no secret executive claims of inherent emergency powers. Presidential emergency action documents (PEADs) originated during the Eisenhower administration to ensure continuity in the wake of a Soviet nuclear attack and have since expanded to address other types of emergencies. We do not know the precise content of current PEADs, but an administration budget request revealed that in 2018, there were fifty-six such documents. Records from the Bush 43 administration released under the Freedom of Information Act suggested that, during a crisis, the president might even claim the power to suspend habeas corpus or turn off the internet. To address this problem, Congress should enact pending legislation that would require the president to disclose PEADs to the relevant oversight committees.[44]

Intelligence Oversight

In the wake of the Iran-contra affair, Congress focused its intelligence-oversight reform efforts on what one former CIA general counsel dubbed "a spate of legislative activity designed to lock the particular barn door in the Iran-Contra Affair."[45] At the time, the CIA's director, general counsel, and inspector general were not subject to Senate confirmation. But that changed after September 11, 2001, when the independent 9/11 Commission proposed sweeping change in the intelligence community to prevent future intelligence failures.[46]

In 2004, Congress followed the adoption of a number of reparative executive orders by President George W. Bush with the enactment of amendments to the National Security Act that strengthened centralized oversight both internally and externally. Unlike other areas of foreign affairs, where considerable room remains for centralization of congressional expertise, little need existed for similar centralization in the intelligence area, where the two select intelligence committees were well established and extensive information sharing already occurred between the committees and the executive branch.[47] But internally, the eighteen intelligence agencies and organizations of the federal government were brought under the centralized supervision of a director of national intelligence. The Office of the Director of National Intelligence itself now has several offices responsible for ensuring legal compliance: the Office of General Counsel, the Office of the Inspector General of the Intelligence Community, and the Office of Civil Liberties, Privacy, and Transparency. Two oversight boards and an advisory board have been created to enhance oversight and preserve privacy and civil liberties.[48]

The CIA whistleblower incident that triggered Trump's first impeachment showed how the internal and external accountability mechanisms created by these institutional reforms can interact to bring potentially impeachable behavior to light.[49] As chapter 8 recounted, Trump turned his conversation with Ukrainian president Zelenskyy on July 25, 2019, into a request for partisan political information relating to the upcoming presidential election and blocked the flow of official aid to pressure Ukraine to comply. Knowledge of these actions led an anonymous CIA whistleblower to write, "In the course of my official duties, I have received information from multiple U.S. government officials that the President of the United States is using the power of his office to solicit interference from a foreign country in the 2020 U.S. election."[50] A few weeks later, the whistleblower's complaint reached the CIA general counsel, who, fearing that a crime had been committed, notified the National Security Council legal adviser and then called the Justice Department's top national security lawyer to recommend a possible criminal referral. By August 12, the whistleblower had filed a formal complaint with the intelligence community's inspector general, who found his complaint "credible." Although White House officials fought to block the acting director of national intelligence from turning the complaint over to relevant committees in Congress, as required by the National Security Act, by the end of August the acting director of national intelligence had sent the Justice Department his own criminal referral based on the whistleblower complaint. The episode revealed that various intelligence reforms have succeeded in creating multiple channels whereby whistleblower complaints can call attention to national security misbehavior. Mindful of this incident, Congress should fill gaps in existing laws by enacting stronger legal protections for other foreign-affairs whistleblowers who are willing to obey their constitutional oath by objecting to lawless actions by senior officials.[51]

Despite these improvements, additional reforms may still be warranted. Congress could assign greater oversight responsibilities within the executive branch to the Justice Department's Office of Intelligence Policy and Review, created in 1980 to assist the attorney general in reviewing the implementation of executive orders by intelligence agencies and carrying out the attorney general's functions under the Foreign Intelligence Surveillance Act. To enforce its regulation of intelligence, Congress could supplement its reform legislation with an appropriations-cutoff device, which would automatically terminate the expenditure of funds for any covert activity with respect to which the president had failed to notify the committees with a signed finding and limit executive power to reprogram appropriations. Violations of these appropriations restrictions could be evaluated by the courts, which would subject intelligence activities to the salutary influence of judicial examination.[52]

Information Control

As suggested in chapters 2 and 3, the National Security Constitution requires that the public, as well as Congress, receive as much information as is necessary to evaluate the wisdom and legality of executive conduct. Professor Eugene Rostow, a strong advocate of executive power, observed that "[i]f the President and the executive branch cannot persuade Congress and the public that a policy is wise, it should not be pursued."[53] My multiple tours in the government have convinced me that executive decisions are far more likely to be made correctly and with full process if all participants are aware that their decision-making will soon undergo public scrutiny.

Still, secrecy reigns across all three branches of government.[54] In part that is because, as Daniel Ellsberg (who leaked the Pentagon Papers to the press more than fifty years ago) has argued, the goal of classification is not just protecting legitimate secrets but "is a protection system against the revelation of mistakes, false predictions, embarrassments of various kinds and maybe even crimes." Within the executive branch, national security information is wildly overclassified. During the Vietnam War, former Supreme Court justice and United Nations ambassador Arthur Goldberg told Congress that in his experience, during five tours in the government, "75 percent of [the classified] documents [I have read] should never have been classified in the first place; another 15 percent quickly outlived the need for secrecy; and only about 10 percent genuinely required restricted access over any significant period of time." Billions and possibly trillions of pages of U.S. documents remain classified. In my own similar experience, I have found that most government documents are overclassified when written, and default classifications endure long after any of the information concealed is of more than historical interest.[55]

At the same time, as Professor David Pozen has chronicled, overclassification and rampant leaking have become chronic and irreducible features of the U.S. information system. The public push for transparency has led to a curious asymmetry: even as "the transparency laws of the 1960s and 1970s placed increasingly onerous demands on the domestic policy process, they grew increasingly detached from the state's most violent and least visible components," which has led to what Pozen calls the "rise and rise of national security secrecy."[56]

Congress should take meaningful and nuanced steps to close this transparency deficit. Although few would dispute the executive's legitimate need to deny sensitive national security information to foreign powers or domestic subversive elements, the question persistently arises "whether the public and Congress receive enough information about defense and foreign policy matters to be able to influence policy decisions and to exercise an effective external check on the power of the executive."[57] The recent classification controversies involving Presidents Trump and Biden and former vice president Pence present an opportunity for Congress to hold new hearings—as a Senate select committee on intelligence oversight (the Church Committee) did after Vietnam—to finally start installing a more nuanced classification system that is better calibrated to genuine national security needs.

Greater transparency is most urgently needed in the area of "secret law." As Elizabeth Goitein and Dakota Rudesill have documented, all three branches use techniques to express secret legal opinions, which they then follow. Congress should pass legislation, such as the DOJ OLC Transparency Act, to require the disclosure of the kind of secret Department of Justice legal memos discussed in chapters 5 and 6.[58] Knowing the executive branch's interpretation would allow both courts and Congress to better challenge self-serving or illegal interpretations.

Most of the current classification system remains governed by executive order.[59] The Freedom of Information Act (FOIA) exemplifies yet another far-reaching post-Vietnam framework statute that has gradually been weakened by executive initiative, congressional acquiescence, and judicial tolerance. Under the statute, national security agencies now enjoy a host of exemptions and exclusions. As originally drafted, the act specified a role for Congress, the executive, the courts, and private individuals in the public release of government information. It required every government agency to disclose documents requested by the public, but its "national security" exemption specifically exempts from disclosure properly classified "matters that are . . . established by an Executive order to be kept secret in the interest of national defense or foreign policy."[60]

To enhance the flow of information to the public and to further the executive branch's external accountability, Congress should amend FOIA to mandate periodic declassification of information that was originally classified under an executive order, unless the executive agency specifically chooses to reinstate that classification. To preserve external accountability, FOIA empowers the district courts to review an agency's refusal to release requested records and, if necessary, to review de novo a decision to withhold information, with the agency bearing the burden to show proper classification. Predictably, however, when executive officials have exercised their statutory discretion to withhold documents, the courts have usually deferred to executive classification decisions and withheld requested information. Congress has acquiesced in these trends by failing to amend the act to preserve its original intent. Congress should now amend FOIA's national security exemption to require the agency to identify the damage to national security likely to result from the release of a particular document and to explain why that agency's need to protect the information outweighs the public interest in disclosure.[61]

National security officials should recall the many ways in which the public release of previously secret information has advanced, rather than harmed, national security interests. The Biden administration's anticipation, in 2021, of the Russia-Ukraine war dramatically revealed the advantages of the strategic release of national security information to the public and our allies. Faced with the looming threat of a Russian invasion of Ukraine, the president took three steps to try to blunt the pending invasion: first, he instructed his director of national intelligence, Avril Haines, to share U.S. intelligence in advance with key allies; second, his team launched a daring plan to declassify and publicize in advance sensitive information about Putin's war plans; and third, they launched a campaign to send lethal weapons to Ukraine. As Director Haines later noted, the centralization of intelligence information allowed the United States to see the big picture earlier. Haines recalled the president saying, "We need to start sharing intelligence and you have got to help [our allies] see that this is a plausible possibility, because that's what's going to help us to engage them in a way that allows us to start planning."[62]

Because information-sharing often requires declassification, overclassification can obstruct the United States' ability to disrupt adversaries and pursue shared goals with allies. As the national security adviser Jake Sullivan acknowledged, regarding Ukraine, intelligence sharing with allies "began in early December [2021] and became a central feature of our approach through the beginning of the invasion—and since." CIA director William Burns, a career diplomat, confirmed that "[w]e shared intelligence quite systematically with the Ukrainians to help them get ready to defend themselves . . . [and this] made a difference, not only in putting Putin on his back foot, but also in shoring up the solidarity and sense of purpose of NATO allies as well." He explained: "The president made the decision to declassify some of our intelligence relatively early on [in the crisis]. . . . I had seen too many instances where Putin had created false narratives that we never caught up to." The White House national security spokesperson further noted that "downgrading intelligence and making it public . . . can [also] really affect the decision-making process of a potential adversary. We were beating Putin's lie to the punch, and we know that by doing so we got inside his decision-making loop."[63]

Democracy and National Security

Finally, as chapter 8 reviewed, interference in elections and presidential transitions must be treated as a severe national security threat. I appreciate that these proposed reforms parallel other recent reform proposals designed to address the broader issue of America's democratic decline.[64] But this overlap only confirms the extent to which today's national security issues have become virtually inseparable from the broader challenges facing our democracy.

The Trump years revealed unique U.S. national security vulnerability, both during our elections and during the transition period between a presidential election and the inauguration of the new president. Tampering during these periods, whether by domestic or foreign actors, directly threatens national security, particularly if it ends up prolonging in office a leader who embraces extreme executive unilateralism. By focusing on a few battleground states that are key to victory in the Electoral College, future election and transition hacking efforts—which could also take the form of gerrymandering and census manipulation—could jeopardize the legitimacy of the U.S. constitutional order.

To address this, Congress should start by further revising the presidential-transition laws to make clear the kinds of activities that both the incoming and outgoing administrations may lawfully engage in during the several-month transition period between an election and inauguration. The Presidential Transition Enhancement Act of 2019 took an important step by including a prohibition on conflicts of interest for members of the transition. At the end of 2022, Congress finally enacted the Presidential Transition Improvement Act, but its main focus was on providing clearer guidelines for when eligible candidates for president and vice president may receive federal resources to support their transition into office and removing the need for the sitting administrator of the General Services Administration to "ascertain" who has won the election during the transition period. The same enactment also amended the Electoral Count Reform Act to reaffirm that the vice president plays only a ministerial role at the joint session of Congress where Electoral College votes are counted, and to raise the threshold necessary for members of Congress to object to a state's electors.[65]

Enactment of a number of other proposals already pending before Congress would meaningfully reduce election insecurity and foreign influence in elections. Congress should now address election security by enacting the Foreign Influence Reporting in Elections (FIRE) Act and the Duty to Report Act, two bipartisan bills that impose sanctions on any entity that attacks a U.S. election. Fortunately, almost all states already use machines that produce paper records that can be recounted and audited. Because hand-marked paper ballots remain the most secure and cost-effective option, better election security means going back to the future: to modern, domestically produced machines; backup paper ballots and optical scanners less vulnerable to foreign interference; and election infrastructure less vulnerable to tampering because it is disconnected from the internet. Most of these changes could be implemented if the Senate simply passed the Securing America's Federal Elections (SAFE) Act, a third law that has already been passed by the House.[66]

Finally, civil society has a critical role to play. Private think tanks, foundations, and cyber experts must identify technologies that enable social media to use disinformation to drive voter preferences. The presidential campaigns themselves bear the responsibility to uphold these standards. All presidential candidates should adhere to a joint statement calling election insecurity a virulent national security threat that merits "zero tolerance." Every presidential campaign and its members should be required to disclose relationships with foreign governments on pain of criminal penalty. In sum, we must protect our national security by protecting the determinants of our democracy. We cannot realistically aspire to democratize the field of foreign relations and national security law unless we also pursue and secure the key reforms needed to democratize constitutional governance more generally.

Conclusion

THIS IS A DAUNTING TO-DO LIST, which could take years to complete. But the journey thus far has taught that our national institutions have not voluntarily preserved *Youngstown*'s vision of balanced institutional participation in foreign affairs. Efforts by the three branches to make the revisions suggested would at least focus national attention on the right questions. What matters more than the adoption of any particular proposal is acceptance of the need to strengthen institutional counterweights to executive unilateralism. More robust principles of internal and external accountability can restrain the executive, revitalize Congress, and reinvolve the courts in the constitutional governance of foreign affairs and national security law. This concluding chapter anticipates and answers questions that could be asked about these proposals.

Don't We Have Enough Laws?

Even if we have too many of the wrong kind of national security laws, we still have too few of the right kind. Too many of our current national security laws are predicated on assumptions that our national institutions will behave in ways that in fact they do not. These laws recall Yogi Berra's famous alleged remark: "We could eliminate all those close plays at first base if we could only move the bag one foot further from home plate."[1] Unlike Berra's, my recommendation is to *reinvolve the first baseman and the umpire in the game.* The new laws that I propose are designed not to clutter the decision-making arena or to hamstring the presidency, but to restore the constitutional roles of Congress and the courts as active players in a system of balanced institutional participation. To do that, we must revise, not ignore, the incentives of the regulated institutions.

The executive branch has an institutional incentive to concentrate operational power within sub-executive entities that can move swiftly, secretly, and without accountability to Congress or other executive-branch actors. My internal-accountability proposals would counteract that incentive by making those sub-executive entities more accountable to the president, the cabinet, and government attorneys charged with maintaining the rule of law. My external-accountability proposals would make executive entities accountable not just to their superiors, but to other governmental actors who do not work for them—including Congress and the courts.

Congress has institutional incentives to acquiesce in presidential judgments. Recent decades have marked an era of intense but unproductive congressional activity. Because Congress's legislative structure is so decentralized, its receipt of legal advice so fragmented, and its access to national security information so irregular, Congress's constant activity has only rarely inserted the legislature beneficially into the process of foreign-policy decision-making.[2] The proposed laws and institutional changes aim to target these structural sources of congressional acquiescence by creating new response centers and expanding information flows to and from them.

The courts are uniquely positioned and structured to police the boundaries of congressional-executive authority in national security matters.[3] Despite a long prior history of foreign-affairs adjudication, since Vietnam, the courts have largely abandoned that function, applying broad deference to the executive and a nationalistic vision in a globalizing world. Courts now defer far more than necessary to protect bona fide separation-of-power concerns. Some federal judges may also betray pro-executive bias because of past executive-branch service.[4] Others proclaim themselves incompetent to decide foreign-affairs cases, which on examination, are no harder than many other on judges' dockets. The doctrinal modifications I propose are designed to counteract this tendency to abstain for unwarranted "prudential" reasons, to ensure that judges play their constitutional role of refereeing recurrent interbranch disputes over foreign-affairs authorities and reconciling our legal standards with those of the rest of the world.

The overriding goal is not to add to the store of rules but to restore a *constitutional process* of national security decision-making. This legal-process approach to national security reform aims to frame a legal structure within which the political system of checks and balances may better operate. Through numerous fixes, this approach seeks to modify the currently ineffective legal structure by making it more conducive to encouraging dialogue, interaction, and political cooperation between the branches. As Justice Brandeis recognized, the purpose of separation of powers is "not to avoid friction, but, by means of the inevitable friction incident to the distribution of the governmental powers among three departments, to save the people from autocracy."[5] Far from denying each branch's institutional incentives and political attributes, these proposals acknowledge them and pit them against one another, to discourage overreaching by any branch and encourage checking behavior by the others. Balanced institutional participation in national security decision-making should be treated not just as a matter of political prudence but as a norm of constitutional stature. It aims not to exalt legalism but to ensure that foreign affairs will be conducted under the rule of law.

Will National Security Reform Ever Happen?

I harbor no illusions that reforms as extensive as those described here will be adopted soon. But the executive and judicial proposals can be adopted by those institutions at any time. There is no current shortage of legislative proposals, only of congressional will to act on them.[6]

Congress has been described as an "organized anarchy" where important policy problems can suddenly resolve when a shifting constellation of linked policies, solutions, and decision makers suddenly coalesce to make positive action possible.[7] Historians and political scientists have demonstrated that the confluence of several factors—public awareness that something has gone wrong with an existing system; a simple policy idea whose time has come; cooperation and competition among powerful political leaders; and activism by self-appointed "policy entrepreneurs"—can bring about sweeping legislative reform, even in the face of the most severe legislative inertia.

In the late 1970s, policy entrepreneurs, key elected public officials, and public receptivity all combined to bring about the deregulation movement.

Similar factors converged to bring about the enactment of the Tax Reform Act of 1986 in defiance of "all the lessons of political science, logic, and history."[8] Since Vietnam, major foreign-affairs reforms—including the War Powers Resolution and the Trade Act of 1974—passed into law without significant presidential guidance or even over presidential opposition. In 1986, the Republican chair of the Senate Foreign Relations Committee led the successful floor fight to override the veto of a South African sanctions bill by a president from his own party.[9] And disasters regularly drive sweeping legislation. After 9/11, Bush 43 received broad legislative mandates to reform intelligence and homeland security. During the Covid-19 and Ukraine crises, Biden received strong legislative support even from a closely divided Congress and, by his second year in office, had achieved a number of unexpected legislative victories.

Political self-interest can also help drive legislative reform. In the late 1960s and 1970s, an era of "competitive credit-claiming" between President Nixon and Senator Muskie spurred dramatic environmental reforms.[10] Under the right circumstances, both political parties could gain politically if they were to compete to lead national security reform as a foreign-policy priority. Were the president and key cabinet and congressional leaders to engage in new rounds of "competitive credit-claiming" to revamp the national security laws, they too could achieve similar aspirational lawmaking. Even if they could not achieve comprehensive national security reform, over time, they could use these guiding principles and specific proposals to reform much or all of the national security regulatory mosaic.

Would These Reforms Tie the President's Hands?

Some might claim that these proposals would weaken the presidency just when our dangerous world situation demands an even stronger president than we already have. According to this claim, national security reform would invite congressional micromanagement and inappropriate judicial involvement in foreign affairs, and thereby drain the presidential energy needed to maintain our precarious global position.

I have long argued that we need a strong chief executive *within* a strong system of internal and external checks and balances.[11] My approach seeks to preserve the respective constitutional roles of the three branches with the president in the lead, Congress in a participating partnership role, and the courts as crucial arbiters of a lawful foreign policy. My proposals seek to constrain the president only to the extent that the president's repeated unilateral conduct disrupts this constitutional equilibrium. At the same time, these proposals preserve that equilibrium by promoting formal institutional procedures for informed interbranch dialogue and power sharing.

Obviously, too many reforms in combination could end up hamstringing a future law-conscious president facing an extreme foreign-policy crisis. Similar concerns were expressed in the 1980s, following the barrage of post-Vietnam and post-Watergate reforms.[12] But if five tours in government have taught me anything, it is this: *in a true crisis, executive power will find a way.* In bona fide emergencies, undeniable proof of a serious national security threat always seems to empower presidents to act decisively despite these accumulated constraints. When authentic threats arise, historically, the president leads, Congress acquiesces, and the courts defer for understandable reasons. The resulting institutional interaction inevitably creates the necessary play in the joints to permit a robust American response.

These proposals nowhere assume that Congress and the courts are somehow better qualified than the president to make foreign policy. Their role is not dictating results but forcing dialogue. History teaches that when Congress and the president embody shared understandings in laws that all three branches can construe, the courts can authoritatively decide whether particular conduct comports with those understandings. When the executive is deciding whether to violate those understandings, the threat of being held in violation of the law will drive the executive toward interbranch dialogue to avert confrontation. And once a court rules, more dialogue will ensue to bring the conduct of the branches into compliance with the judicial decision.

We should not assume that the desirable notion of presidential strength demands that there be no limits on presidential autonomy. Both presidential strength and autonomy are crucial to a successful foreign policy. Restoring Congress's constitutional role may inconvenience the president. A loss of autonomy generally does. Executive energies will doubtless be diverted to testifying before Congress, supplying information, preparing reports, and meeting with the core consultative group. Although steps can and should be taken to reduce redundant or perfunctory consultations, over time, the benefits of these enforced dialogues should far exceed their costs.

Greater congressional participation in foreign affairs should not diminish presidential strength. To the extent that these reform proposals authorize certain presidential activities, clarify zones of constitutional responsibility, promote interbranch dialogue and cooperation, and avert cyclical interbranch conflict, they should strengthen, not weaken, the president's hand vis-à-vis the outside world.[13] As Justice Jackson's *Youngstown* concurrence pointed out, the president's freedom to act alone is not the best measure of presidential strength; on the contrary, the president's constitutional strength in foreign affairs is at its peak when he acts *with the authorization and approval of Congress*. His strength is qualitatively weaker when he acts alone in the face of congressional silence or over congressional objection. Jackson's constitutional reasoning makes good policy sense. The principles and proposals for congressional reform outlined in the previous two chapters would involve Congress in the decision-making process earlier, to make that participation more useful and informed and to avoid the mistrust and confrontation that inevitably follow a presidential fait accompli. They aim to force the president to consult with Congress *before* he acts, and to force Congress to declare approval or opposition to presidential action promptly *after* it happens.

Even if such reforms reduce presidential autonomy in the short term, in the long run, they should enhance presidential strength. History teaches that unilateral American action caused by unilateral presidential action tends to trigger backlash from Congress and America's allies. Unchecked executive discretion engenders cycles of conflict by trading short-term presidential autonomy and "victories" for longer-term strife with domestic and international partners. Some level of congressional-executive conflict in foreign affairs is unavoidable, particularly when the president and the congressional majority hale from different political parties. But the more recent cyclical pattern of conflict and stalemate between the political branches has weakened presidential strength and undermined coherent foreign policy. When the president bears nearly exclusive obligation to respond to all external threats, he eventually stops seeking Congress's advice before responding. As Justice Jackson observed, "[a] crisis that challenges the President equally, or perhaps primarily, challenges Congress. . . . We may say that power to legislate . . . belongs in the hands of Congress, but only Congress itself can prevent power from slipping through its fingers."[14] When the president repeatedly shrinks Congress's role from advice and consent to pro forma rubber-stamping, Congress usually ends up reasserting its prerogative when the president is particularly weak or in need of congressional support. This pattern only reinforces the impression of a Congress myopically pursuing partisan politics at a moment when the president is seeking bipartisan consensus.[15]

Can Constitutionalism and Globalism Coexist?

Some suggest that America's constitutionalism has grown increasingly incompatible with its globalism. Writing during the Iran-contra affair, Charles Krauthammer observed: "[T]he presidency finds itself in the permanent bind: to fulfill its obligations as leader of a superpower or to fulfill its obligations as leader of a democracy."[16] The historian Paul Kennedy added that the United States "may not always be assisted by its division of constitutional and decision-making powers, deliberately created when it was geographically and strategically isolated from the rest of the world two centuries ago . . . but which may be harder to operate when it has become a global superpower, often called upon to make swift decisions vis-à-vis countries which enjoy far fewer constraints."[17]

If America's constitutionalism cannot sustain its globalism, which must give way? Critics of American hegemony respond that America must surrender its global-leadership aspirations if it hopes to sustain its constitutional democracy. To save our constitutionalism, these critics posit, we must abandon an activist foreign policy and scale back expectations that America will function as a dominant world power.[18] *Curtiss-Wright* advocates suggest that external threats require America to revise its Constitution to abandon the *Youngstown* vision and give the president broader unilateral discretion. Yet because many of these same critics also espouse a constitutional jurisprudence of original intent, they must engage in revisionist history to contend that the Framers did not originally draft the Constitution to promote *congressional* dominance in foreign affairs.[19]

Both views share a desire to impose a substantive vision on either globalism or constitutionalism: to resolve the tension between the two by imposing either substantive policy views on global strategy or substantive political views on constitutional interpretation. But as the Trump era showed, the United States cannot simply renounce activism in those international regimes in which it is the leading global participant. Similarly, as much as a president might hope to run foreign policy by himself, sooner or later Congress's power over the purse, its textual role in treaty making and appointments, and its constitutional authority over military and commerce affairs will compel its inclusion in the decision-making process. Although the president and vice president are nationally elected, they are the only executive officials who are, and even they do not face reelection during their second terms. Members of Congress, by contrast, are perennially subject to reelection and are at least as responsive to the popular will. It would be ironic indeed if *Curtiss-Wright's* advocates could use claims of democracy to justify further concentrating the nation's foreign-affairs powers in the hands of a single individual.

If these substantive approaches cannot succeed in reconciling constitutionalism and globalism, why are these national security reform proposals preferable? Because they embody a *procedural* notion that lies at the heart of our National Security Constitution—the principle of balanced institutional participation. That principle leaves it not to the president or Congress alone, but to all three branches acting together to construct a lawful global strategy for a post-hegemonic age.

In too many instances, our national security decision-making process has degenerated into one in which the president's team acts, Congress reacts belatedly (if at all), and the courts validate or defer. Had we any assurance that our presidents would always be omniscient, such a decision-making structure might improve American foreign policy. But as the foregoing history teaches, the president is never omniscient. It was precisely to avoid entrusting too much power to the president that the Framers chose in both foreign and domestic affairs to create the same constitutional process, one based on separated institutions sharing powers. In so doing, the Framers willingly sacrificed speed, secrecy, and efficiency because, as Justice Brandeis explained, "[t]he doctrine of the separation of powers was adopted by the Convention of 1787, not to promote efficiency but to preclude the exercise of arbitrary power."[20]

As the foregoing history has shown, the claim that the world is too unsafe for constitutional democracy was heard at times more precarious than these during America's infancy, when the nation was at its most vulnerable; during its adolescence and adulthood, when America first aggressively stepped into the world arena; and during the height of the Cold War, when the threat of nuclear destruction became a feature of everyday life. The Framers deliberately drafted a constitution of shared powers and balanced institutional participation, aware of the risks that that arrangement posed to the nation's international well-being. By mandating that separated institutions share foreign as well as domestic powers, they deliberately sacrificed short-term gains from speed, secrecy, and efficiency in favor of the longer-term consensus that derives from interbranch participatory decision-making.

Vietnam and Watergate reaffirmed that even in a nuclear age, America would not conduct globalism at the price of constitutionalism. Most foreign-policy decisions are implemented over months and years, not moments. Excepting, perhaps, in the event of a nuclear strike or other extreme crisis that demands an immediate response, requiring the president to consider legality before committing the nation to a course of international action would not jeopardize the nation. Nor, as the Cuban missile and the Iranian hostage crises showed, would requiring the president to act lawfully confine the president to conducting foreign policy through inefficient bureaucracies.[21] Even if more legal restraints were to slow response times, speed and efficiency are not our only foreign-policy values. The Framers knowingly traded losses in efficiency for gains in interbranch consultation and the avoidance of catastrophes by presidents who are evil, foolish, impulsive, or inattentive.

This book has focused on international regimes and constitutional regimes: the relationship between America's constitutional regime and the international regimes to which it belongs at particular historical moments. It has recognized that constitutional regimes may shift depending on the kinds of the international regimes in which America participates. We cannot be certain what forms of global governance will face us in the coming decades. So, we will need a better process for *incrementally amending* the National Security Constitution that remains faithful to its original concept, yet flexible enough to respond to fast-moving times. That external events may require the United States to reform the National Security Constitution does not mean that the Constitution must be reformed solely by executive practice. That national habit puts the task of rewriting constitutional rules in the president's hands alone. The wiser and more enduring method of constitutional reform would be to grant that task to all three branches working together.

The Framers did not consider how constitutional responsibility would be allocated in an age of nuclear weapons, the internet, global pandemics, or radical planetary warming. Those who have argued that a National Security Constitution of checks and balances has become unworkable are welcome to propose its formal amendment.[22] But given the huge obstacles to obtaining formal constitutional amendment, our goal should not be to freeze any particular allocation of institutional power, but to create a dynamic legal process that will allow the National Security Constitution to evolve over time. By supplementing executive action with more nuanced role delineation by Congress and guidance from the judiciary, that process should be flexible enough to respond to unforeseen world events and enduring enough to remain true to the Founders' constitutional vision of balanced institutional participation.

Is This a Bipartisan Approach?

As two secretaries of state from different parties argued in stating bipartisan objectives for U.S. foreign policy, "[a] relationship of trust between the Congress and the White House is essential, even with policy differences."[23] My proposals are about restoring trust between the branches, whoever controls them. These proposals would accept many political, ideological, and economic views of what our foreign policy should be. They would operate equally well with a Republican Congress and a Democratic president (or vice versa), an interventionist president and an isolationist Congress, a free-trade president and a protectionist Congress, or with any other combination. A renewed vision of the National Security Constitution could accommodate many policy visions within a single constitutional framework that viewed the foreign-affairs power as a power shared.

In recent decades, Republican administrations have been more likely to take extreme unilateralist positions, but this could easily change. Historically Democrats have been more skeptical of free trade, entangling alliances, Russian adventurism, and undue fiscal constraint. But during the four years of Trump's presidency, all four of these political orientations suddenly flipped and they could just as quickly flip back again. It would take only one election to return to extreme proactive unilateralism by a president of either party.

These proposals should not be dismissed simply as partisan overreaction to an "aberrational" Trump presidency. This problem did not begin, nor will it end, with Donald Trump. Notwithstanding his extremely grave abuses as president, Trump was hardly the worst national security threat one could envision. As noted earlier, his abuses were many, but he did not succeed in most of his unilateral initiatives, he did not wage lasting wars of choice, and he had only one term to do damage. Many forces—both internal and external to the executive branch—pushed back against his most extreme actions.[24] Courageous members of his own political party stood up inside the government to resist some of his radical initiatives. And more often than not, his bravado thwarted his own policies. But Trump's turbulent presidency offers a cautionary tale of how grave a national security threat could be mounted by a more competent and disciplined unilateralist. The deeper challenge will be preventing the continuing pattern of proactive and reactive executive unilateralism in foreign relations from becoming the new normal.

We cannot avert the next catastrophe without defining and implementing a coherent menu of politically achievable acts for corrective national security reform. If adopted, my proposals should not create internal inconsistencies in the law of U.S. foreign relations. As explained, there are areas in which we must resolve discrepancies to square the law that exists with the law that should be. Twenty-first-century times demand different functional solutions. It should not be easier for the president to bomb another country or to order cyberattacks than to enter into a diplomatic agreement. It should not be simpler for a president to break long-standing international commitments than it is to make them. It should not be easier for Congress to stay silent than to endorse or disapprove particular presidential actions that engage the interests of all Americans and the world. Nor, finally, should it be easier for judges to duck decisions than to make them. As Chief Justice Roberts recognized, in most foreign-affairs cases, the federal courts are "not being asked to supplant a foreign policy decision of the political branches with the courts' own unmoored determination of what United States [foreign policy] should be." When, instead, judges are asked familiar questions of statutory and constitutional interpretation, "[t]his is what courts do."[25]

Let me end on a personal note. After my government experience, some may wonder whether I am the right messenger to deliver this message. They might accuse me, as some have, of changing my views since I first wrote on these topics nearly forty years ago. Others might dismiss this analysis because some presidents based unilateral actions in part on advice that I gave as a government lawyer.

My response is simple. I have now had decades to focus on these issues: as a teacher and academic, as a public servant, as an executive, and as a lawyer for and against governments. Over many decades and many different perspectives, one's views inevitably change, as one lives and learns. To echo Justice Blackmun: "Life is long, and you learn things."

One thing I have learned is that government lawyers and academic lawyers approach the same problems differently. Government lawyers must deal with the real-world situations that confront them and operate under the constraints that exist. The late Walter Dellinger, a distinguished legal scholar who became assistant attorney general for the Office of Legal Counsel and acting solicitor general, was criticized for taking certain legal positions during the Clinton administration. He responded:

> I am not sure I agree with the apparent assumption of [critics] that it would be wrong for me to take a different view [in the government] from the one I would have been expected to take as an academic. It might well be the case that I have actually learned something from the process of providing legal advice to the executive branch—both about the law . . . and about the extraordinary complexity of interrelated issues facing the executive branch in general and the President in particular. Moreover, unlike an academic lawyer, an executive branch attorney may have an obligation to work within a tradition of reasoned, executive branch precedent, memorialized in formal written opinions. Lawyers in the executive branch have thought and written for decades about [these issues, which have been addressed by official o]pinions . . . [which] do count for something. . . . When lawyers who are now at [my] Office . . . begin to research an issue, they are not expected to turn to what I might have written or said in a floor discussion at a law professors' convention. They are expected to look to the previous opinions of the Attorneys General and of heads of this office to develop and refine the executive branch's legal positions. . . . [T]here are powerful and legitimate institutional reasons why one's views might properly differ when one sits in a different place.[26]

Nevertheless, during the four decades since I first entered the government in the 1980s, my legal views and guiding principles have remained largely unchanged. Both inside and outside the government, for example, I have taken the same positions against detentions at Guantánamo and denial of refugees' asylum rights. I have offered detailed legal defenses and have read no persuasive rebuttals of my written opinions as a government lawyer which I continue to believe are correct. I see no inconsistency in fighting against torture, which is always illegal, while defending the selective use of drones under those circumstances in which their use would comport with U.S. and international law.[27]

Finally, I see no hypocrisy in defending, in my role as government lawyer, the legality under the War Powers Resolution of my clients' decision to save tens of thousands of innocent lives in Libya. Looking back as a scholar, I recognize that such a historical incident might have continued the migration of U.S. foreign policy in a unilateralist direction. But in Dellinger's words, "there are powerful and legitimate institutional reasons why one's views might properly differ when one sits in a different place."[28] At the end of the day, as a scholar and public servant, I remain guided by the words of my late teacher, the professor and State Department Legal Adviser Abram Chayes. When after his U.S. government service he sued that same government at the World Court, he said, "[T]here [is] nothing wrong with [a lawyer] holding the United States to its own best standards and best principles."[29]

Americans First

As the millennium approaches its quarter mark, the U.S. government has grown increasingly dysfunctional, even as the world has spun more out of control. While deficits grow and inflation rises, schisms in the House have spawned repeated threats to shut down the U.S. government. Trump has surged in the polls, while defending against multiple criminal charges. As Ukraine's military counteroffensive against Russia has stalled, the brutal illegal attack on Israel by Hamas has triggered a destabilizing war in the Middle East. New Covid variants have resurged, while China expands its global influence, and efforts to revive the Iran nuclear deal and maintain the Paris climate process sputter.

Amid this turmoil, the National Security Constitution remains dangerously off-kilter. Particularly in the last quarter century, it has moved a very long way from its constitutional moorings. Restoring *Youngstown*'s vision of balanced institutional participation in foreign relations will require multiple steps on multiple fronts over an extended period of time. To be meaningful and effective, a national security reform movement will require the many current players in the foreign-policy process to reconceptualize how U.S.

institutions should operate and interact in an increasingly turbulent twenty-first century.

We must candidly acknowledge that institutional reforms can only accomplish so much in a political environment of crippling partisan behavior. Effective reform will demand that all players in the process remember that they are Americans first, and partisans second. Striving to constrain presidential powers cannot fully restrain a president bent on lawlessness. Giving Congress and the courts greater institutional capacities can only accomplish so much if legislators and judges do not also share a nonpartisan commitment to the rule of law. Real change will remain difficult unless our political leaders can act rationally amid today's intensely polarized political environment.

But in the end, we have little choice: our only alternatives are acceptance, despair, or reform. We may be only one election away from another onslaught on our Constitution. There is no excuse for not having sensible reform proposals, even if we do not have politicians who are sensible enough to pass them. If we cannot change, we will be stuck with the National Security Constitution we deserve. And change cannot realistically happen without a considered, achievable roadmap that envisions how best to restore the balanced spirit of our National Security Constitution.

NOTES

Introduction

1. Harold Hongju Koh, *The National Security Constitution: Sharing Power After the Iran-Contra Affair* (1990).
2. This last phrase is Richard Neustadt's. *See* Richard Neustadt, *Presidential Power: The Politics of Leadership with Reflections on Johnson and Nixon* 101 (rev. ed. 1976); *see also The Federalist* No. 75, at 488 (Alexander Hamilton) (Modern Library 1937) ("It must indeed be clear to a demonstration that the joint possession of the [treaty] power . . . by the President and Senate, would afford a greater prospect of security, than the separate possession of it by either of them."). For Justice Jackson's quote, see Youngstown Sheet & Tube Co. v. Sawyer, 343 U.S. 579, 635 (1952) (Jackson, J., concurring).
3. United States v. Curtiss-Wright Exp. Corp., 299 U.S. 304 (1936).
4. *See generally* Harold Hongju Koh, *The Trump Administration and International Law* (2019).
5. Gerhard Casper, "Constitutional Constraints on the Conduct of Foreign and Defense Policy: A Nonjudicial Model," 43 *U. Chi. L. Rev.* 463, 482 (1976) (footnote omitted), https://perma.cc/C7Q9-RK2U; National Security Act of 1947, Pub. L. No. 80-253, 61 Stat. 496 (1947) (codified as amended in 50 U.S.C. § 3001 *et seq.*).
6. *Youngstown*, 343 U.S. at 635 (Jackson, J., concurring).
7. Hans Morgenthau, "Conduct of American Foreign Policy," in *The President: Roles and Powers* 314, 319 (D. Haight & L. Johnston eds., 1965).
8. Myers v. United States, 272 U.S. 52, 293 (1926) (Brandeis, J., dissenting).

Chapter 1. From Founding to National Security Act

1. U.S. Const. art. II, § 2, cl. 2.
2. U.S. Const. art. I, § 8, cl. 11; art. II, § 2, cl. 1.

3. Thomas Franck & Michael Glennon, *Foreign Relations and National Security Law* 431 (1987).

4. *See* Charles Black, *The Working Balance of the American Political Departments*, 1 *Hastings Const. L.Q.* 13 (1974).

5. *See* Kenneth Dam, "The American Fiscal Constitution," 44 *U. Chi. L. Rev.* 271, 279–90 (1977); Kate Stith, "Rewriting the Fiscal Constitution: The Case of Gramm-Rudman-Hollings," 76 *Calif. L. Rev.* 593 (1988) (describing analogous "fiscal constitution" that guides governmental allocation of taxing and spending authority); E. Donald Elliott, "*INS v. Chadha:* The Administrative Constitution, the Constitution, and the Legislative Veto," 1983 *Sup. Ct. Rev.* 125, 169–73 (describing analogous "administrative constitution" that governs operation of American administrative state).

6. Charles Black, *Structure and Relationship in Constitutional Law* 15 (1969) (emphasis added); Charles Black, "Reflections on Teaching and Working in Constitutional Law," 66 *Or. L. Rev.* 1, 11 (1980); *see also* Black, *supra* note 4. For applications of the structural method, see H. Jefferson Powell, "How Does the Constitution Structure Government?: The Founders' Views," in *A Workable Government?* 13 (Burke Marshall ed., 1987), Stephen Carter, "Constitutional Adjudication and the Indeterminate Text," 94 *Yale L.J.* 821, 853–55 (1985), and Akhil Reed Amar, "Of Sovereignty and Federalism," 96 *Yale L.J.* 1425, 1426–29 (1987).

7. *The Federalist* No. 75, at 488 (Alexander Hamilton) (Modern Library 1937) ("It must indeed be clear to a demonstration that the joint possession of the [treaty] power ... by the President and Senate, would afford a greater prospect of security, than the separate possession of it by either of them"); Richard E. Neustadt, *Presidential Power: The Politics of Leadership* 101 (rev. ed. 1976).

8. *See* Louis Henkin, *Constitutionalism, Democracy, and Foreign Affairs* 32 (1990) (reading the Constitution's "[t]ext, context, design, intent and history" to provide the president with "sole and exclusive authority over diplomacy and the diplomatic process, the recognition of states and governments, the maintenance of diplomatic relations, the conduct of negotiations, [and] the gathering of intelligence" through the diplomatic process); *see also H.R. 3822, To Strengthen the System of Congressional Oversight of Intelligence Activities in the United States: Hearings Before the Subcomm. on Legis. of the H. Permanent Select Comm. on Intelligence*, 100th Cong. 356 (1988) (comment of Louis Henkin) (stating that "some means for gathering intelligence—notably through the diplomatic process—may not be subject to comprehensive regulation by Congress").

9. Gerhard Casper, "Constitutional Constraints on the Conduct of Foreign and Defense Policy: A Nonjudicial Model," 43 *U. Chi. L. Rev.* 463, 482 (1976).

10. Gerhard Casper, "The Constitutional Organization of the Government," 26 *Wm & Mary L. Rev.* 177, 187–93 (1985) (including National Emergencies Act of 1976, Congressional Budget and Impoundment and Control Act of 1974, and War Powers Resolution as examples of such framework statutes); *see also* Elliott, *supra* note 5, at 318–19, 361–62 (also including Gramm-Rudman-Hollings Act of 1985 in this category); Dam, *supra* note 5, at 278–82 (treating Budget and Accounting Act of 1921 and Congressional Budget and Impoundment and Control Act of 1974 a

quasi-constitutional); Stith, *supra* note 5, at 1363–64 & n.98 (including as appropriations and spending framework statutes the Anti-Deficiency Act of 1905, the Miscellaneous Receipts statute, and other provisions defining terms in appropriations statutes).

11. *See generally* Louis Henkin, "The President and International Law," 80 *Am. J. Int'l L.* 930, 934 (1986) ("Acts within [the president's sole] constitutional authority may have effect on the law of the United States; they may themselves make law and have effect as law in the United States").

12. *See* Harold Hongju Koh, "Introduction: Foreign Affairs Under the United States Constitution," 13 *Yale J. Int'l L.* 1, 3 & n.7 (1988); *see also* Michael Glennon, "The Use of Custom in Resolving Separation of Powers Disputes," 64 *B.U. L. Rev.* 109, 128–46 (1984) (comparing customary constitutional law and customary international law); Karl Llewellyn, "The Constitution as an Institution," 34 *Colum. L. Rev.* 1, 28–31 (1934) (suggesting requirements for constitutional practice to "be unambiguously a part of the working Constitution"). This body of law also bears some resemblance to what Professor Henry Monaghan has called "constitutional common law": a federal common-law "substructure of substantive, procedural, and remedial rules drawing their inspiration and authority from . . . various constitutional provisions," but "subject to amendment, modification, or even reversal by Congress." Henry Monaghan, "The Supreme Court, 1974 Term—Foreword, Constitutional Common Law," 89 *Harv. L. Rev.* 1, 2–3 (1975); see, e.g., Bivens v. Six Unknown Named Agents, 403 U.S. 388 (1971).

13. Youngstown Sheet & Tube Co. v. Sawyer, 343 U.S. 579, 610–11 (1952) (Frankfurter, J., concurring).

14. *See* Peter Shane, "Legal Disagreement and Negotiation in a Government of Laws: The Case of Executive Privilege Claims Against Congress," 71 *Minn. L. Rev.* 462, 477–81 (1987) (describing nonlegislative means Congress has used to develop customary law of executive privilege).

15. *See, e.g.,* Barnes v. Kline, 759 F.2d 21 (D.C. Cir. 1985) (invalidating pocket veto at intersession adjournment), *vacated as moot sub nom.* Burke v. Barnes, 479 U.S. 361 (1987); Ramirez de Arellano v. Weinberger, 745 F.2d 1500 (D.C. Cir. 1984) (en banc) (enjoining overseas executive action infringing American citizen's enjoyment of private property), *vacated and remanded for reconsideration in light of subsequent legislation,* 471 U.S. 1113 (1985); Goldwater v. Carter, 617 F.2d 697 (D.C. Cir. 1979) (en banc) (upholding presidential termination of treaty in accordance with its terms), *vacated and remanded with directions to dismiss complaint,* 444 U.S. 996 (1979). *Cf. Restatement (Third) of the Foreign Relations Law of the United States* § 339 reporters' note 2, § 444 reporters' note 4 (1987) (treating some of these as rulings with persuasive, although not dispositive, weight).

16. *See infra* chapter 11 (suggesting instead a constitutional "mirror principle" to govern termination of international agreements); *see also Goldwater,* 617 F.2d 697 (upholding presidential termination of treaty in accordance with its terms), *vacated and remanded with directions to dismiss complaint,* 444 U.S. 996 (1979). *Compare Restatement (Third) of the Foreign Relations Law of the United States* § 339 reporters' note 2, § 444 reporters' note 4 (1987) (suggesting that the president has broad

unilateral power to terminate U.S. treaty commitments), *with* Harold Hongju Koh, "Could the President Unilaterally Terminate All International Agreements: Questioning Section 313," in *The Restatement and Beyond: The Past, Present, and Future of U.S. Foreign Relations Law* 67 (Paul B. Stephan & Sarah H. Cleveland eds., 2020) (questioning the accuracy of the claim).

17. Marbury v. Madison, 5 U.S. (1 Cranch) 137 (1803). *See generally* Paul Bator et al., *Hart and Wechsler's The Federal Courts and the Federal System* 30–34 (3d ed. 1988) (describing First Judiciary Act); Akhil Amar, "*Marbury*, Section 13, and the Original Jurisdiction of the Supreme Court," 56 *U. Chi. L. Rev.* 443 (1989).

18. *See* INS v. Chadha, 462 U.S. 919 (1983) (invalidating legislative veto in National Emergencies Act); Dames & Moore v. Regan, 453 U.S. 654 (1981) (sustaining president's exercise of IEEPA authorities during the Iranian hostage crisis on statutory and constitutional grounds).

19. *Youngstown*, 343 U. S. at 635 (Jackson, J., concurring).

20. United States v. Curtiss-Wright Exp. Corp., 299 U.S. 304 (1936). As a U.S. senator and lecturer, Justice Sutherland had previously set forth his ideas in a lengthy article and book. *See* George Sutherland, *The Internal and External Powers of the National Government*, S. Doc. No. 61-417 (1910); George Sutherland, *Constitutional Power and World Affairs* (1919), *criticized in* David M. Levitan, "The Foreign Relations Power: An Analysis of Mr. Justice Sutherland's Theory," 55 *Yale L.J.* 467, 472–78 (1946).

21. *See, e.g.,* Jean Edward Smith, *The Constitution and American Foreign Policy* (1989); Gerald Gunther, *Constitutional Law* 362 (11th ed. 1985); Peter Shane & Harold Bruff, *The Law of Presidential Power* 507 (1988); Geoffrey Stone et al., *Constitutional Law* 413 (1986); John Nowak et al., *Constitutional Law* 191 (3d ed. 1986).

22. *See, e.g.,* Thomas Andrew Bailey, *A Diplomatic History of the American People* (9th ed. 1974); *Modern American Diplomacy* (John M. Carroll & George C. Herring eds., 1986); Jerald A. Combs, *American Diplomatic History: Two Centuries of Changing Interpretations* (1983); Alexander DeConde, *A History of American Foreign Policy* (2d ed. 1971); *Guide to American Foreign Relations Since 1700* (Richard Dean Burns ed., 1983); *Encyclopedia of American Foreign Policy* (Alexander DeConde ed., 1978); Walter LaFeber, *The American Age* (1989); Abraham Sofaer, *War, Foreign Affairs, and Constitutional Power: The Origins* (1976); Henry Cox, *War, Foreign Affairs, and Constitutional Power: 1829–1901* (1984); Arthur Schlesinger, *The Imperial Presidency* (1973); William M. Goldsmith, *The Growth of Presidential Power: A Documented History* (1974).

23. Note, "Developments in the Law—The National Security Interest and Civil Liberties," 85 *Harv. L. Rev.* 1130, 1133 (1972).

24. Although the phrase was first used in the National Security Act of 1947, there is no official definition of the term. The only quasi-official definition, prepared for a dictionary used by the Joint Chiefs of Staff, is "a military or defense advantage over any foreign nation or group of nations, or . . . a favorable foreign relations position or . . . a defense posture capable of successfully resisting hostile or destructive action from within or without, overt or covert." Richard Barnet, "Rethinking National Strategy," *New Yorker*, Mar. 21, 1988, at 107.

25. *See The Federalist, supra* note 7, Nos. 3, 4, 14, 23–32, 34, 36 (military and other external weakness); Nos. 5–8, 18–20 (fear of foreign intervention and dissolution of the union); Nos. 11–12, 22–23 (need to retaliate against foreign restrictions on trade); No. 22 (treaty enforcement); Frederick W. Marks, *Independence on Trial: Foreign Affairs and the Making of the Constitution* 170 (1986) ("Nearly every argument sprang from the concept of a foreign threat."); *see also Documents Illustrative of the Formation of the Union of the American States* 115 (C. Tansill ed., 1927) (remarks of Edmund Randolph) (listing protection against foreign invasion as first priority for new government).
26. *The Federalist* No. 3, *supra* note 7, at 14 (John Jay) (emphasis in original).
27. *See* Articles of Confederation of 1781, arts. VI, IX, *reprinted in* 1 *The Founders' Constitution* 23–24 (P. Kurland & R. Lerner eds., 1987). *See generally* Amar, *supra* note 6, at 1441–51, 1495–96 (describing problems under the Articles of Confederation).
28. *See* Articles of Confederation of 1781, art. VI, *reprinted in* 1 *The Founders' Constitution, supra* note 27, at 23–24; John J. Gibbons, "The Eleventh Amendment and State Sovereign Immunity: A Reinterpretation," 83 *Colum. L. Rev.* 1889, 1899–1920 (1983).
29. *See generally* Daniel George Lang, *Foreign Policy in the Early Republic* 67–82 (1985); Marks, *supra* note 25, at 3–51; Note, "The Framers' Intent and the Early Years of the Republic," 11 *Hofstra L. Rev.* 413, 416–23 (1982).
30. *See* Arthur Schlesinger, "The Constitution and Presidential Leadership," 47 *Md. L. Rev.* 54, 55 (1987). For detailed accounts of the drafting of the provisions of the Constitution regarding foreign affairs, see Charles C. Thach Jr., *The Creation of the Presidency, 1775–1789: A Study in Constitutional History* 55–139 (1922); Leonard Levy, *Original Intent and the Framers' Constitution* 30–53 (1988); Arthur Bestor, "Respective Roles of Senate and President in the Making and Abrogation of Treaties— The Original Intent of the Framers of the Constitution Historically Examined," 55 *Wash. L. Rev.* 1 (1979) [hereinafter Bestor, "Respective Roles of Senate and President"]; Arthur Bestor, "Separation of Powers in the Domain of Foreign Affairs: The Original Intent of the Constitution Historically Examined," 5 *Seton Hall L. Rev.* 529 (1974) [hereinafter Bestor, "Separation of Powers"]; Note, *supra* note 29.
31. Marks, *supra* note 25, at 143 ("Some would differ on the question of how these powers should be exercised and where they should be lodged, but on the question of transferring power in the area of foreign relations from the state to the federal level there was virtual unanimity.").
32. James Madison, Saturday, June 30, in *Notes of Debates of the Federal Convention of 1787* (Publius Marcus ed., 2014) (transcribing remarks of Oliver Ellsworth).
33. *The Federalist* No. 45, *supra* note 7, at 303 (James Madison) (emphasis added).
34. *The Federalist* No. 29, *supra* note 7, at 181 (Alexander Hamilton).
35. Louis Henkin, *Foreign Affairs and the Constitution* 33 (1972); *see also* Levy, *supra* note 30, at 30 ("The Framers simply did not intend the President to be an independent and dominating force, let alone the domineering one, in the making of foreign policy."); *The Federalist* No. 75, *supra* note 7, at 487 (Alexander Hamilton) ("The history of human conduct does not warrant that exalted opinion of human virtue which would make it wise in a nation to commit interests of so delicate and

momentous a kind as those which concern its intercourse with the rest of the world to the sole disposal of . . . a President of the United States.").

36. U.S. Const. art. I, § 8, cls. 1, 3, 4, 10, 11–16, 18 (emphasis added). For a discussion of the "necessary and proper" clause, see William Van Alstyne, "The Role of Congress in Determining Incidental Powers of the President and of the Federal Courts: A Comment on the Horizontal Effect of the Sweeping Clause," *Law & Contemp. Probs.*, Spring 1976, at 102. An early draft of the Constitution gave Congress the exclusive power to "make war," but Madison and Elbridge Gerry jointly moved to substitute the word "declare" for the word "make," in order to allow the president to repel sudden attacks. *See* Levy, *supra* note 30, at 37.

37. *See* U.S. Const. art. II, §§ 2–3; *The Federalist* No. 69, *supra* note 7, at 488 (Alexander Hamilton) (clarifying that the commander-in-chief power "would be nominally the same with that of the king of Great Britain, but in substance much inferior to it"); *see also* Gerhard Casper, "Symposium: Organizing the Government to Conduct Foreign Policy: The Constitutional Questions," 61 *Va. L. Rev.* 777, 778 (1975) (response to Louis Henkin); Amar, *supra* note 6, at 1495–96.

38. *The Federalist, supra* note 7, No. 75, at 448 (Alexander Hamilton), No. 69, at 488 (Alexander Hamilton); *see also* 2 *The Debates in the Several State Conventions on the Adoption of the Federal Constitution* 507 (J. Elliot ed., 1896) (statement of James Wilson) ("Neither the President nor the Senate, solely, can complete a treaty; they are checks upon each other, and are so balanced as to produce security to the people.").

39. *Compare* Charles J. Cooper, "What the Constitution Means by Executive Power," 43 *U. Miami L. Rev.* 165 (1988) (broadly construing Article II, section 1 grant of "executive power"), *with* Phillip Kurland, "Comment on Schlesinger," 47 *Md. L. Rev.* 75, 78 (1987), Bestor, "Respective Roles of Senate and President," *supra* note 30, at 31 ("No serious attempt has ever been made to show that the framers of the Constitution accepted . . . that executive power by its very nature includes control of foreign affairs. As a matter of historical fact, the only utterances made in the Federal Convention of 1787 on the subject were emphatic rejections."), George Winterton, "The Concept of Extra-Constitutional Executive Power in Domestic Affairs," 7 *Hastings Const. L.Q.* 1, 24–29 & n.160 (1979) (rejecting broad view of "executive power" clause), Jules Lobel, "Emergency Power and the Decline of Liberalism," 98 *Yale L.J.* 1385, 1404–05 (1989), *and* Shane & Bruff, *supra* note 21, at 8–12 (Constitutional Convention delegates held a wide variety of views on executive power and therefore "established a Presidency with powers that resist definition").

40. U.S. Const. art. II, § 3; *The Federalist* No. 70, *supra* note 7, at 459 (Alexander Hamilton); *Youngstown*, 343 U.S. at 635 (Jackson, J., concurring) (the "take Care" clause signifies "that ours is a government of laws, not of men").

41. U.S. Const. art. III, § 2; Judiciary Act of 1789, 1 Stat. 73. *See* Bestor, "Separation of Powers," *supra* note 30, at 577 (during first few months of convention only resolution that dealt explicitly with foreign affairs was one that called for judicial enforcement of treaties). For a description of the convention's deliberations regarding federal jurisdiction over foreign relations and the enactment of the First Judiciary Act, see Bator et al., *supra* note 17, at 14–16, 30–34. In particular, the First Judiciary

Act included the Alien Tort Statute, 1 Stat. 77 (1789) (codified as amended at 28 U.S.C. § 1350), which grants federal district courts "original jurisdiction of any civil action by an alien for a tort only, committed in violation of the law of nations." *See generally* Harold Hongju Koh, "Transnational Public Law Litigation," 100 *Yale L.J.* 2347, 2366–75 (1991) (describing suits brought by aliens under that provision against the U.S. government and its officials, challenging the conduct of American foreign policy). The First Judiciary Act did not, however, provide any general "federal question" jurisdiction under which a *U.S. citizen* might sue a U.S. official with regard to similar cases and controversies, but Congress later corrected that discrepancy in the Judiciary Act of 1875. *See* Bator et al., *supra* note 17, at 37, 995–96.

42. Bestor, "Respective Roles of Senate and President," *supra* note 30, at 72 (emphasis added).

43. *See The Federalist* No. 70, *supra* note 7, at 454 (Alexander Hamilton).

44. U.S. Const. art. II, § 2, cl. 1. *Compare* 1 *Records of the Federal Convention of 1787*, at 292 (M. Farrand ed., 1911) (describing proposed constitutional provisions regarding departments), *with* An Act for Establishing an Executive Department, to Be Denominated the Department of Foreign Affairs, 1 Stat. 28–29 (1789), *and* An Act to Establish an Executive Department, to Be Denominated the Department of War, 1 Stat. 49–50 (1789). *See also* U.S. Const. art. I, §8, cl. 18 (Congress may make all laws necessary and proper to execute powers vested "in any Department or Officer" of the government); *id.* art. II, § 2, cl. 2 (Congress may vest appointment of inferior officers in "the Heads of Departments"). Significantly, Congress did not designate the Department of the Treasury, the third cabinet department created at this time, as an executive department. *See* 1 Stat. 65 (1789); Gerhard Casper, "An Essay in Separation of Powers: Some Early Versions and Practices," 30 *Wm. & Mary L. Rev.* 211, 239–42 (1989). *See generally* Jay Caesar Guggenheimer, "The Development of the Executive Departments, 1775–1789," in *Essays in the Constitutional History of the United States in the Formative Period, 1775–1789*, at 116, 172, 176–83 (J. Franklin Jameson ed., 1889).

45. The Declaration of Independence, paras. 2, 14 (U.S. 1776).

46. *Youngstown*, 343 U.S. at 646 (Jackson, J., concurring).

47. U.S. Const. art. I, § 8, cls. 10, 13.

48. *Cf.* Louis Hartz, *The Liberal Tradition in America* 284–309 (1955) (America's separatism fostered political tradition of "liberal absolutism").

49. *The Federalist* No. 41, *supra* note 7, at 263 (James Madison); *see also* Lobel, *supra* note 39, at 1397–98 (America's separatism initially fostered constitutional perspective that took narrow view of executive foreign-affairs powers).

50. Inis Claude, *American Approaches to World Affairs* 4 (1986); *see also* Paul Kennedy, *The Rise and Fall of the Great Powers* 151–58, 178 (1987); Robert Keohane, *After Hegemony* 31, 35–37 (1984). For a similar sentiment, expressed by Washington's attorney general, see Letter from Edmund Randolph to James Monroe, *reprinted in* 1 *American State Papers, Foreign Relations* 706 (W. Lawrie & M. Clark eds., 1883) ("An infant country, deep in debt; necessitated to borrow in Europe; without a land or naval force; without a competency of arms or ammunition; with . . . a constitution more than four years old; in a state of probation, and not exempt from foes [—] such a country can have no greater curse in store for her than war").

51. Woodrow Wilson, *Congressional Government* 43 (15th ed. 1913) ("The early Presidents were men . . . of such a stamp that they would under any circumstances have made their influence felt"); *see also* Theodore Lowi, *The Personal President* 32 (1985) ("During that formative period there was inevitably a stronger role for the presidency and a cabinet than that actually called for in the Constitution"); Black, *supra* note 4, at 20 ("Congress is very poorly structured for initiative and leadership; the presidency is very well structured for such things. The result has been a flow of power from Congress to the presidency.").

52. *See* James T. Patterson, "The Rise of Presidential Power Before World War II," *Law & Contemp. Probs.*, Spring 1976, at 39 (identifying 1810–1829, 1849–1860 as weak periods of presidential power); Shane & Bruff, *supra* note 21, at 12–16 (describing weak period as 1836–1861); David M. Pletcher, "Presidential Powers in Foreign Affairs," in 3 *Encyclopedia of American Foreign Policy*, *supra* note 22, at 805, 807 (period of "slower development" of presidential power from 1815–1845); Clinton Rossiter, *The American Presidency* 83–84 (1960).

53. *See* Shane & Bruff, *supra* note 21, at 12.

54. Arthur Burr Darling, *Our Rising Empire, 1763–1803*, at 130 (1940) (quoting Washington). For accounts of Washington's acts, see Sofaer, *supra* note 22, at 93–129; Note, *supra* note 29, at 458–509.

55. Washington did not seek to withhold those documents from the Senate. *See* Schlesinger, *supra* note 22, at 16–17; Casper, *supra* note 44, at 258 (the dispute "had a somewhat 'academic' character because the Senate had received all the papers and the House members apparently could inspect them at the Senate").

56. Sofaer, *supra* note 22, at 129 (describing actions against Wabash Indians).

57. *Id.* at 103–16; Abraham Sofaer, "The Presidency, War, and Foreign Affairs: Practice Under the Framers," *Law & Contemp. Probs.*, Spring 1976, at 12, 18.

58. Sofaer, *supra* note 22, at 129. Washington ultimately concluded that it "rested with the wisdom of Congress to correct, improve, or enforce" the neutrality policy. *See* Schlesinger, *supra* note 22, at 18–20 (citing 1 *Messages and Papers of the Presidents* 131 (1897)).

59. Act of June 5, 1794, 1 Stat. 381 (codified as amended at 18 U.S.C. §§ 959–961). Hamilton and Jefferson took the lead among Washington's cabinet officers in drafting the statute. *See* Charles Marion Thomas, *American Neutrality in 1793: A Study in Cabinet Government* 13–52 (1931). For histories of that statute, see Jules Lobel, "The Rise and Decline of the Neutrality Act: Sovereignty and Congressional War Powers in United States Foreign Policy," 24 *Harv. Int'l L.J.* 1 (1983); Note, "Nonenforcement of the Neutrality Act: International Law and Foreign Policy Powers Under the Constitution," 95 *Harv. L. Rev.* 1955 (1982); Note, "The Iran-Contra Affair, the Neutrality Act, and the Statutory Definition of 'At Peace,'" 27 *Va. J. Int'l L.* 343 (1987).

60. Louis Fisher, "The Role of Congress in Foreign Policy," 11 *Geo. Mason U. L. Rev.* 153, 158 (1988).

61. *See generally* Casper, *supra* note 44; *id.* at 261 ("Although the special responsibility of the President for the maintenance of foreign relations was understood, neither the President nor the Congress assumed that the Executive had what John Locke

. . . called the 'federative' power, which pertained to foreign relations and was, by him, classified as an executive power."); Edwin Corwin, *The President: Office and Powers, 1787–1984,* at 201 (5th ed. 1984).

62. Albert H. Bowman, "Jefferson, Hamilton and Foreign Policy," 71 *Pol. Sci. Q.* 18, 29 (1956).
63. *See* 1 Goldsmith, *supra* note 22, at 410. For accounts of the Pacificus-Helvidius debate, see Sofaer, *supra* note 22, at 112–16, Levy, *supra* note 30, at 51–52, Corwin, *supra* note 61, at 208–12, and Raoul Berger, "The Presidential Monopoly of Foreign Relations," 71 *Mich. L. Rev.* 1, 17–25 (1972).
64. Sofaer, *supra* note 57, at 36, 37.

> Adams avoided a declaration of war, but sought legislative authority at each stage in the nation's movement toward war with France. Jefferson conducted diplomacy with vigor and secrecy, but moved conservatively in military matters, even when he could have claimed that Congress had approved a full-scale military effort to take West Florida. Madison and Monroe defy simplification; but it can be said of their adventures in the Floridas that they were pursuing popular objectives with minimal commitment of material and military resources. Their efforts cannot be equated with the unpopular, massive engagements in Korea and Vietnam.

Id. at 37; *see also id.* at 15–36; Sofaer, *supra* note 22, at 131–379 (providing greater historical detail in support of these themes); Arthur Schlesinger, *The Cycles of History* 297 (1987) ("Early Presidents, even while they circumvented the Constitution, had a cautious and vigilant concern for consent in a practical if not a formal sense."); 15 Annals of Cong. 19 (1805) (remarks of Thomas Jefferson regarding Spanish West Florida) ("Considering that Congress alone is constitutionally invested with the power of changing our condition from peace to war, I have thought it my duty to await their authority for using force in any degree which could be avoided."); *Youngstown,* 343 U.S. at 638 n.5 (Jackson, J., concurring) ("The Louisiana Purchase had nothing to do with the separation of powers as between the President and Congress, but only with state and federal power. [The criticism was not] that Mr. Jefferson acted without authority from Congress, but that neither had express authority to expand the boundaries of the United States by purchase or annexation.").

65. *See* Act of Mar. 3, 1799, ch. 48, 1 Stat. 749, 750 (repealed 1802).
66. Marshall's speech was supporting not the president's right to *make* treaties without congressional participation but his right to surrender an American for extradition to Great Britain under an existing treaty. *See* 10 Annals of Cong. 596–618 (Mar. 7, 1800); Berger, *supra* note 63, at 16–17. As Professor Corwin recognized, "[c]learly, what Marshall had foremost in mind was simply the President's role as *instrument of communication* with other governments." Corwin, *supra* note 61, at 208 (emphasis in original); *accord* Levy, *supra* note 30, at 52 ("John Marshall's 1800 declaration . . . meant nothing more than that only the President communicates with foreign nations; he is the organ of communication."). For a discussion of congressional acquiescence in these matters, see Alfred H. Kelly, "The Constitution and Foreign Policy," in 1 *Encyclopedia of American Foreign Policy, supra* note 22, at 177, 180. For a detailed historical recounting of the Jonathan Robbins affair, which led to Marshall's full-throated defense of executive power, see generally Ruth Wedgwood,

"The Revolutionary Martyrdom of Jonathan Robbins," 100 *Yale L.J.* 229, 339–54 (1990) (arguing that "Marshall had a far more radical theory of Executive power" than is argued here).

67. *See* Sofaer, *supra* note 22, at 256 n.**.

68. *See generally* Cox, *supra* note 22, at 81–83; Schlesinger, *supra* note 22, at 28–29; Francis D. Wormuth & Edwin Firmage, *To Chain the Dog of War* 79–80 (2d ed. 1989).

69. Patterson, *supra* note 52, at 44.

70. Bas v. Tingy, 4 U.S. (4 Dall.) 37 (1800).

71. Talbot v. Seeman, 5 U.S. (1 Cranch) 1, 28 (1801) (emphasis added); *see also* Note, "Realism, Liberalism and the War Powers Resolution," 102 *Harv. L. Rev.* 637, 643 (1989) (these early decisions "embodie[d] the liberal idea that the executive cannot initiate war or any significant armed conflict without advance congressional approval"); Charles Lofgren, "War-Making Under the Constitution: The Original Understanding," 81 *Yale L.J.* 672, 701 (1972).

72. Little v. Barreme, 6 U.S. (2 Cranch) 170, 177–78 (1804). For accounts of the case, see Sofaer, *supra* note 22, at 162–63, and Michael Glennon, "Two Views of Presidential Foreign Affairs Power: *Little v. Barreme* or *Curtiss-Wright?*" 13 *Yale J. Int'l L.* 5 (1988).

73. Brown v. United States, 12 U.S. (8 Cranch) 110 (1814).

74. United States v. Smith, 27 F. Cas. 1192 (C.C.D.N.Y. 1806) (No. 16,342). For colorful accounts of the case, see Robert J. Reinstein, "An Early View of Executive Powers and Privilege: The Trial of Smith & Ogden," 2 *Hastings Const. L.Q.* 309 (1975), and 7 John Bassett Moore, *A Digest of International Law* 917–19 (1906).

75. *Smith,* 27 F. Cas. at 1218, 1230–31; *see also id.* at 1231 (declaring that the president lacked unilateral war-making authority except where necessary to repel a sudden invasion; if authorized to go beyond that, the president could, "contrary to the constitutional will . . . involve the nation . . . in all the calamities of a long and expensive war").

76. The rulings in *Smith* are in fact fully consistent with all of the later rulings by Judge Gerhard Gesell in the Reagan-era *Oliver North* Iran-contra case, discussed in chapter 3. In another Reagan-era case, a district judge relied heavily on *Smith* to hold that the Neutrality Act prohibited even presidentially authorized paramilitary expeditions that are mounted against a government with whom the United States is at peace. Although the court rejected claims that the Neutrality Act invaded the president's commander-in-chief power and concluded that the matter was justiciable, the judgment was subsequently vacated on appeal on other grounds. *See* Dellums v. Smith, 577 F. Supp. 1449, 1452–54 (N.D. Cal. 1983); Dellums v. Smith, 573 F. Supp. 1489 (N.D. Cal. 1983) (on motion for summary judgment), *vacated on other grounds,* 797 F.2d 817 (9th Cir. 1986).

77. Cox, *supra* note 22, at 85.

78. Walter LaFeber, "The Constitution and United States Foreign Policy: An Interpretation," 74 *J. Am. Hist.* 695, 700 (1987); LaFeber, *supra* note 22, at 103–18; Patterson, *supra* note 52, at 45; Schlesinger, *supra* note 22, at 38–52; Cox, *supra* note 22, at 143–54, 167–72; Jacob Javits, *Who Makes War* 33–103 (1973). Two years after

Congress declared war on Mexico, the House disapproved President Polk's actions by resolving that the war had been "unnecessarily and unconstitutionally begun by the President of the United States." *See* 17 Cong. Globe 95 (1848).

79. Cox, *supra* note 22, at 172.

80. Durand v. Hollins, 8 F. Cas. 111, 112 (C.C.S.D.N.Y 1860) (No. 4,186). For a complete account of the incident, see Moore, *supra* note 74, at 346–54, Martin v. Mott, 25 U.S. (12 Wheat.) 19, 30 (1827) (Story, J.) (sustaining president's authority to call forth the militia to repel invasion and holding that president's decision as to whether an exigency has arisen "is conclusive upon all other persons"), and Fleming v. Page, 50 U.S. (9 How.) 603, 615 (1850) (Taney, C.J.) (reaffirming president's military powers as commander-in-chief "to invade the hostile country, and subject it to the sovereignty and authority of the United States").

81. *See* Kennedy, *supra* note 50, at 179; Albert H.Z. Carr, *The World and William Walker* (1963) (recounting William Walker's use of private army to conquer Nicaragua).

82. *The Political Thought of Abraham Lincoln* 44 (R. Current ed., 1967). In this now-famous letter to his law partner in 1848, Congressman Lincoln wrote: "Allow the President to invade a neighboring nation, whenever *he* shall deem necessary to repel an invasion . . . and you allow him to make war at pleasure. Study to see if you can fix *any limit* to his power in this respect." *Id.* at 43 (emphasis in original).

83. Patterson, *supra* note 52, at 46; Marcus Cunliffe, *American Presidents and the Presidency* 98–102 (2d ed. 1976); Schlesinger, *supra* note 22, at 58–67. *See generally* James Garfield Randall, *Constitutional Problems Under Lincoln* (rev. ed. 1951); William Whiting, *War Powers Under the Constitution of the United States* (43d ed. 1871).

84. *See* The Prize Cases, 67 U.S. (2 Black) 635, 665–71 (1862) (narrowly sustaining Union seizures of ships trading with the Confederacy after Lincoln's blockade of Southern ports); *id.* at 670 (president's decisions in suppressing the insurrection were "question[s] to be decided *by him,* and this Court must be governed by the decisions and acts of the political department of the Government to which this power was entrusted" (emphasis in original)).

85. For a discussion of the illegality of Trump's claim that these laws allowed him to suppress domestic protest actions (discussed in chapter 8), *see* Harold Hongju Koh & Michael Loughlin, *The President's Legal Authority to Commit Troops Domestically Under the Insurrection Act,* American Constitution Society Issue Brief (Sept. 2020), https://perma.cc/Y4LX-4FJZ.

86. *See Prize Cases,* 67 U.S. at 668; John Hart Ely, "Suppose Congress Wanted a War Powers Act That Worked," 88 *Colum. L. Rev.* 1379, 1390 n.34 (1988) ("President Lincoln's actions at the outset of the Civil War are sometimes cited as precedent for presidential military ventures. Although Lincoln did engage in a number of unconstitutional acts during this period . . . usurpation of the war power was not among them. . . . For constitutional purposes a domestic rebellion is quite different from a foreign war.").

87. Ely, *supra* note 86, at 1389–90 & n.34 (1988); Edwin Corwin, "The President's Power," in *The President: Roles and Powers* 360, 361 (D. Haight & L. Johnston eds., 1965) ("the vast majority" of presidential commitments of troops abroad without congressional approval involved fights with pirates, landings on semibarbarous coasts, and dispatches of troops to chase bandits across borders).

88. *See* Patterson, *supra* note 52, at 47; Shane & Bruff, *supra* note 21, at 17; Pletcher, *supra* note 52, at 808.

89. Command of the Army Act, § 2, 14 Stat. 485 (1867); Tenure of Office Act, § 2, 14 Stat. 430 (1867). *See generally* Leonard D. White, *The Republican Era: 1869–1901*, at 20–44 (1958); Michael Les Benedict, *A Compromise of Principle: Congressional Republicans and Reconstruction, 1863–1869*, at 294–314 (1974); Patterson, *supra* note 52, at 46–47 (describing how Johnson's successors in office used their veto and law-enforcement powers to "dis[play] moments of comparable assertiveness").

90. LaFeber, *supra* note 22, at 157–58; *see also* Pletcher, *supra* note 52, at 808.

91. Cox, *supra* note 22, at 312–15.

92. Schlesinger, *supra* note 22, at 80; Patterson, *supra* note 52, at 48. *See generally* W. Stull Holt, *Treaties Defeated by the Senate: A Study of the Struggle Between the President and Senate over the Conduct of Foreign Relations* 121–64 (1933); Daniel S. Cheever and H. Field Haviland, *American Foreign Policy and the Separation of Powers* 48–55 (1952). *But see* T. Alexander Aleinikoff & David Martin, *Immigration Process and Policy* 3–5 (1985) (describing Chinese immigration treaties concluded during this period).

93. Wilson, *supra* note 51, at 50 (emphasis in original); Walter Lippmann, "Introduction" to Woodrow Wilson, *Congressional Government* 8 (Meridian 1956).

94. *See* Kennedy, *supra* note 50, at 179 (before demobilization, the United States was briefly "the greatest military nation on earth"); LaFeber, *supra* note 22, at 161–73; Robert L. Beisner, *From the Old Diplomacy to the New, 1865–1900* (2d ed. 1986); Thomas J. McCormick, *China Market: America's Quest for Informal Empire, 1893–1901* (1967). For accounts of this period, see David M. Pletcher, "1861–1898: Economic Growth and Diplomatic Adjustments," in *Economics and World Power: An Assessment of American Diplomacy Since 1789*, at 120 (W. Becker & S. Wells eds., 1984); Walter LaFeber, *The New Empire: An Interpretation of American Expansionism, 1860–1898* (1963).

95. *See* Kennedy, *supra* note 50, at 246; Charles S. Campbell, *The Transformation of American Foreign Relations, 1865–1900*, at 84–121, 296–318 (1976); Stephen Skowronek, *Building a New American State* 85–120 (1982) (describing restructuring of the army).

96. LaFeber, *supra* note 22, at 158. For accounts of the Brazilian, Chilean, and Venezuelan episodes, see *id.* at 161–67, Cox, *supra* note 22, at 274–75 (Congress rose to Cleveland's support in the Venezuelan affair), and *id.* at 308–12 (Congress failed to respond with regard to Brazil and Chile).

97. Cox, *supra* note 22, at 331.

98. *See id.* at 248–50, 294–95, 326. In *Ex parte Siebold*, 100 U.S. 371, 395 (1880), decided during this period, the Supreme Court sustained the judicial appointment of supervisors of congressional elections pursuant to a statute, but declared in broad dicta that the U.S. government and its agents may exercise on U.S. soil "the power to command obedience to its laws, and hence the power to keep the peace to that extent."

99. *In re* Neagle, 135 U.S. 1 (1890). As Professor LaFeber wryly notes, this was "a question about which [the justices] were hardly disinterested." LaFeber, *supra* note 78 at 702. The facts of this bizarre case are recounted in John E. Semonche, *Charting the Future* 23–27 (1978), and Carl Brent Swisher, *Steven J. Field: Craftsman of the Law* 321–61 (1930).

100. *Neagle,* 135 U.S. at 64 (emphasis added).

101. *See In re* Debs, 158 U.S. 564, 586 (1895) (upholding president's inherent power to obtain injunction against Pullman strike). The Court's broad language in *Debs* was clearly unnecessary to the decision of the case, given that the lower court had already granted the U.S. government injunctive relief against the strike by relying on the Sherman Act. Alternatively, the Court's ruling upholding an implied right of action on behalf of the United States could have been justified as an interstitial judicial remedy supplementing the numerous congressional statutes regulating interstate commerce carried on the railways.

102. *See* Subcomm. on Int'l Sec. & Scientific Affairs of the H. Comm. on Foreign Affairs, 98th Cong., *The War Powers Resolution: Relevant Documents, Correspondence, Reports* 50 para. 2 (Comm. Print 1983) (legal opinion of Lloyd Cutler, president's counsel).

103. Robert L. Beisner, *Twelve Against Empire: The Anti-Imperialists, 1898–1900,* at xv (1968).

104. Schlesinger, *supra* note 22, at 87–89. On the McKinley presidency, see, generally, LaFeber, *supra* note 22, at 181–213. On the Boxer Rebellion, see 134 Cong. Rec. S17,287 (daily ed. Oct. 21, 1988) (remarks of Sen. Biden) ("McKinley [dispatched troops to China] without congressional authorization, using as his pretext the protection of American lives and property. His action aroused no congressional objection."). On the Philippines annexation, see Cox, *supra* note 22, at 315–16 ("McKinley's action in the Philippines was a victory of executive power"), Foster Rhea Dulles, *America's Rise to World Power, 1898–1954,* at 21–81 (1955), and George Kennan, *American Diplomacy, 1900–1950,* at 4–20 (1951). For an argument that the Philippine annexation marked not a new departure but "the last episode of a nineteenth-century pattern of territorial acquisition and direct political rule of subject peoples" that began with U.S. policy toward Native Americans, see Walter L. Williams, "United States Indian Policy and the Debate over Philippine Annexation: Implications for the Origins of American Imperialism," 667 *Am. Hist.* 810, 831 (1980).

105. Theodore Roosevelt, *An Autobiography* 464 (1929); *see also* R. Gordon Hoxie, *Command Decision and the Presidency* 40 (1977).

106. Congress had strongly supported the war against Spain, and the Supreme Court broadly deferred to the judgment of the political branches regarding the new American conquests. In *Neely v. Henkel,* 180 U.S. 109, 124 (1901), the Court declared that "it is not competent for the judiciary to make any declaration upon the question of the length of time during which Cuba may be rightfully occupied and controlled by the United States in order to effect its pacification—it being the function of the political branch of the Government to determine." *See also* the *Insular Cases* (four cases comprising De Lima v. Bidwell, 182 U.S. 1 (1901); Dooley v. United States, 182 U.S. 222 (1901); Armstrong v. United States, 182 U.S. 243 (1901); and Downes v. Bidwell, 182 U.S. 244 (1901)). These decisions effectively ratified McKinley's conquests and held that the newly acquired territories belonged to the United States but were not "incorporated" into it. *See generally* James E. Kerr, *The Insular Cases: The Role of the Judiciary in American Expansionism*

65–97 (1982); Jose Cabranes, "Puerto Rico: Colonialism as Constitutional Doctrine," 100 *Harv. L. Rev.* 450, 453 (1986).

107. Pletcher, *supra* note 52, at 809. Although Roosevelt effectively terminated the Clayton-Bulwer Treaty in building the Panama Canal, the Senate rejected the first version of its successor, the Hay-Pauncefote Treaty. *See* Holt, *supra* note 92, at 184–96.

108. Moreover, the terms of the Root-Takahira Agreement were reaffirmed during World War I by another secret executive agreement, the Lansing-Ishii Agreement of 1917. For discussions of foreign policy during Roosevelt's presidency, see generally Cheever and Haviland, *supra* note 92, at 56–67, Lawrence Margolis, *Executive Agreements and Presidential Power in Foreign Policy* 9–12 (1986), Howard K. Beale, *Theodore Roosevelt and the Rise of America to World Power* (1962), and Ernest May, *Imperial Diplomacy: The Emergence of America as a Great Power* (1961).

109. Kennedy, *supra* note 50, at 248.

110. John P. Roche & Leonard W. Levy, *The Presidency* 23 (1964) (emphasis added).

111. *See generally* Walter V. Scholes & Mary V. Scholes, *The Foreign Policies of the Taft Administration* (1970).

112. Wilson, *supra* note 51, at xi-xii.

113. LaFeber, *supra* note 22, at 261.

114. Patterson, *supra* note 52, at 51.

115. Hoxie, *supra* note 105, at 43; Cheever & Haviland, *supra* note 92, at 80–81; Christopher N. May, *In the Name of War: Judicial Review and the War Powers Since 1918,* at 197–98, 208 (1989).

116. *See* Cheever & Haviland, *supra* note 92, at 68–83.

117. *See generally* Patterson, *supra* note 52, at 52; Cheever & Haviland, *supra* note 92, at 84–92. On the economic diplomacy of the interwar years, see Melvyn P. Leffler, *The Elusive Quest: America's Pursuit of European Stability and French Security, 1919–1933* (1979), and Carl Parrini, *Heir to Empire: United States Economic Diplomacy 1916–1923* (1969).

118. Ely, *supra* note 86, at 1388–91 (emphasis added).

119. Under hornbook U.S. constitutional law, the president may constitutionally enter into three types of executive agreements: international agreements negotiated to carry out existing treaties ("treaty-related executive agreements"); international agreements negotiated pursuant to specific congressional authorization or approval ("congressional-executive agreements"); and international agreements negotiated pursuant to the president's independent constitutional powers (so-called sole executive agreements). *See generally Restatement (Third) of the Foreign Relations Law of the United States* § 303 (1987) ("The prevailing view is that the Congressional-Executive agreement can be used as an alternative to the treaty method in every instance."); *id.* cmt. e, at 161; Myres McDougal & Asher Lans, "Treaties and Congressional-Executive or Presidential Agreements: Interchangeable Instruments of National Policy" (pts. 1 & 2), 54 *Yale L.J.* 181, 534 (1945). *But see* Harold Hongju Koh, "Triptych's End: A Better Framework to Evaluate 21st Century International Lawmaking," 126 *Yale L.J. F.* 338, 339–41 (2017), www.yalelawjournal org/forum/triptychs-end (arguing that this "triptych" is obsolete and does no

capture the current twenty-first-century forms of international lawmaking); *infra* chapter 11 (proposing a better way of addressing agreement making).

120. May, *supra* note 108, at 275.

121. Black, *supra* note 4, at 20.

122. Ackerman identifies the signing of the Constitution and the Reconstruction era as two other constitutional moments. *See generally* Bruce Ackerman, *We The People: Transformations* 7–8, 346 (1998).

123. *Curtiss-Wright*, 299 U.S. 304.

124. *Id.* at 318.

125. *Id.* at 319–20 (emphasis added).

126. *See, e.g.*, Levitan, *supra* note 20, at 493; Berger, *supra* note 63, at 26–33; Glennon, *supra* note 72, at 12–17; LaFeber, *supra* note 78, at 710–14; Charles A. Lofgren, "*United States v. Curtiss-Wright Export Corporation*: An Historical Reassessment," 83 *Yale L.J.* 1 (1973).

127. *See, e.g., Youngstown*, 343 U.S. at 635–36 n.2 (Jackson, J., concurring); Glennon, *supra* note 72, at 12–13.

128. *See generally* Berger, *supra* note 63, at 26–33; Levitan, *supra* note 20; Lofgren, *supra* note 126.

129. These congressional powers include Congress's substantive authorities in Article I, sections 8 and 9 of the Constitution (e.g., Congress's power of the purse and power to declare war); Congress's procedural powers in Article I, § 7 (e.g., Congress's power to override a presidential veto); and Congress's procedural powers in Article II (e.g., the Senate's right to advise and consent to treaty ratification and ambassadorial appointments).

130. Ackerman, *supra* note 122, at 271–74.

131. *See, e.g.*, Brief for the Federal Respondents at 30, 40, 44, 52, 53, Dames & Moore v. Regan, 453 U.S. 654 (1981) (No. 80-2078); Brief for the Appellees at 18, 19, 22, 24, 25, 44, Am. Foreign Serv. Ass'n v. Garfinkel, 490 U.S. 153 (1989) (No. 87-2127).

132. Levitan, *supra* note 20, at 493.

133. The notion of nonjusticiable political questions dates back to *Marbury v. Madison*, 5 U.S. (1 Cranch) 137, 170 (1803) ("Questions in their nature political, or which are, by the constitution and laws, submitted to the executive, can never be made in this court."). But in summarizing the history of that doctrine in *Baker v. Carr*, the Court made clear that "it is error to suppose that every case or controversy that touches foreign relations lies beyond judicial cognizance." 369 U.S. 186, 211 (1962). For further discussion of the political-question doctrine, see generally *infra* chapters 5 and 11.

134. United States v. Belmont, 301 U.S. 324, 330 (1937). For a discussion of the relationship between *Curtiss-Wright and Belmont*, see Stefan Riesenfeld, "The Power of Congress and the President in International Relations: Three Recent Supreme Court Decisions," 25 *Calif. L. Rev.* 643, 665–75 (1937).

135. United States v. Pink, 315 U.S. 203, 229 (1942) (quoting *Curtiss-Wright*).

136. *See* 39 Op. Att'y Gen. 484 (1940). *But see* Edwin Borchard, "The Attorney General's Opinion on the Exchange of Destroyers for Naval Bases," 34 *Am. J. Int'l L.* 690, 690 (1940) (criticizing opinion).

137. *See* Schlesinger, *supra* note 22, at 110–13.

138. *See generally* Stephen Ambrose, *Rise to Globalism: American Foreign Policy Since 1938* (1971); Samuel Huntington, "Coping with the Lippmann Gap," 66 *Foreign Aff.* 453 (1987/88); John A. Vasquez, "Domestic Contention on Critical Foreign-Policy Issues: The Case of the United States," 42 *Int'l Org.* 643 (1988).

139. *See generally* Frederic Kirgis, *International Organizations in Their Legal Setting* (1977).

140. *See* Lowi, *supra* note 51, at 99; Patterson, *supra* note 52, at 39, 56.

141. *See generally* William Leuchtenburg, "Franklin D. Roosevelt: The First Modem President," in *Leadership in the Modern Presidency* 7 (F. Greenstein ed., 1988).

142. *See generally* Stephen Hess, *Organizing the Presidency* 1–2 (1976); Staff of House Comm. on Post Office and Civil Service, Subcomm. on Employee Ethics & Utilization, 95th Cong., *Presidential Staffing—A Brief Overview,* 52–53, 55–61 (1978); Fred Greenstein, "In Search of a Modern Presidency," in *Leadership in the Modern Presidency, supra* note 141, at 347 ("four major changes ... beginning in 1933, produced the modern presidency—increased unilateral policy-making capacity, centrality in national agenda setting, far greater visibility, and acquisition of a presidential bureaucracy").

143. *See* Hilary Stout, "Hide and Seek: How to Keep Your Job When Others About You Are Losing Theirs," *Wall St. J.,* Jan. 20, 1989.

144. Chi. & S. Air Lines, Inc. v. Waterman S.S. Corp., 333 U.S. 103, 111 (1948) (emphasis added). In *Waterman,* the Court held unreviewable a presidential decree approving a Civil Aeronautics Board order that had denied an overseas route.

145. *See Youngstown,* 343 U. S. at 635–36 n.2 (Jackson, J., concurring) (emphasis added).

146. These include the court that tried Oliver North. *See, e.g.,* Memorandum in Support of Motion to Dismiss Counts 1–3, at 32, United States v. North, No. 88-0080-02 (D.D.C. Oct. 11, 1988) (citing *Waterman*) (discussed in chapter 3).

147. *See* John Jackson & William Davey, *Legal Problems of International Economic Relations* 293–96 (1986) (describing International Trade Organization episode); Lawrence LeBlanc, "The United Nations Genocide Convention and Political Groups; Should the United States Propose an Amendment?" 13 *Yale J. Int'l L.* 268, 279–82 (1988) (history of U.S. failure to ratify Genocide Convention). The Connally Reservation stipulated that the United States would not subject itself to the World Court's compulsory jurisdiction with respect to "[d]isputes with regard to matters which are essentially within the domestic jurisdiction of the United States of America as determined by the United States." 92 Cong. Rec. 10,624 (1946) (remarks of Sen. Connally); *see also* Francis O. Wilcox, "The United States Accepts Compulsory Jurisdiction," 40 *Am. J. Int'l L.* 699–736 (1946); Charles Cheney Hyde, "Editorial Comment: The United States Accepts the Optional Clause," 40 *Am. J. Int'l L.* 778, 778–80 (1946).

148. *See* Cheever & Haviland, *supra* note 92, at 100–42; Jay Winik, "Restoring Bipartisanship," *Wash. Q.,* Winter 1989, at 109, 113–15; John Felton, "The Man Who Showed Politicians the Water's Edge," *CQ Weekly,* Feb. 18, 1989, at 336 (describing bipartisan foreign policy under Vandenberg and Truman).

149. For a brief history of these statutes, from which this discussion derives, see Harold Hongju Koh, "Congressional Controls on Presidential Trade Policymaking After *I.N.S.* v. *Chadha,*" 18 *N.Y.U. J. Int'l L. & Pol.* 1191, 1194–1225 (1986).

150. Pub. L. No. 71-361, 46 Stat. 590 (1930). For the classic account of the logrolling that led to Smoot-Hawley, see generally, E.E. Schattschneider, *Politics, Pressures and the Tariff: A Study of Free Enterprise in Pressure Politics, as Shown in the 1929–1930 Revision of the Tariff* (1935). For a description of the impact of the Smoot-Hawley tariff levels on world trade, see Robert Pastor, *Congress and the Politics of U.S. Foreign Economic Policy* 78–79 (1980).

151. Pub. L. No. 73-316, 48 Stat. 943 (1934).

152. *See* Pastor, *supra* note 150, at 93–104; John Jackson et al., *Implementing the Tokyo Round: National Constitutions and International Economic Rules* 141 (1984). The concessions obtained by Congress during this period included the first "legislative veto" found in the trade laws. *See* Trade Expansion Act of 1962, Pub. L. No. 87-794, § 351(a)(2)(B), 76 Stat. 872, 899 (1962).

153. Ambrose, *supra* note 138, at 167; X (George F. Kennan), "The Sources of Soviet Conduct," 25 *Foreign Aff.* 566, 576 (1947); *see also* Walter Lippmann, *The Cold War: A Study in U.S. Foreign Policy* (1947) (criticizing Kennan); George Kennan, *Memoirs: 1925–1950,* at 358 (1967) (conceding his own "failure to make clear that what I was talking about when I mentioned the containment of Soviet power was not the containment by military means of a military threat, but the political containment of a political threat").

154. *See* Lowi, *supra* note 51, at 165–66.

Chapter 2. From National Security Act to *Youngstown*

1. *Youngstown Sheet & Tube Co.* v. *Sawyer (Steel Seizure),* 343 U.S. 579, 634 (1952) (Jackson, J., concurring).

2. *See, e.g.,* John Diggins, *The Proud Decades* (1988); Joyce & Gabriel Kolko, *The Limits of Power* (1972); Saul Landau, *The Dangerous Doctrine: National Security and U.S. Foreign Policy* 33–44 (1988); Walter LaFeber, *America, Russia, and the Cold War, 1945–1971* (1972); Walter Lippmann, *The Cold War: A Study in U.S. Foreign Policy* (1947).

3. R. Gordon Hoxie, *Command Decision and the Presidency* 129–52 (1977); Landau, *supra* note 2, at 36–47. The two planks of the Inter-American System, the Inter-American Treaty of Reciprocal Assistance (the Rio Pact) and the Charter of the Organization of American States, were signed in 1947 and 1948, respectively. The North Atlantic Treaty (creating NATO) was signed in 1949. The pact between Australia, New Zealand, and the United States (ANZUS) was created in 1952; the Southeast Asia Treaty Organization (SEATO) in 1954; and the Central Treaty Organization (CENTO) in 1955. *See generally* Louis Henkin et al., *International Law* 792, 801–02 (2d ed. 1987).

4. *See* Administrative Procedure Act, 5 U.S.C. §§ 551–559, 701–706; Landau, *supra* note 2, at 3–4 ("The National Security Act of 1947 . . . and subsequent amendments and decrees placed the governance of critical foreign and defense policies in

the hands of new institutions: a national security apparatus run by national security managers.").

5. *See* 50 U.S.C. § 3002 ("[E]ach military department shall be separately organized . . . and shall function . . . under civilian control of the Secretary of Defense but [Congress's purpose is] not to merge these departments or services.").

6. *See* 10 U.S.C. § 113(a) ("A person may not be appointed as Secretary of Defense . . . within 10 years after relief from active duty as a commissioned officer of a regular component of an armed force."); *id.* § 132 (deputy secretary); *id.* § 135 (undersecretary).

7. For histories of the executive's intelligence-gathering activities before 1947, see Note, "The Extent of Independent Presidential Authority to Conduct Foreign Intelligence Activities," 72 *Geo. L.J.* 1855, 1856–64 (1984); Loch Johnson, *America's Secret Power: The CIA in a Democratic Society* 3–16 (1989); Gregory Treverton, *Covert Action: The Limits of Intervention in the Postwar World* 31–43 (1987).

8. *See* 50 U.S.C. § 403(a)-(b) (1947) (subsequently revised by 10 U.S. § 528(b)).

9. For taxonomies of covert action, see Johnson, *supra* note 7, at 17–35; Treverton, *supra* note 7, at 13–31.

10. National Security Act of 1947, Pub. L. No. 80-253, § 102(d)(5), 61 Stat. 496, 498 (1947) (subsequently amended and renumbered as section 104A; codified as amended in 50 U.S.C. § 3036(d)(4)) (emphasis added).

11. *See Oversight Legislation: Hearings on S. 1721 and S. 1818 Before the S. Select Comm. on Intelligence,* 100th Cong. 226 (1987) (statement of the Hon. Clark M. Clifford).

12. *See* Pub. L. No. 93-559, § 32, 88 Stat. 1795, 1804 (1974) (repealed in 1991) ("No funds appropriated under authority of this chapter or any other Act may be expended by or on behalf of the Central Intelligence Agency for *operations in foreign countries, other than activities intended solely for obtaining necessary intelligence,* unless and until the President finds that each such operation is important to the national security of the United States." (emphasis added)).

13. *See* Senate Select Comm. to Study Governmental Operations with Respect to Intelligence Activities, *Final Report: Foreign and Military Intelligence (Book I),* S. Rep. No 94-755, at 132 (1976); *id.* at 489 (citing first CIA general counsel's concession that Congress had not intended to authorize covert activity).

14. *See Oversight Legislation: Hearings on S. 1721 and S. 1818 Before the S. Select Comm. on Intelligence,* 100th Cong. 90–93 (1987) (testimony of Charles J. Cooper, assistant attorney general, Office of Legal Counsel) (asserting president's exclusive authority "to initiate, direct, and control extremely sensitive national security activities").

15. *See H.R. 3822, To Strengthen the System of Congressional Oversight of Intelligence Activities of the United States: Hearings Before the Subcomm. on Legis. of the H. Permanent Select Comm. on Intelligence,* 100th Cong. 356–57 (1988) (comment of Louis Henkin); Note, *supra* note 7; Note, "Covert Wars and Presidential Power: Judicial Complicity in a Realignment of Constitutional Power," 14 *Hastings Const. L.Q.* 683 686–97, 710–12 (1987); Note, "Keeping Secrets: The Church Committee, Covert Action, and Nicaragua," 25 *Colum. J. Transnat'l L.* 601, 606–24 (1987) (all suggesting that covert war is subject to concurrent congressional-executive authority). Pro-

fessor Lobel has argued that covert paramilitary action, as a use of force short of declared war, falls within Congress's exclusive authority to issue letters of marque and reprisal under Article I, section 8 of the Constitution. *See* Jules Lobel, "Covert War and Congressional Authority: Hidden War and Forgotten Power," 134 *U. Pa. L. Rev.* 1035 (1986).

16. James Sundquist, *The Decline and Resurgence of Congress* 107 (1981); Joint Committee on the Organization of Congress, *First Intermediate Report: Organization of the Congress*, S. Doc. No. 79-36, at 2 (1945); *see* Legislative Reorganization Act of 1946, 60 Stat. 812 (1946); *see also* Thomas Franck & Edward Weisband, *Foreign Policy by Congress* 218–19, 243–44 (1979).

17. *See generally* Sundquist, *supra* note 16, at 238–314; Franck & Weisband, *supra* note 16, at 61–154 (recounting how Congress legislated a role for itself in virtually every area of foreign policy).

18. *See Youngstown*, 343 U.S. at 635 (Jackson, J., concurring); Dames & Moore v. Regan, 453 U.S. 654, 661 (1981); United States v. Nixon, 418 U.S. 683, 707 (1974). "[T]oday it is almost universally believed that the more narrowly framed concurring opinions in [*Youngstown,* not the Court's opinion] capture what it really 'stands for,'" Paul Gewirtz, "Realism in Separation of Powers Thinking," 30 *Wm. & Mary L. Rev.* 343, 352 (1989); *see also* Nixon v. Adm'r of Gen. Servs., 433 U.S. 425, 443 (1977) (noting that in *Nixon,* 418 U.S. at 707, "the unanimous Court essentially embraced" Jackson's *Youngstown* approach); Mistretta v. United States, 488 U.S. 361, 381 (1989) ("Justice Jackson summarized the pragmatic, flexible view of differentiated government power to which we are heir."); Morrison v. Olson, 487 U.S. 654, 693–94 (1988); Bowsher v. Synar, 478 U.S. 714, 721 (1986).

19. *See* Walter LaFeber, *The American Age* 452–55, 459 (1989).

20. *See* Jules Lobel, "Emergency Power and the Decline of Liberalism," 98 *Yale L.J.* 1385 (1989); John Malcolm Smith & Cornelius Cotter, *Powers of the President During Crises* (1960).

21. Lippmann, *supra* note 2, at 15.

22. Clinton Rossiter, *Constitutional Dictatorship: Crisis Government in the Modern Democracies* 5, 314 (1948) (emphasis omitted). Rossiter recommended that Congress pass framework legislation giving the president statutory emergency powers to deal with the new crisis state. *Id.* at 310–13.

23. *See* Kenneth Waltz, "The Stability of a Bipolar World," *Daedalus,* Summer 1964, at 881, 882 ("Truman, at the time of the Korean invasion, could not very well . . . claim that the Koreans were a people far away in the east of Asia of whom Americans knew nothing. We had to know about them or quickly find out.").

24. Arthur Schlesinger, "The President's Prerogative as Commander-in-Chief," in *The President: Roles and Powers* 353 (D. Haight & L. Johnson eds., 1965); H.R.J. Res. No. 9, 82d Cong. (1951) (introduced by Rep. Coudert) ("[N]o funds heretofore or hereafter appropriated to the support of the Armed Forces shall be available to pay the cost of sending and maintaining abroad additional military forces without the prior consent of the Congress" except if necessary to facilitate the extrication of United States forces now in Korea.). On Truman's decision to commit troops, see generally Glenn Paige, *The Korean Decision* (1968); Thomas Schoenbaum, *Waging*

Peace and War: Dean Rusk in the Truman, Kennedy, and Johnson Years 206–28 (1988); Edwin Hoyt, "The United States Reaction to the Korean Attack: A Study of the Principles of the United Nations Charter as a Factor in American Policy-Making," 55 *Am. J. Int'l L.* 45 (1961); John Hart Ely, "Suppose Congress Wanted a War Powers Act That Worked," 88 *Colum. L. Rev.* 1379, 1391 (1988); Arthur Schlesinger, *The Imperial Presidency* 127–40 (1973).

25. *See* Henry Steele Commager, "Presidential Power: The Issue Analyzed," in *The President: Roles and Powers, supra* note 24, at 354 (citing *Martin v. Mott, The Prize Cases, Durand v. Hollins, In re Neagle,* and *Curtiss-Wright,* all discussed in chapter 1, to support the president's inherent power to seize the steel mills).

26. William Rehnquist, *The Supreme Court: How It Was, How It Is* 64 (1987).

27. *See* Eugene Gerhart, *America's Advocate: Robert H. Jackson* 21 (1st ed. 1958) (discussing Attorney General Jackson's destroyer-for-bases opinion, discussed in chapter 1); *see also Youngstown,* 343 U.S. at 648–49 n.17 (Jackson, J., concurring) (discussing Attorney General Jackson's opinion upholding President Roosevelt's right to seize the North American Aviation plant during a strike shortly before Pearl Harbor); Rehnquist, *supra* note 26, at 62.

28. *But see* Harold Edgar & Benno Schmidt Jr., "*Curtiss-Wright* Comes Home: Executive Power and National Security Secrecy," 21 *Harv. C.R.-C.L. L. Rev.* 349, 352 n.7 (1986) (rejecting this view and noting that *Curtiss-Wright* could equally be characterized as addressing government regulation of domestic arms sales). Significantly in *Dames & Moore,* 453 U.S. 654, the entire Court applied Justice Jackson's reasoning in *Youngstown* to analyze the legality of the Iranian hostage accords, a quintessential foreign-affairs question.

29. *Youngstown,* 343 U.S. at 669, 688, 702 (Vinson, C.J., dissenting).

30. *Id.* at 587–88 (majority opinion).

31. *See id.* at 589. In *INS v. Chadha,* 462 U.S. 919 (1983), a comparably formalistic opinion issued more than three decades later, the Court applied the opposite reasoning. Rather than invalidate an executive act as unlawful legislation, the Court held a congressional act unconstitutional as an unlawful effort to regulate executive action by nonlegislative means. For fuller discussion of *Chadha,* see *infra* chapter 4.

32. *Youngstown,* 343 U.S. at 629–30 (Douglas, J., concurring) (quoting Myers v. United States, 272 U.S. 52, 293 (1926) (Brandeis, J., dissenting)); *id.* at 610, 613 (Frankfurter, J., concurring). In separate concurring opinions, Justices Clark and Burton both reasoned that the president had impermissibly failed to follow statutory procedures previously required by Congress on a matter falling within the concurrent authority of the two branches. *Id.* at 655 (Burton, J., concurring); *id.* at 660 (Clark, J., concurring in the judgment). Justice Clark expressly likened the case to *Little Barreme,* discussed in chapter 1. *See id.* at 660–62.

33. *Youngstown,* 343 U.S. at 635–37 (Jackson, J., concurring).

34. *See, e.g.,* Harold Hongju Koh, "Triptych's End: A Better Framework to Evaluate 21st Century International Lawmaking," 126 *Yale L.J. F.* 338, 339–41 (2017), www.yale lawjournal.org/forum/triptychs-end (discussed in chapter 11); Laurence H. Tribe, "Transcending the *Youngstown* Triptych: A Multidimensional Reappraisal of Sepa-

ration of Powers Doctrine," 126 *Yale L.J. F.* 86 (2016), http://perma.cc/TM4Z-2Q8L; Edward T. Swaine, "The Political Economy of *Youngstown*," 83 *So. Calif. L. Rev.* 263 (2010).

35. *Youngstown*, 343 U.S. at 638, 640.

36. *Id.* at 637.

37. *See, e.g.*, Zivotofsky v. Kerry, 576 U.S. 1 (2015) (applying "*Youngstown* category three" theory to find a legislative enactment unenforceable because it unconstitutionally invaded the president's exclusive recognition powers). For a detailed history and discussion of this issue, see generally David Barron & Martin Lederman, "The Commander in Chief at the Lowest Ebb—Framing the Problem, Doctrine, and Original Understanding," 121 *Harv. L. Rev.* 689, 712–20 (2008), and David Barron & Martin Lederman, "The Commander in Chief at the Lowest Ebb—A Constitutional History," 121 *Harv. L. Rev.* 941 (2008).

38. *Youngstown*, 343 U.S. at 637–38 (Jackson, J., concurring); *see, e.g.*, United States v. Belmont, 301 U.S. 324 (1937) (upholding, pursuant to recognition power in Article II of the Constitution, president's authority to make sole executive agreement without congressional approval).

39. *Youngstown*, 343 U.S. at 637–38 (Jackson, J., concurring) (emphasis added); *id.* at 635–36 n.2, 646–47.

40. *See id.* at 640–47, 653–54.

41. *Cf. infra* chapter 4 (discussing Burger and Rehnquist Courts' growing acceptance of *Curtiss-Wright*'s vision of judicial deference to executive authority).

42. *See* 50 U.S.C. § 3002 (congressional declaration of purpose); *see also* Sundquist, *supra* note 16, at 107.

43. *Cf.* William Draper, "The Rise of the American Junta," *N.Y. Rev. Books,* Oct. 8, 1987, at 47; William Draper, "Reagan's Junta," *N.Y. Rev. Books,* Jan. 29, 1987, at 5 (characterizing the Iran-contra affair as government by junta).

44. *See* U.S. Const. art. II, § 3. *Cf.* Peter Strauss, "The Place of Agencies in Government: Separation of Powers and the Fourth Branch," 84 *Colum. L. Rev.* 573, 599–604, 662–66 (1984) (discussing constitutional requirement that president be unitary, politically accountable head of government with authority to direct all law administrators); Cass Sunstein, "Constitutionalism After the New Deal," 101 *Harv. L. Rev.* 421, 463 (1987) (suggesting wisdom of centralized presidential supervision of federal bureaucracy).

45. *Cf.* Laurence Tribe, *American Constitutional Law* § 5-17, at 363 (2d ed. 1988) ("[A]n agency can assert as its objectives only those ends which are connected with the task that Congress created it to perform."); Hampton v. Mow Sun Wong, 426 U.S. 88, 114 (1976) (Civil Service Commission may not assert foreign-policy ends to defend its challenged regulation, because "[t]hat agency has no responsibility for foreign affairs"); *see also* George Liebmann, "Delegation to Private Parties in American Constitutional Law," 50 Ind. L.J. 650 (1975); Louis Jaffe, "Law Making by Private Groups," 51 *Harv. L. Rev.* 201 (1937) (government may not delegate its official functions to private groups).

46. *Youngstown*, 343 U. S. at 653 (Jackson, J., concurring); *see* Alexander Bickel, *The Morality of Consent* 18 (1975) (citing Edmund Burke) ("Consent will not long be

yielded to faceless officials, or to mere servants of one man, who themselves have no 'connexion with the interest of the people.' . . . [W]e may today oppose excessive White House staff-government by private men whom Congress never sees. It was not for nothing that the American Constitution provided for 'executive Departments' and for Senate confirmation of the appointments of great officers of state."); Strauss, *supra* note 44, at 600 (president and his subordinates must remain accountable to institutions outside executive branch).

47. Eugene Rostow, "Searching for Kennan's Grand Design," 87 *Yale L.J.* 1527, 1534–35 (1978) (emphasis added).

48. *Youngstown,* 343 U.S. at 638 (Jackson, J., concurring) (emphasis added); *accord* Theodore Lowi, *The Personal President* 175 (1985) ("[W]ithout a constitutional balance the presidency flies apart.").

49. Message from the President Vetoing H.R.J. Res. 542, A Joint Resolution Concerning the War Powers of Congress and the President, H.R. Doc. No. 93-171, at 3 (1973); *see also id.* (praising the "constructive measures [in the resolution] which would . . . enhanc[e] the flow of information from the executive branch to the Congress"). For collections of the president's War Powers reports, see Subcomm. on Int'l Sec. & Scientific Affairs of the H. Comm. on Foreign Affairs, 98th Cong., *The War Powers Resolution: Relevant Documents, Correspondence, Reports* 50 (Comm. Print 1983); Note, "The War Powers Resolution: An Act Facing 'Imminent Hostilities' A Decade Later," 16 *Vand. J. Transnat'l L.* 915, 1040–48 & n.831 (1983) (recounting cases of compliance).

50. *See* David Scheffer, "U.S. Law and the Iran-Contra Affair," 81 *Am. J. Int'l L.* 696, 698–713 (1987) (describing these provisions).

51. *See Youngstown,* 343 U.S. at 585 (majority opinion) ("The President's power, if any, to issue the order [under challenge] must stem either from an act of Congress or from the Constitution itself."); *id.* at 635–36 n.2 (Jackson, J., concurring) (*Curtiss-Wright* involved not "the question of the President's power to act without congressional authorization, but the question of his right to act under and in accord with an Act of Congress.").

52. *See* Harold Hongju Koh, "Congressional Controls on Presidential Trade Policymaking After *I.N.S. v. Chadha,*" 18 *N.Y.U. J. Int'l L. & Pol.* 1191, 1197–99 (1986) (describing congressional-executive clashes during the Kennedy round of international trade talks); Radio and Television Report to the American People on the Soviet Arms Buildup in Cuba, 1 Pub. Papers 806–09 (Oct. 22, 1962); Proclamation No. 3504: Interdiction of the Delivery of Offensive Weapons to Cuba 1 Pub. Papers 809–11 (Oct. 23, 1962) (citing joint resolution passed on October 3, 1962); *see also* Dwight Eisenhower, *Waging Peace, 1956–1961,* at 179 (1965).

53. *See, e.g.,* United States v. Robel, 389 U.S. 258, 263 (1967) (refusing to accept executive invocation of congressional war power as "talismanic incantation" to support violation of constitutional rights).

54. Kent v. Dulles, 357 U.S. 116 (1958); *accord* Greene v. McElroy, 360 U.S. 474, 507–08 (1959).

55. *Ex parte* Endo, 323 U.S. 283, 300 (1944) (holding wartime Japanese relocation camps unlawful). *Kent* and *Endo* exemplified what I have elsewhere called the "lib

eral constitutional internationalism" of Justice Douglas: the philosophy that both presidential and American overreaching in international affairs should be checked by both congressional restraints and judicial protection of individual rights. *See* Harold Hongju Koh, "The Liberal Constitutional Internationalism of Justice Douglas," in *He Shall Not Pass This Way Again: The Legacy of Justice William O. Douglas* (Stephen Wasby ed., 1991); *see also* Patrick Gudridge, "Remember *Endo?*," 116 *Harv. L. Rev.* 1933 (2003).

56. Edgar & Schmidt, *supra* note 28, at 355–56.

Chapter 3. From Vietnam to the Iran-Contra Affair

1. H.R.J. Res. 1145, 88th Cong., 78 Stat. 384 (1964), *repealed by* Act of Jan. 12, 1971, Pub. L. No. 91-672, § 12, 84 Stat. 2053; *see also* Department of State, Office of the Legal Adviser, "The Legality of United States Participation in the Defense of Viet Nam," 75 *Yale L.J.* 1085, 1102–06 (1966). On the Tonkin Gulf incident, see David Halberstam, *The Best and the Brightest* 411–14 (1972), Walter LaFeber, *The American Age: United States Foreign Policy at Home and Abroad Since 1750*, at 574 (1989), and Doris Kearns, *Lyndon Johnson and the American Dream* 198–99 (1976). For further discussion of Johnson's decision to escalate the war, see David Barrett, "The Mythology Surrounding Lyndon Johnson, His Advisers, and the 1965 Decision to Escalate the Vietnam War," 103 *Pol. Sci. Q.* 637 (1988).

2. Pub. L. No. 93-148, 87 Stat. 555 (codified at 50 U.S.C. §§ 1541–1548).

3. Charles Black, "The Working Balance of the American Political Departments," 1 *Hastings Const. L.Q.* 13, 18 (1980).

4. These include, for example, former CIA operatives such as Eugene Hasenfus, who later worked during the Iran-contra affair for the "Enterprise" supervised by Oliver North. *Compare* 50 U.S.C. §§ 1542–1543, *with Report of the Congressional Committees Investigating the Iran-Contra Affair*, H.R. Rep. No. 100-433, S. Rep. No. 100-216, at 144–47, 287–88 (1987) [hereinafter *Iran-Contra Report*] (describing Hasenfus affair).

5. On President Ford's actions, see Letter to the Speaker of the House and the President Pro Tempore of the Senate Reporting on United States Actions in the Recovery of the SS Mayaguez, 1 Pub. Papers 669 (May 15, 1975) ("taking note of" rather than complying with the terms of the resolution); *War Powers: A Test of Compliance—Relative to the Danang Sealift, the Evacuation of Phnom Penh, the Evacuation of Saigon, and the Mayaguez Incident: Hearings Before the H. Comm. on Int'l Relations*, 94th Cong. 61 (1975). On President Carter's Iranian operation, see Letter to the Speaker of the House and the President Pro Tempore of the Senate Reporting on the Operation, 1 Pub. Papers 777 (Apr. 26, 1980), and Subcomm. on Int'l Sec. & Scientific Affairs of the H. Comm. on Foreign Affairs, 98th Cong., *The War Powers Resolution: Relevant Documents, Correspondence, Reports* 50 (Comm. Print 1983) (legal opinion of Lloyd Cutler, president's counsel). On President Reagan's actions, see 129 Cong. Rec. 14,610 (Oct. 26, 1983), Michael Rubner, "The Reagan Administration, the 1973 War Powers Resolution, and the Invasion of Grenada," 100 *Pol.*

Sci. Q. 627 (1985–1986), Robert Torricelli, "The War Powers Resolution After the Libya Crisis," 7 Pace L. Rev. 661 (1987), Richard Lugar, Letters to the Next President 47–48 (1988) (consultation on Libyan strike ended twenty-seven minutes before air strike began), Note, "The War Powers Resolution: An Act Facing 'Imminent Hostilities' A Decade Later," 16 Vand. J. Transnat'l L. 915, 964–1013 (1983), and Lowry v. Reagan, 676 F. Supp. 333, 336–37 (D.D.C. 1987), appeal dismissed, No. 87-5426 (D.C. Cir. Oct. 17, 1988) (per curiam) (summarizing Persian Gulf notices). On President George H. W. Bush's actions, see Maureen Dowd, "George Bush, First Year: Likes, Dislikes, Surprises," N.Y. Times, Dec. 31, 1989, at A21.

6. See Multinational Force in Lebanon Resolution, Pub. L. No. 98-119, 97 Stat. 805 (1983) (codified at 50 U.S.C. §§ 1541–1544). For an account of the Lebanon experience, see Cyrus Vance, "Striking the Balance: Congress and the President Under the War Powers Resolution," 133 U. Pa. L. Rev. 79, 94–95 (1984).

7. See War Powers Act Compliance Resolution, S.J. Res. 194, 100th Cong., 133 Cong. Rec. S14,630 (daily ed. Oct. 21, 1987).

8. See Lowry, 676 F. Supp. 333; Statement on the Downing of an Iranian Jetliner by the United States Navy in the Persian Gulf, 24 Weekly Comp. Pres. Doc. 896 (July 3, 1988).

9. See, e.g., S.J. Res. 323, 100th Cong., 134 Cong. Rec. S6239 (daily ed. May 19, 1988) (Byrd-Nunn-Warner-Mitchell proposal); John Hart Ely, "Suppose Congress Wanted a War Powers Act That Worked," 88 Colum. L. Rev. 1379 (1988); Morton Halperin & Gary Stern, "Lawful Wars," 72 Foreign Pol'y 173 (1988); Comm. on Fed. Legislation, "The War Powers Resolution," 44 Rec. of Ass'n of Bar of City of New York 106 (1989).

10. For further explication of these categories, see Harold Hongju Koh, "The Treaty Power," 43 U. Miami L. Rev. 106 (1988).

11. U.S. Const. art. I, § 10, cls. 1, 3; art. II, § 2; art. VI, cl. 2.

12. For historical treatments, see Arthur Bestor, "Respective Roles of Senate and President in the Making and Abrogation of Treaties—The Original Intent of the Framers of the Constitution Historically Examined," 55 Geo. Wash. L. Rev. 1, 135 (1979) ("treatymaking was to be a cooperative venture from the beginning to the end of the entire process"), Jack Rakove, "Solving a Constitutional Puzzle: The Treatymaking Clause as a Case Study," in 1 Perspectives in American History: New Series 23 (B. Bailyn et al. eds., 1984).

13. The Federalist No. 75 (Alexander Hamilton) (Modern Library 1937); 2 The Debates in the Several State Conventions on the Adoption of the Federal Constitution 507 (J. Elliot ed., 1896) (statement of James Wilson) ("Neither the President nor the Senate solely, can complete a treaty; they are checks upon each other, and are so balanced as to produce security to the people."); Leonard Levy, Original Intent and the Framers' Constitution 49 (1988) ("[T]he records of the Convention show that only on delegate . . ., Butler of South Carolina, proposed that the President should possess the treaty power exclusively; the records show, too, that no delegate preferred more important role for the President in foreign affairs than for the Senate."). See generally Koh, supra note 10, at 107–09.

14. The Federalist No. 64, supra note 13, at 420 (John Jay) (remarking that this collaboration "provides . . . our negotiations for treaties [with] every advantage which ca

be derived from talents, information, integrity, and deliberate investigations [of the Senate], on the one hand, and from secrecy and despatch [secured by presidential action] on the other").

15. *See* Missouri v. Holland, 252 U.S. 416, 432 (1920); United States v. Belmont, 301 U.S. 324, 331 (1937); United States v. Pink, 315 U.S. 203, 230–31 (1942).

16. *See* Edwin Borchard, "The Attorney General's Opinion on the Exchange of Destroyers for Naval Bases," 34 *Am. J. Int'l L.* 690, 690 (1940). *See generally* Thomas Franck & Michael Glennon, *Foreign Relations and National Security Law* 379–86 (1987). In concluding the destroyers-for-bases deal, Roosevelt expressly relied on a controversial opinion by then attorney general Robert Jackson that found the transfer supported by two statutes as well as the president's constitutional powers. *See* 39 Op. Att'y Gen. 484 (1940); *see also* Arthur Schlesinger, *The Imperial Presidency* 110–13 (1973) (describing 1941 executive agreements).

17. *See, e.g.,* Myres McDougal & Asher Lans, "Treaties and Congressional-Executive or Presidential Agreements: Interchangeable Instruments of National Policy," 54 *Yale L.J.* 181, 186 (1945).

18. Lawrence Margolis, *Executive Agreements and Presidential Power in Foreign Policy* 30, 101–39 (1986) (listing executive agreements).

19. *See* Dames & Moore v. Regan, 453 U.S. 654 (1981) (upholding Iranian hostage accords); *Pink*, 315 U.S. 203 (upholding Litvinov Assignment); *Belmont,* 301 U.S. 324 ((upholding Litvinov Assignment); *see also* John Jackson, "The General Agreement on Tariffs and Trade in United States Domestic Law," 66 *Mich. L. Rev.* 250, 253 (1967) (describing use of executive agreement by United States to accept the General Agreement on Tariffs and Trade). The most significant congressional-executive disputes over international agreements in the 1950s and 1960s revolved around the so-called Bricker Amendment and international-trade agreements. *See generally* Duane Tananbaum, *The Bricker Amendment Controversy: A Test of Eisenhower's Political Leadership* (1988); Harold Hongju Koh, "Congressional Controls on Presidential Trade Policymaking After *I.N.S. v. Chadha*," *N.Y.U. J. Int'l L. & Pol.* 1191, 1197–1200 (1986); Andreas Lowenfeld, "Roles of the President and Congress," *Yale L. & Pol'y Rev.* 71 (Special Issue No. 1) (1988).

20. S. Res. 85, 91st Cong., 115 Cong. Rec. 3603, 17,245 (1969). The House of Representatives never acted on the measure. Louis Henkin, *Foreign Affairs and the Constitution* 348 n.34 (1972). For the mood of the era, see Henry Steiner & Detlev Vagts, *Transnational Legal Problems* 607 (2d ed. 1976).

21. *See generally Congressional Oversight of Executive Agreements: Hearings on S. 3475 Before the Subcomm. on Separation of Powers of the S. Comm. on the Judiciary,* 92d Cong. (1972).

22. *See* Transmittal Act, Pub. L. No. 92-403, 86 Stat. 619 (1972) (codified at 1 U.S.C. § 112b) (requiring secretary of state to transmit to Congress any international agreement other than a treaty as soon as practicable after its entry into force with respect to the United States). For examples of congressional oversight legislation introduced but not enacted in the years after the Case-Zablocki Act, see the Morgan-Zablocki Bill, H.R. 4438, 94th Cong. (1976); S. 1251, S. 632, 94th Cong. (1975); S. 1286, 93d Cong. (1974).

23. In 2022, Congress mildly strengthened the law by requiring the executive to report and publish certain significant nonbinding instruments after their conclusion. *See* James M. Inhofe National Defense Authorization Act for Fiscal Year 2023, Pub. L. No. 117-263, § 5947, 136 Stat. 2423, 3476 (2022).

24. *See, e.g.,* Consumers Union v. Kissinger, 506 F.2d 136 (D.C. Cir. 1974), *cert. denied,* 421 U.S. 1004 (1975) (upholding President Nixon's voluntary restraint agreement with Japan on steel); John Jackson & William Davey, *Legal Problems of International Economic Relations* 617–22 (2d ed. 1986) (similar Japanese restraints on auto exports); "Administration Announces Import Restraints, Other Measures to Aid Machine Tool Industry," 3 Int'l Trade Rep. (BNA) 1537 (Dec. 24, 1986) (Japanese and Taiwanese restraints on machine tools); Japan—Trade in Semi-Conductors, No. L/6309, 25 I.L.M. 1408 (1986) (similar "arrangement" with Japan regarding semiconductors). Congress received no formal notice of the steel voluntary restraint agreements entered into between 1969 and 1974 or the auto agreement entered into in 1981, all of which took the form of unilateral letters written to U.S. government officials by the industries involved. The remaining Reagan voluntary restraint agreements were all formal, jointly signed documents, but only the 1982 steel accord with the European Community was formally notified to Congress in compliance with the Case-Zablocki Act. For a critique of executive conduct in concluding such agreements, see Kevin Kennedy, "Voluntary Restraint Agreements: A Threat to Representative Democracy," 11 *Hastings Int'l & Comp. L. Rev.* 1 (1987).

25. *See* "Unilateral Policy Declaration by the United States with Respect to the SALT I Treaty," *reported in* 123 Cong. Rec. S31,901 (daily ed. Oct. 3, 1977) (letter from Secretary of State Cyrus Vance to Sen. John Sparkman, chairman, Senate Foreign Relations Committee, dated Sept. 21, 1977).

26. *See* "Over the Top," *Time,* Dec. 8, 1986, at 43; W. Michael Reisman, "The Cult of Custom in the Late Twentieth Century," 17 *Cal. Western Int'l L.J.* 133, 142 (1987) (SALT II exemplified a "new type of executive agreement . . . in which Congress indicates disapproval, but which the Executive respects 'as if there were an agreement on the condition that the other negotiating state lives up to the terms of the unratified treaty.'").

27. *See* United States Ocean Policy, 19 Weekly Comp. Pres. Doc. 383 (Mar. 10, 1983); Proclamation No. 5030, 3 C.F.R. 22–23 (1984); *see also* Proclamation No. 5928, 5 Fed. Reg. 777 (Jan. 9, 1989) (announcing that the United States would henceforth recognize a territorial sea of twelve nautical miles pursuant to customary international law).

28. Reisman, *supra* note 26, at 134; Letter of Transmittal from President Ronald Reagan, Protocol II Additional to the 1949 Geneva Conventions of 12 August 1949 and Relating to the Protection of Victims of Non-International Armed Conflict, S. Treaty Doc. No. 100-2 (1987), *reprinted in* 81 *Am. J. Int'l L.* 910 (1987) (refusing to submit Protocol I of Geneva Convention, which the United States had previously signed, for advice and consent, but accepting some of its provisions as customary international law). For critiques of that decision, see Richard Falk, *Revolutionaries and Functionaries: The Dual Faces of Terrorism* 155–61 (1988); Hans-Peter Gasser, "An Appeal for Ratification by the United States," 81 *Am. J. Int'l L.* 912 (1987).

29. *See* National Defense Authorization Act for Fiscal Years 1988 and 1989, Pub. L. No. 100-180, § 225(a)(2), 101 Stat. 1019, 1056 (1987); H.R. Rep. No. 100-446, at 594 (1987); S. Res. 167, 100th Cong., 133 Cong. Rec. S12,498 (daily ed. Sept. 22, 1987); S. Comm. on Foreign Relations, *The ABM Treaty Interpretation Resolution*, S. Rep. No. 100-164 (1987); "Senate's Condition to Treaty," *N.Y. Times*, May 28, 1988, at A4 (noting exception to Byrd amendment in cases in which the Senate has consented to the new interpretation by subsequent treaty or protocol or through legislative enactment). For accounts of the controversy, see generally Raymond Garthoff, *Policy Versus the Law: The Reinterpretation of the ABM Treaty* (1987); David Koplow, "Constitutional Bait and Switch: Executive Reinterpretation of Arms Control Treaties," 137 *U. Pa. L. Rev.* 1353 (1989); Abram Chayes & Antonia Chayes, "Testing and Development of 'Exotic' Systems Under the ABM Treaty: The Great Reinterpretation Caper," 99 *Harv. L. Rev.* 1956 (1986); Sam Nunn, "The ABM Reinterpretation Issue," *Wash. Q.*, Autumn 1987, at 45. For a defense of the administration's position, see Abraham Sofaer, "The ABM Treaty: Legal Analysis in the Political Cauldron," *Wash. Q.*, Autumn 1987, at 59.

30. Message to the Senate on the Soviet-United States Intermediate-Range Nuclear Force Treaty, 24 Weekly Comp. Pres. Doc. 779, 780 (June 10, 1988).

31. Goldwater v. Carter, 444 U.S. 996, 1006 (1979) (Brennan, J., concurring) (citing president's power under Article II, § 3 of the Constitution to "receive Ambassadors").

32. *See* Beacon Prods. Corp. v. Reagan, 633 F. Supp. 1191, 1199 (D. Mass. 1986), *aff'd*, 841 F.2d 1 (1st Cir. 1987) (dismissing private challenge to State Department's notice of termination of bilateral U.S. Friendship, Commerce, and Navigation Treaty with Nicaragua); Letter from Secretary of State George P. Shultz to U.N. Secretary-General Javier Perez de Cuellar (Oct. 7, 1985), *reprinted in* 24 I.L.M. 1742 (1985) (terminating U.S. acceptance of compulsory jurisdiction of International Court of Justice); Science and Technology, 21 Weekly Comp. Pres. Doc. 336, 338 (Mar. 20,1985) (announcing U.S. withdrawal from UNESCO).

33. *See* Letter from Secretary of State George P. Shultz to U.N. Secretary-General Javier Perez de Cuellar (Apr. 6, 1984), *reprinted in* 23 I.L.M. 670 (1984) (immediately and temporarily "modifying" the 1946 acceptance by the United States of International Court of Justice's compulsory jurisdiction, notwithstanding treaty provision requiring six months' notice of termination).

34. For example, the Reagan administration offered the Genocide Convention to the Senate for advice and consent to ratification with more conditions than had been offered to ratification of a human-rights treaty by any prior administration. *See* Marian Nash Leich, "Contemporary Practice of the United States Relating to International Law," 80 *Am. J. Int'l L.* 612–22 (1986); *see also* Message to the Senate Transmitting the Convention Against Torture and Other Inhuman Treatment or Punishment, 24 Weekly Comp. Pres. Doc. 642 (May 20, 1988); Letter from Secretary of State George P. Shultz to President Ronald Reagan (May 10, 1988), in S. Treaty Doc., No. 100-20, at v (advising transmittal to Senate with seventeen reservations, understandings, and declarations).

35. Garcia-Mir v. Meese, 788 F.2d 1446, 1455 (11th Cir.), *cert. denied,* 475 U.S. 1022 (1986). As Professor Henkin has noted, the Eleventh Circuit's dicta could be read to support an "assertion that . . . the President and lesser executive officials may disregard a treaty or a rule of international law." Louis Henkin, "The Constitution and United States Sovereignty: A Century of *Chinese Exclusion* and Its Progeny," 100 *Harv. L. Rev.* 853, 864 (1987). *See generally* "Agora: May the President Violate Customary International Law?" 80 *Am. J. Int'l L.* 913 (1986); "Agora: May the President Violate Customary International Law? (cont'd)," 81 *Am. J. Int'l L.* 371 (1987); Stuart Malawer, "Reagan's Law and Foreign Policy, 1981–1987: The 'Reagan Corollary' of International Law," 29 *Harv. Int'l L.J.* 85 (1988) (enumerating Reagan administration foreign-policy decisions that have modified or deviated from preexisting international legal rules).

36. Rainbow Navigation, Inc. v. Dep't of the Navy, 699 F. Supp. 339, 349 (D.D.C. 1988) (Greene, J.); *see also* Rainbow Navigation, Inc. v. Dep't of the Navy, 686 F. Supp. 354 (D.D.C. 1988). Mindful of the ABM Treaty controversy, the district judge in *Rainbow Navigation* declared as a matter of domestic constitutional law that the executive branch was bound by authoritative representations that it had made to the Senate regarding the meaning of the agreement in order to secure advice and consent. *See* 699 F. Supp. at 343. *But see* United States v. Stuart, 489 U.S. 353, 373–77 (1989) (Scalia, J., concurring in the judgment) (questioning this ruling).

37. For a discussion of these trends, see generally Norman Ornstein, "The House and the Senate in a New Congress," in *The New Congress* 363 (T. Mann & N. Ornstein eds., 1981), Norman Ornstein, "Interest Groups, Congress, and American Foreign Policy," in *American Foreign Policy in an Uncertain World* 49, 54 (D. Forsythe ed., 1984), and Thomas Franck & Edward Weisband, *Foreign Policy by Congress* 228, 242–45 (1979) (discussing S. Res. 4 staffers and creation of the Congressional Research Service, the General Accounting Office, the Congressional Budget Office, and the Office of Technology Assessment).

38. *See, e.g.,* International Emergency Economic Powers Act, 50 U.S.C. §§ 1701–1706; National Emergencies Act, 50 U.S.C. §§ 1601–1651; Trade Act of 1974, 19 U.S.C. §§ 2101–2487; Export Administration Act of 1979, 50 U.S.C. §§ 2401–2413; Foreign Intelligence Surveillance Act, 50 U.S.C. §§ 1801–1811; International Development and Food Assistance Act of 1975, Pub. L. No. 94-161, 89 Stat. 849 (codified as amended in scattered sections of 7 and 22 U.S.C.); Hughes-Ryan Amendment to the Foreign Assistance Act, Pub. L. No. 93-559, § 32, 88 Stat. 1795, 1804 (1974) (repealed in 1991) (intelligence oversight); International Security Assistance and Arms Export Control Act of 1976, 22 U.S.C. §§ 2751–2796; Section 502B of the Foreign Assistance Act of 1961, 22 U.S.C. § 2304; and the Nuclear Non-Proliferation Act of 1978, Pub. L. No. 95-242, 92 Stat. 120 (codified as amended in scattered sections of 22 and 42 U.S.C.). For descriptions of this intense period of legislative activity, see generally Franck & Weisband, *supra* note 37, and *The Tethered Presidency: Congressional Restraints on Executive Power* (T. Franck ed., 1981).

39. For descriptions of the typical post-Vietnam legislative package, see generally Koh, *supra* note 19, at 1204–08, and Thomas Franck & Clifford Bob, "The Return of Humpty-Dumpty: Foreign Relations Law After the *Chadha* Case," 79 *Am. J. Int'l L.*

912 (1985). One statute that expressly denied the president new delegated authority, however, was the War Powers Resolution. *See* 50 U.S.C. § 1547(d)(2) (providing
that "[n]othing in this [joint resolution] . . . shall be construed as granting any authority to the President with respect to the introduction of United States Armed
Forces").

40. *See* 50 U.S.C. §§ 1701–1706.

41. *See* 50 U.S.C. § 4301 *et seq.* For legislative histories of IEEPA, see Andreas Lowen-
feld, *Trade Controls for Political Ends* 545–46 (2d ed. 1983), *Emergency Controls on
International Economic Transactions: Hearings Before the Subcomm. on Int'l Econ.
Pol'y & Trade of the H. Comm. on Int'l Relations,* 95th Cong 110 (1977) (remarks of
Rep. Bingham), and Note, "The International Emergency Economic Powers Act: A
Congressional Attempt to Control Presidential Emergency Power," 96 *Harv. L. Rev.*
1102, 1104 (1983).

42. Regan v. Wald, 468 U.S. 222, 245–46 (1984) (Blackmun, J., dissenting) (noting
that in 1977, states of emergency originally declared in 1933, 1950, 1970, and 1971
were still in effect).

43. *See* Dames & Moore v. Regan, 453 U.S. 654 (1981); INS v. Chadha, 462 U.S. 919
(1983) (invalidating legislative-veto provision in National Emergencies Act of 1976
that permitted Congress to terminate presidentially declared IEEPA emergencies,
50 U.S.C. § 1622(a)(1)); *Wald,* 468 U.S. 222. For further discussion of the Court's
technique of statutory interpretation in these cases, see *infra* chapter 4.

44. *See* Exec. Order No. 12,170, 44 Fed. Reg. 65,729 (1979) (Iran); Exec. Order No.
12,205, 45 Fed. Reg. 24,099 (1980) (Iran); Exec. Order No. 12,513, 50 Fed. Reg.
18,629 (1985) (Nicaragua); Exec. Order No. 12,543, 51 Fed. Reg. 875 (1986) (Libya);
Exec. Order No. 12,544, 51 Fed. Reg. 1235 (1986) (Libya); Exec. Order No. 12,532, 50
Fed Reg. 36,861 (1985) (South Africa); Exec. Order No. 12,635, 50 Fed. Reg. 12,134
(1988) (Panama). *See generally* Barry Carter, *International Economic Sanctions: Improving the Haphazard U.S. Legal Regime* 191–96 (1988).

45. *See* H. Comm. on Int'l Relations, *Trading with the Enemy Act Reform Legislation,*
H.R. Rep. No. 95-459, at 10 (1977).

46. *See* Jules Lobel, "Emergency Power and the Decline of Liberalism," 98 *Yale L.J.*
1385, 1415 (1989); Carter, *supra* note 44, at 197–203; Note, *supra* note 41, at 1115
("[G]iven the infinite variety of human events, almost any major event in the future
course of the nation's history could be described as 'unusual and extraordinary.'").

47. *See* Beacon Prods. Corp. v. Reagan, 633 F. Supp. 1191 (D. Mass. 1986), *aff'd,* 841
F.2d 1 (1st Cir. 1987) (Nicaragua); Chang v. United States, 859 F.2d 893, 896 n.3
(Fed. Cir. 1988) (Libya).

48. *See* Exec. Order No. 12,444, 3 C.F.R. 168 (1984); Exec. Order No. 12,470, 3 C.F.R.
168 (1985); Joel Harris & Jeffrey Bialos, "The Strange New World of United States
Export Controls Under the International Emergency Economic Powers Act," 18
Vand. J. Transnat'l L. 71 (1985).

49. Carter, *supra* note 44, at 199; *see* Beacon Prods., 633 F. Supp. 1191 (whether a particular country poses sufficient threat to trigger IEEPA declaration of national
emergency constitutes nonjusticiable political question).

50. Exec. Order No. 12,532, 50 Fed. Reg. 36,861 (1985); Lugar, *supra* note 5, at 221 ("The Secretary [of State] said [to the Senate sponsor of the bill], 'This is your bill in exec-utive-order form.'"); Carter, *supra* note 44, at 201 ("It was not clear ... why the threat was so 'unusual and extraordinary' that it was necessary to declare a national emergency, especially since legislation to impose sanctions was already far along in Congress.").

51. *See* "Trade Policy: Administration Weighing Emergency Powers Act Changes, State Department Official Says," 4 Int'l Trade Rep. (BNA) 1300, 1300 (Oct. 21, 1987) (statement of Ambassador-at-Large L. Paul Bremer III).

52. *See* Donald L. Robinson, "The Routinization of Crisis Government," 63 *Yale Rev.* 161 (1973); *see also* Lobel, *supra* note 46, at 1408 (Congress has enacted nearly 470 statutes delegating broad emergency powers to the executive).

53. *See, e.g.,* Laurence Tribe & Jeremy Lewin, Opinion, "$100 Billion. Russia's Treasure in the US Should be Turned Against Putin," *N.Y. Times,* Apr. 15, 2022.

54. *See* Editorial, "This Is Watergate," *New Republic,* Mar. 16, 1987, at 7; Phillip Kur-land, "Comment on Schlesinger," 47 *Md. L. Rev.* 75, 81 (1987) ("[T]he constitutional problem in the Iran-Contra fiasco is essentially not different from the Watergate fiasco."); Kenneth E. Sharpe, "The Real Cause of Irangate," 68 *Foreign Pol'y* 19, 24 (1987) (Watergate arose from Nixon White House efforts to keep the bombing of Cambodia secret from the public, Congress, and other parts of executive branch). For a popular historical account of Watergate, see generally Bob Woodward & Carl Bernstein, *All the President's Men* (1974).

55. "[T]he ultimate responsibility for the events in the Iran-Contra Affair must rest with the President." *Iran-Contra Report, supra* note 4, at 21.

56. *See id.* at 387–88 (statements of witnesses Poindexter and North).

57. In addition to the three investigative bodies discussed in the text, three other legis-lative bodies conducted avowedly preliminary inquiries into the affair. The House and Senate Select Committees on Intelligence separately investigated the affair in November 1986, but only the Senate committee made its report public. *See* Senate Select Comm. on Intelligence, *Preliminary Inquiry into the Sale of Arms to Iran and Possible Diversion of Funds to the Nicaraguan Resistance,* S. Rep. No. 100-7 (1987). The House Foreign Affairs Committee contemporaneously held both closed and open hearings on the matter. *See The Foreign Policy Implications of Arms Sales to Iran and the Contra Connection: Hearings Before the H. Comm. on Foreign Affairs,* 99th Cong. (1986).

58. For the executive order creating the Tower commission, see Exec. Order No. 12,575 § 2, 51 Fed. Reg. 43,718 (1986). The commission was chaired by former senator John Tower and included former senator and secretary of state Edmund Muskie and once and future national security assistant Brent Scowcroft. For the resolution creating the House and Senate select committees, see H.R. Res. 12, 100th Cong. (1987); S. Res. 23, 100th Cong., 133 Cong. Rec. S89 (daily ed. Jan. 6, 1987). Former American Bar Association president and judge Lawrence Walsh was appointed in-dependent counsel by the U.S. Court of Appeals for the District of Columbia Cir-cuit, Independent Counsel Division, pursuant to the independent-counsel provisions of the Ethics in Government Act, 28 U.S.C. § 592(c)(1), and on the basis

of the statutory application of Attorney General Edwin Meese. *See* George Lardner
Jr. & Howard Kurtz, "Iran Inquiry Counsel Selected," *Wash. Post,* Dec. 20, 1986,
at A1.

59. *See* Christopher Madison, "The Arms Sale Say-So," 19 *Nat'l J.* 667, 668–69 (1987);
Henry Kissinger, *White House Years* 1264 (1979); Gary Sick, *All Fall Down: America's Tragic Encounter with Iran* 16 (1986) ("Significantly . . . it was the Department
of Defense that objected vigorously to the notion of selling the shah everything he
wanted.").

60. *See* Pub. L. No. 90-629, 82 Stat. 1320 (codified as amended at 22 U.S.C. §§ 2751–
2796). *See* William Wentz, Note, "The United States Is Moving Farther from Fostering Multilateral Restraint of Conventional Arms Sales," 6 *Dick. J. Int'l L.* 343,
346–49 (1988); Eric Fredland et al., *U.S. Arms Sales Policy: Background and Issues*
6–7 (1982); Franck & Weisband, *supra* note 37, at 98 ("Where once the export of
arms had been a high-minded part of a global strategy to make the world safe for
democracy, now the U.S. appeared to be willing to supply any regime, no matter
how unsavory, so long as the customer professed anti-communism and could pay
cash.").

61. *See* Wentz, *supra* note 60, at 349.

62. Sick, *supra* note 59, at 17. *Compare id.* (quoting Henry Kissinger's memorandum to
the president as stating that "we adopted a policy which provides, in effect, that we
will accede to any of the Shah's requests for arms purchases from us"), *with* William Shawcross, *The Shah's Last Ride: The Fate of an Ally* 168 (1988) ("Never before
in American history had the president ordered the national security bureaucracy to
accept the demands and judgment of a foreign leader on arms transfers.").

63. *See* Nelson-Bingham Amendment to the Foreign Assistance Act of 1974,
Pub. L. No. 93-559, 88 Stat. 1795, 1814 (codified as amended at 22 U.S.C. § 2776);
Franck & Weisband, *supra* note 37, at 98–111 (describing enactment of amendment); *see also* 120 Cong. Rec. 38,073 (1974) (remarks of Sen. Gaylord Nelson)
("The executive branch of this Nation involves the United States in military situations throughout the world without congressional and public debate, discussions,
or deliberations.").

64. *See* Pub. L. No. 94-329, 90 Stat. 729 (1976) (codified as amended at 22 U.S.C. §
2318). The law subjected intergovernmental arms sales to two-house disapproval
only if they exceeded particular dollar thresholds: $14 million for sophisticated
weaponry, called "major defense equipment," and $50 million for defense articles
or services. *See* 22 U.S.C. § 2753(d) (revised after *Chadha* to require a joint resolution of disapproval).

65. *Legislative Veto: Arms Export Control Act: Hearing on S. 1050 Before the Senate Comm.
on Foreign Relations,* 98th Cong. 40 (1983) (statement of Hon. Matthew Nimetz,
former undersecretary of state for security assistance, science, and technology).

66. *See* INS v. Chadha, 462 U.S. 919 (1983).

67. *See* Pub. L. No. 99-247, 100 Stat. 9 (1986); Note, "Congress and Arms Sales:
Tapping the Potential of the Fast-Track Guarantee Procedure," 97 *Yale L.J.* 1439,
1447–49 (1988) (describing events leading to congressional amendment). The

Supreme Court had long validated such report-and-wait provisions. *See Chadha*, 462 U.S. 935 n.9; Sibbach v. Wilson, 312 U.S. 1, 14–15 (1941).

68. *See* 22 U.S.C. §2753(d)(2) (revised after Iran-contra affair); *see generally* David Scheffer, "U.S. Law and the Iran-Contra Affair," 81 *Am. J. Int'l L.* 696, 698 (1987) ("The Reagan administration's covert sale of military arms to Iran falls into a legal quagmire because of the conflict between the laws governing the export of military arms and the laws governing covert activities by the United States Government."); *Iran-Contra Report, supra* note 4, at 451, 539–46 (minority report) (arguing that covert transfers under the National Security Act and the Economy Act can substitute for transfers under the Arms Export Control Act). *But see id.* at 418–19 (majority report) (disputing minority's conclusion).

69. Madison, *supra* note 59, at 669. Congress originally supported the joint resolution of disapproval by votes of 356 to 62 in the House and 73 to 22 in the Senate. *See* Steven Roberts, "Senate Upholds Arms for Saudis, Backing Reagan," *N.Y. Times*, June 6, 1986, at A1.

70. *See* John Felton, "Rare Aid Funding Bill Comes Down to the Wire," 46 *Cong. Q.* 2731 (1988); John Yang, "Reagan Plan to Sell Arms to Kuwait Barred by Senate," *Wall St. J.*, July 8, 1988, at 38.

71. *See* Senator Joseph R. Biden Jr. & Representative Mel Levine, Letter to the Editor, *N.Y. Times*, Apr. 2, 1987, at A30 (supporting S. 419 and H.R. 898, their bills to amend the Arms Export Control Act). Both bills died in the 100th Congress.

72. *See* Robert Pear, "Saudis Seen as Top Mideast Buyer of U.S. Arms," *N.Y. Times*, Feb. 3, 1989, at A3.

73. *See generally Iran-Contra Report, supra* note 4, at 395–407; Note, "The Boland Amendments and Foreign Affairs Deference," 88 *Colum. L. Rev.* 1535, 1567–70 (1988) (describing history of amendments). For the text of the various amendments, see 133 Cong. Rec. H4982–87 (daily ed. June 15, 1987).

74. *Compare* S. Rep. No. 92-431, at 13 (1972), *with Iran-Contra Report, supra* note 4, at 185–86, *and* Kirk Victor, "CIA Counsel's Role Questioned," *Nat'l L.J.*, Feb. 2, 1987, at 3 (describing retroactive finding in Iran-contra affair). *See generally* Jeffrey Meyer, "Congressional Control of Foreign Assistance," 13 *Yale J. Int'l L.* 69, 73–76 (1988) (chronicling presidential abuses of military-aid process from 1961 to 1972).

75. Constitutional Symposium on Indochina War, 116 Cong. Rec. 17,387, 17,392 (May 28, 1970) (remarks of Alexander Bickel). For the text of the Cooper-Church amendment, see S. Rep. No. 91-865, at 15 (1970), *quoted in* Abner Mikva & Joseph Lundy, "The 91st Congress and the Constitution," 38 *U. Chi. L. Rev.* 449, 486 n.107 (1971). For the text of the Hatfield-McGovern amendment, see 116 Cong. Rec. 14,111–12 (1970) (amendment no. 609).

76. *See* Foreign Assistance Act of 1973, Pub. L. No. 93-189, § 30, 87 Stat. 714, 732 (1973) ("No funds authorized or appropriated under this or any other law may be expended to finance military or paramilitary operations by the United States in or over Vietnam, Laos, or Cambodia."); Department of Defense Appropriations Act of 1975, Pub. L. No. 93-437, § 839, 88 Stat. 1212, 1231 (1974); Department of Defense Appropriations Act of 1974, Pub. L. No. 93-238, 87 Stat. 1026 (1973); Department of Defense Appropriations Authorization Act of 1974, Pub. L. No. 93-55, § 806, 87

Stat. 615 (1973); Department of State Appropriations Authorization Act of 1973, Pub. L. No. 93-126, § 13, 87 Stat. 454 (1973); Continuing Appropriations Resolution of 1974, Pub. L. No. 93-52, § 108, 87 Stat. 130 (1973); Fulbright Amendment to Second Supplemental Appropriations Act of 1973, Pub. L. No. 93-50, § 307, 87 Stat. 129 (1973).

77. Pub. L. No. 93-559, §§32, 88 Stat. 1795, 1804–05 (1974) (repealed in 1991).

78. *Compare* Michael Glennon, "Strengthening the War Powers Resolution: The Case for Purse-Strings Restrictions," 60 *Minn. L. Rev.* 1, 21–23 (1975) (objecting to those actions), *with War Powers: A Test of Compliance Relative to the Danang Sealift, the Evacuation of Phnom Penh, the Evacuation of Saigon, and the Mayaguez Incident: Hearings Before the Subcomm. on Int'l Sec. & Scientific Affairs of the H. Comm. on Int'l Relations,* 94th Cong. 16–17, 88–89 (1975) (testimony of State Department Legal Adviser Monroe Leigh) (arguing that Congress did not intend those statutory funding prohibitions to curtail presidential efforts to evacuate Americans).

79. Pub. L. No. 94-329, § 404, 90 Stat. 729, 757–58 (1976), *as amended by* Pub. L. No. 96-533, tit. I, § 118(a)–(d), 94 Stat. 3141 (1980); Cord Meyer, *Facing Reality: From World Federalism to the CIA* 258 (1980).

80. *See* Gregory Treverton, *Covert Action: The Limits of Intervention in the Postwar World* 220 (1987).

81. John Prados, *Presidents' Secret Wars: CIA and Pentagon Covert Operations from World War II Through the Persian Gulf War* 347–48 (rev. ed. 1988).

82. Sanford Ungar & Arnold Kohen, "An Angola Angle to the Scandal?" *N.Y. Times,* Jan. 20, 1987, at A25 (North introduced himself to others as a marine officer who had participated in two American wars: Vietnam and Angola); Michael Maren, "What Congress Didn't Ask," *N.Y. Times,* Nov. 23, 1987, at A23.

83. Oliver North, *Taking the Stand: The Testimony of Lieutenant Colonel Oliver L. North* 270 (1987); *see also id.* at 269–71, 512.

84. *See* North, *supra* note 83, at 284–85, 369, 387; Maren, *supra* note 82 ("Though elements of the Africa connection surfaced on a few occasions during testimony, committee members never pursued the angle, never asked a single question or subpoenaed a single document relating to charges that the Federal Government was arming Unita.").

85. *See* Kissinger, *supra* note 59, at 698–763.

86. *See* 50 U.S.C. § 3021(b)(1) (emphasis added); *see* Joseph Bock, *The White House Staff and the National Security Assistant: Friendship and Friction at the Water's Edge* 12 (1987) (explaining that the act's drafters "worked . . . to limit the authority of the NSC . . . by making it an *advisory* rather than policy-enforcing body" (emphasis in original)).

87. *See* President's Special Review Board, *The Tower Commission Report* 6 (*N.Y. Times* ed., 1987) [hereinafter *Tower Report*].

88. Truman personally attended less than 25 percent of the meetings of the council. *See* Alonzo Hamby, "Harry S. Truman: Insecurity and Responsibility," in *Leadership in the Modern Presidency* 41, 61 (F. Greenstein ed., 1988); *The President and the Management of National Security: A Report by the Institute for Defense Analyses* 58–59 (K. Clark & L. Legere eds. 1969).

89. *See* Thomas Franck, "The Constitutional and Legal Position of the National Security Adviser and Deputy Adviser," 74 *Am. J. Int'l L.* 634, 635 (1980). The only statutory authority given the "executive secretary" was the power to appoint and fix the compensation of the tiny NSC staff. *See* J. Bock, *supra* note 86, at 12.

90. *See* 3 U.S.C. § 105(a)(1); Phillip Henderson, *Managing the Presidency: The Eisenhower Legacy—From Kennedy to Reagan* 74 (1988).

91. Henderson, *supra* note 90, at 81, 85–90 (Eisenhower presided over nearly 90 percent of the 366 NSC meetings held during his tenure); Dean Acheson, *This Vast External Realm* 195 (1973) ("The NSC decides nothing. It is merely a mechanism for preparing and presenting matters for the President's decision.").

92. National Security Act of 1947, Pub. L. No. 80-253, § 102(d)(5), 61 Stat. 496, 498 (1947) (subsequently amended and renumbered as section 104A; codified as amended in 50 U.S.C. § 3036(d)(4)) (emphasis added). For detailed histories of the CIA, see generally Rhodri Jeffreys-Jones, *The CIA and American Democracy* (1989), Prados, *supra* note 81, and Treverton, *supra* note 80. For a description of the CIA's place amid other intelligence agencies, see Jeffrey Richeison, *The U.S. Intelligence Community* 20–34 (1985).

93. *See* National Security Act of 1947 § 102(d)(3), 61 Stat. at 498 (codified as amended at 50 U.S.C. § 3036(d)(1)).

94. *See* Alex Whiting, *Covert Operations and the Democratic Process: The Implications of the Iran/Contra Affair* 8–36, 41–55 (1987).

95. *See* Theodore Sorensen, "The President and the Secretary of State," 66 *Foreign Aff.* 231, 233 (1987/88), www.foreignaffairs.com/print/node/1109554; Bock, *supra* note 86, at 52; Henderson, *supra* note 90, at 127–32; *The President and the Management of National Security, supra* note 88, at 70–98; I.M. Destler, *Presidents, Bureaucrats and Foreign Policy: The Politics of Organizational Reform* 109–12 (1972); Kearns, *supra* note 1, at 319–22.

96. *See* Thomas Schoenbaum, *Waging Peace and War: Dean Rusk in the Truman, Kennedy & Johnson Years* 284 (1988); U.S. Const. art. II, § 2, cl. 2.

97. *See* Franck, *supra* note 89, at 634–39.

98. Kissinger, *supra* note 59, at 38.

99. Zbigniew Brzezinski, "The NSC's Midlife Crisis," 69 *Foreign Pol'y* 80, 86–87 (1987) (emphasis added).

100. Carnes Lord, *The Presidency and the Management of National Security* 73–74 (1988); Joan Hoff-Wilson, "Richard M. Nixon: The Corporate Presidency," in *Leadership in the Modern Presidency, supra* note 88, at 164, 185 (Nixon would point in the direction of the Oval Office and say, "There's the State Department."); Henderson, *supra* note 90, at 135; Bock, *supra* note 86, at 83–100; Destler, *supra* note 95, at 118–32.

101. *See generally* Kissinger, *supra* note 59, at 277–82, 733–87, 823–33, 1124–64; Roger Morris, *Uncertain Greatness: Henry Kissinger and American Foreign Policy* 245–49 (1977); Eugene Wittkopf et al., *American Foreign Policy: Pattern and Process* 242–54, 352 (3d ed. 1987); Sharpe, *supra* note 54, at 24 (Kissinger created an elaborate covert network to keep Cambodian bombing secret even from Strategic Air Command.); Hoff-Wilson, *supra* note 100, at 185–86.

102. *See* James Bill, *The Eagle and the Lion: The Tragedy of American-Iranian Relations* 86–94 (1988); Shawcross, *supra* note 62, at 65–71; Falk, *supra* note 28, at 114–22 (detailing CIA's actions in Iran); Prados, *supra* note 81, at 30–238 (detailing agency's pre-Vietnam activities); Jeffreys-Jones, *supra* note 92, at 90–99 (describing Dominican Republic, Guatemalan, and Cuban activities); *id.* at 118–38 (describing Bay of Pigs fiasco); Treverton, *supra* note 80, at 84–98 (same).

103. Jeffreys-Jones, *supra* note 92, at 143; Prados, *supra* note 81, at 247–50; Halberstam, *supra* note 1, at 411–14. It does not appear, however, that that surveillance unit was under the direction of the CIA.

104. *See generally* Morton Halperin et al., *The Lawless State: The Crimes of the U.S. Intelligence Agencies* 15–57, 135–54 (1976); Jeffreys-Jones, *supra* note 92, at 167; Prados, *supra* note 81, at 171–296; Barton Bernstein, "The Road to Watergate and Beyond: The Growth and Abuse of Executive Authority Since 1940," *Law & Contemp. Probs.*, Spring 1976, at 58, 81–84.

105. Prados, *supra* note 81, at 239–312. Indeed, Cambodia's exiled prince Norodom Sihanouk entitled his 1973 book *My War with the CIA. See* Jeffreys-Jones, *supra* note 92, at 182.

106. *See* Peter Shane & Harold Bruff, *The Law of Presidential Power: Cases and Materials* 137–38 (1988); Jeffreys-Jones, *supra* note 92, at 184–85.

107. Alexander Haig, *Caveat: Realism, Reagan, and Foreign Policy* 141–42, 306–16 (1984); Jeffreys-Jones, *supra* note 92, at 235–51; Lord, *supra* note 100, at 79; Bock, *supra* note 86, at 159–64; Prados, *supra* note 81, at 396–418. For accounts of Casey's role in formulating Central American policy, see Bob Woodward, *Veil: The Secret Wars of the CIA, 1981–1987* (1987), and Roy Gutman, *Banana Diplomacy: The Making of American Policy in Nicaragua: 1981–1987*, at 29–30 (1988).

108. Lord, *supra* note 100, at 81. During his congressional testimony, Oliver North acknowledged that his duties as deputy director for political-military affairs at the NSC had included not merely the coordination of national security policy but "the rescue of American students in Grenada . . . and the US raid in Libya in response to their terrorist attacks." North, *supra* note 83, at 264, 657–58; *see also* Constantine Menges, *Inside the National Security Council: The True Story of the Making and Unmaking of Reagan's Foreign Policy* 54–90, 250–76 (1988) (describing and defending the NSC's role in these incidents).

109. *See* Bill, *supra* note 102, at 409–15.

110. For a discussion of these events, see *Iran-Contra Report, supra* note 4, at 20, 37, 167–68, 208, 271–73.

111. *See* Commission on CIA Activities Within the United States, *Report to the President* (1975) (Rockefeller commission); Prados, *supra* note 81, at 333.

112. *See* Pub. L. No. 93-559, § 32, 88 Stat. 1795, 1804 (1974) (repealed in 1991) (requiring president to report, "in a timely fashion, a description and scope of such operation" to the appropriate congressional committees).

113. *See generally* Loch Johnson, *A Season of Inquiry* (1985) (describing investigations of the most famous of these, the Senate Select Committee to Study Governmental Operations with Respect to Intelligence Activities (the "Church Committee")).

114. Pub. L. No. 96-450, 94 Stat. 1981 (1980), *described in* Thomas Paterson, "Oversight or Afterview?: Congress, the CIA, and Covert Actions Since 1947," in *Congress and United States Foreign Policy: Controlling the Use of Force in the Nuclear Age* 164–65 (M. Barnhart ed., 1987).

115. *See* 50 U.S.C. § 3091(a)(1); *see also* Whiting, *supra* note 94, at 36–41.

116. *See* 50 U.S.C. § 413 (1982) (repealed and replaced in 1991 by Pub. L. No. 102-88, § 602(a)(2)). The eight members to be notified are the chairs and ranking minority members of both intelligence committees, the majority and minority leaders of the Senate, and the Speaker and minority leader of the House. *Id.* § 413(a)(1)(B).

117. Paterson, *supra* note 114, at 165.

118. *See* Exec. Order No. 12,036, § 3-4, 43 Fed. Reg. 3674 (1978), *as amended by* Exec. Order No. 12,139, 44 Fed. Reg. 30,311 (1979); *see also* 126 Cong. Rec. S13,106 (daily ed. June 3, 1980) (remarks of Sen. Moynihan) ("[W]hat we have here is a codification in law of the practice our committee has followed with the administration for the past 3½ years.").

119. Newell Highsmith, Note, "Policing Executive Adventurism: Congressional Oversight of Military and Paramilitary Operations," 19 *Harv. J. on Legis.* 327, 357 (1982).

120. *See* Allan Goodman, "Reforming U.S. Intelligence," 67 *Foreign Pol'y* 121, 123–24 (1987).

121. *Compare* Exec. Order No. 12,036, 43 Fed. Reg. 3674, 3692 (1978) (emphasis added), *with* Exec. Order No. 12,333, 46 Fed. Reg. 59,941 (1981).

122. *See* Memorandum from Assistant Att'y Gen. Charles J. Cooper for the Att'y Gen. 14 (Dec. 17, 1986), *cited in Iran-Contra Report, supra* note 4, at 542 n.** (minority report) ("Activities authorized by the President cannot 'violate' an executive order in any legally meaningful sense.").

123. *See* Morris Fiorina, "Congressional Control of the Bureaucracy," in *Congress Reconsidered* 332, 337 (L. Dodd & B. Oppenheimer eds., 2d ed. 1981). During the 1960s and 1970s, numerous economists and political scientists advanced the notion that regulated entities "capture" the governmental bodies that regulate them. *See generally* Richard Posner, "Theories of Economic Regulation," 5 *Bell J. Econ. & Mgmt. Sci.* 335, 341–44 (1974). Although most versions of the capture theory address cases in which private interests capture their agency regulators, Professor Niskanen has described situations in which a government "bureau and [its congressional] review committee [are] 'in bed with each other.'" William Niskanen, *Bureaucracy and Representative Government* 148 (1971).

124. *See* Leslie Gelb, "Overseeing of C.I.A. by Congress Has Produced Decade of Support," *N.Y. Times,* July 7, 1986, at A1 (remarks of Sen. Moynihan); *see also* Franck & Weisband, *supra* note 37, at 132 ("Senate committees face an unenviable dilemma when they attempt to oversee government secrets. If they expect to get data, the Agencies will expect discretion in return.").

125. Two years later, the International Court of Justice decided that case in Nicaragua's favor. *See* Military and Paramilitary Activities in and Against Nicaragua (Nicar. v. U.S.), 1986 I.C.J. 14 (June 27, 1986). *See generally* "Appraisals of the ICJ's Decision: *Nicaragua v. United States* (Merits), 81 *Am. J. Int'l L.* 77 (1987). For a critique

of the U.S. legal position in the case, see Paul Kahn, "From Nuremberg to The Hague: The United States Position in *Nicaragua v. United States* and the Development of International Law," 12 *Yale J. Int'l L.* 1 (1987).

126. Although the Senate committee vice-chair claimed that he had never been informed, other senators recalled a grudging consultation. *See* R. Lugar, *supra* note 5, at 183 ("My own recollection is that Casey did include mention of the general subject deep in a report which he read in a sometimes inaudible briefing style. While thus fulfilling the bare letter of consultation, he . . . adopted an approach which suggested that if a committee member did not think of the right questions to ask or phrase them in such a way as to dredge up important information, that was his own tough luck.").

127. *See* Scheffer, *supra* note 68, at 722; Woodward, *supra* note 107, at 325; Goodman, *supra* note 120, at 125–26.

128. *See* H.R. 3822, 100th Cong., 133 Cong. Rec. H11,866 (daily ed. Dec. 18, 1987) (introduced by Congressman Stokes); S. 1721, 100th Cong., 133 Cong. Rec. S12,852 (daily ed. Sept. 25, 1987) (introduced by Sen. Cohen). The Senate bill stated, "Each finding shall be in writing, unless immediate action by the United States is required and time does not permit the preparation of a written finding, in which case a written record of the President's decision shall be contemporaneously made and shall be reduced to a written finding as soon as possible but in no event more than forty-eight (48) hours after the decision is made." *Id.* at S12,853. If, however, the president should determine that "it is essential to limit access to the finding to meet extraordinary circumstances affecting vital interests of the United States," the bill authorized the president to report that finding to the "Gang of Eight" described in the text.

129. *See* "The Director: 'We're Not out of Business,'" *Newsweek*, Oct. 12, 1987, at 30 (remarks of CIA director William Webster) ("As far as covert action [is concerned] . . . the procedures are already there. We need only people who will follow the procedures.").

130. *See* David Morrison, "An Eye on the CIA," 20 *Nat'l J.* 1009, 1010 (1988); *Oversight Legislation: Hearings on S. 1721 and S. 1818 Before the S. Select Comm. on Intelligence*, 100th Cong. 90 (1987) (testimony of Charles J. Cooper, assistant attorney general, Office of Legal Counsel) ("We believe . . . that by purporting to oblige the President, under *any and all circumstances*, to notify Congress of a covert action within a fixed period of time, S. 1721 infringes on [a] constitutional prerogative of the President." (emphasis in original)).

131. *Cf.* Stephen Engelberg, "Covert Intelligence: New Glitches and New Eyebrows," *N.Y. Times*, Dec. 15, 1987, at B12 (president's directive to attorney general not to implement provision in annual spending bill for intelligence agencies which required annual report to Congress on certain movements of Soviet diplomats). Members of Congress or private citizens could not have challenged such an action in court without overcoming the numerous obstacles to justiciability described in chapter 4.

132. *See* Covert Action Programs: Letter to the Chairman and Vice Chairman of the Senate Select Committee on Intelligence Regarding Procedures for Presidential

Approval and Notification of Congress, 23 Weekly Comp. Pres. Doc. 910 (Aug. 7, 1987); Gerald Seib, "New Rules for Reporting Covert Actions to Congress Are Announced by Reagan," *Wall St. J.*, Aug. 10, 1987, at 10.

133. *See* Stephen Engelberg, "3 in CIA Expected to Appeal on Jobs," *N.Y. Times*, Dec. 25, 1987, at A19 (announcing disciplinary actions).

134. *See* Michael Oreskes, "Wright, in Gesture to Bush, Shelves Bill on Covert Acts," *N.Y. Times*, Feb. 1, 1989, at A12; Stephen Engelberg, "Bush to Tell Congress of Covert Plans," *N.Y. Times*, Oct. 28, 1989, at A3 (Bush agrees to notify Congress of most, but not all, covert actions).

135. *See* United States v. North, 698 F. Supp. 322, 324 (D.D.C. 1988). Some of North's defenders, including President Reagan, also suggested that no theft had occurred because the U.S. government had received the full, legally required payment for the arms. *See, e.g.,* Phillip Shenon, "North, Poindexter and Two Others Indicted on Iran-Contra Fraud and Theft Charges," *N.Y. Times*, Mar. 17, 1988, at D27 (remarks of President Reagan). But an employee who sells his boss's property worth $100 for $500 is still guilty of embezzlement even if he repays his boss the full $100 and gives the balance to charity. In the same way, the profits of the Iranian arms transaction belonged to the Treasury; North possessed no legal authority to divert them to other unauthorized uses.

136. *See* Defendant's Pretrial Motion No. 40, United States v. North, 708 F. Supp. 375 (D.D.C. 1988) (No. 88-0080-02).

137. *See* Defendant's Pretrial Motion No. 39, United States v. North, 708 F. Supp. 375 (D.D.C. 1988) (No. 88-0080-02). For the text of the Boland amendments, see 133 Cong. Rec. H4982–87 (daily ed. June 15, 1987).

138. *See* North, *supra* note 83, at 256. North's defenders echoed this justification. *See, e.g., Iran-Contra Report, supra* note 4, at 659 (remarks of Sen. James A. McClure) ("Would you lie to save the life of your wife or child?").

139. *See* United States v. North, 708 F. Supp. 375, 379 (D.D.C. 1988) ("Not every matter touching on foreign affairs is barred [from judicial examination] by the political question doctrine."); United States v. Poindexter, 719 F. Supp. 6 (D.D.C. 1989).

140. *See* United States v. North, 708 F. Supp. 380, 382 n.3, 383 (D.D.C. 1988) (emphasis added).

141. *See* Memorandum of Law of the United States as *Amicus Curiae* with Respect to the Independent Counsel's Opposition to the Defendant's Motions to Dismiss or Limit Count One at 6, United States v. North, No. 88-0080-02 (D.D.C. Nov. 18, 1988).

142. *Id.* at 4–6, 12, 18–19 ("'[P]olitical' behavior," the department argued, "is permitted by the Constitution, and the penalties for it should remain within the political process and not be brought to a court for prosecution.") (citations omitted).

143. Jury Instruction on Specific Intent at 6, United States v. North, No. 88-0080-02 (D.D.C. Apr. 21, 1989); *see also id.* ("The conduct of others working with the defendant is not, standing alone, any justification for the defendant's conduct nor is the intent of others necessarily his. You are not to judge defendant's guilt or innocence based solely on the actions of others.").

144. *See Iran-Contra Report, supra* note 4, at 327–74 (describing "The Enterprise").

145. *See generally* Samuel Segev, *The Iranian Triangle: The Untold Story of Israel's Role in the Iran-Contra Affair* (1988) (describing Israel's involvement in the Iran-contra affair).

146. *Tower Report, supra* note 87, at 79 (by his own account, the president then placed "the principal responsibility for policy review and implementation on the shoulders of his advisors"); *see Iran-Contra Report, supra* note 4, at 20 ("At the operational level, the central figure in the Iran-Contra Affair was Lt. Col. North [of the NSC staff], who coordinated all of the activities and was involved in all aspects of the secret operations. . . . [W]e believe that the late Director of Central Intelligence, William Casey, encouraged North, gave him direction, and promoted the concept of an extra-legal covert organization [while] for the most part, insulat[ing] CIA career employees from knowledge of what he and the NSC staff were doing.").

147. *See* Sorensen, *supra* note 95 ("[T]he Iran-contra hearings . . . revealed a pattern of White House disdain for the Department of State so pervasive that Secretary George Shultz's own blunt testimony, while preserving his personal reputation, confirmed his department's emasculation.").

148. *See* North, *supra* note 83, at 741 (statement of Rep. Lee H. Hamilton).

Chapter 4. Why the President Almost Always Wins

1. Charles Black, "The Working Balance of the American Political Departments," 1 *Hastings Const. L.Q.* 13, 17, 20 (1974).

2. *The Federalist* No. 70, at 454 (Alexander Hamilton) (Modern Library 1937). For a more recent discussion of the same concept, see generally Richard Neustadt, *Presidential Power: The Politics of Leadership from FDR to Carter* (rev. ed. 1980).

3. *Cf.* Cass Sunstein, "Constitutionalism After the New Deal," 101 *Harv. L. Rev.* 421, 452–53 (1987) (articulating these three reasons as arguments favoring presidential control of the bureaucracy); *see also* Youngstown Sheet & Tube Co. v. Sawyer, 343 U.S. 579, 629 (1952) (Douglas, J., concurring) ("All executive power—from the reign of ancient kings to the rule of modern dictators—has the outward appearance of efficiency. Legislative power, by contrast, is slower to exercise. . . . [T]he ponderous machinery of committees, hearings, and debates is . . . cumbersome, time-consuming, and apparently inefficient.").

4. United States v. Curtiss-Wright Export Corp., 299 U.S. 304, 319 (1936) (quoting U.S. Senate, Reports, Committee on Foreign Relations, vol. 8, at 24 (Feb. 15, 1816)). *Curtiss-Wright's* language appears to derive from the *Federalist* No. 75, in which Hamilton referred to the treaty process as one requiring "decision, *secrecy* and despatch." But significantly, Hamilton used that reason to justify the *House's* exclusion from the treaty ratification process, not to justify the president's monopoly over it. *See The Federalist* No. 75, *supra* note 2, at 488 (Alexander Hamilton) (emphasis in original).

5. For a political scientist's attempt to untangle the intricate relationship between domestic politics and international relations, see Robert Putnam, "Diplomacy and Domestic Politics: The Logic of Two-Level Games," 42 *Int'l Org.* 427 (1988).

6. *See* Michael Roskin, "From Pearl Harbor to Vietnam: Shifting Generational Paradigms and Foreign Policy," 89 *Pol. Sci. Q.* 563 (1974).

7. Ole Holsti & James Rosenau, *American Leadership in World Affairs: Vietnam and the Breakdown of Consensus* 29–78 (1984); Bruce Russett, "The Americans' Retreat from World Power," 90 *Pol. Sci. Q.* 1, 5 (1975); John Vasquez, "Domestic Contention on Critical Foreign-Policy Issues: The Case of the United States," 39 *Int'l Org.* 643, 646 (1988); John Vasquez, "A Learning Theory of the American Anti-Vietnam Movement," 13 *J. Peace Res.* 299 (1976); Ernest May, *"Lessons" of the Past: The Use and Misuse of History in American Foreign Policy* 143–71 (1973).

8. For claims of declining American hegemony, see David Calleo, *Beyond American Hegemony: The Future of the Western Alliance* (1987), Robert Gilpin, *The Political Economy of International Relations* (1987), Robert Gilpin, *War and Change in World Politics* (1981), Robert Gilpin, *U. S. Power and the Multinational Corporation* (1975), Paul Kennedy, *The Rise and Fall of the Great Powers* (1987), Mancur Olson, *The Rise and Decline of Nations: Economic Growth, Stagnation, and Social Rigidities* (1982) (explaining U.S. economic decline as a function of special-interest-group government fostered in part by nation's hegemonic status), Charles Kindleberger, "Systems of International Economic Organization," in *Money and the Coming World Order* 15, 33 (D. Calleo ed. 1976), Stephen Krasner, "Transforming International Regimes: What the Third World Wants and Why," 25 *Int'l Stud. Q.* 119 (1981), Robert Gilpin, "American Policy in the Post-Reagan Era," *Daedalus*, Summer 1987, at 42–43, and Robert Keohane, *After Hegemony* (1984) (recognizing decline of American postwar hegemony but questioning whether hegemony constitutes either necessary or sufficient condition for stable international order). But see Samuel Huntington, "The U.S.—Decline or Renewal?" 67 *Foreign Aff.* 76–96 (1988), Joseph Nye, "Short-Term Folly, Not Long-Term Decline," *New Perspectives Q.*, Summer 1988, at 33, Joseph Nye, "Understating U.S. Strength," 72 *Foreign Pol'y* 105–29 (1988), Joseph Nye, "Before the Fall," *New Republic*, Feb. 13, 1989, at 37–39, Bruce Russett, "The Mysterious Case of Vanishing Hegemony: Or, Is Mark Twain Really Dead?" 39 *Int'l Org.* 207 (1985), and Susan Strange, "The Persistent Myth of Lost Hegemony," 41 *Int'l Org.* 551 (1987), all questioning notion of America's lost hegemony. For policy analysis, see also David Hendrickson, *The Future of American Strategy* (1989), and Barry Bosworth & Robert Lawrence, "America's Global Role: From Dominance to Interdependence," in *Restructuring American Foreign Policy* 12 (J. Steinbruner ed., 1989), all making policy recommendations based on lost hegemony assumption.

9. These regimes have been the subject of intensive political-science analysis. For general accounts, see Keohane, *supra* note 8, *International Regimes* (S. Krasner ed. 1983), and Stephan Haggard & Beth A. Simmons, "Theories of International Regimes," 41 *Int'l Org.* 491 (1987). For descriptions of particular political regimes, see, for example, Robert Keohane & Joseph Nye, "Two Cheers for Multilateralism," 60 *Foreign Pol'y* 148 (1986) (describing debt, peacekeeping, and exchange rate regimes), Jack Donnelly, "International Human Rights: A Regime Analysis," 40 *Int'l Org.* 599 (1986), and Richard Bilder, "An Overview of International Dispute Resolution Settlement," 1 *Emory J. Int'l Dispute Res.* 1 (1986) (describing international

dispute-settlement regime without using regime terminology). For descriptions of particular economic regimes, see, for example, Robert D. Putnam & Nicholas Bayne, *Hanging Together: The Seven-Power Summits* (rev. ed. 1987) (studying cooperation and conflict in the Seven-Power summits), Timothy Aeppel, "The Evolution of Multilateral Export Controls: A Critical Study of the CoCom Regime," 9 *Fletcher Forum* 105–24 (1985), Miles Kahler, "Politics and International Debt: Explaining the Crisis," 39 *Int'l Org.* 357 (1985), and Karen Hudes, "Coordination of Paris and London Club Reschedulings," 17 *N.Y.U. J. Int'l L. & Pol.* 553 (1985).

10. For a discussion of developments in the trade area, see, for example, Harold Hongju Koh, "Congressional Controls on Presidential Trade Policymaking After *INS v. Chadha*," 18 *N.Y.U. J. Int'l L. & Pol.* 1227 (1986) [hereinafter Koh, "Congressional Controls"], Harold Hongju Koh, "The Legal Markets of International Trade: A Perspective on the Proposed United States–Canada Free Trade Agreement," 13 *Yale J. Int'l L.* 240–48 (1987), and Robert Gilpin, *The Political Economy of International Relations* 171–230 (1987). For a description of the legal structure of the antiterrorism regime, see, for example, Harold Hongju Koh, "Civil Remedies for Uncivil Wrongs: Combatting Terrorism Through Transnational Public Law Litigation," 22 *Tex. Int'l L.J.* 169, 170–73 (1987). For a discussion of the international debt problem and regime, see, for example, Harold Lever & Christopher Huhne, *Debt and Danger* (1986), Kahler, *supra* note 9, and Keohane & Nye, *supra* note 9 at 165–66.

11. On the rise of congressional activism, see Koh, "Congressional Controls," *supra* note 10, at 1211–21 (discussing enhanced powers of the House Ways and Means and Senate Finance Committees under the 1984 Trade and Tariff Act), Richard Fenno, *Congressmen in Committees* 26–35 (1973) (discussing the power of the foreign-affairs committees), and Paul Hammond, "Congress in Foreign Policy," in *The President, the Congress, and Foreign Policy* 81 (E. Muskie et al. eds., 1986) (listing informal congressional foreign policy caucuses). On the decentralization of Congress, see Norman Ornstein, "The Constitution and the Sharing of Foreign Policy Responsibility," in *The President, the Congress, and Foreign Policy, supra*, at 35, 57.

12. On the South African sanctions battle, see Exec. Order No. 12,532, 50 Fed. Reg. 36,861 (1985) (South African sanctions order), and Richard Lugar, *Letters to the Next President* 208–47 (1988). On the PLO mission controversy, see Designation of Palestine Information Office as a Foreign Mission, 52 Fed. Reg. 37,035 (Oct. 2, 1987) (executive decision to close Palestinian office to forestall enactment of the Anti-Terrorism Act of 1987, Pub. L. No. 100-204, §§ 1001–1005, 101 Stat. 1331, 1406–07), and "United States Department of State, Statement on the Visa Application of Yassir Arafat," 83 *Am. J. Int'l L.* 253–54 (1989). On presidential preemptive actions in the trade field, see Koh, "Congressional Controls," *supra* note 10, at 1225–33, Patricia I. Hansen, Note, "Defining Unreasonableness in International Trade: Section 301 of the Trade Act of 1974," 96 *Yale L.J.* 1122–26 (1987) (describing Reagan administration's use of section 301 of the Trade Act of 1974 to open foreign markets), and Statement on United States Action Against Foreign Trade Barriers, 25 Weekly Comp. Pres. Doc. 777 (May 26, 1989) (naming Brazil, India, and Japan as "priority" unfair trading countries under "Super 301" of Omnibus Trade and Competitiveness Act of 1988). On the role of the Kassebaum amendment in the U.N. funding crisis,

see Pub. L. No. 99-93, § 143, 99 Stat. 405, 424 (1985) (imposing preconditions on U.S. payment of assessed contributions to United Nations and specialized agencies), and Richard W. Nelson, "International Law and U.S. Withholding of Payments to International Organizations," 80 *Am. J. Int'l L.* 973 (1986).

13. *See* Theodore Lowi, *The Personal President* 173 (1985).

14. The political-science literature on each of these phenomena is massive. On ideology, see, for example, Michael H. Hunt, *Ideology and U.S. Foreign Policy* (1987). On the role of realism in Kissinger's thought, see Michael Joseph Smith, *Realist Thought from Weber to Kissinger* 192–217 (1986). On the role of bureaucratic politics and foreign policy, see Graham Allison, *Essence of Decision: Explaining the Cuban Missile Crisis* (1971), Morton Halperin, *Bureaucratic Politics and Foreign Policy* (1974), and Robert Art, "Bureaucratic Politics and Foreign Policy: A Critique," 4 *Pol'y Sci.* 467–90 (1973).

15. *See* Lowi, *supra* note 13, at 173. For descriptions of President Carter's actions during the Iranian hostage crisis, see Koh, "Congressional Controls," *supra* note 10, at 1229 n.112, Opinions of the Attorney General and of the Office of Legal Counsel Relating to the Iranian Hostage Crisis, 4A Op. O.L.C. 71–333 (1980), and Gaddis Smith, *Morality, Reason, and Power* 180–207 (1986).

16. *See* "Shultz's 'Battle Royal,'" *Newsweek*, Aug. 3, 1987, at 16 (statement of Secretary of State Shultz, quoting President Reagan); Oliver North, *Taking the Stand: The Testimony of Lieutenant Colonel Oliver L. North* 12, 256 (1987) ("This is a nation at risk in a dangerous world. . . . [W]e all had to weigh . . . the difference between lies and lives.").

17. *Cf.* Henry Kissinger, *White House Years* 806 (1979) ("[President] Nixon feared leaks . . .; he thus encouraged procedures unlikely to be recommended in textbooks on public administration that, crablike, worked privily around existing structures."). When Nixon ordered the Cambodian bombings, for example, he explicitly instructed the NSC that the "State [Department] is to be notified only after the point of no return." *Id.* at 245. When Henry Kissinger returned from his secret mission to China, Nixon instructed him to give the secretary of state only a "sanitized" account of the trip. *Id.* at 756–57.

18. *See generally* Irving L. Janis, *Victims of Groupthink: A Psychological Study of Foreign-Policy Decisions and Fiascoes* (1972).

19. "Excerpts from Interview with Nixon About Domestic Effects of Indochina War," *N.Y. Times*, May 20, 1977, at A16, https://perma.cc/RPN9-MV8Q.

20. The phenomenon is not restricted to the American legislature. *See, e.g.,* Alan Watson, "Legal Evolution and Legislation," 1987 *B.Y.U. L. Rev.* 375–79 (1987) (providing cross-cultural explanation for why legislatures often reject revolutionary proposals).

21. *See* Morris Fiorina, *Retrospective Voting in American National Elections* (1981).

22. For general discussions of the role of interest groups in the legislative process, see Jonathan Macey, "Promoting Public-Regarding Legislation through Statutory Interpretation: An Interest Group Model," 86 *Colum. L. Rev.* 223–68 (1986), and Cass R. Sunstein, "Interest Groups in American Public Law," 38 *Stan. L. Rev.* 29 (1985). On interest-group politics in international trade, see generally Raymond A.

Bauer et al., *American Business and Public Policy: The Politics of Foreign Trade* (1963), Stephen D. Cohen, *The Making of United States International Economic Policy* 121–39 (1988), I. M. Destler, *American Trade Politics: System Under Stress* (1986), Robert Pastor, *Congress and the Politics of U.S. Foreign Economic Policy* (1980), E.E. Schattschneider, *Politics, Pressure and the Tariff* (1935), and Edward John Ray, "Changing Patterns of Protectionism: The Fall in Tariffs and the Rise of Non-Tariff Barriers," 8 *Nw. J. Int'l L. & Bus.* 285–327 (1987) (arguing that U.S. trade policy results from political equilibrium struck between national-policy and interest-group pressures). The recurring battle between business interests for and against the restriction of textile imports forms a particularly fascinating case study. *See, e.g.,* John Felton, "President Vetoes Textile Import-Quota Bill," 46 *Cong. Q.* 2754 (1988). For an economic modeling of the role of interest-group politics in the creation of voluntary restraint agreements, see Arye L. Hillman & Heinrich W. Urspring, "Domestic Politics, Foreign Interest, and International Trade Policy," 78 *Am. Econ. Rev.* 729 (1988).

On the role of the defense lobby, see, for example, Christopher Madison, "The Arms Sale Say-So," 19 *Nat'l J.* 667 (1987), and Hedrick Smith, *The Power Game* 173–215 (1988) (describing "iron triangle" between the military services, defense contractors, and members of Congress). On the influence of the Israel lobby, see Thomas Franck & Edward Weisband, *Foreign Policy by Congress* 200–09 (1979), Kennan Teslik, *Congress, The Executive Branch, and Special Interests* (1982) (discussing role of Israel lobby in the enactment of Arab anti-boycott legislation), Smith, *supra,* at 216–31 (discussing role of American Israel Public Affairs Committee (AIPAC) in opposing Arab arms sales), and Christopher Madison, "Arms-Sale Armistice," 19 *Nat'l J.* 2607 (1987). See generally *Ethnic Groups and U.S. Policy* (M. Ahrari ed., 1987), describing the influence of pro-Israel, Black, Polish-American, Mexican-American, Cuban-American, and Irish-American lobbies on foreign policy. On interest-group influence on the intelligence committees, see Loch Johnson, *America's Secret Power: The CIA in a Democratic Society* 219–20 (1989).

23. On interest-group influence on U.S. human-rights policy, see generally David Forsythe, *Human Rights and U.S. Foreign Policy* (1988), and Pastor, *supra* note 22, at 301–21. On the Vietnam lobby, see Norman Ornstein, "Interest Groups, Congress, and American Policy," in *American Foreign Policy in an Uncertain World* 49, 52–55 (D. Forsythe ed., 1984).

24. David Mayhew, *Congress: The Electoral Connection* 138 (1974). For Senator Eagleton's proposal, see 119 Cong. Rec. 25,079–86 (1973).

25. *See generally* Mayhew, *supra* note 24, at 126–40. For examples of legislative "fixes" easily comprehended by the public, see Balanced Budget and Emergency Deficit Control Act of 1985, Pub. L. No. 99-177, 99 Stat. 1037 (1985) (codified as amended in scattered sections of 2, 31, and 42 U.S.C.) (Gramm-Rudman-Hollings budget-balancing act), which employed a numerical approach to domestic deficit reduction; Trade and International Economic Policy Reform Act of 1987, H.R. 3, 100th Cong. § 126, 133 Cong. Rec. 2,755–57 (1987) (Gephardt amendment to 1988 act, subsequently dropped in conference), which required the president to retaliate against countries running excessive and unwarranted trade surpluses with the

United States by forcing those countries to reduce their surpluses by 10 percent annually; and Christopher Madison, "It's Congress's Move," 19 *Nat'l J.* 2014, 2017–18 (1987), which describes "forty-eight-hour notice" intelligence reform bill.

26. I am grateful to Robert J. Kurz of the Brookings Institution (who served on the staff of the House Subcommittee on Western Hemisphere Affairs when the Boland amendments were enacted) for this observation. On the problems of coalition formation within committees, see Barry Weingast & William Marshall, "The Industrial Organization of Congress; or, Why Legislatures, Like Firms, Are Not Organized As Markets," 96 *J. Pol. Econ.* 146–47 (1988).

27. *See Standing Rules of the Senate Revised to June 1, 1988,* S. Doc. No. 100-33, at 15 (1988) (rule XXII(2)); *see also* Irvin Molotsky, "A Senator Is Captured, but Not His Mind," *N.Y. Times,* Feb. 25, 1988, at A26, https://perma.cc/F2LH-L2QW (describing Republicans' use of that rule, along with the quorum requirement, to defeat Democratic-supported campaign-reform bill).

28. *Compare* 50 U.S.C. § 1542, *with* Jimmy Carter, *Keeping Faith* 518 (1982) ("I had planned on calling in a few members of the House and Senate . . . before the rescue team began its move into Tehran. . . . But I never got around to that."). Most presidents, however, have complied in some form or another with the resolution's consultation requirement. *See generally* Note, "The War Powers Resolution: An Act Facing 'Imminent Hostilities' A Decade Later," 16 *Vand. J. Transnat'l L.* 915–1052 (1983) (citing examples).

29. *Compare* 50 U.S.C. § 1542 (1982), *with* Robert Torricelli, "The War Powers Resolution After the Libya Crisis," 7 *Pace L. Rev.* 666 (1987), *and* Lugar, *supra* note 12, at 47–48 ("consultation" of key senators began two hours after planes were in the air and concluded less than thirty minutes before bombing began).

30. *See* 50 U.S.C. §§ 1543(a)(1)-(3), 1544(b).

31. Michael Glennon, "The War Powers Resolution Ten Years Later: More Politics Than Law," 78 *Am. J. Int'l L.* 571 (1984).

32. Mayhew, *supra* note 24, at 122.

33. Compare the "in every possible instance" phrase in 50 U.S.C. § 1542 (1982) with the identical phrase in IEEPA, 50 U.S.C. § 1703(a). For a cross-cultural discussion of how and why such "legal transplants" occur, see generally Alan Watson, *Legal Transplants* 21–30 (1974).

34. *See* Comprehensive Anti-Apartheid Act of 1986, Pub. L. No. 99-440, 100 Stat. 1086 (1986); Richard Messick, Former Counsel to the Senate Foreign Relations Committee, Remarks at the Yale Law School Symposium on Human Rights Advocacy and the U.S. Political Process (April 9, 1988) (on file with author). For a description of the law's loopholes, see generally Raymond Paretzky, "The United States Arms Embargo Against South Africa: An Analysis of the Laws, Regulations, and Loopholes," 12 *Yale J. Int'l L.* 133 (1987).

35. *See, e.g.,* Lowry v. Reagan, 676 F. Supp. 333 (D.D.C. 1987), *appeal dismissed,* No. 87-5426 (D.C. Cir. Oct. 17, 1988) (dismissing suit seeking to compel president to comply with reporting requirement of War Powers Resolution with regard to U.S. military activities in Persian Gulf); Crockett v. Reagan, 720 F.2d 1355 (D.C. Cir. 1983) (dismissing similar suit with regard to U.S. military activities in El Salvador).

36. Guido Calabresi, *A Common Law for the Age of Statutes* 61, 62 (1982).

37. *See* Thomas Franck & Clifford Bob, "The Return of Humpty-Dumpty: Foreign Relations Law After the *Chadha* Case," 79 *Am. J. Int'l L.* 934 (1985).

38. For accounts of the use or threatened use of the legislative veto in the areas of arms control and the transfer of nuclear materials, see Michla Pomerance, "United States Foreign Relations Law After *Chadha*," 15 *Cal. W. Int'l L.J.* 262 (1985). For descriptions of Congress's efforts to use appropriations cutoffs in foreign affairs, see Louis Fisher, *Constitutional Conflicts Between Congress and the President* 221–51, 318–23 (1985), Gregory Treverton, *Covert Action* 156–60 (1987) (describing legislative cutoff of funds for covert activities in Angola under the Clark amendment), and Franck & Bob, *supra* note 37, at 944–48.

39. For a fuller description, see Koh, "Congressional Controls," *supra* note 10, at 1196 n.16.

40. INS v. Chadha, 462 U.S. 919 (1983).

41. *See* Bowsher v. Synar, 478 U.S. 714 (1986); N. Pipeline Constr. Co. v. Marathon Pipe Line Co., 458 U.S. 50 (1982); Buckley v. Valeo, 424 U.S. 1 (1976). *But see* Morrison v. Olson, 487 U.S. 654 (1988); Mistretta v. United States, 488 U.S. 361 (1989).

42. *See* Clinton Rossiter, *The American Presidency* 157 (1956) ("The President often feels compelled to sign bills that are full of dubious grants and subsidies rather than risk a breakdown in the work of whole departments.").

43. *See* Stephen Engelberg, "Contra Aid: Loose Law?" *N.Y. Times,* Jan. 15, 1987, at A12, https://perma.cc/M2QS-CBM8 (describing claimed loopholes in Boland amendments).

44. United States v. Lovett, 328 U.S. 303 (1946). For an intriguing account of the decision, see John Hart Ely, "*United States v. Lovett:* Litigating the Separation of Powers," 10 *Harv. C.R.-C.L. L. Rev.* 10 (1975).

45. *See, e.g.,* L. Gordon Crovitz, "Crime, the Constitution, and the Iran-Contra Affair," *Commentary,* Oct. 1987, at 23, 28; Vicki Quade, "The President Is His Only Client," *Barrister,* Winter/Spring 1988, at 5, 7 (interview with A. B. Culvahouse Jr., counsel to the president) ("[I]t was clear in our mind and remains clear that the Boland Amendment could not circumscribe the efforts of the President to speak with foreign leaders about supporting the Nicaraguan freedom fighters.").

46. *See, e.g.,* Louis Henkin, *Constitutionalism, Democracy, and Foreign Affairs* 33 (1990); Kate Stith, "Congress' Power of the Purse," 97 *Yale L.J.* 1351 & n.32 (1988).

47. *See* Nat'l Fed'n of Fed. Emps. v. United States, 688 F. Supp. 671, 685 (D.D.C. 1988), *vacated and remanded sub nom.* Am. Foreign Serv. Ass'n v. Garfinkel, 490 U.S. 153 (1989) (per curiam). Shortly before the district court's ruling in this case, another district judge declared that "[w]e are aware of no case striking down federal legislation as an encroachment of the executive's authority to conduct foreign affairs." Mendelsohn v. Meese, 695 F. Supp. 1474, 1483 (S.D.N.Y. 1988) (Palmieri, J.).

48. *See Report of the Congressional Committees Investigating the Iran-Contra Affair,* H.R. Rep. No. 100-433, S. Rep. No. 100-216, at 16 (1987) (emphasis added); Stith, *supra* note 46, at 1358 (only monies receivable by the U.S. government *and* subject to its control and expenditure are subject to Congress's appropriations power). Congress sought to redress this problem by passing an appropriations rider (which the president later

vetoed) that would punish U.S. officials who solicit funds from foreign countries to carry out activities for which Congress has cut off aid. *See* 135 Cong. Rec. S8107–09 (daily ed. July 18, 1989) (Moynihan amendment (amendment no. 268) to the fiscal year 1990 State Department Authorization Act); H.R. 2939, § 577, 101st Cong., 135 Cong. Rec. H4071–72 (daily ed. July 21, 1989) (parallel provision in House foreign-aid bill).

49. North, *supra* note 16, at 473 (1987) (emphasis added).

50. For descriptions of presidential devices to control spending, see Louis Fisher, *President and Congress: Power and Policy* 110–32 (1972), Louis Fisher, *Presidential Spending Power* (1975), and Jeffrey Meyer, "Congressional Control of Foreign Assistance," 13 *Yale J. Int'l L.* 74–75 (1988).

51. Kenneth E. Sharpe, "The Real Cause of Irangate," 68 *Foreign Pol'y* 33–34 (1987).

52. During the Trump administration, Congress largely denied the president's request to fund construction of a border wall, which led the president to announce plans to transfer that amount from other funds. When the Democratic-led House challenged that action as unconstitutional under the appropriations clause, the D.C. Circuit panel concluded that the House had the right to sue. But Trump then lost, and Biden stopped, then resumed, the spending, after the Supreme Court had vacated that ruling as moot. *See* Yellen v. U.S. House of Representatives, 142 S. Ct. 332 (2021) (mem.). *See* Todd Ruger, "Supreme Court Ends Legal Clash over Border Wall Spending," *Roll Call*, Jan. 12, 2021, https://perma.cc/T229-7LKN.

53. *See, e.g.,* U.S. Army Corps of Eng'rs v. Ameron, Inc., 809 F.2d 979 (3d Cir. 1986), *cert. dismissed,* 488 U.S. 918 (1988) (dismissing a constitutional challenge to the comptroller general's statutory authorities, leaving unresolved whether Congress may constitutionally direct the comptroller general to enforce executive compliance with spending limitations in foreign affairs); Stith, *supra* note 46, at 1390–92 & nn. 232–47 (describing constitutional difficulties of using comptroller general to enforce appropriations requirements against the executive); Note, "The Role of the Comptroller General in Light of *Bowsher* v. *Synar*," 87 *Colum. L. Rev.* 1539–64 (1987).

54. *See* Meghan M. Stuessy, Cong. Research Serv., RS22188, *Regular Vetoes and Pocket Vetoes* (2021), https://perma.cc/2V73-CKH8. *See generally* Robert Spitzer, *The Presidential Veto: Touchstone of the American Presidency* (1988).

55. *See* J. William Fulbright, "Congress and Foreign Policy," in 5 *Appendices: Commission on the Organization of the Government for the Conduct of Foreign Policy* 58–59 (1975) [hereinafter *Appendices to Murphy Commission Report*].

56. *See* 133 Cong. Rec. S15,011 (daily ed. Oct. 23, 1987) (Bork vote); Gerald Seib & John J. Fialka, "Advise and Reject: Tower Fiasco Hurts Bush, but It Also Puts Congress on Defensive," *Wall St. J.*, Mar. 10, 1989, at A1 (Tower vote), https://perma.cc/3UNB-Z8CE; "Trade Policy: New Trade Legislation Expected in Congress as Senate Sustains Reagan's Veto of HR 3," 5 Int'l Trade Rep. (BNA) 879 (June 15, 1988) [hereinafter "New Trade Legislation"]. The president defeated an override of his trade-bill veto because the Senate failed to gain the unanimous consent necessary to bring to a vote a concurrent resolution stripping an Alaskan-oil-export limitation from the bill. By retaining that single provision in its one-thousand-page bill, Congress lost the critical override votes of both Alaskan senators. *See* "Trade Policy:

Trade Bill Goes to Reagan This Week for Certain Veto; Override Unlikely," 5 Int'l Trade Rep. (BNA) 678 (May 11, 1988).

57. Jennifer E. Manning, Cong. Research Serv., R47470, *Membership of the 118th Congress: A Profile* (2023), https://crsreports.congress.gov/product/pdf/download/R/R47470/R47470.pdf/ (in the 118th Congress, the House had 222 Republicans versus 212 Democrats).

58. *Cf.* Bob Eckhardt & Charles Black, *The Tides of Power* 62–65 (1976) (statement of Prof. Charles Black) (proposing that Congress simply follow convention of overriding all presidential vetoes, regardless of substance).

59. *See* Girardeau A. Spann, "Spinning the Legislative Veto," 72 *Geo. L.J.* 813–18 (1984).

60. *See* Note, *supra* note 28, at 1008–14.

61. *See, e.g.,* Jonathan Feuerbringer, "Senate Defers Vote on Gulf Escort Policy," *N.Y. Times,* Oct. 22, 1987, at A3, https://perma.cc/A6TG-XMV4.

62. "New Trade Legislation," *supra* note 56, at 880 (describing such an action by Senate majority leader, who led drive to override president's veto of trade bill). It would be highly unlikely, however, that a congressional leader would cast such a vote if it would be decisive in securing an override.

63. Louis Henkin, "'A More Effective System' for Foreign Relations: The Constitutional Framework," in 5 *Appendices to Murphy Commission Report, supra* note 55, at 9, 16. *Accord* Thomas Eagleton, *War and Presidential Power* 146 (1974).

64. *See* Cyrus Vance, "Striking the Balance: Congress and the President Under the War Powers Resolution," 133 *U. Pa. L. Rev.* 79, 94–95 (1984) (describing events leading to enactment of Multinational Force in Lebanon Resolution, Pub. L. No. 98-119, 97 Stat. 805 (1983)).

65. *See Youngstown,* 343 U.S. at 585 ("The President's power, if any, to issue the order [under challenge] must stem either from an act of Congress or from the Constitution itself."); *id.* at 635–36 n.2 (Jackson, J., concurring) (stating that *Curtiss-Wright* involved not "the question of the President's power to act without congressional authorization, but the question of his right to act under and in accord with an Act of Congress").

66. N.Y. Times Co. v. United States, 403 U.S. 713 (1971) (*Pentagon Papers* case).

67. *See id.* at 753, 756 (Harlan, J., joined by Burger, C.J., and Blackmun, J., dissenting); *id.* at 718–19 (Black, J., joined by Douglas, J., concurring); *id.* at 726–27 (Brennan, J., concurring).

68. *See id.* at 728–29 (Stewart, J., joined by White, J., concurring).

69. *See* United States v. Progressive, Inc., 467 F. Supp. 990 (W.D. Wis. 1979), *dismissed summarily,* 610 F.2d 819 (7th Cir. 1979) (regarding an effort to enjoin publication in article which was dropped after similar information appeared elsewhere). One year after the *Pentagon Papers* case, in *United States v. U.S. District Court (Keith),* 407 U.S. 297 (1972), the Supreme Court similarly ruled against the president by invalidating warrantless wiretaps for domestic intelligence gathering that had been authorized only by the attorney general. But the *Keith* Court carefully declined "judgment on the scope of the President's surveillance power with respect to the activities of foreign powers, within or without this country." *Id.* at 308; *see also id.*

at 322 (reiterating that case did not involve issues "with respect to activities of foreign powers or their agents").

70. *Curtiss-Wright,* 299 U.S. at 320 (emphasis added).

71. For a statement of this view by the former assistant attorney general in charge of the Office of Legal Counsel, see Charles J. Cooper, "Comment on Schlesinger," 47 *Md. L. Rev.* 84, 91 (1987) ("[*Curtiss-Wright*] emphatically declared . . . that congressional efforts to act in this area must be evaluated in the light of the President's constitutional ascendancy.").

72. During the Carter administration, the Court decided three significant cases concerning the foreign-affairs power and declined to hear two others. *See* Warren Christopher, "Ceasefire Between the Branches: A Compact in Foreign Affairs," 60 *Foreign Aff.* 989 (1982) (discussing *Edwards v. Carter, Dole v. Carter, Goldwater v. Carter, Haig v. Agee,* and *Dames & Moore v. Regan*). As even President Carter's former deputy secretary of state conceded, the only unifying feature of these cases was that "the outcome in all instances was to let the President have his way." *Id.* at 995.

73. *See* Snepp v. United States, 444 U.S. 507, 510 n.3 (1980) (citing director's authority under 50 U.S.C. § 403(d)(3), which at the time made him "responsible for protecting intelligence sources and methods from unauthorized disclosure" but specified no remedies for such disclosure). For criticism of *Snepp,* see Anthony Lewis, "Limits on Presidential Power," 49 *U. Pitt. L. Rev.* 750 (1988). *See also* Kent v. Dulles, 357 U.S. 116 (1958).

74. *See* Dames & Moore v. Regan, 453 U.S. 654 (1981). Justice Rehnquist declined to hold that either IEEPA or the Hostage Act of 1868 specifically authorized the president to suspend claims, but found both statutes "highly relevant in the looser sense of indicating congressional acceptance of a broad scope for executive action." *Id.* at 677.

75. *Compare id.* at 674 n.6 & 688–90, *with id.* at 690–91 (Powell, J., concurring in part and dissenting in part) (dissenting from Court's decision with respect to attachments).

76. *Id.* at 661 (majority opinion); *see also id.* at 660 ("[We are] acutely aware of the necessity to rest decision on the narrowest possible ground capable of deciding the case."); *id.* at 661 ("[We] attempt to confine the opinion only to the very questions necessary to decision of the case."); *id.* at 688 ("[W]e re-emphasize the narrowness of our decision.").

77. Compare *id.* at 675–79, *with Youngstown,* 343 U.S. at 669, 683–700 (Vinson, C.J., dissenting). For other critiques of the Court's technique of statutory construction in *Dames & Moore,* see William Eskridge & Phillip Frickey, *Legislation: Statutes and the Creation of Public Policy* 317–21 (1987); Laurence Tribe, *Constitutional Choices* 38–39 (1985).

78. *See* William Rehnquist, *The Supreme Court: How It Was, How It Is* 45–60 (1987) (recalling national mood during *Youngstown*).

79. *See, e.g.,* Abner Mikva & Gerald Neuman, "The Hostage Crisis and the 'Hostage Act'" 49 *U. Chi. L. Rev.* 292 (1982) (arguing that President Carter sought to use the previously unknown Hostage Act of 1868, 22 U.S.C. § 1732, as a blank check au-

thorizing the president to use any means to rescue hostages). *See* North, *supra* note 16, at 503–04; *id.* at 606 (remarks of Rep. Henry Hyde) (claiming that the Hostage Act provided the executive branch with "the authority to do whatever (was) necessary" during the Iran-contra affair).

80. For examples of executive-branch lawyers "finding-the-statute," as with the Hostage Act, see Harold Hongju Koh, "War and Responsibility in the Dole-Gingrich Congress," 50 *U. Miami L. Rev.* 14–15 (1995).

81. Haig v. Agee, 453 U.S. 280, 291 (1981). *Compare id.* at 309 (upholding secretary's act as "'an inhibition of *action*' rather than of speech" (emphasis in original) (citation omitted)), *with id.* at 318 (Brennan, J., dissenting) ("The point . . . today's opinion should make, is that the Executive's authority to revoke passports touches an area fraught with important constitutional rights, and that the Court should therefore 'construe narrowly all delegated powers that curtail or dilute them.'" (citing *Kent v. Duties*)).

82. Regan v. Wald, 468 U.S. 222 (1984); *see id.* at 255 (Blackmun, J., dissenting) (The Court's construction "loses all sight of the general legislative purpose of the IEEPA and the clear legislative intent behind the grandfather clause. . . . Ironically, the very pieces of legislative history that the Court cites to justify its result clearly support the contrary view.").

83. *Id.* at 243 (majority opinion) (citation omitted). *Compare id., with* Wald v. Regan, 708 F.2d 794, 800 (1st Cir. 1983) (Breyer, J.).

84. *See* Leonard Boudin, "Economic Sanctions and Individual Rights," 19 *N.Y.U. J. Int'l L. & Pol.* 809 (1987).

85. INS v. Chadha, 462 U.S. 919, 952 (1983).

86. Despite the *Chadha* Court's sweeping suggestion that all legislative vetoes are unconstitutional, some have argued that section 5(c) of War Powers Resolution survives *Chadha. See, e.g.,* Stephen Carter, "The Constitutionality of the War Powers Resolution," 70 *Va. L. Rev.* 101, 129–33 (1984). In the first six years after *Chadha,* Congress still enacted more than 140 legislative vetoes, most of them in appropriations bills. *See* Martin Tolchin, "The Legislative Veto: An Accommodation That Goes On and On," *N.Y. Times,* Mar. 31, 1989, at A11, https://perma.cc/SR7A-2YTS. President Reagan usually signed those bills into law, but with an express declaration that he was not legally bound by their legislative veto provisions. *See, e.g.,* Department of Housing and Urban Development—Independent Agencies Appropriation Act, 1985, 20 Weekly Comp. Pres. Doc. 1040 (July 18, 1984).

87. *See generally* Pomerance, *supra* note 38.

88. *See, e.g.,* United States v. Guy W. Capps, Inc., 204 F.2d 655 (4th Cir. 1953) (refusing to give effect to sole executive agreement regulating trade because agreement was inconsistent with statute regulating same subject matter enacted under Congress's foreign-commerce power), *aff'd on other grounds,* 348 U.S. 296 (1955).

89. *See* Bowsher v. Synar, 478 U.S. 714 (1986). For criticism of *Chadha* and *Bowsher's* formalistic approach, see generally Cass Sunstein, "Constitutionalism After the New Deal," 101 *Harv. L. Rev.* 493–500 (1987), and Peter Strauss, "Formal and Functional Approaches to Separation-of-Powers Questions—A Foolish Inconsistency?" 72 *Cornell L. Rev.* 488 (1987).

90. *Dames & Moore*, 453 U.S. at 686–87 (relying on "history of acquiescence in executive claims settlement" and the fact that "Congress has not enacted legislation, or even passed a resolution, indicating its displeasure with the [Hostage] Agreement").

91. Morrison v. Olson, 487 U.S. 654, 691 (1988); Mistretta v. United States, 488 U.S. 361, 382 (1989) ("It is this concern of encroachment and aggrandizement that has animated our separation-of-powers jurisprudence."). *But see Morrison*, 487 U.S. at 697 (Scalia, J., dissenting); *Mistretta*, 488 U.S. at 413 (Scalia, J., dissenting) (continuing to apply formalistic approach to argue for invalidation of statute and guidelines).

92. *See* Franck & Bob, *supra* note 37, at 951 n.274.

93. *See* Bipartisan Accord on Central America, 25 Weekly Comp. Pres. Doc. 420 (Mar. 24, 1989); Robert Pear, "Baker Plan: A New Deal," *N.Y. Times*, Mar. 25, 1989, at A1, https://perma.cc/7E6S-BJZZ. This accord simply illustrated Louis Fisher's observation that *Chadha* did not so much kill the legislative veto as it "drove underground a set of legislative and committee vetoes that used to operate in plain sight." Louis Fisher, *Constitutional Dialogues: Interpretation as Political Process* 288 (1988).

94. *See, e.g.*, Koh, "Congressional Controls," *supra* note 10, at 1200–03, 1216–17 (describing fast-track regulatory device used in international-trade statutes).

95. *Compare* Weinberger v. Catholic Action of Hawaii/Peace Educ. Project, 454 U.S. 139 (1981), *with* 5 U.S.C. § 552(a)(4)(B); *see also* Morton Halperin, "The National Security State: Never Question the President," in *The Burger Years: Rights and Wrongs in the Supreme Court, 1969–1986*, at 50–54 (H. Schwartz ed., 1987).

96. Japan Whaling Ass'n v. Am. Cetacean Soc'y, 478 U.S. 221 (1986).

97. *See* 22 U.S.C. § 1978(a)(1) (Pelly amendment to the Fishermen's Protective Act of 1967); 16 U.S.C. § 1821(e)(2) (Packwood amendment to the Magnuson Fishery Conservation and Management Act).

98. *Japan Whaling*, 478 U.S. at 246 (Marshall, J., dissenting). *Compare id., with id.* at 227–29 (majority opinion).

99. In *Webster v. Doe*, 486 U.S. 592 (1988), the Court read the National Security Act of 1947 to permit judicial review of a CIA decision to terminate an employee but did not pass on the merits of the employee's constitutional claim. *Id.* at 604 n.8. Two justices dissented from *Webster's* modest finding of reviewability, not surprisingly citing *Curtiss-Wright*. *See id.* at 605–06 (O'Connor, J., dissenting in part); *id.* at 614–15 (Scalia, J., dissenting).

100. Dep't of the Navy v. Egan, 484 U.S. 518, 527 (1988) (emphasis added).

101. *Id.* at 536 (White, J., dissenting). The dissent cited the Warren Court's decision in *Greene v. McElroy*, 360 U.S. 474 (1959), which had held that, without express congressional authorization, the executive branch could not deprive a person of a security clearance without a full hearing. *See Egan*, 484 U.S. at 536 (White, J. dissenting) ("Such [congressional] decisions cannot be assumed by acquiescence or non-action. They must be made explicitly . . . to assure that individuals are not deprived of cherished rights under procedures not actually authorized." (citing *Greene*, 360 U.S. at 507)).

102. *See, e.g.,* Zemel v. Rusk, 381 U.S. 1, 17 (1965) ("Congress—in giving the President authority over matters of foreign affairs—must of necessity paint with a brush broader than that it customarily wields in domestic affairs."). As many as five Justices on the current Supreme Court seem to endorse this view. *See* Gundy v. United States, 139 S. Ct. 2116, 2137 (2019) (Gorsuch, J., joined by Roberts, C.J., and Thomas, J., dissenting) (questioning the constitutionality of agency rulemaking about "private conduct," but not so long as it overlapped with "authority the Constitution separately vests in another branch," such as executive power over "foreign affairs"); *id.* at 2130–31 (Alito, J., concurring in the judgment); Paul v. United States, 140 S. Ct. 342, 342 (2019) (Kavanaugh, J., respecting the denial of certiorari) (approving of Gorsuch *Gundy* opinion); *see also* Harlan Grant Cohen, "The National Security Delegation Conundrum," *Just Security,* July 17, 2019, https://perma.cc/PEC4-UXXS ("The opinion Justice Alito presumably would have joined was the dissent authored by Justice Gorsuch and joined by Chief Justice Roberts and Justice Thomas.").

103. *See Dames & Moore,* 453 U.S. at 684–86.

104. *See Wald,* 468 U.S. at 240–42; *Agee,* 453 U.S. 280; *Snepp,* 444 U.S. 507.

105. *Chadha,* 462 U.S. 919; *Bowsher,* 478 U.S. 714.

106. Goldwater v. Carter, 444 U.S. 996 (1979). The justices voted to reject Senator Goldwater's challenge to the president's treaty termination on a variety of grounds: ripeness, *id.* at 997–98 (Powell, J., concurring in the judgment); the political question doctrine, *id.* at 1002–03 (Rehnquist, J., concurring in the judgment); and the merits, *id.* at 1006–07 (Brennan, J., dissenting).

107. Burke v. Barnes, 479 U.S. 361 (1987).

108. The Vietnam cases include Schlesinger v. Reservists Comm. to Stop the War, 418 U.S. 208 (1974), Holtzman v. Schlesinger, 414 U.S. 1316 (1973) (Douglas, J.) (opinion in chambers), Laird v. Tatum, 408 U.S. 1 (1972), Samoff v. Shultz, 409 U.S. 929 (1972), DaCosta v. Laird, 448 F.2d 1368 (2d Cir. 1971), *cert. denied,* 405 U.S. 979 (1972), Orlando v. Laird, 443 F.2d 1039 (2d Cir.), *cert. denied,* 404 U.S. 869 (1971), Massachusetts v. Laird, 400 U.S. 886 (1970), Holmes v. United States, 391 U.S. 936 (1968), Hart v. United States, 391 U.S. 956 (1968), Shiffman v. Selective Serv. Bd., 391 U.S. 930 (1968), Epton v. New York, 390 U.S. 29 (1968), Zwicker v. Boll, 391 U.S. 353 (1968), Luftig v. McNamara, 387 U.S. 945 (1967), Mora v. McNamara, 389 U.S. 934, 935(1967), and Mitchell v. United States, 386 U.S. 972 (1967). *See generally* Robert P. Sugarman, "Judicial Decisions Concerning the Constitutionality of United States Military Activity in Indo-China: A Bibliography of Court Decisions," 13 *Colum. J. Transnat'l L.* 470 (1974) (collecting cases).

Cases arising out of the Central American conflict include Dellums v. Smith, 797 F.2d 817 (9th Cir. 1986), Sanchez-Espinoza v. Reagan, 770 F.2d 202 (D.C. Cir. 1985), Ramirez de Arellano v. Weinberger, 745 F.2d 1500 (D.C. Cir. 1984) (en banc), *vacated and remanded for reconsideration in light of subsequent legislation,* 471 U.S. 1113 (1985), and Crockett v. Reagan, 720 F.2d 1355 (D.C. Cir. 1983). *See generally* David Cole, "Challenging Covert War: The Politics of the Political Question Doctrine," 26 *Harv. Int'l L.J.* 155 (1985); Note, "Covert Wars and Presidential Power: Judicial Complicity in a Realignment of Constitutional Power," 14 *Hastings Const. L.Q.* 683 (1987) (reviewing decisions).

109. In *Kleindienst v. Mandel,* 408 U.S. 753, 762 (1972), the Supreme Court ruled that because an excluded foreigner seeking entry into the United States has no right to enter, he or she lacks standing to challenge the exclusion. Consequently, challenges to ideological exclusions of aliens have generally been raised not by the excluded foreigners, but by American citizens who want to hear their message. *See, e.g.,* Abourezk v. Reagan, 785 F.2d 1043, 1050–51 (D.C. Cir. 1986), *aff'd by an equally divided Court,* 484 U.S. 1 (1987); Harvard Law Sch. Forum v. Shultz, 633 F. Supp. 525 (D. Mass. 1986), *vacated,* No. 86-1371 (1st Cir. June 18, 1986). Decisions denying standing on the basis of citizenship include Schlesinger v. Reservists Comm. to Stop the War, 418 U.S. 208 (1974), United States v. Richardson, 418 U.S. 166 (1974), Laird v. Tatum, 408 U.S. 1 (1972), and Velvel v. Nixon, 415 F.2d 236 (10th Cir.), *cert. denied,* 396 U.S. 1042 (1969). The courts rejected taxpayer standing in *Richardson,* 418 U.S. 166, and *Phelps v. Reagan,* 812 F.2d 1293 (10th Cir. 1987). In *Raines v. Byrd,* 521 U.S. 811 (1997), the Supreme Court held that individual members of Congress do not automatically have standing to challenge the constitutionality of laws that affect Congress as a whole.

110. For decisions recognizing official immunity, see Anderson v. Creighton, 483 U.S. 635 (1987), Mitchell v. Forsyth, 472 U.S. 511 (1985), Harlow v. Fitzgerald, 457 U.S. 800 (1982), and Nixon v. Fitzgerald, 457 U.S. 731 (1982).

111. For decisions barring suits by members of the armed forces, see, for example, United States v. Johnson, 481 U.S. 681 (1987), and Feres v. United States, 340 U.S. 135 (1950); also see Note, "From *Feres* to *Stencel:* Should Military Personnel Have Access to FTCA (Federal Tort Claims Act) Recovery?" 77 *Mich. L. Rev.* 1099 (1979). On government contractor immunity, see *Boyle v. United Technologies Corp.,* 487 U.S. 500 (1988), which created federal common-law immunity barring a serviceman's estate from suing an independent contractor that had allegedly supplied a defective military helicopter to the United States.

112. *See, e.g.,* Smith v. Reagan, 844 F.2d 195 (4th Cir. 1988); Sanchez-Espinoza v. Reagan, 770 F.2d 202 (D.C. Cir. 1985); United States v. Stanley, 483 U.S. 669 (1987) (barring a former serviceman from maintaining *Bivens* constitutional-tort action against military officers and civilians who administered experimental drug to him without his consent).

113. *See, e.g., Sanchez-Espinoza,* 770 F.2d at 207–09; Crockett v. Reagan, 558 F. Supp. 893, 902–03 (D.D.C. 1982), *aff'd,* 720 F.2d 1355 (D.C. Cir. 1983) (per curiam), *cert. denied,* 467 U.S. 1251 (1984). *See generally* Thomas Franck & Michael Glennon, *Foreign Relations and National Security Law* 824–27 (1987) (discussing equitable-discretion doctrine).

114. *See, e.g.,* Johnson v. Weinberger, 851 F.2d 233 (9th Cir. 1988) (dismissing for lack of standing suit challenging U.S. "Launch on Warning" policy, which district court had dismissed under political-question doctrine); Smith v. Reagan, 844 F.2d 195 (4th Cir. 1988) (dismissing suit under Hostage Act as political question and for want of cause of action); Americans United for Separation of Church & State v. Reagan, 786 F.2d 194 (3d Cir.) (dismissing establishment-clause challenge to dispatch of ambassador to Vatican on mixed standing and political-question grounds).

cert. denied, 479 U.S. 914 (1986); *Sanchez-Espinoza,* 770 F.2d. 202 (dismissing suit on grounds of sovereign immunity, equitable discretion, absence of *Bivens* constitutional-tort remedy or implied statutory causes of action, mootness, and political-question doctrine); Crockett v. Reagan, 720 F.2d 1355 (D.C. Cir. 1983) (rejecting congressional suit for declaratory judgment requiring president to remove U.S. armed forces from El Salvador, reasoning that whether War Powers Resolution's sixty-day cutoff provision had been triggered was political question), *cert. denied,* 467 U.S. 1251 (1984); Lowry v. Reagan, 676 F. Supp. 333 (D.D.C. 1987) (dismissing suit brought by members of Congress to compel president to report on U.S. military activities in Persian Gulf on mixed political-question and equitable-discretion grounds), *appeal dismissed,* No. 87-5426 (D.C. Cir., Oct. 17, 1988) (dismissing on political-question grounds); Chaser Shipping Corp. v. United States, 649 F. Supp. 736 (S.D.N.Y. 1986) (dismissing as political question suit by shipowner whose vessels were damaged by U.S. mines in Nicaraguan port), *aff'd,* 819 F.2d 1129 (2d Cir. 1987) (mem.), *cert. denied,* 484 U.S. 1004 (1988); Cranston v. Reagan, 611 F. Supp. 247 (D.D.C. 1985) (dismissing suit brought by members of Congress seeking determination that bilateral treaties violate Atomic Energy Act, as nonjusticiable political question and, alternatively, on grounds of remedial discretion).

115. *See, e.g., Chadha,* 462 U.S. 919 (ruling for president on merits after rejecting intervenor House and Senate's claim that president's challenge to constitutionality of legislative veto raised political question).

116. *See* Erwin Chemerinsky, "A Paradox Without a Principle: A Comment on the Burger Court's Jurisprudence in Separation of Powers Cases," 60 *S. Calif. L. Rev.* 1084 (1987).

117. *See, e.g.,* Narenji v. Civiletti, 617 F.2d 745, 748 (D.C. Cir. 1979) (Robb, J.), *cert. denied,* 446 U.S. 957 (1980) ("[I]t is not the business of courts to pass judgment on the decisions of the President in the field of foreign policy.").

118. *See, e.g., Egan,* 484 U.S. 518; *Agee,* 453 U.S. 280; *Snepp,* 444 U.S. 507 (citing considerations of "national security"); Korematsu v. United States, 323 U.S. 214 (1944) ("military necessity"); United States v. Johnson, 481 U.S. 681 (1987); Chappell v. Wallace, 462 U.S. 296, 301–02 (1983); Brown v. Glines, 444 U.S. 348, 354–57 (1980); Schlesinger v. Councilman, 420 U.S. 738, 757 (1975) ("military discipline"); Orloff v. Willoughby, 345 U.S. 83, 93–94 (1955); Bums v. Wilson, 346 U.S. 137, 142, 144 (1953); Gilligan v. Morgan, 413 U.S. 1 (1973); Goldman v. Weinberger, 475 U.S. 503, 507–08 (1986); Rostker v. Goldberg, 453 U.S. 57, 64–68 & n.6 (1981); Parker v. Levy, 417 U.S. 733, 743, 756–57 (1974) (citing need to defer to executive discretion in "military affairs").

119. *See, e.g.,* Chi. & S. Air Lines, Inc. v. Waterman S.S. Corp., 333 U.S. 103 (1948); *Phelps,* 812 F.2d 1293; *Crockett,* 720 F.2d 1355; *Lowry,* 676 F. Supp. 333; *Chaser Shipping,* 649 F. Supp. 736; Dole v. Carter, 569 F.2d 1109 (10th Cir. 1977).

120. *See Japan Whaling,* 478 U.S. at 230 ("Under the Constitution, one of the judiciary's characteristic roles is to interpret statutes, and we cannot shirk this responsibility merely because our decision may have significant political overtones.").

Chapter 5. Bush 41 and Clinton

1. John Lewis Gaddis, "And Now This: Lessons from the Old Era for the New One," in *The Age of Terror: America and the World After September 11*, at 1 (Strobe Talbott & Nayan Chanda eds., 2001).

2. *See* Harold Hongju Koh, "The Globalization of Freedom," 26 *Yale J. Int'l L.* 305 (2001).

3. "Power of Progressive Economics: The Clinton Years," *Center for American Progress*, Oct. 28, 2011, https://perma.cc/BZC3-D9VU.

4. "Modest Bush Approval Rating at War's End," *Pew Research Center*, Apr. 18, 2003, https://perma.cc/Q4J9-X67P.

5. George H. W. Bush, Inaugural Address (Jan. 20, 1989), https://perma.cc/876A-QA4K.

6. George H. W. Bush, Address Before a Joint Session of the Congress on the Persian Gulf Crisis and the Federal Budget Deficit (Sept. 11,1990), https://perma.cc/JDX6-5WUK.

7. George H. W. Bush, Address to the Nation Announcing Allied Military Action in the Persian Gulf (Jan. 16, 1991), https://perma.cc/PGK4-8ZC4.

8. Authorization for the Use of Military Force Against Iraq Resolution, Pub. L. No. 102-1, 105 Stat 3 (1991), *reprinted in* 137 Cong. Rec. S403–04 (daily ed. Jan. 12, 1991).

9. Dellums v. Bush, 752 F. Supp. 1141 (D.D.C. 1990).

10. I was co-author of the law professors' memorandum. *See, e.g.,* Harold Hongju Koh, "Presidential War and Congressional Consent: The Law Professors' Memorandum in *Dellums v. Bush*," 27 *Stan. J. Int'l L.* 247 (1991).

11. *Dellums*, 752 F. Supp. at 1149. For an example of a soldier suit, see Ange v. Bush, 752 F. Supp. 509 (D.D.C. 1990).

12. *Dellums*, 752 F. Supp. at 1145.

13. Extraterritorial Apprehension by the Federal Bureau of Investigation, 4B Op. O.L.C. 543, 549 (1980) (citation omitted).

14. Benjamin Runkle, "Remembering Manuel Noriega and his Capture," *War on the Rocks*, June 6, 2017, https://perma.cc/4F3C-MFBL.

15. Steven Arrigg Koh, "Foreign Affairs Prosecutions," 94 *N.Y.U. L. Rev.* 340 (2019); Steven Arrigg Koh, "The Criminalization of Foreign Relations," 90 *Ford. L. Rev.* 737 (2021).

16. Authority of the Federal Bureau of Investigation to Override Customary International Law, 13 Op. O.L.C. 163 (1989), https://perma.cc/5AKS-WMEH. This incident is reviewed in Harold Hongju Koh, "Protecting the Office of Legal Counsel from Itself," 15 *Cardozo L. Rev.* 513, 518–19 (1993–94).

17. *FBI Authority to Seize Suspects Abroad: Hearing Before the Subcomm. on Civil & Constitutional Rights of the H. Comm. on the Judiciary*, 101st Cong. 5 (1989) (statement of William P. Barr, Office of Legal Counsel, U.S. Dep't of Justice) [hereinafter Barr Statement], https://perma.cc/45H4-YGEU.

18. United States v. Alvarez-Machain, 504 U.S. 655 (1992).

19. *See* Barr Statement, *supra* note 17, at 4.

20. *See* Transcript, *Anderson Cooper 360 Degrees* (CNN television broadcast Apr. 16, 2019), https://perma.cc/EME8-ZFKQ; *see also* Ryan Goodman, "Barr's Playbook: He Misled Congress When Omitting Parts of Justice Dep't Memo in 1989," *Just Security*, Apr. 15, 2019, https://perma.cc/EZ7H-PLEC.

21. *See generally* Mark Bowden, *Black Hawk Down: A History of Modern War* (2010); Michael J. Durant, *In the Company of Heroes* (2003) (noting that the pilot who transported Noriega was also the pilot of the ill-fated Black Hawk helicopter in Somalia).

22. I served as counsel of record to the Haitian plaintiffs in this litigation. *See generally* Harold Hongju Koh, "The 'Haiti Paradigm' in United States Human Rights Policy," 103 *Yale L.J.* 2391 (1994) (detailing the history of the Haitian-refugee episode).

23. Convention Relating to the Status of Refugees art. 33, July 28, 1951, 19 U.S.T. 6259, 6276, 189 U.N.T.S. 150, 176 [hereinafter Refugee Convention]. The United States became party to the Refugee Convention when it acceded to the United Nations Protocol Relating to the Status of Refugees, Jan. 31, 1967, 19 U.S.T. 6223, 606 U.N.T.S. 267. *See also* Proposed Interdiction of Haitian Flag Vessels, 5 Op. O.L.C. 242, 248 (1981); Memorandum from Larry L. Simms, Deputy Assistant Att'y Gen., Office of Legal Counsel, to the Associate Att'y Gen. (Aug. 5, 1981) ("Those who claim to be refugees must be given a chance to substantiate their claims [under Article 33]."), *quoted in* Joint App. at 222, Sale v. Haitian Ctrs. Council, Inc., 509 U.S. 155 (1993); Installation of Slot Machines on U.S. Naval Base, Guantanamo Bay, 6 Op. O.L.C. 236, 237 (1982) (construing Anti-Slot Machine Act, 15 U.S.C. § 1175).

24. *See* Haitian Ctrs. Council, Inc. v. McNary, 969 F.2d 1326 (2d Cir. 1992), *vacated as moot sub nom.* Sale v. Haitian Ctrs. Council, Inc., 509 U.S. 918 (1993); Haitian Ctrs. Council, Inc. v. McNary, 969 F.2d 1350 (2d Cir. 1992), *rev'd sub nom.* Sale v. Haitian Ctrs. Council, Inc., 509 U.S. 155 (1993); Haitian Ctrs. Council, Inc. v. Sale, 823 F. Supp. 1028 (E.D.N.Y. 1993) (permanent injunction ordering release of Haitians being held on Guantánamo) (subsequently vacated by settlement).

25. William J. Clinton, Address Before a Joint Session of the Congress on the State of the Union (Jan. 27, 2000), https://perma.cc/LTS6-EA9X.

26. Russell D. Covey, "Adventures in the Zone of Twilight: Separation of Powers and National Economic Security in the Mexican Bailout," 105 *Yale L.J.* 1311, 1311 (1996) ("It is far from clear that the President had the authority to take this action.").

27. *Compare* Laurence Tribe, "Taking Text and Structure Seriously: Reflections on Free-Form Method in Constitutional Interpretation," 108 *Harv. L. Rev.* 1221 (1995) (arguing that NAFTA is unconstitutional), *with* Bruce Ackerman & David Golove, "Is NAFTA Constitutional?," 108 *Harv. L. Rev.* 799 (1995) (arguing that it is not).

28. *See generally* Bill Clinton, *My Life* 506, 807–08, 857, 936–38 (2004).

29. *See generally* Richard Holbrooke, *To End a War: The Conflict in Yugoslavia* (1999); Prosecutor v. Milošević, Case No. IT-01-50-I, Indictment (Int'l Crim. Trib. for the Former Yugoslavia Sept. 27, 2001), https://perma.cc/5P5U-NW5Y.

30. *See generally* Koh, *supra* note 22; Harold Hongju Koh, "The Enduring Legacies of the Haitian Refugee Litigation," 61 *N.Y.L. Sch. L. Rev.* 31 (2016–2017) (describing Cuban refugee litigation, in which I also served as plaintiffs' counsel); David Maraniss, *First in His Class: A Biography of Bill Clinton* 577 (1995) (describing Fort Chaffee incident).

31. *See Haitian Ctrs. Council,* 823 F. Supp. at 1041–45.

32. *See* Sale v. Haitian Ctrs. Council, Inc., 509 U.S. 155 (1993).

33. Haitian Refugee Ctr. v. Baker, 953 F.2d 1498 (11th Cir.), *cert. denied,* 502 U.S. 1122 (1992). Altogether, the Court thrice intervened to stay lower-court rulings favoring the Haitians. *See* Baker v. Haitian Refugee Ctr., 502 U.S. 1083 (1992); McNary v. Haitian Ctrs. Council, Inc., 503 U.S. 1000 (1992); McNary v. Haitian Ctrs. Council, Inc., 505 U.S. 1234 (1992). Moreover, the Court had twice denied stay requests from Haitian-refugee groups, *see* Haitian Refugee Ctr. v. Baker, 502 U.S. 1084 (1992); Haitian Refugee Ctr. v. Baker, 502 U.S. 1122 (1992), had granted certiorari over the Haitians' opposition, *see* McNary v. Haitian Ctrs. Council, Inc., 506 U.S. 814 (1992), and had denied their motions both to expedite briefing, *see* McNary v. Haitian Ctrs. Council, Inc., 505 U.S. 1236 (1992), and to suspend briefing until after Inauguration Day, *see* McNary v. Haitian Ctrs. Council, Inc., 506 U.S. 996 (1992).

34. McNary v. Haitian Ctrs. Council, Inc., 505 U.S. 1234 (1992) (staying the Second Circuit's ruling over the dissent of Justices Blackmun and Stevens).

35. *See Sale,* 509 U.S. at 188–89 (Blackmun, J., dissenting). Justice Blackmun's conference notes composed on the day of oral argument made plain his view that "Resp[onden]ts' case on t[he] *merits* is *very* strong. Nothing ambig[uous] [about] t[he] lang[uage] or t[he] st[andar]d forbids [the] U.S. from returning any alien to his persecutor." Notes of Justice Harry A. Blackmun on Oral Argument in Sale v. Haitian Ctrs. Council, Inc., No. 92-344 (Mar. 1, 1993) (on file at U.S. Library of Congress).

36. *Compare* "Le bourbier haïtien," *Le Monde,* May 31–June 1, 1992, *quoted in Sale,* 509 U.S. at 192 (Blackmun, J., dissenting) (emphasis added), *with* Exec. Order No. 12,807, 57 Fed. Reg. 23,133, 23,133-34 (June 1, 1992) (appropriate directives will be issued "providing for the Coast Guard . . . to *return* the vessel and its passengers to the country from which it came" (emphasis added)). The majority accepted the government's unpersuasive argument that the term *"refouler"* meant "to expel," not "to return," and hence barred only the forced expulsion of Haitian refugees who had already landed in the United States, not the forced return of those refugees intercepted en route. The government's reading of "refouler" as "to expel" flouted the ordinary French meaning of the term. *See* Jean-Michel Caroit, "L'exode continue," *Le Monde,* May 29, 1992, at 4 ("La décision du président Bush d'ordonner à la garde côtière américaine de *refouler* les boat-people haïtiens vers leur île pour tenter de mettre fin à un véritable exode a suscité." ["President Bush's decision to order the U.S. Coast Guard to *return* the Haitian boat people to their island was an attempt to put an end to a genuine exodus."] (emphasis added)). That misreading also effectively rewrote article 33 to create a pointless redundancy: "no Contracting State shall expel *or expel* a refugee" to conditions of persecution.

37. *See* Refugee Convention, *supra* note 23, art. 33; *Sale,* 509 U.S. at 200–01 (Blackmun, J., dissenting) (quoting 8 U.S.C. § 1103(a)); *see also id.* at 201 ("Even the challenged Executive Order places the Attorney General 'on the boat' with the Coast Guard."). As the statute notes, "The officers of the Coast Guard insofar as they are engaged . . . in enforcing any law of the United States shall . . . be deemed to be acting as agents of the particular executive department . . . charged with the admin

NOTES TO PAGES 140–146

istration of the particular law . . . and . . . be subject to all the rules and regulations promulgated by such department . . . with respect to the enforcement of that law." 14 U.S.C. § 522(b) (previously codified at 14 U.S.C. § 89(b)). The government's argument recalled the Reagan administration's hollow claim during the Iran-contra affair that the Boland amendments' restriction on U.S. agencies "involved in intelligence activities" somehow did not bind the National Security Council, even when it engaged in intelligence activities. *See* Harold Hongju Koh, "Boland Amendments," in 1 *Encyclopedia of the American Presidency* 111 (Leonard Levy & Louis Fisher eds., 1994); *supra* chapter 3 (discussing Boland amendments).

38. *See* Youngstown Sheet & Tube Co. v. Sawyer, 343 U.S. 579, 637 (1952) (Jackson, J., concurring); *Sale,* 509 U.S. at 188 (citing *Curtiss-Wright* to claim that presumption against extraterritoriality "has special force when we are construing treaty and statutory provisions that may involve foreign and military affairs for which the President has unique responsibility"). *But see id.* at 190 (Blackmun, J., dissenting) ("Vulnerable refugees shall not be returned. The language is clear, and the command is straightforward; that should be the end of the inquiry.").

39. *See generally* Koh, *supra* note 22, at 2424–25.

40. Deployment of United States Armed Forces into Haiti, 18 Op. O.L.C. 173 (1994) [hereinafter Dellinger Opinion].

41. *See generally* Harold Hongju Koh, "The War Powers and Humanitarian Intervention," 53 *Hous. L. Rev.* 971, 976–80 (2016).

42. Dellinger Opinion, *supra* note 40.

43. War Powers Resolution, Pub. L. No. 93-148, 87 Stat. 555 (1973) (codified at 50 U.S.C. §§ 1541–1548 (2012)).

44. *See* 50 U.S.C. § 1547(a)(1) (2000); Authorization for Continuing Hostilities in Kosovo, 24 Op. O.L.C. 327, 339 (2000). The OLC memo, signed by Randolph Moss (currently a federal judge), reasoned that the Congress that enacted the emergency supplemental appropriation could not constitutionally be bound by the terms of the earlier War Powers Resolution and that the legislative history of the supplemental appropriation sustained the inference that Congress implicitly meant, in appropriating the funds President Clinton had requested, to provide the legal authority for the operation he intended to pursue. *Id.* at 340–58.

45. *Compare* Michael J. Matheson, "Justification for the NATO Air Campaign in Kosovo," 94 *Am. Soc'y Int'l L. Proc.* 301 (2000), *with* U.K. Foreign & Commonwealth Office, FRY/Kosovo: The Way Ahead; U.K. View on the Legal Base for Use of Force (1998), *quoted in* Adam Roberts, "NATO's 'Humanitarian War' over Kosovo," *Survival,* Autumn 1999, at 102, 104, 106; Legality of Use of Force (Serb. v. Belg.), Verbatim Record (May 10, 1999, 3 p.m.), https://perma.cc/A29C-QE5H (arguing that NATO's use of force was lawful); Indep. Int'l Comm'n on Kosovo, *The Kosovo Report* 4 (2000), https://perma.cc/KC3R-9Z9P.

46. Louis Henkin, Commentary, "Kosovo and the Law of 'Humanitarian Intervention,'" 93 *Am. J. Int'l L.* 824, 827 (1999). During the Kosovo episode, I was serving in the State Department not as a lawyer but as assistant secretary of state for democracy, human rights, and labor under Secretary of State Madeleine Albright.

47. Dawn Johnsen, "When Responsibilities Collide: Humanitarian Intervention, Shared War Powers, and the Rule of Law," 53 *Hous. L. Rev.* 1065, 1073, 1092 (2016); Harold Hongju Koh, "The Legal Adviser's Duty to Explain," 41 *Yale J. Int'l L.* 189 (2016).
48. *See* Chelsea O'Donnell, "The Development of the Responsibility to Protect: An Examination of the Debate over the Legality of Humanitarian Intervention," 24 *Duke J. Comp. & Int'l L.* 557, 560–63 (2014).

Chapter 6. Bush 43

1. *See generally* Lawyers Committee for Human Rights, *Imbalance of Powers: How Changes to U.S. Law and Security Since 9/11 Erode Human Rights and Civil Liberties* (2003), https://perma.cc/ZW2M-PQ5B; Lawyers Committee for Human Rights, *A Year of Loss: Reexamining Civil Liberties Since September 11* (2002), https://perma.cc/75UD-LB3M.
2. James Mann, *Rise of the Vulcans: The History of Bush's War Cabinet* (2004).
3. *See generally* Charlie Savage, *Takeover: The Return of the Imperial Presidency and the Subversion of American Democracy* (2007).
4. Franklin Delano Roosevelt, Eighth Annual Message to Congress (Jan. 6, 1941), in *The State of the Union Messages of the Presidents, 1790–1966*, at 2855 (Fred L. Israel ed., 1966); *See generally* Mary Ann Glendon, *A World Made New: Eleanor Roosevelt and the Universal Declaration of Human Rights* (2001).
5. Ronald Reagan, Promoting Democracy and Peace, Address to British Parliament (June 8, 1982), www.reaganlibrary.gov/archives/speech/address-members-british-parliament. *See generally* Thomas Carothers, *Aiding Democracy Abroad: The Learning Curve* 30–32 (1999); Tony Smith, *America's Mission: The United States and the Worldwide Struggle for Democracy in the Twentieth Century* (1994); Harold Hongju Koh, "A United States Human Rights Policy for the 21st Century," 46 *St. Louis U. L.J.* 293 (2002).
6. *See generally* Harold Hongju Koh, "Foreword: On American Exceptionalism," 55 *Stan. L. Rev.* 1479, 1499 (2003). During the Clinton administration, a large cast of characters engaged daily in the Middle East peace process: President Clinton; Vice President Gore; Secretary of State Madeleine Albright; Sandy Berger, the national security adviser; Martin Indyk, the assistant secretary for Near Eastern affairs; and Dennis Ross, who served as special Middle East envoy for both Republican and Democratic administrations. On North Korea, see Paul Krugman, "Games Nations Play," *N.Y. Times*, Jan. 3, 2003, at A21 (the "axis of evil" speech forced Kim to shift his own policies to counter new American hostility).
7. *Cf.* Hillel Neuer, "Aharon Barak's Revolution," https://perma.cc/4UG3-L5ZX ("[T]he world is filled with law. . . . Wherever there are living human beings, law is there. There are no areas in life which are outside of law." (quoting Aharon Barak of the Israeli Supreme Court)). Under the clear-statement doctrine of *Kent v. Dulles* 357 U.S. 116 (1958), courts must carefully scrutinize statutes cited by the executive not only for signs that Congress has consented to the president's actions, but also to determine whether the president and Congress acting together have made a

clear determination to infringe on individual rights. When individual rights are at stake, courts should "construe narrowly all delegated powers that curtail or dilute them." *Id.* at 129; *accord* Greene v. McElroy, 360 U.S. 474, 507–08 (1959); Graham v. Richardson, 403 U.S. 365, 371–72 (1971) ("[T]he Court's decisions have established that classifications based on alienage, like those based on nationality or race, are inherently suspect and subject to close judicial scrutiny. Aliens as a class are a prime example of a 'discrete and insular' minority for whom such heightened judicial solicitude is appropriate.")

8. Authorization for Use of Military Force, Pub. L. No. 107-40, 115 Stat. 224 (codified at 50 U.S.C. § 1541 note).

9. *See generally* Harold Hongju Koh, "Presidential War and Congressional Consent: The Law Professors' Memorandum in *Dellums v. Bush*," 27 *Stan. J. Int'l L.* 247 (1991) (reviewing resolutions that led to the First Gulf War). For the 1990 Iraq resolution, see S.C. Res. 678, U.N. SCOR, 45th Sess., at 28, U.N. Doc. S/RES/678 (1990), *reprinted in* 29 I.L.M. 1565 (1990). In its national-security-strategy white paper, issued in September 2002, the White House declared, "To forestall or prevent such hostile acts by our adversaries, the United States will, if necessary, act preemptively." The National Security Strategy of the United States of America ch. 5 (Mar. 2006), https://perma.cc/V7NC-W9DD.

10. *See* Ron Suskind, *The One Percent Doctrine: Deep Inside America's Pursuit of Its Enemies Since 9/11*, at 62 (2007) ("The Cheney Doctrine [after 9/11 became] 'Even if there's just a one percent chance of the unimaginable coming due, act as if it is a certainty.'"); Errol Morris, "The Certainty of Donald Rumsfeld," *N.Y. Times*, Mar. 28, 2014, https://perma.cc/K8KR-PNWE (quoting August 5, 2003 press briefing by Secretary of Defense Rumsfeld regarding the discovery in Iraq of a Russian-built fighter aircraft).

11. Matthew Waxman, "The 'Caroline' Affair in the Evolving International Law of Self-Defense," *Lawfare*, Aug. 28, 2018, https://perma.cc/6JK8-5PWK (reviewing traditional law of self-defense); *see also* Harold Hongju Koh, "Comment," in Michael W. Doyle, *Striking First: Preemption and Prevention in International Conflict* 99 (2008).

12. H.R.J. Res. 114, 107th Cong. (2002). The authorization for the use of military force against Iraq that Congress passed in October 2002 authorized the president "to use the Armed Forces of the United States as he determines to be necessary and appropriate in order to (1) defend the national security of the United States against the continuing threat posed by Iraq; and (2) enforce all relevant United Nations Security Council resolutions regarding Iraq." *Id.*

13. *See generally* Koh, *supra* note 6 at 1515–25.

14. Security Council Resolution 1441 (1) decided that "Iraq has been and remains in material breach of its obligations" through its failure to cooperate with inspectors and its failure to disarm; (2) afforded Iraq "a final opportunity to comply with its disarmament obligations under relevant resolutions" by setting up an enhanced inspection regime and ordering Iraq to submit an accurate and complete declaration of its chemical, biological, and nuclear-weapons programs; and (3) "warned Iraq that it will face serious consequences as a result of its continued violations of its obligations." U.N. SCOR, 57th Sess., U.N. Doc. S/Res/1441 (2002).

15. The United States provided its most complete legal justification for the Iraq War in a letter from U.N. ambassador John Negroponte to the president of the Security Council. *See* Letter from U.N. Ambassador John Negroponte to Ambassador Mamady Traore, President of the Security Council (Mar. 20, 2003). The Legal Adviser of the State Department, William Howard Taft IV, made a similar argument in a speech before the National Association of Attorneys General. *See* Peter Slevin, "U.S. Says War Has Legal Basis: Reliance on Gulf War Resolutions Is Questioned by Others," *Wash. Post*, Mar. 21, 2003, A14.

16. *See infra* chapters 7 and 8.

17. *See generally* Harold Hongju Koh, "Can the President Be Torturer-in-Chief?," 81 *Ind. L. Rev.* 1145 (2006).

18. George W. Bush, Statement on the U.N. International Day in Support of Victims of Torture (June 26, 2004), https://perma.cc/XEJ4-D5WA.

19. Human Rights Watch, *Leadership Failure: First Hand Accounts of Iraqi Detainees by the U.S. Army's 82nd Airborne Division* (2005), https://perma.cc/7QSQ-UEU4; *see, e.g., Commission of Inquiry into the Actions of Canadian Officials in Relation to Maher Arar: Report of Professor Stephen J. Toope* (2005), https://perma.cc/TT29-RQUC (reporting on the alleged torture of a Canadian citizen in Syria following extraordinary rendition by U.S. officials).

20. Memorandum from Jay S. Bybee, Assistant Att'y Gen., Office of Legal Counsel, to Alberto R. Gonzales, Counsel to the President (Aug. 1, 2002) [hereinafter Bybee Opinion], https://perma.cc/PC9A-KH7J (construing 18 U.S.C. §§ 2340–2340A, which provide that a person who commits torture may be subject to a fine or imprisonment for up to twenty years, or both, and that if the victim should die from the torture, the torturer may be sentenced to life imprisonment or death). The USA PATRIOT Act also makes conspiracy to commit torture a crime. *See* Uniting and Strengthening America by Providing Appropriate Tools Required to Intercept and Obstruct Terrorism Act (USA PATRIOT Act) of 2001, Pub. L. No. 107-56, 115 Stat. 272 (amending generally 18 U.S.C. §§ 3121–3127). The Bybee opinion was partly withdrawn by a subsequent memo. *See* Memorandum from Daniel Levin, Acting Assistant Att'y Gen., Office of Legal Counsel, to James B. Comey, Deputy Att'y Gen. (Dec. 30, 2004) [hereinafter Levin Opinion], https://perma.cc/AC64-RKH2. For a discussion of the appropriate role of the Office of Legal Counsel, see Harold Hongju Koh, "Protecting the Office of Legal Counsel from Itself," 15 *Cardozo L. Rev.* 513 (1993).

21. Bybee Opinion, *supra* note 20, at 1, 35, 39. The White House, "Saddam Hussein's Repression of the Iraqi People," in *A Decade of Deception and Defiance* (2002), https://perma.cc/7EUX-YEFA; David E. Sanger, "The State of the Union: Diplomacy; Emphasis on Iraq but from a Different Angle," *N.Y. Times*, Jan. 21, 2004, at A17.

22. Levin Opinion, *supra* note 20, at 2; Bybee opinion, *supra* note 20, at 39.

23. *See* David S. Cloud, "Private Gets 3 Years for Iraq Prison Abuse," *N.Y. Times*, Sept. 28, 2005, at A20. Abu Ghraib photos came to light through releases in the Australian press. *See* David Stout, "More Abu Ghraib Pictures Broadcast on Australian TV," *N.Y. Times*, Feb. 16, 2006, at A18, https://perma.cc/A57V-6SPD; *Final Report of the Independent Panel to Review DoD Detention Operations* (Aug. 2004), https://

perma.cc/SP76-7S74; Anthony R. Jones & George R. Fay, *Investigation of Intelligence Activities at Abu Ghraib,* https://perma.cc/582E-KPLX; Tim Golden & Eric Schmitt, "Detainee Policy Sharply Divides Bush Officials," *N.Y. Times,* Nov. 2, 2005, at A1; Eric Schmitt, "Senate Moves to Protect Military Prisoners Despite Veto Threat," *N.Y. Times,* Oct. 6, 2005, at A22.

24. In *In re Yamashita,* 327 U.S. 1 (1946), the U.S. Supreme Court recognized the doctrine of command responsibility, under which commanding officers are liable if they exercised effective control over subordinates who engaged in torture or other mistreatment of detainees in violation of the law of nations, knew or had reason to know of their subordinates' unlawful conduct, but failed to take reasonable measures to prevent their subordinates' conduct. *Cf.* Statute of the International Criminal Tribunal for the Former Yugoslavia art. 7(4), May 25, 1993, 32 I.L.M. 1192, 1194 (1993) ("The fact that an accused person acted pursuant to an order of a Government or of a superior shall not relieve him of criminal responsibility."), https://perma.cc/XZG9-V79K.

25. *See* ACLU v. Dep't of Defense, 389 F. Supp. 2d 547 (S.D.N.Y. 2005); Eric Schmitt, "House Defies Bush and Backs McCain on Detainee Torture," *N.Y. Times,* Dec. 15, 2005, at A14 (reporting that the House voted 308 to 122 and that the Senate voted 90 to 9 to support the McCain amendment); Statement on Signing H.R. 1815, the National Defense Authorization Act for Fiscal Year 2006, 42 Weekly Comp. Pres. Doc. 23 (Jan. 6, 2006); Interview by Bob Schieffer of CBS News with George W. Bush (Jan. 27, 2006), https://perma.cc/PX8C-F3BZ. For a critique of presidential signing statements, see generally ABA Task Force on Presidential Signing Statements and the Separation of Powers Doctrine, *Report and Recommendations* (2006).

26. U.S. Const. art. I, § 8, cl. 14.

27. In 1950, Congress passed the Uniform Code of Military Justice (UCMJ), 10 U.S.C. §§ 801–946 (2000), to ensure fairness and openness in the trials and treatment of military defendants. The unambiguous text of articles 49 and 50 of the UCMJ applies not just to defendants in courts-martial, but also defendants before military commissions. *See* 10 U.S.C. § 849(d) (explicitly covering "any military court or commission"); *id.* § 850(a) (explicitly referring to "a court-martial or military commission"). Article 31 further requires that "[n]o person subject to this chapter may compel any person to incriminate himself or to answer any question the answer to which may tend to incriminate him." *Id.* § 831(a). On offenses against the law of nations see U.S. Const. art. I, § 8, cl. 10. For other congressional actions, see U.S. Senate Resolution of Advice and Consent to Ratification of the Convention Against Torture and Other Cruel, Inhuman or Degrading Treatment or Punishment, 136 Cong. Rec. S17, 486–501 (1990); Torture Victim Protection Act, Pub. L. No. 102-256, 106 Stat. 73 (1992) (codified at 28 U.S.C. § 1350 note (2000)); 18 U.S.C. § 2441 (2000) (War Crimes Act); Defense Authorization Act, Pub. L. No. 109-148, div. A, tit. X, § 1003, 119 Stat. 2739–40 (2005) ("It is the policy of the United States to—(1) ensure that no detainee shall be subject to torture or cruel, inhuman, or degrading treatment or punishment that is prohibited by the Constitution, laws, or treaties of the United States."). For the quotation from the Second Circuit, see Filártiga v. Peña-Irala, 630 F.2d 876, 890 (2d Cir. 1980) ("[F]or purposes of civil liability, the

torturer has become—like the pirate and slave trader before him—*hostis humani generis,* an enemy of all mankind.").

28. Authorization for Use of Military Force, Pub. L. No. 107-40, § 2 (a), 115 Stat. 224, 224 (2001); *see also* J.E.M. Ag. Supply, Inc. v. Pioneer Hi-Bred Int'l, Inc., 534 U.S. 124, 141–42 (2001) ("[T]he only permissible justification for a repeal by implication is when the earlier and later statutes are irreconcilable." (quoting Morton v. Mancari, 417 U.S. 535, 550 (1974))). Aharon Barak, Israel Supreme Court, *Judgments of the Israel Supreme Court: Fighting Terrorism Within the Law* 51–52 (2005) (internal citations omitted).

29. Youngstown Sheet & Tube Co. v. Sawyer, 343 U.S. 579, 635 (Jackson, J. concurring). See *supra* chapter 3 for a discussion of the Tonkin Gulf Resolution, Joint Resolution of Aug. 10, 1964, Pub. L. No. 88-408, 78 Stat. 384 (1964).

30. Committee of U.S. Citizens Living in Nicaragua v. Reagan, 859 F.2d 929, 941 (D.C. Cir. 1988); Sosa v. Alvarez-Machain, 542 U.S. 692, 725 (2004); *see also id.* at 732–33 ("This limit upon judicial recognition is generally consistent with the reasoning of many of the courts and judges who faced the issue before it reached this Court. And the determination whether a norm is sufficiently definite to support a cause of action should (and, indeed, inevitably must) involve an element of judgment about the practical consequences of making that cause available to litigants in the federal courts." (citations and footnote omitted)); *id.* at 762 (Breyer, J. concurring) (arguing that norms actionable under the Alien Tort Statute "include[] *torture,* genocide, crimes against humanity, and war crimes" (emphasis added)); Rasul v. Bush, 542 U.S. 466, 485 (2004) ("[I]ndeed, 28 U.S.C. § 1350 explicitly confers the privilege of suing for an actionable 'tort . . . committed in violation of the law of nations or a treaty of the United States' on aliens alone. The fact that petitioners in these cases are being held in military custody is immaterial to the question of the District Court's jurisdiction over their nonhabeas statutory claims.").

31. Shane O'Mara, *Why Torture Doesn't Work: The Neuroscience of Interrogation* (2015); *see also* Harold Hongju Koh, "Pain Versus Gain," *Just Security,* June 20, 2016 https://perma.cc/D3ZQ-ZJUP.

32. In 2005, I testified to that conclusion before the Senate Judiciary Committee. *See* Harold Hongju Koh, Testimony Before the Senate Judiciary Committee Regarding The Nomination of the Honorable Alberto R. Gonzales as Attorney General of the United States (Jan. 7, 2005), https://law.yale.edu/sites/default/files/documents pdf/KohTestimony.pdf; *see also* Harold Hongju Koh, "A World Without Torture," 4 *Colum. J. Transnat'l. L.* 641, 647 (2005) ("[T]he Bybee Opinion is perhaps the most clearly erroneous legal opinion I have ever read.").

33. U.S. Const. art. 2, § 4 ("The President, Vice President and all civil Officers of the United States, shall be removed from Office on Impeachment for, and Conviction of, Treason, Bribery, or other high Crimes and Misdemeanors."); *see also* Al Shimari v. CACI Premier Tech., Inc., 840 F.3d 147, 162 (4th Cir. 2016) (Floyd, J concurring) ("[W]hile executive officers can declare the military reasonableness of conduct amounting to torture, it is beyond the power of even the President to declare such conduct lawful.").

34. Memorandum from Patrick F. Philbin & John C. Yoo, Deputy Assistant Att'ys Gen., Office of Legal Counsel, to William J. Haynes II, Gen. Counsel, U.S. Dep't of Def. 1 (Dec. 28, 2001), https://perma.cc/YRF6-E7QA.

35. Military Order of Nov. 13, 2001: Detention, Treatment, and Trial of Certain Noncitizens in the War Against Terrorism § 1(e), 66 Fed. Reg. 57,833 (Nov. 16, 2001). For a critique of that order, see Harold Hongju Koh, "The Case Against Military Commissions," 96 *Am. J. Int'l L.* 337 (2002). The four cases were Rasul v. Bush, 542 U.S. 466 (2004); Hamdi v. Rumsfeld, 542 U.S. 507 (2004); Hamdan v. Rumsfeld, 548 U.S. 557 (2006); Boumediene v. Bush, 553 U.S. 723 (2008). *See generally* Harold Hongju Koh, "Setting the World Right," 115 *Yale L.J.* 2350, 2360 (2006) (analyzing *Hamdan*); Martin S. Flaherty, *Restoring the Global Judiciary: Why the Supreme Court Should Rule in U.S. Foreign Affairs* 204–19 (2019) (arguing that *Hamdi, Hamdan, Rasul,* and *Boumediene* should have been read together to reduce judicial deference to government national security arguments).

36. *See* Hamdi v. Rumsfeld, 542 U.S. 507, 510, 536 (2004).

37. Rasul v. Bush, 542 U.S. 466, 476, 480 (2004); *id.* at 487 (Kennedy, J., concurring).

38. Hamdan v. Rumsfeld, 548 U.S. 557, 567, 593 n.23 (2006); *see also id.* at 637, 638–39 (Kennedy, J., concurring in part) (citing *Youngstown*); UCMJ, 10 U.S.C. §§ 801–946 (2000). The UCMJ is discussed further in note 27. For a discussion of this case, see generally Hamdan v. Rumsfeld: *Establishing a Constitutional Process: Hearing Before the S. Comm. on the Judiciary,* 109th Cong. 50–52 (2006) (statement of Harold Hongju Koh, Dean, Yale Law School), www.govinfo.gov/content/pkg/CHRG-109shrg43111/pdf/CHRG-109shrg43111.pdf.

39. *Hamdan,* 548 U.S. at 637, 641 (Kennedy, J., concurring in part).

40. Guaranty Trust Co. v. York, 326 U.S. 99, 101 (1945).

41. *Hamdan,* 548 U.S. at 635; *id.* at 636 (Breyer, J., concurring).

42. *Id.* at 630–32 (majority opinion). Geneva Convention Relative to the Treatment of Prisoners of War, art. 3, August 12, 1949, 6 U.S.T. 3316, 75 U.N.T.S. 135 [hereinafter Common Article 3]; Murray v. Schooner Charming Betsy, 6 U.S. 64 (1804) (courts must construe statutes consistently with international law).

43. *Hamdan,* 548 U.S. at 636 (Breyer, J., concurring). See the discussion of *Kent v. Dulles* in note 7.

44. *See, e.g., Hamdi,* 542 U.S. at 535–36 (rejecting the president's claim that courts may not inquire into the factual basis for the detention of a U.S. citizen "enemy combatant" and reasoning that "[w]hatever power the United States Constitution envisions for the Executive in its exchanges with other nations or with enemy organizations in times of conflict, it most assuredly envisions a role for all three branches when individual liberties are at stake"); *Rasul,* 542 U.S. at 476, 480; *id.* at 487 (Kennedy, J., concurring) (rejecting the president's claim that it would be an unconstitutional interference with the president's commander-in-chief power to interpret the habeas corpus statute to encompass actions filed on behalf of Guantánamo detainees); *Youngstown,* 343 U.S. at 586 (invalidating the president's seizure of the steel mills when Congress had previously "rejected an amendment which would have authorized such governmental seizures in cases of emergency"); *Ex parte* Milligan, 71 U.S. 2 (1866) (holding that the executive had violated the

Habeas Corpus Act by failing to discharge from military custody a petitioner charged, inter alia, with violation of the laws of war); Little v. Barreme, 6 U.S. (2 Cranch) 170 (1804) (invalidating the seizure of a ship during a conflict with France as implicitly disapproved by Congress); United States v. Smith, 27 F. Cas. 1192, 1230 (Paterson, Circuit Justice, C.C.D.N.Y. 1806) (No. 16,342) ("The president of the United States cannot control the statute, nor dispense with its execution, and still less can he authorize a person to do what the law forbids.").

45. Foreign Intelligence Surveillance Act, 18 U.S.C. § 2511(2)(f) (2000).

46. For development of this argument, see *Wartime Executive Power and the National Security Agency's Surveillance Authority II: Hearing Before the S. Comm. on the Judiciary*, 109th Cong. 425–27 (2006) (statement of Harold Hongju Koh, Dean, Yale Law School), https://perma.cc/8PC2-SDHL (rebutting arguments in U.S. Dep't of Justice, Legal Authorities Supporting the Activities of the National Security Agency Described by the President 34–35 (Jan. 19, 2006), https://perma.cc/JF5C-8NLE).

47. Military Commissions Act of 2006, Pub. L. No 109-366, 120 Stat. 2600 (codified at 10 U.S.C §§ 948–949).

48. Boumediene v. Bush, 553 U.S. 723, 764–65, 770 (2008).

49. *See generally* Stephen I. Vladeck, "The D.C. Circuit After *Boumediene*," 41 *Seton Hall L. Rev.* 1451 (2011).

50. United States v. Husayn (Zubaydah), 142 S. Ct. 959, 994 (2022) (Gorsuch, J., dissenting). In April 2023, the en banc D.C. Circuit continued a Guantánamo detainee's long-term detention, without charge or trial. In a one-paragraph order, the court continued to leave the due-process issue unresolved, ruling that, "assuming due process protections apply to Guantanamo detainees, the District Court's rejection of Mr. al-Hela's substantive due process challenge based solely on the length of his detention be affirmed; and that Mr. al-Hela's claim that continuing to detain him if he no longer presents an ongoing threat violates substantive due process be remanded to the District Court for further proceedings." Al-Hela v. Biden, No. 19-5079 (D.C. Cir. Apr. 4, 2023) (en banc) (per curiam), https://pacer-documents.s3 amazonaws.com/207/19-05079/01208506932.pdf. Thus, after three decades, this constitutional issue still remains unresolved. *See* Charlie Savage & Carol Rosenberg, "Appeals Court Punts on Due Process Rights for Guantánamo Detainees," *N.Y. Times*, Apr. 4, 2023, www.nytimes.com/2023/04/04/us/politics/guantanamo appeals-court-due-process.html.

Chapter 7. Obama

1. Barack Obama, Remarks by the President at Cairo University (June 4, 2009) https://perma.cc/XH9H-9GZ8.

2. *See, e.g.*, Hillary Rodham Clinton, U.S. Sec'y of State, Smart Power Approach to Counterterrorism, Remarks at the John Jay School of Criminal Justice (Sept. 9, 2011) https://2009-2017.state.gov/secretary/20092013clinton/rm/2011/09/172034.htm. *See generally* Hillary Rodham Clinton, *Hard Choices* (2014); Harold Hongju Koh, *The Trump Administration and International Law* 9–13 (2018).

3. I participated regularly in the group as State Department Legal Adviser during Obama's first term. *See generally* Harold Hongju Koh, "National Security Legal Advice in the New Administration," *Just Security*, Nov. 16, 2016, https://perma.cc/3UZ8-E4AR.

4. Abram Chayes, *Cuban Missile Crisis: International Crises and the Role of Law* 103 (1974).

5. *See* Charlie Savage, *Power Wars: The Relentless Rise of Presidential Authority and Secrecy* 62–74 (2017); Barack Obama, Remarks by the President at the National Defense University (May 23, 2013), https://perma.cc/E9VU-YECP.

6. Barack Obama, Remarks by the President on National Security at the National Archives (May 21, 2009), https://perma.cc/9C99-KSMV.

7. *See generally* Harold Hongju Koh, "The Emerging Law of 21st Century War," 66 *Emory L.J.* 487 (2017); Obama, *supra*, note 6; Barack Obama, Remarks on Accepting the Nobel Peace Prize in Oslo, 2 Pub. Papers 1799 (Dec. 10, 2009) [hereinafter Obama, Nobel Lecture], https://perma.cc/HTG7-5UC4; Barack Obama, Inaugural Address (Jan. 21, 2009), https://perma.cc/YNL8-DFLT; Authorization for Use of Military Force, Pub. L. 107-40, § 2(b), 115 Stat. 224, 224 (2001).

8. Hamdan v. Rumsfeld, 548 U.S. 557 (2006). In *Hamdan*, the justices acknowledged that Common Article 3 of the Geneva Conventions, which governs the minimum humanitarian standard in all armed conflicts, should apply. *See, e.g., id.* at 629 ("[Common Article 3] applies here even if the relevant conflict is not one between signatories."); *id.* at 641–42, 646 (Kennedy, J., concurring in part) (referring to "our Nation's armed conflict with Al Qaeda in Afghanistan" and to "our Nation's armed conflict with the Taliban and Al Qaeda—a conflict that continues as we speak").

9. For a more detailed discussion of the administration's legal theory for using force against ISIS (also called ISIL (Islamic State of Iraq and the Levant), or Da'esh), see *Report on the Legal and Policy Frameworks Guiding the United States' Use of Military Force and Related National Security Operations*, at i, 4, 11 (Dec. 2016) [hereinafter *Frameworks Report*], https://perma.cc/LVZ4-MDA7; Harold Hongju Koh, "Obama's ISIL Rollout: Bungled, Clearly. But Illegal? Really?," *Just Security*, Sept. 29, 2014, https://perma.cc/L3HX-KM8V.

10. *See Frameworks Report, supra* note 9, at 12–14 (describing how the United States works with others in an armed conflict).

11. On the need for an elongated notion of imminence, see Daniel Bethlehem, "Self-Defense Against an Imminent or Actual Armed Attack by Nonstate Actors," 106 *Am. J. Int'l L.* 770, 770–72, 774, 776 (2012).

12. *Compare* Al-Bihani v. Obama, 590 F.3d 866, 871 (D.C. Cir. 2010) (Kavanaugh, J.) (The "premise that the war powers granted by the AUMF and other statutes are limited by the international laws of war . . . is mistaken."), *with* Al-Bihani v. Obama, 619 F.3d 1, 1 (D.C. Cir. 2010) ("We decline to en banc this case to determine the role of international law-of-war principles in interpreting the AUMF because . . . the panel's discussion of that question is not necessary to the disposition of the merits."). *See also* Brief of the United States in Response to Petition for Rehearing En Banc at 5–6, Al-Bihani v. Obama, 590 F.3d 866 (May 13, 2010) (No. 09-5051),

https://perma.cc/7MUW-C83M ("The [Obama administration] agrees that [the majority's] broad statement does not properly reflect the state of the law. *The Government interprets the detention authority permitted under the AUMF, as informed by the laws of war.* That interpretation is consistent with the Supreme Court's decision in *Hamdi* . . . and with longstanding Supreme Court precedent that statutes should be construed as consistent with applicable international law." (emphasis added)).

13. Geneva Convention Relative to the Treatment of Prisoners of War art. 3, Aug. 12, 1949, 6 U.S.T. 3316; *see* Hamdan v. Rumsfeld: *Establishing a Constitutional Process: Hearing Before the Senate Committee on the Judiciary,* 109th Cong. 51 (2006) (statement of Harold Hongju Koh, Dean, Yale Law School), www.govinfo.gov/content/pkg/CHRG-109shrg43111/pdf/CHRG-109shrg43111.pdf; Protocol Additional to the Geneva Conventions of 12 August 1949, and Relating to the Protection of Victims of Non-International Armed Conflicts (Protocol II) art. 4, ¶ 2, June 8, 1977, 1125 U.N.T.S. 609; National Defense Authorization Act for Fiscal Year 2016, Pub. L. No. 114-92, § 1045, 129 Stat. 726, 977 (2015); Marty Lederman, "The President's NDAA Signing Statement re: GTMO and Anti-Torture Provisions," *Just Security,* Nov. 25, 2015, https://perma.cc/VJH2-VXDG.

14. Exec. Order No. 13,732, 81 Fed. Reg. 44,485 (July 1, 2016), https://perma.cc/V5Y6-GFAX; *see also* Charlie Savage & Scott Shane, "U.S. Reveals Death Toll from Airstrikes Outside War Zones," *N.Y. Times,* July 1, 2016, https://perma.cc/HWR8-KGDX; Harold Hongju Koh, How to End the Forever War?, Remarks at the Oxford Union 14 (May 7, 2013), https://perma.cc/U2T4-XZBF ("[T]he real issue . . . is not drone technology per se, but the need for transparent, agreed-upon domestic and international legal process and standards." (emphasis omitted)).

15. These public explanations began with a speech that I gave to the American Society of International Law in 2010. *See* Harold Hongju Koh, The Obama Administration and International Law, Speech at the Annual Meeting of the American Society of International Law (Mar. 25, 2010), https://perma.cc/R739-ADC8. The trend continued with speeches given by Attorney General Eric Holder at Northwestern, the deputy national security adviser John Brennan at Harvard, and Defense Department general counsels Jeh Johnson and Stephen Preston at Yale and the American Society of International Law, respectively. *See* Savage, *supra* note 5 at 238. On the legality of some forms of targeted killing, see HCJ 769/02 Pub. Comm. Against Torture in Israel v. Gov't of Israel (2) IsrLR 459, 473 (2006). On the legality of the bin Laden raid, see Harold Hongju Koh, "The Lawfulness of the U.S. Military Operation Against Osama bin Laden," *Opinio Juris,* May 19, 2011, https://perma.cc/V7XR-T48R.

16. Just before leaving office, the Obama administration issued a comprehensive report detailing how, under President Obama, the United States sought to "ensure[] that our uses of force overseas are supported by a solid domestic law framework and consistent with an international legal framework predicated on the concepts of sovereignty and self-defense embedded in the United Nations Charter." Barack Obama, "Foreword" to *Frameworks Report, supra* note 9, at i. In an effort to "encourage[] future Administrations to build on this report and carry forward the principles of transparency it represents," *id.* at ii, President Obama issued a memorandum

asking the National Security Council staff to update the report at least annually, *see* Presidential Memorandum—Steps for Increased Legal and Policy Transparency Concerning the United States Use of Military Force and Related National Security Operations (Dec. 5, 2016), https://perma.cc/Z5DM-UUBY. The report was also accompanied by President Obama's last national security speech. *See* Barack Obama, Remarks by the President on the Administration's Approach to Counterterrorism (Dec. 6, 2016), https://perma.cc/7NDK-LVWW.

17. Harold Hongju Koh, "International Law in Cyberspace," 54 *Harv. Int'l. L.J. Online* 1, 2–7 (2012), https://harvardilj.org/2012/12/online_54_koh/. For the follow-on speech by Brian Egan, my successor as State Department Legal Adviser, see Brian J. Egan, Remarks on International Law and Stability in Cyberspace (Nov. 10, 2016), https://perma.cc/M7MD-FPVH. For expert efforts to elaborate cyber norms, see, for example, Michael N. Schmitt, "International Law in Cyberspace: The Koh Speech and Tallinn Manual Juxtaposed," 54 *Harv. Int'l. L.J. Online* 13 (2012), https://harvardilj.org/2012/12/online-articles-online_54_schmitt/, Elaine Korzak, "The 2015 GGE Report: What Next for Norms in Cyberspace?," *Lawfare*, Sept. 23, 2015, https://perma.cc/FSJ4-YSRE, and Louise Marie Hurel, "The Rocky Road to Cyber Norms at the United Nations," *Council on Foreign Relations*, Sept. 6, 2022, https://perma.cc/QX4V-SPLT.

18. For a review of this issue with respect to Syria, and a suggested international legal framework, see Koh, *supra* note 2, at 127–40; *see also* Obama, Nobel Lecture, *supra* note 7, at 1801. *See generally* Harold Hongju Koh, "The War Powers and Humanitarian Intervention," 53 *Hous. L. Rev.* 971 (2016) [hereinafter Koh, "War Powers"].

19. *See* Jeffrey Goldberg, "The Obama Doctrine," *Atlantic,* Apr. 2016, https://perma.cc/2FDJ-TPD6 (interviewing President Obama regarding, inter alia, his policies in Syria).

20. *See generally* Harold Hongju Koh, "The Legal Adviser's Duty to Explain," 41 *Yale J. Int'l L.* 189 (2016); Authorization for Continuing Hostilities in Kosovo, 24 Op. O.L.C. 327, 339 (2000).

21. Koh, *supra* note 18, at 981; Press Statement, Hillary Rodham Clinton, Secretary of State, Sexual Violence in Libya, the Middle East and North Africa (June 16, 2011), https://perma.cc/VWX3-VJ6T; Transcript, *This Week:* Hillary Clinton, Robert Gates, and Donald Rumsfeld (ABC News television broadcast Mar. 27, 2011), https://perma.cc/GG62-4FQN.

22. The President's Weekly Address, 1 Pub. Papers 293, 293 (Mar. 26, 2011), https://perma.cc/3GGN-DLXW; Address to the Nation on the Situation in Libya, 1 Pub. Papers 306 (Mar. 28, 2011), https://perma.cc/3GGN-DLXW. Caroline Krass, the acting assistant attorney general for OLC, followed the Dellinger approach in Haiti and Kosovo, concluding that the president could constitutionally initiate military action without prior congressional approval if (a) the use of force served significant national interests that have historically supported unilateral actions—here, promoting regional stability and preventing destruction of the near-century-old ban on chemical weapons—and (b) the operations were not expected to be "sufficiently extensive in 'nature, scope, and duration' to constitute a 'war' requiring prior specific congressional approval under the Declaration of War Clause." Authority to Use Military Force in Libya, 35 Op. O.L.C. 1 (2011).

23. Charlie Savage of the *N.Y. Times* later reported that around day fifty-seven,

> the message came back that there was no political appetite to enact an authorization. McCain and Kerry, seeing that there was no chance of getting a resolution through the House anyway, had shelved their plans to push one in the Senate. . . . [T]here was a widespread understanding within the Obama administration that congressional leaders of both parties in each chamber had separately and privately told the president that they did not think authorization was legally necessary.

> Savage, *supra* note 5, at 641, 643. As I later noted in Senate testimony,

> few Members of Congress asserted that our participation in the NATO mission would trigger or had triggered the War Powers Resolution's pullout provision. House Speaker [John] Boehner stated on June 1, 2011, that "[l]egally, [the Administration has] met the requirements of the War Powers Act." House Minority Leader Nancy Pelosi reported, that "[t]he limited nature of this engagement allows the President to go forward," as "the President has the authority he needs." Senate Majority Leader [Harry] Reid stated on June 17, 2011, that "[t]he War Powers Act has no application to what's going on in Libya." Senate Foreign Relations Committee Chairman [John] Kerry stated on June 21, 2011, that "I do not think our limited involvement rises to the level of hostilities defined by the War Powers Resolution," and on June 23, 2011, that "[w]e have not introduced our armed forces into hostilities. No American is being shot at. No American troop is at risk of being shot down today. That is not what we're doing. We are refueling. We are supporting NATO."

> *Libya and War Powers: Hearing Before the S. Comm. on Foreign Relations*, 112th Cong. 7-13 n.8 (2011) [hereinafter Koh, Libya Testimony] (statement of Harold Hongju Koh, Legal Adviser, U.S. Dep't of State). Savage reports that the Senate majority leader, Republican Mitch McConnell, also made public comments suggesting that he did not think the administration was violating the War Powers Resolution. *See* Savage, *supra* note 5, at 643; Tom Cohen, "Key Senate Republicans Disagree with House GOP on War Powers Debate," *CNN*, June 19, 2011, https://perma.cc/Z86S-C7K4.

24. U.S. government lawyers had similarly generated a fourth option of quarantine during the Cuban missile crisis. *See generally* Abram Chayes, *supra* note 4; Graham Allison & Phillip Zelikow, *Essence of Decision: Explaining the Cuban Missile Crisis* (1971); Robert F. Kennedy, *Thirteen Days: A Memoir of the Cuban Missile Crisis* (1969). Savage reports that another option would have been to reduce "military activity . . . to a purely supporting role, like refueling allied warplanes and providing surveillance." Savage, *supra* note 5, at 643–44. But the U.S. military disfavored that option (although put forward by the Defense Department's own general counsel) because it would have created an unacceptable operational risk: "[w]ithout the availability of the United States' unique weapons systems, the risk would go up that pro-Gadhafi forces would shoot down a NATO aircraft" and NATO would be barred from using its Predator drones to strike at Qadhafi forces seeking to exploit chemical weapons depots. *Id.*

25. Lowry v. Reagan, 676 F. Supp. 333, 341 n.53 (D.D.C. 1987); H.R. Rep. No. 93-287, at 7 (1973) (emphasis omitted); *War Powers Legislation: Hearings on S. 731, S.J. Res. 18, and S.J. Res. 59 Before the S. Comm. on Foreign Relations*, 92d Cong. 28 (1971) (statements of Sen. Jacob K. Javits and Henry Steele Commager, Prof., Amherst College).

26. *See* Koh, Libya Testimony, *supra* note 23, at 8.

27. *War Powers: Hearings Before the Subcomm. on Nat'l Sec. Policy & Sci. Devs. of the H. Comm. on Foreign Affairs*, 93d Cong. 22 (1973) (statement of Sen. Jacob K. Javits).

28. *See* Letter from Monroe Leigh, Legal Adviser, U.S. Dep't of State, & Martin R. Hoffmann, Gen. Counsel, U.S. Dep't of Def., to Clement J. Zablocki, Chairman, H. Foreign Affairs Comm. (June 3, 1975), *reprinted in* War Powers: A Test of Compliance Relative to the Danang Sealift, the Evacuation of Phnom Penh, the Evacuation of Saigon, and the Mayaguez Incident: Hearings Before the Subcomm. on Int'l Sec. & Scientific Affairs of the H. Comm. on Int'l Relations, 94th Cong. 38 (1975) [hereinafter Leigh-Hoffmann Letter]; *see also* Koh, Libya Testimony, *supra* note 23, at 12, 14 ("By Presidential design, U.S. forces are playing a constrained and supporting role in a NATO-led multinational civilian protection operation, which is implementing a U.N. Security Council resolution tailored to that limited purpose. This is a very unusual set of circumstances, not found in any of the historic situations in which the "hostilities" question was previously debated. . . .").

29. *See* Richard F. Grimmett, Cong. Research Serv., R41199, *The War Powers Resolution: After Thirty-Six Years* 13–27 (2010); John H. Kelly, "Lebanon: 1982–1984," in *U.S. and Russian Policymaking with Respect to the Use of Force* 85, 96–99 (Jeremy R. Azrael & Emil A. Payin eds., 1996); Ben Bradlee Jr., "A Chronology on Grenada," *Bos. Globe*, Nov. 6, 1983, at 24; John L. Hirsch & Robert B. Oakley, *Somalia and Operation Restore Hope: Reflections on Peacemaking and Peacekeeping* 112, 124–27 (1995).

30. Koh, Libya Testimony, *supra* note 23, at 10.

31. Savage, *supra* note 5, at 643; *see also id.* at 638–49 (reviewing the internal administration legal debate).

32. *See, e.g.*, Morrison v. Nat'l Austl. Bank Ltd., 561 U.S. 247, 266 (2010). As President Obama later put it,

> when you look at the history of the War Powers resolution, it came up after the Vietnam War in which we had half a million soldiers there, tens of thousands of lives lost, hundreds of billions of dollars spent, and Congress said, you know what, we don't want something like that happening again. So if you're going to start getting us into those kinds of commitments, you've got to consult with Congress beforehand. And I think that such consultation is entirely appropriate.

The President's News Conference, 1 Pub. Papers 715, 718–19 (June 29, 2011), https://perma.cc/3GGN-DLXW.

33. *See* Leigh-Hoffman Letter, *supra* note 28, at 38–39; *see also* Letter from Wendy R. Sherman, Assistant Sec'y of State for Legislative Affairs, to Rep. Benjamin Gilman, Member, H. Comm. on Foreign Affairs (Sept. 28, 1993), *reprinted in* 139 Cong. Rec. 22,752–53 (1993) ("[N]o previous Administration has considered that intermittent

military engagements involving U.S. forces overseas, whether or not constituting 'hostilities,' would necessitate the withdrawal of such forces pursuant to section 5(b) of the Resolution."); Presidential Power to Use the Armed Forces Abroad Without Statutory Authorization, 4A Op. O.L.C. 185, 194 (1980), https://perma.cc/XR64-RFAE.

34. Koh, Libya Testimony, *supra* note 23, at 9 (emphasis added).

35. Compare Savage, *supra* note 5, at 644–45 (discussing positions of Donilon and Bauer) with Bob Bauer, "Power Wars Symposium: The Power Wars Debate and the Question of the Role of the Lawyer in Crisis," *Just Security*, Nov. 18, 2015, https://perma.cc/DH86-TXH6. Former White House counsel Bauer later wrote to me and said:

> Charlie [Savage] reports someone's belief that I advised the President that the view you and I shared about the interpretation of hostilities was "available." . . . That belief is mistaken: I never have used that standard—"availability"—for judging a legal theory. This is a topic—the boundaries of acceptable legal advice under national security pressures—that I have spent time thinking about in arriving at a conclusion much like the one you put forward effectively to the Senate, *I believed it to be a reasonable, good faith interpretation*, and I recognized that there would be disagreement with it, some of it strong.

Email from Bob Bauer to author (Mar. 4, 2016, 8:07 AM EST) (on file with author) (emphasis added).

36. Koh, Libya Testimony, *supra* note 23, at 12.

37. Obama, *supra* note 32, at 719 ("[D]o I think that our actions in any way violate the War Powers Resolution? The answer is no. So I don't even have to get to the constitutional question. There may be a time in which there was a serious question as to whether or not the War Powers Resolution Act was constitutional. So I don't have to get to the question."); Savage, *supra* note 5, at 649; *id.* at 643 ("[T]here was a widespread understanding within the Obama administration that congressional leaders of *both* parties in each chamber had separately and privately told the president that they did not think authorization was legally necessary" and repeated those positions publicly after the sixty-day deadline had passed. (emphasis in original) (discussing positions of Boehner, Pelosi, Reid, and McConnell)). For the unsuccessful House resolutions challenging the interpretation, see H.R. Res. 1212, 112th Cong. (2011); H.R. Res. 6290, 112th Cong. (2011); H.R. Con. Res. 31, 112th Cong. (2011). As in Kosovo, Congress continued to fund the Libyan operation. *See* Kathleen Hennessey, "House Rebukes Obama on Libya, but Won't Cut Funds, *L.A. Times*, June 24, 2011, http://articles.latimes.com/2011/jun/24/nation/la-na-congress-libya-20110625.

38. For academic criticism of the administration's legal reasoning, see, for example Bruce Ackerman, "Legal Acrobatics, Illegal War," *N.Y. Times*, June 20, 2011, https://perma.cc/29T9-5XSA, and Dawn Johnsen, "When Responsibilities Collide: Humanitarian Intervention, Shared War Powers, and the Rule of Law," 53 *Hous. L. Re* 1065, 1073 (2016). Although Professor Johnsen suggests that her view was share at the time by a "consensus" of "most commentators," *id.* at 1099–1100, no con

mentary that I have seen—including hers—has adequately grappled with either the factual account of the use of force in Libya or the legal analysis of the statutory term "hostilities" that I have offered here. Professor Johnsen acknowledges that my "Senate testimony made a strong and appropriately narrow case" for why "hostilities" were not occurring in Libya on the sixtieth day. *Id.* at 1074. She further concedes that the text of the War Powers Resolution is ambiguous, inasmuch as "[t]he statute does not define" "hostilities," a term she clarifies only to the extent of calling it "more expansive than 'war' in the constitutional sense." *Id.* at 1097–98. But she offers no test to clarify what level or nature of military activity would constitute "hostilities" in a statutory sense. Nor does she explain why Congress had not acquiesced in Obama's construction of the word "hostilities" when the Speaker, former Speaker, and the Senate majority and minority leaders each made clear that they did not think the administration was violating the War Powers Resolution. *See supra* note 23. Finally, she concedes that "[i]n any particular instance, the President clearly possesses the authority to make the final call about which legal analysis seems correct and will inform action," which President Obama clearly did here. Johnsen, *supra,* at 1075. For commentary supporting the administration's legal position, see, for example, Richard Pildes, "Power Wars Symposium: What Role Should Law Play in Areas of Vital National and International Affairs?," *Just Security,* Nov. 13, 2015, https://perma.cc/R6PT-EEVM, and Akhil Amar, "Bomb Away, Mr. President," *Slate,* June 29, 2011, https://perma.cc/2JW3-65GX. Professor Laurence Tribe, of Harvard Law School, initially questioned the administration's legal position in Libya, *see* Paul Starobin, Opinion, "A Moral Flip-Flop? Defining a War," *N.Y. Times,* Aug. 6, 2011, http://nyti.ms/1HFFmt4, but later wrote me in October 2011 to say, "It's true that I was among the people who were unpersuaded by your and the W[hite] H[ouse]'s legal view of what constitute 'hostilities,' and I know hindsight can be 20/20, but in retrospect I have to say that your view of the matter may have been the wiser one." Email from Laurence H. Tribe, Carl M. Loeb Univ. Professor, Harv. Law Sch., to author (Oct. 20, 2011, 10:33 PM EST) (on file with author).

9. *See* Jo Becker & Scott Shane, "A New Libya, with 'Very Little Time Left,'" *N.Y. Times,* Feb. 27, 2016, https://perma.cc/ZQ9P-HC3S; Jo Becker & Scott Shane, "Hillary Clinton, 'Smart Power' and a Dictator's Fall," *N.Y. Times,* Feb. 27, 2016, https://perma.cc/XPX4-X3ZE; Shadi Hamid, "Everyone Says the Libya Intervention Was a Failure. They're Wrong," *Vox,* Apr. 5, 2016, https://perma.cc/TM4U-2NBU; Kim Ghattas, "Hillary Clinton Has No Regrets About Libya," *Foreign Pol'y,* Apr. 14, 2016, https://perma.cc/FP72-J822 ("A European diplomat told me recently the choice was between rivers of blood or a mess.").

0. For a discussion of the Syria case study, see Savage, *supra* note 5, at 627–54. For a discussion of the humanitarian crisis, see Michael Ignatieff & Leon Wieseltier, "Enough Is Enough—U.S. Abdication on Syria Must Come to an End," *Wash. Post,* Feb. 9, 2016, https://perma.cc/DSJ3-N9WJ.

1. *See* Barack Obama, Remarks by the President to the White House Press Corps, 2012 Daily Comp. Pres. Doc. 6 (Aug. 20, 2012), https://perma.cc/95XV-EW7M; "Major Powers Hold UN Talks on Syria," *Al Jazeera Am.,* Aug. 28, 2013, https://

perma.cc/5BRW-JMWE; Joshua Rosenberg, "Syria Intervention: It May Not Be
Wise, but Using Force May Be Lawful," *Guardian,* Aug. 28, 2013, https://perma.
cc/4T94-WQUY. For the U.K. Foreign and Commonwealth Office's formal legal
position to the House of Commons Foreign Affairs Committee on the international lawfulness of humanitarian intervention, see Letter from Right Hon. Hugh
Robertson MP, Minister of State, Foreign & Commonwealth Office, to House of
Commons, Foreign Affairs Comm. (Jan. 14, 2014), https://perma.cc/7CMX-QPL7
(following the Syria crisis in August 2013). The Danish government similarly con-
cluded that use of force for humanitarian purposes would be justifiable under in-
ternational law under exceptional circumstances. *See* Memorandum from the
Ministry of Foreign Affairs of Denmark to the Members of the Foreign Policy
Comm. (Aug. 30, 2013), https://perma.cc/XH2A-8VBK; *see also* Ernesto Londoño,
"Obama Says U.S. Will Take Military Action Against Syria, Pending Congress's
Approval," *Wash. Post,* Aug. 31, 2013, https://perma.cc/K6KK-RB97; Barack
Obama, Remarks by the President in Address to the Nation on Syria (Sept. 10,
2013), https://perma.cc/M7QT-ACCQ.

42. *See* Koh, "War Powers," *supra* note 18, at 999–1000 ("[T]he [White House] Counsel
explained that, while an attack on Syria 'may not fit under a traditionally recognized legal basis under international law,' given the novel factors and circumstances, such an action would nevertheless be 'justified and legitimate under
international law' and so not prohibited. As a matter of domestic law, the Administration also apparently concluded that congressional approval was not required.
As the *N.Y. Times* reported, '[A]dministration lawyers decided that it was within Mr.
Obama's constitutional authority to carry out a strike on Syria as well, even without
permission from Congress or the Security Council, because of the "important national interests" of limiting regional instability and of enforcing the norm against
using chemical weapons. . . .'").

43. *See* Koh, *supra* note 2, at 127–40.

44. Jonathan Karl, "John Kerry Promises 'Unbelievably Small' U.S. Strike Against
Syria," *ABC News,* Sept. 9, 2013, https://perma.cc/M9V5-URDT.

45. Vladimir V. Putin, Opinion, "A Plea for Caution from Russia," *N.Y. Times,* Sept. 11
2013, https://perma.cc/3XG9-PBWP.

46. Barack Obama, Remarks to the United Nations General Assembly in New York
City, 2013 Daily Comp. Pres. Doc. 2, 4 (Sept. 24, 2013), https://perma.cc/JHW7
FD9B.

47. Chayes, *supra* note 4, at 44.

48. *See generally* Harold Hongju Koh, "Triptych's End: A Better Framework to Evaluate
21st Century International Lawmaking," 126 *Yale L.J. F.* 338, 339–41 (2017), www.
yalelawjournal.com/forum/triptych's-end [hereinafter Koh, "Triptych's End"]; Har
old Hongju Koh, "Remarks: Twenty-First-Century International Lawmaking," 101
Geo. L.J. 725, 726–27 (2013).

49. According to the assistant legal adviser of the State Department for treaty affairs
since 2009 the Senate has advised and consented to only eighteen treaties, less
than one-third of the average approved since 1960 in any four-year presidential
term. *See* Michael J. Mattler, "Observations on Recent U.S. Practice Involving

Treaties and Other International Agreements and Arrangements" 2 (Oct. 15, 2016) (unpublished paper presented at 2016 Yale-Duke Foreign Relations Law Roundtable).

50. Louis Henkin, *Foreign Affairs and the United States Constitution* 217 (2d ed. 1996) ("[I]t is now widely accepted that the Congressional-Executive agreement is available for wide use, even general use, and is a complete alternative to a treaty."); Myres S. McDougal & Asher Lans, "Treaties and Congressional-Executive or Presidential Agreements: Interchangeable Instruments of National Policy: I," 54 *Yale L.J.* 181 (1945). *See generally* Oona A. Hathaway, "Treaties' End: The Past, Present, and Future of International Lawmaking in the United States," 117 *Yale L.J.* 1236, 1244–48 (2008) (describing "the interchangeability debate"). *Compare* Laurence H. Tribe, "Taking Text and Structure Seriously: Reflections on Free-Form Method in Constitutional Interpretation," 108 *Harv. L. Rev.* 1221 (1995), *with* Bruce Ackerman & David Golove, "Is NAFTA Constitutional?," 108 *Harv. L. Rev.* 799 (1995). *See also* Peter J. Spiro, "Treaties, Executive Agreements, and Constitutional Method," 79 *Tex. L. Rev.* 961 (2001); North American Free Trade Agreement Implementation Act, Pub. L. No. 103-182, 107 Stat. 2057 (1993) (repealed in 2020); Uruguay Round Agreements Act, Pub. L. No. 103-465, 108 Stat. 4809 (1994) (enacted to implement the Agreement Establishing the World Trade Organization, http://perma.cc/2DU3-FJB9); Ackerman & Golove, *supra,* at 891 (discussing Bretton Woods Agreements Act, Pub. L. No. 79-171, 59 Stat. 512 (1945) (codified at 22 U.S.C. § 286)).

1. *Cf.* Karoun Demirjian & Carol Morello, "State Department Gets Some Nominees, After Cruz Clears His Roadblock," *Wash. Post,* Feb. 12, 2016, http://perma.cc/R284-59NZ (describing how, in the context of executive confirmations, a single senator placed a blanket hold on all State Department nominees for several months by preventing a voice vote).

2. United States v. Pink, 315 U.S. 203, 222 (1942) (confirming the holding in *Belmont*); United States v. Belmont, 301 U.S. 324, 330–33 (1937) (upholding the constitutionality of an executive agreement made as part of a transaction that included recognition of the Soviet Union). *See generally Restatement (Third) of Foreign Relations Law of the United States* § 303 (1987) ("[T]he President, on his own authority, may make an international agreement dealing with any matter that falls within his independent powers under the Constitution."); Henkin, *supra* note 50, at 219–24; Agreement Respecting Naval and Air Bases (Hull-Lothian Agreement), U.S.-Gr. Brit., Sept. 2, 1940, 54 Stat. 2405; *see also* William Casto, "Advising Presidents: Robert Jackson and the Destroyers for Bases Deal," 52 *Am. J. Legal Hist.* 1 (2012) (describing the role that President Roosevelt and his advisers played in negotiating the agreement).

. *See, e.g.,* David Golove, "Constitutionalism and the Non-Binding International Agreement" 2 (Oct. 15, 2016) (unpublished paper presented at 2016 Yale-Duke Foreign Relations Law Roundtable).

. Anti-Counterfeiting Trade Agreement, Dec. 3, 2010, 50 I.L.M. 243. *See, e.g.,* Jack Goldsmith & Lawrence Lessig, Op-Ed, "Anti-Counterfeiting Agreement Raises Constitutional Concerns," *Wash. Post,* Mar. 26, 2010, http://perma.cc/F93C-

MANH ("Binding the United States to international obligations of this sort without congressional approval would raise serious constitutional questions."); Oona A. Hathaway & Amy Kapczynski, "Going It Alone: The Anti-Counterfeiting Trade Agreement as a Sole Executive Agreement," *Am. Soc. Int'l L.: Insights,* Aug. 24, 2011, http://perma.cc/J4ZA-BB5U.

55. Koh, "Triptych's End," *supra* note 48, at 321–22.

56. Dames & Moore v. Regan, 453 U.S. 654 (1981).

57. *Id.* at 678–79.

58. Confirmation Hearing of John G. Roberts Jr. to be Chief Justice of the United States Before S. Comm. on the Judiciary, 109th Cong. 370 (2005).

59. *See, e.g.,* Michael Ramsey, "Is the Iran Deal Unconstitutional?," *Originalism Blog,* July 15, 2015, http://perma.cc/U43L-CQ5H; David A. Wirth, "Is the Paris Agreement on Climate Change a Legitimate Exercise of the Executive Agreement Power?," *Lawfare,* Aug. 29, 2016, http://perma.cc/R46X-K3GF.

60. Daniel Bodansky & Peter J. Spiro, "Executive Agreements+," 49 *Vand. J. Transnat'l L.* 885 (2016).

61. U.N. Conference of the Parties of the Framework Convention on Climate Change. Addendum to Part Two: Action Taken by the Conference of the Parties at Its Seventeenth Session, p. 2, U.N. Doc. FCCC/CP/2011/9/Add.1 (Mar. 15, 2012), http:// perma.cc/LLV2-ZF4A.

62. *See* Koh, "Triptych's End," *supra* note 48, at 329–31; Global Climate Protection Act 15 U.S.C. § 2901 (2012); Clean Air Act, 42 U.S.C. §7415 (2012) (held by the Supreme Court in *Massachusetts v. EPA,* 549 U.S. 497, 498–501 (2007), to regulate carbon dioxide emissions as a pollutant); Convention on Long-Range Transboundary Air Pollution (1979 CLRTAP) 1302 U.N.T.S. 217 (adopted Nov. 13, 1979, entered into force Mar. 16, 1983); Protocol to the 1979 CLRTAP on the Reduction of Sulphur Emissions or Their Transboundary Fluxes by at Least 30 Percent 1480 U.N.T.S. 21 (adopted July 8, 1985, entered into force Sept. 2, 1987); Protocol to the 1979 CLRTAP on Further Reduction of Sulphur Emissions 2030 U.N.T.S. 122 (adopted Jun 14, 1994, entered into force Aug. 5, 1998); Protocol to the 1979 CLRTAP to Abat Acidification, Eutrophication and Ground-Level Ozone 2319 U.N.T.S. 81 (adopted Nov. 30, 1999, entered into force May 17, 2005); Protocol to the 1979 CLRTAP Concerning the Control of Emissions of Nitrogen Oxides or Their Transboundary Fluxes 1593 U.N.T.S. 287 (adopted Oct. 31, 1988, entered into force Feb. 14, 1991); Protocol to the 1979 CLRTAP Concerning the Control of Emissions of Volatile Organic Compounds or Their Transboundary Fluxes 2001 U.N.T.S. 187 (adopted Nov. 18, 1991, entered into force, Sept. 29, 1997); Protocol to the 1979 CLRTAP on Heavy Metal 2237 U.N.T.S. 4 (adopted June 24, 1998, entered into force Dec. 29, 2003); Protocol to the 1979 CLRTAP on Persistent Organic Pollutants 2230 U.N.T.S. 79 (adopted June 24, 1998, entered into force Oct. 23, 2003); Agreement on Air Quality, U.S.-Can., 30 I.L.M. 676 (Mar. 13, 1991); Minamata Convention on Mercury (adopted Oct. 11, 2013 entered into force Aug. 16, 2017), https://perma.cc/8JR3-R9HP.

63. Conditions Regarding U.N. Framework Convention on Climate Change, S. Rep No. 105-54 (1997); Kyoto Protocol to the United Nations Framework Convention on Climate Change, 2303 U.N.T.S. 162 (Dec. 10, 1997).

4. Daniel Bodansky, "The Legal Character of the Paris Agreement," 25 *Rev. Eur. Comp. & Int'l Envtl. L.* 142, 142 (2016).

5. For the full text and annexes of the Iran nuclear agreement, see Joint Comprehensive Plan of Action, U.S. Dep't of State, http://perma.cc/7ECU-MJSV. The annexes include: Annex I—Nuclear Related Commitments; Annex II—Sanctions Related Commitments; Annex III—Civil Nuclear Cooperation; Annex IV—Joint Commission; and Annex V—Implementation Plan.

6. For a detailed enumeration of statutory authorities, see generally Dianne Rennack, Cong. Research Serv., R43311, *Iran: U.S. Economic Sanctions and the Authority to Lift Restrictions* (2016). *Cf.* Youngstown Sheet & Tube Co. v. Sawyer, 343 U.S. 579, 635–37 (1952) (Jackson, J., concurring) ("When the President acts pursuant to an express or implied authorization of Congress, his authority is at its maximum, for it includes all that he possesses in his own right plus all that Congress can delegate.")

7. Duncan B. Hollis & Joshua J. Newcomer, "'Political' Commitments and the Constitution," 49 *Va. J. Int'l L.* 507 (2009) (citing, inter alia, precedents in the "six-party talks" applied to promote denuclearization in North Korea in 1994 and 2006); *see also* Letter from Denis McDonough, Assistant to the President and Chief of Staff, to Hon. Bob Corker, Chairman, Senate Comm. on Foreign Relations (Mar. 14, 2015), http://perma.cc/2XBT-SZS3 (reviewing a broad range of bilateral and multilateral cooperative arrangements regarding arms control and nonproliferation that have been developed by nonbinding political commitments).

8. Iran Nuclear Agreement Review Act, Pub. L. No. 114-17, 129 Stat. 201 (2015). The act requires the president to submit any agreement with Iran to Congress, delays implementation of any agreement for sixty days so that Congress can decide whether to act on it, and provides Congress with an opportunity to vote its disapproval. For an argument that the Iran Nuclear Review Act authorizes the president to enter into a legally binding agreement with Iran, see David Golove, "Congress Just Gave the President Power to Adopt a Binding Legal Agreement with Iran," *Just Security*, May 14, 2015, http://perma.cc/9B24-7EF6, and Marty Lederman, "Congress Hasn't Ceded Any Constitutional Authority with Respect to the Iran JCPOA," *Balkinization*, Aug. 8, 2015, http://perma.cc/JJ4C-P7B3.

9. *See, e.g.,* Curtis A. Bradley et al., "The Rise of Nonbinding International Agreements: An Empirical, Comparative, and Normative Analysis," 90 *U. Chi. L. Rev.* 1281 (2023)

10. Robert Putnam & Nicholas Bayne, *Hanging Together: Cooperation and Conflict in the Seven-Power Summits* (rev'd and enlarged ed. 1988); Peter M. Haas, "Introduction: Epistemic Communities and International Policy Coordination," 46 *Int'l Org.* 1 (1992).

11. *See* Harold Hongju Koh, "Why Do Nations Obey International Law?," 106 *Yale L.J.* 2599, 2650–51 (1997) (discussing the "positive transformational effects of repeated participation in the legal process" and how "[t]o the extent that [international] norms are successfully internalized, they become future determinants of . . . why nations obey").

12. *See, e.g.,* James M. Inhofe National Defense Authorization Act for Fiscal Year 2023, Pub. L. No. 117-263, § 5947, 136 Stat. 2423, 3476 (2022) (seeking to promote greater

transparency with regard to international agreements and nonbinding instruments by requiring the executive to report and publish certain significant nonbinding instruments after their conclusion).

Chapter 8. Trump

1. *See* Ben Protess et al., "Trump Is Indicted: The First Ex-President to Face Criminal Charges," *N.Y. Times*, Mar. 31, 2023, www.nytimes.com/2023/03/30/nyregion/trump-indictment-hush-money-charges.html (New York state-court indictment relating to hush-money payment to Stormy Daniels); Amy O'Kruk & Curth Merrill, "Donald Trump's Criminal Cases, in One Place," *CNN.com*, Aug. 4, 2023, www.cnn.com/interactive/2023/07/politics/trump-indictments-criminal-cases/ (Florida and Washington, D.C., federal-court indictments for hoarding classified documents and conspiring to obstruct joint session of Congress). For further discussion of these criminal cases, see *infra* chapter 9, note 62.

2. Rafi Schwartz, "Here's Trump Screaming in Front of a Plane About How He Has Unlimited Power," *Splinter*, July 12, 2019, https://perma.cc/R29L-CDF6 ("Nobody ever mentions Article II. It gives me all of these rights at a level that nobody has ever seen before."); *see also* Michael Brice-Saddler, "While Bemoaning Mueller Probe, Trump Falsely Says the Constitution Gives Him 'the Right to Do Whatever I Want,'" *Wash. Post*, July 23, 2019, https://perma.cc/B3M6-C4GU ("I have an Article II, where I have to [*sic*] the right to do whatever I want as president.").

3. *See* Harold Hongju Koh, "Is Preemptive Assassination the New Trump Doctrine?" *Foreign Pol'y*, Jan. 9, 2020, https://perma.cc/LRJ6-C5KN.

4. On July 25, 2019, facing pressure from Russian military action in the Donbas, Ukraine's new president Volodymyr Zelenskyy asked Trump for "great[er] support in the area of defense" and said that "we are almost ready to buy more Javelins [anti-tank weapon systems] from the United States for defense purposes." (Ukraine later received those weapons systems) from the Biden administration after Russia's invasion in 2022.) But instead of addressing this national security question, Trump asked Zelenskyy to help him with a partisan political priority: gathering opposition research to use against Biden for the forthcoming 2020 presidential election. "I would like you to do us a favor though . . . [w]ork with Rudy Giuliani," Trump said. Memorandum of Telephone Conversation with President Zelenskyy of Ukraine, July 25, 2019, 9:03–9:33 a.m. EDT, at 3, www.nytimes.com/interactive/2019/09/25/us/politics/trump-ukraine-transcript.html (emphasis added). Trump went on to abuse his foreign-affairs authority by freezing $320 million in U.S. aid to Ukraine to pressure Zelenskyy to comply. Joshua Yaffa, "How Donald Trump Is Making It Harder to End the War in Ukraine," *New Yorker*, Dec. 6, 2019, https://perma.cc/F9EF-W44W. For a discussion of the Iran-contra affair, see *supra* chapter 3.

5. Donald Ayer, "Why Bill Barr Is So Dangerous," *Atlantic*, June 30, 2019, https://perma.cc/CDT6-CRVM.

6. *See* Charlie Savage, "Trump's Claim of Executive Privilege in the Jan. 6 Inquiry Explained," *N.Y. Times*, Oct. 19, 2021, www.nytimes.com/2021/10/19/us/politics

trump-executive-privilege.html; Corinne Ramey, "Trump Fires Back in New York Subpoena Fight," *Wall St. J.*, Feb. 1, 2022, www.wsj.com/articles/trump-fires-back-in-new-york-subpoena-fight-11643756993; Harold Hongju Koh, Opinion, "The Arrogance of Trump's Enablers," *N.Y. Times*, Jan. 8, 2020, www.nytimes.com/2020/01/07/opinion/trump-impeachment-congress.html. On January 20, 2021, eleven hours before Trump was to leave office, he issued 143 pardons and commutations. *But see* Harold Hongju Koh et al., "Is the Pardon Power Unlimited?" *Just Security*, July 11, 2020, https://perma.cc/GZ9X-LAQK (arguing that pardons could independently form the basis for criminal charges of obstruction of justice, in both state and federal courts, after Trump leaves office); Devlin Barrett et al., "FBI Searched Trump's Home to Look for Nuclear Documents and Other Items, Sources Say," *Wash. Post*, Aug. 12, 2022, https://perma.cc/TJ25-6SG6; Glenn Thrush et al., "Trump Search Said to Be Part of Effort to Find Highly Classified Material," *N.Y. Times*, Aug. 11, 2022, www.nytimes.com/2022/08/11/us/politics/trump-fbi-subpoena.html.

7. Aaron Blake, "Stephen Miller's Authoritarian Declaration: Trump's National Security Power 'Will Not Be Questioned,'" *Wash. Post*, Feb. 13, 2017, https://perma.cc/G5K2-65AY.

8. For a description of Trump's approach to the Covid-19 pandemic, see Chris Whipple, *The Fight of His Life: Inside Joe Biden's White House* 13–15 (2023).

9. *See* Jessica Bolter et al., Migration Policy Institute, *Four Years of Profound Change: Immigration Policy During the Trump Presidency* (Feb. 2022), https://perma.cc/4KGD-KPGM (breaking hundreds of changes down by issue area).

10. *See generally* Adam Cox & Cristina Rodríguez, *The President and Immigration Law* (2020).

11. Dep't of Homeland Sec. v. Regents of the Univ. of Cal., 140 S. Ct. 1891 (2020).

12. These issues are discussed in greater detail in chapter 9.

13. *See* Trump v. Hawaii, 138 S. Ct. 2392 (2018) (upholding Muslim travel ban); Korematsu v. United States, 323 U.S. 214 (1944) (upholding Japanese internment). *See generally* Harold Hongju Koh, "*Trump v. Hawaii*—*Korematsu*'s Ghost and National-Security Masquerades," *SCOTUSblog*, June 28, 2018, https://perma.cc/H29W-EGLT; *see also* Theodore Schleifer, "Donald Trump: 'I think Islam Hates Us,'" *CNN*, Mar. 10, 2016, https://perma.cc/27SF-ESQ9; Meghan Keneally, "Donald Trump Cites FDR Policies to Defend Muslim Ban," *ABC News*, Dec. 8, 2015, https://perma.cc/C8AC-S4QL.

14. Convention Relating to the Status of Refugees, art. 3, July 28, 1951, 19 U.S.T. 6259, 6276, 189 U.N.T.S. 150, 176 [hereinafter Refugee Convention]; International Covenant on Civil and Political Rights, art. 26, S. Exec. Doc. No. E. 95-2, 999 U.N.T.S. 171 (1976). The United States became party to the Refugee Convention when the country acceded to the United Nations Protocol Relating to the Status of Refugees, Jan. 31, 1967, 19 U.S.T. 6223, 606 U.N.T.S. 2.

15. *See, e.g.*, 8 U.S.C. § 1152(a)(1)(A) ("[N]o person shall receive any preference or priority or be discriminated against in the issuance of an immigrant visa because of the person's race, sex, *nationality*, place of birth, or place of residence" (emphasis added)).

16. I served as counsel of record for an amicus brief on behalf of former national-security officials in support of the respondents in *Trump v. Hawaii*. That brief noted that "the Proclamation targets eight countries whose nationals have committed *no deadly terrorist attacks on U.S. soil in the last forty years*. Although [the Government] initially invoked the September 11 attacks as rationale for Travel Ban 1.0, none of the September 11 hijackers were citizens of the countries listed in any of the Orders." Brief of Amici Curiae Former National Security Officials in Support of Respondents at 18, Trump v. Hawaii, 138 S. Ct. 2392 (2018) (No. 17-965) (emphasis in original), https://perma.cc/3TDD-NU3A.

17. *See* Evan Perez et al., "Inside the Confusion of the Trump Executive Order and Travel Ban, *CNN*, Jan. 30, 2017, https://perma.cc/4ZEB-T39S.

18. *See* Trump v. Hawaii, 138 S. Ct. at 2423; *see id*. at 2435 (Sotomayor, J., dissenting).

19. *Compare id*. at 2421 (majority opinion), *with* National Security Officials' Amicus Brief, *supra* note 16, at 29 ("From the beginning, this has always been a ban in search of a threat, not vice versa.").

20. *See* Trump v. Hawaii, 138 S. Ct. at 2402 (noting that the travel ban "reflects the results of a worldwide review process undertaken by multiple Cabinet officials and their agencies"); United States v. Fordice, 545 U.S. 717, 746–47 (1992) (Thomas, J., concurring).

21. For the majority's articulation of its rational-basis review, see Trump v. Hawaii, 138 S. Ct. at 2402, and Adam Cox et al., "The Radical Supreme Court Travel Ban Opinion—But Why It Might Not Apply to Other Immigrants' Rights Cases," *Just Security*, June 27, 2018, https://perma.cc/EP5P-ALXV (describing the Court's unrealistically high standard). For the freedom-of-religion case, see Masterpiece Cakeshop, Ltd. v. Colorado Civil Rights Comm'n, 138 S. Ct. 1719 (2018) (invalidating under the First Amendment's free-exercise clause a Colorado commission's actions against a baker who refused to serve gay couples).

22. Trump v. Hawaii, 138 S. Ct. at 2408; National Security Officials' Amicus Brief, *supra* note 16, at 24 ("In their long collective experience, [the 52 amici] know of no case where a President has invoked authority under [8 U.S.C. § 1182(f)] to suspend admission of such a sweeping class of people.").

23. Trump v. Hawaii, 138 S. Ct. at 2408 (observing that the travel ban set forth "extensive findings" that supported the president's determination that "it was in the national interest to restrict entry of [designated] aliens . . . both to protect national security and public safety"); *id*. at 2448 (Sotomayor, J., dissenting).

24. *Id*. at 2423 (majority opinion); *Korematsu*, 323 U.S. 214.

25. *See* Trump v. Hawaii, 138 S. Ct. at 2417 (despite the record of Trump's tweets announcing that his intent was to target Muslims, accepting the government's contention that the intent of the ban was to address national security issues that Trump had been talking about "for years now, from the campaign trail to the White House" (internal quotations omitted)); Charlie Savage, "*Korematsu*, Notorious Supreme Court Ruling on Japanese Internment, Is Finally Tossed Out," *N.Y. Times*, June 26, 2018, www.nytimes.com/2018/06/26/us/korematsu-supreme-court-ruling.html. *Compare* Regina Jefferies, "Tragedy of Errors: The Solicitor General, the Supreme Court and the Truth," *Just Security*, May 23, 2018, https://perma.

cc/8CX8-ERYL, *with* Office of the Solicitor General, "Confession of Error: The Solicitor General's Mistakes During the Japanese-American Internment Cases," May 20, 2011, https://perma.cc/X9FL-54GM.

26. Trump v. Hawaii, 138 S. Ct. at 2433 (Sotomayor, J., dissenting); Luke Harding, "'It had a big impact on me'—Story Behind Trump's Whirlwind Missile Response," *Guardian,* Apr. 7, 2017, https://perma.cc/8P2Q-X2M6 (quoting President Trump as saying, "I will tell you that attack on children yesterday had a big impact on me—big impact . . . My attitude toward Syria and Assad has changed very much").

27. *See generally* Dara Lind, "We Should Give Up on the Fantasy of Solving the Border Crisis," *N.Y. Times,* Mar. 14, 2023, www.nytimes.com/2023/03/14/opinion/immigration-border-crisis-asylum.html.

28. *See generally* Harold Hongju Koh, *The Trump Administration and International Law* 54–61 (2019).

29. *See generally* Harold Hongju Koh, "Congressional Controls on Presidential Trade Policymaking After *INS v. Chadha,*" 18 *N.Y.U. J. Int'l. L. & Pol.* 1191–1234 (1986).

30. *See generally* Harold Hongju Koh, "Trump Change: Unilateralism and the 'Disruption Myth' in International Trade," 44 *Yale J. Int'l L. Online* 98 (2019), https://perma.cc/R84L-CA5V.

31. *See* Koh, *supra* note 28, at 59–60.

32. *See generally* Koh, *supra* note 30, at 98.

33. *See* Robert Farley, "Trump Wrong About WTO Record," *Factcheck.org,* Oct. 27, 2017, https://perma.cc/Z349-WB8M.

34. *See* Gregory Shaffer, "A Tragedy in the Making? The Decline of Law and the Return of Power in International Trade Relations," 44 *Yale J. Int'l L. Online* 39 (2019), www.yjil.yale.edu/features-symposium-international-trade-in-the-trump-era/.

35. Koh, *supra* note 30, at 101–02.

36. Paul Krugman, "Bumbling into a Trade War," *N.Y. Times,* Mar. 22, 2018, www.nytimes.com/2018/03/22/opinion/trade-war-china-trump.html.

37. Trump reportedly signaled his desire to withdraw from the United States–Korea Free Trade Agreement (KORUS), NAFTA, the WTO, and NATO. *See* Bob Woodward, *Fear: Trump in the White House* 135 (2018) ("Just do it. Just do it. Get out of NAFTA. Get out of KORUS. And get out of the WTO. We're withdrawing from all three." (quoting President Trump)).

38. Koh, *supra* note 30, at 99–100.

39. Trump withdrew from, among other global arrangements, the Paris climate agreement; the Joint Comprehensive Plan of Action (the Iran nuclear deal); the United Nations Educational, Scientific, and Cultural Organization (UNESCO); the Global Compact for Safe, Orderly, and Regular Migration; the United Nations Human Rights Council; the Trans-Pacific Partnership; the Treaty of Amity, Economic Relations, and Consular Rights with Iran (1955); the Optional Protocol Concerning the Compulsory Settlement of Disputes (to the Vienna Convention on Diplomatic Relations); the Universal Postal Union Treaty; the Open Skies Treaty; and the Intermediate-Range Nuclear Forces Treaty. As previously noted (*see supra* note 37), Trump also began withdrawal from WHO and threatened to withdraw from NAFTA, KORUS, the WTO, and NATO.

40. "Agreement" is used here as an umbrella term used by U.S. law to describe Article II treaties, congressional-executive agreements, sole executive agreements, and other agreements made by the United States. Nearly all of these function as "treaties" that create binding obligations under international law, subject to the Vienna Convention on the Law of Treaties. "Withdrawal," "suspension," "abrogation," and "termination" are related but not identical concepts. When one or two partners lawfully terminate or abrogate a bilateral agreement, it is dead. But when one partner lawfully withdraws from, or abrogates its legal duties to comply with, a multilateral treaty, the agreement continues, minus that partner. When one partner says that it is "suspending" its commitment to a bilateral or multilateral agreement, it is not saying that it is leaving, just not fulfilling its agreement duties for now, with the consequence that it could later be held in breach or resume fulfillment of its international obligations. *See generally* Harold Hongju Koh, "Presidential Power to Terminate International Agreements," 128 *Yale L.J. F.* 432, 432–33 (2018), https://perma.cc/85LD-5S9F.

41. Goldwater v. Carter, 444 U.S. 996 (1979) (per curiam). The justices splintered around several rationales, with only one justice reaching the merits. Four justices—Chief Justice Burger and Justices Rehnquist, Stewart, and Stevens—found that the case raised a political question. Justice Powell agreed that the case should be dismissed, but because it was not ripe and it remained unknown "whether there ever will be an actual confrontation between the Legislative and Executive branches" constituting a "constitutional impasse." *Id.* at 998 (Powell, J., concurring). Justice Brennan voted on the merits to uphold the president's power to terminate the Taiwan treaty given the peculiar fact that the case involved derecognition of a foreign government, an issue over which, he argued, the president exercises textual plenary constitutional power. Justice Marshall simply concurred in the dismissal without explaining why. Only Justices Blackmun and White dissented, voting that the Court should set the case for oral argument.

42. *Id.* at 1006–07 (Brennan, J., dissenting).

43. *Id.* at 1003 (Rehnquist, J., joined by Burger, C.J., and Stewart and Stevens, JJ., concurring in the judgment).

44. *Restatement (Fourth) of the Foreign Relations Law of the United States* § 313 & cmt. (2018) [hereinafter *Restatement (Fourth)*] ("According to established practice, *the President has the authority to act on behalf of the United States in suspending or terminating U.S. treaty commitments and in withdrawing the United States from treaties* either on the basis of terms in the treaty allowing for such action (such as a withdrawal clause) or on the basis of international law that would justify such action. (emphasis added)); Curtis A. Bradley, "Exiting Congressional-Executive Agreements," 67 *Duke L.J.* 1625, 1644 (2018). For a critique of this *Fourth Restatement* provision and suggested substitute, see Harold Hongju Koh, "Could the President Unilaterally Terminate All International Agreements?: Questioning Section 313 in *The Restatement and Beyond: The Past, Present, and Future of U.S. Foreign Relations Law* 67 (Paul B. Stephan & Sarah H. Cleveland eds., 2020).

45. *See* Curtis Bradley, "Treaty Termination and Historical Gloss," 92 *Tex. L. Rev.* 77 773 (2014); Louis Henkin, *Foreign Affairs and the U.S. Constitution* 214 (2d ed. 1996).

46. *Restatement (Fourth), supra* note 44, § 313 cmt. d, at 128.

47. *Id.* at § 313, reporters' note 6, at 135.

48. Youngstown Sheet & Tube Co. v. Sawyer, 343 U.S. 579, 610 (1952) (Frankfurter, J., concurring) (emphasis added).

49. *Restatement (Fourth), supra* note 44, § 313 reporters' note 3. As the reporter of the *Restatement (Third)*, Louis Henkin, put it, "[c]ontroversy as to who has authority to terminate treaties has been infrequent, if only because the United States has not often been disposed to terminate treaties." Henkin, *supra* note 45, at 213.

50. *Compare* Brief for the United States in Opposition to Certiorari at 28, Goldwater, 444 U.S. 996 (No. 79-856), *with* Petition for Writ of Certiorari at 38 n.20, Goldwater, 444 U.S. 996 (No. 79-856). In December 1979, Judge MacKinnon argued that there had only been two genuinely unilateral terminations up to that point. *See* Goldwater v. Carter, 617 F.2d 697, 734 (D.C. Cir. 1979) (MacKinnon, J., dissenting in part and concurring in part).

51. *See* Koh, *supra* note 40, at 448–49.

52. *Id.* at 450.

53. *Id.* at 459–60.

54. *Id.* at 452–67 (citing comparative constitutional practice, including from the United Kingdom, in support of a "mirror principle" for exiting agreements).

55. Brief of the United States as Amicus Curiae Supporting Reversal at 1, Jam v. Int'l Fin. Corp., 139 S. Ct. 759 (2019) (No. 17-1011), https://perma.cc/9ENZ-GLGM ("The United States participates in or supports nearly 200 international organizations and other multilateral entities, including major international financial institutions such as the International Monetary Fund (IMF) and the World Bank. The United States contributes billions of dollars annually to those organizations and entities. In recognition of the United States' leadership role, nearly 20 international organizations are headquartered in the United States, and many others have offices here.").

56. Jean Galbraith, "Rejoining Treaties," 106 *Va. L. Rev.* 73 (2020) (arguing that if a president withdraws from a treaty, a future president can rejoin that treaty without needing to return to the Senate for advice and consent).

57. *Goldwater*, 617 F.2d at 739 (MacKinnon, J., dissenting in part and concurring in part) (emphasis omitted).

58. *See, e.g.,* Kucinich v. Bush, 236 F. Supp. 2d 1 (D.D.C. 2002) (dismissing a challenge by thirty-two congressmen to President George W. Bush's decision to withdraw from the Anti-Ballistic Missile Treaty with Russia, on the ground that the challenge raised a nonjusticiable political question); Beacon Products Corp. v. Reagan, 633 F. Supp. 1191, 1199 (D. Mass. 1986), *aff'd on other grounds,* 814 F.2d 1 (1st Cir. 1987) (holding with regard to President Ronald Reagan's unilateral termination of the Treaty of Friendship, Commerce, and Navigation with Nicaragua that a "[constitutional] challenge to the President's power vis-a-vis treaty termination raise[s] a nonjusticiable political question").

59. Zivotofsky v. Clinton (*Zivotofsky I*), 566 U.S. 189, 194–95 (2012) (quoting Baker v. Carr, 369 U.S. 186, 217 (1962)). Section 214 of the Foreign Relations Authorization Act, enacted in 2002, allowed passports issued by the U.S. State Department to list

"Jerusalem" or "Jerusalem, Israel" as the place of birth. The parents of a boy born in Jerusalem sued Secretary of State Hillary Clinton, invoking § 214 to challenge the State Department's long-held policy that no country holds sovereignty over Jerusalem. The D.C. Circuit held that the case presented a nonjusticiable political question, but the Supreme Court disagreed and remanded. *Zivotofsky I,* 566 U.S. at 201–02. The D.C. Circuit then held on the merits that the statute was unconstitutional, and in *Zivotofsky v. Kerry (Zivotofsky II),* 576 U.S. 1 (2015), the Supreme Court affirmed.

60. *Goldwater,* 444 U.S. at 1000 (Powell, J., concurring).
61. In 2018, two members of Congress introduced the No NATO Withdrawal Act, H.R. 6530, 115th Cong., § 3 (2018), which states: "It is the sense of Congress that (1) the President shall not unilaterally withdraw the United States from NATO; and (2) the case Goldwater v. Carter is not controlling legal precedent with respect to the unilateral withdrawal of the United States from a treaty." Just days later, a bipartisan group of six senators introduced the Defending American Security from Kremlin Aggression Act of 2018, S. 3336, 115th Cong. (2018), which, among other things, would require a two-thirds vote of the Senate to leave NATO. *See also* Karoun Demirjian, "Bipartisan Bill Would Prevent Trump from Exiting NATO Without Senate Consent," *Wash. Post,* July 26, 2018, www.washingtonpost.com/powerpost/bipartisan-bill-would-prevent-trump-from-exiting-nato-without-senate-consent/2018/07/26/4ca1b206-9106-11e8-bcd5-9d911c784c38_story.html.
62. *Goldwater,* 444 U.S. at 997 (Powell, J., concurring).
63. *Id.* at 1003 (Rehnquist, J., joined by Burger, C.J., and Stewart and Stevens, JJ., concurring in the judgment).
64. Special Counsel Robert S. Mueller III, *Report on the Investigation into Russian Interference in the 2016 Presidential Election* (2019) (two volumes), https://perma.cc C5Q3-9NVH (vol. 1); https://perma.cc/F254-N79U (vol. 2); *see also* "Trump Responds to Mueller Report: 'Complete and Total Exoneration,'" Reuters, Mar. 24 2019, https://perma.cc/8TK7-2BHM; Interview by George Stephanopoulos of ABC News with President Trump (June 16, 2019), https://perma.cc/J2NX-7CD3 (stating in response to hypothetical question whether he would look at oppositional research provided by Russia or China without alerting the FBI, "I think you might want t listen . . . there's nothing wrong with listening. . . . I think I'd take it.").
65. H.R. Res. 755, 116th Cong. (2019) (articles of impeachment); *see* Amanda Seitz et al., "As Trial Nears, Trump Keeps Discredited Ukraine Theory Alive," *AP,* Jan. 1: 2020, https://apnews.com/article/us-news-ap-top-news-elections-internationa news-donald-trump-893415ed7acb069604566149630abdb8.
66. "Full Transcript: Mueller Testimony Before House Judiciary, Intelligence Committees," *NBC News,* July 25, 2019, https://perma.cc/RS8R-C9LM (statement of Special Counsel Mueller) ("The [Russians are] doing it as we sit here, and they expe to do it during the next campaign."); National Intelligence Council, *Foreign Threa to the 2020 U.S. Federal Elections* (Mar. 10, 2021), https://perma.cc/M7KU-KDML
67. *See* Peter Baker, "Trump Is Depicted as a Would-Be Autocrat Seeking to Hang on Power at All Costs," *N.Y. Times,* June 9, 2022, www.nytimes.com/2022/06/0 us/politics/trump-jan-6-hearing.html. *See generally* Susan B. Glasser & Pet

Baker, "Inside the War Between Trump and His Generals," *New Yorker,* Aug. 8, 2022, https://perma.cc/9TPR-LMWQ ("At the end of the administration . . . [t]he Chair of the Joint Chiefs had two great fears: One was that Trump might spark an external crisis, such as a war with Iran, to divert attention or to create a pretext for a power grab at home. The other was that Trump would manufacture a domestic crisis to justify ordering the military into the streets to prevent the transfer of power."); *id.* ("Trump kept asking for alternatives, including an attack inside Iran on its ballistic-weapons sites. Milley explained that this would be an illegal preemptive act: 'If we do what you're saying,' [Milley] said, 'we are all going to be tried as war criminals in The Hague.'").

68. Ashton Carter et al., Opinion, "All 10 Living Former Defense Secretaries: Involving the Military in Election Disputes Would Cross into Dangerous Territory," *Wash. Post,* Jan. 3, 2021, https://perma.cc/6D3D-BJ2H; H.R. Res. 24, 117th Cong. (2021) (article of impeachment); Donald J. Trump (@realDonaldTrump), TruthSocial (Dec. 3, 2022, 7:44 AM); *see also* Kristen Holmes, "Trump Calls for the Termination of the Constitution in Truth Social Post," *CNN Politics,* Dec. 4, 2022, https://perma.cc/XU96-55WG (emphasis added).

69. H.R. Res. 755, 116th Cong. (2019).

70. As Congressman Adam Schiff put it in his closing statement during Trump's first impeachment: "He has betrayed our national security, and he will do so again. . . . You cannot constrain him. He is who he is." Dareh Gregorian, "Schiff's Powerful Closing Speech: 'Is There One Among You Who Will Say, Enough!'?," *NBC News,* Feb. 3, 2020, https://perma.cc/2TB7-CR53.

Chapter 9. Biden

1. Chris Megerian, "Few Laughs, Tough Questions as Biden Chats with Kimmel," *AP News,* June 9, 2022, https://perma.cc/3W7K-VCBE (quoting statement by President Biden while he was in Los Angeles for the Summit of the Americas).

2. On the length of Biden's Senate service, see www.senate.gov/senators/longest_serving_senators.htm.

3. Jonathan Martin & Carl Hulse, "Democrats Have Their Doubts About Biden's Bipartisan Bonhomie," *N.Y. Times,* Aug. 20, 2020, www.nytimes.com/2020/08/20/us/politics/biden-congress.html.

4. These observations derive from my personal service on the Biden foreign-policy and national security transition team and service as senior adviser, the only political appointee, in the Office of the Legal Adviser at the State Department, from inauguration to October 2021.

5. *See generally* Chris Whipple, *The Fight of His Life: Inside Joe Biden's White House,* 60–76 (2023); Apoorva Mandavilli, "'We Were Helpless': Despair at the C.D.C. as the Pandemic Erupted," *N.Y. Times,* Mar. 21, 2023, www.nytimes.com/2023/03/21/health/covid-cdc.html; David Leonhardt, "A Conversation with Joe Biden," *N.Y. Times,* Dec. 24, 2020, www.nytimes.com/2020/12/24/briefing/stella-tennant-the-midnight-sky-rebecca-luker.html.

6. Remarks by President Biden at the Dedication of the Dodd Center for Human Rights (Oct. 15, 2021), https://perma.cc/6NPY-6PA5.

7. Daniel Bodansky & Peter J. Spiro, "Executive Agreements+," 49 *Vand. J. Transnat'l L.* 885 (2016).

8. Mike Berardino, "Mike Tyson Explains One of His Most Famous Quotes," *So. Fla. Sun Sentinel,* Nov. 9, 2012, https://perma.cc/7W2A-2YJM.

9. "The Guantánamo Docket," *N.Y. Times,* updated Mar. 8, 2023, www.nytimes.com/interactive/2021/us/guantanamo-bay-detainees.html.

10. Remarks by President Biden, *supra* note 6.

11. Harold Hongju Koh, "The 2001 Richard Childress Memorial Lecture: A United States Human Rights Policy for the 21st Century," 46 *St. Louis U. L.J.* 293 (2002); Associated Press, "Blinken Ends Trump Admin's Human Rights Plan to Promote Conservative Agenda Abroad," Mar. 30, 2021, https://perma.cc/D8XB-NCAC; Statement by President Joe Biden on Armenian Remembrance Day, Apr. 24, 2021, https://perma.cc/2ML7-MA3H (honoring "all those Armenians who perished in the genocide that began 106 years ago today").

12. Press Statement, Antony J. Blinken, Sec'y of State, U.N. Office of the High Commissioner for Human Rights Report on the Human Rights Situation in Xinjiang (Sept. 1, 2022), https://perma.cc/QUG3-B2HS; Matthew Lee, "US: War Crimes on All sides in Ethiopia's Tigray Conflict," *AP News,* Mar. 20, 2023, https://perma.cc/5MCB-SL9Z; Jaclyn Diaz, "The U.S. Says Russian Actions in Ukraine Are 'Crimes Against Humanity,'" *NPR,* Feb. 18, 2023, https://perma.cc/6G3C-WV7S.

13. *See generally* Harold Hongju Koh, "International Criminal Justice 5.0," 38 *Yale J. Int'l L.* 515 (2013).

14. Developments in the Biden administration's relationship with the International Criminal Court are discussed in Adam Keith, "Is the Pentagon Relenting? A Close Study of Opposition to the Int'l Criminal Court's Ukraine Investigation," *Just Security,* July 26, 2023, www.justsecurity.org/87231/is-pentagon-opposition-to-the-international-criminal-courts-ukraine-investigation-relenting/, and Beth Van Schaack, Remarks to the Cardozo Law School on Sexual and Gender Based Crimes in the Case of *Prosecutor v. Dominic Ongwen* (Apr. 21, 2023), www.state.gov/ambassador-at-large-beth-van-schaacks-remarks-to-the-cardozo-law-school.

15. Charlie Savage, "Biden Orders U.S. to Share Evidence of Russian War Crimes with Hague Court," *N.Y. Times,* July 26, 2023, www.nytimes.com/2023/07/26/us politics/biden-russia-war-crimes-hague.html.

16. *Id.*

17. Immanuel Kant, *Toward Perpetual Peace: A Philosophical Essay* (1795) (calling for a "federation of free states" in accordance with the idea of "the law of nations"); George Orwell, *1984* (1949). For the strategy of Trump and other authoritarians, see Harold Hongju Koh, *The Trump Administration and International Law* 142–47 (2019).

18. Amy Mackinnon, "Defining the Biden Doctrine," *Foreign Pol'y,* Jan. 18, 2022 https://perma.cc/LLL7-7KAN (interview with Jake Sullivan, national security adviser) (We want to "mak[e] sure that it is democracies who are writing the rules of the road for trade and technology going forward, so that the technologies that will shape our future are more rights-respecting and less subject to authoritarian con

trol and domination. It's a comprehensive agenda, and you saw every element of it at play in the Summit for Democracy, which brought together more than 100 governments, as well as private sector leaders, civil society, activists.").

19. Antony Blinken, The Administration's Approach to the People's Republic of China, Speech at the George Washington University (May 26, 2022), https://perma.cc/2V78-CZWN.

20. *See* Harold Hongju Koh, "Triptych's End: A Better Framework to Evaluate 21st Century International Lawmaking," 126 *Yale L.J. F.* 338, 339–41 (2017), www.yalelawjournal.com/forum/triptych's-end; *see generally* Brianna Rosen, "Ending Perpetual War," *Just Security*, Oct. 25, 2022, https://perma.cc/D4BC-8RV4.

21. Michael J. Glennon, *National Security and Double Government* 7 (2015).

22. *The Budget, Diplomacy, and Development, Hearing Before the H. Comm. on Foreign Affairs*, 115th Cong. 32 (2017) (statement of William J. Burns), https://perma.cc/LR94-D97R.

23. Remarks by President Biden Before the 76th Session of the United Nations General Assembly (Sept. 21, 2021), https://perma.cc/DH3K-JN29.

24. WHO Coronavirus (Covid-19) Dashboard, accessed Mar. 25, 2023, https://perma.cc/4SN9-Z2NJ; "History of 1918 Flu Pandemic," CDC, Mar. 21, 2018, https://perma.cc/VX8V-KCFX (the United States lost about 675,000 people to the Spanish flu).

25. *See* Antony Blinken & Xavier Becerra, "Strengthening Global Health Security and Reforming the International Health Regulations: Making the World Safer from Future Pandemics," 326 *JAMA* 1255 (2021).

26. Whipple, *supra* note 5, at 165–75; *see generally* Helen Mountford et al., "COP26: Key Outcomes from the UN Climate Talks in Glasgow," World Resources Inst., Nov. 17, 2021, https://perma.cc/GTW6-BDVU.

27. *See* Emily Cochrane et al., "Manchin, in Reversal, Agrees to Quick Action on Climate and Tax Plan," *N.Y. Times*, July 31, 2022, www.nytimes.com/2022/07/27/us/politics/manchin-climate-tax-bill.html.

28. *See generally* Stephen Biddle, "Afghanistan and the Future of Warfare," *Foreign Aff.*, Mar.–Apr. 2003, at 31; Ann Devroy & Dana Priest, "Clinton Aides Debate Size of U.S. Peacekeeping Force for Bosnia," *Wash. Post.*, Sept. 21, 1995, at A24; Carlotta Gall, "Threats and Responses: Karzai's Progress," *N.Y. Times*, Dec. 25, 2002, at A1; Dexter Filkins, "The Anxiety of Postwar Afghans," *N.Y. Times*, Mar. 31, 2002, at D5; Carlotta Gall, "Afghan Leader Swears in 5 Deputies With an Eye to Balance," *N.Y. Times*, June 28, 2002, at A6 (explaining Hamid Karzai's attempts to negotiate a political alliance with powerful regional-ethnic warlords and Rashid Dostum's ongoing resistance to a centralized Afghan state); Press Release, Human Rights Watch, Anti-Pashtun Violence Widespread in Afghanistan (Mar. 3, 2002), https://perma.cc/LWX2-78HB. For an account of competing hegemonic influences in postwar Afghanistan, see Michael Ignatieff, "Nation-Building Lite," *N.Y. Times*, July 28, 2002, at F26, and Paul Krugman, "The Martial Plan," *N.Y. Times*, Feb. 21, 2003, at A27.

29. Whipple, *supra* note 5, at 77–101.

30. *Id.* at 102–10 (citing statistics); *see* Joe Biden, *Promises to Keep: On Life and Politics* 317 (2007) (When told by a 13-year-old Afghan girl, "America can't go," Biden told her "No. No. No, honey. America is going to stay.").

31. The Roberts Court ultimately accepted the Biden administration's effort to repeal Trump's "remain in Mexico" policy. *See* Biden v. Texas, 142 S. Ct. 2528 (2022).

32. Whipple, *supra* note 5, at 125–36, 258. The Title 42 policy was established under 42 U.S.C. § 265 in March 2020. *See* Control of Communicable Diseases; Foreign Quarantine: Suspension of Introduction of Persons into United States from Designated Foreign Countries or Places for Public Health Purposes, 85 Fed. Reg. 16,559, 16,563 (Mar. 24, 2020). On April 1, 2022, the CDC terminated the policy, effective May 23, 2022, explaining that because of the end of the pandemic emergency, "the extraordinary measure of an order under 42 U.S.C. 265 is no longer necessary," and that as a result, the agency lacked statutory authority to continue the policy. 87 Fed. Reg. 19941, 19944, 19954–55 (Apr. 6, 2022).

33. Huisha-Huisha v. Mayorkas, 27 F.4th 718, 733–34 (D.C. Cir. 2022).

34. *See* 8 U.S.C. § 1231(b)(3)(A). Article 3 of the Convention Against Torture categorically prohibits state parties from expelling, returning, or extraditing any person, *without exception*, to any state where there are "substantial grounds for believing that he would be in danger of being subjected to torture." Article 33 of the Refugee Convention, subject to certain narrow exceptions, flatly prohibits state parties from expelling or returning ("refouler") "a refugee *in any manner whatsoever* to the frontiers of territories where his life or freedom would be threatened" on one of the designated grounds (emphasis added).

35. Annika Kim Constantino, "Biden Condemns Border Patrol Agents' Treatment of Haitian Migrants, Vows They Will Face Consequences," *CNBC*, Sept. 24, 2021, https://perma.cc/D8HU-ZRZE.

36. Harold Hongju Koh, "Ending Title 42 Return Flights to Countries of Origin, Particularly Haiti," *Politico*, Oct. 2, 2021, https://perma.cc/W7U8-L5FB; *see also* Jaya Ramji-Nogales, "How an Internal State Department Memo Exposes 'Title 42' Expulsions of Refugees as Violations of Law," *Just Security*, Oct. 5, 2021, https://perma.cc/6MJV-732B (noting that Koh memo paralleled a similar letter signed by Senator Kamala Harris); Alexander Ward & Quint Forgey, "Departing State Lawyer: Biden's Title 42 Use 'Illegal' and 'Inhumane,'" *Politico Nat'l Security Daily*, Oct. 4, 2021, https://perma.cc/CJ9Z-KGQW.

37. *See, e.g., Huisha-Huisha*, 27 F.4th at 735 (finding plaintiffs likely to succeed on the merits of their statutory claim that the executive cannot expel them to places where they face persecution or torture); Huisha-Huisha v. Mayorkas, No. 1:21-cv-00100 (D.D.C. Nov. 15, 2022), https://perma.cc/BW2R-KTWN (granting partial summary judgment against Title 42 policy as arbitrary and capricious and permanently enjoining the U.S. government from applying it to plaintiff class members). *But see* Louisiana v. CDC, No. 22-cv-885, 2022 WL 1604901 (W.D. La. May 20, 2022) (enjoining CDC's nationwide termination of Title 42 on the ground that the order was issued without sufficient notice and comment). Adam Liptak, "Supreme Court Cancels Arguments in Title 42 Immigration Case," *N.Y. Times*, Feb. 16, 2023, www.nytimes.com/2023/02/16/us/politics/supreme-court-title-42-immigration.html.

38. Liptak, *supra* note 37; Press Release, Dep't of Homeland Security, DHS Continues to Prepare for End of Title 42; Announces New Border Enforcement Measures

and Additional Safe and Orderly Processes (Jan. 5, 2023), https://perma.cc/N2X7-6G64.

39. Harold Hongju Koh, "The 'Haiti Paradigm' in United States Human Rights Policy," 103 *Yale L.J.* 2391 (1994).

40. *See* Suggestion of Immunity by the United States, Cengiz v. Muhammed bin Salman, No. 1:20-cv-3009 (D.D.C. Nov. 17, 2022), ECF No. 53-1, https://perma.cc/G3JC-CRYH (recognizing head-of-state immunity "[u]nder common law principles of immunity articulated by the Executive Branch in the exercise of its Constitutional authority over foreign affairs and informed by customary international law"); Stephanie Kirchgasessner, "Biden Administration 'Dragged Feet' on Mohammed bin Salman Immunity Ruling," *Guardian,* Nov. 23, 2022, https://perma.cc/A69C-UUDQ; Harold Hongju Koh, "Foreign Official Immunity After *Samantar:* A United States Perspective," 44 *Vand. L. Rev.* 1141, 1159–61 (2021) (discussing precedents that allow the United States to use the "sound of silence" in immunity cases to advance its foreign-policy goals).

41. *See generally* Whipple, *supra* note 5, at 229–44, 263–83.

42. *See* International Trade Administration, Russia—Country Commercial Guide: Sanctions Framework, July 21, 2022, https://perma.cc/4F3Y-FWE4 (listing sanctions imposed).

43. *Compare* Laurence Tribe & Jeremy Lewin, Opinion, "$100 Billion. Russia's Treasure in the US Should Be Turned Against Putin," *N.Y. Times,* Apr. 15, 2022, www.nytimes.com/2022/04/15/opinion/russia-war-currency-reserves.html, *with* Paul Stephan, "Giving Russian Assets to Ukraine—Freezing Is Not Seizing," *Lawfare,* Apr. 26, 2022, https://perma.cc/A7SM-WU96. *Compare* IEEPA, 50 U.S.C. § 1702 (a)(1)(B), *with* TWEA, 50 U.S.C. § 4301 *et seq.* (authorizing seizure and vesting of enemy assets).

44. *See* Jill Goldenziel, "An Alternative to Zombieing: Lawfare Between Russia and Ukraine and the Future of International Law," 108 *Cornell L. Rev. Online* 1 (2023), https://perma.cc/93FR-MZP4. I have served as counsel for Ukraine since 2016 in two International Court of Justice cases and one law of the sea case before the Permanent Court of Arbitration.

45. *See generally* Harold Hongju Koh, "International Law in the Russia-Ukraine War," 84 *Ohio St. L.J.* — (2024).

46. Bel Trew, "100,000 Ukrainian Civilian Deaths: Shocking Toll of Putin's Bloody Invasion," *Independent,* Feb. 23, 2023, https://perma.cc/X48H-DCRJ; U.N. General Assembly, Furtherance of Remedy and Reparation for Aggression Against Ukraine, A/ES-11/L.6, Nov. 7, 2022, https://perma.cc/4XYA-XURV; Press Release, United Nations, General Assembly Adopts Text Recommending Creation of Register to Document Damages Caused by Russian Federation Aggression Against Ukraine, Resuming Emergency Special Session (Nov. 14, 2022), https://perma.cc/P7LK-5M78; Chiara Giorgetti et al., "Historic UNGA resolution Calls for Ukraine Reparations," *Just Security,* Nov. 16, 2022, https://perma.cc/M9BW-EWVA.

47. Eric Lutz, "Ron DeSantis Calls Russia's War in Ukraine a 'Territorial Dispute,'" *Vanity Fair,* Mar. 14, 2023, www.vanityfair.com/news/2023/03/ron-desantis-donald-trump-ukraine-aid (reporting that as the two top Republican presidential

contenders cast doubt on support for Ukraine, polls have shown more and more Republican voters tiring of U.S. aid for the country under siege by Vladimir Putin).

48. *See generally* Rosen, *supra* note 20.

49. Karoun Demirjian, "Decades Later, Senate Votes to Repeal Iraq Military Authorization," *N.Y. Times*, Mar. 29, 2023, www.nytimes.com/2023/03/29/us/politics/congress-iraq-war-powers-authorization.html.

50. *See generally* Harold Hongju Koh, "Presidential Power to Terminate International Agreements," 128 *Yale L.J. F.* 432 (2018), https://perma.cc/85LD-5S9F; Mica Rosenberg and Nandita Bose, "Biden to Build More U.S. Border Wall Using Trump-Era Funds," *Reuters*, October 6, 2023.

51. Jim Cooper, "Fixing Congress," *Bos. Rev.*, June 26, 2012, https://perma.cc/B6PW-ZNXA. Biden's first two years witnessed only a few pieces of foreign-policy legislation: the climate-change bill, enacted along party lines and based on negotiations between Senate majority leader Chuck Schumer and Democratic holdout Joe Manchin, H.R. 5376, 117th Cong. (2022), the bipartisan China competitiveness bill, H.R. 4346, 117th Cong. (2022), and the NATO expansion resolution, S. Res. 646, 117th Cong. (2022).

52. Cooper, *supra* note 51; *see also* John Bresnahan, "The Demise of One of the Best Gigs in Congress," *Politico*, Jan. 30, 2018, https://perma.cc/9EXU-VUCH; Juliet Eilperin, *Fight-Club Politics: How Partisanship Is Poisoning the U.S. House of Representatives* 32 (2007).

53. Cooper, *supra* note 51.

54. Alexander Ward et al., "The Natsec Implications of the Speaker Fight," *Politico Nat'l Security Daily*, Jan. 5, 2023, https://perma.cc/6AWX-AV5V.

55. Ronald Brownstein, "Why the Senate Doesn't Work Anymore," *CNN*, Oct. 5, 2021, https://perma.cc/4FX5-LZQZ (quoting Thomas E. Mann). Recall, for instance, the roles of "swing" Democratic senators Joe Manchin and Kyrsten Sinema in paring back Biden's 2022 climate and tax legislation. *See* Cochrane, *supra* note 27.

56. *See* Koh, *supra* note 20, at 340 ("Under the political deadlock between the President and Congress during the Obama Administration, the number of Senators needed to block consideration of [an agreement or nomination] has declined over time from fifty-one (a majority of the Senators), to forty-one (the number needed to sustain a filibuster), to ten (the number usually needed to prevent [the agreement or nomination] from being voted out of the relevant committee), to one (a single Senator or staffer preventing an otherwise uncontroversial [nomination or agreement] from getting unanimous consent).").

57. *See* Rasul v. Bush, 542 U.S. 466 (2004); Hamdi v. Rumsfeld, 542 U.S. 507 (2004); Hamdan v. Rumsfeld, 548 U.S. 557 (2006); Boumediene v. Bush, 553 U.S. 723 (2008). *See generally* Martin S. Flaherty, *Restoring the Global Judiciary: Why the Supreme Court Should Rule in U.S. Foreign Affairs* 204–19 (2019) (arguing that *Hamdi, Hamdan, Rasul,* and *Boumediene* should have been read together to reduce judicial deference to government national security arguments).

58. Bond v. United States, 564 U.S. 211 (2011); Zivotofsky v. Clinton (*Zivotofsky I*), 566 U.S. 189 (2012); *see, e.g.,* Ganesh Sitaraman & Ingrid (Wuerth) Brunk, "The Normalization of Foreign Relations Law," 128 *Harv. L. Rev.* 1897, 1903 (2015) ("In

Zivotofsky v. Clinton and *Bond v. United States* (*Bond I*) . . . the Court rejected the exceptionalist approach and declared the issues in those cases as suitable for adjudication.").

59. *See generally* Curtis Bradley & Eric A. Posner, "The Real Political Question Doctrine," 75 *Stan. L. Rev.* 1031 (2023) (arguing that lower courts have nonetheless continued to apply the political-question doctrine). *See, e.g.,* El-Shifa Pharm. Indus. Co. v. United States, 378 F.3d 1346 (Fed. Cir. 2004) (invoking political-question doctrine to dismiss a takings suit arising out of the destruction of a Sudanese pharmaceutical plant because it had been erroneously identified as "enemy property"), *cert. denied,* 545 U.S. 1139 (2005); *see also* Stephen I. Vladeck, "The New National Security Canon," 61 *Am. U. L. Rev.* 1295 (2012); Janko v. Gates, 741 F.3d 136 (D.C. Cir. 2014), *cert. denied,* 575 U.S. 902 (2015). For examples of the dispositions mentioned in the text, see Carmichael v. Kellogg, Brown & Root Servs., Inc., 572 F.3d 1271 (11th Cir. 2009), *cert. denied,* 561 U.S. 1025 (2010); Harris v. Kellogg Brown & Root Servs., Inc., 724 F.3d 458 (3d Cir. 2013), *cert. denied,* 574 U.S. 1120 (2015); Taylor v. Kellogg Brown & Root Servs., Inc., 658 F.3d 402 (4th Cir. 2011); Lane v. Halliburton, 529 F.3d 548 (5th Cir. 2008); *In re* Assicurazioni Generali, 592 F.3d 113 (2d Cir. 2010), *cert. denied,* 562 U.S. 952 (2010); and United States v. Husayn (Zubaydah), 142 S. Ct. 959 (2022) (plurality opinion ruling that the state-secrets privilege required dismissal of the plaintiff's claim).

60. *See* Zivotofsky v. Kerry (*Zivotofsky II*), 576 U.S. 1 (2015). *See* Note, "Nondelegation's Unprincipled Foreign Affairs Exceptionalism," 134 *Harv. L. Rev.* 1132 (2021). The five justices who support the broad theory of statutory delegation are Chief Justice Roberts and Justices Thomas, Alito, Gorsuch, and Kavanaugh. *See* Gundy v. United States, 139 S. Ct. 2116, 2135–37 (2019) (Gorsuch, J., dissenting); *id.* at 2130–31 (Alito, J., concurring in the judgment); Paul v. United States, 140 S. Ct. 342, 342 (2019) (Kavanaugh, J., respecting the denial of certiorari); Dep't of Transp. v. Ass'n of Am. R.Rs., 575 U.S. 43, 80 & n.5 (2015) (Thomas, J., concurring in the judgment). Yet in the domestic realm, ironically, the same justices, led by Justice Gorsuch in *Gundy,* are trying to revive the *non*delegation doctrine while conspicuously taking the opposite approach when foreign-affairs-related statutes are at issue. *See Gundy,* 139 S. Ct. at 2137 (Gorsuch, J., dissenting) (accepting the constitutionality of agency rulemaking so long as it overlapped with "authority the Constitution separately vests in another branch," such as executive power over "foreign affairs"); *see also* Harlan Grant Cohen, "The National Security Delegation Conundrum," *Just Security* July 17, 2019, https:// perma.cc/PEC4-UXXS; Curtis A. Bradley, "*Chevron* Deference and Foreign Affairs," 86 *Va. L. Rev.* 649 (2000) (citing cases); Elad D. Gil, "Rethinking Foreign Affairs Deference," 63 *B.C. L. Rev.* 1603 (2022).

61. *Final Report of the Select Committee to Investigate the January 6th Attack on the United States Capitol,* H.R. Rep. No. 117-663, at 75, 78–85, 103–12 (2022), www.govinfo. gov/app/details/GPO-J6-REPORT/context; *see* Peter Baker, "Trump Is Depicted as a Would-Be Autocrat Seeking to Hang onto Power at All Costs," *N.Y. Times,* June 9, 2022, www.nytimes.com/2022/06/09/us/politics/trump-jan-6-hearing. html (summarizing the committee's description of Trump's alleged "seven-part conspiracy" to subvert democracy).

62. *See* Tom Joscelyn, "Comparing the Trump Indictment and the January 6th Select Committee's Final Report," *Just Security*, Aug. 3, 2023, www.justsecurity.org/87473/ comparing-the-trump-indictment-and-the-january-6th-select-committees-final-report/. Just a few weeks after the federal indictment, in a sweeping set of forty-one state charges from which Trump could not be federally pardoned, a Georgia state grand jury invoked state racketeering charges to accuse Trump and eighteen co-defendants of leading a criminal enterprise to overturn his 2020 loss in Georgia. *See* Richard Fausset & Danny Hakim, "Trump Indicted in Georgia: Ex-President Accused of Leading Push to Overturn 2020 Vote," *N.Y. Times*, Aug. 15, 2023, www. nytimes.com/live/2023/08/15/us/trump-indictment-georgia-election. In a fourth case, also immune from federal pardon, Trump was indicted by a Manhattan, N.Y., grand jury for allegedly making illegal hush-money payments to cover up a sex scandal that arose during his 2016 presidential campaign. For the status of each of these four criminal cases against Trump, see generally "Keeping Track of the Trump Investigations," *N.Y. Times* (updated Aug. 15, 2023), www.nytimes.com/interactive/2023/us/trump-investigations-charges-indictments.html.

Chapter 10. A Strategy for Reform

1. For example, in 1984, the Reagan administration hastily modified the U.S. declaration, from 1946, accepting the compulsory jurisdiction of the International Court of Justice, in an effort to divest the court of jurisdiction over a suit being brought against the United States by Nicaragua. Not only was that unilateral decision later held to be legally ineffective, but it weakened the United States' argument that the court lacked jurisdiction without the modification. Once the court rejected the United States' argument at the jurisdictional phase of the suit, the Reagan administration had little choice but to withdraw from the ICJ's compulsory jurisdiction altogether, breaking an acceptance issued nearly four decades earlier. Predictably, the court then ruled against the United States on the merits, laying the groundwork for Nicaragua's new claim that the United States had breached its international obligation to respect World Court judgments and triggering domestic lawsuits against U.S. officials by U.S. citizens living in Nicaragua. This wave of executive treaty breaking fostered the impression of a United States contemptuous of its treaty partners at the same moment that the administration was seeking to mobilize those same partners to advance a Central American peace process. *See generally* Abram Chayes, "Nicaragua, the United States, and the World Court," 85 *Colum. L. Rev.* 1445 (1985).

2. Oliver North, *Taking the Stand: The Testimony of Lieutenant Colonel Oliver L. North* 745 (1987) (statement of Rep. Lee Hamilton); *see also* Louis Henkin, "International Law and National Interest," 25 *Colum. J. Transnat'l L.* 1 (1986) (enumerating ways in which following the law in foreign affairs serves American national interests).

3. For decades, scholars have acknowledged the dangers of greater executive dominance in foreign affairs. *See, e.g.,* Arthur M. Schlesinger Jr., *The Imperial Presidency* (1973); Paul Gewirtz, "Realism in Separation of Powers Thinking," 30 *Wm. & Mary*

L. Rev. 343 (1989); John Hart Ely, *War and Responsibility: Constitutional Lessons of Vietnam and its Aftermath* (1993); Michael P. Van Alstine, "Executive Aggrandizement in Foreign Affairs Lawmaking," 54 *UCLA L. Rev.* 309, 314–15 (2006); Rebecca Ingber, "Congressional Administration of Foreign Affairs," 106 *Va. L. Rev.* 395 (2020).

4. *See generally* Gerhard Casper, *Separating Power: Essays on the Founding Period* (1997); Curtis A. Bradley & Martin S. Flaherty, "Executive Power Essentialism and Foreign Affairs," 102 *Mich. L. Rev.* 545 (2004); Curtis A. Bradley & Trevor W. Morrison, "Historical Gloss and the Separation of Powers," 126 *Harv. L. Rev.* 411 (2012).

5. Korematsu v. United States, 323 U.S. 214, 246 (1944) (Jackson, J., dissenting).

6. *See* Harold Hongju Koh, *The National Security Constitution: Sharing Power After the Iran-Contra Affair* 156–84 (1990) (urging passage of a comprehensive national-security charter that would reenact, in five separate titles, the War Powers Resolution, the International Emergency Economic Powers Act, the arms-export-control laws, the Intelligence Oversight Act, and the National Security Council provisions of the National Security Act of 1947; address modes of congressional-executive consultation in international agreement making, internal and external agency control procedures, and provisions for judicial review of executive action; create new congressional structures; and effect revisions in internal House and Senate rules).

7. *See* National Security Powers Act of 2021, S. 2391, 117th Cong. (2021), https://perma.cc/22U8-GWES; National Security Reforms and Accountability Act, H.R. 5410, 117th Cong. (2021), https://perma.cc/P3L2-FDSF. For analysis of this legislation, see Tess Bridgeman & Stephen Pomper, "A Giant Step Forward for War Powers Reform," *Just Security*, July 20, 2021, https://perma.cc/VJ83-WNLN.

8. *Cf.* Louis Fisher, *Constitutional Dialogues: Interpretation as Political Process* 3 (1988) (arguing that "constitutional law is not a monopoly of the judiciary" but "a process in which all three branches converge and interact with their separate interpretations").

9. *Cf.* Neal Kumar Katyal, "Internal Separation of Powers: Checking Today's Most Dangerous Branch from Within," 115 *Yale L.J.* 2314 (2006) (arguing for separate and overlapping cabinet offices, mandatory review of government action by different agencies, civil-service protections for agency workers, reporting requirements to Congress, and an impartial decision-maker to resolve interagency conflicts). At times, entrenched national security bureaucracies (the "deep state") can act as internal checks and balances, resisting rash political impulses; but at others, these bureaucracies may simply obstruct new presidents from carrying out campaign promises that arguably are part of their electoral mandate.

10. *See, e.g.,* Philip Odeen, *National Security Policy Integration: Report of a Study Requested by the President Under the Auspices of the President's Reorganization Project* (Sept. 1979); Graham Allison & Peter Szanton, *Remaking Foreign Policy* (1976); *Commission on the Organization of the Government for the Conduct of Foreign Policy* (1975) [hereinafter *Murphy Commission Report*]; Cecil Crabb & Kevin Mulcahy, *Presidents and Foreign Policy Making: From FDR to Reagan* (1986); *see also* Leslie Gelb, "Why Not the State Department?," in *Decisions of the Highest Order: Perspectives on the National Security Council* 229, 240–41 nn.1 & 16 (K. Inderfurth & L. Johnson eds., 1988) (listing twelve other studies dating back to the Hoover Commission report on foreign affairs in 1949).

11. Alexander George, "The Case for Multiple Advocacy in Making Foreign Policy," 66 *Am. Pol. Sci. Rev.* 751 (1972). The Bush 41 administration sought to apply this multiple-advocacy approach with regard to domestic-policy decision-making. *See* Michael Duffy, "Mr. Consensus," *Time*, Aug. 21, 1989, at 16–18 ("On domestic matters . . . Bush [41] relies on a highly structured decisionmaking process . . . [k]nown to government-school types as multiple advocacy").

12. In addition to the "torture opinion" discussed in chapter 6 and the Barr opinion on extraordinary rendition discussed in chapter 5, two other such legal opinions helped drive the Iran-contra affair discussed in chapter 3: one by the CIA's general counsel permitting the president to make an intelligence finding retroactively and another by the counsel to the Intelligence Oversight Board, which declared the Boland amendments inapplicable to NSC activities. Apparently, neither of these legal opinions was ever subjected to centralized executive-branch review. As President Reagan's White House counsel later recalled, "[o]ne of the real problems with the entire Iran-contra episode was that not only was it not well-lawyered, but it was *not lawyered* in most respects." Vicki Quade, "The President Is His Only Client," *Barrister*, Winter/Spring 1988, at 7 (interview with Arthur B. Culvahouse Jr., counsel to the president) (emphasis added); *see also Report of the Congressional Committees Investigating the Iran-Contra Affair*, H.R. Rep. No. 100-433, S. Rep. No. 100-216, at 185–86 (1987) [hereinafter *Iran-Contra Report*]; Kirk Victor, "CIA Counsel's Role Questioned," *Nat'l L.J.*, Feb. 2, 1987, at 3 (both describing the CIA general counsel's unlawful "retroactive finding" in the Iran-contra affair).

13. Harold Hongju Koh, "National Security Legal Advice in the New Administration," *Just Security*, Nov. 16, 2016, https://perma.cc/HX5Z-B9J6.

14. Rebecca Ingber, "Good Governance Paper No. 17: How to Use the Bureaucracy to Govern Well," *Just Security*, Oct. 31, 2020, https://perma.cc/U6VT-BQEX ("When the question on the table is the legality of action, and there are differing views on the appropriate legal rationale, this may result in a decision to act but with no clear consensus on why it is lawful. *In fact, this may mean that the government takes action even when a majority of the relevant officials are opposed to any one legal rationale for doing so.*" (emphasis added)).

15. *Cf.* Cass Sunstein, "Constitutionalism After the New Deal," 101 *Harv. L. Rev.* 421, 454–60 (1987) (enumerating advantages of such centralized review); Colin Diver, "Presidential Powers," 36 *Am. U. L. Rev.* 519 (1987) (such centralized review does not create imbalance in constitutional order).

16. Harold Hongju Koh, "The Legal Adviser's Duty to Explain," 41 *Yale J. Int'l L.* 189 195 (2016) ("Providing a public justification is a necessary step to explain why others should agree that actions taken by those government officials are consistent with international law. As a prudential matter, such public explanations prove to be critically important in bringing along the rest of the country and prospective allies in establishing the legitimacy of a public action."); Ingber, *supra* note 14 ("[M]aking the [legal] output *public* (or as much of it as possible) incentivizes clarity of output and allows for broader debate and accountability when the legal rationale for government action is overly generalized or otherwise weak." (emphasis in original)).

17. *See* Ingber, *supra* note 14 ("Group decisionmaking is often hailed for bringing to-gether all the relevant players with expertise and interest, and for allowing the full airing of views. But it can also stifle dissent, promote group think, and . . . dilute the relevant expertise in the room, for example when the entire group is asked to weigh in on a matter on which only a small subset have expertise—such as a ques-tion of international law.").

18. Alexandra H. Perina, "Black Holes and Open Secrets: The Impact of Covert Action on International Law," 53 *Colum. J. Transnat'l L.* 507 (2015); *see, e.g.,* Thomas Ehrlich, "Remarks," in 5 Appendices to *Murphy Commission Report, supra* note 10, at 26–27 (urging that the State Department Legal Adviser conduct such review). The State Department Legal Adviser's Office was created in 1931 by the Moses-Linthicum Act, Pub. L. No. 71-715, § 30, 46 Stat. 1207, 1214 (1931), and has existed in some form dating back to 1848. Harold Hongju Koh, "The State Department Legal Adviser's Office: Eight Decades in Peace and War," 100 *Geo. L.J.* 1747 (2012); *see generally* Michael P. Scharf & Paul R. Williams, *Shaping Foreign Policy in Times of Crisis: The Role of International Law and the State Department Legal Adviser* (2010).

19. *See* 28 U.S.C. §§ 510, 512–513; 28 C.F.R. § 0.25(a).

20. For articles about OLC, see Trevor W. Morrison, "Stare Decisis in the Office of Le-gal Counsel," 116 *Colum. L. Rev.* 1448 nn.4–7 (2010). In the 1980s, I had the privi-lege of serving as an attorney-adviser in that fine office, but I have long expressed hesitations about the ways in which its actual and desired prominence is exagger-ated by its academic alumni from both parties. *See, e.g.,* Harold Hongju Koh, "Pro-tecting the Office of Legal Counsel from Itself," 15 *Cardozo L. Rev.* 513 (1993). OLC attorneys may have expertise in constitutional law, but they generally have far less expertise in international law (which I also lacked when working as an attorney there more than four decades ago). *Cf.* Harold Hongju Koh, "Can the President be Torturer-in-Chief?," 81 *Ind. L.J.* 1145 (2006) (analyzing, among other things, inter-national-law errors in OLC's infamous torture memo).

21. For such a "best practices" statement, see Walter Dellinger et al., *Principles to Guide the Office of Legal Counsel* (2004), *reprinted in* Dawn E. Johnsen, "Faithfully Execut-ing the Laws: Internal Legal Constraints on Executive Power," 54 *UCLA L. Rev.* 1559, 1603 app. 2 (2007) (drafted by attorneys who worked in OLC during the Clinton, George W. Bush, and Obama administrations); Morrison, *supra* note 20; Memorandum from David J. Barron, Acting Assistant Att'y Gen., Office of Legal Counsel, to Attorneys of the Office 1 n.* (July 16, 2010), https://perma.cc/VV9K-TJK7 ("This memorandum updates a prior memorandum, 'Best Practices for OLC Opinions,' issued May 16, 2005."). Prime candidates for disavowal are the OLC legal opinions that justified, after the fact, the killing of Iranian general Qassim Suleimani, which was illegal when ordered in 2020. *See* Harold Hongju Koh, "Is Preemptive Assassination the New Trump Doctrine?," *Foreign Pol'y,* Jan. 9, 2020, https://perma.cc/TJR9-KBTZ; Brian Finucane, "Time for the Biden Administra-tion to Disavow the Dangerous Soleimani Legal Opinions," *Just Security,* Jan. 3, 2022, https://perma.cc/8RTR-ETPQ.

22. *See* Charlie Savage, "Can the President Be Indicted? A Long-Hidden Legal Memo Says Yes," *N.Y. Times,* July 22, 2017, www.nytimes.com/2017/07/22/us/politics /can-president-be-indicted-kenneth-starr-memo.html.

23. Richard Willard, "Law and the National Security Decision-Making Process in the Reagan Administration," 11 *Hous. J. Int'l L.* 129, 132 (1988) ("The cumulative effect of these restrictions was to minimize the ability of the Attorney General to partici- pate in the deliberations or to render meaningful legal advice. He was even asked at times to render off-the-cuff oral advice on complex legal situations. The obvious desire was to be able to claim that the Attorney General had given a legal seal of approval to various proposals without permitting them to undergo real legal scrutiny.")

24. *See* Exec. Order No. 11,030 § 2(b), 3 C.F.R. § 610 (1959–1963).

25. *See, e.g.,* Margaret Colgate Love, "Trump's Self-Serving Pardons Should Renew Calls for a Reckoning with Presidential Power," *Wash. Post,* Jan. 20, 2021, www. washingtonpost.com/opinions/trumps-self-serving-pardons-should-renew-calls- for-a-reckoning-with-the-presidential-power/2021/01/20/04b4c65e-5b48-11eb- a976-bad6431e03e2_story.html ("[A] desire to regain firearms rights accounts for nearly half of the pardon applications filed. It is beyond absurd to make the presi- dent a one-person gun-licensing bureau for people convicted of nonviolent federal crimes who want to go hunting again.").

26. Independent counsel Alexia Morrison's investigation into Ted Olson led to the Su- preme Court decision in *Morrison v. Olson,* 487 U.S. 654 (1988). That case recog- nized certain limitations on the president's power to appoint and remove executive-branch officials, at least in the case of independent counsel. Even after *Morrison,* Ken Starr's Whitewater investigation ventured far afield from its original purposes.

27. *See generally* Andrew Weissman, *Where Law Ends: Inside the Mueller Investigation* (2020); Andrew Weissman, "Some Advice for Jack Smith, the New Special Coun- sel for the Trump Investigations," *N.Y. Times,* Nov. 22, 2022, www.nytimes. com/2022/11/22/opinion/trump-special-counsel-mueller.html (urging a more "sensible approach to communicating where needed with the American public").

28. U.S. Const. art. I, § 9, cl. 8 (emphasis added).

29. These allegations were made in *Blumenthal v. Trump,* 949 F.3d 14 (D.C. Cir. 2020) which involved suspicious transactions in Saudi Arabia, China, and Argentina. *See also* Richard Painter, "2022 Update: Good Governance Paper No. 15: Enforcing the Emoluments Clauses," *Just Security,* Jan. 20, 2022, https://perma.cc/43ZQ-H7XH.

30. *See* Presidential Tax Filings and Audit Transparency Act of 2022, H.R. 9640, 117th Cong. (2022). *See generally* Joshua D. Blank, "Presidential Tax Transparency," 4 *Yale L. & Pol'y Rev.* 1 (2021). Many applicable principles are set forth in American Law Institute, *Principles of the Law: Government Ethics* (tent. drafts nos. 1–4, 2015 2023), https://perma.cc/9LRD-9Z5K, which focuses on ethical standards applica- ble to the operations of the legislative and executive branches.

31. Exec. Order No. 11,905, 3 C.F.R. § 90 (1976); Exec. Order No. 12,333, 3 C.F.R. § 200 (1981); *see also* Michael N. Schmitt, "Assassination in the Law of War," *Lieber Inst. West Point,* Oct. 15, 2021, https://perma.cc/D4LS-EY7F; Koh, *supra* note 21.

32. Exec. Order No. 13,732, https://perma.cc/WF8B-FJBB.
33. *See, e.g.,* Tom Cotton, Opinion, "Tom Cotton: Send in the Troops," *N.Y. Times,* June 3, 2020, www.nytimes.com/2020/06/03/opinion/tom-cotton-protests-military.html.
34. Susan Glasser & Peter Baker, "Inside the War Between Trump and His Generals," *New Yorker,* Aug. 8, 2022, www.newyorker.com/magazine/2022/08/15/inside-the-war-between-trump-and-his-generals ("The President wanted to invoke the Insurrection Act of 1807 and use active-duty military to quell the protests. He wanted ten thousand troops in the streets and the 82nd Airborne called up. He demanded that [General] Milley take personal charge. When Milley and the others resisted[,] . . . [t]urning to Milley, Trump said, 'Can't you just shoot them? Just shoot them in the legs or something?'").
35. *See* Harold Hongju Koh & Michael Loughlin, *The President's Legal Authority to Commit Troops Domestically Under the Insurrection Act,* American Constitution Society Issue Brief (Sept. 2020), https://perma.cc/BC8E-PDA9.
36. *See* Dakota Rudesill, "Nuclear Command and Statutory Control," 11 *Harv. J. Nat'l Security L.& Pol'y* 1 (2020), Saikrishna Bangalore Prakash, "Deciphering the Commander-in-Chief Clause," 133 *Yale L.J.* 1, 87 (2023) (suggesting consultation and approval requirements for nuclear strikes would be constitutional); *see also* David S. Jonas & Bryn McWhorter, "Nuclear Launch Authority: Too Big a Decision for Just the President," *Arms Control Assoc.,* June 2021, https://perma.cc/92FX-LBCZ; Michael J. Glennon, *National Security and Double Government* 7 (2015); Dakota Rudesill, "2022 Update: Good Governance Paper No. 20: Repairing and Strengthening Norms of Nuclear Restraint," *Just Security,* Feb. 16, 2022, https://perma.cc/7PN6-99BJ.
37. *See generally* Glennon, *supra* note 36; Rebecca Ingber, "Bureaucratic Resistance and the National Security State," 104 *Iowa L. Rev.* 139, 220–21 (2018). And so it took the Biden administration nearly two years to issue new governing rules on drones and detention. *See* Charlie Savage, "White House Tightens Rules on Counterterrorism Drone Strikes," *N.Y. Times,* Oct. 7, 2022, www.nytimes.com/2022/10/07/us/politics/drone-strikes-biden-trump.html. Biden himself had to weigh in to overrule the Pentagon's resistance to intelligence sharing with the International Criminal Court. *See* Charlie Savage, "Biden Orders U.S. to Share Evidence of Russian War Crimes with Hague Court," *N.Y. Times,* July 26, 2023, www.nytimes.com/2023/07/26/us/politics/biden-russia-war-crimes-hague.html; Adam Keith, "Is the Pentagon Relenting? A Close Study of Opposition to the Int'l Criminal Court's Ukraine Investigation," *Just Security,* July 26, 2023, www.justsecurity.org/87231/is-pentagon-opposition-to-the-international-criminal-courts-ukraine-investigation-relenting/.
38. Ingber, *supra* note 14.
39. John Hart Ely, *supra* note 3, at 52.
40. *Cf.* Roberta Romano, "Are There Empirical Foundations for the Iron Law of Financial Regulation?," *Am. L. & Econ. Rev.* (forthcoming 2024), https://papers.ssrn.com/sol3/papers.cfm?abstract_id=4340042, at 9–10 (empirical study demonstrating that, with respect to financial crises, "i) Congress, like clockwork, will not

permit a financial crisis to go unanswered, whereas there is no determinant timing for when it might enact financial legislation in noncrisis times; and ii) crisis-driven legislation is unidirectional and significantly greater in regulatory impact than noncrisis-driven legislation").

41. As discussed in chapter 9, Biden's initial years saw only rare success in foreign-policy legislation: the bill on climate change, H.R. 5376, 117th Cong. (2022), the bipartisan bill on China competitiveness, H.R. 4346, 117th Cong. (2022), and a resolution on NATO expansion, S. Res. 646, 117th Cong. (2022).

42. *See* Michael Fitts, "The Vices of Virtue: A Political Party Perspective on Civic Virtue Reforms of the Legislative Process," 136 *U. Pa. L. Rev.* 1567, 1628–33 (1988) (tracing history of power diffusion in Congress); Norman Ornstein, "The Constitution and the Sharing of Foreign Policy Responsibility," in *The President, the Congress, and Foreign Policy* 35, 57 (E. Muskie et al. eds., 1986) (to the extent that Congress has been able to reassert itself in foreign affairs, it has done so in a decentralized manner, which has given too much power to the congressional rank and file and insufficient power to the leadership); Thomas Franck & Edward Weisband, *Foreign Policy by Congress* 210–26, 228 (1979).

43. The Joint Committee on Taxation, which has existed since 1926, is a nonpartisan committee of Congress with five members from the Senate Finance Committee and five from the House Ways and Means Committee. It is supported by a nonpartisan staff of economists, lawyers, and other tax professionals. The committee staff "enjoys a high-level of trust from both sides of the political aisle and in both houses of Congress. . . . Because the . . . staff is independent, [expert,] and involved in all stages of the . . . legislative process, the staff is able to ensure consistency" as bills move through Congress. "About the Joint Committee on Taxation," Joint Committee on Taxation, https://perma.cc/M95C-VA56.

44. *See* Byrd-Nunn-Warner-Mitchell Bill, S.J. Res. 323, 100th Cong., 134 Cong. Rec. S6, 239 (daily ed. May 19, 1988) (text on file with author). Congressman Hamilton introduced the same bill on the House side. *See* H.R. J. Res. 601, 100th Cong. (1988); Lee Hamilton, Opinion, "War Powers: Revise Resolution to Make It Work," *Wall St. J.,* Mar. 20, 1989, at 14. The bill was reintroduced in the 101st Congress, but never enacted. *See* S.J. Res. 2, 101st Cong., 135 Cong. Rec. S167, S184–85 (daily ed. Jan. 25, 1989); *see also* Morton Halperin, "Lawful Wars," 72 *Foreign Pol'y* 173, 176 (1988) (endorsing creation of a special leadership committee); John Felton, "Will Bush-Hill Honeymoon Bring Bipartisanship?," *Cong. Q.,* Feb. 18, 1989, at 332, 335 (describing proposal of six senators, led by Senators Boren and Danforth).

45. Alton Frye, "Congress and President: The Balance Wheels of American Foreign Policy," 49 *Yale Rev.* 1, 11–15 (1979) (urging creation of a congressional "monitor" on foreign-policy matters).

46. *See, e.g.,* Gerald Ford, *A Time To Heal* 252 (1979) (president could not consult with key congressional leaders about 1975 Da Nang evacuation, because ten were abroad and twelve were scattered throughout the United States).

47. Compare the Boren-Danforth proposal described in note 44. *See* Cyrus Vance, *Hard Choices* 14 (1983) (pointing out that during the Iranian hostage crisis, the

secretary of state or his deputy spent up to two hours each day in meetings or briefing sessions with members of Congress).

48. Frye, *supra* note 45, at 15 .

49. The Boren-Danforth proposal for an informal consultative group also incorporated such an agreement. *See* Felton, *supra* note 44, at 335.

50. *See* Fitts, *supra* note 42, at 1603–07 (because centralized institutions tend to represent broad constituencies and experience fewer collective-action problems, they are more likely to promote public-regarding action).

51. *Compare* Roger Davidson, "Congress and the Dispersion of Powers," in *Mr. Madison's Constitution and the Twenty-First Century: A Report from the Williamsburg Conference* 25–28 (1988) ("The average tenure of senators and representatives is about 10.5 years," with some members serving several times that length.), *with* Frye, *supra* note 45, at 3–4 (cabinet officers currently average only two years' consecutive service and assistant secretaries serve an average of only eighteen months).

52. *See* Richard Lugar, *Letters to the Next President* 51 (1988) (six future presidents, nine vice presidents, and nineteen secretaries of state have served on the Senate Foreign Relations Committee).

53. *See* "Introduction to CBO," Congressional Budget Office, https://perma.cc/EAJ2-CDYC (The Congressional Budget Office, which has existed since 1975, "is strictly nonpartisan; conducts objective, impartial analysis; . . . hires its employees solely on the basis of professional competence without regard to political affiliation;" and has a "commitment to objectivity and transparency."); Richard Falk, "Remarks," in 5 Appendices to *Murphy Commission Report, supra* note 10, at 29 (urging the creation of a similar congressional unit).

54. *See* Franck & Weisband, *supra* note 42, at 245.

55. *See* Continuing Appropriations for Fiscal Year 1987, Pub. L. No. 99-500, § 213, 100 Stat. 1783, 1783-305 to 1783-306 (1986) (creating Central American "Kissinger Commission"); *see also* Jeffrey Meyer, "Congressional Control of Foreign Assistance," 13 *Yale J. Int'l L.* 69, 88 (1988).

56. *See generally* William Eskridge et al., *Cases and Materials on Legislation: Statutes and the Creation of Public Policy* 829–43 (6th ed. 2020) (presenting nine drafting commandments).

57. To ensure that Congress will have sufficient information to express its views before executive action becomes a fait accompli, prior notice of proposed covert actions and uses of force should be given in every case, rather than "in every possible instance," to afford the core group a meaningful opportunity to argue with the president before the president irreversibly commits the United States to a covert or forceful course of action.

58. See section 8 of the War Powers Resolution, 50 U.S.C. § 1547.

59. Accordingly, the chairman of the Senate Armed Services Committee, Senator Nunn, opted to test the administration's interpretation through extensive and adversarial congressional hearings. *See The ABM Treaty and the Constitution: Joint Hearings before the S. Comm. on Foreign Relations and the S. Comm. on the Judiciary,* 100th Cong. (1987); *see also Iran-Contra Report, supra* note 12, at 408 n.15, 421 n.37, 542 n.** (discussing various executive-branch legal opinions); Abram Chayes &

Antonia Chayes, "Testing and Development of 'Exotic' Systems Under the ABM Treaty: The Great Reinterpretation Caper," 99 *Harv. L. Rev.* 1956, 1971 (1986).

60. To protect against inadvertent congressional disclosures, the new law could incorporate similar provisions from both Senate Standing Rule 36 and the resolution establishing the Senate Iran-contra committee. *See generally* John Grabow, *Congressional Investigations: Law and Practice* 167–92 (1988) (describing congressional rules for demanding executive-branch information); Standing Rule of the Senate 36.4, *reprinted in* Frank Cummings, *Capitol Hill Manual* 180 (1976) ("Any Senator or officer of the Senate who shall disclose the secret or confidential business or proceedings of the Senate shall be liable, if a Senator, to suffer expulsion from the body; and if an officer, to dismissal from the service of the Senate, and to punishment for contempt."); S. Res. 23, 100th Cong. § 6, 133 Cong. Rec. S89, S91 (daily ed. Jan. 6, 1987) (resolution establishing Senate Iran-contra committee) (requiring all committee staff members and consultants, as conditions of employment, to obtain security clearances and sign nondisclosure agreements, with immediate removal as sanction for disclosure, and providing that any senator who violates security procedures of committee may be referred to Senate Select Committee on Ethics for imposition of sanctions in accordance with Senate rules).

61. *See supra* chapter 4 (discussing INS v. Chadha, 462 U.S. 919 (1983)). *See generally* Stephen Breyer, "The Legislative Veto After *Chadha*," 72 *Geo. L.J.* 785, 794 (1984); Harold Bruff & Ernest Gellhorn, "Congressional Control of Administrative Regulation: A Study of Legislative Vetoes," 90 *Harv. L. Rev.* 1309 (1977) (recounting inefficiencies and constitutional defects of the legislative veto).

62. *See* Trade Act of 1974, 19 U.S.C. §§ 2191–2193 (1982); Harold Hongju Koh, "The Fast Track and United States Trade Policy," 18 *Brook. J. Int'l L.* 143 (1992); "Congressional Controls on Presidential Trade Policymaking After *INS v. Chadha*," 18 *N.Y.U. J. Int'l L. & Pol.* 1191, 1211–21 (1986) [hereinafter Koh, "Congressional Controls"]. The fast-track procedure has also been included in several other foreign-affairs statutes, including the foreign-assistance and war-powers legislation. *See* Meyer, *supra* note 55, at 78–79 & n.38, 86–88 (citing statutes). For proposals to incorporate fast-track provisions into other foreign-affairs statutes, see, for example, Note, "Reinterpreting Advice and Consent: A Congressional Fast Track for Arms Control Treaties," 98 *Yale L.J.* 885 (1989); Note, "Congress and Arms Sales: Tapping the Potential of the Fast-Thick Guarantee Procedure," 97 *Yale L. J.* 1439, 1448, 1453–57 (1988).

63. *See* U.S. Const. art. I, § 5, cl. 3 ("[T]he Yeas and Nays of the Members of either House on any question shall, at the Desire of one fifth of those Present, be entered on the Journal."); Breyer, *supra* note 61, at 794.

64. As a congressional control device, the fast-track procedure has two disadvantages that the legislative veto lacked. First, in cases in which the president's action will take effect unless Congress expresses fast-track disapproval, both houses must disapprove that act by supermajorities in order to override a presidential veto (as opposed to the one- or two-house majority sufficient to sustain a legislative veto). Second, because fast-track procedures are simply statutory modifications in internal house rules and Article I, section 5, clause 2, of the Constitution authorize

"[e]ach House [to] determine the Rules of its Proceedings," each house theoretically retains discretion to change those rules at any time. *See* Koh, "Congressional Controls," *supra* note 62, at 1217 n.79; Meyer, *supra* note 55, at 98–99.

65. For a similar proposal, see Charles Tiefer, "Can the President and Congress Establish a Legislative Veto Mechanism for Jointly Drawing Down a Long and Controversial War?," 6 *J. Nat'l Sec'y L. & Pol'y* 131 (2012); S.J. Res. 323, 100th Cong., 134 Cong. Rec. S6,239 (daily ed. May 19, 1988) (reintroduced in 101st Congress as S.J. Res. 2, 135 Cong. Rec. S167, S184–85 (daily ed. Jan. 25, 1989)). Former secretary of state Cyrus Vance had earlier proposed that Congress amend the War Powers Resolution to declare that "no funds made available under any law may be obligated or expended for any presidential use of force not authorized by Congress" under the terms of the amended act. *See* Cyrus Vance, "Striking the Balance: Congress and the President Under the War Powers Resolution," 133 *U. Pa. L. Rev.* 79, 93–94 (1984).

66. Such a gatekeeping procedure, the fast-track provision of the Trade and Tariff Act of 1984, afforded the House Ways and Means and Senate Finance Committees extensive input into the negotiation of the United States–Canada Free Trade Agreement. *See* 19 U.S.C. § 2112(b)(4)(A). For a description of the role played by the procedure in negotiating the agreement, see Koh, "Congressional Controls," *supra* note 62, at 1211–21; Harold Hongju Koh, "The Legal Markets of International Trade: A Perspective on the Proposed United States–Canada Free Trade Agreement," 12 *Yale J. Int'l L.* 193, 208–18 (1987).

67. *See Procedure in the U.S. House of Representatives* ch. 31, § 1, at 697 (looseleaf ed. 1982) (describing point-of-order procedure); Thomas Franck & Clifford Bob, "The Return of Humpty-Dumpty: Foreign Relations Law After the *Chadha* Case," 79 *Am. J. Int'l L.* 912, 942–43 (1985) (suggesting that each chamber could adopt rules triggering point of order against such a bill). For descriptions and illustrations of how point-of-order procedures have been used in each of the houses, see Stephen Ross, "Legislative Enforcement of Equal Protection," 72 *Minn. L. Rev.* 311, 359–62 (1987).

68. *See Hearings on the Separation of Powers before the Subcomm. on Separation of Powers of the S. Comm. on the Judiciary*, 90th Cong. 43 (1967). Appropriations authorizations are statutes enacted under internal House and Senate rules that permit Congress to appropriate certain sums or monies for certain activities but bar Congress from appropriating larger sums or monies for any activities that have not been authorized. Kate Stith, "Congress' Power of the Purse," 97 *Yale L.J.* 1343, 1370 n.135 (1988).

69. The president may, with clearance from the appropriate legislative committees, "reprogram" funds for different purposes within a particular appropriations account. In 1977, Congress added a provision to the Foreign Assistance Act that denied the president authority to reprogram appropriated funds unless he first notified the two authorizing committees (the Foreign Relations Committee in each house) *and* the Appropriations Committees in each house of his intent to do so and received no disapproval. In the Good Friday accords in March 1989, Congress apparently authorized the president to use reprogrammed funds to support the contras for seven months. In exchange, the president informally promised to return to

the four authorizing committees for notice and approval as a prerequisite to tapping the last three months of reprogrammed funds. The Good Friday accords illustrate the kind of informal, nonstatutory legislative veto that has proliferated since the Supreme Court's legislative-veto decision, *INS v. Chadha*, 462 U.S. 919 (1983). Because they are not embodied in legislation, such nonstatutory vetoes alter no legal rights or duties of persons outside the executive branch and thus do not run afoul of *Chadha*. At the same time, they benefit both branches. Presidents gain assurance of continued congressional funding as long as they abide by the informal accord; Congress retains its freedom to appropriate in successive lump sums while using both its power of the purse and its expert committees to monitor executive compliance with the accord through the reprogramming process. For descriptions of the accords, see Michael Glennon, "The Good Friday Accords: Legislative Veto by Another Name?," 83 *Am. J. Int'l L.* 544 (1989). As Louis Fisher notes, more than 140 legislative vetoes were signed into law in the years immediately after *Chadha*, and many of them were honored on an informal basis. *See* Martin Tolchin, "The Legislative Veto, an Accommodation That Goes On and On," *N.Y. Times*, Mar. 31, 1989, at A11 (quoting Louis Fisher).

70. Stith, *supra* note 68, at 1361.

71. *See H.R. 3822, To Strengthen the System of Congressional Oversight of Intelligence Activities in the United States: Hearings Before the Subcomm. on Legis. of the H. Permanent Select Comm. on Intelligence*, 100th Cong. 56–57 (1988) (statement of Hon. Clark M. Clifford).

72. Congress could also authorize departmental inspectors general or an independent branch of the Justice Department analogous to the Office of Special Investigations to conduct such prosecutions. *See* Official Accountability Act of 1987, H.R. 3665, 100th Cong., 133 Cong. Rec. H10,723 (daily ed. Nov. 20, 1987) (introduced by Rep. Conyers) (authorizing independent counsel to indict and convict U.S. government officials who "order or engage in the planning of, preparation for, initiation or conduct of intelligence activity which violates any statute or Executive Order in force or international agreements to which the United States is a party"); *cf.* Dellums v. Smith, 573 F. Supp. 1489 (N.D. Cal. 1983), *motion to alter judgment denied*, 577 F. Supp. 1449 (N.D. Cal. 1984) (holding Neutrality Act applicable to actions of government officials and enforceable by independent counsel), *vacated on other grounds*, 797 F.2d 817 (9th Cir. 1986); H.R. 2522, 100th Cong., 133 Cong. Rec. E2987–88 (daily ed. July 22, 1987) (remarks of Rep. Mel Levine) (proposing to amend Neutrality Act, 18 U.S.C. §§ 959, 960–961 (criminalizing organization or initiation of hostile expeditions on U.S. territory against a foreign country with which U.S. is "at peace")).

73. U.S. Const. art. II, § 4 (emphasis added); *id.* art. I, §§ 2–3; *id.* art. II, § 2. For historical and constitutional analysis of the impeachment remedy, see generally Charles Black & Phillip Bobbitt, *Impeachment: A Handbook* (new ed. 2018); Raoul Berger, *Impeachment: The Constitutional Problems* (1973).

74. *See* House Comm. on the Judiciary, *Impeachment of Richard Nixon, President of the United States*, H.R. Rep. No. 93-1305, at 217–19 (1974).

75. U.S. Const. art. I, § 3, cls. 6–7. Dean Choper, for example, argues against the need for judicial review of presidential action in foreign affairs in part because Congress

retains the political remedy of impeachment. *See* Jesse Choper, *Judicial Review and the National Political Process: A Functional Reconsideration of the Role of the Supreme Court* 286 (1980).

76. Because the fast-track procedure requires bicameral action and presentment to the president, albeit on an expedited basis, it does not constitute a legislative veto for purposes of *Chadha,* 462 U.S. at 955 n.20. The addition of committee gatekeeping provisions does not render such procedures unconstitutional. Point-of-order procedures and impeachments exploit a different loophole in *Chadha,* which specifies that each house of Congress, acting alone, retains the power to determine its own rules and procedures. U.S. Const. art. I, § 5, cl. 2 ("Each House may determine the Rules of its Proceedings"). The House's authority to initiate impeachments and the Senate's power to try them are similarly exempt from *Chadha*'s requirements.

77. Jim Cooper, "Fixing Congress," *Bos. Rev.,* June 26, 2012, https://perma.cc/B6PW-ZNXA. During Speaker Gingrich's tenure, the House approved unlimited travel by representatives back to their home districts, which meant that members did not need to stay in Washington, D.C., or develop cross-party friendships through regular social interaction. Repealing or modifying this rule could be one of many small but salutary changes, with real-world consequences. *See, e.g.,* Thomas B. Langhorne, "Congress Doesn't Live Here Anymore | Secrets of the Hill," *Courier & Press,* Oct. 14, 2018, https://perma.cc/XQL7-W899.

78. *See, e.g.,* Ramirez de Arellano v. Weinberger, 745 F.2d 1500, 1511, 1512–15 (D.C. Cir. 1984) (en banc) (both D.C. Circuit majority and Judge Scalia's dissent reject U.S. officials' political-question defense); Tel-Oren v. Libyan Arab Republic, 726 F.2d 774, 803 n.8 (D.C. Cir. 1984) (Bork, J., concurring) (rejecting political-question defense), *cert. denied,* 470 U.S. 1003 (1985).

79. Zivotofsky v. Clinton, 566 U.S. 189, 194 (2012) (quoting Cohens v. Virginia, 19 U.S. (6 Wheat.) 264, 404 (1821)); *id.* at 196, 201 ("Resolution of [that] claim demands careful examination of the textual, structural, and historical evidence put forward by the parties regarding the nature of the statute and of the passport and recognition powers. This is what courts do.").

80. Baker v. Carr, 369 U.S. 186, 211–13 (1962) (finding that courts had historically construed treaties and statutes that conflicted with treaties, applied statutes to recognized territories, construed proclamations of belligerency abroad and executive determinations of foreign diplomatic status, and evaluated claims of foreign sovereign immunity). Significantly, the Court in *Baker* also declined to apply the political-question doctrine to the particular facts before it. *Id.* at 226–37.

81. *See, e.g.,* United States v. Belmont, 301 U.S. 324 (1937) (construing executive agreement); Sumitomo Shoji America v. Avagliano, 457 U.S. 176 (1982) (construing treaty); The Paquete Habana, 175 U.S. 677 (1900) (ruling on matter of customary international law); New York Times Co. v. United States, 403 U.S. 713 (1971); Kent v. Dulles, 357 U.S. 116 (1958); Faruki v. Rogers, 349 F. Supp. 723, 732 (D.D.C. 1972) ("Where constitutionally protected rights are at stake . . . notions of automatic deference disappear"); *Chadha,* 462 U.S. at 942 ("Resolution of litigation challenging the constitutional authority of one of the three branches cannot be evaded by courts because the issues have political implications."). Although greater judicial

deference to the executive may be warranted when no interbranch dispute exists, such a rationale would not apply when a constitutional impasse arises between two political branches. *See* Barnes v. Kline, 759 F.2d 21 (D.C. Cir. 1985), *vacated as moot sub nom.* Burke v. Barnes, 479 U.S. 361 (1987).

82. Marbury v. Madison, 5 U.S. (1 Cranch) 137, 177 (1803).

83. *See* Louis Henkin, "The Supreme Court, 1967 Term—Foreword: On Drawing Lines," *82 Harv. L. Rev.* 63, 91 (1968) (questioning Supreme Court's refusal to hear cases challenging constitutionality of the Vietnam War and writing, "I should be happier . . . if the Court would demonstrate that the decision to hear or not to hear a constitutional claim is based on something sturdier than caprice."). My late colleague Robert Cover's outrage at what he viewed as "judicial complicity in the crimes of Vietnam" similarly sparked his research about slavery and the judicial process. *See* Robert Cover, *Justice Accused: Antislavery and the Judicial Process,* at xi (1975).

84. Japan Whaling Ass'n v. Cetacean Soc'y, 478 U.S. 221, 230 (1986); *accord* INS v. Cardoza-Fonseca, 480 U.S. 421, 447 (1987) (reiterating that even in the immigration context the "judiciary is the final authority on issues of statutory construction" (quoting Chevron U.S.A. v. Natural Res. Def. Council, 467 U.S. 837, 843 n.9 (1984))); Trans World Airlines, Inc. v. Franklin Mint Corp., 466 U.S. 243 (1984) (adjudicating challenge based on federal regulations to liability limitations in a treaty); Romer v. Carlucci, 847 F.2d 445, 461–63 (8th Cir. 1988) (en banc) (environmental impact statements filed with Air Force's deployment of MX missiles, allegedly in violation of National Environmental Policy Act of 1969, involve statutory interpretation and thus raise no political question); Comm. of U.S. Citizens Living in Nicaragua v. Reagan, 859 F.2d 929, 932 (D.C. Cir. 1988) (deeming "reliance on the political question doctrine . . . misplaced" in case in which individuals claimed deprivations stemming from war in Nicaragua).

85. Webster v. Doe, 486 U.S. 592 (1988) (National Security Act did not intend to preclude judicial review of a constitutional challenge to CIA employment termination decision); Dames & Moore v. Regan, 453 U.S. 654 (1981); *Chadha,* 462 U.S. 919.

86. *See* Daniel Meltzer, "Deterring Constitutional Violations by Law Enforcement Officials: Plaintiffs and Defendants as Private Attorneys General," *88 Colum. L. Rev.* 247, 295–327 (1988) (describing utility of such provisions in deterring constitutional violations by government officials).

87. *See* United States v. Johnson, 481 U.S. 681, 692 (1987) (Scalia, J., dissenting); *see also* Note, "Making Intramilitary Tort Law More Civil: A Proposed Reform of the *Feres* Doctrine," 95 *Yale L.J.* 992 (1986). Although the *Feres* doctrine was originally predicated on the existence of a statutory compensation scheme and concerns about military discipline, it could also be applied to bar suits by members of the armed forces against superiors who order them to participate in illegal wars. This barrier to adjudication is particularly significant because members of the armed forces under orders to report to a war zone for battle are the individuals who most clearly have standing to sue their superiors under current doctrine. *See, e.g.,* Massachusetts v. Laird, 451 F.2d 26 (1st Cir. 1971); Berk v. Laird, 429 F.2d 302 (2d Cir. 1970).

88. *See* Nixon v. Fitzgerald, 457 U.S. 731, 748–49 (1982); Harlow v. Fitzgerald, 457 U.S. 800, 818 n.31 (1982). *See generally* Peter Schuck, *Suing Government: Citizen Remedies for Official Wrongs* (1983).

89. *See* 5 U.S.C. § 553(a)(1) (foreign-affairs exception); *id.* § 702 (right of review); *id.* § 706 (scope of review); *cf.* Sanchez-Espinoza v. Reagan, 770 F.2d 202, 207, 209 (D.C. Cir. 1985) (finding discretionary nonmonetary relief "arguably available" under the APA against federal officials for unlawful actions in foreign affairs).

90. *See, e.g., Ramirez,* 745 F.2d 1500; *See* U.S. Const. amend. V ("nor shall private property be taken for public use, without just compensation"); Dames & Moore v. Regan, 453 U.S. 654, 691 (1981) (Powell, J., concurring in part and dissenting in part) ("The Government must pay just compensation when it furthers the Nation's foreign policy goals by using as 'bargaining chips' claims lawfully held by a relatively few persons and subject to the jurisdiction of our courts. The extraordinary powers of the President and Congress . . . cannot . . . displace the Just Compensation Clause of the Constitution.") (footnote omitted). *See generally* Alex Cohen & Joseph Ravitch, "Economic Sanctions, Domestic Deprivations, and the Just Compensation Clause: Enforcing the Fifth Amendment in the Foreign Affairs Context," 13 *Yale J. Int'l L.* 146 (1988).

91. *Cf.* Foreign Sovereign Immunities Act of 1976, 28 U.S.C. § 1391(f)(4) (laying venue in the district courts of the D.C. Circuit for suits against foreign sovereigns).

92. *See, e.g.,* American Society of International Law, *Benchbook on International Law* (Diane Marie Amann ed., 2014), https://perma.cc/2PRP-P5MA.

93. *See* Ganesh Sitaraman & Ingrid (Wuerth) Brunk, "The Normalization of Foreign Relations Law," 128 *Harv. L. Rev.* 1897, 1970–74 (2015).

94. Trump v. Hawaii, 138 S. Ct. 2392, 2433 (2018) (Sotomayor, J., dissenting).

95. Dep't of Commerce v. New York, 139 S. Ct. 2551, 2575–76 (2019) (dealing with the 2020 U.S. census).

96. West Virginia v. EPA, 142 S. Ct. 2587, 2609 (2022); *see also* Mila Sohoni, "The Major Questions Quartet," 136 *Harv. L. Rev.* 263, 310, 335 (2022) (One reading of this case and related decisions is that "Congress may not delegate the power to make legally binding rules for important subjects *unless foreign affairs is involved,*" without explaining when a case genuinely implicates foreign affairs. (emphasis added)).

97. The decision has already been widely and harshly criticized, on and off the Court. *See, e.g., Biden v. Nebraska,* 600 U.S. —, slip op. at 14 (U.S. June 30, 2023) (Kagan, J., dissenting) (charging the Court majority with "substitut[ing] itself for Congress and the Executive Branch—and the hundreds of millions of people they represent—in making this Nation's most important, as well as most contested, policy decisions"); Thomas W. Merrill, "Major Questions about *West Virginia v. EPA*— and the Future of the *Chevron* Doctrine," *Marquette Lawyer,* Fall 2022, at 39, 44 ("The major questions doctrine inverts the *Chevron* doctrine, is indeterminate, and as a practical matter, will encourage courts to engage in something more akin to political punditry than law."); E. Donald Elliott, "How *West Virginia v. EPA* Changed the Administrative State," *Am. Spectator,* July 27, 2022, https://perma.cc/ XKF7-6HDM ("Chief Justice Roberts did not need to write a major opinion of constitutional and historical significance. He could have decided the case on conventional grounds under existing law.").

98. *See* Harold Hongju Koh, "Civil Remedies for Uncivil Wrongs: Combatting Terrorism through Transnational Public Law Litigation," 22 *Tex. Int'l L.J.* 169, 202–08 (1987) (discussing these doctrines); *see also* Harold Hongju Koh, "Transnational Public Law Litigation," 100 *Yale L.J.* 2347, 2382–94 (1991); Harold Hongju Koh, *Transnational Litigation in United States Courts* 247–60 (2008) [hereinafter Koh, *Transnational Litigation*]; Pamela K. Bookman, "Litigation Isolationism," 67 *Stan. L. Rev.* 1081, 1086 (2015) (arguing that judicially adopted avoidance doctrines in transnational litigation have proliferated to the point at which they "fail to serve or positively undermine the values that the doctrines purport to advance," for example, separation of powers, international comity, U.S. sovereign interests, and fairness and efficiency for all parties).

99. *See generally* Steven Arrigg Koh, "Foreign Affairs Prosecutions," 94 *N.Y.U. L. Rev.* 340 (2019) (discussing how in transnational criminal cases, federal courts have managed the presumption against extraterritoriality and other doctrines, such as the rule of lenity, in U.S. prosecutions with foreign-affairs implications).

100. United States v. Husayn (Zubaydah), 142 S. Ct. 959, 999 (2022) (Gorsuch, J., dissenting).

101. *See*, for example, the second brief of the United States in *Kiobel*. Supplemental Brief for the United States as Amicus Curiae in Partial Support of Affirmance, Kiobel v. Royal Dutch Petroleum Co., 569 U.S. 108 (2013) (No. 10-1491). That brief's authors argued without persuasive proof and without the participation of the State Department's Legal Adviser that foreign-affairs interests are being damaged by Alien Tort Statute litigation against foreign corporations. But see the Supreme Court of Canada's decision in *Nevsun Resources Ltd. v. Araya* (Can. S. Ct. 2020) (Abella, J.), https://perma.cc/9RFG-86AW, holding that Canadian corporations may be sued in tort for violations of international human-rights law that occur abroad.

102. Sale v. Haitian Centers Council, Inc., 509 U.S. 155 (1993); EEOC v. Arabian Am. Oil Co., 499 U.S. 244, 260–78 (1991) (Marshall, J., dissenting) (noting that the House report made it clear that the statute was intended to apply to discrimination by U.S. employers against U.S. employees employed abroad). *See generally* Koh, *Transnational Litigation, supra* note 98, at 58–59, 71–83; Harold Hongju Koh, "The 'Haiti Paradigm' in United States Human Rights Policy," 103 *Yale L.J.* 2391, 2418–19 (1994).

103. Morrison v. Nat'l Austl. Bank Ltd., 561 U.S. 247, 255–66 (2010). *Morrison* and *Kiobel* held, respectively, that the presumption against extraterritoriality applies to section 10(b) of the Securities Exchange Act and to the federal common-law cause of action recognized under the Alien Tort Statute by *Sosa v. Alvarez-Machain*. As one commentator has noted, "It is certainly possible that a Supreme Court bent on restricting private litigation in transnational cases might read [the recent case law regarding the presumption against extraterritoriality] broadly to require domestic injury in every case." William S. Dodge, "The New Presumption Against Extraterritoriality," 133 *Harv. L. Rev.* 1582, 1620 (2020).

104. Hartford Fire Ins. Co. v. California, 509 U.S. 764, 814–15 (1993) (Scalia, J., dissenting).

105. *Kiobel,* 569 U.S. at 127–28 (Breyer, J., concurring in the judgment); Hannah L. Buxbaum & Ralf Michaels, "Reasonableness as a Limitation on the Extraterritorial Application of U.S. Law," in *The Restatement and Beyond: The Past, Present, and Future of U.S. Foreign Relations Law* 295 (Paul B. Stephan & Sarah H. Cleveland eds., 2020) (noting that the Supreme Court has not rejected a case-by-case reasonableness requirement and that "the practice of reasonableness analysis has wide application in the lower courts.") For the counterargument that a reasonableness balancing approach gives judges too much discretion to indulge their isolationist instincts, see, for example, *In re Vitamin C Antitrust Litig.,* 8 F.4th 36 (2d Cir. 2021); William S. Dodge, "Cert Petition Challenges Second Circuit's Comity Abstention Doctrine," *Transnational Litigation Blog,* Apr. 7, 2022, https://perma.cc/8ZA7-NB5R.

106. Medellín v. Texas, 552 U.S. 491, 505 n.3 (2008). *See generally* Carlos Manuel Vázquez, "Treaties as Law of the Land: The Supremacy Clause and the Judicial Enforcement of Treaties," 122 *Harv. L. Rev.* 599 (2008).

107. Buxbaum & Michaels, *supra* note 105, at 295; Harold Hongju Koh, "International Law as Part of Our Law," 98 *Am. J. Int'l L.* 43 (2004); Harold Hongju Koh, "Keynote Address, A Community of Reason and Rights," 77 *Fordham L. Rev.* 583 (2008); Martin S. Flaherty, *Restoring the Global Judiciary: Why the Supreme Court Should Rule in U.S. Foreign Affairs* 250 (2019) ("[T]he Court has long and consistently drawn upon international law to interpret constitutional rights. . . . [T]he range is truly wide.").

108. In addition to Justices Alito, Gorsuch, and Kavanaugh, over the years nine other Justices—Blackmun, Breyer, Ginsburg, Kennedy, O'Connor, Scalia, Souter, Stevens, and Rehnquist—have all referenced constitutional practice from other democratic countries in support of particular arguments. *See* Harold Hongju Koh, "Presidential Power to Terminate International Agreements," 128 *Yale L.J. F.* 432, 456–57 and accompanying notes (2018), www.yalelawjournal.org/forum/presidential-power-to-terminate-international-agreements (citing cases). Despite Justice Alito's confirmation testimony that he did not think it "appropriate or useful to look to foreign law in interpreting the provisions of our Constitution," his majority opinion in *Dobbs v. Jackson Women's Health Org.,* 142 S. Ct. 2228, 2270 (2022), found it "telling that other countries almost uniformly eschew" using viability as a line for determining the legality of abortion. *Compare Confirmation Hearing on the Nomination of Samuel A. Alito Jr. to Be an Associate Justice of the Supreme Court of the United States: Hearing Before the S. Judiciary Comm.,* 100th Cong. 471 (2006), www.govinfo.gov/content/pkg/GPO-CHRG-ALITO/pdf/GPO-CHRG-ALITO.pdf, *with Dobbs,* 142 S. Ct. at 2270 (noting also that *Casey* and *Roe* "allowed the States less freedom to regulate abortion than the majority of western democracies enjoy"). In his confirmation hearing, Justice Gorsuch testified: "I do not know why we would look to the experience of other countries rather than to our own." Adam Liptak, "Conservatives, Often Wary of Foreign Law, Embrace It in Census Case," *N.Y. Times,* Apr. 29, 2019, www.nytimes.com/2019/04/29/us/politics/foreign-law-census.html. But, dissenting in *Buffington v. McDonough,* he wrote: "[C]ourts in other countries that often consult American administrative

law practices have declined to adopt the [*Chevron*] doctrine." 143 S. Ct. 14, 22(2022) (Gorsuch, J., dissenting from denial of certiorari). Asking during oral argument about a citizenship question on the U.S. census questionnaire in the census case, *Department of Commerce v. New York*, 139 S. Ct. 2551 (2019), Justice Gorsuch further noted, "Virtually every other English-speaking country and a great many others besides ask this question in their censuses." Liptak, *supra*. Justice Kavanaugh, who had previously written that "international-law norms are not domestic U.S. law," added: "The United Nations recommends that countries ask a citizenship question on the census. And a number of other countries do it. Spain, Germany, Canada, Australia, Ireland, Mexico ask a citizenship question. It's a very common question internationally." *Id.*

109. As the Court has repeatedly recognized, the concept of "ordered liberty" is not uniquely American but rather, is "enshrined" in the legal history of "English-speaking peoples," as well as other legal systems. In *Lawrence v. Texas*, 539 U.S. 558 (2003), the Supreme Court acknowledged that the concept of privacy is not American property, unique to the United States, but rather, part of a privacy concept recognized and shared in other countries. In asking a question under U.S. law—whether there is a compelling governmental interest in preventing people from having sex with same-sex partners—the *Lawrence* Court found that that claimed compelling governmental interest had not been found elsewhere, in countries with whom the United States arguably shared a common heritage of privacy. *Id.* at 577.

110. Justice Breyer elaborated, "Of course, we are interpreting our own Constitution, not those of other nations, and there may be relevant political and structural differences between their systems and our own," *Printz v. United States*, 521 U.S. 898, 977 (1997) (Breyer, J., dissenting). But if somebody else has considered a constitutional question before, why shouldn't U.S. courts look to what those countries have decided to determine whether the sister country's solution has led to a good outcome? *See generally* Stephen Breyer, *The Court and the World: American Law and the New Global Realities* (2015).

111. Murray v. Schooner Charming Betsy, 6 U.S. (2 Cranch) 64, 118 (1804) (Marshall, C.J.). The roots of the canon can be traced back at least two decades earlier, to *Rutgers v. Waddington* (N.Y. City Mayor's Ct. 1784), *reprinted in* 1 *The Law Practice of Alexander Hamilton: Documents and Commentary* 392 (Julius Goebel Jr. ed., 1964), a case argued by Alexander Hamilton, and then another two decades before that in principles of statutory interpretation stated in Blackstone's *Commentaries*. *See* William S. Dodge, "*The Charming Betsy* and *The Paquete Habana* (1804 and 1900)," in *Landmark Cases in Public International Law* 11, 15–16 (Elrik Bjorge & Cameron Miles eds., 2017).

112. Société Nationale Industrielle Aérospatiale v. U.S. Dist. Ct. for the S. Dist. of Iowa 482 U.S. 522, 555, 567 (1987) (Blackmun, J., concurring in part).

113. Some have pejoratively analogized this to letting a justice "look over the heads of the crowd and pick out . . . friends." Antonin Scalia, *A Matter of Interpretation: Federal Courts and the Law* 36 (1997) (quoting Judge Harold Leventhal). But if a justice may already look at persuasive law-review articles written by publicists

which happen to be a subsidiary source of international law under article 38 of the Statute of the International Court of Justice, why shouldn't a justice also be allowed to consult international or foreign-law decisions that express reasoned, enlightened views that cast light on community standards, parallel rules, or empirical lessons from other legal systems?

114. McCulloch v. Maryland, 17 U.S. 316, 498 (1819).

115. *Ramirez*, 745 F.2d at 1514.

116. *See, e.g.,* Buckley v. Valeo, 424 U.S. 1 (1976) (per curiam) (declaring unconstitutional portions of the Federal Election Campaign Act); Bowsher v. Synar, 478 U.S. 714 (1986) (invalidating portions of Gramm-Rudman-Hollings budget-balancing act).

117. *See* Northern Pipeline Constr. Co. v. Marathon Pipe Line Co., 458 U.S. 50 (1982) (declaring bankruptcy statute unconstitutional, but staying judgment until Congress could repair constitutional defects).

118. Martin Redish, "Judicial Review and the Political Question," 75 *Nw. U. L. Rev.* 1031, 1052 (1985).

119. Narenji v. Civiletti, 617 F.2d 745, 748 (D.C. Cir. 1979) (Robb, J.), *cert. denied,* 446 U.S. 957 (1980).

120. *Compare Ramirez,* 745 F.2d at 1566 (Scalia, J., dissenting), *with id.* at 1543–44 (Wilkey, J.) (emphasis in original) (footnote omitted). Judge Wilkey, formerly the assistant attorney general for the Office of Legal Counsel of the Department of Justice, later served as U.S. ambassador to Uruguay and an independent counsel during the Bush 41 administration.

121. *See generally* Harold Hongju Koh, *The Trump Administration and International Law* 6–37 (2019).

122. United States v. Belmont, 301 U.S. 324, 331 (1937) (additionally stating that, in foreign affairs, "state lines disappear"). The Court held in *American Insurance Ass'n v. Garamendi* that a presidential policy of settling the claims of Holocaust survivors through international agreements preempted a California statute. 539 U.S. 396 (2003). *See also* United States v. Pink, 315 U.S. 203, 230 (1942) (quoting *Belmont*); Zschernig v. Miller, 389 U.S. 429, 441 (1968) (barring Oregon from "establish[ing] its own foreign policy"); Crosby v. National Foreign Trade Council, 530 U.S. 363 (2000).

123. For example, after Trump withdrew from the Paris Agreement, an international climate-change treaty, a coalition of twenty-four state governors committed to the Paris goals enacted policies on behalf of 55 percent of the U.S. population. Composing by GDP the equivalent of the third-largest national economy in the world, these states enacted policies that they estimated would achieve a combined 26 to 28 percent reduction in greenhouse-gas emissions from 2005 levels by 2025. U.S. Climate Alliance Fact Sheet (Sept. 2022), https://perma.cc/8M3Y-GAWV. Although some of their policies were challenged by the Trump administration, those challenges were ultimately rejected by the courts. *See* United States v. California, No. 2:19-cv-02142, 2020 WL 4043034 (E.D. Cal. July 17, 2020, appeal dismissed); No. 20-16789 (9th Cir., Apr. 22, 2021).

124. These lawsuits were generally filed by cities, counties, and states. *See, e.g.,* Cnty. of San Mateo v. Chevron Corp., 294 F. Supp. 3d 934 (N.D. Cal. 2018), *aff'd in part,*

appeal dismissed in part, 960 F.3d 586 (9th Cir. 2020), *cert. granted, judgment vacated,* 141 S. Ct. 2666 (2021), *and aff'd,* 32 F.4th 733 (9th Cir. 2022); City of Oakland v. BP PLC, 960 F.3d 570 (9th Cir. 2020), *opinion amended and superseded on denial of reh'g,* 969 F.3d 895 (9th Cir. 2020), *cert. denied sub nom.* Chevron Corp. v. City of Oakland, 141 S. Ct. 2776 (2021); City of New York v. BP PLC, 325 F. Supp. 3d 466 (S.D.N.Y. 2018), *aff'd sub nom.* City of New York v. Chevron Corp., 993 F.3d 81 (2d Cir. 2021); Rhode Island v. Chevron Corp., 393 F. Supp. 3d 142 (D.R.I. 2019), *aff'd sub nom.* Rhode Island v. Shell Oil Prod. Co., 979 F.3d 50 (1st Cir. 2020), *cert. granted, judgment vacated,* 141 S. Ct. 2666 (2021), *and aff'd sub nom.* Rhode Island v. Shell Oil Prod. Co., 35 F.4th 44 (1st Cir. 2022); Mayor & City Council of Baltimore v. BP PLC, 952 F.3d 452 (4th Cir. 2020), *vacated and remanded,* 141 S. Ct. 1532 (2021); City & Cnty. of Honolulu v. Sunoco LP, 39 F.4th 1101 (9th Cir. 2022); Connecticut v. Exxon Mobil Corp., No. 3:20-cv-1555, 2021 WL 2389739 (D. Conn. June 2, 2021). Although the move to state courts holds more favorable prospects for plaintiffs, should their cases be heard before state juries, there is a circuit split on preliminary venue and preemption issues. *See generally* Matthew Blaschke et al., "The Widening Circuit Split on State Court Climate Claims," *Law360,* July 11, 2022, www.law360.com/articles/1509964/the-widening-circuit-split-on-state-court-climate-claims (reviewing decisions).

125. Turkish president Recep Tayyip Erdogan's allies in parliament recently presented a "disinformation law" that criminalizes "fake news"—without defining the term. Emre Kizilkaya, "In Turkey, Erdogan's Crackdown on the Free Press Intensifies," *Nieman Reports,* June 22, 2022, https://perma.cc/6D5E-7SET. Similarly, Russian president Vladimir Putin has blocked foreign news and social-media access in the country and signed a law criminalizing "false information" regarding his war of aggression in Ukraine. *See* Anton Troianovski & Valeriya Sfronova, "Russia Takes Censorship to New Extremes, Stifling War Coverage," *N.Y. Times,* Mar. 4, 2022, www.nytimes.com/2022/03/04/world/europe/russia-censorship-media-crackdown.html. Since then, foreign news media have left, Russian outlets have closed, and journalists have fled the country. Elahe Izadi & Sarah Ellison, "Russia's Independent Media, Long Under Siege, Teeters Under New Putin Crackdown," *Wash. Post,* Mar. 4, 2022, www.washingtonpost.com/media/2022/03/04/putin-media-law-russia-news.

126. *See* Anupam Chander, "Trump v. TikTok," 55 *Vand. J. Transnat'l L.* 1143, 1147 (2022) (arguing that "the failed TikTok ban . . . demonstrated . . . the 'National Security Constitution' at work—the checks and balances between the three branches of government in the context of what the President deems to be a national emergency"). At the end of 2022, Congress waded into this battle by enacting legislation that would ban TikTok from U.S. government devices. At this writing fourteen states have passed bans on having the service on their government-issued devices. *See* Sapna Maheshwari et al., "Bans on TikTok Gain Momentum in Washington and States," *N.Y. Times,* Dec. 20, 2022, www.nytimes.com/2022/12/20/technology/tiktok-ban-government-issued-devices.html.

127. *See* Koh, *supra* note 108, at 453–60; *see also* Goldwater v. Carter, 444 U.S. 996, 1003 (1979) (Rehnquist, J., joined by Burger, C.J., and Stewart and Stevens, JJ., concurring in the judgment) ("[D]ifferent termination procedures may be appropriate for different treaties."); Crosby v. Nat'l Foreign Trade Council, 530 U.S. 363, 385 (2000) (discussing Barclays Bank PLC v. Franchise Tax Bd. of Cal., 512 U.S. 298 (1994)) ("In *Barclays,* we had the question of the preemptive effect of federal tax law on state tax law with discriminatory extraterritorial effects. *We found the reactions of foreign powers and the opinions of the Executive irrelevant in fathoming congressional intent because Congress had taken specific actions rejecting the positions both of foreign governments . . . and the Executive. . . .* Here, however, Congress has done nothing to render such evidence beside the point." (emphasis added) (citations omitted)).

128. *See* Oversight Board, "Oversight Board Upholds Former President Trump's Suspension, Finds Facebook Failed to Impose Proper Penalty," May 2021, https://perma.cc/T66A-6VXW.

129. *See, e.g.,* Oxford Inst. for Ethics, Law & Armed Conflict, "The Oxford Process on International Law Protections in Cyberspace," https://perma.cc/6SNG-N3PL (last visited Dec. 2, 2023).

130. The ALI has published two full restatements and one partial restatement on the "foreign relations law of the United States": the first was a single volume published in 1965, when the ALI was issuing its "second" restatement series, hence called the *Restatement (Second) of the Foreign Relations Law of the United States* (1965). That was followed twenty-two years later by a two-volume edition called the *Restatement (Third) of the Foreign Relations Law of the United States.* My fellow former State Department Legal Adviser John Bellinger and I are co-chairs for the ongoing *Restatement (Fourth);* also participating in the project are the reporters Curtis Bradley, William Dodge, and Oona Hathaway. *See* Harold Hongju Koh, "Could the President Unilaterally Terminate All International Agreements: Questioning Section 313" in *The Restatement and Beyond, supra* note 105, at 67.

Chapter 11. Rethinking Foreign-Affairs Law

1. INS v. Chadha, 462 U.S. 919 (1983); 50 U.S.C. § 1544(c) (legislative veto in War Powers Resolution).

2. Charles Black, "The Working Balance of the American Political Departments," 1 *Hastings Const. L.Q.* 13, 18 (1980).

3. *See* Richard Pildes, "Power Wars Symposium: What Role Should Law Play in Areas of Vital National and International Affairs?," *Just Security,* Nov. 13, 2015, https://perma.cc/QGM6-6PXP.

4. *See, e.g.,* War Powers Consultation Act of 2014, S. 1939, 113th Cong. (2014). For a now-classic proposal explaining how Congress could broadly modify the War Powers Resolution to make it more effective, see generally John Hart Ely, *War and Responsibility: Constitutional Lessons of Vietnam and Its Aftermath* (1993).

5. *See* S. 440, 93rd Cong. (1973), *reprinted in* Thomas Franck & Michael Glennon, *Foreign Relations and National Security Law* 590 (1987); S. 2956, 92d Cong., 117 Cong. Rec. 44,794–95 (1971) (similar bill proposed by Sen. Javits).

6. The current War Powers Resolution already provides expedited fast-track procedures for considering certain joint resolutions introduced after a presidential report on "hostilities" is submitted or "required to be submitted" to Congress. *See* 50 U.S.C. §§ 1544(b), 1545 (1982). Reasoning that a presidential report was required to be submitted after U.S. forces had destroyed an Iranian oil platform, Senator Brock Adams attempted in 1988 to invoke this procedure to force a vote on the president's compliance with the War Powers Resolution in the Persian Gulf. *See* Allan Adler, "Senator Adams' Gambit Paves the Way for Vote on Tanker-Escort in the Persian Gulf," First Principles, Feb.–Mar. 1988, at 4.

7. *See, e.g.,* Robbie Gramer, "Lawmakers Redouble Push to Stop Trump from Going to War with Iran," *Foreign Pol'y,* Aug. 5, 2019, https://foreignpolicy.com/2019/08/05/lawmakers-redouble-push-to-stop-trump-from-going-to-war-with-iran-defense-policy-bill-armed-services-commitee-war-powers-congress-trump-middle-east-tensions/; Tess Bridgeman & Brianna Rosen, "Still at War: The United States in Syria," *Just Security,* Apr. 29, 2022, https://perma.cc/L843-MLRL; Brian Finucane, "An Unauthorized War: The Shaky Legal Ground for the U.S. Operation in Syria," *Foreign Aff.,* Jan. 11, 2022, www.foreignaffairs.com/articles/syria/2022-01-11/unauthorized-war; Oona Hathaway & Luke Hartig, "Still at War: The United States in Somalia," *Just Security,* Mar. 31, 2022, https://perma.cc/3L75-CL53; Luke Hartig & Oona Hathaway, "Still at War: The United States in Yemen," *Just Security,* Mar. 24, 2022, https://perma.cc/9PZE-V2C2.

8. *See* Harold Hongju Koh, "The Fast Track and United States Trade Policy," 18 *Brook. J. Int'l L.* 143 (1992) (describing use of the fast-track expedited legislative process in the trade field).

9. Ely, *supra* note 4, at 61. For rulings in the human-rights area, see, for example, Filártiga v. Peña-Irala, 630 F.2d 876 (2d Cir. 1980); Forti v. Suarez-Mason, 672 F. Supp. 1531 (N.D. Cal. 1987); Von Dardel v. U.S.S.R., 623 F. Supp. 246 (D.D.C. 1985). For commercial rulings under the "act of state" doctrine and the Foreign Sovereign Immunities Act, see generally Gary Born & Peter Rutledge, *International Civil Litigation in United States Courts* (7th ed. 2022).

10. *See* Zadvydas v. Davis, 533 U.S. 678, 699 (2001) (reading an implicit time frame into a statute whose terms were silent on the limits on detention, finding "nothing in the history of these statutes that clearly demonstrates a congressional intent to authorize indefinite, perhaps permanent, detention").

11. *See* 50 U.S.C. §§ 1801–1811. Under the Foreign Intelligence Surveillance Act of 1978 (FISA), the executive branch may not engage in certain forms of electronic surveillance for national security purposes unless it has received advance approval from the attorney general and presented in camera, ex parte applications for warrants to the Foreign Intelligence Surveillance Court (FISC). That court entertains applications submitted by the government for approval of electronic surveillance, physical search, and other investigative actions for foreign-intelligence purposes. The court is composed of eleven federal district judges appointed by the chief justice for a maximum

of seven years, and conducts proceedings under the strictest security. The chief justice also designates three federal appeals-court judges to review government appeals when initial warrants have been denied. The court also assesses the sufficiency of foreign-intelligence procedures and receives compliance reports regarding possible violations. *See generally* Americo Cinquegrana, "The Walls (and Wires) Have Ears: The Background and First Ten Years of the Foreign Intelligence Surveillance Act of 1978," 137 *U. Pa. L. Rev.* 793 (1989); Stephen Saltzburg, "National Security and Privacy: Of Governments and Individuals Under the Constitution and the Foreign Intelligence Surveillance Act," 28 *Va. J. Int'l L.* 129 (1987); Jack Boeglin & Julius Taranto, "Stare Decisis and Secret Law: On Precedent and Publication in the Foreign Intelligence Surveillance Court," 124 *Yale L.J.* 2189 (2015); Andrew Nolan & Richard M. Thompson II, Cong. Research Serv., R43362, *Reform of the Foreign Intelligence Surveillance Courts: Procedural and Operational Changes*, 2 (2014), https://perma.cc/2U92-YMPU.

12. *See supra* p. 298.

13. *See* U.N. General Assembly Security Council, Annex to the Letter Dated Oct. 2, 2008 from the Permanent Representative of Switzerland to the Secretary-General: Montreux Document on Pertinent International Legal Obligations and Practices for States Related to Operations of Private Military and Security Companies During Armed Conflict, U.N. Doc. A/63/467-S/2008/636 (2008); International Code of Conduct for Private Security Service Providers, Int'l Code of Conduct Ass'n, https://perma.cc/B7JV-TZZQ.

14. Bureau of Arms Control, Verification & Compliance, U.S. State Dep't, Political Declaration on Responsible Military Use of Artificial Intelligence and Autonomy (Feb. 16, 2023), https://perma.cc/T299-PEXL; Charlie Dunlap, "The Law and the U.S.'[s] New Declaration on Military Uses of AI: Some Observations," *Lawfire*, Feb. 18, 2023, https://perma.cc/U2QN-AR2P.

15. *See Report on the Legal and Policy Frameworks Guiding the United States' Use of Military Force and Related National Security Operations*, at i, 4, 11 (Dec. 2016), https://perma.cc/LVZ4-MDA7 (discussed in chapter 7).

16. Harold Hongju Koh, *The Trump Administration and International Law* 105–26 (2018).

17. *See* Charlie Savage, "White House Tightens Rules on Counterterrorism Drone Strikes," *N.Y. Times*, Oct. 7, 2022, www.nytimes.com/2022/10/07/us/politics/drone-strikes-biden-trump.html.

18. Eli Okun, "Will Washington Close a Chapter on Iraq?," *Politico Playbook PM*, Mar. 16, 2023, https://perma.cc/3MEF-SZPV; National Security Powers Act of 2021, S. 2391, 117th Cong., https://perma.cc/3U5A-26QM; National Security Reforms and Accountability Act, H.R. 5410, 117th Cong., https://perma.cc/9PTJ-BHY4. For analysis of this legislation, see Tess Bridgeman & Stephen Pomper, "A Giant Step Forward for War Powers Reform," *Just Security*, July 20, 2021, https://perma.cc/V8HR-PEYH, Tess Bridgeman & Stephen Pomper, "Good Governance Paper No. 14: War Powers Reform & 2022 Update," *Just Security*, Jan. 21, 2022, https://perma.cc/XSA7-6C5C, and Tess Bridgeman, "In Support of Sunsets: Easy Yes Votes on AUMF Reform," *Just Security*, July 13, 2022, https://perma.cc/872E-PAC2.

19. Laurence H. Tribe, "Transcending the *Youngstown* Triptych: A Multidimensional Reappraisal of Separation of Powers Doctrine," 126 *Yale L.J. F.* 86 (2016), http://perma.cc/TM4Z-2Q8L (Jackson's tripartite *Youngstown* framework created a "flat" two-dimensional space that lacks "an analytical guide for navigating what is in truth the multidimensional universe of relevant constitutional values and relationships.").

20. *See, e.g.,* Zivotofsky v. Kerry (*Zivotofsky II*), 576 U.S. 1 (2015) (exclusive presidential recognition power overrides congressional disapproval); *see also* United States v. Belmont, 301 U.S. 324 (1937); United States v. Pink, 315 U.S. 203 (1942) (both holding that president's recognition power supports sole executive agreement); Goldwater v. Carter, 444 U.S. 996, 1006–07 (Brennan, J., dissenting) (arguing that President Carter had sufficient constitutional authority to exit a particular bilateral treaty pursuant to his recognition power).

21. *See, e.g.,* United States v. Guy W. Capps, Inc., 204 F.2d 655 (4th Cir. 1953) (executive agreement was void because it contravened a statute in the area of foreign commerce, which is subject to regulation by Congress alone), *aff'd*, 348 U.S. 296 (1955).

22. *Cf.* Consumers Union v. Kissinger, 506 F.2d 136 (D.C. Cir. 1974) (upholding legality of executive undertakings to restrain steel imports because they were not legally binding and did not conflict with any explicit congressional statute regulating imports enacted under Congress's exclusive authority over foreign commerce).

23. *See* Louis Henkin, "'A More Effective System' for Foreign Relations: The Constitutional Framework," in 5 *Appendices: Commission on the Organization of the Government for the Conduct of Foreign Policy* 19 (1975).

24. The extent of information sharing between the House Ways and Means and Senate Finance Committees and the executive branch during the Tokyo round of talks was so extensive that they signed an interbranch memorandum of understanding under which the president's trade representative agreed to provide the committees with classified cables relating to the negotiations. *See* Harold Hongju Koh, "Congressional Controls on Presidential Trade Policymaking After *I.N.S. v. Chadha*," 18 *N.Y.U. J. Int'l L. & Pol.* 1191, 1214 n.65 (1986). For the INF Treaty, see S. Res. 86, 99th Cong., *reprinted in* 131 Cong. Rec. S2,437–38 (daily ed. Feb. 28, 1985), and Edmund Muskie, "Congress and National Security," 28 *Va. J. Int'l L.* 949, 958–59 (1988) (describing Senate observer group's activities).

25. Goldwater v. Carter, 617 F. 2d 697, 697 (D.C. Cir. 1979) (en banc) (per curiam), *dismissed as nonjusticiable and vacated*, 444 U.S. 996 (1979).

26. Head Money Cases, 112 U.S. 580, 599 (1884); Whitney v. Robertson, 124 U.S. 190, 194 (1888).

27. In May 2018, Trump announced that the United States was withdrawing from the Iran nuclear deal and on August 6, 2018, Trump issued an executive order reimposing certain sanctions against Iran that had been lifted as a part of that deal Exec. Order No. 13,846, 83 Fed. Reg. 38,949 (Aug. 7, 2018); *see* OFAC FAQs: Iran Sanctions, U.S. Dep't of the Treasury, https://perma.cc/P2TK-T2DF. But in a joint statement, France, Germany, and the United Kingdom all noted that the U.N. Security Council resolution endorsing the deal "remained the binding international

legal framework for the resolution of the dispute," which "raise[d] the possibility
that the United States will be found to be in violation of the Security Council."
Mark Landler, "Trump Abandons Iran Nuclear Deal He Long Scorned," *N.Y. Times,*
May 8, 2018, www.nytimes.com/2018/05/08/world/middleeast/trump-iran-
nuclear-deal.html. The Biden administration has tried to revive the deal.

28. *See* Printz v. United States, 521 U.S. 898, 977 (1997) (Breyer, J., dissenting); Stephen Breyer, *The Court and the World: American Law and the New Global Realities*
245 (2015) ("At most, cross-referencing will speed the development of 'clusters' or
'pockets' of legally like-minded nations whose judges learn things from one another, either as a general matter or in particular areas of law, such as security, commerce, or the environment.").

29. In *R v. Secretary of State for Exiting the European Union,* [2017] UKSC 5, [36], [77–93],
[2017] 2 WLR 583 (appeal taken from England and Northern Ireland), the court
reasoned that prior parliamentary approval was required because Brexit would require fundamental constitutional changes, including the repeal of the European
Communities Act 1972, which expressly allowed for E.U. treaties to take effect
within U.K. domestic law. Since the British executive would not have had domestic
legal authority to effect the removal of the act unilaterally, the court reasoned, neither should the prime minister have the power to unilaterally withdraw from the
treaty without legislative participation. Similarly, in *Democratic Alliance v. Minister of
International Relations and Cooperation,* 2017 (3) SA 212 (GP) (S. Afr.), the court held
that South Africa could withdraw from the Rome Statute only upon approval of
parliament and after the repeal of the statute implementing the treaty. In Canada,
where legislation limits the prerogative, the prerogative power to withdraw from a
treaty must be exercised in accordance with the legislated limits. *See* Maurice Cop-
ithorne, "National Treaty Law and Practice: Canada," in *National Treaty Law and
Practice: Canada, Egypt, Israel, Mexico, Russia, South Africa* 1, 11–12 (Monroe Leigh et
al. eds., 2003); *see also* Pierre-Hugues Verdier & Mila Versteeg, "Separation of Powers, Treaty-Making, and Treaty Withdrawal: A Global Survey" 4 (Univ. of Va. Sch. of
Law Pub. Law & Legal Theory Paper Series, Research Paper No. 2018-56, 2018),
https://perma.cc/J2ZG-DPDV ("In recent decades, several national legal systems
have introduced constraints on that [executive] power, usually by requiring parliamentary approval of withdrawal from treaties whose conclusion required such approval."); *id.* at 15 (citing such provisions from Belgium, China, Denmark, and the
Netherlands). A recent survey reports that parliamentary approval for withdrawal is
required by organic laws in ten Eastern European countries (Belarus, Bosnia and
Herzegovina, Estonia, Latvia, Lithuania, Russia, Slovenia, Tajikistan, Turkmenistan,
and Ukraine) and Mexico, *id.* at 16 n.47, and by constitutional or administrative interpretation or presidential decree in nine others (Austria, Czechia, Ethiopia, Hungary, Iran, Japan, Norway, Slovakia, and South Africa), *id.* at 16 n.48.

30. *See, e.g.,* Zivotofsky v. Clinton (*Zivotofsky I*), 566 U.S. 189 (2012).

31. For a comparable provision, see No NATO Withdrawal Act, H.R. 6530, 115th Cong.
(2018).

32. Youngstown Sheet & Tube Co. v. Sawyer, 343 U.S. 579, 650 (1952) (Jackson,
J., concurring). *See generally* Elizabeth Goitein, "The Alarming Scope of the

President's Emergency Powers," *Atlantic*, Jan.–Feb. 2019, www.theatlantic.com/
magazine/archive/2019/01/presidential-emergency-powers/576418/;   Elizabeth
Goitein, "Good Governance Paper No. 18: Reforming Emergency Powers," *Just Se-curity*, Oct. 31, 2020, https://perma.cc/T7QZ-F5SU.

33. *See generally* Scott Anderson et al., "What Sanctions Has the World Put on Russia?," *Lawfare*, Mar. 4, 2022, www.lawfaremedia.org/article/what-sanctions-has-
world-put-russia (blocking central bank assets has previously only been applied to
Iran, North Korea, and Syria). For a discussion of Trump's "emergencies," see Harold Hongju Koh, "Presidential Power to Terminate International Agreements,"
128 *Yale L.J. F.* 432 (2018), https://perma.cc/85LD-5S9F, Harold Hongju Koh,
"Symposium: *Trump v. Hawaii—Korematsu*'s Ghost and National-Security Masquerades," *SCOTUSblog*, June 28, 2018, https://perma.cc/2VZY-3B7A; Adjusting
Imports of Aluminum into the United States, Proclamation No. 9758, 83 Fed. Reg.
25,849, 25,850 (May 31, 2018), https://perma.cc/C6XH-ZV76 (Canada is import-
ing aluminum and steel imports "in such quantities and under such circumstances
as to threaten to impair the national security of the United States."); and Dov S.
Zakheim, "Canada as a National Security Threat to the United States," *The Hill*,
June 4, 2018, https://thehill.com/opinion/national-security/390527-canada-as-a-
national-security-threat-tothe-united-states.

34. For a comprehensive recommendation for restructuring the current U.S. statutory
regime governing international economic sanctions, see Barry Carter, *International
Economic Sanctions: Improving the Haphazard U.S. Legal Regime* (1988).

35. *See* "Declared National Emergencies Under the National Emergencies Act," *Brennan Center for Justice* (last updated Feb. 17, 2023), https://perma.cc/396W-LS4M.
The oldest emergency still in effect is the one declared by President Carter in 1979
concerning Iran.

36. For a helpful primer on how U.S. sanctions are developed by the interagency process, see Brian O'Toole & Samantha Sultoon, "Sanctions Explained: How a Foreign
Policy Problem Becomes a Sanctions Program," *Atlantic Council*, Sept. 22, 2019,
https://perma.cc/63FS-BVJE. On the role of the State Department sanctions coor-
dinator, see Dan Fried & Eddie Fishman, "The Rebirth of the State Department
Office of Sanctions Coordination: Guidelines for Success," *Atlantic Council*, Feb.
12, 2021, https://perma.cc/5BN2-954D; Ambassador James C. O'Brien, Coordina-
tor for Sanctions Policy, U.S. Dep't of State, "Keeping the Pressure on Russia and
Its Enablers: Examining the Reach of and Next Steps for U.S. Sanctions," Testimony Before the Senate Foreign Relations Committee (Sept. 28, 2022), https://
perma.cc/9MQY-6NVL; and James C. O'Brien, "The Role of Sanctions in US Foreign Policy," *Institute for Human Sciences* (Feb. 16, 2023), https://perma.cc/DM94-
9CJK (urging the creation of "common law of sanctions").

37. In connection with these amendments, Congress could follow the recommendation of the Iran-contra committees and amend or repeal the so-called Hostage Act
of 1868, 22 U.S.C. § 1732, an obscure statutory provision that Oliver North claimed
provided the executive branch with "the authority to do whatever [was] necessary"
during the Iran-contra affair. Oliver North, *Taking the Stand: The Testimony of Lieutenant Colonel Oliver L. North*, 503–04 (1987); *see also id.* at 606 (remarks of Rep

Henry Hyde). Despite powerful arguments that the Congress of 1868 had never intended that law to be a blank check authorizing all future presidents to use any means to rescue hostages, President Carter regularly invoked that statute, along with IEEPA, as legislative authorization for virtually all of his actions during the Iranian hostage crisis. *See generally* Opinions of the Attorney General and of the Office of Legal Counsel Relating to the Iranian Hostage Crisis, 4A Op. O.L.C. 155–56, 227 (1980). For a thorough historical examination of the narrow legislative intent underlying the statute, see Abner Mikva & Gerald Neuman, "The Hostage Crisis and the 'Hostage Act,'" 49 *U. Chi. L. Rev.* 292 (1982), and Dames & Moore v. Regan, 453 U.S. 654, 677 (1981).

38. The ARTICLE ONE Act, introduced by Senator Mike Lee, would require any presidentially declared national emergency to expire after thirty days unless approved by Congress, in which case the emergency could remain in effect for up to a year, but subsequent renewals would also require congressional approval. Significantly, the bill exempts emergency declarations that rely solely on IEEPA from the congressional-approval requirement because it would be burdensome for Congress to have to vote on several dozen sanctions programs each year. *See* S. 241, 117th Cong. (2021), www.congress.gov/bill/117th-congress/senate-bill/241.

39. *See* 50 U.S.C. § 1702(a)(1)(B).

40. *See* Alan Rappeport & David E. Sanger, "Seizing Russian Assets to Help Ukraine Sets Off White House Debate," *N.Y. Times,* May 31, 2022, www.nytimes.com/2022/05/31/us/politics/russia-sanctions-central-bank-assets.html. Professor Laurence Tribe and Jeremy Lewin have read this IEEPA language to allow the United States to seize and transfer Russian Central Bank assets. *See* Laurence Tribe & Jeremy Lewin, Opinion, "$100 Billion. Russia's Treasure in the U.S. Should be Turned Against Putin," *N.Y. Times,* Apr. 15, 2022, www.nytimes.com/2022/04/15/opinion/russia-war-currency-reserves.html; Laurence Tribe, et al., "Making Putin Pay," Sept. 17, 2023, https://perma.cc/E267-595F. *But see* Paul Stephan, "Giving Russian Assets to Ukraine—Freezing Is Not Seizing," *Lawfare,* Apr. 26, 2022, https://perma.cc/7RJX-9ZNK; Philip Zelikow & Simon Johnson, "How Ukraine Can Build Back Better," *Foreign Aff.,* Apr. 19, 2022, www.foreignaffairs.com/articles/ukraine/2022-04-19/how-ukraine-can-build-back-better; Scott R. Anderson & Chimène Keitner, "The Legal Challenges Presented By Seizing Frozen Russian Assets," *Lawfare,* May 26, 2022, https://perma.cc/B3YH-G42T.

41. *See* Japan Whaling Ass'n v. American Cetacean Soc'y, 478 U.S. 221, 230 (1986) ("Under the Constitution, one of the judiciary's characteristic roles is to interpret statutes, and we cannot shirk this responsibility merely because our decision may have significant political overtones.").

42. *See* William Dodge, "Why Terrorism Exceptions to State Immunity Do Not Violate International Law," *Just Security,* Aug. 10, 2023, www.justsecurity.org/87525/why-terrorism-exceptions-to-state-immunity-do-not-violate-international-law/ (discussing Iran-Canada and Iran-U.S. cases before the ICJ).

43. *See* C-72/15, Rosneft Oil Company and Others v. Council (March 28, 2017). The two Iran-U.S. cases are Certain Assets (Iran v. USA) (Judgment), 2023 I.C.J., March 30,

2023, www.icj-cij.org/sites/default/files/case-related/164/164-20230330-JUD-01-00-EN.pdf; and Alleged Violations of the 1955 Treaty of Amity, Economic Relations, and Consular Rights (Iran v. U.S.), Judgment of Feb. 2021, 2021 I.C.J., www.icj-cij.org/sites/default/files/case-related/175/175-20210203-JUD-01-00-EN.pdf (challenging U.S. sanctions).

44. "Presidential Emergency Action Documents," *Brennan Center for Justice* (last updated May 26, 2022), https://perma.cc/P6JM-EFER; Benjamin Waldman, "New Documents Illuminate the President's Secret, Unchecked Emergency Powers," *Brennan Center for Justice,* May 26, 2022, https://perma.cc/WLJ2-UV4R. Senator Ed Markey has introduced legislation to require that all such PEADs be made public. *See* REIGN Act of 2020, S. 4279, 116th Cong. (2020), www.congress.gov/bill/116th-congress/senate-bill/4279/.

45. *See* Daniel Silver, "The Uses and Misuses of Intelligence Oversight," 11 *Hous. J. Int'l L.* 7, 16 (1988).

46. *The 9/11 Commission Report: Final Report of the National Commission on Terrorist Attacks Upon the United States* (2004), www.govinfo.gov/content/pkg/GPO-911REPORT/pdf/GPO-911REPORT.pdf.

47. *See* Loch Johnson, *America's Secret Power: The CIA in a Democratic Society* 223, 263 (1989) (noting that division of intelligence committees has proved to be a source of strength to the Congress in the performance of its oversight duties); Michael O'Neil, "Remarks of Michael O'Neil," 11 *Hous. J. Int'l L.* 211, 217 (1988).

48. President Bush nominated career diplomat John Negroponte as the first director of national intelligence. Executive Order No. 12,333 prescribed general principles to govern intelligence collection, retention, and dissemination. Office of the Director of National Intelligence, "Organization," https://perma.cc/X8A6-AHLQ. The Iran-contra report recommended more oversight boards. *See Report of the Congressional Committees Investigating the Iran-Contra Affair,* H.R. Rep. No. 100-433, S. Rep. No. 100-216, at 426 (1987). And the 9/11 Commission Report led to the President's Intelligence Advisory Board, a group of distinguished citizens from outside the government that provides the president with independent advice on the intelligence community's effectiveness. Four members drawn from the advisory board make up the standing Intelligence Oversight Board, which is charged with overseeing the intelligence community's legal compliance. The "9/11 implementation act" also created the Privacy and Civil Liberties Oversight Board (with four part-time members and a full-time chair, to provide oversight and advice to ensure that intelligence activities are consistent with privacy and civil-liberties laws.

49. Greg Miller et al., "How a CIA Analyst, Alarmed by Trump's Shadow Foreign Policy, Triggered an Impeachment Inquiry," *Wash. Post,* Nov. 16, 2019, www.washingtonpost.com/national-security/how-a-cia-analyst-alarmed-by-trumps-shadow-foreign-policy-triggered-an-impeachment-inquiry/2019/11/15/042684a8-03c3-11ea-8292-c46ee8cb3dce_story.html.

50. Letter from Anonymous Whistleblower to Hon. Richard Burr & Hon. Adam Schiff House Homeland Security Committee (Aug. 12, 2019), https://perma.cc/3SPW5WST.

51. For a review of current federal whistleblower laws, and the gaps within them, see generally National Whistleblower Center, "Whistleblower Protection Laws for Federal Employee Whistleblowers," https://perma.cc/6KST-C4Z2.

52. See *H.R. 3822, To Strengthen the System of Congressional Oversight of Intelligence Activities in the United States: Hearings Before the Subcomm. on Legis. of the H. Permanent Select Comm. on Intelligence*, 100th Cong. 56 (1988) (statement of Hon. Clark M. Clifford); Kate Stith, "Congress' Power of the Purse," 97 *Yale L. J.* 1343, 1387 n.213 (1988) (collecting cases in which courts have determined whether the executive has exceeded specified appropriations limitations). For a description of the Justice Department's Office of Intelligence Policy and Review, *see* "Office of Intelligence Policy and Review," www.justice.gov/archive/jmd/mps/2006omf/manual/oipr.htm.

53. Eugene Rostow, "Searching for Kennan's Grand Design," 87 *Yale L.J.* 1527, 1536 n.35 (1978).

54. Exec. Order No. 12,356, 3 C.F.R. 166 (1986), revoking and superseding Exec. Order No. 12,065, 3 C.F.R. 190 (1979). *See generally* Sudha Setty, *National Security Secrecy: Comparative Effects on Democracy and the Rule of Law* 1–72 (2017) (providing an overview of national security secrecy practices across the three branches of government); Dana Priest & William M. Arkin, "A Hidden World, Growing Beyond Control," *Wash. Post*, July 19, 2010, www.washingtonpost.com/investigations/top-secret-america/2010/07/19/hidden-world-growing-beyond-control-2 (estimating that some "1,271 government organizations and 1,931 private companies work on programs related to counterterrorism, homeland security[,] and intelligence in about 10,000 locations across the United States" and that over 850,000 individuals hold top-secret security clearances); *Report of the Commission on Protecting and Reducing Government Secrecy*, S. Doc. No. 105-2, at 19–46 (1997); Elizabeth Goitein & David M. Shapiro, "Reducing Overclassification Through Accountability," *Brennan Center for Justice*, https://perma.cc/PGK2-RN4J.

55. Alex Kingsbury, "The Man Who Leaked the Pentagon Papers Is Scared," *N.Y. Times*, Mar. 24, 2023, www.nytimes.com/2023/03/24/opinion/international-world/ellsberg-nuclear-war-ukraine.html; *U.S. Government Information Policies and Practices—The Pentagon Papers (Part 1): Hearings Before a Subcomm. of the House Comm. on Gov't Operations*, 92d Cong. 12 (1971) (statement of Hon. Arthur J. Goldberg); *see also id.* at 97 (statement of William Florence, retired civilian security-classification-policy expert) (estimating that 99.5 percent of all Defense Department classified information could be released without prejudicing defense interests); *id.* (part 3) at 791 (statement of then assistant attorney general William Rehnquist) (agreeing that government officials have persistent tendency to overclassify); Peter Galison, "Removing Knowledge," 31 *Critical Inquiry* 229, 230 (2004) (estimating as of 2004 that around "8 billion pages" had been classified in the United States since 1978 and noting that "[s]ome suspect as many as a trillion pages are classified").

56. David Pozen, "The Leaky Leviathan: Why the Government Condemns and Condones Unlawful Disclosures of Information," 127 *Harv. L. Rev.* 512, 529, 630 (2013) (noting the apparent proliferation of such leaks). David Pozen, "Transpar-

ency's Ideological Drift," 128 *Yale L.J.* 100, 156 (2018), https://perma.cc/U8AH-868R.

57. Note, "Developments in the Law—The National Security Interest and Civil Liberties," 85 *Harv. L. Rev.* 1130, 1190 (1972).

58. *See generally* Elizabeth Goitein, *The New Era of Secret Law* (2016); Dakota S. Rudesill, "Coming to Terms with Secret Law," 7 *Harv. Nat'l Sec. J.* 241 (2015); DOJ OLC Transparency Act, S. 3334, 116th Cong. (2020), https://perma.cc/AD57-EGUX.

59. Exec. Order No. 13,526, 3 C.F.R. § 298 (2010).

60. *See* 5 U.S.C. §§ 552(a)(3), 552(b)(1); *see also Litigation Under the Federal Freedom of Information Act and Privacy Act* 21–36 (A. Adler ed., 13th ed. 1988).

61. *See* 5 U.S.C. § 552(a)(4)(B); S. Rep. No. 93-1200, at 11–12 (1974) (articulating standards of judicial deference to agency affidavits under national security exemption); *see also, e.g.,* Miller v. Casey, 730 F.2d 773 (D.C. Cir. 1984); Taylor v. Dep't of the Army, 684 F.2d 99 (D.C. Cir. 1982). *Cf.* Goldberg v. U.S. Dep't of State, 818 F.2d71, 77 (D.C. Cir. 1987) (stating that under FOIA, courts should accord "substantial weight" to agency affidavits "without relinquishing their independent responsibility" to determine the propriety of classification decisions) (emphasis omitted).

62. Chris Whipple, *The Fight of His Life: Inside Joe Biden's White House* 210–24 (2023); Erin Banco et al., "'Something Was Badly Wrong': When Washington Realized Russia Was Actually Invading Ukraine," *Politico,* Feb. 24, 2023, https://perma.cc/QGR6-GUVU.

63. Banco et al., *supra* note 62. As Director Haines recalled, "[t]here were things that really made this a much more compelling case—budget decisions that were taken, other forms of intelligence surrounding it, the information campaign that they were playing. It wasn't until you brought it all together, you start to see how the picture pulls together." *Id.*

64. *See, e.g.,* E. J. Dionne Jr. et al., *One Nation After Trump: A Guide for the Perplexed, the Disillusioned, the Desperate, and the Not-Yet Deported* (2018); Robert Bauer and Jack Goldsmith, *After Trump: Reconstructing the Presidency* (2020); Commission on the Practice of Democratic Citizenship, *Our Common Purpose: Reinventing American Democracy for the 21st Century* (2020), https://perma.cc/X5UE-YDS7.

65. Electoral Count Reform and Presidential Transition Improvement Act, Consolidated Appropriations Act, 2023, Pub. L. No. 117-328, div. P, 136 Stat. 4459, 5233–46 (2022), www.congress.gov/117/plaws/publ328/PLAW-117publ328.pdf. For a discussion of the Presidential Transition Enhancement Act of 2019, Pub. L. No. 16-121, 134 Stat. 138 (2020), see Amy B. Wang & Liz Goodwin, "Congress Moves Ahead on Electoral Count Act Reforms in Response to January 6," *Wash. Post,* Dec. 20, 2022, www.washingtonpost.com/politics/2022/12/19/electoral-count-reform-omnibus/.

66. *See* Turquoise Baker et al., "Voting Machines at Risk in 2022," *Brennan Center for Justice,* Mar. 1, 2022, https://perma.cc/4LCX-LSQS; *Secure Our Vote,* https://perma.cc/CVH9-M7WK; Kim Zetter, "Exclusive: Critical U.S. Elections Systems Have Been Left Exposed Online Despite Official Denials," *Vice,* Aug. 8, 2019, https://perma.cc/4R2A-X6E8. The three bills are the Foreign Influence Reporting in Elections (FIRE) Act, S. 1562, 116th Cong. (2019), https://perma.cc/68MA-

SF4Q; the Duty to Report Act, S. 1247, 116th Cong. (2019), https://perma.cc/8E5Y-L8LF; and the Securing America's Federal Elections (SAFE) Act, H.R. 2722, 116th Cong. (2019), https://perma.cc/4J53-M69M.

Conclusion

1. Thanks to Burt Neuborne for this "Berraism."
2. *See* J. William Fulbright, *The Price of Empire* 72 (1989) ("The trouble with the resurgent legislature of the late 1970s is that it went in the wrong directions too often, carping and meddling, in the service of special interests, not engaging in reflective deliberation on basic issues of national interest. . . . What executive branch officials choose to ignore is that Congress has been driven to this from the years of ignored advice.")
3. Asking who should safeguard the Republic from future foreign-policy disasters, Oregon Supreme Court justice Hans Linde summarized:

   We are looking . . . for something with these characteristics: (1) It must be a permanent institution, with authority beyond that of its changing members; (2) it must be nonpartisan and independent of Congress and the President, and seen to be so; (3) it must explain its conclusions publicly, not advise in secret; (4) it must have some factfinding procedures if facts are decisive; (5) it must maintain a long view, beyond the exigencies of the immediate case; and (6) it must have enough other work so that a constitutional case is the exception rather than its *raison d'être*. . . . We do not have to search far for a body that meets these criteria. It is a court.

   Hans Linde, "A Republic . . . If You Can Keep It," 16 *Hastings Const. L.Q.* 295, 307–08 (1989).
4. Four members of the current Supreme Court—Chief Justice Roberts and Justices Alito, Kagan, and Kavanaugh—previously held high-level executive-branch positions.
5. Myers v. United States, 272 U.S. 52, 293 (1926) (Brandeis, J., dissenting); *see also* Akhil Amar, "Of Sovereignty and Federalism," 96 *Yale L.J.* 1425, 1495 (1987) ("Vest power in different sets of agents who will have personal incentives to monitor and enforce limitations on each other's power.").
6. *See, e.g.*, National Security Powers Act of 2021, S. 2391, 117th Cong., https://perma.cc/3U5A-26QM (introduced July, 20, 2021); National Security Reforms and Accountability Act, H.R. 5410, 117th Cong., https://perma.cc/9PTJ-BHY4 (introduced Sept. 29, 2021).
7. *See, e.g.*, Michael Cohen et al., "A Garbage Can Model of Organizational Choice," 17 *Admin. Sci. Q.* 1 (1972).
8. *See, e.g.*, Jeffrey Birnbaum & Alan Murray, *Showdown at Gucci Gulch: Lawmakers, Lobbyists, and the Unlikely Triumph of Tax Reform* 285–88 (1987); John Kingdon, *Agendas, Alternatives, and Public Policies* (1984).
9. *See* 132 Cong. Rec. S14,629 (daily ed. Oct. 2, 1986); Richard Lugar, *Letters to the Next President* 208–47 (1988).

10. *See generally* E. Donald Elliott et al., "Toward a Theory of Statutory Evolution: The Federalization of Environmental Law," 1 *J.L. Econ. & Org.* 313 (1985).

11. *See generally* Harold Hongju Koh, *The National Security Constitution: Sharing Power After the Iran-Contra Affair* 7 (1990) ("Today's world demands not simply a strong president, but one who operates within an institutionally balanced constitutional structure of decision making."); *see also* Arthur Schlesinger, *The Imperial Presidency*, at xxviii (We need "to devise means of reconciling a strong and purposeful Presidency with equally strong and purposeful forms of democratic control. . . . [W]e need a strong Presidency—but a strong Presidency *within the Constitution*.") (emphasis in original).

12. *See, e.g., The Tethered Presidency: Congressional Restraints on Executive Power* (Thomas M. Franck ed., 1981).

13. *See, e.g.,* Thomas Friedman, "Baker Says Accord on Contra Aid Enhances Powers of the President," *N.Y. Times,* Mar. 27, 1989, at A10.

14. Youngstown Sheet & Tube Co. v. Sawyer, 343 U.S. 579, 637, 654 (1952) (Jackson, J., concurring) ("When the President takes measures incompatible with the expressed or implied will of Congress, his power is at its lowest ebb, for then he can rely only upon his own constitutional powers minus any constitutional powers of Congress over the matter.").

15. Historical examples date back to well before the Senate's rejection of the Versailles Treaty in 1919. A later example is the Senate's imposition of the Byrd amendment as a condition for ratification of the Intermediate-Range Nuclear Forces Treaty. *See* Message to the Senate on the Soviet-United States Intermediate-Range Nuclear Force Treaty, 24 Weekly Comp. Pres. Doc. 779, 780 (June 10, 1988); Michael Oreskes, "An 'Imperial Congress' in Conservatives' Sights," *N.Y. Times,* Mar. 27, 1989, at B13.

16. Charles Krauthammer, "Divided Superpower," New Republic, Dec. 22, 1986, at 14, 16, 17; Kenneth Sharpe, "The Real Cause of Irangate," 68 *Foreign Pol'y* 41 (1987) ("It is not national security but pursuit of empire that clashes with constitutional democracy."); Jules Lobel, "Emergency Power and the Decline of Liberalism," 98 *Yale L.J.* 1385, 1426–27 (1989).

17. Paul Kennedy, *The Rise and Fall of the Great Powers* 524–25 (1987); Susan Strange, "The Persistent Myth of Lost Hegemony," 41 *Int'l Org.* 551, 572 (1987) ("The United States is ill-suited to sustaining . . . consistency in policymaking, partly by reason of its constitutional provisions.").

18. *See, e.g.,* Lobel, *supra* note 16, at 1426–27 (arguing that the United States should discard "pervasive anti-communism[,] . . . relinquish the prevailing assumption that our national security requires the prevention or overthrow of leftist revolutionary governments throughout the world[,] . . . move to end the cold war" with the Soviet Union, and increase "reliance on multilateral political, economic, and judicial institutions to resolve international problems").

19. *See, e.g.,* Robert Bork, "Foreword" to *The Fettered Presidency, Legal Constraints on the Executive Branch*, at i, ix (L. Crovitz & J. Rabkin eds., 1989) ("America has usually prospered most in eras of strong presidents, and the state of today's world makes the capacity for strong executive action more important than ever."); Robert Turner

"Separation of Powers in Foreign Policy: The Theoretical Underpinnings," 11 *Geo. Mason U. L. Rev.* 114, 116 (1988) ("We live in a dangerous world. . . . [Congress's] botched efforts to tie the president's hands and seize control of the nation's foreign policy have produced many tragic consequences [which] should make all of us realize how wise our Founding Fathers really were in vesting primary responsibility for foreign intercourse to the president."); *see also* Lawrence Block et al., "The Senate's Pie-in-the-Sky Treaty Interpretation: Power and the Quest for Legislative Supremacy," 137 *U. Pa. L. Rev.* 1481 (1989); Bruce Fein & William Bradford Reynolds, "Don't Constrain Presidential Diplomacy," Legal Times, July 31, 1989, at 18; Charles Cooper, "What the Constitution Means by Executive Power," 43 *U. Miami L. Rev.* 165 (1988); Eugene Rostow, "What the Constitution Means by Executive Power," 43 *U. Miami L. Rev.* 188 (1988); John Norton Moore, *Government Under Law and Covert Operations* (1980), *reprinted in Report of the Congressional Committees Investigating the Iran-Contra Affair*, H.R. Rep. No. 100-433, S. Rep. No. 100-216, at 614 (1987) (minority report); *cf.* Phillip Trimble, "The President's Foreign Affairs Powers," 83 *Am. J. Int'l L.* 750 (1989) (more moderate statement of this position). *Compare* Cooper, *supra*, at 177 ("[T]he understanding of article II displayed by Washington, Madison, Hamilton, and Jefferson indicates that the conduct of foreign relations is an aspect of the executive power entrusted to the President, subject only to narrowly defined exceptions."), *with* Leonard Levy, *Original Intent and the Framers' Constitution* 53 (1988) ("Nowadays, leading supporters of a constitutional jurisprudence of original intent are advocates of inherent presidential powers in the field of foreign relations, a stance that sheds light on either their ignorance or their hypocrisy.").

20. Myers v. United States, 272 U.S. 52, 293 (1926) (Brandeis, J., dissenting).
21. *See generally* Abram Chayes, *The Cuban Missile Crisis: International Crises and the Role of Law* (1974); "Introduction and Summary," Opinions of the Attorney General and of the Office of Legal Counsel Relating to the Iranian Hostage Crisis, 4A Op. O.L.C. 71–114 (1980) (describing role of legal opinions in Iranian hostage crisis).
22. *See, e.g.,* Lloyd Cutler, "To Form a Government," 59 *Foreign Aff.* 126, 139 (1980); Committee on the Constitutional System, *A Bicentennial Analysis of the American Constitutional Structure* 12 (1987); James Sundquist, *Constitutional Reform and Effective Government* 224–38 (1986).
23. *See, e.g.,* Henry Kissinger & Cyrus Vance, *Bipartisan Objectives for American Foreign Policy,* 67 *Foreign Aff.* 899, 901 (1988).
24. *See generally* Harold Hongju Koh, *The Trump Administration and International Law* 8–54 (2019).
25. Zivotofsky v. Clinton, 566 U.S. 189, 196, 201 (2012).
26. Walter Dellinger, "After the Cold War: Presidential Power and the Use of Military Force," 50 *U. Miami L. Rev.* 107, 109–10 (1995).
27. *See, e.g.,* Harold Hongju Koh, "The War Powers and Humanitarian Intervention," 53 *Hous. L. Rev.* 971 (2016); Harold Hongju Koh, "The Emerging Law of 21st Century War," 66 *Emory L.J.* 487 (2017) Harold Hongju Koh, "Triptych's End: A Better Approach to 21st Century International Lawmaking," 126 *Yale L.J. F.* 338 (2017), www.yalelawjournal.org/forum/triptychs-end; Harold Hongju Koh, "International

Law in Cyberspace" 54 *Harv. Int'l L.J. Online* 1 (2012), harvardilj.org/2012/12/online_54_koh; Harold Hongju Koh, "The Crime of Aggression: The United States Perspective" (with T. F. Buchwald), 109 *Am. J. Int'l L.* 257 (2015); Harold Hongju Koh, "International Criminal Justice 5.0," 38 *Yale J. Int'l L.* 525 (2013); Harold Hongju Koh, "The Legal Adviser's Duty to Explain," 41 *Yale J. Int'l L.* 189 (2016); Harold Hongju Koh, How to End the Forever War?, Remarks at the Oxford Union (May 7, 2013), https://perma.cc/6MPS-5A6R; Harold Hongju Koh, "Finally Ending America's Forever War, Part I: Diagnosis," *Just Sec.*, Sept. 11, 2023, https://www.justsecurity.org/88131/finally-ending-americas-forever-war-part-i-diagnosis/ [https://perma.cc/7HRG-NMKC]; Harold Hongju Koh, "Finally Ending America's Forever War, Part II: Prescription," *Just Sec.*, Sept. 12, 2023, https://www.justsecurity.org/88164/finally-ending-americas-forever-war-part-ii-prescription/ [https://perma.cc/BP34-JL4B]. Harold Hongju Koh, The Obama Administration and International Law, Keynote Speech at the Annual Meeting of the American Society of International Law (Mar. 25, 2010), https://2009-2017.state.gov/s/l/releases/remarks/139119.htm; Harold Hongju Koh, "Can the President be Torturer-in-Chief?," 81 *Ind. L. Rev.* 1145 (2007).

28. Dellinger, *supra* note 26, at 110. For fuller discussion of the matters in text, see Harold Hongju Koh, "On Academic Lawyers in the U.S. Government: Walter's Wisdom," 102 *N.C. L. Rev.* — (2024).

29. Stuart Taylor, "The American Accuser," *N.Y. Times,* Apr. 11, 1984, at A8, https://perma.cc/ASW8-MKQQ ("When he was asked by Nicaragua to sue his own country, Mr. Chayes . . . said, . . . '[I]n the end I thought that there was nothing wrong with holding the United States to its own best standards and best principles.'").

INDEX

Plan linked to, 289; as "executive agreement plus," 197–98, 234; existing agreements duplicated by, 197–98, 199–200
parliamentarians, 278
Passport Act (1926), 115–16
Paterson, William, 26
Patriot Act (2001), 148
peacekeeping, 96, 97, 143, 242
Pearl Harbor attack (1941), 39
Pelosi, Nancy, 189
Pence, Mike, 227, 322
Pentagon Papers case, 112, 322
Permanent Court of International Justice, 34
Persian Gulf, 61, 97, 104, 184
Philippines, 31, 32, 34, 60, 154
Pike Committee, 272
Pildes, Richard, 189, 301
Poindexter, John, 71, 81, 85, 90
Poland, 137
policy entrepreneurs, 329
political-question doctrine, 26, 28, 35, 61, 86, 123, 130, 255, 287, 294, 315; criticisms of, 285; emergency declarations and, 69; in *Goldwater v. Carter*, 121, 217; six-factor test for, 224
Polk, James, 21, 27
Pompeo, Mike, 236
Powell, Colin, 129, 148, 160
Powell, Lewis, 225
Power, Samantha, 173, 231
Pozen, David, 322
preemption doctrine, 296–97
president of the United States: almost always wins in foreign affairs, 92–122, 123; as "defender in chief," 2; groupthink around, 99; as national security threat, 6, 225–29; plebiscitary, 40, 45, 97, 111, 128; reactivity of, 96–99; structural superiority of, 93–94; as "torturer-in-chief," 163
presidential emergency action documents (PEADs), 319

Presidential Transition Enhancement Act (2019), 325
Presidential Transition Improvement Act (2022), 325
President's Committee on Administrative Management, 40
President's Emergency Plan for AIDS Relief, 151
Printz v. Unted States (1997), 314
Prize Cases (1863), 28, 50
Prohibition, 35
Puerto Rico, 31
Pullman railroad strike (1894), 31
Putin, Vladimir, 192, 236, 248–49, 324
Putnam, Robert, 202

Qadhafi, Muammar, 180–82, 185, 189–90
Qaeda, al, 163, 171, 174, 252, 306
Quadrilateral Security Dialogue (QSD), 238
quasi-constitutional customary law, 12–13, 131, 196, 223, 265

railroads, 30, 31
Ramirez v. Weinberger (1984), 295
Rasul v. Bush (2004), 162, 164, 165
Reagan, Ronald, 41, 61, 108, 116, 143, 268, 272; attorney general's foreign-policy role diminished by, 269; democracy promoted by, 150; emergency powers abused by, 69–70; national security process subverted by, 89–90, 98, 99; Nicaraguan contras backed by, 70, 121; "nonagreement agreements" employed by, 63–64; unilateralism of, 60, 64–66, 97, 102, 107, 109, 184, 252. *See also* Iran-contra affair
Reciprocal Trade Agreements Act (1934), 42–43
recognition power, 11, 20, 265, 286, 310; contrary congressional statutes vs., 224, 315; expansive reading of, 9, 24, 39, 65, 111, 239; in Jackson's